Tanzania

Social Sector Review

The World Bank
Washington, D.C.

11-10-99

World Bank Country Studies are among the many reports originally prepared for internal use as part of the continuing analysis by the Bank of the economic and related conditions of its developing member countries and of its dialogues with the governments. Some of the reports are published in this series with the least possible delay for the use of governments and the academic, business and financial, and development communities. The typescript of this paper therefore has not been prepared in accordance with the procedures appropriate to formal printed texts, and the World Bank accepts no responsibility for errors. Some sources cited in this paper may be informal documents that are not readily available.

ISBN: 0-8213-4585-0
ISSN: 0253-2123

Cover photo taken in 1996 of girls who received scholarships to attend secondary school in a pre-test of the program, which was a direct result of the analysis of this document. This first cohort of girls will graduate from lower secondary school in December 1999.

Library of Congress Cataloging-in-Publication Data

Tanzania : social sector review.
        p.   cm. — (World Bank country study)
    Includes bibliographical references.
    ISBN 0-8213-4585-0
    1. Human services—Tanzania.   2. Tanzania—Social conditions.   I. World Bank.   II.
Series.
HV448.5.T36   1999
362.9678—dc21   99-047476

CONTENTS

vi

TABLES

FIGURES

BOXES

Acronyms and Abbreviations

ADB	African Development Bank
AIDS	Acquired Immune Deficiency Syndrome
BMI	Body Mass Index
CBD	Community-Based Distribution
CIDA	Canadian International Development Agency
CMS	Central Medical Stores
CPI	Consumer Price Index
CPR	Contraceptive Prevalence Rate
CSPD	Child Support, Protection and Development
DEO	District Education Officer
DHMT	District Health Management Team
DM	Deutschmark
DMO	District Medical Officer
DSM	Dar es Salaam
DWD	Department of Water Development
EDP	Essential Drugs Program
EKWSP	East Kilimanjaro Water Supply Project
EPI	Expanded Program on Immunization
ESR	Education for Self-Reliance
FAO	Food and Agriculture Organization
FAST	Focused Area Studies Technique
FINNIDA	Finland International Aid Organization
FY	Fiscal Year
GDP	Gross Domestic Product
GTZ	German Technical Assistance Agency
HC	Health Center
HESAW	Health through Sanitation and Water
HH	Household
HIV	Human Immunodeficiency Virus
HMIS	Health Management Information System
HRDS	Tanzania Human Resources Development Survey
ICD	Institute for Curriculum Development
IDD	Iodine Deficiency Disease
IEC	Information, Education and Communication
IFC	International Finance Corporation
IMR	Infant Mortality Rate
IUD	Intrauterine Device
JICA	Japan International Cooperation Agency
JNSP	Joint Nutrition Support Project
KAP	Knowledge, Attitudes and Practices

Acronyms and Abbreviations (continued)

MCH/FP	Maternal and Child Health/Family planning
MOE	Ministry of Education (Zanzibar)
MOEC	Ministry of Education and Culture
MSTHE	Ministry of Science, Technology and Higher Education
NCHS	National Center for Health Statistics
NGO	Nongovernmental Organization
NORAD	Norwegian Agency for International Development
NUWA	National Urban Water Authority
OC	Oral Contraceptive
ODA	Overseas Development Agency
PCM	Protein-Calorie Malnutrition
PER	Public Expenditure Review
PHCC	Primary Health Care Center
PHCU	Primary Health Care Unit
PMO	Prime Minister's Office
PSLE	Primary School Leaving Examination
RDD	Regional Development Director
REO	Regional Education Officer
RHMT	Regional Health Management Team
RMO	Regional Medical Officer
RWMP	Regional Water Master Plan
SIDA	Swedish International Development Authority
SSR	Social Sector Review
TB	Tuberculosis
TBA	Traditional Birth Attendant
TDHS	Tanzania Demographic and Health Survey
TES	Tanzania Elimu Supplies
TFNC	Tanzania Food and Nutrition Center
TFR	Total Fertility Rate
TIE	Tanzania Institute of Education
TKAP	Tanzania Knowledge, Attitude and Practice
Tsh	Tanzanian Shilling
TTC	Teacher Training College
UK	United Kingdom
UMATI	National Family Planning Organization
UN	United Nations
UNDP	United Nations Development Program
UNFPA	United Nations Population Fund
UPE	Universal Primary Education
US$	United States Dollar

Acronyms and Abbreviations (continued)

USAID	United States Agency for International Development
VAD	Vitamin A Deficiency
WDR	World Development Report
WHO	World Health Organization
WTP	Willingness to Pay

ABSTRACT

This report was prepared by The World Bank cooperatively with the Government of Tanzania to provide a comprehensive review of Tanzania's social sector activities, including education, health, water and sanitation, nutrition, and family planning. It has contributed materially to The World Bank's social sector policy dialogue with the Government of Tanzania, precipitated the restructuring of the World Bank's portfolio in health and education, and led to improved cooperation in the social sectors both within the donor community and between donors and the Government. The report is based on the Human Resources Development Survey of 1993/94, qualitative surveys, community case studies, and other population-based surveys, such as the Tanzania Demographic and Health Survey 1991/92 and the Tanzania Knowledge, Attitudes and Practices Survey 1994.

The report describes trends in the social sectors and analyzes the factors that influence these trends, including the performance of the economy, government social sector spending and policy, household behavior and incomes, and demographic trends. Findings from the surveys and case studies are synthesized to provide a comprehensive picture of the demand for and supply of education, health, water and sanitation, nutrition, and family planning services. Tanzania's social indicators remain among the poorest in the world. The report reviews these trends, presents issues, assesses past government policies in the social sectors, and provided both the data and framework for the development and implementation of the Government's Social Sector Strategy.

This document is part of a series of analytical pieces on poverty and the social sectors in Tanzania, including *Tanzania: A Poverty Profile,* Report No. 12298-TA (1993); *Tanzania: The Challenge of Reforms: Growth, Incomes, and Welfare,* Report No. 14982-TA (1996); and *Technical and Higher Education and Training in Tanzania: Investments, Returns, and Future Opportunities,* Report No. 15327-TA (1997).

ACKNOWLEDGMENTS

This report was prepared by a team under the guidance of Charles C. Griffin. Members included Anil Deolalikar, Nicholas Kessy, Faustin Mukyanuzi, Issa M. Omari, Perran Penrose, Liberatus L. Shirima and Dale Whittington (consultants); Michael Kiernan and Jens Pedersen (DANIDA); Larry Forgy (USAID); Margaret Grosh; Emmanuel Malangalila; R. Paul Shaw; Sverrir Sigurdsson; Maria Luisa Ferreira; Young Hoy Kimaro; Ruth E. Levine; and Lynn Tsoflias. Amit Dar and Ruth Levine assembled and analyzed most of the information on post-secondary education. Lynn Tsoflias took primary responsibility for assembling information on the social sectors in Zanzibar. Tamara Fox assisted with the collection and cataloguing of background materials. The authors are grateful for the many background papers that were prepared for this report. The papers are listed in the bibliography. The authors are also grateful for the thoughtful comments on earlier drafts. In particular, we thank Elizabeth Morris-Hughes, Mark Blackden and Chitra Bhanu for a thorough gender review of the previous draft. Ruth Levine took primary responsibility to pull the work of many different authors together into a cohesive report. R. Marisol Ravicz and Andrew Follmer updated the budget numbers for this publication. Oscar Picazo, under Ruth Kagia's direction, pushed the report to production, with final editing by Suzanne Gnaegy.

The report was prepared under the general supervision of Jacob van Lutsenburg Maas, Division Chief, AF2PH, and James W. Adams, Director for Tanzania and Uganda. Motoo Konishi and Ronald Brigish, Resident Representatives, provided support throughout the process of developing this report. The peer reviewers were Jeffrey Hammer (EAPVP) and William McGreevey (PHN), and the Lead Economist was Shahid Yusuf.

The household survey data used for this report were collected as part of a collaborative project of the World Bank with the University of Dar es Salaam and the President's Office Planning Commission, partially financed by the Government of the United Kingdom. The survey forms, training materials, and data from the Human Resources Development Survey 1993/94 are available in electronic form at The World Bank's web site, http://www.worldbank.org/html/prdph/lsms/guide/select.html.

The authors would like to acknowledge, with thanks, the support provided by Yordi Seium, Lourdes Cuadro-Meliotes, and Helen Taddese at World Bank Headquarters, and Betty Sakaya, Maryanne Mwakangale, Rosalie Ferrao, Lorraine James and Mercy Sabai at the World Bank Resident Mission, Dar es Salaam.

The authors would also like to express gratitude for the leadership provided by the President's Office Planning Commission in overseeing this work. In particular, we would like to thank F. Kazaura, Principal Secretary; J. Kipokola, Deputy Principal Secretary; and J. Zayumba, Director, Social Services. The Steering Committee and Technical Subcommittee provided guidance at all stages. Members included: J. Kipokola, M. Konishi, A. Chiduo, P. Hiza, H. Kamote, E. Malangalila, R. Man'genya, F. Mrisho, L.K. Msaki, M. Mvungi, H.K. Mwenisongole, F. Ndaba, G. Upunda, and J. Zayumba.

PREFACE

The core material for the report was drawn from the 1994 Human Resources Development Survey and supplemented with background reviews of specific sector issues. The report discusses the situation and trends in the social sector and identifies ways that the government, the private sector, and households can use their respective resources most effectively. Chapter 1 provides the background and objectives of the social sector review. Chapter 2 traces the evolution of the social sector in Tanzania and the issues engendered by different policy regimes since the country gained independence. Chapter 3 presents the characteristics of the Tanzanian household; from this characterization, the report draws innovative household-focused, demand-driven policy recommendations. The succeeding chapters review the performance and issues in specific subsectors (Chapter 4 on education, 5 on health, 6 on family planning, 7 on nutrition, and 8 on water and sanitation) and draws conclusions and appropriate responses to deal with these issues. Chapter 9 reviews these same sectors for Zanzibar.

The enthusiasm by which the results of this report have been embraced by the government and its partners is demonstrated by the quick adoption of its prescriptions. In education, two recent initiatives - the community education fund and the scholarship for girls in secondary schools - illustrate the way the study's recommendations are being implemented.

Community Education Fund (CEF) – This is a program designed to help communities improve their primary schools. A participating school community conducts an annual fund-raising campaign and deposits the resources generated in the bank. The government provides a matching grant to the community-generated resources on a ratio of 1:1 or 1:1.5 for poorer communities. The community, through a village committee and the schoolteacher, plans and executes the use of these combined resources to improve school instruction, based on an agreed list of allowable expenditures. Under the roll-out program, by 1999 a total of 357 schools are expected to have established functioning CEFs.

Girls Secondary Education Support (GSES) Program – GSES is a pilot program which provides bursaries for selected secondary-school girls. It aims to increase the enrollment rates of currently under-represented girls in secondary schools by targeting bright students coming from poor families who would otherwise not be able to continue their studies beyond Standard VII. Girls' education is an important investment in Tanzania, as this Social Sector Review shows, for it has important linkages in the improvement of household income, reduction in fertility, and improvement in women's health status. The GSES pilot sites now cover nine districts in six regions. More than a thousand girls are currently enrolled, with the first batch expected to graduate in December 1999.

Since the results of the Social Sector Review were disseminated, the Ministry of Health has revitalized its fee-based cost sharing program, pretested the concept of community health funds, initiated a drug capitalization program for hospitals, reexamined its health policies in light of its burden of disease and cost-effectiveness review, and is launching a health insurance program for civil servants with the enabling Act of Parliament passed in April 1999.

Drug Capitalization Program – Under this program, the Medical Stores Department procures drugs for government health facilities and supplies hospital pharmacies with drugs that they manage as revolving funds based on patient fees. Twenty-three hospitals have been selected for the initial set of participating hospitals and capitalized with an initial stock of 2- to 4-months' supply of drugs. The fee and demand-driven elements of the program are intended to provide a more sustainable arrangement and to inculcate discipline among hospital managers who are now mandated to determine their actual pharmaceutical needs and not reduced to being passive recipients of supplies.

National Health Insurance – Tanzania is in the process of launching a health insurance program that will cover initially 92,000 civil servants or 552,000 persons including dependents. The program will be funded by a mandatory contribution (3% of salary) from the employee and an equal contribution from the government as employer. The program was motivated by the need to increase financial resources to the health sector; to facilitate private financing of curative care; and by allowing members' choice of accredited providers, to introduce demand elements into the historically supply-driven and ill-funded government health facilities. The program is expected to assist the further development of the Tanzanian health care market.

Cost Sharing Program – This user-fee program, formally launched in July 1993, underpins the other initiatives in the health sector. One of the key results of the Social Sector Review was the policy focus on user fees at the hospital level, to be accompanied by a program for dispensaries and clinics that strengthens community participation and moves towards a risk-sharing system (see Community Health Funds below). The Cost Sharing Program has since been expanded to cover all hospitals and in 1998, national policy also allowed dispensaries and health centers to charge modest fees. The program now contributes around 13% of total recurrent costs of the Ministry of Health budget, from a modest contribution of under 1% in 1993/94. There are anecdotal evidence suggesting a variety of efficiency improvements (more reliable supplies at hospitals, better facility upkeep, improved morale of providers, etc.), but there continues to be issues with respect to waivers and exemptions that need to be resolved and for the system to be improved so as not to prevent access to care by the truly indigent.

Community Health Fund (CHF) – This is a village prepayment scheme for health services pretested in Igunga District in 1996; it has since attracted national attention for its ability to mobilize communities to generate revenues for health, identify service needs, and plan for their funding and delivery. Under a typical scheme, a participating household voluntarily prepays Tsh 5,000 a year for the benefit of consultations and drugs provided at the dispensary, health center, or the district hospital outpatient department. Non-CHF members pay the usual Tsh 500 per visit at the dispensary or health center and Tsh 1,000 at the district hospital outpatient department. Those without capacity to pay are protected through community-determined exemptions. As of November 1998, CHFs in five pretest districts already cover some 269,000 household members who have contributed Tsh 131 million in the form of prepayments and user fees. The government plans to replicate these schemes in other districts nationwide.

At the macro level, the Government of Tanzania has also taken major initiatives supportive of the social sector prescriptions made in this study. The budget reform program, through the medium-term expenditure framework, seeks to improve the predictability, sustainability, allocative efficiency, transparency, and accountability of the budget (especially education and health) through a variety of public expenditure management mechanisms such as better sector programming, stricter enforcement of budgetary ceilings, expenditure tracking, and greater performance or results orientation.

The Local Government Reform Program is intended to devolve education and health services to local councils. The implementation will be carried out in three phases beginning January 1999, each phase comprising one third (around 35) of all districts and urban councils. The devolution process is expected to involve a complex set of activities including organizational restructuring, staff retrenchments and hiring under the Civil Service Reform Program, design and use of new fiscal instruments to provide funds to devolved district services, installation of new financial and personnel management systems, and capacity building at central, regional and district levels.

It certainly would take some time before the results of these and other policy reforms in the social sector would be fully realized. And there is always an initial cost involved in the transitory period. But this Social Sector Review has taken a close and candid look at the past and the past left much to be desired. The review has catalyzed the process of change. Perhaps more important than the document itself is the critical catalyzing role that the participatory process played in helping key actors in the government to review the situation, identify key bottlenecks in the system, and take action in innovative ways to implement key changes in the system of financing and providing social services. Now five years into the implementation process, much progress has been made, but the reforms themselves have opened new challenges.

EXECUTIVE SUMMARY

THE MESSAGES

The two main messages of this review echo throughout the document:

- <u>Message 1</u>: Basic education is fundamental to Tanzania's efforts to speed up economic growth and distribute the benefits of growth widely throughout the society. Basic education is a catalyst that increases the impact of other investments in health, nutrition, family planning, and water.

- <u>Message 2</u>: Women in Tanzania are the primary agents of human capital investment. The litmus test of an effective social investment is whether it improves the ability of women to carry out this task.

Put these two messages together, and three recommendations result:

- <u>Recommendation 1</u>: A renewed commitment in Tanzania to getting every child through primary school and improving the quality of the schooling.

- <u>Recommendation 2</u>: A new commitment to getting a large share of the next generation of girls through secondary school.

- <u>Recommendation 3</u>: That other interventions in health, water, nutrition, and family planning be carefully targeted, and if possible, should support these two initiatives.

No institution or country can do everything. Thus our recommendations are selective and focus on a few key commitments by the public sector to human capital investments whose impacts will ripple through the economy and improve the lives of every Tanzanian.

In order to meet the challenges posed by these recommendations, the Government must solve the problems that inhibit the education sector and have existed in Tanzania for at least a decade. These include under-performance, inequitable subsidy patterns, inefficient production, lack of accountability, inadequate choices for users, poor resource mobilization, insufficient local authority and responsibility. In one way or another, the same problems are faced by the other sectors that are reviewed in this document. There is no need to wait to act in these other sectors. However, improving access to, and quality of, primary education, and advancing girls farther through the system, are the top priorities, and will require the concerted efforts of the best minds and managers in Tanzania. Simply allowing parents and communities to take greater responsibility for decisions will go far towards improving the management and efficacy of the limited resources that are available.

THE SOCIAL SECTOR REVIEW

The *Tanzania Social Sector Review* is a product of the Government of Tanzania and The World Bank, plus experts and other interested parties from Tanzania, NGOs, and other bilateral and multilateral donors. The process of producing it has been led by a Government Steering Committee and Technical Committee that worked closely with Tanzanian consultants and Bank staff. Consultants and products were managed by The World Bank.

However imperfect, this process has been uniquely successful in advancing the Government's policy process in the social sectors. In late November 1994, the Government prepared a *Social Sector Strategy*, a direct result of the background work underlying this *Review*. The *Strategy* was presented to donors at the Consultative Group Meeting in Paris in March 1995. In addition, Bank staff have been working with the government to develop pilot projects to test new approaches to human capital investment that follow directly from its *Strategy*.

The main purpose of this report is to focus on social sector outcomes (as opposed to inputs to sector ministries) from a human capital investment perspective. Thus the *Review* is oriented to the demand for social services by households, where most decisions affecting the formation of human capital are made. Treating households as the main producers of human capital, rather than as passive consumers of social services provided by sector ministries, provides an opportunity to consider how inputs from social services combine to produce a healthy, knowledgeable, and skilled population. For comprehensive coverage, however, information on the supply of social services is also provided, and the report is organized along sectoral lines. The reader who persists to the end of the document will find an exhaustive review of the education, health, water, nutrition, and family planning sectors.

ECONOMIC GROWTH AND POVERTY

Economic Growth Since 1980

Figure S.1 shows annual growth rates in GDP for the Tanzanian economy since 1980. Since structural adjustment began in 1984, there has been steady positive growth in the economy, with a large surge in the late 1980s and a period

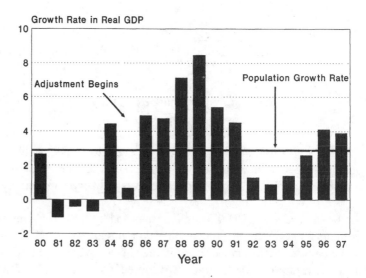

Figure S.1: Tanzania's Record of Growth Since 1980
Source: World Bank Data

of slower growth in the first half of the 1990s. If population growth of about 2.8 percent per year is taken into account, there was substantial improvement in per capita income in the last half of the 1980s, with much slower growth prevailing in the 1990s.

A nationally representative survey conducted for this *Review*, the Tanzania Human Resource Development Survey of 1993/94 (HRDS), asked detailed questions about expenditures to estimate household welfare levels[1]. In addition to information on overall household spending, the survey provides estimates of use and spending patterns for health, education, family planning, and water/sanitation services in Tanzania. The survey is used throughout this report to describe household behavior.

Estimates of household expenditures from the survey suggest that income in Tanzania is probably substantially higher than is measured by national accounts. Figure S.2 compares estimated GDP per capita from the national accounts (the left-most bar) with expenditure estimates from the survey (the remaining bars). For the nation as a whole, cash expenditures are about a third higher than GDP estimates. If nonmarket consumption is included, consumption per capita is about double the estimate of GDP per capita[2]. The bars for rural, urban (other than Dar es Salaam), and Dar es Salaam households show the much higher per capita expenditure levels and greater share of cash in expenditures in urban areas.

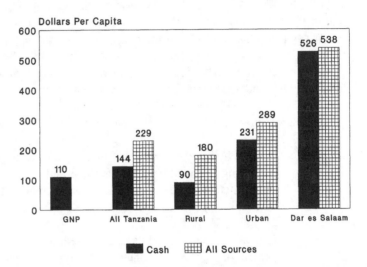

Figure S.2: Estimated Consumption per Capita Compared to GDP Estimate for 1993
Source: HRDS 1993/94

Poverty in Tanzania

The Tanzania Poverty Profile, based on household data from 1991 (it is therefore comparable to the HRDS survey results, not to the GDP estimates), shows that 51 percent of the population had incomes

---

[1] The survey covered approximately 5,000 households from the National Master Sample and was carried out during late 1993 and early 1994 by the Faculty of Economics at the University of Dar es Salaam, the Planning Commission, and the World Bank. It was financed by The World Bank, ODA, and the Government of Japan.

[2] In each pair of bars from the survey, the left bar is cash expenditures, and the right bar is cash plus noncash expenditures, including consumption from own production. GDP estimates are adjusted for estimated own-consumption, so the right bar of each pair, which includes cash plus noncash expenditures, is probably more comparable to GDP estimates. As consumption expenditures are only one of the components of GDP (which also includes investment, government expenditures, and exports minus imports), there is little question that the national accounts substantially underestimate per capita GDP.

of less than $1 per day per person in 1991. Forty-two percent had incomes of less than $0.75 per day[3]. The Poverty Profile suggests that poverty in Tanzania is almost exclusively a rural phenomenon. While 59 percent of the population live in rural areas, about 85 percent of the below-$1-a-day poor, and 90 percent of the below-$0.75-a-day poor, live in the countryside.

A comparison of the 1991 data with another survey from 1983, just before the first structural adjustment program, shows that the resumption of economic growth over the past decade has substantially improved the lot of the poor in Tanzania. In 1983, 65 percent of the population was living on less than $1 a day equivalent, compared to 51 percent in 1991, using prices in 1991 for both years. In terms of the lower poverty line of $0.75 per day, the percent of the population in poverty fell from 51 percent in 1983 to 42 percent in 1991. As a result, there are nearly 2 million fewer people living below $0.75 per day today than in 1983. If there had been no growth in the economy, population growth alone would have swelled the ranks of the poor from 11 million in 1983 to at least 14 million in 1991. Tanzania's success in poverty reduction through growth is an impressive achievement. In fact, the analysis probably understates the improvement that actually took place (Ferreira, 1994).

There are three problems with this picture of general economic improvement:

- Poverty in Tanzania remains primarily a problem of growth. To say the least, it is disturbing to have 50 percent of the population living on less than $1 per day, and the only way to change this situation is to accelerate the rate of economic growth far beyond current levels.

- Growth has been accompanied by greater inequality. The really poor — the bottom 10 percent or so of the income distribution — appear to have fallen behind. They need special attention. Income inequality between cities and the countryside, and even within the countryside, has increased. These problems are probably related to the inequitable distribution of human capital and uneven access to markets, rather than to a maldistribution of other productive assets.

- Tanzania missed a golden opportunity during this period of growth to do a much better job in the social sectors. Children who should be in primary school are not enrolled. The gross primary school enrollment rate should be well over 100 by now (it reached nearly 100 percent in 1979-80), but it has dropped to less than 70 percent[4]. The average age of entry to primary school is far too old, 9 years for girls and almost 10 years for boys in 1993. Tanzania's secondary-school enrollment rate is among the lowest in the entire world. The infant mortality rate has hardly changed over the last decade (Figure S.3).

---

[3] These poverty lines are based on income, but they are adjusted for purchasing power parity and family composition (children require less food than adults to sustain themselves, for example). Poverty lines based on consumption, a more reliable measure of welfare, put 51 percent of the population below the equivalent of $1 per day and 36 percent below the equivalent of $0.75 per day (World Bank 1993, Tanzania: A Poverty Profile, Report No. 12298, December).

[4] The gross primary enrollment rate could exceed 100 percent because it is the total number of children in primary school divided by the number of children in the normal primary school age groups.

These problems cannot be solved by increased per capita income alone. But sustained growth in the economy gives Tanzania some breathing room to begin addressing these problems in the social sectors. Solving them will add to the growth potential of the economy and will contribute directly to improved welfare and an improved distribution of income. These concerns are the starting point for this review, and comprise the principal reason for the government's dedication to finding a new approach in social sector development.

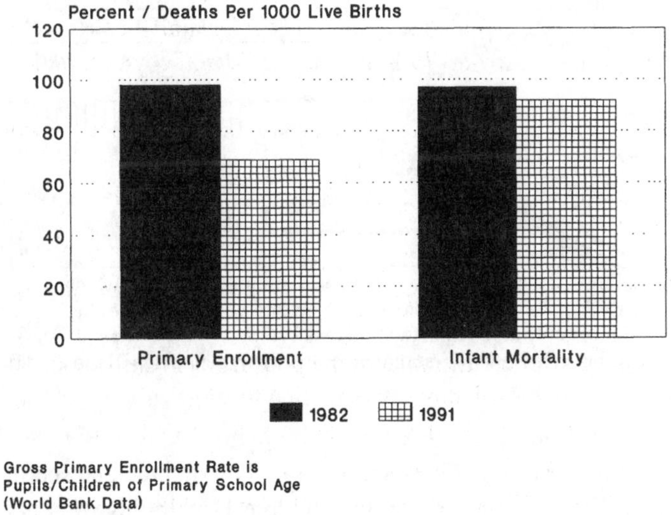

Percent / Deaths Per 1000 Live Births

■ 1982   ▦ 1991

Gross Primary Enrollment Rate is
Pupils/Children of Primary School Age
(World Bank Data)

Figure S.3: Reversal in Education Enrollment and Stagnation in Health Indicators

HUMAN CAPITAL AND ECONOMIC DEVELOPMENT

For *individuals and households*, it is now clear that there are very high private rates of return to investments in schooling and health. The private internal rate of return to schooling in Sub-Saharan Africa is estimated to be 41 percent to primary, 27 percent to secondary, and 28 percent to higher education. For *countries*, the social rate of return to schooling in Sub-Saharan Africa is estimated to be 24, 18, and 1 percent to primary, secondary, and higher education, respectively. There are few investments that governments or parents could make that could compete with the high returns from primary and secondary schooling.

Much of the success of the "East Asia Miracle" in achieving unprecedented rates of growth over the past three decades has been attributed to heavy investment in primary and secondary education by both households and governments. Those economies reduced poverty at rates of up to 7 percent per year growth in per capita GDP. They employed huge pools of previously underemployed labor and spread the benefits of growth widely throughout society. They allowed people to seek internationally competitive returns to these human capital investments by following export-led growth strategies.

Beyond the direct economic benefits, investment in human capital also improves the welfare of individuals and the society as a whole. Even single inputs, such as education, can create several types of benefits. Table S.1 illustrates what we know about these impacts. It shows social services down the left side and human capital-related outcomes across the column headings. Each cell shows the impacts of social services on outcomes. Only the stronger "cross effects" are shaded. Additional education, for example, increases the ability of couples to space their children optimally, which invariably results in lower birthrates. Education also contributes to improved health, better nutrition, and the ability to take advantage of better water and sewerage services to create more healthful living conditions.

Table S.1: Interactions among Social Sector Investments and Human Capital Outcomes

INPUTS FROM SOCIAL SERVICES	IMPACTS ON HUMAN CAPITAL FORMATION				
	Knowledge	Family Size and Child Quality	Health Status	Nutritional Status	Healthful Living Conditions
Education		▓	▓	▓	▓
Family planning			▓	+	
Health	+	+		▓	+
Nutrition	+		▓		
Water and Sanitation			▓	+	

Note: The strongest cross-sector effects are shaded. The two cells surrounded by heavy lines with no shading indicate high potential for carefully targeted interventions. All of the diagonal cells could be shaded, of course, but in this table only cross-effects are considered.

Source: This is the authors' summary of the general findings of the empirical literature.

Similar cross effects are generated by other social sector services. Family planning investments improve the health of mothers and children. Health investments improve nutritional status because of the link between a high disease burden and nutritional failure. This link works in the other direction as well: improved nutrition raises the body's resistance to disease. A healthier environment resulting from better water and sanitation services can have positive health impacts and are complementary to many other investments, such as education and nutrition. In addition, targeted health and nutrition interventions before and during the primary school years have positive impacts on educational outcomes.

Four messages emerge from this framework. First, *education is the key producer of cross benefits*. It has large impacts across the board for the individual receiving the investment in terms of higher earning potential, cross effects in generating additional human capital investments, and improved welfare for the individual. Second, *education for women has large external or "multiplier" benefits*. Because women bear children and care for them in the crucial early years, but also because of women's traditional role as cultivators in Tanzania, investments in schooling for women have the largest impact in creating additional human capital and in improving living conditions. Third, *targeted health, nutrition, and sanitation investments can have high cross-benefits*, especially for school children. Fourth, *health is the major "user" of cross benefits*. Almost all of the other sectors have strong impacts on improved health outcomes because better health is the result of many different inputs.

Human capital investments provide a stream of returns for their whole lives even if they do not own other property. In fact, human capital is often the only asset the poor and women own. It cannot be sold or stolen from them once they get it. For women, schooling and good health provide a stream of returns not only for themselves but also for their families, and especially for their young children. Because education has strong cross effects, it is possible to get large payoffs across the board by emphasizing primary and secondary education, especially education for girls.

THE TANZANIAN HOUSEHOLD

The production of human capital is managed by the household, especially by mothers, and the money the government spends in the social sectors is absorbed by households in pursuit of their goals. What do Tanzanian households look like? How are they using social services? How much are they spending to accomplish their objectives in human capital formation? How are they using government subsidies? How do they view the social services available to them? In this section, we start with a few general facts about households.

Household Expenditures

Consumption of purchased and home-produced goods and services in Tanzania is shown in Table S.2 in Tsh and in Table S.3 in US dollars[5]. A high proportion of expenditures for the average household in 1993, about 72 percent, was for food. Health accounted for only 1.9 percent, and education only 1.4 percent, of expenditures. Urban residents and the rich spent a lot more on *health* in both absolute and percentage terms than did the rural poor. However, *education* is different. It accounted for only 1.2 percent of expenditures in both rural areas and Dar es Salaam, but 2.0 percent in other cities.

Although we provide per capita expenditures, we prefer discussing expenditures per adult equivalent, because it standardizes across households by taking into account that children consume less than adults. Household expenditure per adult equivalent was Tsh

Table S.2: Annual Household Expenditures in 1994/95 (Cash and Consumed Production) in Tanzania (Tsh)

		Rural	*Urban*[a]	*DSM*	*All*
Expenditures		664,116	910,905	1,487,092	776,604
	Food	76.1%	66.4%	61.1%	71.5%
	Health	1.7%	2.2%	2.3%	1.9%
	Education	1.2%	2.0%	1.2%	1.4%
	Other	21.0%	29.3%	35.4%	25.2%
Per Capita Expenditures		119,425	191,375	356,657	152,063
Per Adult Equivalent		186,917	281,846	523,328	231,421
	Poorest 20%	68,378	94,365	187,889	74,048
	Richest 20%	366,519	568,451	1,053,901	484,295

[a] Urban means cities other than Dar es Salaam (DSM)
Source: HRDS, 1993/94 inflated to 1994/95 levels, World Bank 1997

Table S.3: Annual Household Expenditures (Cash and Consumed Production) in Tanzania, 1993 (US$)

	Rural	*Urban*	*DSM*	*All*
Expenditures	1,001	1,373	2,242	1,171
Food	762	1,045	1,706	891
Health	17	23	38	20
Education	12	16	27	14
Other	210	288	471	246
Per Capita Expenditures	180	289	538	229
Per Adult Equivalent	282	425	789	349
Poorest 20%	103	142	283	112
Richest 20%	551	857	1,589	730

Note: Exchange rate: Tsh. 495 per dollar
Source: HRDS, 1993/94.

172,702 in 1993, or about $350. The poorest 20 percent of the population had adult equivalent expenditures equal to only 32 percent of this amount, the richest about 210 percent. In short, the poor are extremely poor, and tend to live in rural areas, while the rich are heavily concentrated in Dar es Salaam.

---

[5] The population surveyed was ranked by total household expenditures, then divided into five groups, or expenditure quintiles, each representing 20 percent of the national population. The data in Table S.2 and Table S.3 have already been summarized in Figure S.2.

Demographics

All national averages in Tanzania are driven by the characteristics of the rural population (59 percent of the total). For example, the average household in 1993 was composed of about 6 people; 6.3 in rural households, 5.0 in Dar es Salaam, and 5.8 in other cities. The richest households were about one person smaller (5.0) than the average, and the poorest households were about one person larger (7.2).

The head of the household averaged about 44 years of age. The poorest household heads were about 2 years older than the average, and the richest household heads were about 2 years younger. This is the reverse of the typical pattern throughout the world, which is for younger household heads to be poorer. However, poor households in Tanzania do follow world patterns in having more children who are below the age of 15, as compared to the richest households (3.4 versus 2.1 youngsters).

There are fewer men than women in Tanzania, with 0.97 men for every woman. In Dar es Salaam, there are only 0.9 men for every woman. About 15 percent of all households were headed by a woman in 1993/94, but female-headed households were 18 percent of the highest income households and only 13 percent of the poor households, the reverse of what we observe in other countries.

GOVERNMENT SOCIAL SECTOR SPENDING

Domestic Resources

Government spending in the social sectors is widely acknowledged to be inadequate for operating the extensive public network of health facilities, water systems, and schools. The poor performance of the social sectors has not been due to a lack of fiscal effort. The social sector's share of recurrent government spending grew from 24 percent in 1991/92 to 39 percent in 1994/95. However, the Government's approved expenditure estimates indicate that the social sector's share of spending likely dropped back to about 23 percent in 1995/96.

Table S.4: Total Government Budget Estimates, 1994/95

	Actual Expenditures (Tsh billion)	Share of Recurrent Expenditures (%)
Gross Recurrent Expenditures	372.7	100
Social Sectors	149.7	39
Education	83.0	22
Health	57.0	15
Water	5.4	1
Other	4.3	1
Development Expenditures	20.0	
Total Expenditures	392.7	

Source: Follmer and Kessy, 1996; World Bank, 1997.

Approximate recurrent spending per capita was US$4.99 in education, US$3.43 in health, and US$3.78 in water[6]. While these amounts may look small, they are high for eastern Africa. In education, Tanzania's recurrent spending in 1990 was estimated to be 5.8 percent of GNP, compared to 4.9 percent in Ethiopia, 6.8 percent in Kenya, and 2.9 percent in Uganda. In health, Tanzania's recurrent government spending on health accounts for 2.4 percent of GDP in 1993/94, compared to 0.9 percent in Eritrea, 1.9 percent in Ethiopia, 1.3 percent in

---

[6] These figures are based on an exchange rate of Tsh 575 per dollar and an estimated population of 28.9 million. The health and education figures were taken from Follmer and Kessy (1996). The water figure was estimated by inflating data from World Bank (1994a) to 1995 levels.

Kenya, and 0.6 percent in Uganda.

Further proof of Tanzania's high level of commitment to the social sectors is growth in the number of civil service personnel devoted to health and education (Figure S.4). In fact, in education during the 1980s, enrollments declined as the supply of teachers continued to expand. During the period of civil service reform during the 1990s, service providers in education and health were exempted. Notwithstanding this high degree of commitment, three characteristics of the social sectors have severely distorted the budget and the distribution of benefits from that budget, including a huge social infrastructure, a large civil service to operate it, and a commitment to provide comprehensive services free to every citizen.

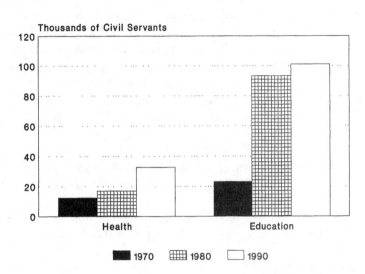

Figure S.4: Growth in Civil Service Personnel in Health and Education
Source: See Tables 2.1 and 2.2.

Salary and examination expenditures dominate the recurrent social sector budget. The government currently allocates Tsh 13,100 (about $22.80) per primary school student (including donor supplements). This expenditure pays for little more than Tsh 8,842 ($15.38) for salaries and emoluments, Tsh 3,353 ($5.83) for primary school exams, materials, and a handful of other non-instructional items. Furthermore, our investigation in 8 districts suggests that only about 68 percent of allocated funds actually get to the primary schools for instruction. In health, at the health center and dispensary level, personal emoluments absorb about 67 percent of government recurrent spending.[7]

Because of the government's commitment to a comprehensive system, high-cost institutions absorb a very large share of spending. In education, thousands of primary schools absorb 58 percent of the budget, while a handful of technical schools and colleges absorb 23 percent of the budget. Throughout the 1990's, primary and university spending has increased as a share of total education expenditures while secondary school's share of the budget has declined. In health, about 1,500 dispensaries and health centers consume 31 percent of the recurrent budget, compared to 59 percent consumed by fewer than 100 referral, regional, and district hospitals. Over the course of the 1990's, funding to health centers has steadily increased as a share of the health budget, and despite a slight dip in 1995, is projected to continue to do so. Regional and district hospitals' share of spending has dropped considerably.

The high-cost colleges and hospitals are not lavishly funded institutions. They are run on a

---

[7] Figures for health and education spending are based on Follmer and Kessy (1996). Figures for water spending are based on World Bank (1997).

shoestring. But the resulting distortion in the allocation of resources to low-return investments is extraordinary. In education, for example, the government and donors together annually spend (apart from the Tsh 13,100 (US$23) per primary student discussed above), Tsh 95,300 (US$165.74) per secondary student and Tsh 3,324,200 (US$5,781) per college student. Given the high social rate of return to primary school investment, each shilling of subsidy transferred from a college student to a primary school student by the government would generate a 23 percent greater return. In health, the internal rate of return to expensive curative interventions provided principally by hospitals is estimated at -21 percent. Each shilling transferred from these services to community interventions to reduce malaria, for example, would increase the rate of return by 32 percent, to a positive rate of 11 percent.

Finally, the government is inefficient as a provider of these services. The average unit costs (recurrent only) in public secondary schools were estimated at Tsh 73,000 per year in 1992, and Tsh 60,000 in private institutions. Yet a study based on data from 1981 found that a private secondary-school student would be expected to perform 16 percent better on mathematics and verbal examinations than would a public secondary-school student with comparable family background. In short, the same amount of learning in private schools was found to cost only 59 percent of the cost in public schools.

Donor Spending

Net official development assistance in recent years has comprised approximately 40 percent of Tanzania's GDP. In 1991, external assistance represented about US$43 on a per capita basis, making Tanzania one of the world's most dependent countries.

In 1994/95, donors funded about 5 percent of all government expenditures in education, 13 percent of expenditures in health, and 48 percent of expenditures in water and sanitation. In education, however, only 41 percent of external assistance is devoted to primary education. In health, donors do better. Approximately 70 percent of the donor supplement goes to preventive services and 30 percent to curative services, principally to basic services delivered in dispensaries and health centers[8].

Summary

Overall, the expenditure statistics paint a bleak picture of a public system that is far more extensive than the budget can fund under almost any reasonable scenario. Despite the government's emphasis on basic education and health services, their allocations to comprehensive, highly subsidized services result in actual expenditures that have a different emphasis. High-cost institutions crowd out low-cost basic services. High personnel costs crowd out all other inputs, so that basic education and health services function poorly. In both sectors, substantial claims on the budget are made by activities with very low investment payoffs to the economy. Donors supplement domestic spending in a fairly positive way in health, but they distort education spending away from primary education.

Spending more money alone will not solve the budgetary problems in these sectors, as spending is already high for such a poor country. Even if social sector spending were doubled to 78 percent of the government's recurrent budget, which is impossible, this would not be enough money to adequately fund

---

[8] Figures for health and education spending are based on Follmer and Kessy (1996). Figures for water spending are based on World Bank (1997).

everything the government has promised to do or to adequately fund the system that now exists. In education, for example, doubling the public expenditure per primary student would have a large impact, but it would only return real spending per student to the level reached in 1970. It would still be only about one-half of what Kenya spends per student. Moreover, because the real salaries of teachers in 1990 was the same as in 1980, and their salaries are among the lowest in Africa, it is likely that doubling spending would not result in a substantially improved mix of inputs. Higher spending would not eliminate the need for rationalization of social sector spending and for greater selectivity. The government is spread too thin, and as a result, the budget does not reflect its stated priorities.

EXPENDITURES IN THE SOCIAL SECTORS

Table S.5 summarizes the overall picture for social sector spending by showing estimates for total spending on education, health, and water from all sources for 1994/95. Almost all household spending in this table is cash, rather than in-kind. Tanzania was devoting about 5 percent of GDP to both education and health, and about 1 percent to water. The water data does not include the imputed cost of labor required for fetching water, which would dwarf all other expenditures in the table. Government was providing about 70 percent of the current cost of education, 51 percent of the cost of health care, and nearly 40 percent of the cash cost of water. Donors contributed from 4 to 34 percent of funds to each sector, favoring water over health and education in terms of their share of total sector spending. Households provided 30 percent of the cash costs of water, 26 percent of education costs, and 42 percent of health costs directly out of their pockets.

Table S.5: Total Expenditures on the Social Sectors from All Sources, 1994/95

	Expenditures (Tsh billion)	Percent of GDP	Percent of Sector Expenditures
Education			
Total	120.510	5.3	100
Government	84.350	3.7	70
Household	31.209	1.4	26
Donor	4.952	0.2	4
Health			
Total	114.764	5.0	100
Government	58.579	2.6	51
Household	47.803	2.1	42
Donor	8.382	0.4	7
Water			
Total	18.651	0.8	100
Government	6.787	0.3	36
Household	5.556	0.2	30
Donor	6.308	0.3	34
Total			
Total	253.925	11.1	100
Government	149.715	6.6	59
Household	84.567	3.7	33
Donor	19.642	0.9	8

Source: Government and donor health and education data from Follmer and Kessy, 1996; household data estimated from HRDS (1993/94) and inflated to 1995 levels; water data from World Bank (1997).

Households devote about 68 percent of their education expenditures to primary schooling and 32 percent to secondary schooling. They spend very little for higher levels of education because those levels are most heavily subsidized and because few households are able to take advantage of those opportunities. Virtually all household expenditures on health are for acute care for simple health problems. The exact nature of household spending will be explored in more detail in the next several sections, but the important points to bear in mind are that (a) households contribute a substantial share of resources, even in this heavily subsidized system, for all types of social services; (b) households have their priorities right — they are making high return investments in basic education and health care; and (c) as the system is currently structured, they have very little voice in how their contributions, both out-of-pocket and government subsidies, are channeled. Thus they have little opportunity to influence the productive efficiency or quality of the social services that they consume.

WHO BENEFITS FROM GOVERNMENT AND DONOR SUBSIDIES?

Table S.6 presents the distribution of benefits from public spending in Tanzania's social sectors. These estimates are derived from household expenditure patterns for social services, plus total government and donor expenditures for each type of government service. If benefits were distributed equally, each quintile would receive a 20 percent share of each row item[9].

Table S.6: Distribution of Benefits of Social Sector Expenditures, by Sector, Recurrent and Development Budgets by Expenditure Quintile, FY93/94

	Lowest	<<<	Quintile	>>>	Highest
	1	2	3	4	5
Education					
Primary	19	22	21	20	18
Secondary	8	14	17	24	36
University	0	0	0	0	100
Overall	14	16	16	17	38
Health					
Preventive	20	20	20	20	20
Health Center/Dispensary	19	27	18	18	19
Hospital	16	16	15	20	34
Overall	17	21	16	19	27
Water	11	11	15	23	41
Total for Social Sectors	15	18	16	17	34

Source: HRDS, 1993/94; World Bank, 1994a.

Education. The benefits of primary education expenditures are fairly evenly distributed across expenditure groups, but the upper two quintiles capture 60 percent of secondary school, and 100 percent of university subsidies[10]. The overall incidence of subsidies for education is consequently quite skewed toward the rich, as the highest expenditure quintile captures almost 40 percent of government spending, and the lowest only 14 percent. For the middle three groups, however, the distribution is fairly equal.

Health. The benefits of health services are also skewed to the highest expenditure quintile, but not as much as for education. This is partly due to the fairly equitable distribution of health center and dispensary subsidies, and the fact that the rich can opt out of the government system and pay for mission or private-sector services. They typically do not have that option in education because of the government monopoly at the primary and university levels. The highest quintile does, however, capture the largest share of the overall health budget, principally because it is the heaviest user of expensive hospital services.

---

[9] In making these estimates, we were conservative in the sense that we tried rounding off so as to make the distribution look more equal rather than less equal.

[10] The university line is based on a sample of only a few people.

Water Subsidies. The distribution of public subsidies for water is highly skewed toward the rich because prices for water are among the most highly subsidized in the world. Most access comes through the municipal water systems in Dar es Salaam, Arusha, and other secondary cities where the bulk of the higher- income population lives. As a result, the lowest expenditure quintile receives only about 11 percent of the subsidy placed on water, while the highest quintile receives 41 percent of the subsidy.[11]

Overall. The health sector performs relatively well in distributing its expenditures evenly across the population, while the education and water sectors appear increasingly distorted in favor of the rich. The result is a distribution of benefits overall that leaves the poorer 60 percent of the population with 49 percent of the benefits, and the top 40 percent of the population with 51 percent of the benefits. The highest expenditure quintile alone captures 34 percent of all subsidies, principally through education and water. The main reason for the skewed result at the upper level is the ability of the urban high-income population to capture the more expensive public subsidies that come through urban-based facilities – hospitals, universities, water systems, and secondary schools.

In short, the government's scarce resources are targeted disproportionately to the richest segment of the population. Donors improve the distribution of benefits in health, but worsen it in education and water. Achieving an even distribution of subsidies, 20 percent to each quintile, would be one way to improve the current system. That could be accomplished by leaving the system as it stands and adding new resources to basic services in education, health, and rural water. But skewing the distribution toward the poor would be more in line with government policies. That could be achieved by increasing resources at the lower levels, plus moving resources from the upper levels to the lower levels of the system, either through reallocation or charging user fees in the more expensive parts of the systems (hospitals and the university). The government has begun to do just that.

Improving equity in the distribution of benefits also improves the efficiency of the system. Using the earlier example, moving a shilling from university education to primary education increases the rate of return by 23 percent. It also increases the likelihood that the shilling will be captured by a poor household. We estimate that in health, a reform package that raises spending by $1 per capita and redistributes it to cost-effective community and preventive interventions would eliminate 12 percent of life years currently lost, and would tilt the distribution of subsidies toward the poor (World Bank, 1995b).

The next sections discuss major issues in each social sector covered by the *Review*. The emphasis is on household use, expenditure patterns, and outcomes.

---

[11] Water figures for 1994/95 were not available. Estimates of the distribution of benefits for health and education in 1994/95 were calculated based on the 1994/95 division of expenditures across subsectors assuming that each quintile's share of subsector benefits had not changed. For example, assuming that the distribution of benefits across quintiles for primary school, secondary school, and university had not changed, the distribution of total education benefits was recalculated using the 1994/95 distribution of expenditures across levels of education. Using this approach, it is estimated that the lowest expenditure quintile received 13 percent of education expenditures in 1994/95, the second lowest 16 percent, the middle quintile 15 percent, the second highest 15 percent, and the highest 41 percent of the benefits. Thus, the highest expenditure quintile appears to have increased their share of total education benefits. Using this same technique to estimate the distribution of health expenditures, the lowest quintile received approximately 17 percent of health spending in 1994/95, the second lowest 19 percent, the middle quintile 16 percent, the second highest 19 percent, and the highest quintile of the population 28 percent. Thus, the distribution of health benefits appears not to have changed from the previous year.

EDUCATION

Primary School Enrollment

In the household survey, we found that most children are attending school between the ages of 10 and 14. Between ages 7 and 9, only 32 percent of the children are in school, between ages 10 and 14, 82 percent, and between ages 15 and 19, attendance drops to 36 percent. In each age group, the poor are least likely to attend. Of those children starting school in 1993, the average age was 9.8 and 9.0 for boys and girls, respectively, and with little variation across income groups. Ninety-nine percent of children attend government schools. Approximately equal numbers of boys and girls are in primary school.

Expenditures on Primary Education

On average, Tanzanian families spend Tsh 5,148 per pupil in primary school. Rural households spend the least (Tsh 3,950 per pupil) and households in Dar es Salaam spend the most (Tsh 13,368 per pupil). Per-pupil expenditures vary across the welfare distribution as one might expect, with wealthier households paying about 3 to 4 times as much per student as poorer households. As shown in Table S.7, for example, a very poor household in a rural area spends Tsh 2,663 per student per year, while a wealthy rural household spends an estimated Tsh 7,295 per student.

Table S.7: Estimated Household Expenditures per Student Enrolled in Primary School, 1995 (Tsh)

Residence	Lowest Expenditure Quintile	Highest Expenditure Quintile	All
Dar es Salaam	8,916	27,639	13,368
Other Urban	3,926	14,408	7,314
Rural	2,663	7,295	3,950
All	2,692	10,973	5,148

Source: HRDS, 1993/94, inflated to 1995 levels.

Public spending of about US$22.78 per primary student is allocated almost entirely to teachers' salaries and emoluments. Parents add Tsh 5,123 (US$8.91) to this amount for a total of about Tsh 18,223 (US$31.69). It is hard to detect, however, what they get for this money in terms of schooling for their children. Fifty percent of the parents' contribution goes for uniforms. Another 19 percent goes for fees and other assessments, for which there is little or no

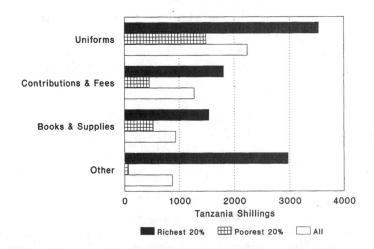

Figure S.5: Components of Per Student Primary Expenditures
Source: HRDS 1993/94

accountability. The school fee, essentially a sales tax on primary education, accrues to the district, where it is lost in the pool of general revenue. The final 20 percent of parents' expenditure is for school supplies. For the poor, these three categories account for 99 percent of spending, but for the rich, they account for 74 percent. The rich are able to add an additional amount on tutors and other expenses (such as clubs, extracurricular activities, pocket money, and so on). The relative size of these components can be seen in Figure S.5.

Thus, Tanzania has a primary school system of teachers and students, and not much more. The teacher is paid by the central government, and is often no more than a primary-school leaver with a little extra in-service training. Government and parents add a bit over Tsh 1,100 in school supplies. The school facilities are run down, since nearly nothing is spent on maintenance. There are 5 students per desk, the average teacher does not have a chair and a desk, and children typically eat little or no food all day. It is illegal for a child to own a textbook, yet the government cannot get textbooks to the schools.

For whatever reason, primary schooling in Tanzania is characterized by a long-term declining enrollment rate with quite late entry and early exit. Virtually everyone attends a government school. Tanzania has achieved parity at the primary level for boys and girls. Some of the richer parents are using tutors to supplement the schooling of their primary-age children. The problems of how to get more children, especially girls, into school earlier, and how to make schools more effective, are of paramount importance.

Consumers' Evaluation of Primary Education Services

The household survey asked respondents to rank characteristics of primary schools according to their importance to the household and to evaluate the closest government primary school relative to the same characteristics. Table S.8 contains descriptive statistics on these rankings. Parents agree that the quality of personnel is important, and they rate the quality of personnel as relatively good, with only 14 to 21 percent of the sample thinking that the teachers are either poor or very poor[12]. Parents consider school supplies to be as important as teachers in the evaluation of schools. The foregoing evidence shows that these items have been squeezed out of the government budget by salaries.

Table S.8: Households' Priorities and Perceptions of Government Primary Schools

Primary School Characteristic	Ranking [a]	Percent Very Poor or Poor	Percent Good or Very Good
Quality of Teachers	5.0	21	33
Adequate Supplies	4.9	49	13
Quality of Headmaster	3.8	14	49
Physical Infrastructure	3.3	44	16
Self Reliance Work	3.0	19	30
Primary School Curriculum:			
Math and Science	4.2	21	22
English	4.1	39	16
Kiswahili	3.7	12	35
Good Behavior	3.4	27	19

[a] The ranking can range from 0 to 20. This column shows the average across the national sample.
Source: HRDS, 1993/94.

---

[12] The household survey responses are much more favorable towards personnel than responses derived from qualitative studies. Typically, focus-group respondents vehemently complain about the lack of conscientiousness and integrity of the teaching staff in local primary schools. Focus groups conducted for this Review found that the most prevalent complaints raised by parents were about personnel when asked about problems with primary schools in eight districts.

Forty-nine percent of households say that school supplies are either poor or very poor. Parents indicate that math, science, and English are the highest priorities in the curriculum. On English, though, 39 percent rate the schools as either poor or very poor.

Willingness to Pay for Primary Schools

Figure S.6 shows how much respondents were willing to pay for a primary school that delivered the types of services they thought were important. The average amount the whole sample would be willing to pay for one student for one year is Tsh 11,486, a few thousand shillings more than the current average household expenditures per primary student. About 18 percent of the respondents indicate that they would pay nothing. About 31 percent of the sample would pay Tsh 1,340 to 4,020 for all school costs, another 31 percent would pay between Tsh 6,700 and 17,420, and a full 22 percent would pay over Tsh 26,800, with most of those over Tsh 33,500.

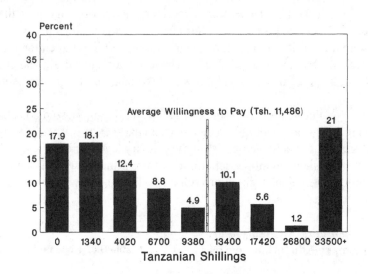

Figure S.6: Willingness to Pay All Costs, One Year, for Primary School
Source: HRDS 1993/94

That a fifth of the sample gives a response higher than the maximum asked in the survey is surprising because the assumption of such questionnaires is that we are getting *lower bound* responses on willingness to pay, as households sensibly make offers lower than what they would actually pay.

In the context of the willingness-to-pay questions, we should address the issue of cost recovery from users. If there is any expansion of the quantity or quality of services, the government will have to pay attention to how the improvements are financed, including the roles of both government and households in footing the bill. Households pay the bill whether through taxes or direct payments, so cost sharing in this context is really a question of clarifying who benefits and who pays.

These responses also tell us a lot about how households might react to very costly investments in specific characteristics such as the physical condition of school buildings. It is clear that parents value the inputs that make schools work, namely teachers and supplies. They want to see the schools teach basic numeracy and literacy, plus English. They do not think the schools perform very well in most of these areas, but they would highly value, and would be willing to contribute more to, schools that provide these services adequately.

Secondary Education

Very few Tanzanian children have the opportunity to attend a secondary school, whether government or private (only 7 percent of children entering Standard I make it through to Form I, or eighth grade). In the whole of Tanzania, there were only about 176,000 secondary students in 1992[13]. Of those in the survey attending secondary school in 1993/94, 39 percent attended a government school, 17 percent a church-related school, 32 percent a private secular school, and 12 percent a community school. The rich dominated all types of secondary schools except community schools, where 11 percent of the students were from the poorest households and 9 percent came from the richest. The rest came from the middle three expenditure groups. About one-half of the students were in boarding school, the remainder in day school, and there was virtually no difference across the sexes.

Gender is an important concern at the secondary level. The gender ratio of secondary students for the whole country is fairly even, at 46 percent girls and 54 percent boys. While there is near-gender parity in enrollments at entry into government secondary schools, girls are far less likely than boys to continue on to upper secondary school (Forms V and VI). They enter secondary school at a deficit, since the cut-off point for girls' selection into government secondary school is approximately 10 points lower than for boys. As a result, they do worse during secondary school and are more likely to drop out. In upper secondary schools, only about 25 percent of the students are female. The top 10 ranking schools in the national Form IV examinations in 1992 were all-male seminaries. Out of the total enrollment in the 30 top-performing schools on Form IV exams, only 17 percent of the students are female. At the university, only 13 percent of students were female in 1990, compared to 18 percent in 1980.

Expenditures on Secondary School

Parents with children in secondary school spent an average of Tsh 55,527 (US$97) per student in 1994/95. In rural areas, a poor household with a child in secondary school pays somewhat less per student than the richest households (Tsh 45,058 and 59,977, respectively). However, the urban poor spend much less than the rural poor, and they spend only one-half to one-fourth of what the rich spend (see Table S.9).

Table S.9: Average Household Expenditures per Student Enrolled in Secondary School per Year, by Expenditure Quintile, 1994/95 (Tsh)

Residence	Lowest Expenditure Quintile	Highest Expenditure Quintile	All
Dar es Salaam	35,803	117,140	65,901
Other Urban	35,412	77,985	55,867
Rural	45,058	59,977	53,650
All	38,039	71,902	55,527

Source: HRDS, 1993/94, inflated to 1994/95 levels.

About 36 percent of household expenditures on secondary school are for fees and contributions. Transportation and boarding costs account for 28 percent of expenditures. Sixteen percent of expenditures are for uniforms, 13 percent for books and supplies, and 7 percent for miscellaneous costs (Mason and Khandker, 1997).

---

[13] There were approximately 2,338,560 children aged 14-17, the age that typically attends Forms I-IV, and another 1,088,640 aged 18-19, the age of children in Forms V and VI. Thus, 176,000 students represent only 5 percent of the total number eligible for all 6 levels of secondary school.

Summary

Entry to secondary school in Tanzania has historically been rationed in the interest of manpower planning, to avoid producing more students than could be absorbed by the public sector, and to increase equality of opportunity in the population. Thanks to the law of unintended consequences, this policy has had many negative effects on human capital formation. Tanzania has succeeded in producing so few secondary students that it shares with Malawi the distinction of having the lowest secondary-school gross enrollment rate in the world. Comparisons with almost any other country are alarming. Uganda, despite being racked by civil violence for almost two decades and spending only a fraction as much on education, raised its gross secondary enrollment rate from 3.7 percent in 1970 to 13.0 percent in 1992[14]. Over the same period, Tanzania's rate rose from 2.7 to 5.0 percent. Rationing has deprived the country of a huge stock of human capital, channeled public subsidies for secondary school to the rich, and distorted its income distribution (World Bank, 1994b). The failure to get girls through secondary school has reduced the impact of other costly investments Tanzania has made in health, nutrition, family planning, water, and sanitation.

The de facto liberalization of secondary schooling in 1986 has begun to relieve this constraint. Up to 1985, the gross secondary enrollment rate was 3.3 percent, and it did not rise to 4.7 percent until after private schools started opening for business. The supply response to this change in policy has been incredible, despite continuing price controls on secondary-school fees, taxation of fees, absorption of the best students by government schools, and other roadblocks put in the way of private schools. The public sector now enrolls less than one-half of all secondary students. The change is due not to a decline in the number of spaces in public sector schools but to growth in private non-public secondary schools. The high expenditures of the rural poor for the few places they are able to capture in secondary schools is surprising, and is an indicator of the importance they attach to education as a way out of poverty. It will take many years, however, for Tanzania to recover from its original decision to ration education.

HEALTH

Burden of Disease and Health Spending

Table S.10 shows the top ten causes of mortality in Tanzania and eastern Africa (Eritrea, Ethiopia, Kenya, Tanzania, and Uganda).[15] These ten diseases alone account for nearly 77 percent of the life years lost annually in Tanzania. The mortality profile of Tanzania is similar to that of the region, although malaria and AIDS are more serious problems in Tanzania, and diseases among children under 5 and pregnant women account for a much smaller share of total life years lost in Tanzania relative to the other countries in the region. Cardiovascular disease and injury are gaining slightly in importance.

---

[14] In purchasing power parity equivalents, Uganda spent US$148.9 million on education in 1970, US$39.1 million in 1980, and US$106.3 million in 1985. Tanzania spent US$392.6, US$439.5, and US$386.6 million in each of those years (International Institute for Educational Planning, 1994; World Bank, 1995a).

[15] This section is based on information from World Bank 1995 "Health Policy in Eastern Africa: A Structured Approach to Resource Allocation," Report No. 14040 AFR, March 14.

This success is not accidental, as Tanzania has devoted considerable resources over the past two decades to providing basic health services through the public sector. Table S.11 shows this in absolute terms for FY1993/94. The table includes spending from all sources, including households, government, and donors. Because of the high labor element in health care costs, and to compare expenditures across countries, this table converts half of expenditures to the purchasing power parity equivalent in dollars. Tanzania spends more per capita than Eritrea, Ethiopia, and Kenya, and about double the amount per capita recommended by *The World Development Report 1993* (WDR). It distributes the expenditures across intervention categories in nearly the same proportion as recommended by the WDR. Thus its relatively good performance in the health sector can be explained partially by its high spending and effective allocations of expenditures. However, much of the spending on community and preventive interventions is driven by donors.

The relative position of the government's own health sector budget is shown in Table S.12. Tanzania's recurrent budget is skewed toward curative services, and close to the regional average. Tanzania has used high total spending to "buy down" avoidable mortality due to childhood diseases. However, the most effective spending in this regard is being provided by donors. While this role is a common one for donors to play, it leaves Tanzania and the region dependent on outside funds for its high-impact health care spending.

Perhaps more importantly, Tanzania appears to have a very inefficient system. With a lower overall level of spending and about the same

Table S.10: Eastern Africa Regional Comparison of Burden of Disease, 1993

Cause of Death	Percent of Life Years Lost	
	Tanzania	Eastern Africa
Perinatal/Maternal	22.9	23.3
Malaria	18.2	9.8
Diarrhea	7.5	12.7
AIDS	6.0	4.7
Injury	5.9	2.3
Pneumonia	5.7	11.7
Tuberculosis	4.8	4.2
Cardiovascular	3.5	2.4
Measles	1.0	2.3
Protein-Calorie Malnutrition	0.9	3.3
Total Target Causes	76.5	76.9
All Other Causes	23.5	23.1
Total	100.0	100.0
Diseases of Children < 5 and pregnant women	38.0	53.4

Source: Ravicz 1996

Table S.11: Purchasing Power Parity Adjusted Per Capita Health Care Expenditures, by Type of Intervention

Country	Purchasing Power Parity Adjusted US$ Per Capita			
	Community	Preventive	Curative	Total
Eritrea	0.17	0.85	7.27	8.28
Ethiopia	0.33	1.01	4.97	6.31
Kenya	1.41	4.44	15.13	20.98
Tanzania	2.63	7.92	14.02	24.58
Uganda	5.70	5.89	21.72	33.31

Note: This table adjusts one-half of the expenditure by the PPP. adjustment factor for that country.
Source: Ravicz, 1996

Table S.12: Government Health Care Expenditures, by Type of Intervention

Country	Share of Total Government Expenditures			
	Community	Preventive	Curative	Total
Eritrea	1.3	8.3	90.4	100.0
Ethiopia	8.5	13.0	78.5	100.0
Kenya	7.9	15.5	76.6	100.0
Tanzania	6.7	15.4	77.9	100.0
Uganda[1]	13.4	24.5	62.1	100.0
E. Africa	8.1	15.3	76.6	100.0

[1] Note that if water expenditures were omitted from the Ugandan data, the Community share of total government spending would decline from 13 percent to 10 percent.
Source: Ravicz, 1996

pattern of government allocations, Kenya is able to achieve 8 years' longer life expectancy, over a third lower infant mortality rate, over a third lower child mortality rate, and a total fertility rate that is an average of one child lower. Table S.13 shows the results of a simulation of how each country in the region would fare if part of the government budget were reallocated and an additional exogenous infusion of US$2 per capita were spent by the government on the most effective community and

Table S.13: Simulated Impact of Reallocation and Spending Increase on Under-Five Mortality Rate

	East Africa	Eritrea	Ethiopia	Kenya	Tanzania	Uganda
Current Under-5 Mortality Rate per 1,000	172	203	205	102	148	205
Percent Reduction with Reallocation and Additional $2 Per Capita Spending	40	38	37	82	14	44
Post-Reform Under-5 Mortality Rate per 1,000	104	125	130	19	127	116

Source: Ravicz, 1996.

preventive interventions. If we ignore Kenya and just compare Tanzania with other east African countries, Tanzania achieves only a 14 percent reduction in under-five mortality. With this small additional expenditure, the other countries meet or exceed Tanzania's child mortality rate. Why? Because there are a dearth of cost effective interventions in Tanzania relative to the other countries. The system is relatively ineffective in producing the desired outcomes, even with reallocations and additional spending.[16]

Based on the results, Tanzania should pay attention to increasing the impact of the health system. The health system is consuming a large volume of resources relative to other countries in the region and relative to what it is able to produce. The remainder of the health section reviews how households interact with the system.

Illness and Use of Health Services

About 15 percent of Tanzanians reported being ill or injured during the month prior to the HRDS survey, and two-thirds of those sought care. In a pattern seen in many countries, individuals in the poorest 20 percent of households were about half as likely as the richest 20 percent to report being sick (11 versus 21 percent), and were less likely to seek care if sick (57 versus 74 percent).

---

[16] An extra US$5 is added per capita in Kenya in this simulation because of the high rate of return to the additional investment there.

The government system is the most important source of care for the poor by far (Table S.14). Approximately 70 percent of sick individuals in the poorest 20 percent of households who sought care first went to a government facility, compared to 46 percent of the richest 20 percent. About 36 percent of the richest households seek nongovernment, non-voluntary agency, private-sector care.

Despite the fact that the government operates about half (52 percent) of the hospital beds in Tanzania, government hospitals are used by only about one-third (35 percent) of those who reported being admitted for at least one night (Table S.15). Better-off individuals are more likely than the poor to use government hospitals for both outpatient and inpatient services, which accounts for why they are able to capture such a large share of the government's subsidy at this level of health care.

Health Expenditures

On average, Tanzanians spent Tsh 1,118 per short-illness episode when health care was sought (Table S.16). Rural households spent more than urban ones for care at a hospital, but substantially less for care at a health center or dispensary, principally because of high rural transport costs.

Table S.14: First Source of Curative Outpatient Care, by Expenditure Quintile (%)

Source of Care	Lowest Expenditure Quintile	Highest Expenditure Quintile	All
Government Hospital	15	20	17
Voluntary Agency / Private Hospital	5	9	6
Government Health Center or Dispensary	55	26	40
Voluntary Agency Health Center or Dispensary	10	9	10
Private Health Center or Dispensary	6	24	14
Other (traditional and pharmacy)	9	12	13

Source: HRDS, 1993/94.

Table S.15: Use of Inpatient Services, by Welfare Level (%)

Source of Care	Lowest Expenditure Quintile	Highest Expenditure Quintile	All
Government Hospital	35	44	35
Other	65	56	65

Table S.16: Expenditures per Illness Episode Among Those Seeking Care, by Residence in 1994/95 (Tsh)

	Dar es Salaam	Other Urban	Rural	All
Hospital	2,897	1,404	4,332	2,751
Health Center	2,856	784	531	663
Dispensary	2,458	1,596	741	1,009
Other	1,337	2,291	1,395	1,715
All	2,641	1,495	1,361	1,498

Source: HRDS, 1993/94, inflated to 1994/95 levels.

Table S.17 shows expenditure per visit by type of provider and welfare quintile. The poorest group pays about one-third what the richest group spends on a visit overall, but the patterns are not consistent. In the government system, the poor pay much less at the dispensary level, but they pay more than the rich for services at government health centers and hospitals. The rich pay significantly more for non-governmental services at each level.[17]

Figure S.7 shows the distribution of expenditures among visits, drugs, and transportation for the lowest and highest expenditure quintiles. The main reason for much higher spending overall by the rich is that they spend about 8 times more on drugs than do the poor. For visit costs, the poor are spending about half as much as the rich, but for transportation, expenditures are similar for both groups. The poor pay more for transport than for any other expense item.

Table S.17: Expenditures per Visit, by Type of Provider and Expenditure Quintile, 1994/95 (Tsh)

Source of Care	Lowest Expenditure Quintile	Highest Expenditure Quintile	All
Dispensary			
Government	107	322	229
Other	1,258	2,759	2,021
Health Center			
Government	804	531	667
Other	1,731	2,362	2,052
Hospital			
Government	1,611	1,522	1,276
Other	2,467	7,172	7,267
Total	878	2,399	1,572

Source: HRDS, 1993/94, inflated to 1994/95 levels.

Use of health services in Tanzania is quite high by international standards among the rich and poor alike. The rich are more likely than the poor to perceive themselves as sick and to seek care from expensive public institutions like hospitals. In data not reported here, very high percentages of women seek prenatal care, primarily from the government. These are major accomplishments of the health system. Yet the impact on health statistics, such as infant mortality, has been small, which suggests that despite a good record of deploying medical resources, some of the other inputs to good health in Table S.1 may not have been available in adequate quantities (especially higher levels of female education and investments in effective preventive health programs).

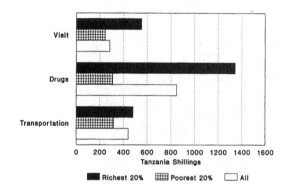

Figure S.7: Components of Expenditures per Visit Source: HRDS 1993/94

Consumers' Evaluation of Health Services

The household survey asked respondents to rank characteristics of an ideal dispensary or health center according to their importance to the household, then to evaluate the closest government health center/dispensary relative to the same characteristics. Table S.18 contains descriptive statistics on these rankings. By far the highest priorities are availability of drugs and quality of personnel. The most important item, adequate drugs, is the one that respondents think the government performs worst in delivering (63 percent rated the system as poor or very poor). The least important items to households

---

[17] Total spending of Tsh 1,572 in Table S.17 is higher than in Table S.16 because S.17 includes self care.

are the ones the World Bank typically finances: additional facilities to reduce the distance from the household, and improved physical plant and conditions.

Willingness to Pay for Primary Health Services

Households were also asked how much they value a dispensary or health center that embodies the characteristics the respondent himself or herself values. Nearly one-half the sample (47 percent) indicated that they would pay Tsh 134 shillings or less for all the costs associated with a visit to such a dispensary. However, the distribution, which can be seen in Figure S.8, is quite skewed. While half the responses lie at Tsh 134 or below, and two-thirds are at Tsh 2,680 or below, the remaining one-third would pay Tsh 5,360 and up for a visit. The result of the skewed distribution is that the average willingness to pay is quite high, at Tsh 4,401 (about triple the average expenditure per visit to any source of care today, and 30 times higher than average expenditures for a dispensary visit)[18]. However, most people fall far below this amount.

Table S.18: Households' Priorities and Perceptions of the Local Government Health Center or Dispensary

Characteristic	Ranking[a]	Percent Very Poor or Poor	Percent Good or Very Good
Adequate Drugs	5.2	63	10
Quality of Personnel	4.5	25	35
Community and Preventive Health	3.8	26	37
Distance from Home	3.3	44	28
Physical Plant/Clean Toilet/Water	3.1	30	25

[a] The ranking can range from 0 to 20. This column shows the average across the national sample.
Source: HRDS, 1993/94.

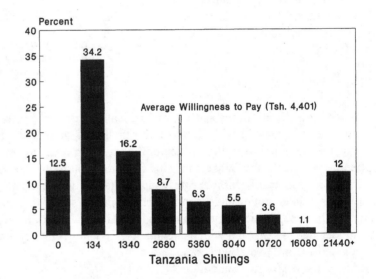

Figure S.8: Willingness to Pay for Health Center/Dispensary Visit Including All Costs
Source: HRDS 1993/94

Figure S.9 shows how willingness to pay varies by each 10 percent of the expenditure distribution, further disaggregated by urban and rural population. Average willingness to pay in rural areas is actually slightly higher than in urban areas despite the fact that the urban population is substantially richer than the rural population. This is especially true at the lower end of the scale.

---

[18] Average willingness to pay for a health visit is Tsh 3,284; for a year of primary school, it is Tsh 8,572.

Many people use such figures to justify increased cost sharing for health services, as the average willingness to pay is much higher than current charges in the facilities. However, the highly skewed distribution is significant. One-half the sample would pay very little, even though the rest of the sample would pay Tsh 1,340 and more for a visit at a government clinic that offers drugs and good care. The best-off, urban segment of the population is willing to pay by far the most for health services, yet is the most heavily subsidized group of healthcare consumers.

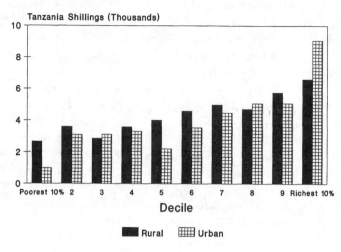

Mean Value: 4450 (R), 4292 (U)

Figure S.9: Willingness to Pay for One Visit, Health Center or Dispensary, by Decile and Residence
Source: HRDS 1993/94

Summary

Tanzania is a heavy spender on the health sector, and Tanzanians are heavy users of health services. Spending on health care by government and donors has the most pro-poor impact of any social sector spending in the country. Much of the spending is "right" in the sense of being targeted to cost-effective interventions. What is missing from the picture is impact. Why is Tanzania not getting better results? Is it a lack of complementary inputs that produce health, such as education and improved environmental conditions? Is it an ineffective public sector that consumes resources with little to show for it? Or is the physical environment in Tanzania so bad for health that the country must spend as much as it does just to stay even with its neighbors? Whatever the reason, the result is that the largest potential gains in the health sector will come not from increased government spending, but by making existing spending more effective, and by enabling consumers to get more for the money they spend on services.

WATER AND SANITATION

Water and Sanitation Sources

Water. Only about 11 percent of households in Tanzania have a private water connection inside their home or yard (Table S.19). Even these households must sometimes collect water from other sources due to the unreliability of the municipal

Table S.19: Household Water Sources, by Residence (%)

Type of Water Source	Dar es Salaam	Other Urban	Rural	All
Private Connection (inside or outside dwelling unit)	50.0	28.6	1.8	11.3
Distributing Water Vendor	2.7	0.36	0.0	0.3
Tanker Truck Vendor	0.1	0.14	0.0	0.0
Neighbor	32.9	17.3	1.2	7.1
Public Standpipe	8.7	26.1	19.7	20.6
Handpump	0.7	9.6	8.8	8.6
Open Well	3.9	10.6	27.8	22.2
Surface Water Source (river, stream, lake, pond)	0.4	7.2	41.0	29.9
Other	0.4	0.1	–	0.1
Total	100	100	100	100

Source: HRDS, 1993/94.

water supply system in most towns. Fifty percent of residents of Dar es Salaam and 29 percent in other cities now have a private water connection in their dwelling or yard, but 47 percent of households in Dar es Salaam collect water from outside their home (from a neighbor, public standpipe, handpump, open well, or surface water source). In other cities, 71 percent get water from these sources, principally from public taps and public wells.

In the rural areas of Tanzania, very few households have private water connections in their home or yard, and the vast majority of households collect water from sources outside the home. Sixty-nine percent still rely on traditional surface water sources or open wells. These sources are often a considerable distance from people's homes.

The urban figures track the sources of water by expenditure quintile. The richest 20 percent of all households have almost two-thirds of the private connections in Tanzania and buy more than half the water sold by tanker trucks and distributing water vendors. However, in rural areas, unimproved surface water sources are used by households in all income groups because many rural areas have no improved sources available. Conversely, when improved water sources such as public standpipes and handpumps are available in rural areas, they are used by all income groups.

Sanitation. Approximately 12 percent of the population have no sanitation facility at all (Table S.20). The most prevalent form of household sanitation system in both urban and rural areas is a traditional pit latrine. Data from the HRDS show that between 90 and 95 percent of households in urban and rural areas use traditional pit latrines.

Table S.20: Type of Sanitation Facility, by Residence (%)

Sanitation Facility	Dar es Salaam	Other Urban	Rural	All
Own or Shared Flush Toilet	8.1	4.9	1.1	2.5
Traditional or Improved Pit Latrine	90.2	92.4	92.3	92.2
No Facility, Bush, Pan, Bucket	1.7	2.7	6.6	5.3
Total	100	100	100	100

Source: HRDS, 1993/94.

In Dar es Salaam and other urban areas, only about 3 percent of the population have either a flush toilet for their own use or one that is shared with other households. Eight towns on mainland Tanzania have limited sewerage systems. In these towns, some of the few households with flush toilets have connected to the sewer system, while others empty into septic tanks and drainage fields.

Household Expenditures on Water

Only a small percentage of Tanzanian households (15 percent) pay any significant amount of cash for drinking water. On average, households with private connections and those buying from neighbors spend about the same amount annually, slightly more than Tsh 6,000 per year. Few households use vendors as their main source of drinking water, but those that do spend almost 10 times as much for water as a household with a private connection or a household purchasing from neighbors. Virtually no households in the lower 40 percent of the welfare distribution buy water from distributing vendors.

In short, the majority of Tanzanian households do not incur any monetary costs to obtain their domestic water supply. They pay instead with their labor by committing a significant share of their human capital resources to the daily task of obtaining small amounts of water for domestic use. In rural areas, for example, an average household spends about three hours a day to collect water, or over 1000 hours per year. Even in urban areas, the average household collecting water from outside the home spends about 1.5 hours a day (500 hours per year) on such activities.

Huge sums have been spent on water and sanitation services in Tanzania, but much of that investment is standing idle in the country, producing little or no water for the intended beneficiaries. A major question is whether any of the investment can be salvaged to reduce the burden of water gathering on the population. The fundamental problem the country faces in the water sector is not how to fund new investments, but to find viable organizational structures through which existing assets can be given economic value or new, sustainable systems can be developed. In the water sector, perhaps more than any other, the need for decentralization, local responsibility, pricing that is related to costs, and a stronger connection between the demand for, and supply of, services are essential elements of a new approach.

NUTRITION

The review of household nutrition generated some surprising and provocative results. Levels of malnutrition in Tanzania are surprisingly low, relative to other Sub-Saharan African countries, and relative to other developing countries with comparable living standards. The incidence of moderate wasting (low weight for height) among children is around 6 percent, compared to 9 to 11 percent in neighboring countries. The major determinants of child malnutrition are low per capita income and inadequate schooling of women. Economic growth in hand with early and long schooling for girls would go far towards reducing the undernutrition that exists in Tanzania.

It is clear from expenditure patterns in the household survey that the poor currently consume a wide variety of foods not normally found in the diets of the poor in other countries, including eggs, meats, and dairy products. The latter comprise about 14 percent of the lowest quintile's food budgets, well over half of what they spend on the staple food (maize). As the poor increase their incomes, they will tend to switch even more toward "luxury" foods rather than to devote all of the additional funds to purchasing more staples. This suggests that the poor probably consider themselves fairly well fed, but that higher incomes alone will not reduce the significant malnutrition problems that exist.

There is consequently plenty of room for carefully targeted interventions to improve nutrition status among vulnerable groups. The mean duration of breast feeding is excessively long (21 months), but rarely are babies exclusively breast fed for the first 6 months. Supplementary foods are introduced for over half the infants during the first month of life. These foods are low in energy and nutritionally inadequate. There are also some specific micronutrient problems, most of which are closely associated with a high incidence of infectious and parasitic diseases. From the household survey, we also know that about 45 percent of primary school students do not receive any food before going to school, and 89 percent receive no food while at school.

So, while the overall nutrition picture looks surprisingly good, there is great potential for targeted interventions to improve human capital formation, particularly during pregnancy, for women at birth, and for children through primary school. Apart from the need for more educated mothers, the benefits of short-term but well-targeted nutritional interventions could be high.

FAMILY PLANNING

In family planning, as in all other sectors, there is much to be positive about in terms of services available but much to be concerned about in terms of results. Family planning shares most of the same health system that draws almost all pregnant women in for prenatal checkups. Overall, 80 percent of health facilities provide mother-and-child health services, and 69 percent offer family planning services. This system has achieved high levels of awareness of family planning methods and a reasonable supply of contraceptives throughout most of the country. Some areas are not covered as well as others, and many women must travel long distances for supplies, but an analysis of the 1992 Demographic and Health Survey (TDHS) suggests that supply of services is not the main constraint.

If there is a failure in the system, it is at the household level in that families are not demanding family planning services. Current use of effective modern contraceptives is, according to the TDHS, well below 10 percent. The high prevalence of sexually transmitted diseases and endemic HIV infections add to the importance of increasing demand for family planning. Analysis of the TDHS survey suggests that the major factor increasing demand for contraception is female education. While some levels of primary education can increase the demand, demand is strongly affected by secondary education. The relatively high impact of secondary education has been demonstrated in countries with low levels of contraception. As the prevalence of contraception increases, the impact of primary education for women also increases. Tanzania can expect continued high rates of fertility unless it can affect a real change in the environment within which family size decisions are made.

"Unmet need," or demand for contraception, is determined by subtracting the number of desired births from actual births. In the HRDS, we asked respondents how much they would have to be compensated (or would pay) to delay the birth of their next child by an additional year[19]. Responses to the question ranged from the respondent *paying* at least Tsh 67,000 to space the next child, to a *subsidy* of Tsh 335,000 or more to delay the birth. If the individual would not accept Tsh 335,000 to space the next birth, we do not know the actual amount she or he would accept, only that it is higher[20]. The relevant questions were asked to about 5,000 people, but the results reported here are only for 2,516 women between 15 and 45 who are married, widowed, divorced, or have a partner (93 percent are married).[21]

Figure S.10 shows the distribution of responses for these women (HRDS, 1993/94). The group would require an average subsidy of Tsh 170,717 (US$297) to delay the birth of the next baby by one year. However, the distribution is quite skewed. About 45 percent of the women would pay to delay the next birth. Another 15 percent would space the next birth if subsidized by Tsh 67,000 (US$117). For all practical purposes, the remaining 40 percent of women appear to have little or no interest in contraception to space births, as most of them say they would require a subsidy of over Tsh 335,000

---

[19] Spacing children more widely results in a lower fertility rate.

[20] In the analysis discussed here, we assume that the maximum subsidy is Tsh 350,000, but that is arbitrary. It could well be infinite, and we chose this value so as not to overstate the subsidy that would really be required.

[21] The exact survey question was: "The choice we would like you to think about is whether to delay a birth by a year in exchange for a sum of money. The money would be paid to the woman whose pregnancy is delayed. Please understand that this question is about delaying a birth, not stopping it altogether." The question was introduced by a longer explanation, including the fact that the question was not about abortion, and that the woman would not be paid if she became pregnant during the year.

(US$583) to space for one year.

Table S.21 shows characteristics of these women. They differ very little in age and only moderately in whether they use any contraceptive. About one-third of the women in each willingness-to-pay category are using contraceptives, but given their responses to this question, many are probably doing so for reasons other than child spacing. The women who would pay are quite serious about it, however, as they are much more likely than the others to use effective modern contraceptives. They are also, on average, better educated by about 1 year. The expenditure patterns are a bit surprising, since the women who are most willing to pay for spacing their children pay more overall for contraceptives, but they spend the least for modern contraceptives. The ones who say they would need the highest subsidy are paying the most.

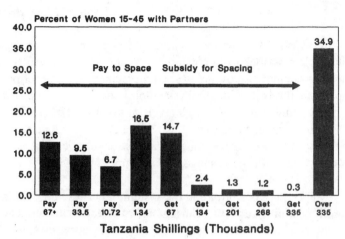

Mean Value: Receive 170,717
Observations: 2,516

Figure S.10: Willingness to Pay, or Accept a Subsidy, for Spacing the Next Child an Additional Year
Source: HRDS 1993/94

We estimate that about 266,000 women were using modern contraceptives at a direct program cost of about Tsh 1,200 (US$2.42) per woman in 1992. Much of this is spent by women who would be willing to pay to space their next births. However, this subsidy level is nowhere near what it would take to induce most women who are not currently spacing to begin doing so. The women who most value child spacing are capturing public subsidies for family planning, but are the ones whose behavior is probably least affected by the subsidy.

Table S.21: Characteristics of Women between 15 and 45 Responding to Contingent Valuation Question of Child Spacing

	Would Pay Tsh 1,340 or more	*Would Require Subsidy of Tsh 67,000*	*Would Require Subsidy Greater than Tsh 67,000*
Years of schooling	5.4	4.4	4.7
Age	29.2	29.5	28.8
Currently use any contraceptive	49.6	36.8	31.4%
Currently use modern contraceptives	20.1%	8.5%	8.3%
Expenditure on family planning	Tsh 236.5	Tsh 71.8	Tsh 115.9
Expenditure on family planning if using modern contraceptives	Tsh 420.5	Tsh 574.2	Tsh 1,306.9

Source: HRDS, 1993/94, inflated to 1994/95 levels.

In Tanzania, according to the 1992 Demographic and Health Survey, the difference in actual fertility between a woman aged 40-49 with a secondary education relative to one with a primary education is almost 2 births. For Tanzanian girls in the 15-19 age group, only 5 percent of those in secondary school have begun to have children. However, 34 percent of those who left school having completed only the primary level have had at least one child.

Four years of additional schooling, at a rate of subsidy of US$152 per year from the government, costs the government approximately US$309 to avert one birth. This investment reduces the infant mortality rate by about 30 percent, and creates many other benefits, not the least of which is improving the girl's education. For the 25 percent of secondary-school girls in Tanzania who are enrolled in nongovernment schools at the parents' expense, the country gets the same benefits for free. Worldwide, it costs about US$65 to avert one birth through family planning programs.

Referring to Figure S.10, what Tsh 335,000+ subsidy would induce the large group of women clustered in the "over Tsh 335,000" group to space the next child? The existing Tsh 403,286 subsidy for four years of public secondary education would do the trick. In fact, the required subsidy would probably amount to much less than that, as parents and girls would contribute to schooling. Because 63 percent of the women saying they would require this high subsidy are 30 years old or less, and 36 percent are 25 or less, appreciating and acting on this information just 10 years ago (in 1985) could have had a tremendous impact on the fertility of this cohort today.

A demand-side intervention like secondary education for girls may not be as high profile as a contraceptive program, but it can be every bit as effective at lowering costs, and has a high immediate negative impact on fertility for girls while they are in school. The effects of secondary education on fertility are both immediate and long lasting, and produce a range of other benefits. For the time being, it may be the only family planning intervention for which there is plenty of in-built but un-met demand.

SUPPLY-SIDE CONSTRAINTS

The foregoing has focused on public finance in the social sectors and on the household side of the equation. Supply-side and management issues in the government system are serious but are well known and discussed in many other reports. We will do little more here than to summarize them (see Table S.22). The government has already put in place many reforms aimed at removing some of these constraints, primarily through decentralization of authority in the government and liberalization of the economy. Giving households more choice over social-service providers, and a stronger voice in the operation of the governing system (by moving authority and funds farther down into the system), would go far towards changing incentives and improving performance in the system.

LOCAL GOVERNMENTS AND THE SOCIAL SECTORS

At present, the delivery of basic education, health, and water and sanitation services in Tanzania involves regional and district governments and administration. The main problems at this level are related to the confused role of the local government in the system of governance as an administrative unit of the central government but also as a representative unit of the people in its jurisdiction. Ownership of primary-level facilities ostensibly lies with the community, but there are few privileges of ownership, as there is no local control over inputs. In addition, there are severe budgetary constraints and problems of accountability in local government. Four major issues include:

- Extensive central control: Social services are funded almost entirely by the central government, and the present revenue instruments available to district councils are not sensitive to growth in the local economy. As a consequence, the ability of the local government to fund social services

Table S.22: Constraints on the Supply of Social Services

Sector	Financial	Managerial/Human Resource/Institutional	Non-Government Providers
Education	• under-funding, with personnel costs squeezing out complementary inputs • high recurrent cost burden for extensive primary school infrastructure • disproportionate allocation of resources to university • dependence on donor support for essential nonsalary inputs • public funding of boarding forces rationing of secondary and tertiary slots • UPE contribution goes to district government • resources poorly matched to demand	• heavy central control but little supervision or incentives for good performance • low accountability to parents or students • large numbers of teachers with relatively low qualifications • remuneration structure discourages well-qualified entrants into teaching • low morale among teachers • split and unclear responsibilities between ministries, with multiple ministries and levels of government involved at all points of service • headmasters typically lack managerial discretion	• legal constraints at the primary level • competition from subsidized public schools for secondary, university, and training institutions • lack of financing mechanisms for nongovernment education (credit markets, capitation grants) • exam system reduces access to best students • inadequate information sources for parents to make choices among schools and decisions on educational investments • price controls on, and taxation of, secondary-school fees • training by all ministries and parastatals crowds out private sector
Health, Nutrition, and Family planning	• disproportionate allocation of resources to hospitals • high recurrent cost burden for extensive network of facilities • dependence on donor support for essential nonsalary inputs • free public provision of all services (with nominal cost sharing now in hospitals)	• heavy central control but little supervision or incentives for good performance • low morale among health workers • low accountability to consumers • multiple ministries and levels of government involved at all points of service	• competition from subsidized public hospitals and clinics • inadequate financing mechanisms for nongovernment services (insurance, capitation grants) • inadequate information sources for patients
Water and Sanitation	• high recurrent cost burden for large capital projects • free or very low-cost public provision of services	• lack of beneficiary involvement • poor intersectoral communication and cooperation	• historical central government monopoly • lack of contracting mechanisms or experience in outsourcing

is poorly connected to the community's demand for those services. Central-government control and nationally set prices for water, education, and health services limit the ability of local government, or for that matter the service providers themselves, to finance the services they deliver.

• <u>Separation between budget decisions and local needs</u>: During various stages of the budgeting process, cuts may be made at the center that reflect central-government constraints and priorities, but they do not reflect local needs. Under the current system, local authorities have little room to affect what actually happens on the ground as a result of these central decisions, as they have virtually no capacity themselves to make up the shortfalls.

- Inefficiency: Much of the reluctance of the center to give up control stems from the perceived lack of political and administrative accountability and efficiency on the part of local governments. Many local authorities have failed to produce their accounts on a regular basis, external audits are often delayed, and only a few councils have a functioning internal audit unit. In addition, many local authorities encounter serious difficulties and are ineffective in collecting taxes, fees, and charges that are due.

- Lack of capital or labor markets for local social services: Local governments are unable to borrow money for improvements in physical capital, such as water delivery systems, schools, and health facilities. These investments are centrally controlled. Local governments have little or no control over personnel posted by the center to these facilities, as all professional employees in health and education are part of a national cadre that rotates throughout the country.

In short, local governments are at the mercy of the central government for all inputs, including policy, management, capital, personnel, the budget, even books and other supplies. The district hospital, for example, is funded by local government, but its pharmaceutical budgets are managed by the Central Medical Stores Unit. The hospital must requisition drugs from the center, and may not purchase them elsewhere if they are unavailable from the Unit. District administrations, not schools, are shipped books from the central government. School libraries are stocked with a list of books predetermined by the central government, yet on paper, local communities are responsible for these services.

The result is a system in which responsibility is so fragmented that there is no accountability at any level. The center maintains control over almost all resources, but has delegated almost all of the responsibility to the local governments. The local governments have all the responsibility in principle, but are fully dependent on the largesse of the center. Local governments can always put the blame elsewhere when the system fails, and the central ministries blame the local units for incompetence.

CONCLUSIONS

The conclusion of the many parties involved in the production of this *Review* was an appreciation for the new facts put on the table, but a desire to jump to action quickly. Tanzanians are concerned about fixing the problems that jeopardize the future of their children. They are prepared to take bold steps to improve the situation. The following conclusions are shared by all who have participated in this process.

First, there is general agreement about the importance of primary and secondary education as a prerequisite for fast economic growth and creating a flexible and well trained work force. Similarly, there is agreement about the strong impact of women's education in improving growth prospects and in facilitating improved health and nutrition, as well as smaller families and better educated children. Investing in early childhood care and development and basic education, especially for girls, will have high payoffs in Tanzania.

Second, the traditional mode of investment by the government and especially The World Bank must be adjusted to the realities of the situation. The traditional approach of putting investments into publicly owned schools, health dispensaries, water systems, and training with minimal input by beneficiaries, will probably do little to increase the stock of human capital in the country. One of Tanzania's main strengths is its development of a widely dispersed system of local social infrastructure in education, health, and water. But many of these investments have depreciated heavily through lack of maintenance or use because the intended beneficiaries' needs were either not met by the supply system, or it was simply not sustainable with the resources available. The last ten years have seen a deterioration of primary school enrollments, persistently poor health indicators, and abandonment of rural water systems. Additional investments in bricks and mortar are not justified without the assurance of increased demand for those services. The liberalization of secondary schools and primary medical care has revealed a huge potential supply (and demand) response when choices are made available to the public. Additional investments in social infrastructure take into account the fact that the public system is already too extensive to be supported by available resources and in many cases responds poorly to the felt needs of the population. Further investment should not occur in the absence of an incentive system that gives clear responsibility for operation and maintenance to local owners (including nongovernment owners). Finally, rationalization of existing public-sector plant and equipment cannot be maintained under any incentive system for want of adequate local resources or demand.

Third, Tanzania has tried for several decades to channel resources to the poor through direct provision of health and education services. The strategy of accomplishing this goal must be reconsidered in light of the fact that the rich are capturing a large share of public subsidies through the current system. It is time to re-examine how to better target the benefits from public sector spending to the poor. Such reallocations would be difficult, but they are feasible.

TANZANIA'S SOCIAL SECTOR STRATEGY

The Government of Tanzania has now prepared a *Social Sector Strategy* that proposes the following strategies:[22]

- Strategy 1: Concentrate public-sector resources on core activities of the government. This strategy involves increasing the relative budgetary allocations to the social sectors, and focusing spending within the social sectors on basic education and health.

- Strategy 2: Balance personnel and other inputs within the social sectors. This strategy includes altering the number and structure of personnel in the social sectors and allocating funds to inputs that have been given too little attention in the past.

---

[22] These six strategies are extracted from the Government of Tanzania's *Social Sector Strategy*, October 1994, pp. 17-20.

- Strategy 3: Decentralize authority to the local level. This strategy extends beyond the social sectors, and applies to the overall structure of the central-local government relationship. It is likely that this will entail revision of the Local Government Act of 1983.

- Strategy 4: Eliminate constraints to private-sector participation in the provision of social services. Several actions have already been taken, including the liberalization of secondary-school ownership and the legalization of private medical practice. In addition, implementation of the user fee program in the health sector is likely to shift some users to the private sector. Additional actions can also be taken to broaden the supply of social services.

- Strategy 5: Promote high quality standards. There are two aspects to this element of the strategy. First, quality-related problems must be addressed within the public system. Second, among the government's core functions is the appropriate regulation of health, education, and water services. The implementation of this function will be consistent with the changing role of the government in the economy.

- Strategy 6: Move resources closer to the household and promote household investment in human capital. This element of the strategy represents a full departure from the supply-side approach to the social sectors that has prevailed since Independence. In the long run, it will be the most effective way to finance important inputs into human capital.

IMPLEMENTATION OF THE SOCIAL SECTOR STRATEGY

The government, with assistance from The World Bank, has now begun to implement the *Social Sector Strategy* through pilot projects. The pilot schemes are being financed through existing IDA credits, and successful programs will be extended nationally and financed through IDA and other donor assistance. The four pilots are briefly described below.

- Pilot 1: Community Education Funds. These funds collect local contributions that are being matched by additional funds from the outside. Matching grants to supplement existing primary-school budgets, to be administered by local communities, are being forwarded by these funds to the schools. When primary education is liberalized, these matching grants will follow the student to the school of choice.

- Pilot 2: Scholarships for Girls to Attend Secondary School. This program may also include nonmonetary assistance to improve the performance of girls in secondary school.

- Pilot 3: Community Health Fund. This is a quasi-insurance system that collects premiums from households to finance a prepayment system for health care. It is a capitation system, under which families choose a single provider for a specified period.

- <u>Facility-Based Management</u>. The community education and community health pilots provide for a local management board that manages public-sector facilities that participate in the pilot scheme.

- <u>Pilot 4: Early Childhood Care and Development</u>. Today, there are 7.2 million children from age 0 to 6 years or roughly 23% of the population. Investments in Tanzanian human capital begin at this early age, and the goal of this pilot is to enhance the quality and quantity of these investments. This is a community-based program aimed at preparing children from birth to age six for a healthy and productive life through community-organized interventions for mothers and care givers. These interventions will include practical mother-child activities aimed at better nutrition, education for better parenting, preparing the child for school by beginning to teach the rudiments of literacy, teaching mothers to identify various danger signals in their children (e.g. swollen bellies for worm infestation, white spots on pupils for Vitamin A deficiency, etc.), and providing community-based care.

As stated at the outset, the key recommendations flowing from the background work contained in this *Review* are to invest in expanding the quantity and quality of primary schooling, and to advance many more girls through lower secondary school. Through the *Strategy* and the pilot projects, the government is acting on these recommendations and is doing so in a way that puts decision-making at the parental and community levels. These changes are likely to result in new problems, and they will turn out to be imperfect fixes for what ails the system. As pilots, it is expected that the most serious problems can be corrected before nationwide implementation begins.

The process of getting started is now complete. The enormity of the problems Tanzania faces in the social sectors has been documented by this *Review*. The government has enunciated principles in its *Strategy* that will guide its efforts to find solutions for these problems. Finally, the government is trying to implement workable solutions on a pilot basis. Getting to this point has been a tremendous achievement for Tanzania's social sectors.

1
BACKGROUND

Tanzania is experiencing a crisis in the social sectors that threatens the country's future economic and social development. After encouraging progress up to about 1980, education and health outcomes have stagnated or even worsened in recent years. The government system of social service delivery, once a model envied by other countries, is ill suited to today's budget constraints and growing demands. The weaknesses of the current health, education, water, and other social services have been recognized by the government, donors and, most importantly, the Tanzanian people.

The World Bank has made investments in the social sectors in Tanzania since Independence. In general, Bank operations have supported the government's social services delivery system. Schools, health facilities and central institutions have been constructed, rehabilitated and supported. Government managers and service deliverers have been trained, and public water systems have been created. Experience has shown, however, that World Bank investments have yielded minimal results and have had an undetectable impact on human capital. Implementation constraints have limited the size of the total resource transfer, so the Bank has been able to invest only a tiny sum per capita annually. In addition, public infrastructure, financed by the Bank and others, has depreciated rapidly due to lack of maintenance. Little actual improvement in the quality of health and education services can be documented, and the lack of improvement in outcome indicators documented in this report should be disturbing to any organization, and not the least, parents, who have been investing in these systems.

The Government of Tanzania and the World Bank have made a commitment to change. Investments in human capital, ensuring that the next generation of Tanzanian children will be healthier and better educated, have risen to the top of the government's agenda, and also drive the World Bank's strategy. As a first step toward developing a collaborative work program, the World Bank and the Government of Tanzania agreed in 1993 to prepare a review of the social sectors that would bring together a common, objective set of information from which to design future operations. The *Social Sector Review* (SSR) was to have an explicit focus on the household, an often-neglected but vital actor in human capital investment. Without duplicating existing studies, the SSR was designed to present the results of the 1994 Human Resources Development Survey, supplemented with information from a set of background reviews on specific sectoral issues.

OBJECTIVES OF THE SOCIAL SECTOR REVIEW

This *Social Sector Review* has the goal of highlighting the role of the families and household members as the most important investors in human capital. At the same time, recognizing the importance of characteristics of the supply of social services in determining health and education outcomes, the SSR also seeks to synthesize information about how the government and other institutions deliver and finance services.

Specifically, the SSR seeks to:

- present indicators of the status of human capital in Tanzania;

- describe patterns of use of, and spending on, social services at the household level, with specific attention to differences according to welfare, income level, and gender of the beneficiary of social services;

- estimate the demand for social services, both under existing conditions and under the conditions induced by policy change and improvements in the provision of services;

- describe patterns of government and non-governmental provision of, and spending on, social services; and

- identify the major constraints affecting the provision of social services.

This document reviews issues concerning the social sectors in Tanzania, but we try not to duplicate information readily available from other sources. For example, the education sections of this report emphasize primary and secondary education. A more complete analysis of post-secondary education is contained in Higher and Technical Education in Tanzania: Investments, Returns and Future Opportunities (World Bank Report No. 15327-TA).

This analysis is intended to provide readers with insights about how specific interventions can work in synergy with household-level behaviors to increase the quantity and effectiveness of investments in human resource development in Tanzania. It is intended to provide readers with insights about the potential for partnership between the government and an emerging private sector, and about specific interventions that could ease the constraints now impeding the effectiveness of social service delivery.

This document is the result of a participatory process that took place between July 1993 and September 1995. It was a fully cooperative effort of the government and the World Bank, with most of the data collection, analysis, and discussion carried out by Tanzanians for Tanzania. Other donors and representatives of NGOs also participated. One of the key concerns of the government and other donors was that the Bank not make recommendations on policy, but rather, facilitate a process whereby the government would prepare its *Strategy*, a longstanding commitment it had made to the donor community. The government (using the background papers and surveys produced for this report, along with the initial draft produced in June 1994, workshop discussions, its own policy pronouncements as embodied in its *Rolling Plan for the Budget*, and other sources) completed the *Strategy*, and presented it to donors at the Consultative Group Meeting in Paris in February, 1995.

This document, unlike most Bank reports, is not filled with recommendations, although it has a clear purpose and themes. Portions of the government's *Strategy* are quoted throughout this report in boxes, allowing the reader to see what the government proposes to do in response to the findings of our joint research and analysis. As has been the case with this work from the beginning, the participatory process has caused action to race ahead of the production of the analysis. Since August 1994, soon after the workshop to review the background work for this report and the production of a first draft of the government's strategy, we have been working with the Planning Commission, the Ministry of Education and Culture, the Ministry of Health, and the Prime Minister's Office, to review and reorient existing World Bank-funded projects in education and health in order to implement elements of the reforms envisaged in the government's *Strategy*. Three pilot projects were implemented in August, 1995.

KEY DEFINITIONS

For our purposes, we define *human capital* as the productive assets that are embodied within individuals. Principally, these are formal and informal education, and good health. We define *investments* in human capital as the inputs (or payment for inputs) that increase human capital. These include, for example, schooling, use of preventive and curative health services, and child nutrition. The greatest potential for increasing human capital occurs during childhood, so our emphasis is largely on inputs that directly affect children. By design, therefore, we pay less attention to adult health, literacy, and technical education than to child health and primary and secondary schooling.

We define *household* as a group of individuals sharing cooking facilities. In most cases, these individuals are related by marriage and kinship ties. Households often also include unrelated individuals and may have close financial and other types of links to other households. Thus, while the primary context for decision making is the household, as defined above, we also pay attention to the larger community of households that influence decisions. It is essential to acknowledge that household members may (and typically do) have differential access to resources, and "household decisionmaking" may not reflect a uniform set of preferences among all household members. To the extent possible, therefore, we provide analyses that distinguish among age groups and between genders within the household.

DATA SOURCES

The primary source of data on household characteristics, use of social services, and spending is the Human Resources Development Survey 1993/94 (HRDS). The HRDS is a nationally representative survey of approximately 5,000 households based on the National Master Sample created by the Bureau of Statistics in the Planning Commission. It was conducted with the objective of obtaining detailed information about investments in human capital within the context of overall household expenditures. We also use data from other population-based surveys, specifically the Tanzania Demographic and Health Survey 1991/92 (TDHS), and the 1994 Tanzania Knowledge, Attitudes and Practices Survey (TKAP).

Insights from community case studies carried out for the *Social Sector Review* are also presented in this volume. The qualitative and quantitative research (using the Focused Area Study Technique, or FAST) involved focus group discussions and in-depth interviews with parents, children, teachers, and health care workers. It also employed time-use studies of children in and out of school, and the collection of data on the personnel and material inputs available in schools and health facilities.

Data on government facilities and expenditures come from government reports and previous budget analyses carried out for 1996's *Tanzania Social Sector Expenditures Review* (Follmer and Kessy, 1997). Analyses of the main constraints in each sector are derived from a set of sector-specific "overview papers" and several small-scale studies prepared as background for the SSR.

Many earlier studies have analyzed the financial and managerial difficulties facing social service delivery in Tanzania. In addition, donor agencies have documented implementation of specific interventions in the education, health and other sectors. Information from these reports is incorporated in this volume. However, this report is not intended to be a comprehensive review of all aspects of each element within the social sectors.

ORGANIZATION OF THE REPORT

Organizing this immense volume of information into a sensible structure that systematically highlights the role of household-level behavior and choices proved to be a significant challenge to the authors. The dividing line between the demand and supply sides of the equation are not as simple to define in practice as they are to discuss in theory. For example, it is difficult to describe patterns of school enrollment and household spending without referring to the structure and constraints of the school system. In addition, some elements of the social sectors (nutrition, for example) do not have an obvious "supply" side, although government actions can and do affect the supply and use of nutritious food within households.

Given these complexities, the *Social Sector Review* is organized as follows. This chapter continues with the conceptual framework for the rest of the report. Chapter 2 describes the government's approach to the social sectors since Independence, presents information on public spending, and emphasizes the critical role of the local government in social service operation. Chapters 3 through 7 present information on the demand for and supply of education, health, nutrition, family planning, and water sectors, respectively. Those chapters emphasize outcomes and the role of the household first. Then they present background information on characteristics of the supply of services.

IMPORTANCE OF HUMAN CAPITAL AND HUMAN RESOURCES TO DEVELOPMENT IN TANZANIA

Growth and Human Welfare

Figure 1.1 shows the growth in the Tanzanian economy since 1980. Since structural adjustment began in 1984, there has been steady growth in the economy in gross terms. However, if population growth is taken into account, there has been little growth in per capita income. While this is one of the better growth records in Africa over the period, growth at this pace is not adequate to achieve rapid poverty reduction and broad improvement in the welfare of the population.

Consider a child born in 1994 in Tanzania who will be six years old in the year 2000. What kind of economic prospects will that child face, depending on the ability of the Tanzanian economy to grow? Figure 1.1

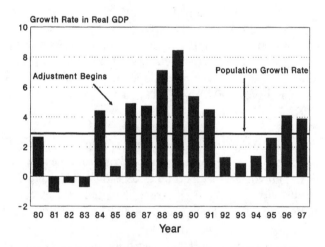

**Figure 1.1: Tanzania's Record of Growth Since 1980
Source: World Bank Data**

shows a few scenarios. If the economy can sustain a growth rate in per capita income of 10 percent annually, when this child is 56 years old and officially retired, Tanzania will be richer than the United States is today. That child will have quite a life – he or she will see Tanzania get wealthier every single year by such a large amount that the improvements could probably be noticed almost monthly. No economy, however, has sustained such a high growth rate in per capita income over such a long period. If the economy can sustain a growth rate every year of 7 percent, which is approximately what has been done in East Asia, Tanzania will have a GDP per capita that would put it at the high middle-income level by 2050. A growth rate of 5 percent yields respectable results, but at a rate of only 1 or 2 percent per annum, which is above Tanzania's sustained rate of growth over the past 15 years, the country will still be extremely poor in 2050. The child born today will live in a fairly stagnant world and face many of the same problems of poverty endured by his or her parents and grandparents. Tanzania is a wonderful place, and this individual could have a good life, but this will not happen unless high sustained rates of growth in per capita GDP can be achieved.

What does this have to do with human capital? Simple. There are basically three resources available to create wealth: land, people, and capital. We are focusing on the *people* dimension. Economic research into the determinants of economic growth suggests that 40 to 60 percent of growth rates in per capita GDP can be attributed to accumulation of human capital and increased productivity of people. In economic development, and this is certainly the case in Tanzania, the emphasis has been on accumulating physical capital and increasing the productivity of land, often neglecting *investments in people*. We are now beginning to understand that people are the key ingredient in economic growth, and investing in them can have huge payoffs. Thus, this Review is much more than just a review of social sector welfare programs for the poor. Close attention to the amount of resources being invested in the social sectors, the

Table 1.1: Compound Rates of Growth and per Capita Income in 2050

Annual Growth Rate in GDP Per Capita (%)	GDP Per Capita in 2050
10	US$23,478
7	US$5,891
5	US$2,293
2	US$538
1	US$329

Note: Assumes US$200 per capita GDP in 2000
Source: Author's calculations

efficiency of social programs, and the quality of the outputs can have a major impact on Tanzania's growth prospects. Decisions the government makes in the social sectors will have much to do with the sort of lives today's Tanzanian children will face when they are adults, and with their ability to further improve the prospects for their own children.

Human Resources as Capital

What is human capital? We cannot see it or touch it, but it is something we create in our minds and our bodies. It is like building a dam inside our heads or a railroad in our bones. A dam or a railroad can be seen and touched, but the economic value of those investments is every bit as intangible as the human capital that each of us has accumulated. Both can become worthless or even a drag on the economy even though they are still physically in view. We usually think of human capital as the bundle of knowledge, health, skills, energy, creativeness, and other such characteristics that each of us brings to solving problems and earning a living. It is an economic phenomenon that becomes embodied in each of us. We can earn money from it. It has economic value.

Human capital is acquired not solely to make money, of course. Greater knowledge and skills make life better, and each of us benefits in innumerable ways when the person next to us is also well educated and healthy. While these other types of direct "welfare" benefits are important, the point of this document is that even without them, only looking at the economic investment aspects of human capital, a very strong case can be made for greater investment in human beings. The indirect benefits that are not measured in GNP statistics make a very strong case even stronger.

The latest regional estimates of rates of return to education are shown in Table 1.2. There are wide variations by region and level of schooling, as would be expected. However, by any standard, these rates of return are high and competitive with other uses of investable funds. A recent review of 1,200 World Bank and IFC projects showed rates of return of from 3 to 17 percent for public-sector agricultural projects, and 10 to 15 percent for private-sector projects. The range depends on macroeconomic policies that accompany the investments (World Bank, 1991b, p. 82). The average social rate of return to primary education in Africa, Asia, and Latin America lies well above these rates, and even higher levels of schooling are very competitive. In Sub-Saharan Africa, in particular, the social rate of return to primary education is nearly 25 percent and to secondary education, 18 percent. The private rates of return are much higher, and these are the rates that parents face when they make schooling decisions for their children[1]. While there has been considerable controversy over the last two decades about estimating rates of return for education, there is now little question that investments in education, especially primary and secondary education, are very profitable for parents and for nations.

Table 1.2: Returns to Investment in Education, by Level and Region, Latest Year

Region	Social Return in Percent			Private Return in Percent		
	Primary	Secondary	Higher	Primary	Secondary	Higher
Sub-Saharan Africa	24.3	18.2	1.2	41.3	26.6	27.8
Asia	19.9	13.3	11.7	39.0	18.9	19.9
Europe, Middle East, North Africa	15.5	11.2	10.6	17.4	15.9	21.7
Latin America, Caribbean	17.9	12.8	12.3	26.2	16.8	19.7
OECD	14.4	10.2	8.7	21.7	12.4	12.3
World	18.4	13.1	10.9	29.1	18.1	20.3

Note: Social and private returns are the internal rate of return to another dollar spent on education at each level.
Source: Psacharopoulos, 1993, p. 7.

From an investment standpoint, Table 1.2 contains another important piece of information. Rates of return to education fall very slowly as more people become educated. Cross-sectionally, this is easy to see. The social rate of return to secondary education falls from 15.2 percent for low-income countries (US$610 per capita or less) to 10.3 percent for high-income countries (US$7,620 per capita). This is a drop of only one-third in the rate of return across groups of countries that differ in incomes by a factor of over 12 (Psacharopoulos, 1993). The net secondary-school enrollment rate in low-income countries was 37 percent in 1988, compared to 95 percent in OECD countries (World Bank, 1991b). For Africa, where the stock of educated people is relatively low compared to OECD countries, the social rate of return to primary education is 24.3 percent, compared to 14.4 percent for OECD countries. Thus, additional investments in primary education could be expected to earn high returns well into the future. Although

---

[1] Private rates of return exceed the social rate of return because the social rate of return includes the public subsidy at each level of education.

we do not have similar information for returns to health, we would expect that there would also be high economic returns to investments in better health, especially in high-mortality areas.

Human capital can also be safely assumed to share a number of features with physical capital. Increasing the level of human capital should yield diminishing returns. The previous paragraph suggests that on an economy-wide basis, diminishing returns set in slowly. However, for individuals this is not the case. Those with a lot of human capital begin to reach a point where it makes little sense to invest more in themselves. Conversely, those with little capital can benefit relatively more from small investments.

Unique Features of Human Capital

Everyone owns some human capital. Not everyone owns land, buildings, and machines. Thus land and physical capital is often very inequitably distributed. In contrast, every person gets an initial endowment of human capital at birth. These endowments may not be equal, they may come with defects, but everyone has some. Females are not discriminated in this, and in fact, they start out with a little more health capital than do males. For many people, human capital is the only capital they will ever own. What happens to the endowment after birth is a matter of private and public investment choices, which is what this report is all about.

Human capital cannot be bought or sold. Human capital depreciates, like any investment, but it cannot be given away, lost to a swindler, gambled away, or misplaced. It is a form of capital that can only be rented by others, usually for a wage. There may be imperfections in the rental or wage market, but human capital can be an equity-enhancing source of wealth in a society if subsidies for it are properly targeted.

It is slow to depreciate. In industrial countries, earnings for college-educated people tend to rise continuously after college up to their late 50s, and many well-educated people continue to enjoy very high earnings into their 60s or 70s if they continue to work. In contrast, those with lower levels of education, especially those in manual jobs, see their earnings peak in their early 50s. Investments in general knowledge and skills have very long payoffs because they result in greater flexibility, adaptability, and mobility, among other things. Even our health tends to be slow to degenerate, and we now know that we have considerable control over the rate of depreciation of our physical and mental capacities by virtue of how we live.

It is possible to catch up. It is also possible to catch up quickly if investments are targeted to basic services. Richer countries have literacy rates closing in on 100 percent. It takes only a few decades to close the gap that exists in literacy rates between poorer and richer countries. Figure 1.2 shows how the trajectory has steepened during the last four decades as countries have striven for higher levels of literacy. Sweden and other OECD countries have been slowly moving toward 100 percent from a much higher starting point over the last century. In health, diminishing returns to additional investments means that poorer countries can close that gap as well, and a few have done so quickly. However, many countries, including those of eastern Africa, have not yet effectively begun to exploit high-return options for improving health outcomes. Poorer countries like Tanzania can catch up quickly to countries much richer than they are by investing selectively in high-return human capital investments.

Producing Human Capital

Most production of education capital in a person takes place during the first two decades of life, while that of health capital comes before age five. People continue to invest in themselves throughout life, but much of that investment is re-tooling and maintenance.

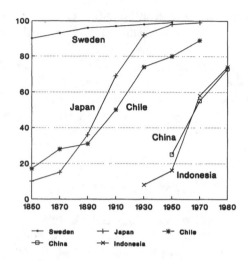

Figure 1.2: Increases in Literacy in Selected Countries, 1850-1980
Source: World Bank, 1991b

Virtually all human capital investment in children is produced in the home, in schools, environmental health investments, or through the use of medical services. The range of investment opportunities for adults is somewhat wider, including on-the-job training, experience in a job, and other little tricks each of us has learned to upgrade our skills and continually invest in ourselves. This report is focused primarily on investments in children, because they are the key to future economic development, and they are the focus of present concerns about social welfare and poverty in Tanzania. Children depend on the household, particularly their mothers, for the mothers are the agents that contract for, or produce, most of the capital that children take into their adult years. A very large share of the investment in children is produced through social sector services.

One of the key features of human capital production is the complementary nature of the various investments that can be made. Table 1.3 provides an illustration of the types of interactions that are known to exist across the social sectors. The diagonal elements are suppressed on the assumption that there is a positive effect of each type of investment on its own outcome, such as health investments on health status.

Look first at education. We know that it increases the ability of couples to choose their level of fertility and achieve their goals. We also know that better educated people are considerably healthier than less educated people. People with higher levels of schooling eat better, and tend to take greater advantage of safe water and sewerage services. These effects are true for educated men and educated women. However, education for women has an even broader impact in that education for them generates strong additional benefits for their families, especially the children. Educated women have fewer, healthier, better-fed, and better-educated children. A father's education matters in many ways (particularly in adding to household income), but a mother's education is the most important input to improved human capital formation in her children.

Table 1.3: Interactions among Social Sector Investments and Human Capital Outcomes

INPUTS FROM SOCIAL SERVICES	IMPACTS ON HUMAN CAPITAL FORMATION				
	Knowledge	Family Size and Child Quality	Health Status	Nutritional Status	Healthful Living Conditions
Education		+	+	+	+
Family planning			+	+	
Health	+	+		+	+
Nutrition	+		+		
Water and Sanitation			+	+	

Note: The strongest cross-sector effects are shaded. The two cells surrounded by heavy lines with no shading indicate high potential for carefully targeted interventions. All of the diagonal cells could be shaded, of course, but in this table only cross-effects are considered.

Source: This is the authors' summary of the general findings of the empirical literature.

To look at the other shaded cells, family planning investments improve the health of mothers and children. Health investments improve nutrition outcomes because of the strong links nutrition has to disease from parasites, endemic diseases, and nutritional failures. The links also work in the opposite direction. A more healthful living environment resulting from investments in water and sanitation is complementary to many other investments such as education and nutrition. In addition, targeted health and nutrition interventions before and during the primary-school years have been shown to have important positive impacts on educational outcomes.

Four clear messages emerge from this chart. First, *education is the key producer of cross benefits to increasing the stock of human capital*. It has strong impacts across the board for the individual receiving the investment. Second, *education for women has large external benefits in increasing the stock of human capital*. Because women bear children, but also because of their traditional roles in the household and as cultivators in Africa, investments in the schooling of women directly affect the quality of the lives of children and others in the household. Third, *targeted health, nutrition, and sanitation* investments can have high cross-benefits, especially for school children. Fourth, *health is the major "user," or beneficiary, of other social sector inputs*.

To illustrate, let's examine one important example from Tanzania of the relationships among education, health, and population growth. As indicated above, female education is strongly correlated with lower demand for children and higher rates of child survival. According to the Demographic and Health Survey 1991/92, Tanzanian women with no education have an average of 6.5 children during their lifetimes, while women who have at least some secondary education have 4.2 children. The same survey estimated infant mortality in the past 10 years to be 103 per 1,000 live births for mothers with no education but 72 per 1,000 live births for mothers with secondary or higher education. These same relationships exist in industrialized and less-developed countries alike. A World Bank study of 13 African countries between 1975 and 1985 found that a 10 percent increase in female literacy rates reduced child mortality by 10 percent, while changes in male literacy had little influence.

It appears, however, that in Tanzania, female primary education does not have a large negative impact on fertility but secondary schooling does. This is a typical finding in countries that have high levels of fertility and low use of contraceptives. In Tanzania, total fertility and the mean number of children born to one woman falls only slightly with increasing education, until secondary school (see Table 1.4). Much of the impact is direct in that it comes from delayed childbearing while girls are still attending school[2]. One problem for Tanzania is that girls are starting primary school so late (an average of almost age 10 in our 1993/94 survey) that they may complete only a few years before child-bearing begins. Very few are advancing at all to secondary school, and there the drop out rate for girls is at least double that for boys. For Tanzania to reap the health and population-control benefits of improved schooling of women will require large and sustained investments in female education. These investments may be one of the most effective investments towards increasing the rate of accumulation of human capital in the country because of the cross-effects shown in Table 1.3.

Table 1.4: Fertility and Education in Tanzania

Education	Total Fertility Rate for Women Age 15-49	Mean Number of Children Ever Born to Women Age 40-49	Teenagers 15-19 Who Have Begun Child-Bearing (%)
No Education	6.11	7.08	39.9
Primary Incomplete	5.21	6.47	14.1
Completed Primary	5.17	6.26	30.0
Secondary/Higher	4.2	4.8	9.6

Note: All information is for 1994 from the Knowledge, Attitudes and Practices Survey except for information about total fertility and mean number of children born for women with a secondary or higher education. These data for these women are from the 1991/92 TDHS.
Source: TKAP, 1993 and TDHS, 1991/92, p. 23.

Paying for Investments in Human Capital

Most of the costs of human capital formation are up front. We generally pay for an entire education long before we start to see the economic payoffs to it, although many of the non-economic benefits become obvious quite early. The development of human educational capital takes a very long time, 6 or 7 years of primary school, plus an additional 2 to 12 years of secondary or higher education. The cash and opportunity costs of time in school are usually quite high, especially beyond primary school, and they make up most of the costs born by the household. Even if the cash costs are paid by the government, households pay the taxes that make such subsidies possible, so there is no escaping the high cost of such investments.

The problem of financing human capital, with high up-front costs and long-term pay-back, is compounded by poverty. While everyone can benefit from human capital investments, not everyone is equally capable of making them. The poor often have to make tragic choices between today's consumption and productive investments in their children. They simply cannot afford to do both.

Once a child finishes about three or four years of primary school, he or she is passably literate and numerate. Another four years, and the child is competent in all basic intellectual processes. In Tanzania, completion of primary school cost the government about US$153 in FY 1995 in direct subsidies, and cost parents about US$80. One year of secondary school cost about US$575 in FY 1995. Of this total, the government paid approximately US$167, and parents paid about US$408 (Follmer and Kessy, 1996; Dar and Levine, 1996). One year of university education costs about US$5,781, paid

---

[2] Although Table 1.4 contains simple correlations, the pattern is supported by multivariate work and is robust across many developing countries.

entirely by the government.

Government recurrent spending in FY 1995 was about US$48 million on primary education, US$8 million on secondary education, and US$22 million on primary health care, a total of about US$78 million. Households pay approximately double this amount. The key message of this report is that public sector spending on human capital investment is very low relative to the needs of the economy and its potential to absorb such investments. Public subsidies are provided inefficiently, and the distribution of the subsidies is inequitable.

Summary

The payoffs to human capital investment in Tanzania are large even if we only look at the impact they can have on earnings capacity and economic growth. Because of the synergistic effects of investing in one type of human capital on another, it is clear that the highest priority investments should be in basic education and education for girls. Targeted health and nutrition subsidies can also substantially improve the stock of human capital.

Perhaps most importantly, efficient investments in human capital are powerful poverty-reduction tools. When all of the benefits, both direct and indirect, of investing in people are tallied up, it is hard to find a loser in the process. The benefits extend across all productive sectors of the economy, tend to improve the relative position of the poor, and offer high payoffs to future growth potential. This is a win-win situation. Tanzania will only benefit by reviewing its social sectors, improving its human capital investment policies, and constantly monitoring those policies to make sure the goals are being achieved.

2
DEVELOPMENT AND STRUCTURE OF THE SOCIAL SECTORS

The conditions of the social sectors in Tanzania are, in large measure, a result of policies that have been in place for the past several decades. This chapter provides an overview of the development of the social sectors in Tanzania. It begins by describing the general policies, practices and problems in the social sectors since Independence. It then presents information on the implementation of social sector policies through the local government structure. The chapter concludes with a review of public spending levels and patterns.

THREE ERAS[1]

The Government of Tanzania, recognizing that the country's development depends on the education and well-being of the citizenry, has had a long and enduring history of progress in the social sectors. From the time Tanzania gained its independence, the delivery of a wide range of social services has been viewed as the government's responsibility, and policymakers have sought to extend health, education, water, and other social services to the largely rural population. In light of the low income levels in most of Tanzania, the government historically provided services at no direct charge.

Bilateral and multilateral donors have played an important role in the development of Tanzania's social service infrastructure. Much of the capital for construction of service delivery points (dispensaries, health centers, primary schools, and water systems) has come from external sources. In addition, basic inputs such as essential drugs for rural health units and primary school textbooks have been provided by donor agencies. Both short- and long-term technical assistance have been offered in the form of managerial and technical support for social services.

Non-governmental organizations, particularly those associated with religious organizations, also have contributed to the development of the social sectors in Tanzania. Religious missions have supplemented government-provided services with hospitals, dispensaries and schools in many areas of the country.

Phase I: Independence to Early-1980s

In 1961, upon gaining its independence, Tanzania inherited the British colonial economic and public sector structure. The health system consisted of a few hospitals and private doctors in urban areas,

---

[1] This section is adapted from the *Social Sector Strategy* prepared by the Government of Tanzania Planning Commission for the Consultative Group meeting, February 1995.

religious mission services, and traditional healers in rural areas. The education system was stratified according to race, and the quality and accessibility of African schools were poor. In the water sector, most households obtained water at no charge from natural sources (surface water) or purchased it at kiosks.

Recognizing the fundamental inadequacies of the colonial system, and the needs of the population and the economy, the government sought to increase access to basic health, education and other social services. Much of this was done with the generous assistance of bilateral and multilateral donor agencies willing to support the newly-independent country.

The government's approach was to provide both basic and specialized social services using uniform, population-based standards for construction and staffing. It sought to provide those services at no charge to the users, and to finance the services using tax revenues and donor support.

Table 2.1: Expansion of the Health Sector: 1969, 1978, and 1992

Input	*1969/70*	*1978/79*	*1992*
Civil Servants	12,400 (1971)	17,036 (1981)	32,650 (1988)
Health Centers	50	183	267
Dispensaries	1,444	2,282	2,393
Civil Servants per Unit	8.7	6.9	12.3

Sources: MOH, 1993; World Bank, 1994a.

The expansion of social service infrastructure and service provision during this period was impressive. In the health sector, for example, the number of government-operated rural health centers more than tripled between 1969 and 1978, and the number of dispensaries nearly doubled (see Table 2.1). Most of the 107 institutions now training health personnel were opened during this period, and large numbers of rural medical aides, medical assistants, medical officers, and nurses were trained and deployed in rural areas. As a result, the number of doctors increased more than three-fold and the number of medical assistants, rural medical aides, and health assistants increased by an order of 10. This expansion resulted in about 90 percent of the population living within 10 kilometers of a health facility, and nearly three-quarters within 5 kilometers of health services.

In the education sector, expansion was even more rapid. As shown in Table 2.2, both the number of enrollees in primary schools and the number of education sector workers increased by nearly four-fold during the 1970s. The majority of the 10,900 primary schools now in operation were constructed during the 1970s, allowing each village to have its own primary school. Most of the 40 teacher-training colleges now in operation were opened during this period.

Table 2.2: Expansion of the Education Sector: 1971, 1981, and 1991

Inputs and Enrollees	*1971*	*1981*	*1991*
Civil Servants Working in Education	23,131	93,318	101,042 (1988)
Primary School Enrollments	902,619	3,530,622	3,512,347
Secondary-school Enrollments	43,352	67,002	166,812
Civil Servants per Student	41	39	36

Sources: MOEC, various years; World Bank, 1994a.

Secondary-school enrollments expanded at a much slower pace. This was due to deliberate rationing of secondary schooling as part of a government effort to coordinate student enrollment with the nation's manpower requirements. Between 1971 and 1981, enrollment in secondary schools grew by only about 24,000 students, and the enrollment rate remained stagnant, at only about 4 percent of the cohort of children in the relevant age range.

Water delivery systems were expanded greatly during the 1970s. Under Regional Water Master Plans, donor-financed blueprints for improved water schemes were created in nearly all regions, and large-scale construction was initiated. As shown in Table 2.3, between 1971 and 1980, the proportion of the population with access to improved water sources increased from 12 to 47 percent.

Table 2.3: Expansion of the Water Sector: 1971, 1980, and 1991

Water Supply Indicator	*1971*	*1980*	*1992*
Population Covered by "Safe" Water ('000s)	1,440	7,644	7,474
Share of Population Covered by "Safe" Water (%)	12	47	46[a]

[a] Recent figures are widely thought to overestimate access. Currently, only about 25 percent of households are thought to use improved water sources.

Source: Mutalemwa, 1994.

As the water sector improved, centrally-planned activities were initiated to expand access to sanitation facilities. In 1973, the government introduced the "latrinization" campaign, "Mtu ni Afya." This campaign, which required that each household should have and use a latrine, was accelerated following a cholera outbreak in 1977. As a result, latrine coverage in the rural areas increased from 20 percent to 50 percent between 1973 and 1980.[2]

Phase II: Early-1980s to Early-1990s

The impressive investments and accomplishments of the 1970s were not sustained through the 1980s. The government encountered difficulties in financing and managing the social services that had been put in place. At the same time, the expectations of the population increased. By the end of the decade and into the 1990s, the system that had promised rapid improvement in human welfare had not met its ambitious targets. Progress toward improved outcomes was lagging. A brief examination of the problems that emerged during the 1980s illustrates the weaknesses in the system.

Three basic supply-side problems emerged as the government sought to increase social services' coverage of the population.

First, the *recurrent cost burden*, following large capital investments in health, education and water services, and training of large numbers of personnel, was enormous. While donors had been willing to finance much of the capital cost of developing the infrastructure, financing of the recurrent cost was largely left to the government, which in turn depended on a small tax base.

The problems resulting from an overextension of the health, education, and water systems were compounded by rapid increases in the costs of imported materials, including petroleum, by the financial demands of other sectors, and by unfavorable international trading conditions. In 1972, the total oil import bill of Tanzania was Tsh 269 million, but by 1977, despite a 20 percent cut in oil consumption, the cost was Tsh 835 million. Among other consequences, the skyrocketing oil bill cut deeply into the health and education systems' supervision and referral functions.

---

[2] Figures on latrine coverage may be slightly misleading because of a broadened definition of improved sanitation facilities in recent years.

At the same time, government revenues declined. The prices of three of the nation's major exports (coffee, tea and tobacco) fell by 40, 29 and 12 percent, respectively, between 1976/77 and 1981/82. The unfavorable import-export market placed severe financial strains on the government's capacity to support social and other services. Purchase of items such as spare parts for water pumps became nearly impossible.

The second major problem faced by the government was that centralized *management* of the vast networks of water systems, health facilities, schools and associated staff was severely limited by the high cost of transportation and communication in rural areas. Accountability was inadequate, and consumers felt little or no ownership of the social services upon which they depended. The problems were made worse by the lack of coordination and changing lines of authority between central and local governments. Standard plans and norms established by ministries in Dar es Salaam were expected to be implemented by local governments, but the local administrations had relatively few financing options. Health and education sector employees, technically accountable to and supervised by central ministries and regional authorities, were formally employed by local governments.

The third problem was that both central and local governments were relatively passive toward the initiatives of donor agencies. These agencies had been essential to the positive developments in the social sectors. The *lack of coordination of donor efforts* led to a situation in which some donor-funded vertical programs drew attention away from core supervisory and service delivery functions in the health sector. External technical assistance in some sectors, especially the water sector, was poorly integrated into the government's existing structure, and too little indigenous capacity was developed to maintain the systems after the termination of consultant contracts. Some districts tended to receive considerable foreign assistance, while others were left with little or none.

None of the problems described above were insoluble. However, the Government of Tanzania did relatively little to improve the situation during the 1980s, in the face of a severe crisis throughout the economy. Without altering the fundamental definition of the government's role and near-monopoly position in the social sectors, policymakers attempted to stretch shrinking resources over expanding needs. The government's commitment did not wane. Table 2.1 and Table 2.2 show that by the end of the 1980s, manpower in the social sectors had continued to increase. However, the high cost of personnel tended to crowd out other necessary expenditures.

As a result, the quality of most social services declined. In the health sector, difficulties were manifested in decreased attention to supervision at the regional and district level, critical shortages of basic pharmaceutical and other medical supplies, and dissatisfaction of workers with their salaries. In the education sector, where the expansion had been most dramatic, textbooks and basic teaching materials were in short supply, as were qualified and motivated teachers in rural primary schools. In the water sector, implementation of the Regional Water Master Plans faltered. Over time, those systems required maintenance, spare parts, and ongoing operational support that was not forthcoming. Within several years, a large share of the pumps, wells, and other schemes that had been installed were non-operational. In some regions, up to two-thirds of the schemes went out of service. Some systems were started and never completed, leaving communities with partially constructed wells and pumping systems, and no access to improved water sources.

On the demand side, the population grew by about 3 percent annually during the 1980s. As a result, population growth alone placed increasing pressure on the government's ability to deliver social services. Graduates from the first Universal Primary Education cohort placed severe pressure on the limited number of spaces available in secondary schools.

In part as a result of early successes in the social sectors, expectations about what the government should provide rose. The rise in living standards, at least in some areas of the country, created growing demand for better health care, education, and piped water – in short, for greater state spending. Despite faltering growth in the late 1970s and early 1980s, sustained growth in incomes began again under structural adjustment in 1984, further fueling demands for services that the government could not adequately supply.

Phase III: Current Era (early-1990s)

The stresses placed on the system of social services and the economy, and the inability of the system to adapt to those stresses during the 1980s, can be seen in health, education, and other outcomes during the 1990s. Overall, progress has been disappointingly slow. Enrollments in primary school have declined while illiteracy rates have at best remained stagnant. Basic health conditions, including those related to water supply and nutrition interventions, have improved very little, while the AIDS epidemic has added critical new challenges to the system. Continued rapid population growth has only added to the problem.

The government's current position, as articulated in its *Social Sector Strategy* (Government of Tanzania Planning Commission, 1994) is that the country's future development depends on a well-educated, healthy population. In Africa, as in the rest of the world, the engine of development will be the skills and productivity of the population. The experience of East Asia shows most clearly the potential for sound investments in basic education, in particular to support rapid rates of poverty-reducing growth.

A recognition that effective human capital investment has stagnated for 15 years has prompted new thinking about the government's role in the social sectors. Experiences of the 1980s show the need for greater flexibility, diversification, and responsiveness to demand in social service delivery, attention to sustainable financing, and explicit priorities for government and donor spending.

As part of this new thinking, the government is consolidating and focusing its role in the delivery of basic health and education services. At the same time, it is liberalizing the environment for private-sector participation in high-demand services that provide individual benefits. The government is defining its core (and non-core) functions and seeking to allocate the vast majority of public monies toward core functions. In addition, it is identifying the highest-payoff investments within and across the social sectors.

The government recognizes the role of households in investment decisions regarding health, education, and the well-being of its members. Household members are seen as active participants in choosing and supporting the services that offer concrete benefits to the population. This recognition has the potential both to improve the quality of social services and place them on a sounder and more sustainable financial base. As part of this effort, the state has plans to shift some management decisions for primary schools to committees. Further, a pilot project is currently underway in which community representatives participate in the management of basic health service facilities (see Box 5.2).

DELIVERY OF SOCIAL SERVICES THROUGH LOCAL GOVERNMENT

Abolished in 1972, elected local governments were reintroduced in Tanzania in 1983 and charged with the responsibility of delivering basic health services (district hospital and below) and primary education services. This mandate is wide-reaching, and includes responsibility for the operation and maintenance of health facilities and schools, employment and supervision of health cadres and teaching personnel, maintenance of local water systems, and so forth (Shirima 1994).

Local Government Institutions

The functions of the existing three tiers of government are complex and often overlapping. The central government prepares guidelines for economic policy and management, human resource planning, investment guidelines, manpower management policies, and budgets (including centrally prepared investment and recurrent budgets). Regional governments are responsible for

---

Box 2.1: Principles of the *Social Sector Strategy*

The government proposes the following as principles for investments and action in the social sectors.

Priority Attention to Development of Human Capital. As the key to Tanzania's future, the social sectors will receive priority attention from the highest levels of decision makers. Public investments in human capital will be consistent with the country's development goals.

Private Sector Partnership. The public sector (government and donors) will serve as agents to stimulate private investment, ensuring that basic services are adequately financed while not necessarily directly providing those services.

Defining the Public Sector Role. The government has a special role to play in complementing, not substituting for, investments in human capital that are made by the household. In particular, the government has the responsibility of investing in the priority areas that have the greatest social payoffs and that disproportionately benefit the poor. This is true along several dimensions: Across all sectors, the government will seek the optimal allocation between social sectors and other types of projects; within the social sectors as a whole, the government will identify the types of investments that generate the greatest long-term returns; and within each of the social sectors, the government will seek to concentrate resources on the inputs and programs that are most appropriate for public financing. In briefest form, this means concentrating public resources on preventive and basic curative health services, and basic education.

Targeted External Assistance. Donors will be asked to concentrate their activities and support in areas that are of high priority to the government, and that do not divert scarce human or material resources toward lower priority objectives. At the same time, donors will be asked to complement investments being made by the government.

Orientation toward Outcomes. Progress toward objectives will be measured in terms of improved measurable outcomes, rather than expansion of the number of schools, water systems, facilities, and personnel.

Local Control. The government will be accountable to the communities and households served. In the final analysis, it will be the consumers of social services themselves who must be satisfied with the quality and quantity of services and choices that are available to them. The means to do this is through further decentralization of authority and movement toward facility-based management.

Cross-Sectoral Linkages. Investments in the social sectors will be made more efficient by taking into account linkages across the sectors. Specifically, available evidence strongly suggests that improvements in one area—female education—is the surest route to significant improvements in household welfare in the next generation.

---

interpreting locally implemented central government plans and policies for the benefit of local governments, supervising their implementation, and providing technical advice to local governments in the execution of their development plans. The local governments, as stated above, are responsible for the implementation of services, employment of personnel, and (in concept) preparation of budget requests.

Administratively, local governments are weak due to shortages of qualified staff, compounded by the loss of experience and institutional continuity during the period 1972-83. The structure and organization of local governments is currently based on an elaborate committee structure, inherited from the one-party era that prevailed from Independence to the early 1990s. The three types of committees generally recognized include political committees, administrative-political committees, and technical committees. These committees are also multi-tiered, ranging from the Village Council (the lowest formal committee in the local government system) to the Regional Development Committee. Currently, the district and village councils are elected, but all district-level officials are appointed by the central government. In general, members of the decision-making committees and councils are predominantly male. However, the government has made some efforts to increase female participation in these decision-making bodies.

Local governments are the owners of primary schools and dispensaries and are responsible for their maintenance. Their authority is severely circumscribed, however. Procurement of supplies and equipment for health and water schemes is usually done through central government stores, and the costs are debited from the respective district account. While some attempt has been made to increase local governmental authority, household and community members are otherwise virtually uninvolved in facility or systems operations.

Local governments are the *de facto* employers of staff in the social sectors in that they issue letters of appointment and pay salaries and related benefits. However, local governments have little say in the selection, motivation and discipline of their staff. They have to accept staff provided through central government allocations, and local governments are neither permitted to identify candidates nor to fire them. Disciplinary measures for professional misconduct and recognition for outstanding performance are largely handled by the sectoral ministries through their regional arms (see Box 2.2).

There are few incentives for staff to perform and few disincentives not to perform. Given the distance between supervisory and implementation levels, and constraints within the central ministries, there is virtually no assessment of performance, and promotions are usually awarded on the basis of length of service or patronage. On the other hand, only gross negligence is considered grounds for firing. A vacant post is normally filled by appointment rather than open competition.

Box 2.2: Hiring and Firing of School Teachers

The hiring and firing of school teachers illustrates the complexity of the relationship between central planning and local implementation. Teachers are centrally supplied to the local government system without local governments having any say in the selection of individuals. In the case of severe teacher misconduct, parents are expected to lodge their complaint with the local school committee. If the committee agrees on a probable cause for action, the District Executive Director within the local government is notified, and he or she passes the matter on to the Teachers Service Commission in the Ministry of Education and Culture, which in turn prepares a recommendation to the Regional Service Commission. The matter is finally decided and settled by a national committee, which hands down a verdict; the verdict then cascades back through the system to the local school. The Regional Service Commission is the body with the authority to hire, fire and discipline staff. Recognition of exceptionally good performance follows the same process and is understandably rare.

Local governments are heavily dependent on central government financing, in particular for the agency services that cover education, health, and water and sanitation. Development projects are almost wholly funded by annual block grants from the center, and about 70 percent of the recurrent budget is similarly funded.

The sources from which local governments in Tanzania can raise money to finance services are well articulated in statutes, and include taxes, licenses and fees, user charges, rental income from council properties, government grants, and donations. Despite being empowered by existing statutes to raise revenues from a variety of sources, however, the actual performance in generating revenues has been low.

An examination of the potential revenue sources shown in Table 2.4 suggests that most are inflexible and cannot keep up with inflation. The development levy, a head tax, is the most important, especially in rural areas. Businesses and liquor license fees are relatively more important to municipal governments. For both urban and rural councils, these two taxes account for approximately 60 percent of the revenues.

Locally raised resources are inadequate in part because the central government proscribes increases in license fees, and because user fees are fixed at very low levels. Consumers are unwilling to pay for poor quality services, as described below:

- The central government sets the minimum and maximum license fees for each business. About 80 percent of these license fees (ranging from Tsh 40,000 to 400,000 per annum) are collected by the central government, leaving only about 20 percent of the collectable fees to the local governments. Local government agencies are not legally empowered to further raise the collection fees.

Table 2.4: Source of Funds for Rural and Urban Councils (%)

Source	Type of Council	
	Urban	Rural
Development Levy	35	50
Business/Liquor Licenses	24	9
Market Dues	7	–
Property Tax	7	–
Produce Cess	–	10
Livestock Cess	–	3
Others	27	28
Total	100	100

Source: Shirima, 1994.

- User charges for social services were abolished in the early 1970s. Their recent reintroduction has been problematic, especially given the low quality of the services provided by the government. Local governments are caught in a vicious circle: declining revenues affect the quality of services, which in turn undermines the willingness to pay.

Local Government Allocation Process and Accountability

The decisions about how much to spend and how to allocate funds are embedded in a local authority's budget. Thus, the degree of discretion over spending may be evaluated at several stages through the planning and budgeting process. The local authority planning/budgeting process is iterative and lasts a full year from July to June. It involves both the administrative and the political systems at successively higher levels, as well as local governments, regional administrations, and the central government (see Box 2.3).

Local governments have occasionally expressed concern over the role of the regional administration in the planning process. In particular, they have identified the following problems, which indicate that financial decision making and technical knowledge are disconnected:

- local government budgets are assessed and amended at the regional level before they are forwarded for approval to the Prime Minister's Office;

- regional administrations unilaterally carry out development works within the jurisdictions of the councils, regardless of councils' perceived priorities;

- regional administrations divert council resources for activities which have not been budgeted for by the councils;

- regional administrators undermine council decisions on the setting of tariffs and rates; and

- urban councils are at a disadvantage because regional development priorities are determined by the regional development councils on which urban council representatives are greatly outnumbered by rural council representatives.

The accountability of local governments in Tanzania is seriously deficient, for the following reasons.

- External audits for the most recently available fiscal year (1991-92) were more than 40 percent in arrears on account of delayed submission by local governments and staff shortages in the Auditor General's Department. External audits of some accounts have been in arrears for more than three years.

- Internal controls are neither feasible nor operational because of a lack of qualified and experienced staff. By the end of 1993, there were only two fully-qualified accountants working as treasurers in the entire local government system. These (and others, less qualified) had only limited and unclear decision-making authority.

Box 2.3: Transfer of Funds

Development Expenditures.

Step 1.   Councils prepare quarterly progress reports on project implementation, which are forwarded to the Regional Development Director (RDD).

Step 2.   RDD consolidates district project reports and forwards them to the Planning Commission through the Department of Local Governments in the Prime Minister's Office (PMO).

Step 3.   Planning Commission reviews report and approves release of funds through the PMO.

Step 4.   PMO channels funds to the districts through the RDD.

Recurrent Expenditures.

Step 1.   Funds to meet expenditures for grant services are released to districts through the RDD.

Step 2.   Reports are prepared by councils highlighting how funds were applied. These are checked by the PMO before the next quarterly release.

In short, the role of the RDD can be viewed either as that of an unnecessary administrative layer, or that of a post office box, depending on how each RDD views his/her function.

- Annual accounts are kept in a variety of forms (cash, accrual, or modified accrual), submissions are irregular, and principles of accounting are applied inconsistently from one year to the next.

- Budgetary controls suffer from major anomalies in the budgeting system, with the recurrent budget running from January to December and the development budget running from July to June. Budget proposal changes are subject to arbitrary cuts at higher levels without reference to local priorities.

- Internal audits are constrained by shortages of qualified staff and the lack of audit guidelines. Few councils have functioning internal audit units.

The principal issues in resource allocation relate to a disconnect between spending authority and accountability. Local government budgets are assessed and amended at different stages, and arbitrary cuts are made by other tiers of government without consultation and regardless of local priorities. Assessments of spending priorities for development are made without a financial and economic appraisal of the proposed investment, and without an assessment of the associated recurrent budget implications. Recurrent expenditure budgets are prepared on an incremental basis, without an assessment of spending priorities, and the resources to control and account for expenditures are woefully inadequate.

PUBLIC SPENDING AND THE DISTRIBUTION OF BENEFITS

This section provides a broad overview of public spending on the social sectors. Two basic questions are posed: How much does the government spend on health, education and water services? How does the population benefit from these investments? We first present information on the levels and trends of government spending on the social sectors. Next, we examine how the benefits of public spending are distributed across the population, by income category. This is intended as an overview. In the chapters that follow, resource allocations and benefit incidence for each sector are examined in detail.

Government Spending

The levels of spending in the social sectors are widely acknowledged to be inadequate to operate even the existing health facilities, water systems, and schools (see Box 2.4). In 1994/95, the Government of Tanzania budgeted 40 percent of recurrent expenditures, about Tsh 150 billion, for the social sectors, broadly defined to include education, health, water and sanitation (see Table 2.5). Education absorbed 22 percent of the budget. On average, direct central government expenditures through sector ministries constituted slightly more than one-third of the total, while the remainder was disbursed through the regional government and district councils. Almost all of the

Table 2.5: Total Government Expenditures, 1994/95

	Budgeted Estimate 93/94 (Tsh billion)	Share of Total Recurrent (%)
Gross Recurrent Expenditures	372.7	100
Of Which:		
Education	83.0	22
Health	57.0	15
Water	5.4	1
Other	4.3	1
Total Development Expenditures	20.0	
Total Expenditures	392.7	

Source: Follmer and Kessy, 1996; World Bank, 1997.

money was raised by the central government.

Box 2.4: How Much is Enough? Underfunding in the Social Sectors

In each of the social sectors, chronic underfunding has been identified by the government and donors alike as a severe problem. As Lawson (1993) points out, however, the concept of underfunding is rarely defined. At times, references to underfunding are meant to indicate that government funding of education and health services is inadequate to meet the demand for those services. This is the broadest sense of the concept of underfunding, and it accepts the premise that it is the government's responsibility to provide all services to the full population. At other times, "underfunding" means that the budget does not stretch to meet the government's current targets for coverage, given certain staffing and other input norms. Given the ever-expanding targets in health, education and water, and the use of staffing norms that were not based on economic analyses, this definition of underfunding is also broad. A narrower definition of underfunding is interpreted to mean that the health facilities, schools, and water systems *now in operation* cannot function at capacity because of lack of financial resources.

In his analysis of underfunding, Lawson drew from past estimates of the cost of fully supplying, staffing, and maintaining existing schools and health facilities. He concluded that "to operate *existing* services effectively, the government would require additional recurrent funding of at least Tsh 15.5 billion for health and Tsh 17.5 billion for education."

In a separate analysis of the magnitude of underfunding, the World Bank (1994a) estimated that to provide quality education to the current enrollees in 1993/94 throughout the primary school system would cost the government nearly 20 percent more than is currently devoted to primary education. If the enrollment were to expand to universal coverage of appropriately-aged children, the education budget would have to increase by about 76 percent. In the health sector, the World Bank roughly estimated that the health budget would have to nearly triple to meet the funding requirements for the essential health care package recommended in the *World Development Report* (World Bank, 1994c).

Whichever analysis is used as an indicator, there is no doubt that the funding of the social sectors is in a state of crisis. The gap between current expenditures and requirements is vast. The skewed allocation of funds toward higher-level services means that conditions are even worse for basic health and education, which provide most of the services to the poor. The matter of where additional money should come from (reallocations within the sectors, reallocation of the central government budget, greater local tax capacity, users, or donors, or a mixture of all) is a major problem to be solved.

The high recurrent costs of the overextended social service network, combined with severe economic constraints, resulted in the government spending most of its funds on the relatively expensive elements of the system, namely secondary schools, universities, hospitals, and so forth. Few resources have remained for maintenance, non-personnel inputs, and quality improvements. Very little money has been mobilized for new capital investments in the water sector, which has suffered from many years of inadequate maintenance.

The share of total government spending that is devoted to the social sectors has been falling over the past several years. While total government expenditures have grown in real terms at an annual average rate of 18 percent, social sector expenditures have grown by only 11 percent. In the social sectors, development expenditures have increased more rapidly than have recurrent expenditures (see Table 2.6). Social sector spending as a share of overall government spending at the regional and council levels fell from 43 percent in 1991/92 to 36 percent in 1993/94.

Donor Spending

Net official development assistance has comprised approximately 40 percent of Tanzania's gross domestic product in recent years. In 1991, external assistance amounted to about US$43 per capita, making Tanzania one of the countries most dependent on external funds. A large share of this assistance is allocated to the social sectors, though the relative shares that different sectors have received have changed over time.

Each of the social sectors depends heavily on donor aid. Donors fund about 78 percent of development expenditures, and 5 percent of all government expenditures in education. Only 41 percent of external assistance is devoted to primary education, while 53 percent is allocated to higher and technical education, adult education, science and cultural programs, and ministry and regional administration.

In the health sector, donors fund a full 84 percent of development expenditures. Donors do relatively better in focusing on basic services in health as compared to education. Approximately 70 percent of all donor funds in the health sector go toward preventive services (including vertical immunization programs). Another 30 percent is devoted to curative services, principally those delivered in dispensaries and health centers.

Table 2.6: Trends in Social Sector Spending: 1990-93

	Average Share FY90-FY93	Change in Share between FY90 and FY93	Average Real Growth per Annum FY90-FY93
Net Public Expenditures	100.0	0.0	17.5
Total Expenditures in Social Sectors	30.2	-2.7	11.3
Net Recurrent Expenditures	100.0	0.0	10.3
Recurrent Expenditures in Social Sectors	36.3	-2.1	6.1
Total Development Expenditures	100.0	0.0	54.6
Development Expenditures in Social Sectors	14.0	+3.9	74.4

Source: World Bank, 1994a.

Donor investment in water and sanitation has been declining since 1982. External funding for the sector decreased by about 78 percent, from US$49.6 million in 1989 to US$11.0 million in 1995. Spending on water and sanitation as a share of all foreign assistance declined during that same period from about 5.4 to about 1.1 percent.

The dependence of Tanzania's social sectors, even at the current unsatisfactory level of service, places the country in an extraordinarily vulnerable position. It is fully dependent on donor support for key inputs. Most training activities are fully funded by external assistance. Recent budget crises have forced the government to curtail all official travel, even routine supervision trips, unless donor support is provided. Numerous institutions, including the Institute for Management Training of Education Personnel, the Tanzania Food and Nutrition Center, the National Family Planning Program and others, are heavily (or fully) dependent on donor funding for their survival.

Incidence of the Benefits of Public Spending

As noted earlier in this chapter, an overriding and consistent theme of Tanzania's social policy since the Arusha Declaration has been to ensure that basic social services are available equitably to all members of society. The extent to which this is achieved can be assessed, in rough terms, by examining how the benefits of public spending are distributed across the population. The basic question is whether government spending is targeted toward the needy population. To answer this question, data on household use of social services were combined with information on how the government and donors spend their resources on health (including family planning and nutrition), education, and water.

The analyses
show that the benefits of
public spending accrue
disproportionately to the
best-off households (see
Table 2.7)[3]. The richest
20 percent of
households capture 34
percent of the benefits
of recurrent public
spending on health,
education and water.
The poorest 20 percent
capture 14 percent of
the benefits.[4]

Table 2.7: Aggregation of Public Social Expenditure Incidence, 1993

Sector	Welfare Group					Total
	Lowest Expenditure Quintile	Second	Third	Fourth	Highest Expenditure Quintile	
Education	14	16	16	16	37	100
Health	17	20	16	18	29	100
Water	11	11	15	23	40	100
Combined Education, Health, and Water	14	18	16	17	34	100

Source: HRDS, 1993/94, and World Bank, 1994a.

This distribution of the benefits of public spending can be explained quite simply. The government has made a commitment to provide all levels of health, education, and other services at highly subsidized prices and to restrict the private sector. The distribution of subsidies from basic health and education services are fairly even across income groups. But they are also cheap. The highest levels of services (hospitals and universities, for example) are far more costly on a per capita basis. They are also more accessible to the relatively well off urban population. In education, the relatively few, typically wealthier students who are selected for secondary or university schooling receive the benefits of a sizeable share of government and donor investment. In health, better-off populations use nearby district, regional and consultant hospital services, and therefore consume a disproportionate share of the health budget. In water, where the distribution of benefits is highly skewed, huge investments have been made in urban water systems, benefitting the well off populations almost exclusively.

The systematic inhibition of the private sector in Tanzania greatly contributes to the distribution of the benefits of public spending. In settings where the private sector is more active in providing social services, the better-off populations are likely to meet a large share of their demand by purchasing services in the market.

---

[3] Water figures for 1994/95 were not available. Estimates of the distribution of benefits for health and education in 1994/95 were calculated based on the 1994/95 division of expenditures across subsectors assuming that each quintile's share of subsector benefits had not changed. For example, assuming that the distribution of benefits across quintiles for primary school, secondary school, and university had not changed, the distribution of total education benefits was recalculated using the 1994/95 distribution of expenditures across levels of education. Using this approach, it is estimated that the poorest income quintile received 13 percent of education expenditures in 1994/95, the second poorest received 16 percent, the middle quintile received 15 percent, the second richest received 15 percent, and the richest received 41 percent of the benefits. Thus, the richest quintile appears to have increased their share of total education benefits. Using this same technique to estimate the distribution of health expenditures, the poorest quintile received approximately 17 percent of health spending in 1994/95, the second poorest received 19 percent, the middle quintile received 16 percent, the second richest received 19 percent, and the richest quintile of the population received 28 percent. Thus, the distribution of health benefits appears not to have changed from the previous year.

[4] It is important to note that we have no information on the incidence of taxes. However, because government revenue is heavily dependent on indirect taxes, it is quite likely that tax incidence is regressive, compounding the regressivity of social spending. Moreover, conservative assumptions were made in estimating incidence of expenditures, so we expect that Table 2.7 actually *understates* the regressivity of the benefit structure.

CONCLUSION

The social sectors in Tanzania are entering a new era, in which the government and donors are learning, from successes and failures of the past, to restructure the delivery of services through the government and to ease the constraints on private-sector participation. Increasingly, there is recognition that the government cannot provide all services to all people, given the tight budget constraints and limitations in implementation capacity. The government is committed to targeting public funds toward the investments that yield the greatest positive results for society in general, and for the poor in particular.

The current division of responsibilities between the central and local government authorities is now a significant part of the problem. Ambiguity in management roles, overexpansion of infrastructure, lack of revenue-generating authority at the local level, and general underfunding have created a situation in which local authorities cannot adequately operate and maintain the institutions that were centrally planned. More effective decentralization, combined with greater accountability at the local level, is a requirement for progress in the delivery of social services.

The fundamental reason that the government should ease constraints on the private sector and foster more effective decentralization is to increase opportunities for households to invest in their children's human capital. Under the current system, households are severely constrained in their ability to make investments in health and education that will yield greater welfare for their families in future generations. Given that households have the greatest stake in human capital investment, it is essential that the government alleviate those constraints.

3
CHARACTERISTICS OF THE TANZANIAN HOUSEHOLD

The household's role in determining the outcomes in the social sectors has often been neglected in Tanzania. Regardless of the education, health, water, and other services available, the impact of those services depends heavily on the choice that parents and other household members make to use, or not to use, the services. In addition, many of the preconditions for successful education and good health are determined within the household, and are relatively insensitive to government intervention.

This chapter summarizes information about the characteristics of the Tanzanian household. How many children and adults live in a Tanzanian household? How much does a typical household consume, within and outside of the market, and how do consumption patterns vary? How much does a typical household spend on health, education, and other types of human capital investments? We highlight the differences between poorer and better-off households, as well as been those in urban and rural areas of the country. The information presented comes from analyses of the Human Resources Development Survey 1993/94.

HOUSEHOLD STRUCTURE

Overall, the average family size in Tanzania is 6.1 persons. Poorer households tend to be larger than better-off households (7 versus 5 household members for the lowest and highest income quintile, respectively). On average, rural households are larger than urban households.

Rural households and low-income households are characterized by a higher dependency ratio than urban and/or better-off households. That is, low-income households tend to have more children and more older people, relative to the number of individuals in the working age groups. The dependency ratio for the poorest one-fifth of households is 1.3, compared to 0.9 for the best-off households. Most of this difference is the result of differentials in fertility and the number of young children. On average, there are 3.4 children under 15 years of age in the lowest-income households, compared to 2.1

Table 3.1: Demographic Characteristics of the Household, by Expenditure Level

Characteristic	Lowest 20%	Highest 20%	All
Average Household Size	7.2	5.0	6.1
Dependency Ratio	1.3	0.9	1.2
Average Age of Household Head	46.3	41.1	43.6
Female-Headed Households (%)	13.2	18.0	15.1
Average Number of Children Under 15	3.4	2.1	2.8
Average Number of Adults Over 64	0.20	0.14	0.15
Male-Female Ratio	0.94	0.93	0.97

Source: HRDS, 1993/94.

children in better-off families (see Table 3.1).

According to the HRDS 1993/94, 15 percent of Tanzanian households are headed by a woman. There is a higher proportion of female-headed households among the better-off households, and female-headed households are no more likely to be found in poverty than male-headed households. Despite this, there are indications that women's legal and social status is lower than men's (see Box 3.1).

Box 3.1: Gender Issues in Tanzania

Despite the measures taken by the Tanzanian government since Independence to ensure that women and men are equal partners in the nation's development, there is a general consensus that some of the existing religious and traditional norms and attitudes assign women a subordinate position in the society. This has proven very resistant to change, especially in the rural areas (Meena, 1994).

Women continue to carry the dual burden of caring for their families while providing the main labor on the family farm. The following facts highlight the disadvantaged position of Tanzanian women with respect to their male counterparts.

(a) The land is allocated to the households, but it is the husband who retains claim to it for both legal and practical purposes. In terms of land ownership, women continue to be regarded as legally incompetent. Moreover, under customary law, land is inherited through the male line. Thus, as a rule, women are unable to own land in their own right, borrow money using land as collateral, or grow cash crops for their own gain unless they have saved enough cash to purchase such land outright.

(b) Women are seldom in charge of cash crops. (The HRDS indicates that female-headed households in rural areas are significantly less likely to be cultivating at least one cash crop). However, by and large women are expected to do much of the day-to-day work. In addition, most women have the responsibility to raise all food consumed by the family.

(c) According to the present Employment Act, women employed in the private sector have the right to paid maternity leave for 12 weeks every three years, and 30-minute breaks for breastfeeding. In the absence of laws against discrimination, employers discriminate against women because labor costs can be higher.

(d) The bride price is acknowledged in the law, and discriminates against women in the event that they wish to divorce their husbands. A woman cannot obtain a divorce without returning the bride price.

SOURCES OF INCOME AND LIVING CONDITIONS

According to the HRDS, the most important source of income is from agriculture. Crop production was mentioned as the most important source of income for 60 percent of households on the mainland, but for the rural and the poor this percentage is 75 and 77, respectively. The next most important source of income is monetary savings, followed by livestock income.

Ownership of Goods

Table 3.2 shows the percent of the population owning at least one of the goods in each category, those being a bicycle, watch, and book. Patterns of ownership reflect strong differences in ownership of these goods across the population. While 36 percent of the males older than 15 own a watch, only 15 percent of women among the same age group claim to do so. Men are far more likely than women to own bicycles

Table 3.2: Ownership of Some Assets by Gender Among Population 15 Years and Older (%age)

Item	Male	Female	Total
Bicycle	24.5	1.7	12.5
Watch	36.5	15.5	25.5
Book	51.1	34.1	42.2

Source: HRDS, 1993/94.

and books. Among all the goods for which information was collected in the HRDS, none was more likely to be owned by women than by men.

Patterns of ownership of durable goods reflect strong differences in access to these types of goods across poor and better-off households, as well as between rural and urban residents. Durables such as cameras and refrigerators are owned by only a very small proportion of the population, and only by rich households in Dar es Salaam or other urban areas. Still, even among these groups, the proportion of households that claim to own any of these assets is very low, revealing low standards of living for the overall population.

Housing Conditions

The poor are identified not only by lower expenditures, but also by distinct differences in the condition of their houses. In general, there is a clear distinction between a rich and poor household, as well as between a rural and an urban household. The average number of people per room is lower in the rural areas of Tanzania than in the urban area, including Dar es Salaam. However, overall housing conditions in rural areas are much worse. Only 1.4 percent of households in rural Tanzania have access to any source of electricity. This affects not only the poor rural households but the better-off as well. Overall, 74 percent of households live in a house with an earth floor. Among the poor, 95 percent live in houses with earth floors, compared to 46 percent among the better-off. There were no significant differences in most housing characteristics between male- and female-headed households of similar income levels.

Ownership of Land and Livestock

The survey analysis found no remarkable quantitative or qualitative differences in ownership of land or livestock to distinguish better-off from poorer households in Tanzania. Unlike many other developing countries, access to land is not the factor that distinguishes between poor and better-off households. About 88 percent of *both* poor and better-off households own land. Even among urban residents, whether in Dar es Salaam or other towns, ownership of land is prevalent. The average amount of land owned per rural household is 5.9 acres, with poor rural households owning about 5 acres and better-off households owning 6.4 acres, on average. Female-headed households have only about 60 percent as much land as male-headed households.

Based on the survey respondents' ranking of the physical quality of their land, neither quality not quantity of land can explain the differences in the incomes obtained from the land (as reflected in different levels of consumption). However, quality of land may be interpreted more broadly to include any factor that may influence the returns of the physical capital. In this sense, access to roads may be a key element in determining the overall (non-physical) quality of land, and help explain the differentials in income.

Among rural households, the likelihood of a better-off household owning some livestock is similar to that of lower-income households. The average number of owned livestock of low-income rural households (6.9 animals) is similar to that of high-income rural households (7.4 animals).

Human Capital

According to the estimates of the HRDS, the literacy rate in 1993 was 75 percent. The survey indicates that women, and people older than 14 years of age living in poor rural households, are more likely to be illiterate than other groups. The literacy rate is 63 percent among the poor, 84 percent among the better-off. In Dar es Salaam, the literacy rate is 88 percent, compared to 82 percent in other urban areas, and 72 percent in rural areas. About 84 percent of all males older than 14 can read and write, while only about 67 percent of women older than 14 can do so.

Although Tanzania is performing relatively well in terms of the percentage of the population who are literate or numerate, the level of education achieved is rudimentary. Approximately 94 percent of the population over 21 years of age does not have any education beyond the primary level.

Very few of those who go beyond primary education live in poor households. Among the lowest-income households, less than 1.5 percent have any secondary education, while among the better-off, more than 11 percent have some secondary-school training. The gap is even more pronounced if we compare rural households with urban households. Approximately 16 percent of the population older than 21 living in Dar es Salaam has some secondary education, while in rural areas of Tanzania this value is as low as 3 percent. Among the better-off households in Dar es Salaam, about 30 percent had secondary education among their members. (These issues are discussed in greater detail in Chapter 4.)

EXPENDITURE AND CONSUMPTION PATTERNS

The HRDS allowed estimation of per capita expenditures at Tsh 166,917 for 1993. In the rural areas, average expenditure per capita was estimated at Tsh 119,425, as compared to Tsh 191,375 in the urban areas. The average per capita expenditure of the richest households is 7.3 times greater than that of the poorest group in Tanzania.

Patterns of expenditure reveal that all households in Tanzania, even the comparatively well off ones, are performing poorly. The share of food in total expenditures, which is an indicator of household welfare, is high even among the highest-income households. The survey estimated that in 1993, an average Tanzanian household spends 72 percent of their total outlay on food, 2 percent on health, and 1.4 percent on education (see Table 3.3). The share of expenditures on food is higher in rural areas than in the urban areas, and lowest in Dar es Salaam.

The main food item consumed is cereals, comprising an average of 27 percent of all food expenditures. In the rural areas, 65 percent of cereal consumption is from own production (among the poorest rural households it is 78 percent). Among low-income

Table 3.3: Annual Household Expenditures (Cash and Consumed Production), 1994/95

	Rural	*Urban* [a]	*DSM*	*All*
Expenditures	664,116	910,905	1,487,092	776,604
Food	76.1%	66.4%	61.1%	71.5%
Health	1.7%	2.2%	2.3%	1.9%
Education	1.2%	2.0%	1.2%	1.4%
Other	21.0%	29.3%	35.4%	25.2%
Per Capita Expenditures	119,425	191,375	356,657	152,063
Per Adult Equivalent	186,917	281,846	523,328	231,421
Poorest 20%	68,378	94,365	187,889	74,048
Richest 20%	366,519	568,451	1,053,901	484,295

[a] Cities other than Dar es Salaam (DSM).

Source: HRDS, 1993/94, inflated to 1994/95 levels.

groups, a large share of food expenditure is on maize, pulses, and seeds. At higher levels of income, households switch from maize to rice, and start spending relatively more on meat, fruits, and vegetables.

Urban residents (whether in towns or in Dar es Salaam) and better-off households spend more on health in both absolute and percentage terms than do the rural and the poor. While a rich household spends more than 2 percent of its total outlay on health, a poor household spends about 1 percent of theirs.

The share of total expenditures devoted to education is remarkably similar across locations and income groups. In absolute terms, however, this corresponds to a better-off household spending 4.4 times more than a poor household. This gap is much smaller in Dar es Salaam, where a rich household spends about 57 percent more than a poor household.

CONCLUSION

This brief analysis of household characteristics emphasizes that the vast majority of the Tanzanian population resides in rural areas, living in poor housing, and dependent on basic agricultural output for own consumption and for a limited income. While there are significant differences in disposable income, human capital, and other resources between the poorest and better-off households, even the well-off population may be having a difficult time making ends meet.

4
EDUCATION

Households have the most to gain from investing in the education of children, and the most to lose if the productive time lost during school is not compensated in higher future earnings. Given access to educational opportunities for their children and the right signals from the market, most parents will invest in schooling. However, when opportunities are constrained and education is substandard, parents may make other choices. Poorer parents are always the most constrained, and for them the choice between the future earning capacity of their children and immediate survival are often cruelly straightforward.

This chapter reviews education issues in Tanzania. However, an effort is made not to duplicate information available from other sources. For that reason, this chapter emphasizes primary and secondary education. A more complete analysis of post-secondary education is contained in *Higher and Technical Education in Tanzania: Investments, Returns and Future Opportunities* (World Bank Report No. 15327-TA).

We will examine both sides of the complex interaction between the demand for education and the supply of school services in Tanzania. On the one hand, we use household survey data to study patterns of enrollment and household perceptions of the quality of schooling. On the other, we summarize existing information about the constraints within the educational system. The picture that emerges is one of parents who are investing moderate-to-large amounts of money, relative to their income, in their children's education, but who are faced with a system that offers few choices and uneven quality. Poor households are particularly disadvantaged, with more children to educate, fewer resources, and scarcer opportunities.

OUTCOMES AND ENROLLMENT

Tanzania is far from achieving universal enrollment in primary school, and enrollment in secondary schools is much lower than in most developing countries. The gross enrollment ratio (GER) for primary education (the number of children in school divided by the number of children in the age groups that should be in school) was estimated to be 82 percent in 1993[1]. The GER for girls is slightly more than for boys. Only about 7 percent of secondary-school-age children were enrolled in secondary school.

---

[1] These rates are from the 1993/94 Tanzania Human Resources Development Survey (HRDS). The government estimates the gross primary enrollment rate in 1991 to be 81 percent and the net rate to be 59 percent. The net rate is the percent of the relevant age group attending primary school.

Most Tanzanian children attend some primary school, but data suggest that the quality of that education is uneven. Official illiteracy rates rose from 10 percent in 1986 to 16 percent in 1992. Household survey data indicate that the self-reported illiteracy rate might be twice as high as the official reports, and that women are considerably more likely than men to be illiterate. Approximately 33 percent of women and 16 percent of men reported that they could not read or write (HRDS, 1993/94).

While Sub-Saharan Africa has low secondary-school enrollment rates by global standards, Tanzania's performance is poor relative even to that standard. Tanzania is now outperformed by its neighbors and falls below the average for Africa for secondary enrollment rates. Tanzania is matched only by Malawi in having the lowest secondary-school enrollment rate in the world.

Table 4.1: Gross Enrollment Rates, 1993

Country	Primary School	Secondary School
Ethiopia	23	12
Kenya	92	26
Tanzania	82	10
Uganda	91	14
Sub-Saharan Africa	71	more than 23[a]

[a] The enrollment rate for women was 23 percent. The enrollment rate for men was not available.
Source: HRDS, 1993/94; World Bank, 1996.

Primary School

Educational enrollment in Tanzania has fallen precipitously since the quantitative gains of the Universal Primary Education (UPE) movement. After UPE was implemented, gross primary-school enrollment rose to 95 percent in 1982. Nearly fifteen years later, enrollment had fallen to 82 percent. This means that, despite rapid population growth, the absolute number of children enrolled in primary school was almost the same in the early-1990s as it was a decade earlier.

Gross primary-school enrollment rates are low for all income quintiles. Low-income households appear to be less likely to send their children to school than more affluent households. The average gross enrollment rate for households in the lowest income quintile was 77 percent, while that of the highest quintile was 87 percent (Table 4.2). However, when the figures for all income quintiles are reviewed, the pattern of the probability of enrollment increasing with income is clearer for boys than girls. Furthermore, Mason and Khandker (1997) did not find a statistically significant correlation between income and enrollment.

Table 4.2: Primary School Enrollment Rates, by Expenditure Quintile, Gender, and Location, 1993

	Lowest Quintile		Highest Quintile		Average	
	Male	Female	Male	Female	Male	Female
Gross Enrollment Rates						
Dar es Salaam	n/a	n/a	74	72	75	73
Other Urban	79	94	88	92	89	93
Rural	77	74	90	87	79	80
All	77	76	87	86	81	82
Net Enrollment Rates						
Dar es Salaam	n/a	n/a	51	53	50	54
Other Urban	54	60	69	68	62	68
Rural	50	52	66	65	53	56
All **Tanzania**	50	53	65	65	55	59

Source: Mason and Khandker, 1997.

Enrollment rates vary by geographic location. The nation's highest enrollment rates are in urban areas other than Dar es Salaam. On average, the gross enrollment rate in these areas is more than 90 percent. The rate is 80 percent on average in rural areas, and about 74 percent in Dar es Salaam. The especially low rate in Dar es Salaam is surprising considering that the city is relatively well endowed with school infrastructure, and household income is high by national standards (see Table 4.2).

Primary-school enrollment rates for boys and girls are relatively equal. However, in urban areas excluding Dar es Salaam, girls are somewhat more likely than boys to be enrolled. Girls are slightly less likely than boys to be enrolled in Dar es Salaam.

In Tanzania, 84 percent of children start school later than the statutory age of 7 years. In 1993, over one-half of children enrolled in primary school had started school at the age of 10 or older, and almost 13 percent of children had started school at the age of 12 or older (Table 4.3). The modal age for initial enrollment in primary school is 9 years. Girls are slightly less likely than boys to start school late. Parents and teachers report that one reason children start school late is that schools are overcrowded. As a coping strategy,

Table 4.3: Incidence of Late Enrollment Among Current Primary School Enrollees

	Boys	Girls	Total
% of Students Who Enrolled Late	85.3	82.3	83.7
% of Whom Enrolled [a]:			
1 Year Late	18.1	22.9	20.6
2 Years Late	26.8	30.9	28.9
3 Years Late	21.8	24.2	23.1
4 Years Late	17.5	12.1	14.7
5 Years Late	15.8	9.9	12.7

[a] Columns may not add up to 100 due to rounding error.
Source: Mason and Khandker, 1997

schools fill up Standard 1 spots with the oldest children who have not yet begun school. Parents, especially in rural areas, also report keeping young children out of school to assist with agricultural and household tasks. Mason (1996) found that the presence of electricity in a village also reduced the likelihood of late starting. He hypothesized that this occurred because electricity was indicative of a more sophisticated economic infrastructure and that the returns to education in electrified areas were probably higher than the returns in areas in which economic activities were more traditional.

Gross enrollment rates by grade, shown in Table 4.4, indicate that enrollment drops off sharply after Standard 5. This corresponds to age patterns of attendance. The peak in attendance is in the very early teenage years. According to the HRDS, between ages 7 and 9, only 32 percent of children are in school, but between age 10 and 14, 82 percent are attending. Between ages 15 and 19, attendance drops back to about 36 percent. The gross enrollment rate is higher for boys than for girls in some grades; in other grades, the reverse is true.

Table 4.4: Gross Enrollment Rates, by Grade

Grade	Gross Enrollment Rates (%)		
	All	Boys	Girls
Standard 1	72	76	67
Standard 2	90	96	85
Standard 3	94	91	97
Standard 4	78	78	77
Standard 5	89	84	93
Standard 6	47	42	52
Standard 7	26	26	26
Form I	14	13	14
Form II	11	13	9
Form III	8	9	6
Form IV	7	8	6

Source: HRDS, 1993/94.

Girls tend to start school slightly earlier than boys. The HRDS found that the average age of children starting school in 1993 was 9.0 years for girls, and 9.7 years for boys. This gender differential was confirmed in FAST interviews with parents. Parents reported that they preferred daughters to start school early so that they could complete primary school before reaching puberty and risking pregnancy. In contrast, they preferred their sons to start school a little later so that they were old enough to enter the workforce when they completed primary school.

Children from lower-income households start school at a later age than do better-off children. Among 7- to 9-year-olds, almost one-half of the children from the 20 percent of households at the top of the welfare distribution are in school, while only one-quarter of the young children from the poorest 20 percent of households attend school. At age 10 to 14, however, attendance is more uniform across the population. These differentials hold true for both girls and boys (HRDS, 1993/94).

Having started school at 9 or 10 years of age, children are 13 or 14 when they first reach the Standard 4 diagnostic examination, which is intended to indicate to students, parents and teachers whether the child is prepared to advance, or should repeat the fourth year of school. At this point, about 80 percent of students are allowed to continue to Standard 5. Three-quarters of the remaining students (15 percent of the total) repeat Standard 4, and the rest (about 5 percent of the total) drop out (MOEC, various years). Differences between boys and girls with respect to dropping out and repeating are minimal.

By the time they complete primary school most boys and girls are 15 years old. However, because of late starts and repetition of Standard 4, a significant portion are much older. In 1992, 15.6 percent of students in the final year of primary school were 17 years or older (MOEC, various years).

A high proportion of students drop out of school, and that proportion has increased since the UPE movement. Among the 1978/84 cohort, 28 percent of students dropped out before completing Standard 7. Among the 1983/89 cohort, 47 percent dropped out. Among the 1984/90 cohort, 42 out of every 100 entrants into Standard 1 did not complete Standard 7 (MOEC, various years). Although the rate of dropping out is similar for boys and girls, female students who do complete primary school score lower on the Primary School Leaving Exam than do boys. As a result, the cut-off point for girls' selection into government secondary school is approximately 10 points lower than for boys.

Children from poor households leave school at an earlier age than do better-off children. By age 15 to 19, about two-thirds of poor children (in the lowest 20 percent of the welfare distribution) are out of school (HRDS, 1993/94). The higher opportunity cost of remaining in school at older ages may help to explain this. The FAST time-use study found that boys older than 12 who are out of school split their time between farm work and working for money. Not surprisingly, because of later starts and higher levels of primary school drop-out, the total time in primary school for the poor is significantly less than for the rich. Thus, the primary school enrollment rate is low in Tanzania because, if children enroll, they frequently start late and drop out before completion. Mason and Khandker (1997) found that the direct monetary cost of attending school does not strongly affect student enrollment (see Box 4.1). In contrast, the opportunity cost of children's time was found to be quite significant in influencing enrollments. School enrollments were also positively correlated with school supply and parental education. Enrollment was not significantly correlated with income.

Box 4.1: Factors Influencing Primary School Enrollment

Mason and Khandker (1997) analyzed two recent household surveys to explore why primary-school enrollment rates are low in Tanzania and have fallen over the last 15 years. Their findings indicate that neither the direct monetary cost of attending school nor family income strongly affect the likelihood of enrollment.

The opportunity cost of children's time is significant in influencing enrollments. An increase in the opportunity cost of girls' time is correlated with reduced female enrollments in school. The distance to school is also negatively correlated with enrollment, possibly because a further distance to school increases the opportunity cost of attending. Furthermore, an increase in female wages or female labor force participation reduces the likelihood of enrollment for boys. This crossover effect likely indicates that if girls are working outside the home, their brothers are more likely to be kept out of school to help with housework. Finally, when household income is held constant, an increase in the number of adults in a household results in an increased likelihood that children will attend school. This indicates that if adults are available to perform household tasks, children's opportunity costs are probably lower and they are therefore more likely to attend school.

School enrollments are also positively correlated with school supply. Holding distance to school constant, the greater the number of schools per capita, the more likely children are to enroll. This finding is in keeping with the FAST study in which parents and teachers said that schools were frequently overcrowded and younger children were delayed from entering until spaces became available. Mason and Khandker also found that in Tanzania, as in many other countries, parental education is positively associated with children attending school. Children living with their parents or grandparents are more likely to be in school than children living with more distant relatives. There was insufficient data to ascertain whether school quality was correlated with enrollments.

Secondary School

There were approximately 547 secondary schools in Tanzania in 1994, 344 of which were private. Most of these only cover lower secondary school (Dar and Levine, 1996). The number of government-owned secondary schools increased by 100 percent from 1987 to 1994. The number of private schools increased by 150 percent over the same period. Despite this rapid growth in the number of secondary schools, it is still the case that only a small fraction of those who complete primary school are accepted into secondary school, or have opportunities for post-primary education (Box 4.2). The proportion of primary-school leavers selected for government secondary school has been 5 to 7 percent since Independence. If places in secondary schools and in vocational training institutions are considered together, there is one place in a government institution for every 12 primary-school leavers (Dar and Levine, 1996). Because private secondary schools have grown so rapidly over the past decade, secondary-school enrollments have also increased sharply. Since the *de facto* liberalization of secondary education from 1984-85, enrollments in secondary schools grew at double-digit rates for nearly a decade.

Table 4.5: Secondary-school Enrollment Rates, by Expenditure Quintile, Gender, and Location, 1993

	Lowest Quintile		Highest Quintile		Average	
	Male	*Female*	*Male*	*Female*	*Male*	*Female*
Gross Enrollment Rates						
Dar es Salaam	n/a	n/a	23	21	18	19
Other Urban	1	2	31	28	15	17
Rural	3	2	15	7	8	4
All Tanzania	3	2	23	17	11	8
Net Enrollment Rates						
Dar es Salaam	n/a	n/a	18	19	13	17
Other Urban	1	2	22	24	11	14
Rural	2	2	7	5	5	3
All Tanzania	2	2	15	14	7	7

Source: Mason and Khandker, 1997.

Box 4.2: Selection to Secondary Schools

By far the most important examination in the school system is the Primary School Leaving Examination. On the basis of that examination, students are selected into government secondary schools. The examination is also used as an entry exam for many private secondary schools.

The secondary-school selection process has multiple steps. First, the government has established regional and district quotas, based on enrollments and available places in so-called national schools. There are also gender-based quotas, to equalize the numbers of boys and girls selected. Following selection for the national schools (boarding schools), there is selection for regional (mostly day) schools. Some private schools conduct their own examinations. However, virtually all private schools select students after the government schools have been assigned students (a few prestigious seminaries are exceptions to this rule). For the transition from lower- to upper-secondary school, selection is based on the results of the national Form IV examination.

The selection process is not transparent. Pupils and parents receive no information about their scores. Thus the students cannot choose, but are assigned schools by the government. As a result, some students may be sent to schools in regions far away from home (Dar and Levine, 1996).

Student enrollments more than doubled from 74,208 in 1984 to 196,375 in 1995. Primarily as a result of private-sector participation, the overall proportion of primary-school leavers able to enter secondary school has grown to about 15 percent. The gross enrollment rate for secondary school was about 10 percent in 1993 (Table 4.5).

In 1992, only 5.5 percent of students leaving primary school were selected for Form I in a government secondary school, and another 7.4 percent were selected for private secondary schools. While some alternative post-primary opportunities such as vocational training do exist, the vast majority of individuals who are not selected into secondary school receive no more formal education.

As secondary-school students progress through Forms, many drop out. In 1985, for example, 21,057 pupils were enrolled in Form I (public and private enrollments). By the time they reached Form IV (the completion of lower secondary), 14,806 (70 percent) were still in school. But five years after the 1985 cohort started secondary school, only 3,953 (19 percent) were in Form VI (to be precise, these figures do not refer exactly to the 1985 cohort because a small proportion are repeaters from other cohorts). Children who attend private schools appear to be less likely to continue from lower to higher secondary schools. The high drop-out rate between lower- and upper-secondary school is partially due to the limited supply of upper secondary-school places. In fiscal 1994, there were about 5.5 students who successfully completed lower secondary school for each place in the first year of upper-secondary school in public and private institutions (Dar and Levine, 1996).

Gender Differences. On average, gross secondary-school enrollment rates are higher for boys than for girls. Net enrollment rates for the two genders are approximately equal. This indicates that boys are more likely than girls to remain in secondary school after they pass the "standard" secondary-school age if they have not yet completed their studies. In Dar es Salaam and in other urban areas, gross and net enrollment rates are slightly higher for girls than for boys. In rural areas, girls have significantly lower enrollment rates than boys (see Table 4.5).

Girls may be more likely to be pulled out of school for family reasons. Pregnancy itself is often grounds for dismissal of students. Up to about one-third of all girls enrolled in secondary school are expelled due to pregnancy (World Bank, 1991a).

Students' subject choices in secondary schools are tightly constrained and influenced by gender stereotyping. Many specialists have identified biases in the teaching methods and materials used. For example, only one school offers advanced levels of the agricultural curriculum, and this school is open only to boys. In contrast, the home economics curriculum is offered in 122 secondary schools, of which 23 are single-sex (girls) and the rest are coeducational (Meena, 1994).

The Tanzanian government is understandably concerned about the country's very low secondary-school enrollment rates and about the gender inequity in enrollments. Furthermore, the government is aware of the fact that the rate of return to educating girls is higher than the return to educating boys. For these reasons, the government has recently initiated the Girls' Secondary Education Support Program (GSES) which provides bursaries for poor girls to attend secondary school (see Box 4.3).

Box 4.3: Girls' Secondary Education Support Program (GSES)

Tanzania's gross secondary-school enrollment rate is only about 10 percent. Enrollments are particularly low for girls, while the rate of return to educating girls is higher than the return to educating boys. The Girls' Secondary Education Support Program (GSES) seeks to raise enrollments and maximize the social return to education investments by providing secondary-school bursaries to poor girls. The program's aim is to provide a bursary each year to at least one girl in each participating primary school. The Government of Tanzania and the World Bank designed the program through a participatory process involving extensive consultations with the beneficiary villages and other stakeholders.

For each participating primary school, the school and the relevant village council advertise the program in their community. Interested girls enrolled in Standard VII submit applications. The school lists all the girls who submitted applications and would not be able to afford secondary school unless assisted by a bursary. From these they select up to 6 of the most academically able students. The village council chooses one nominee to be eligible for the bursary. The village gathers in a community meeting to vote on whether they agree with the decision of the village council. The parents of the nominated girl sign a memorandum of understanding (contract) with the community and the bursary program. The secondary school the girl will attend signs a memorandum of understanding with the bursary program. The girl attends school and reports back to the village council on her progress. Her progress is also monitored by the GSES program.

Each primary school selected by the program is allocated an annual bursary of Tsh 300,000 (approximately US$ 500). The families of the selected girls are expected to contribute any amount that is not covered by the bursary. The girls must attend secondary schools that are qualified to participate in the GSES program. Conditional on performance, participating girls receive an annual bursary for all four years of their lower secondary education. When the girls enroll in schools, the bursaries are directly deposited into segregated bank accounts opened by the secondary schools. The girls and the schools must account for funds entrusted to them.

The program has functioned well in its first two years, although some problems have arisen. Villagers are excited about the program and, through their participation, have taken an increased interest in girls' education. The participating girls are performing approximately as well as other students in their schools. In the short run, the program may crowd out financially better off students due to constraints on school places. Therefore, it is possible that though the economic strata in a school will change, it may not increase total enrollment. As the program continues however, it is expected that there will be a supply response to the increased demand for secondary education. Day-school attendees have experienced some difficulties in transportation, which is expensive and time consuming. Some students stay with families close to school to avoid transport problems. However, some complain of being treated like servants. There have also been reported cases of pregnancy. Nevertheless, of the 392 girls who obtained a bursary in the first year, 364 continued for the second year.

Economic Differences. Gross secondary-school enrollment rates are low for all income quintiles. Nevertheless, low-income households are much less likely to send their children to secondary school than the more affluent. The average gross enrollment rate for households in the lowest-income quintile was 2 to 3 percent, while for the highest quintile it was approximately 20 percent (Table 4.5).

Government secondary schools are the main source of secondary schooling, but they tend to serve the better-off households disproportionately. According to results of the HRDS, of those attending secondary school in 1993/94, 39 percent attended a government school, 17 percent a church-related school, 32 percent a private secular school, and 12 percent a community school. Of those in government secondary schools, only 8 percent came from the poorest 20 percent of the population, while 34 percent came from the richest 20 percent.

These differentials are reflected in the composition of the student bodies. At the secondary level, more than half (60 percent) of the students in government schools come from the wealthiest 40 percent of the population. In the secondary church-related and private secular schools, nearly three-quarters of the students are in the upper 40 percent (HRDS, 1993/94).

Among the poorest group, girls made up 64 percent of the students attending government schools, but parents offset this by enrolling boys in other secondary schools so that the overall ratio of girls to boys at that level of income was 48 versus 52 percent (HRDS, 1993/94).

Geographic Differences. Secondary-school enrollment rates also vary significantly by geographic location. The gross enrollment rate is approximately 16 percent in other urban areas, and about 6 percent in rural areas.

Mason and Khandker (1997) found that a number of factors contribute to the probability of children enrolling in secondary school. The greater the distance between home and school, the less likely were children to be enrolled. This is probably due to the fact that families must pay more for travel (and possibly for boarding) if schools are distant. As is the case for primary-school enrollment, secondary-school enrollment for girls declines as girls' opportunity costs increase. In contrast to primary-school enrollment, secondary- school enrollment is highly correlated with family income. Secondary-school enrollment is also significantly correlated with the education level of the head of the household. Finally, girls are more likely to attend secondary school if they live with their immediate family than if they live with more distant relations. Mason and Khandker's results did not show that the direct costs of secondary school significantly influenced the probability of enrollment. However, they hypothesized that data limitations may have masked this link. Similarly, data limitations did not allow Mason and Khandker to ascertain whether supply constraints or school quality were associated with the probability of enrollment.

Mason and Khandker undertook simulations to estimate how reducing the distance to schools and introducing bursaries to cover tuition fees and children's opportunity costs might impact enrollment rates. According to their simulations, bursaries covering the direct and opportunity costs of attending secondary school would increase the rate of initial enrollment in secondary school from its current level of 13 percent to 16 percent. Thus, according to Mason and Khandker's calculations, these policy changes would have positive but very modest effects on enrollment levels.

Higher and Tertiary Education and Training

Currently about 6,000 students take the Form VI examination each year. There are approximately 2,000 university-level spots, or one for every 3 secondary-school leavers. After Form VI, students may also enter diploma or similar programs in various public institutions. Each year, there are about 3,200 spots in these post-Form VI institutions. In addition, a small number of Tanzanian students go abroad for study. In all, almost all individuals finishing Form VI have the opportunity to continue on with academic or professional training. The number of students completing tertiary-level education increased by about 45 percent from 1985 to 1991, the most recent year for which reasonably complete data are available (Dar and Levine, 1996).

Individuals who have completed primary school can enter vocational training at either government or private institutions. About 25,000 primary-school leavers enroll in vocational training programs that include handicrafts, carpentry, masonry, mechanics, painting, tailoring, and a variety of practical skills.

Increasing Post-Primary Education Opportunities

As the previous sections illustrate, post-primary educational opportunities are very limited in Tanzania. The government is aware of this, and increasing enrollment rates remains an important priority for the state. However, increasing post-primary enrollment rates is expensive. Table 4.6 estimates required increases in government recurrent expenditures if the government implements a policy of increasing secondary and/or tertiary enrollments assuming that unit costs

Table 4.6: Increasing Enrollment Rates Without Altering Unit Costs

Scenarios	Enrollment	As a % of Current Costs
Current Situation	146,058	100
Alternative Scenarios in 2000		
Doubling Secondary	273,085	159
Doubling Secondary and Tertiary	354,660	238
Tripling Secondary	368,965	198
Tripling Secondary and Tertiary	539,749	372

Source: Dar and Levine, 1996.

remain the same in the year 2000 (in real terms) as they are today. Enrollments are adjusted to take into account a 2.8 percent annual population growth rate (Dar and Levine, 1996).

If the government doubled secondary enrollment rates (without altering tertiary enrollment rates or per student expenditures on tertiary education[2]), its recurrent expenditure on post-primary education would increase by 59 percent (in real terms). If both secondary and tertiary enrollments were doubled, costs would rise by 138 percent. Real costs would rise by almost 200 percent if secondary-school enrollments were tripled by the year 2000, and costs would rise by 272 percent if secondary and tertiary enrollment rates were tripled.

As Table 4.7 indicates, an increase in enrollment rates without altering cost structures would have very large budget repercussions for a government that already faces significant fiscal constraints. Given the government's budget constraints, significantly increased post-primary enrollments probably cannot be achieved if the government does not reduce unit costs and does not actively encourage the private sector in the provision of educational services. The following scenarios review simulations of post-primary school enrollments under alternative budget reallocation assumptions. First, the impact of reallocation from tertiary vocational/training institutions and the university to secondary education is considered. This is followed by an examination of the impact of reducing unit costs on enrollments. In all the simulations, total expenditure on post-primary education remains constant.

---

[2] Even though tertiary enrollment rates remain constant, total tertiary enrollment will rise slightly simply due to population growth. Thus, while per capita expenditures remain fixed, overall expenditures on tertiary-level education will also rise.

Table 4.7: Increasing Enrollments Through Reallocation

Program	Current	Scenario A	Scenario B	Scenario C
Policy Changes	NA	Resources shifted to secondary	Cost sharing	Resources shifted to secondary
		Close cost ineffective institutions	Efficient welfare, personnel expenditures	Close cost ineffective institutions
		Encourage private training		Cost sharing
				Efficient welfare, personnel expenditures
				Encourage private training
Enrollment				
Secondary	79,027	153,394	98,784	191,743
Tertiary	63,011	31,506	90,106	45,168
Training/ University	4,020	2,680	5,950	3,966
Total	146,508	187,580	194,839	240,877
% change in enrollment				
Secondary	NA	94	25	142
Tertiary	NA	-50	43	-29
Training/ University	NA	-33	48	-2
Total	NA	28	33	64

Source: Dar and Levine, 1996.

Scenario A: The government reallocates one-half of its budget currently devoted to tertiary training institutions, and one-third of its university budget to general secondary education. This will involve closing down some institutions that are a drain on government resources. Even though the enrollment in public tertiary institutions will decline, the private sector can step in and supply training if demand exists. If the current cost structure is maintained, secondary-school enrollments will approximately double.

Scenario B: More efficient use of teaching staff, and a reduction in government contributions towards student boarding and welfare, could potentially reduce government recurrent expenditures per student by 20 percent at the secondary level and almost 40 percent at the tertiary level. If these efficiency gains were achieved, enrollments would increase at all levels. However, this scenario may prove the least beneficial and most costly in the long run. The government would be forced to support an even greater number of tertiary institutions, many of which are of relatively poor quality.

Scenario C: If both changes outlined in scenarios A and B were made, Tanzania could afford to educate nearly 112,000 more secondary students, maintain university enrollments at the current level, and reduce enrollments in training institutions. Again, if demand exists, we assume that the private sector will step in and provide training services.

In all these scenarios, recurrent expenditures on education remain constant while enrollments rise. Scenario C seems to be the most optimal.

HOUSEHOLD EXPENDITURES ON EDUCATION

Overall Expenditures

Households across Tanzania spend a little more than one percent of their total expenditures on education (see Table 4.8). Overall, the poorest households spend a greater percentage, but rural households spend a smaller percentage (of a smaller amount) than urban households. Interpretation of the ratio should take into account the fact that education expenditures are nearly all cash expenditures, while total household expenditures are not all cash. Roughly 53 percent of expenditures in the bottom 20 percent of the welfare distribution are cash, while in the top 20

Table 4.8: Share of Total Expenditures on Education, by Expenditure Quintile (%)

Residence	Lowest 20%	Highest 20%	All
Dar es Salaam	2.0	0.9	1.2
Other Urban	1.7	1.8	1.8
Rural	1.5	1.0	1.1
All	1.4	1.4	1.3

Source: HRDS, 1993/94.

percent the vast majority (80 percent) of household expenditures are cash. Consequently, the poorest group spends almost 4 percent of cash income for schooling compared to just over 1 percent for the richest 20 percent of households. There is virtually no difference in total spending on education between male- and female-headed households.

There are two ways to consider household expenditures on education. First, one can look at the total amount spent on education (for all children) in a household. Second, one can examine the amount spent per student in a household. Given the differentials in the number of children of school age, two households can spend the same absolute amount and yet be making qualitatively different investments in their children. We examine both in the following tables.

On average, households spend a total of Tsh 18,211 per year on the education of children. As shown in Table 4.9, there is great variation in the total expenditures on education across the welfare distribution. The poorest households spend a total of about Tsh 6,869 on education annually, while the 20 percent of households at the top of the income distribution spend more than four times as much, or Tsh 41,320.

Table 4.9: Total Household Expenditures on Education per Year, by Households with at Least One Child in School (Tsh)

Residence	Lowest Quintile	Highest Quintile	Ratio (High/ Low)	All
Dar es Salaam	19,741	103,266	5.2	42,738
Other Urban	10,963	64,430	5.9	29,744
Rural	7,145	23,770	3.3	12,722
All	6,869	41,320	6.0	18,211

Source: HRDS, 1993/94, inflated to FY95 levels.

While the differentials are seen in all areas of the country, the gap between rich and poor spending is greatest in urban areas outside of Dar es Salaam, and least in Dar es Salaam. For all households except those in the highest income category, education expenditures on sons exceed expenditures on daughters (see Table 4.10).

On average, households spend Tsh 5,148 per pupil. Rural households spend the least (Tsh 3,950 per pupil) and households in Dar es Salaam spend the most (Tsh 13,368 per pupil). Per-pupil expenditures vary across the welfare distribution, as one might expect, with wealthier households paying about 3 to 5 times as much per student as poorer households. A very poor household in a rural area spends on average Tsh 2,663 per student per year, while a wealthier rural household spends an estimated Tsh 7,295 per student. The differential across the welfare distribution is greatest in urban areas outside of Dar es Salaam (see Table 4.11).

Table 4.10: Total Annual Household Expenditures on Education by Households with at Least One Child in School, by Gender (Tsh)

Expenditure Quintile	Expenditures on Boys	Expenditures on Girls	Total Household Expenditures
1 (Lowest)	4,043	2,826	6,869
2	5,154	4,903	10,057
3	8,308	6,404	14,712
4	9,832	9,336	19,167
5 (Highest)	20,016	21,306	27,920
Total	9,364	8,847	18,211

Source: HRDS, 1993/94, inflated to FY 1995 levels.

Primary School Expenditures

The three largest expense categories for primary school were uniforms, contributions and fees, and books and supplies, which accounted for 48, 19 and 20 percent of expenditures, respectively. These three categories accounted for 99 percent of spending by the poor, but only 80 percent by the rich. The best-off households spent

Table 4.11: Government and Household Expenditures per Student Enrolled in Primary School (Tsh)

Residence	Government Recurrent Expenditures	Household Expenditures			
		Lowest 20%	Highest 20%	Ratio (High/Low)	All
Dar es Salaam	8,844	8,916	27,639	3.1	13,368
Other Urban	8,844	3,926	14,408	3.7	7,314
Rural	8,844	2,663	7,295	2.7	3,950
All	8,844	2,692	10,973	4.1	5,148

Source: HRDS, 1993/94 inflated to 1994/95 levels; Follmer and Kessy, 1996.

a substantial amount on tutors and other expenses (such as clubs, extracurricular activities, pocket money, and so on). The relative distribution of expenditures was similar for boys and girls.

Secondary School Expenditures

Cost-sharing has been in place in government secondary schools since the late 1980s when schools started charging nominal tuition fees. Since 1993/94, students have been required to buy their own uniforms, stationery, books, personal hygiene items, and bedding. Students are also expected to pay for transportation costs and part of food expenses. Typically, food, clothing and transportation account for 60 percent or more of students' secondary-school expenses (Dar and Levine, 1996).

Parents with children in secondary school spent an average of Tsh 55,527 per student in 1994/95. In rural areas, if poor households have a child in secondary school, they pay somewhat less per student than do the richest households (Tsh 45,058 and 59,977, respectively). However, the urban poor spend much less than the rural poor, and they spend only one-half to one-fourth of what the rich spend (Table 4.12). Expenditures on boarding schools across the population are fairly constant except among the richest group, which spends considerably more than the other groups. On average, sending a child to secondary school costs an upper-income family about 21 percent of their annual per capita expenditures. A family in the lowest expenditure quintile pays 81 percent of per capita expenditures to send a child to secondary school (Mason and Khandker, 1997).

Because public schools are heavily subsidized by the government, they are significantly less expensive for parents than private schools (Table 4.13). In 1993, parents spent 63 percent more to send their children to private schools than to public schools. The spending differences required for sending a child to private school are particularly large for the poor. Poor households spent 124 percent more when they sent their children to private schools than they did when their children attended government schools. Households in Dar es Salaam spent on average 16 percent more to enroll children in private schools. In other urban areas, households spent 84 percent more for private schooling (Mason and Khandker, 1997).

Table 4.12: Government and Household Expenditures per Student Enrolled in Secondary School per Year, by Expenditure Level, 1994/95 (Tsh)

Residence	Government	Household Expenditures			
		Lowest 20%	Highest 20%	Ratio (High/Low)	All
Dar es Salaam	100,500	35,803	117,140	3.3	64,901
Other Urban	100,500	35,412	77,985	2.2	55,867
Rural	100,500	45,058	59,977	1.3	53,650
All	100,500	38,039	71,902	1.9	55,527

Source: HRDS, 1993/94, updated by inflation to 1994/95 levels ; World Bank, 1994a.

Table 4.13: Average Household Expenditure per Student Enrolled in Government and Private Secondary Schools (Tsh per year in 1994/95)

	Lowest 20%	Highest 20%	Ratio (High/Low)	All
Annual Household Spending for Government Schools				
Dar es Salaam	26,146	95,322	3.6	62,149
Other Urban	40,763	53,193	1.3	37,917
Rural	24,828	41,245	1.7	40,409
All Tanzania	24,072	52,292	2.2	40,956
Annual Household Spending for Private Schools				
Dar es Salaam	46,310	141,231	3.0	72,231
Other Urban	40,698	94,856	2.3	69,868
Rural	62,487	70,591	1.1	62,808
All Tanzania	53,868	85,208	1.6	66,587
Percent for Difference in Household Spending: Private vs. Government Schools				
Dar es Salaam	77%	48%		16%
Other Urban	0%	78%		84%
Rural	152%	71%		55%
All Tanzania	124%	63%		63%

Source: Mason and Khandker, 1997, based on HRDS, 1993/94, then inflated to 1994/95 levels.

When comparing expenditures on primary versus secondary schooling, rural households spend on average 9 times as much on secondary education as on primary, while in Dar es Salaam the differential is only a factor of 4.6. The poorest households pay 8 times as much for secondary education (Table 4.14).

Poor households tended to spend about the same on girls as on boys at the primary-school level, but much less on girls than on boys at the secondary-school level. Higher-income households spent somewhat more on daughters than on sons in primary school, but this pattern is reversed in secondary school (Table 4.15). It is unclear why households spend more on boys than on girls in secondary school. Mason and Khandker (1997) hypothesize that this is because boys are more likely than girls to attend upper secondary school and so a larger percentage of the boys in secondary school are in the upper standards. This would result in higher average expenditure per boy than per girl because the cost of upper secondary school is higher than the cost of lower secondary school. It is also possible that schools to which households send boys are more expensive than the schools in which households enroll girls.

Table 4.14: Ratio of Expenditures on Secondary to Primary School, by Expenditure Level (%)

Residence	Lowest 20%	Highest 20%	All
Dar es Salaam	2.9	4.6	4.6
Other Urban	5.4	4.3	5.3
Rural	9.8	4.9	8.9
All	8.0	4.9	7.5

Source: HRDS, 1993/94.

Table 4.15: Household Expenditures on Education per Student in Households with at Least One Child in School, by Gender, 1994/95 (Tsh)

Type of Spending	Lowest 20%	Highest 20%	All
Primary School			
Boys	2,734	9,391	4,843
Girls	2,764	11,955	5,406
Secondary School			
Boys	56,367	17,756	60,962
Girls	80,901	72,848	55,531

Source: HRDS, 1993/94, updated by inflation to 1994/95 levels.

Because poor households have, on average, more children, the burden of financing education is unevenly distributed across the population. Almost one-half of the poorest households have more than three children, implying that they could not finance all their children in school even if they wanted to. Across the population as a whole, nearly one-half (46 percent) of the households with five children of school age are in the poorest 40 percent of households. However, on a per student basis, the rich spend far more than the poor on primary education. For example, the richest 20 percent of households in Dar es Salaam spend more than 10 times the amount per student as the poorest households in rural areas (Table 4.11).

Opportunity Cost of Education

As the above section illustrates, households are making cash investments in their children's educations. In addition, keeping children in school has an opportunity cost. Households with children in school forego their children's wages in the labor force and/or their help with agricultural and household tasks. Mason and Khandker (1997) reviewed the opportunity cost of children's time in school based on the results from two recent studies.

On average, children not in school work 20 hours per week or more from the age of 7 (Table 4.16). The number of hours that they work increases as they grow older. At every age level, children (especially girls) in school work fewer hours than do children not in school. Furthermore, the number of hours worked by children in school does not increase as they grow older. Thus, families incur a significant opportunity cost by sending even their very young children to school, and this cost increases as their children grow up. For children ages 7 to 9 who are in school, households lose from 9 to 19 hours per week of work. They lose from 26 to 37 hours of work per week for children ages 16 to 18 who are in school.

Table 4.16: Children's Weekly Time Use in Tanzania, by Gender and Age Cohort, 1993

Average Hours Per Worked per Week, Based on HRDS Timelog Data

Age	Males				Females			
	Hours Worked, Children not in School	*Hours Worked, Children in School*	*Hours in School or on School Work*	*Hours Work Foregone by School Children*	*Hours Worked, Children not in School*	*Hours Worked, Children in School*	*Hours in School or on School Work*	*Hours Work Foregone by School Children*
	(1)	(2)	(3)	(4)=(1)-(2)	(5)	(6)	(7)	(8)=(5)-(6)
7-9	24.0	5.9	38.4	18.1	31.5	12.3	35.8	19.2
10-12	32.9	9.7	39.3	23.2	36.6	10.0	42.5	26.6
13-15	33.8	8.5	47.3	25.3	48.6	11.8	47.9	36.8
16-18	45.5	9.3	49.7	36.3	47.5	10.2	48.6	37.3
19-21	36.1	13.6	39.6	22.4	50.5	31.0	21.2	19.5

Average Hours Worked Per Week, Based on FAST Survey Data

Age	Males				Females			
	Hours Worked, Children Not in School	*Hours Worked, Children in School*	*Hours in School or on School Work*	*Hours Work Foregone by School Children*	*Hours Worked, Children Not in School*	*Hours Worked, Children in School*	*Hours in School or on School Work*	*Hours Work Foregone by School Children*
	(1)	(2)	(3)	(4)=(1)-(2)	(5)	(6)	(7)	(8)=(5)-(6)
7-9	21.3	12.4	27.2	8.9	35.2	21.1	24.7	14.1
10-12	34.3	17.0	30.1	17.3	49.0	17.4	31.8	31.6
13-15	36.8	12.1	39.3	24.7	54.0	17.5	40.1	36.5
16-18	34.8	8.7	41.0	26.1	56.6	20.9	40.6	35.7
19-21	46.4	10.0	43.8	36.4	54.6	n/a	n/a	n/a

Source: Mason and Khandker, 1997.

Attending school also has an opportunity cost for children. At every age level, children in school spend significantly more time engaged in productive activities (school work, labor market activities, and household tasks) than do children not in school. Indeed, even children ages 7 to 9 who are in school are spending 40 to 48 hours per week on productive activities. Children ages 7 to 9 not in school spend from 21 to 35 hours per week on productive activities.

Households incur significant opportunity costs sending all of their children to school. However, for children under 18 years of age, the opportunity cost of sending girls to school is significantly higher than the opportunity cost of sending boys. For example, if boys ages 13 to 15 are in school, households lose about 25 hours of work per week. For girls of the same age, they lose about 37 hours of work.

DEMAND FOR EDUCATION

Parents' Perceptions of the Quality of Education

Late entry enrollments and early exits suggest that many parents perceive that schooling has less value than alternative ways for children to spend time. Particularly startling is the finding from time logs that young boys who are not in school tend to spend their time playing rather than working. This implies that the perceived value of schooling is very low.

In the HRDS, respondents were asked for their opinions about various quality-related features of the nearest government primary school. Because the government has retained a monopoly on primary schooling, this is the only option available. The features reviewed included (a) qualifications of teaching staff, (b) qualifications of head teacher, (c) adequacy of supplies, (d) state of physical infrastructure, and (e) self-reliance work. Responses suggest that households are dissatisfied with several aspects of the educational services. The most obvious shortcoming is in supplies and infrastructure (see Table 4.17). Overall, only about 13 percent of respondents who had children in primary school stated that the adequacy of supplies was "good" or "very good," and a full 57 percent said that supplies were "poor" or "very poor."

Table 4.17: Ratings of Government Primary School Quality (%)

Characteristic	Very Good or Good	Adequate	Poor or Very Poor	Total
Teachers' Qualifications	33.8	44.2	22.0	100
Quality of Head teacher	39.1	46.7	14.2	100
Adequate Supplies	13.3	29.3	57.4	100
Physical Infrastructure	17.6	38.7	43.7	100
Self-Reliance Work	31.2	46.7	22.1	100

Source: HRDS, 1993/94.

About 44 percent of respondents rated the infrastructure as "poor" or "very poor." In contrast, teachers and headmasters generally were viewed as adequate or better, although a significant minority of the respondents (about 22 percent) had strong negative opinions about teacher qualifications and self-reliance work. There were very few differences in perceptions among regions (rural and urban), or across expenditure groups.

Cooksey et al. (1993) found that focus-group respondents vehemently complained about the lack of conscientiousness and integrity of the teaching staff in local primary schools. Omari, Sumra and Levine (1994) similarly found that complaints about personnel were the most prevalent issues raised by parents when asked about the problems with primary schools in eight districts selected for the FAST study.

Willingness to Pay for Improved Education Services

HRDS respondents were asked a series of structured questions designed to determine how much they would be willing to pay for the full-costs of one year of primary school, if the school provided the sort of education that the respondent values[3]. Such questions solicit information on willingness to pay, but are used primarily to investigate how to improve welfare through public action. The contingent-valuation responses are influenced by the variables that economic theory implies should explain variations across households. Households with more educated heads showed a greater willingness to pay bids than those with less educated heads. Higher income households bid higher than those living in less affluent households. Male respondents, older respondents, married respondents, and more educated

---

[3] The determinants of the willingness to pay for primary education can be divided into four categories: characteristics of the game, characteristics of the respondent, characteristics of the household, and characteristics of the community.

respondents were willing to give higher bids. Clearly income and education measures are significant determinants of the responses.

The main reason for asking the question, however, was to determine how bids from households respond to the characteristics of the local primary school, as measured by an index of quality. This is a subjective measure of quality, but we are also interested in the impact of government district per capita education expenditures as a proxy for objective quality. We simulated the effects of increasing the quality of school, separate from those of increasing government expenditures. Our results showed that increases in the quality index would have a strong impact on how much the household would be willing to pay for one year in primary school[4]. Thus, consumers will pay more, or feel their welfare is enhanced, when specific characteristics they value are improved.

THE SUPPLY OF EDUCATION SERVICES

Policy Framework

Historical Background. Since the time of the Arusha Declaration, Tanzania has recognized the central role of education in the development of people and the nation. The approach taken, in which emphasis was given to expanding access to primary education in rural areas, has had several distinctive elements (see Box 4.4).

At Independence, the education sector was small and fragmented along racial and ethnic lines. There were European, Asian and African schools, with resources grossly skewed away from the latter. The resources expended per student-year in European schools was five times those in Asian schools, and 60 times those in African schools.

Policy changes starting in 1961 were largely designed to promote national unity and eradicate existing inequities. This included abolition of the three racially-defined (Caucasian, Asian, and African) types of schools, and the introduction of a unified system where pupils from all backgrounds were educated together. At the secondary-school level, students were selected to attend boarding schools far from their homes in order to attend school with classmates from other regions. Kiswahili was introduced as the language of instruction in government primary schools, with the explicit intent of promoting a single national

> **Box 4.4: Features of the Tanzanian Educational System**
>
> ❑ The government has been virtually the only provider of educational services, from primary through tertiary and vocational.
>
> ❑ The government sought to make primary education universally available, compulsory, and affordable to the poorest households by subsidizing all costs.
>
> ❑ Large-scale increases in the numbers of primary schools and teachers were brought about through campaign-style programs.
>
> ❑ The structure and staffing of government facilities was based on uniform, enrollment-based standards.
>
> ❑ The government oriented the curriculum and structure of primary-school education to rural life.
>
> ❑ The government limited the number of secondary school and university slots based on projected needs in the formal sector in general, and the civil service in particular.
>
> ❑ The government tried to increase the equity of admissions into the limited number of secondary schools through a quota system that gave preferential treatment to certain disadvantaged groups (e.g., children from disadvantaged districts, girls).
>
> [from the *Social Sector Strategy*, November 1994]

---

[4] Simulations were for an increase in the quality index by 5 and 10 points, compared with the initial conditions.

identity.

The policy of Education for Self-Reliance was introduced in 1967, followed in 1974 by the introduction of the Universal Primary Education (UPE) policy. Together, the policies drastically altered the characteristics and size of the educational system. They led to large-scale increases in access to primary schools, and reduced access among primary-school leavers to secondary and higher education. The UPE (1974-1980) virtually ensured that each viable village in the country had a primary school. Thus, primary schools now exist within walking distance from almost all households (see Box 4.5).

Recent Policy Initiatives. In early 1997, the Tanzanian government developed a Basic Education

---

Box 4.5: Physical Access to Schools

The level of physical access to schools is very high at the primary level, lower for private secondary schools, and very low for government secondary schools. For primary schools, for example, the FAST field study concluded, "In all the eight sites visited, schools were located within walking distance for children. In some areas, like Masangula in Mbozi, parents were able to choose between schools where they would send their children. Similarly, on the road to Lwati, a stretch of six kilometers, there were three primary schools" (Omari, Sumra and Levine, 1994). According to the HRDS, the distance from household to government primary schools averaged about 5 to 7 kilometers in both rural and urban areas.

Secondary schools are far from households in rural areas and highly concentrated in Dar es Salaam. Survey respondents reported that government secondary schools were nearly 52 kilometers away, on average, in rural areas, 14 kilometers away in urban areas outside of Dar es Salaam. In Dar es Salaam, government secondary schools were only about 5 kilometers away (or closer than the nearest primary school).

Private secondary schools, in contrast, were closer to all households than were government schools. This was most apparent in urban areas outside of Dar es Salaam. In rural areas, for example, respondents estimated that the nearest private secondary school was about 34 kilometers away, and in urban areas outside of Dar es Salaam the nearest secondary school was only about 8 kilometers away.

Master Plan (BEMP) to guide education policy for the 1997-2002 period. This plan is budgeted to require approximately US$375 million.

The BEMP's main goal is to increase primary-school completion rates and improve student performance. It seeks to achieve this by enhancing educational quality, improving access to education, introducing better educational planning, management, and monitoring, and instituting teacher service rationalization. Many of the BEMP reforms enhance local ownership and management of basic education. Approximately 40 percent of the BEMP budget would be managed by schools. An additional 40 percent of the budget is earmarked for teacher rationalization and training. The major BEMP proposals are summarized below:

- Divestiture of school ownership to village and urban ward authorities.

- Enhanced district and school discretion over school management and resource allocations. District authorities and school committees will play a much greater role in recruiting, monitoring, and evaluating teachers. They will also receive block grants that will be used to purchase school inputs (including teaching and textbooks). Authorities will specify what share of the grant should be reserved for non-salary expenses.

- Cost recovery for specific inputs will be introduced to encourage parental contributions and improve accountability to parents concerning how resources are spent. Matching grant programs will be implemented to further stimulate cost recovery.

- Increased administrative focus on helping communities to deliver education services rather than on providing services directly. The MOEC will focus on policy formulation, planning, and performance monitoring rather than on directly providing education services. Deployment of academic officers, inspectors, and ward education officers will be rationalized. These staff will also increase their efforts in administering advice and information to schools rather than simply reporting school performance to central authorities.

- Augmented teacher quality and instruction time, especially in rural areas. Many "Grade B" and "Grade C" teachers with limited education and training will be replaced with more highly qualified staff. This will be accomplished by implementing a departure plan for teachers with limited skills, providing incentives for more qualified teachers to move to rural areas, increasing districts' and school committees' roles in recruiting, monitoring, and evaluating teachers, and increasing allocations to, and the cost-effectiveness of, teacher training. It is anticipated that instructional time will be increased through the enhanced role of school and district authorities in teacher management.

- Increased availability of private provision of basic education.

- Increased government and donor resources available for primary education. A modest increase in education's share of total recurrent government expenditures, and an increase in primary education's share of government education spending. Significantly increased donor support of primary education.

- Grants to schools in low-income areas and/or to poor families earmarked for educational inputs.

- Measures to improve girls' academic performance. For example, the Girls' Secondary Education Support Project.

- Introduction of a simplified curriculum that will emphasize basic literacy and computation skills.

- Increased community involvement in school construction and rehabilitation. Expansion of multi-grade and multi-shift teaching.

Legal and Regulatory Framework. The legal basis for provision of education is mainly statutory law. The Education Act of 1978 empowers the government to ensure "the promotion of the education of the people of Tanzania and the progressive development of institutions devoted to that purpose, and for securing the effective execution by local authorities under this guidance, control and direction, of the national policy for providing a varied, comprehensive, and nationally beneficial educational service in their respective jurisdiction." Under that statute, regulations have been created to make primary education compulsory, to ensure the rights of students, to place a ceiling on fees that can be charged in the public and private schools, and to prevent transfers from private to public schools.

The education system suffers from a lack of enforcement of existing laws and regulations designed to improve quality and increase enrollments. For example, Nditi (1994) reports that statutes protecting the rights of students are not rigorously enforced, and teachers often administer corporal punishment with little regard for students' rights. In addition, compulsory attendance of children over age 7 is not enforced, as evidenced by low enrollment rates and the advanced ages of children in primary school.

Many of the provisions in education sector laws and regulations constrain the delivery of educational services by the non-governmental sector. For example, Section 23 of the Education Act states that a private school must impart education "wholly or mainly in technical fields of learning." This implies that private primary schools are prohibited, as are private teacher-training colleges that prepare teachers for primary schools. Section 32 of the Act empowers the government to take over private schools and constitute them as regional or national schools under certain circumstances. In addition, students in private schools are not permitted to transfer to government schools. Prices in private schools are controlled and tuition is taxed.

Relatively recent policy changes have begun to loosen the constraints on the private-sector provision of both primary and secondary education. Responding to high demand for secondary education and low transition rates between primary and secondary levels, and in the face of tight fiscal constraints, private secondary schools were allowed to operate starting in 1984.

Between 1984 and 1994 the number of non-governmental secondary schools increased from 85 to 298 (Table 4.18). Enrollment in private schools increased from 33,591 in 1984 to 102,805 in 1994. By comparison, the number of state-owned secondary schools increased from 85 in 1984 to 193 in 1994, while enrollment grew from 40,617 to 83,441. In 1994, the 298 private schools accounted for 61 percent of upper, and 57 percent of lower, secondary-school enrollment. Private enrollment in Forms V and VI were only 4,584 in 1994 out of a total of 12,626 (GOT Ministry of Education, 1996).

Table 4.18: Expansion of Private Schools

Year	Number of Private Secondary Schools	Share of Total Secondary School Enrollment (%)
1978	71	35
1980	71	42
1982	82	44
1984	85	45
1986	124	53
1988	175	57
1990	213	57
1992	258	58
1994	298	55

Source: Government of Tanzania, Ministry of Education, Basic Education Statistics, various years.

Organization and Structure of the Education System

The educational system in Tanzania is highly centralized and uniform. Primary education in Tanzania is universal, nominally free (with the exception of a Tsh 200 UPE fee) and, on paper, compulsory. School-aged children are expected to begin primary school at 7 years. Public secondary education is not compulsory and, as stated earlier, tightly rationed. Movement through the educational system is determined directly by students' performance on national examinations (see Box 4.6). The curriculum is established nationally, under the auspices of the Tanzania Institute for Education (formerly the Institute for Curriculum Development).

Primary Education. For primary education, policy is made by the Ministry of Education and Culture (MOEC), and implemented through the local government administration. The MOEC provides teachers, sets standards for physical facilities, formulates sector policies, sets the curriculum, administers nationwide exams, provides textbooks, and posts ministry staff to manage the education system from the districts. It also operates the teacher training colleges in which primary-school teachers are produced.

Box 4.6: Examination System

Advancement from one education level to the next is based on nationwide examinations and continuous assessments. The first examination is encountered in Standard 4. That exam, designed to be diagnostic, informs the teacher and parents about the ability of students to progress further in primary school. Students failing the examination can repeat Standard 4. No other primary-school grades can be repeated. The Primary School Leaving Exam (PSLE) is taken in the last year of primary school (Standard 7) and, in conjunction with district-based quotas, determines advancement to secondary school (Form I).

A similar pattern of diagnostic and then achievement examination is followed in secondary school. A diagnostic exam in Form II leads either to progression to Form III or repeat of Form II. The Form IV exam punctuates the transition from lower to upper secondary school. The Form VI examination is required for University entrance, with some allowances made for mature-age applicants or equivalents. Private candidates, many of whom study in unregistered schools, are also allowed to take national examinations.

District governments nominally own the primary schools and are responsible for maintaining them and for paying the centrally-established teacher salaries. As in all the social sectors, the local government depends on the central government, rather than its own resource base, for funds. Education is represented at District and Ward Development Committees by the District Education Officer (DEO) and Ward Education Coordinators, respectively. School inspectors work at the headquarters of MOEC, as well as in zones and districts.

As of 1993, there were 10,879 government primary schools, or about 100 per district, and slightly more than one per village, on average. Primary schools typically have about 340 students. Only three regions (Dar es Salaam, Kigoma and Singida) have schools with an average size of more than 500 students. Dar es Salaam has, by far, the largest average school size (1,154 students).

As shown in Table 4.19, a typical primary school has about 9 teachers, each with about 36 students. Classrooms, furniture, and teacher housing are thinly spread. There are 5 children to a desk, only 2 regions out of 20 have more than one table per teacher, and only 5 out of 20 regions have 1 or more chairs per teacher on average.

The for-profit private sector is prohibited from operating primary schools, and to date there are no guidelines to ensure registration and quality control of private primary schools. A limited number of non-profit organizations, including the Aga Khan Foundation and religious missions, have been permitted to run schools. As of 1993, there were 13 privately-operated primary schools. These have an enrollment of just over 5,000 pupils.

Table 4.19: Profile of the Average Primary School

Indicator	Average Number
Students per school	336.1
Students per classroom	66.8
Students per teacher	35.7
Students per desk	4.7
Teachers per school	9.4
Housing per school	2.8
Tables per teacher	0.7
Chairs per teacher	0.7

Source: MOEC, 1994.

The primary-school curriculum in 1993 included arithmetic, Kiswahili, English (from Standard 3 onward), general science (from Standard 3), social studies, work skills, health, and religious studies. Most classroom time beginning with Standard 4 is devoted to predictors of secondary-school success, such as arithmetic and English.

There are 101,816 primary-school teachers in Tanzania, according to the most recent count. About two-thirds of those now in service are trained at the relatively low Grade B or C (see Box 4.7). The remainder are Grade A teachers. Overall, teachers are quite evenly distributed throughout the country, though there are somewhat fewer teachers in rural districts compared to urban areas. Teachers in rural areas also tend to have less preparation than do urban teachers. For example, in 1989, the most recent year for which district-level data could be found, more than 40 percent of the teachers in Iringa Urban District primary schools were Grade A, while only 25 percent of the teachers in Iringa Rural District primary schools had achieved that qualification level. In Kigoma Urban District, 49 percent of the primary-school teachers were Grade As, but in Kigoma Rural, only 21 percent were Grade A. The same pattern is found in nearly all regions.

Across regions, there are large variations in the distribution of Grade A versus other (less well-

---

Box 4.7: Structure of the Teaching Workforce

There are five basic types, or levels, of teachers in Tanzania, differing by degree of preparation: primary-school teachers can be Grade C, B or A, depending on their pre-service qualifications and training. Higher-level teachers include diploma holders and graduates. Grade C, B and A teachers are eligible to teach in primary school, while secondary-school teachers include Grade A, diploma, and graduate-level teachers.

Grade C school teachers were trained during the period of Universal Primary Education. They have a primary education, and received a "crash course" in teaching methodology before being deployed to teach the lower grades in primary schools throughout the country. Many Grade C teachers subsequently have been "upgraded" to Grade B through intensive in-service training. Teachers are no longer being hired at this level.

Grade B school teachers enter teacher training with no more than a primary-school leaving certificate (having successfully completed Standard VII). Training consists of two years of general education (essentially the equivalent of a Form II education) and then two years of training in primary-school subjects. Grade B teachers can teach in primary schools.

Grade A school teachers enter teacher training with O-levels (Form IV), and having passed at least four subjects at the Form IV level. The training program is two years, and students study 11 primary subjects, as well as teaching methods. The course includes teaching practice.

Grade B teachers can also be upgraded to Grade A, in a two-step process. First, they must upgrade to O-level, which often is done through an "in-service" correspondence course or private secondary schooling. Once they pass their O-level examinations as private candidates, they are eligible for a one-year course in training methodology to attain Grade A status.

Most Grade A teachers teach in primary schools. A few have in the past taught in secondary schools, and a very small number are employed at teacher-training institutions.

Diploma-level teachers enter teacher training with A-levels (Form VI). Individuals completing the two-year course, which includes practice teaching, are hired to teach in lower secondary schools and teacher-training colleges.

Grade A teachers can also be upgraded to diploma level in an intensive two-year course. The training covers material for A-levels in the first year, and then the diploma-level training in the second. To upgrade from Grade A, teachers must have at least three credits at O-level and 3 years of teaching experience.

Graduate teachers, trained in the Faculty of Education at the University of Dar es Salaam, go through a three-year program. Most teach in secondary schools, but some also teach in teacher-training colleges.

prepared) primary-school teachers. The regions that are relatively well-endowed with better-prepared teachers are Dar es Salaam, Kilimanjaro, and Arusha, while the poorer regions of the country have far smaller relative numbers of Grade A teachers.

About one-half of primary-school teachers are female. A disproportionately large number of the female teachers are employed in urban areas. For example, in Dar es Salaam, about 84 percent of primary-school teachers are women, while in Lindi, only 25 percent are female. In all except two regions (Mwanza and Singida), the female teachers are disproportionately the less well-prepared and lower-paid teachers. In Tanga, for example, about 45 percent of Grades B and C, but only 35 percent of Grade A, teachers are female. The same pattern is repeated throughout the country. Female teachers also tend to be less educated than their male counterparts.

During the UPE decade, the focus of education administrators was almost exclusively on increasing the quantity of primary schools. In more recent years, attention has shifted to improving school quality (see Box 4.8). Improvements have been slow in coming, however, and intra- and inter-regional disparities are profound. Even within the same district, there are large differences in performance on examinations. In 1990, for example, performance on the Standard 7 examination varied from a mean of 39.9 percent in Kinondoni Urban to 18.6 percent in Kilosa.

In an attempt to understand why some schools performed better than others, Omari and Mosha (1987) divided a large sample of schools into high- and low-quality and performed in-depth analyses. Results indicated that urban schools consistently performed better than rural schools. The main explanatory variables included higher academic qualifications of teachers, stability of teaching staff (more than five years in one position), better provision of learning and teaching materials, experienced and more academically prepared head teachers, and regularity of inspection.

Secondary Education. In contrast to primary education, government secondary schools are administered directly by the MOEC's Department of Secondary Schools. Secondary-school teachers are employees of the Ministry, and operating funds come directly from the central administration. The Ministry is also responsible for ensuring the quality of the education provided in registered private schools.

As the private secondary-school sector expanded rapidly, several patterns and characteristics emerged:

- The regional disparity in the provision of private schooling is pronounced. There is a heavy concentration of private secondary schools in three regions; Kilimanjaro, Dar es Salaam and Iringa. Very little private provision of secondary schooling is found in Mtwara (less than 3 percent) and Pwani (less than 10 percent).

- Most of the private schools are located in rural areas, while most state-owned schools are located in urban areas and district centers.

- Most of the newer private schools are day schools, rather than boarding schools.

- The majority of the schools under the ownership and management of churches, mosques, and parent organizations are community-initiated. This also includes schools funded by

---

Box 4.8: Community Education Fund (CEF)

The Community Education Fund (CEF) is a matching grant program that empowers communities to improve their primary schools. The program addresses problems of underfunding and lack of accountability in schools. The Government of Tanzania and the World Bank designed the program through a participatory process involving extensive consultations with beneficiary villages and other stakeholders.

The residents of villages decide by majority vote in a meeting whether to participate in the CEF. If they decide to participate, they establish school funding priorities and set an amount for parents to contribute to the CEF during the first year of the program. The school committee, which is elected by parents, prepares a detailed Three-Year School Plan that includes objectives, a three-year budget, and, for the first year, implementation and procurement plans. The School Plan is cleared by the parents who vote on whether to accept the plan. One-half of the agreed annual village contribution is collected and deposited in the primary school's CEF bank account. After verifying that the community's contribution is in the account, the government deposits a matching grant into the same account. The government matches the money raised by the community on a 1-to-1 basis, currently up to Tsh. 6,000 per pupil (about US$10). Provisions have also been made for matching on a 1.5-to-1 basis for targeted schools in poorer districts.

Over the course of the following year, the village council and the government conduct periodic reviews of the program. For example, halfway through the year, the village holds a community meeting for the school committee to show progress against the School Plan, account for funds spent, and solicit the second half of pledged parental contributions (which are also matched by the project).

The initial pre-tests have yielded very promising results. Parental contributions have been 10-20 times more than had previously been committed to the schools, largely due to the transparency of the process. In most cases, communities have spent CEF funds on infrastructure and desks. Construction activities under this project have generally been less expensive and faster than those under previous IDA-financed projects. In one school, parents were able to enroll 90 more children in the school without adding teachers, once additional classroom space was made available through the CEF investment.

Previous projects have suffered theft of donated desks and equipment. However, one CEF community reported that under this project there is no fear of having new desks stolen because parents contributed to their purchase. Thus any such thefts would be viewed as neighbors stealing from neighbors. Schools are also keeping careful records of financial transactions. Headmasters value this record keeping so that probity can be established, and parents use the information to monitor program performance. An independent evaluation could not find a single parent in 4 pre-test villages who did not know about and understand the program. Villages have successfully handled subsidies for parents who cannot pay, but no one has been exempted from making some contribution. Finally, teachers have been empowered. For most of them, this is the first time they have been able to help decide what should happen in schools and to assume responsibility for the implementation of plans.

---

the Cash Crop Cooperatives, Development Trust Funds and Development Associations.

Private schools have come under considerable criticism for providing lower-quality education at a substantially higher cost to households. In an early attempt to address this issue, a study based on 1981 data found that a private secondary-school student would be expected to perform 16 percent better on mathematics and verbal examinations than would a public secondary-school student with comparable family background. The same study found that private secondary schools have unit costs that are only 69 percent of public school costs. Given the performance advantage of private schools, the ratio of relative cost to effectiveness was found to be 59 percent. That is, the same amount of learning in private schools was found to cost only 59 percent of the cost of an equivalent education in public schools (Jimenez et al., 1991). These estimates are rough because of the small sample size, and refer to the universe of private schools in 1981. While they suggest that the private schools may have the potential to offer more education at lower cost, it is important to note that the universe of private schools in 1995 is far different, and probably of lower average quality, than that in 1981. Nevertheless, the impact of private schools cannot be ascertained from overall averages, if only for the simple reason that public schools pick the best students.

Lower-secondary education (Form I to IV) is segmented into four streams for commercial, agricultural, technical, and domestic science. There are four technical secondary schools (Moshi, Tanga, Mtwara and Ifunda) and four "talented" schools, or schools for pupils who perform particularly well on the Standard 7 examination (Mzumbe, Kilakala, Ilboru and Msalato). Under the draft Integrated Education and Training Policy of 1993, these streams will be abandoned due to high cost, disappointing outcomes, and logistical problems in implementation.

Forms V and VI are not diversified, but instead adhere to traditional subjects. These include physics, chemistry, mathematics, geography, biology, accountancy, bookkeeping, education, Kiswahili, literature and commerce. Pupils take a combination of three subjects, designated as science and arts streams. There are three technical high schools (Arusha, Mbeya and Dar es Salaam Technical Colleges) with small enrollments.

There were 9,568 secondary-school teachers in Tanzania in 1993. Twenty percent of the secondary-school teachers are female. Of all secondary teachers, the vast majority hold diplomas, and a small number are graduates of the University of Dar es Salaam Faculty of Education. Private schools have a somewhat heavier concentration of graduate teachers than do government schools (Table 4.20).

Table 4.20: Qualifications of Teachers in Government and Private Secondary Schools

Type of Secondary-school Teacher	School Ownership		
	Government	Private	Total
Diploma	4,064	1,759	5,823
Graduate	833	681	1,514
All	4,897	2,440	7,337

Source: MOEC, 1992.

Performance varies widely among the different types of secondary schools in Tanzania. Based on examination results, all-male seminaries typically are top-performers, closely followed by single-sex government boarding schools. Co-educational boarding schools also perform relatively well. The schools that perform most poorly are private and community day schools. These comparisons are made hesitantly, as they do not account for the variety of factors that should be considered in assessing a school's impact on performance.

Other Vocational, Technical and Academic Opportunities. Vocational and technical training opportunities exist, but are very limited in number. For primary-school leavers, about 114 government-owned basic vocational training centers and institutes offer a total of 25,000 places to learn practical skills such as handicrafts and tailoring. This level of training includes the 52 Folk Development Colleges that were established to provide rural-based training opportunities to literate primary-school graduates. For the most part, these basic vocational training centers are designed to provide skills for informal sector workers.

Students with at least some O-level secondary schooling may attend a vocational training institute operated by a government ministry. The 153 vocational training institutions have traditionally trained agricultural, engineering, medical, and education workers for government employment. These institutions grant certificates and/or advanced certificates, and a few also grant diplomas. A dozen of the training programs are closely affiliated with parastatal enterprises, and the rest are directly under ministerial control. The Ministry of Education's teacher-training colleges constitute the largest number of institutions in a single category. About 11,000 students (or 38 percent of all trainees) are enrolled in institutions that grant certificates for A- or B-level teachers. The Ministry of Health, with about 4,800 students in certificate programs (or 17 percent of all trainees), has the second largest set of training activities.

Students who have successfully completed their A-level education with high passes on the examination may enroll in one of 14 technical-training institutions, or one of the three universities, all of which are relatively autonomous organizations operated under the auspices of MOSTHE. The technical institutions, which grant diplomas, advanced diplomas, and professional degrees, provide technical training in management, business, secondary-school teaching, journalism and similar fields. At the universities (University of Dar es Salaam, Muhimbili University College of Health Sciences, Sokoine University of Agriculture, and the Open University of Tanzania) students can earn baccalaureate and higher degrees.

Teachers, Textbooks, and Management in Primary Education

The problems facing the educational system in Tanzania are myriad. In this section, we cover three of the constraints that most severely affect the sector's ability to meet its goals for high-quality universal primary education. These are problems related to primary-school teachers and their training, the production and distribution of textbooks, and education management.

Teachers. There is no shortage in the absolute number of teachers in Tanzania[5]. However, there are clear problems in the recruitment and deployment of qualified primary- and secondary-school teachers. Most of these problems are linked to the underlying structure of the workforce. For instance, relative to the number of Grade B teachers, there are too few Grade A primary-school teachers. The Grade B teachers are more likely to be found in rural areas and are more likely to be female, while the Grade A teachers are disproportionately found in urban schools and are more likely to be male. In secondary schools, there appears to be a mismatch between the subject-area requirements within secondary schools and the availability of trained teachers with relevant specializations.

- MOEC is responsible for assigning recent graduates of teaching-training colleges to the various regions. The assignment attempts to match graduates' stated preferences with the requirements submitted by the Regional Education Officer (REO). Once the regional assignment is made, the responsibility for district placement falls to the REO. The District Education Officer (DEO) assigns new teachers to specific schools and classes. Although the DEO submits specific requests for teachers, he or she does not know in advance how many teachers will arrive at the start of a term.

- MOEC compiles no statistics on whether teachers show up at their assigned posts. One study found that in the Morogoro Region in 1989, only 118 out of 174 teachers assigned to that region actually arrived (World Bank, 1991, p.10). It is likely that an even higher proportion of teachers fail to arrive at less desirable regions, such as the Mtwara and Lindi regions.

- Within primary schools, there is little room for flexibility in staff deployment. The official formula permits one teacher per stream, an additional teacher for schools

---

[5] This statement is made on the basis of the relatively low pupil-teacher ratios prevailing in the country, and analyses in the study, "Teachers and Financing of Education" (World Bank, 1991). It is important to note, however, that MOEC consistently stresses that a shortage exists.

offering Standards 5 to 7, a head teacher, and a teacher specialized in music and crafts or vocational and technical training. For relatively large schools (with more than 14 streams), an assistant head teacher is allowed.

● The financial pressures associated with a large teaching workforce prevent the government from providing teachers with salaries commensurate with a valued profession. While the government's total wage bill has grown, the real wages of individual teachers have failed to keep up with inflation. Teachers are demoralized, as reflected in recent strikes in some parts of the country. Unfortunately for the system's long-term prospects, the teachers who are the most satisfied with their pay and work are those who have the least amount of training, and are the least likely to contribute to improvements in the quality of Tanzanian education.

Two basic problems related to teacher compensation are worth highlighting:

● *Teachers' salaries are too low to attract high-quality workers.* As has been widely reported, the salaries offered to teachers generally are too low to sustain a household. Low wages, combined with low prestige of the occupation, contributes to the inability of the sector to attract the highest-quality candidates. The vast majority of primary teachers fall into the lowest categories and are paid less than Tsh 10,000 per month (now valued at US$20).

   o A 1991 study determined that the average gross salary of primary and secondary teachers was insufficient to feed the average household. It was recommended that "to ensure a reasonable standard of living and to increase productivity significantly in the public service would probably require salary increases by a factor of 3 to 5 times their existing levels" (World Bank, 1991, p. 18).

   o The teachers surveyed in 1991 who were the most dissatisfied with their jobs were the more highly educated secondary-school teachers, and younger Grade A primary-school teachers. For example, only about 45 percent of secondary-school teachers said that they were satisfied with their jobs, and only 43 percent stated that they were planning to stay in their positions. These are individuals who are likely to have alternative career opportunities. This is consistent with some limited data on attrition of teachers. Attrition rates among primary-school teachers is low (estimated at 3-5 percent annually), while attrition rates among secondary-school teachers are at least twice as high (World Bank, 1991).

   o The concern that teaching is an unattractive profession is also backed up by the *decline* in the number of graduate-level teachers from about 1,600 to 1,500 between 1989 and 1992. These findings indicate that few strong candidates are entering the profession, or are being retained in their posts. As stated by the Task Force on the Education System for the 21st Century, "The teaching profession does not attract the highest achievers. It is among the last professional choices of able secondary-school graduates" (MOEC, 1992b).

● *The wage "signals" sent to teachers do not encourage change in the right direction, toward higher quality trainees and teachers*. The salary adjustments of the late 1980s sent the "wrong signals about the value of teachers with higher qualifications" (World Bank, 1991, p.18). That is, the least qualified primary-school teachers (Grade B) were given the largest relative increase in wages during the adjustment. As a consequence, the differentials in salary between teachers with the lowest and highest qualifications declined from 2.4 to 1.6 between 1978 and 1990 (World Bank, 1991). The minimum salary (including monetary allowances) for a teacher who has had only a primary-school education and four years of government-financed teacher training is Tsh 6,592 per month, while the salary for a two-year trainee who started with a Form IV education is only Tsh 8,107. Given that the lower-level Grade B teacher can move into a higher salary range simply by accruing time on the job, there is little difference in the expected lifetime earnings of Grade B and Grade A teachers. The economic "signal," then, is that it makes sense for individuals to enter teacher-training college with little academic preparation, obtain a government-financed education to the equivalent of Form II, and then leave training to a secure job.

Textbooks. Since Independence, the state has had an effective monopoly over the preparation, production, and distribution of textbooks, closing out private investment in the subsector. As a result of well-documented inefficiencies, a tight budget, and several donor projects that supported the government's policies (including World Bank projects), the shortage of textbooks is precipitating major policy change.

- Manuscript preparation has been under the domain of the Tanzania Institute for Education (formerly the Institute for Curriculum Development), and has been seen as a natural adjunct to the Institute's responsibilities for curricular development. The Institute has been widely criticized for frequent curriculum changes, slow manuscript production and, in many cases, poor quality of curricular products. Among the problems at TIE are financial constraints, low staff motivation, inability to develop medium- and long-term manuscript preparation programs, lack of pilot testing and evaluation, and a limited pool of authors (Zayumba, 1994).

- Nearly all publishing has been done by the government and parastatal publishing houses using donor-supplied paper. Lack of funds, unpredictable payments by the government to the parastatals for work completed, lack of expertise, and a host of related problems have led to a situation in which delays in publishing manuscripts are typically three to eight years (Zayumba, 1994).

- Once published, the books are distributed very slowly. For many years, Tanzania Elimu Supplies (TES), a parastatal organization, was the sole distributor of primary-school textbooks and other school materials. This effectively "crowded out" the private distribution networks, including most booksellers. Once printed, books would be delivered to TES warehouses and would then be distributed to districts and schools. Because of financial difficulties, however, this system broke down and the government took over the distribution role through the Ministry of Education and Culture and the Prime Minister's Office. Commonly cited problems with the system are lack of coordination, leakage of goods out of the storage and distribution system, and a simple inability to move sufficient numbers of textbooks into the rural schools and the hands of students (Zayumba, 1994).

- A 1995 survey assessed the availability of teaching materials (Hedkvist, 1996). The study concluded that for the education system as a whole, the government's target of a book to student ratio of 1:3 for each subject in each standard is largely met. However, textbooks are distributed somewhat unequally across districts. Thus, many individual districts fail this standard for some subjects. Further, even when districts achieve the 1:3 ratio at the school level, they fail to achieve this standard at the classroom level. Indeed, only a few districts in the survey were meeting the 1:3 ratio at the classroom level in more than one subject area (see Box 4.9).

The result of this system has been to make private procurement of most textbooks illegal, and access to publicly-provided textbooks difficult. Parents who seek to purchase textbooks for their children can technically be deemed criminals. In addition, teachers have incentives to hoard, rather than use, the few textbooks that make their way to the schools. In short, the system has been a failure, a fact that is widely recognized by specialists, teachers and parents. It has essentially removed a key educational input from the school system. It is important to note that the problem of textbook production and distribution is being given intensive attention, particularly with the assistance of the Swedish International Development Authority.

Management. The problems in the education sector are exacerbated by constraints in the institutional framework and by weaknesses in managerial operations. The fragmentation of institutions, in the form of five Ministries involved directly in education (Ministry of Education and Culture, Ministry of Science, Technology and Higher Education, Ministry of Labor and Youth, Ministry of Regional Administration and Local Government, and the Ministry of Community Development, Women and Children's Affairs), is arguably the most serious constraint as it hinders rational planning and efficient utilization of resources. It does not allow for the reallocation of resources according to national priorities because each ministry defends its own agenda and priorities.

- Within ministries there are a number of organizational constraints. The Planning Directorates are mostly concerned with budgeting problems and are not engaged in program and policy development, setting program targets, evaluating strategies, and carrying out cost-benefit and cost-effectiveness exercises. Data collection and analysis is carried out under the Directorates of Planning. However, while good data are collected, in many instances they are not analyzed in relation to the pervasive problems affecting the ministry concerned. Most of the implementation Directorates are concerned with routine administrative matters to the detriment of professional development activities.

- The school inspectorate system is well established in Tanzania but has very little impact on qualitative improvements in education. The major constraint can be traced to the issue of accountability. Inspectors have no professional responsibilities for the schools they supervise, apart from routine reports made to the Commissioner of Education.

- In primary and basic education, the roles and inter-relationships between MOEC, the Prime Minister's Office, and local governments are unclear and frequently dysfunctional. Local governments are charged with the delivery of educational services, but are dependent almost totally on central level funds. When these funds are eventually

---

Box 4.9: Availability of Textbooks in Primary Schools

In 1995, a random sample of 203 schools in 30 districts was surveyed to assess whether learning materials were available to schools and, within schools, to students (Hedkvist, 1996).[a]

The government's objective for textbook availability is a book to student ratio of 1:3 for each subject in each standard. This study demonstrated that the 1:3 ratio is being met in a large number of schools. On average, the 1:3 book to student ratio is maintained or exceeded for all subjects except Kiswahili which has a ratio of 1:3.2. The ratio is 1:2 or better for science, history and mathematics.

Book availability within individual districts is relatively good. If books from all subjects are counted together, 27 of the 30 districts surveyed achieve a 1:3 book to student ratio. Within subjects, the results are mixed. Twenty-one of the 30 surveyed districts do not achieve the 1:3 standard for Kiswahili, 13 districts miss the standard for Kilimo, 14 do not meet the standard for home economics, and 12 fail the standard for geography. Of the 30 districts surveyed, Rufiji had the poorest book to student ratios despite being located relatively close to the nation's central store for textbooks in Dar es Salaam.

The availability of books in classrooms is much lower than the availability of books in schools. Four of primary school's eight subjects, Kiswahili, geography, Kilimo, and home economics, have classroom availability ratios of one book for every ten or more students. The other four subjects, English, mathematics, science, and history, have classroom availability ratios of 1 book for every 5 to 6 students. Availability of textbooks in classrooms is poor in virtually all of the districts surveyed. Only a few districts in the survey were meeting the 1:3 book to student ratio at the classroom level in more than one subject area.

The availability of teaching guides is poorer than the availability of books. Many guides are not available in schools and often guides available in schools are not available in classrooms. The subjects and districts with the lowest availability of books are also those with the lowest availability of guides.

[a] _The urban/rural population distribution for the sampled schools reflected the country's distribution. The sampling framework was developed such that the results of the survey are assumed to be relevant for 92 of the country's 104 districts._

---

transferred to local authorities, they are already earmarked, and thus give local authorities no opportunity to respond to local conditions and priorities. The revenue base of local governments is so inadequate that funds levied specifically for education (for example, the UPE contribution) are often not invested in educational services.

- The next level of organization and management is the region. Again the lack of clear and defined relationships between central government education administrators and local authorities constrains effective regional planning and implementation. The Regional Education Office is meant to supervise the implementation of, and supply technical advice to, educational programs in the region. While regional offices are constrained by underfunding, they are constrained even more by not having the authority to set regional priorities and allocate budgets for targeted programs.

- Many would argue that the source of all the institutional and managerial weaknesses in the system is to be found at the school level. Here the constraints hinge on two critical factors: the relationship between schools and their communities, and the quality of school management itself. The issue of accountability is best illustrated in the problems relating to school boards and committees. Schools are essentially accountable to the district and central authorities, and the parents have no real say in the development of their own schools. Even the question of who owns primary schools is unclear. It seems that due to the fact that local communities do not constitute legal entities, they cannot legally own schools despite their responsibility for the schools. The districts own the primary schools, and this distances the institutions, villages, or wards from a sense of ownership. While head teachers are meant to be the executive secretaries of school committees, it is most often the case that the committees are actually controlled by the head teachers. In addition, school committees tend to concern themselves with student discipline rather than the operation of the school.

GOVERNMENT AND DONOR SPENDING ON EDUCATION

Recurrent Expenditures

In 1994/95, the Government of Tanzania spent about Tsh 83 billion on recurrent education expenditures. Education's share of total government spending was approximately 14 percent annually from 1989/90 to 1992/93. This share increased in 1993/94 and 1994/95, to approximately 22 percent. However, estimates for 1995/96 indicate that education has dropped back to about 15 percent of total social-sector spending.

Education expenditures' share of government spending, net of debt repayment, declined marginally from 21 percent in 1989/90 to less than 19 percent in 1992/93, then increased dramatically to approximately 30 percent in 1994/95. Education was estimated to be about 3.6 percent of GDP in 1994/95, up from 2.7 percent two years earlier. Education's share of total social sector spending has declined slightly from 62 percent in 1989/90 to 58 percent in 1994/95.

Expenditure by Program

While primary education has been the explicit focus of the Tanzanian educational system, this is only weakly reflected in spending patterns. Primary education was budgeted at about 58 percent of total education-recurrent expenditures in 1994/95. Primary education's share of recurrent expenditures has risen over the 1990's, from 46 percent in 1989/90 to an estimated 59 percent in 1995/96. Secondary education absorbed 10 percent of recurrent education spending in 1994/95, down from its 1989/90 level of 16 percent. This downward trend is expected to continue through 1996/97. Teacher training accounted for 2 percent of spending in 1994/95, down from its 1989/90 level of 8 percent. Higher education absorbed 23 percent of expenditures, up from 19 percent in 1989/90. Ministerial administration and other education-related programs accounted for about 5 percent of total recurrent education spending, down from the 1989/90 level of 11 percent.

Inclusion of the development budgets in this analysis has a minor impact on the distribution of resources across education sector programs. Table 4.21 shows the 1994/95 recurrent and development budget expenditures by program. Inclusion of the development budget decreases primary education's

Table 4.21: Distribution of Recurrent and Development Expenditures Among Education Sector Programs, 1994/95

| Category | Recurrent | | Development | | | | Total | |
	Govt. (Tsh million)	Share (%)	Govt. (Tsh million)	Share (%)	Donor (Tsh million)	Share (%)	Govt. and Donor (Tsh million)	Share (%)
Total	82,956	100	1,393	100	4,952	100	89,302	100
Primary	47,756	58	475	34	2,020	41	50,251	56
Total Secondary	7,955	10	210	15	157	3	8,322	9
Technical Secondary	2,265	3	210	15	157	3	2,632	3
Commercial Secondary	2,753	3	0	0	0	0	2,753	3
Agricultural and Other Secondary	2,936	4	0	0	0	0	2,936	3
Teacher Education	2,129	2	33	2	167	3	2,329	3
Adult and Literacy	1,249	2	13	1	0	0	1,262	1
Higher and Technical	19,082	23	371	27	2,160	44	•21,614	24
Other Education	2,133	2	67	5	0	0	2,200	3
Ministry and Regional Administration	2,653	3	224	16	448	9	3,325	4

Source: Follmer and Kessy, 1996.

share of total budgeted expenditures from 58 to 57 percent. Secondary education's share of total expenditures and that of higher and technical education are virtually unchanged. Ministerial and regional administration's share of total expenditures also remain roughly the same.

Expenditure by Input

Table 4.22 shows spending by inputs. Without question, personnel costs dominate spending at the primary-school level, accounting for approximately 70 percent of all expenditures. School examination expenses account for about 20 percent of expenditures, and materials, boarding costs, and other expenditures another 10 percent. Spending on operation and maintenance is not broken down in the local budget, but accounts for less than 3 percent of total primary-school expenditures.

In the budget for 1996/97, the share of total spending on wages increased sharply. On average, personal emoluments accounted for 91 percent of all recurrent costs in the 1996/97 budget estimates for primary schools.

The large share of spending on personal emoluments at the primary level is not due to high teacher salaries, but rather to the size of the teaching workforce in combination with the fact that the education sector as a whole is seriously underfunded. The implications of the budget distortions caused by a large

Table 4.22: Input Use in Education Sector Programs, 1994/95 (shares of total program expenditures)

| Input | Primary | Secondary School | | | | Teacher Training |
		Technical	Commercial	Agricultural	Total	
Total	100	100	100	100	100	100
Personal Emoluments	70	26	41	40	37	44
Travel and Visits	0	1	2	2	2	3
Operation and Maintenance	0	6	1	2	3	4
Staff Training	0	0	0	0	0	5
Pupil Transport	0	0	0	1	0	0
Student Boarding/Welfare	1	54	43	42	46	36
Materials	7	5	5	5	5	2
Exam Expenses	20	5	4	4	4	5
Hospital Services	0	0	0	0	0	0
Other	2	3	3	5	4	0

Source: Follmer and Kessy, 1996.

Box 4.10: Uses of Funds for Sample of Government and Private Schools

Table 4.23 estimates expenditures by use of funds for a sample of government and private secondary schools in Tanzania. Analyzing expenditures for specific schools provides a higher assurance of the accuracy of these estimates, and performing these calculations for private schools allows for a comparison of the two types of institutions. These estimations were made for 4 government and 2 private secondary schools in fiscal 1994 (Dar and Levine, 1996). While this very small sample cannot be assumed to be representative of all secondary schools, it nonetheless may provide indications of more general patterns.

For the sampled schools, total expenditures per child in FY94 were 50 percent higher in government schools than in private schools. Furthermore, 57 percent of government- school expenditures were for student welfare and boarding. These expenses accounted for only 23 percent of private-school expenditures. On a per student basis, these expenses were four times as high in government schools as in private schools.

The government schools spent slightly more per student than the private schools on staff salaries. However, because total spending in the government schools was higher per student than in the private schools, staff salaries accounted for 33 percent of total government school expenses, versus 43 percent for private schools.

Private schools spent 24 percent of their budgets on teaching and learning materials. These supplies accounted for only 7 percent of government-school budgets. On a per student basis, private schools spent more than twice as much as government schools on materials.

Private schools had 11 students per staff member, whereas public schools had 10. Government schools had a ratio of 14.6 students to each academic staff member, whereas private schools had a ratio of 17.9. Private schools had lower student-to-staff ratios for non-academic staff than did government schools.

This analysis indicates that the government schools in this sample spent far more per student than did the private schools. Furthermore, more than one-half of government school expenses were used for student boarding, whereas boarding accounted for less than one-fourth of expenditures for the sample private schools. The government and private schools had relatively low student-to-staff ratios, and staff expenses per student were relatively equal across the two types of schools. This small study indicates important similarities and differences between government and private schools. If this same analysis were done on a regular basis for a representative sample of schools, and if the results were combined with assessments of students' academic performances, the results could be very useful in helping improve school quality and efficiency.

teacher workforce are profound. By all measures, the size of the government's wage bill in the education sector (as well as expenditures on student boarding in secondary schools) is squeezing out expenditures on complementary inputs. These include books, school supplies, and school maintenance. The shortages of basic educational inputs in both primary and secondary schools has been well documented (Planning Commission, 1991; UNESCO, 1989). For example, MOEC estimates that there is a shortage of nearly

Table 4.23: Expenditures for Sample Government and Private Secondary Schools

	Percent of Expenditures		Expenditures per Student, FY94 (Tsh)	
	Public Schools	*Private Schools*	*Public Schools*	*Private Schools*
Staff				
Salaries	20%	21%	12,571	8,472
Other	13%	22%	8,411	9,029
Total	33%	43%	20,983	17,501
Students				
Food and Boarding	56%	22%	36,297	9,090
Other	1%	1%	457	433
Total	57%	23%	36,754	9,523
Other Expenditures				
Teaching\Learning Materials	7%	24%	4,251	9,833
Others	3%	10%	2,011	4,143
Total	10%	34%	6,263	13,976
TOTAL	100%	100%	64,000	41,000
Student to Academic Staff Ratio	14.6	17.9		
Student to Non- academic Staff Ratio	34.2	29.5		
Total Student Staff Ratio	10.2	11.2		

Source: Dar and Levine, 1996.

850,000 student desks in primary schools (MOEC, various years). Despite many studies drawing attention to the problems, and despite significant, targeted donor contributions, many classrooms still have few or no textbooks (see Box 4.9), and chairs, desks, and buildings are in disrepair.

At the secondary-school level, the largest expenditures are on boarding costs. Student welfare (room and board) accounts for about 46 percent of total spending. Personnel costs account for another 37 percent. In teacher-training schools, student boarding and welfare expenditures account for 36 percent of total spending, and personal emoluments, 44 percent. The secondary schools and teacher-training colleges are as much student hostels as they are educational institutions. Box 4.10 examines the expenditures of a small sample of government and private secondary schools, using data presented in Table 4.23.

Donor Spending

Donors in the education sector concentrate their spending on post-secondary and primary education. Donors were budgeted to spend Tsh 4,952 million (approximately 5 percent of total non-household expenditures) in the sector in 1994/95. Donor funds accounted for approximately 13 percent of non-household higher-education spending, 4 percent of non-household primary-school spending, and 2 percent of non-household secondary-school spending. In general, donor funds are allocated to construction and rehabilitation of facilities, provision of textbooks, equipment and materials, and training of managers.

The major bilateral donors in primary education are Denmark, Ireland and Sweden, with the UK planning a large-scale increase in the near future. At the secondary level, major bilateral donors include Denmark, the UK, Germany and Norway, and at the tertiary level, Sweden, Denmark, Norway, Germany and Ireland. Among multilateral donors, the European Union is active on all three levels, the World Bank focuses on the primary and secondary sub-sectors, and UNICEF concentrates its funding on the primary level (DANIDA, 1994a and b). For a more detailed review of donor funding in the education sector, see Box 4.11 on the next page.

Unit Costs

In 1995, the government's recurrent budget expenditures were Tsh 12,600 per pupil for primary schools, Tsh 95,300 for secondary schools, Tsh 131,000 per pupil in teacher training colleges, Tsh 716,700 in technical institutions, and Tsh 3,324,200 at the two universities (including study abroad).

Inclusion of recurrent expenditures funded through the development budget results in a small increase in total per-unit expenditures in some programs. Per-unit primary-school expenditures remained constant at 12,600 Tsh, but secondary-school expenditures increased from Tsh 95,300 to Tsh 96,300. Teacher-training and technical college expenditures remained constant, but university expenditures increased from Tsh 3,324,200 to Tsh 3,332,800.

Primary Schools. The 1994 small-scale FAST study of the costs of education found that approximately Tsh 5,000 was expended annually by the government on each primary-school student in each of eight districts visited. Compared to the per-student expenditure derived from government budgets for that year, this suggests that about one-quarter of primary-school expenditures are devoted to administrative expenses from the district on up.[6]

Secondary Schools. Another small study found that unit costs at private secondary schools were 59 percent of those at public secondary schools (Jimenez et al., 1991). Similarly, a 1992 study in the Lake Zone found that the total unit costs in public schools were Tsh 13,000 (or 18 percent) higher than those in private schools. The average unit (recurrent) cost in public secondary schools was estimated at Tsh 73,000 per year, as compared to Tsh 60,000 in private institutions (Babyegeya, 1993, quoted in Galabawa, 1994).[7]

Teacher-Training Colleges. Costs per trainee-year in teacher training colleges vary widely, depending on the size of the class and type of training. By far the most costly programs are those which offer only in-service training. The next most expensive programs are those which train Grade B teachers, either with or without in-service adjunct courses. Remarkably, the colleges that produce the most highly trained teachers (both Grade A and diploma courses) are the least expensive. In fact, one year of training in a Grade A/Diploma teacher-training college is estimated to be approximately one-tenth the cost of one year of in-service training.

---

[6] Readers are cautioned to interpret these numbers cautiously, as they are based on a small sample.

[7] Note that these figures include private contributions. In the case of government schools, an average of Tsh 19,000 was contributed by households, while that for private institutions averaged Tsh 25,000.

Box 4.11: Recent Donor Initiatives in the Education Sector

Donors fund 6 percent of all non-private expenditures in the education sector, with 41 percent of their funding going directly to primary (basic) education. This support accounts for approximately 8 percent of all non-private expenditures on primary education. Donor countries support improvements in the quality of, and access to, basic education. They also seek to improve cooperation and centralization of individual programs. In higher education, donors seek to improve teaching skills in training for trades and professions in both vocational and university programs.

DANIDA (the Danish government's aid agency) is the largest donor in the education sector. It is currently embarking on a three-year support and expansion phase of its Primary Education Program (PEP). A pilot program focusing on improvement of teacher and student performance levels, PEP is now budgeted at approximately US$ 3 million per year. On the secondary-school level, Danida funds a nationwide school rehabilitation project, maintaining and improving the physical plants and facilities of these schools. Danida works closely with Sweden's aid agency (SIDA) and the Vocational Education and Training Authority (VETA) on the tertiary and vocational levels of education, contributing to various regional vocational and training schools throughout Tanzania. Total DANIDA spending in the education sector has risen from US$ 3.6 million in 1991 to US$ 7.7 million in 1993. DANIDA expects to increase funding levels for education in the coming years.

The Overseas Development Agency (**ODA**) is planning to substantially increase its support to the education sector by focusing on government initiatives in basic education, such as improving the primary-school curricula, the training of teachers, and the efficiency of examinations. O.D.A. is also promoting an increase in the number of English language courses taught in primary schools. In secondary education, O.D.A. focuses on improvement and extension of the teaching of the English language to students and teachers. O.D.A.'s focus on the tertiary level is to increase funding to the Ministry of Education and Culture (MoEC), thereby insuring coordinated efforts. It is also pushing to improve the quality of European aid to education by strengthening its own ties and activities with the European Union (EU), as well as by promoting coordination with the government's Planning Commission. O.D.A. also seeks to improve the quality and availability of education to girls.

The International Development Agency (**IDA**) sponsors the Community Education Fund (CEF) which has the specific goal of improving community and parental involvement in primary-school planning and budgeting. IDA also sponsors the Girls' Secondary Education Support Project (GSES), a US$ 4.1 million effort that targets girls in poorer communities and attempts to improve their chances of successfully completing secondary school. However, IDA's largest initiative in the education sector is its Education Planning and Rehabilitation Project, budgeted over six years at a total of US$ 67.5 million. With US$ 38.3 million of that total amount designated as a loan, the Project has three goals: to strengthen the planning and implementing capacity of institutions to allow for the improvement of training of education managers; to improve the overall quality of primary- and secondary-school education by strengthening the Institute of Curriculum Development and improving school libraries; and to improve the utilization of non-government resources and support for education by establishing the National Education Trust Fund (NETF). The NETF was designed to provide matching grants to communities that give priority to increasing the enrollment levels of girls, and that demonstrate efforts at decreasing the inequalities girls face at the secondary-school level. All-boy schools are not eligible to receive any NETF funding.

SIDA focuses its efforts on the production of textbooks for primary schools. It is the predominant financier of the book management unit in the MOE, and helped to increase the number of textbooks in circulation from 632,000 in 1988 to more than 4 million in 1994. SIDA also funds a program aimed at improving training for primary-school teachers. In vocational schools, SIDA is heavily involved in many regional projects, attempting to improve the quality of the country's skilled workforce. It also works closely with VETA in this area.

NORAD (Norway's aid agency) is a major donor to tertiary education, funding numerous programs in Tanzanian universities and technical schools. NORAD's efforts are aimed at everything from training students in maritime skills, to enhancing an animal science program in hopes of making post-graduate work possible in this field. NORAD also funds the National Education Trust Fund (NETF) that seeks to support and promote community initiatives undertaken to enhance the quality and availability of secondary schools.

The **Dutch** have announced their intentions to increase support for basic education in many developing countries. This represents a break from their traditional support that was aimed at tertiary education. They will promote this new strategy through multinational and bilateral channels. Two-thirds of all of Holland's increased aid will be given to the Sub-Saharan Africa region. The initiatives range from a children's book project focused on the Kiswahili region, to a teaching-methodology improvement project. Although specific program funding is not yet available, the Dutch have committed US$ 7.8 million to the Tanzanian education sector for the years 1995 through 1998, and approximately US$ 1.7 million to local government training programs from 1995 to 1997.

Irish Aid has an education project slated to last until 2000. Its objective is to improve the teaching of math and sciences at the primary level through direct support to teachers and regional schools at the district level, and indirect support through zonal and national programs. Irish Aid also funds various vocational- and university-level programs aimed at improving engineering skills, agricultural techniques, and mathematical skills. The Irish spend approximately US$0.9 million annually on education projects in Tanzania.

GTZ offers a combination of technical and financial assistance to the Christian Social Service Commission (CSSC) for the improvement of services in secondary schools run by churches. The main focus of GTZ however, is on the tertiary and vocational level, where they support many programs. After assisting with the creation of the Technical College in Arusha until 1986, GTZ is now supporting the foundation of a training course there for road technicians. Other projects receiving GTZ support include the establishment of the Institute of Product Innovation at the University of Dar es Salaam (UDSM), and aid to agricultural and orthopaedic training universities.

UNICEF has declared that universal primary education is its education priority in Tanzania, targeting girls and women specifically. The organization includes much of its funding for primary schools in its umbrella-like *Programme for Child Survival Protection and Development in Tanzania*. Aiming at strengthening the ability of local communities to provide care and education for children, this program provides funding to various regional and local projects, espousing grassroots educational planning as opposed to the traditional top-down method. Examples of this include the training of school committees, support to teacher centers, and the strengthening of district and ward support systems. UNICEF also supports an AIDS education program in primary schools throughout Tanzania. Adult education and early childhood development are promoted as supporting strategies to UNICEF's primary-school efforts.

The European Union (**EU**) supports the Government of Tanzania (GOT) initiatives in general, as opposed to funding specific programs on their own. Accordingly, the EU has recently approved programs designed to support GOT efforts in all levels of education by providing funding which allows the GOT to evaluate programs in detail and budget for them accordingly. The EU also advocates the coordination of donor efforts in the education sector, calling for cooperation with GOT and MOEC initiatives.

RETURNS TO EDUCATION

To estimate the net gains from education, it is necessary to compare costs and benefits. The most tangible benefits of education are the higher earnings that accrue to individuals with more education. Education may also bring many non-monetary benefits to households and societies. For example, increased education may convey a general increase in household and societal welfare, a reduction in crime, better health and hygiene, and lower fertility rates. However, these benefits are difficult to estimate and are therefore excluded from this analysis. This implies that the benefits used in this exercise are lower-bound estimates of the true benefits to individuals and society that accrue from education.

Excluding non-earnings benefits, the private rate of return to a level of education is estimated by comparing the present value of the earnings differential between two levels of education[8] with the economic (out of pocket and opportunity) cost incurred by a household in obtaining the higher level of education. For example, a rate of return of 3.6 percent on primary education implies that if an individual invested Tsh 100,000 on an additional year of primary school, his or her annual income would be Tsh 3,600 higher than it would have been if the individual had not undertaken the additional year of education.

This analysis also excludes non-earnings benefits from social rates of return. Thus the social benefits to education are also assumed to be the earnings differential between people with different levels of education. These are compared to the societal costs of education, including the full direct and indirect costs (including opportunity costs) of education borne by households, businesses, and the government.

This section reviews estimates of the private and social rates of return to education in Tanzania. Because non-monetary benefits are excluded from this analysis, the results are lower-bound estimates of actual returns. These results should be interpreted with caution for several reasons. First, the number of observations, particularly at the university level, are few. Second, due to data limitations, this analysis is confined to formal sector workers who account for less than 10 percent of the overall workforce. This is likely to bias upwards the rates of return, especially at lower levels of education[9]. Third, the rates of return may also be biased because over 65 percent of the sample analyzed is employed in the public sector where pay scales are set administratively and may have little relationship to productivity. However, the general trends in this rate of return analysis are similar to those found for other countries (Psacharopoulos, 1993).

Private Returns

Private rates of return to education in 1990/91 have been computed by estimating an earnings function that controls for human capital characteristics (education and training) along with individual, regional, and labor market characteristics (Dar and Levine, 1996).

---

[8] Private rates of return should be based on net (after tax) earnings. However, this information was not available. Thus, the earnings used in this analysis are gross (before tax).

[9] This is especially the case because several studies have found that the return to education for people engaged in traditional agricultural production is significant but relatively low (Mason, 1996).

On average, private rates of return are 3.6 percent for primary school, 6.9 percent for secondary school, and 9.0 percent for University. Rates of return are significantly higher for women than for men at all three levels of general education, but especially at the primary-school level. Private rates of return increase sharply with education levels for men but are relatively flat for women (Table 4.24).

On-the-job training has by far the highest rate of return. Rates of return are also much higher for vocational training than for general education. Training, like general education, has higher rates of return for women than for men.

The private rates of return to education estimated for 1990/91 are lower than those reported by Psacharopoulos (1994) for seven sub-Saharan African countries (including Tanzania) in the 1970s and 1980s. Returns for these countries ranged from 8 percent in Ethiopia to 20 percent in Cote d'Ivoire. Psacharopoulos reports that the average return to education in Tanzania was 11.9 percent in 1980 (Mason and Khandker, 1997). This return is slightly higher than the rates estimated above for formal education for women, and significantly above those rates for men.

Table 4.24: Private and Social Annual Rates of Return to Education and Training (1990/91)

Group	Education Level			Training	
	Primary	**Secondary**	**University**	**Vocational**	**On-the-job**
Private Rates					
All	3.6 (2,113)	6.9 (609)	9.0 (41)	19.4 (814)	35.2 (514)
Male	1.9 (1,612)	6.6 (360)	9.9 (28)	17.8 (523)	33.0 (416)
Female	10.8 (501)	9.0 (249)	11.4 (13)	20.2 (291)	35.0 (98)
Social Rates					
All	3.6	1.5	0.0	0.0	

Note: Numbers in parentheses are the number of observations.
Source: Dar and Levine (1996), based on 1990/91 Labor Force Survey.

It is difficult to speculate on the implications of these differences in returns. Tanzania has lower returns to education than many other Sub-Saharan African countries, and its returns may have fallen between 1980 and 1990. However, Mason and Khandker (1997) report that it is likely that earnings' premiums to lower secondary graduates in Tanzania increased from 1980 to 1990. He therefore speculates that the apparent decline in returns to education indicated above may be wholly attributable to declines in the returns to primary education.

It is possible that the differences in returns are attributable to differences in the methods used to make these estimates. Indeed, Mason and Khandker (1997) used the same data as that used by Dar and Levine to estimate private returns to primary and secondary education, but Mason and Khandker's results differ significantly from those by Dar and Levine presented above. Dar and Levine estimated an average rate of return for primary school of 3.6 percent, whereas Mason and Khandker computed a 7.9 percent return. Dar and Levine's average return to secondary school of 6.9 percent was also below Mason and Khandker's 8.8 percent return.

Social Returns

Taking into account the costs incurred by the government, and continuing to exclude non-earnings benefits, lower-bound estimates for social rates of return are negligible for secondary education, and zero for vocational training and higher education. This is mainly due to high public expenditures per pupil in post-primary education as a result of inefficient resource allocation. Thus the economic cost of the public provision and financing of vocational training and higher education are as great as the net present value of economic benefits.

In an era of tight budget constraints, the government has to rationalize its expenditure on education so that social returns are maximized. Since social returns decline by education level, efficiency gains will be realized if the government progressively increases cost-sharing (and hence reduces its investment) at higher levels of education, and reallocates resources to lower levels of education. The government should foster private and employer-based training which, in any case, is usually more relevant to market needs than government-managed programs. The fact that the private returns to post-primary education and training are high implies that households should be willing to pay far more than they are currently doing to obtain these services. Loan programs for individuals who do not have the resources to fund their post-primary education could be created or expanded. The high private returns to this education imply that students should be able to repay the loans once their education is completed.

Private rates of return to education are significantly higher for women than for men. However this has not been realized by communities, as evidenced by low enrollment rates of women. Parents should be made aware of the benefits of educating their daughters. Furthermore, because the social rates of return to education are also higher for women than for men, the government could make a greater effort to target education sector resources to programs that benefit women.

THE DISTRIBUTION OF BENEFITS FROM EDUCATION SPENDING

Total Spending on Education

Any estimate of the total amount spent on education in Tanzania necessarily depends on imprecise estimates. However, such an exercise is worth doing to discern, even in rough terms, the absolute and relative spending on critical investments in human capital.

An estimated Tsh 128 billion were spent on education in Tanzania in 1994/95. Households contributed about 30 percent of these funds in the form of fees, expenditures on uniforms, and other inputs[10]. Government and donors provided the remainder (about 70 percent).

Distribution of Public Subsidies

Who benefits from government spending on education? According to an analysis of the incidence of the benefits of public spending, a disproportionate share of the benefits are captured by the best-off households. Given the relatively large share of the public budget devoted to secondary schools, the high unit costs of secondary-school education, the limited access to government secondary schools, and the lack of gender parity in enrollment, the government de facto subsidizes the children from better-off households more than those from poor households, and male children more than female children. While this result is not an intentional outcome of the Tanzanian educational system, it nonetheless

---

[10] These estimates were derived as follows: government and donor expenditures were taken from the total recurrent and development budgets, as reported in Follmer and Kessy (1997). Household expenditures were taken from 1993/94 per student levels and updated by inflation and the new number of students for 1994/95. Household expenditures were estimated based on estimated average expenditures of Tsh 6,578 per primary-school student (for the approximately 3.8 million primary-school students) and Tsh 71,704 per secondary-school student (for the approximately 196,375 secondary-school students).

occurs.

In 1993/94, the richest 20 percent of households received about 1.8 times the share of government spending on education received by the poorest 20 percent of households. In 1994/95, the richest 20 percent of households received about 3 times the share of government spending

Table 4.25: Distribution of the Benefits of 1993/94 Public Spending on Education, by Expenditure Quintile

	Lowest 20% (1)	(2)	(3)	(4)	*Highest 20%* (5)	*All*
Primary Education	20.0	21.0	21.0	20.0	19.0	100.0
Secondary Education	7.6	12.7	19.1	26.6	34.1	100.0

Source: HRDS, 1993/94; World Bank, 1994a.

on education as that received by the poorest 20 percent of households. The benefits of government spending on primary schools are quite uniformly distributed across the population. However, because better-off households are most likely to obtain entrance into government secondary schools, the benefits of the significant public expenditures at that level are primarily captured by households in the upper end of the welfare distribution. In fact, the poorest 20 percent of households realized only 8 percent of the benefits of public spending on secondary schools in 1993/94, while the richest 20 percent captured 34 percent of the benefits (see Table 4.25).[11]

CONCLUSION

Education is by far the most important avenue through which families and nations can invest in human capital. Unfortunately, the current state of the education sector that emerges from this analysis of the demand for, and supply of, education is grim. Educational outcomes in Tanzania are poor and, in many areas, worsening. Parents are withholding children from school, and even when children do attend, the quality of the education is jeopardized by ill-prepared, poorly motivated teachers and a severe shortage of basic learning materials. The education of girls, arguably the most essential ingredient for the improved welfare of the next generation, faces the greatest risk.

Based on the preceding analysis, it appears that if little or nothing is done to alter the current course of the education sector, we can expect:

- falling enrollments and increasing illiteracy;
- declining quality at all levels of education;
- continued deterioration in teacher morale and the quality of education infrastructure;
- a rapidly growing number of poorly educated, unemployed youth;
- perpetuation of the already established gender gap in primary education achievement and secondary education enrollment;
- markedly reduced chances for the nation to compete in the international economy; and
- an increasing divide between the education of the wealthy and the poor.

---

[11] Estimates for 1994/95 figures were arrived at by multiplying the 1993/94 quintile shares for education subsectors by each subsector's share of 1994/95 education expenditures.

However, the government has a strong commitment to education which, if implemented effectively, could greatly strengthen the sector. To realize this goal, there are policy initiatives that the government has already begun, or which it might choose to undertake in the future, that would improve the allocative efficiency of government education funding and the operating efficiency of government owned and operated schools. These initiatives are outlined below.

Primary Education. The social rates of return to primary education are higher than the social returns to other types of schooling. Yet primary education is woefully underfunded. Despite very low gross enrollment rates, government expenditure was only about US$22 per student in fiscal 1995. To ameliorate this problem, the government could speed its practice of increasing primary education's share of total education funding. Indeed, primary education's share of education funding could climb from it's current level of about 57 percent to 65 percent within a few years.

Continuing to increase primary education's share of total sector spending will have only a modest impact on primary education funding because other types of education also have relatively small budgets. There is a huge and growing stock of children waiting to go to school. Finally, there has been significant under-investment in maintaining and expanding infrastructure, furniture, books, and equipment. Thus, reversing the decline in primary education will also depend on parents contributing more to local schools. For substantial improvements at the local level to take place, the government can begin to implement policies to decentralize primary education and empower teachers and parents to turn the system around. The government has initiated this effort through a pilot program to increase local communities' financial support for, and administrative and policy management of, primary schools.

As stated in the government's Basic Education Master Plan (BEMP), the government could continue this effort by transferring the title of government-owned primary schools to the local authorities closest to the schools, such as villages or urban wards. In addition, the government could prepare a time-bound action plan to decentralize management and financing of primary education. Under this plan, head teachers could assume primary responsibility for school management, including managing school accounts, hiring and firing teachers, establishing remuneration of teachers, preparing annual school plans, and making decisions about curriculum and textbooks. Head teachers could be chosen through consultation between the school committee and the DEO. School committees could supervise and manage the head teacher and approve his or her decisions.

As identified in the Basic Education Master Plan, the central government could expand its pilot program under which the states make financial contributions directly to schools. This practice would allow school committees to determine their schools' greatest needs and spend funds efficiently to maximize their benefit. The central government could also review the regulatory structure for private primary schools to increase the private sector's ability to enter this market. The central government could modify the roles of the school inspectorate and the ward education coordinators to encourage them to provide general advice to schools concerning ways to make information available to schools about best practice, to help schools prepare good plans, and to help them improve procurement, maintenance, and construction. Finally, the central government could complete its review of the current system of multi-ministerial management of education. It could then determine whether efficiency could be realized by consolidating management of the education system.

Secondary Education. Tanzania has one of the world's lowest secondary-school enrollment rates. To rectify this situation, the government, in collaboration with non-government school operators, could develop a five-year plan to radically increase enrollments in lower secondary schools. The plan might address the following three areas:

- *Non-government Schools*: Secondary-school enrollment rates have grown steadily since 1986 primarily due to the legalization of non-government schools. For the upward trend in secondary enrollments to accelerate, non-government provision of secondary schooling must expand considerably faster than it has in the recent past. The government could increase incentives for private school creation by removing controls on fees and replacing these with indicative guidelines, by providing good information to schools on unit costs, and by widely distributing information to parents on availability, costs, and performance of secondary schools. A number of other simple reforms would accelerate the creation of private secondary schools. These reforms include eliminating taxes on secondary tuition, allowing free movement between private and government schools, opening up the exam and secondary-school selection system, making available excess capacity in government institutions for non-government operators, and expanding and improving the National Education Trust Fund.

- *Government Secondary Schools:* To expand secondary-school enrollments in government schools, the government could (a) consider secondary and teacher-training colleges as alternatives, and bring the costs of the latter in line with the former, (b) review the feasibility and desirability of converting secondary schools into self-managing, self-financing institutions, removing all restrictions on their ability to accept tuition-paying students, and (c) convert the current system of selection to, and support of, secondary education into a bursary program in which government-funded bursaries are awarded partially for merit and partially to support disadvantaged students, allowing the students to choose the school they want to attend.

- *Secondary Education for Girls:* Secondary enrollment for girls is rising, yet girls remain under-represented in secondary education, particularly in upper-secondary schools. The government could address this issue by evaluating its Girls' Secondary Education Support Program to see if this program could be expanded on a nationwide basis. If the program is not found to be satisfactory, another plan for augmenting girls' enrollments and performance in secondary schools could be developed.

Post-Secondary and Technical Education. Tanzania needs a comprehensive post-secondary and technical education system. However, the social returns to primary and secondary education are much higher than the social returns to post-secondary education. Furthermore, the overwhelming share of the benefits of higher levels of education accrue to better off households. The government could increase the social returns to its education investment by reallocating some of its higher education investments to primary- and secondary-school funding. Students receiving post-secondary education could assume a significant share of the costs currently borne by the government. For households without sufficient savings to immediately meet these costs, a loan system could be developed. The high private returns to these levels of education imply that students who assumed these loans would be able to repay them upon completing their education. To reduce funding for higher levels of education, the government might increase cost sharing in state-owned institutions to a level that would fully fund transportation and boarding costs. Preferably however, the government could convert public schools to autonomous trusts that would receive government subsidies earmarked to only the poorest students. If subsidies to publicly-owned institutions were reduced or narrowly targeted to the poor, the supply of higher education would probably increase, as private institutions would be able to compete with state facilities.

Other Education Programs and Education Administration. To further free up resources for reallocation to primary and secondary education, many of the non-formal vocational and training programs managed by the Ministry of Community Development, Women, and Children and the Ministry of Labor could be eliminated or the subsidies for them withdrawn. These programs have very high unit costs and are a much lower priority for the government than basic education. Furthermore, the government could simplify the educational administration system by concentrating administration of all education activities within the Ministry of Education.

5
HEALTH

Most health-related investment in human capital takes place outside of the organized medical system through nutrition, proper child care, hygienic cooking and waste disposal practices, healthful behaviors, and so forth. In other words, most of the responsibility for maintaining good health lies within the household. Moreover, it is the household members who have the greatest interest in getting better when they fall ill, and they often make significant payments in time, foregone income, and money costs for curative care.

The results of many health-related investments can be seen in the patterns of disease. In Tanzania, these basic investments have been insufficient to conquer persistent causes of disease and death. Persistent infectious diseases due to poor sanitation, exposure to vectors, and generally unhealthful conditions affect both children and adults in large numbers. New problems, most notably the AIDS pandemic, threaten to reverse improvements that have been achieved in both infant and adult mortality.

In subsequent chapters, we examine the family planning, nutrition, and water and sanitation sectors. In this Chapter, we look specifically at the demand and supply sides of a more narrowly defined health sector. We use household survey data to review patterns of utilization of, and spending on, government and other health services. We then summarize existing information about the characteristics of the Tanzanian health service delivery system.

The picture that emerges is mixed. While access to health services in the narrowest sense is relatively good, the costs have been high and the impact on health limited. As government resources have been pulled toward higher-cost, urban-based facilities, funding has become more constrained for the drugs, personnel, supervision and other inputs required to maintain the function of peripheral facilities. Most seriously, government funding priorities have tended to favor services that benefit individuals over services that have community-wide benefits. Many of the basic preventive services have been funded in large part by external donors. Households invest moderate (and sometimes large) percentages of their incomes on health care. Households show a preference for non-governmental curative services over government-provided ones, when the choice is available.

OUTCOMES AND UTILIZATION

Mortality Levels

Infant and Child Mortality. Infant mortality rates are high, and reductions have been slow in coming. According to the Tanzania Demographic and Health Survey (TDHS, 1991/92), 92 out of every 1,000 children die before age 1, and an estimated 141 per 1,000 children die before their fifth birthday. Analyses of the TDHS indicate that during the 15 years preceding the survey (1977-91), under-five mortality declined from 163 to 141 deaths per 1,000. Essentially all of that improvement is attributable to declines in mortality between ages 1 and 4, as infant mortality appears to have been unchanged over the period.

Levels of infant and childhood mortality in Tanzania are high, but consistent with those in the Sub-Saharan African region and among very low-income countries (see Table 5.1). Surveys currently estimate that infant mortality in the region averages 99 per 1,000 live births, reflecting poor environmental conditions, scarce maternal resources, and the high prevalence of communicable diseases. Similarly, Tanzania's under-five mortality rate is not outside of the range expected, given the country's low income level.

Table 5.1: Infant Mortality per 1,000 Live Births, 1992

Country	Infant Mortality Rate
Ethiopia	122
Kenya	66
Tanzania	92
Uganda	122
Zambia	107
Sub-Saharan Africa	99

Source: World Bank, 1994c.

Adult Mortality. Without functioning death registration or reporting systems, estimation of adult mortality rates are only speculative. However, a recent study in three districts (Dar es Salaam, Morogoro Rural, and Hai) that attempted to measure adult mortality disclosed interesting patterns (ODA, 1994).

Using the United Kingdom as a rough standard for adult survivorship and longevity, age-specific mortality rates were at least twice as high in each of the three study sites than in England and Wales. While the largest differential was found in the youngest ages (Tanzanian childhood mortality was 7 to 20 times as high as infant mortality in the UK), adult mortality was also far higher in Tanzania[1]. For example, among young adults, ages 15-34, for every 1 death per 1,000 in the U.K., there were about 8 to 10 deaths in Tanzania.

The pattern of women's mortality is typical of countries in which women experience high levels of reproductive mortality. Unlike the developed world, in which a woman's risk of dying is far lower than that of a man of the same age, in Tanzania adult women's risk of dying approaches men's. The maternal mortality rate, which is notoriously difficult to measure accurately, is estimated to be 342 deaths per 100,000 births in Tanzania (World Bank, 1994c).

The distribution of the risk of death throughout the life span highlights the relatively high level of adult mortality in Tanzania. In middle- and upper-income countries, nearly all deaths occur in the

---

[1] The range of these estimates is wide because the patterns of mortality varied substantially among the three study areas. Therefore, this summary of complex data is necessarily imprecise.

earliest years of life and, even more importantly, after 55 years of age. For example, in England and Wales in 1990, only about 9.7 percent of all deaths among males and 5.4 percent of all deaths among females occurred between ages 15 and 54. In Tanzania, however, young and middle-aged adults are at far higher risk. The study of adult mortality found that in Dar es Salaam, for example, a full 38 percent of male deaths and 48 percent of female deaths occur between ages 15 and 54.

AIDS is becoming an increasing threat to adult mortality in Tanzania. It is estimated that between one-half million and one million individuals are currently infected with HIV, and AIDS is expected to become the major cause of death among adults within the next several years. Women and men are equally affected. Life expectancy at birth in 1985-90 was estimated to be 1.8 years less than it would have been in the absence of AIDS. In addition, because of the AIDS epidemic, life expectancy is now expected to decline by about 1 year between now and the year 2000 (United Nations, 1993).

Causes of Illness and Death

Infectious Disease. Community-based studies and healthcare-provider reports indicate that virtually all major health problems of infants, young children, and other vulnerable groups in Tanzania are preventable. Major diseases affecting the population include malaria, HIV/AIDS, respiratory infections, water-borne and water-washed diseases (such as typhoid, cholera, dysentery, and parasites). A recent study by the MOH (1994) estimated that malaria is responsible for about 17 percent of all deaths, perinatal and maternal causes about 15 percent, and diarrheal disease, pneumonia, tuberculosis and AIDS about 5 to 6 percent each (see Table 5.2).

Table 5.2: Total Deaths and Life Years Lost, by Disease

Cause	Deaths	Share of Deaths	Life-Years Lost	Share of Life-Years Lost
Perinatal or Maternal	60,050	14.8	1,781,512	17.5
Malaria	69,174	17.0	1,956,234	19.3
Diarrhea	19,756	4.9	587,147	5.8
Pneumonia	20,744	5.1	616,505	6.1
AIDS	24,441	6.0	639,387	6.3
Tuberculosis	19,334	4.8	513,706	5.1
Protein Calorie Malnutrition	3,254	0.8	96,707	1.0
Measles	3,486	0.9	103,614	1.0
Injury	23,980	5.9	637,155	6.3
Cardiovascular	15,884	3.9	379,712	3.7
All Other Causes	146,262	36.0	2,84,874	28.0
Total	406,365	100.0	10,153,553	100.0

Source: MOH, 1994.

The prevalence of preventable diseases places large burdens on the curative health system. According to spotty epidemiological information from the MOH reporting sites, malaria constitutes the most common reason for attendance at outpatient clinics and hospital admissions. In Iringa region in 1991, for example, 29 percent of patients coming to outpatient facilities were diagnosed with malaria, and 39 percent of inpatients were said to have malaria[2] (MOH, 1993).

---

[2] It is important to note that it is likely that malaria is over-diagnosed. A recent study examined the accuracy of clinical diagnoses of febrile episodes, the most common presentation of malaria. It found the following: rural medical aides generally diagnose all febrile illnesses as malaria. In fact, they diagnose only 13 percent of non-malarial febrile episodes correctly. Medical doctors are more likely to arrive at correct diagnoses of non-malarial illness, but even they are wrong in about one-half of the non-malarial cases.

Respiratory infections, including pneumonia, also consume a large proportion of curative resources. In the Iringa reporting sites, for example, about 29 percent of outpatient visits and 17 percent of hospital admissions were for treatment of upper respiratory tract infections and pneumonia (MOH, 1993).

Diarrheal diseases, nearly all of which are associated with exposure to contaminated food and water (particularly during the vulnerable stage when children are weaning), account for another large share of outpatient visits. In Iringa for example, 16 percent of all outpatient visits to government facilities were diagnosed as diarrheal disease.

Throughout the 1980s, the HIV/AIDS pandemic became an increasing problem in Tanzania. The country now ranks sixth among Sub-Saharan countries in HIV prevalence. While precise estimates are difficult to obtain, the National AIDS Control Program estimates that about 800,000 people in Tanzania are infected with HIV, and AIDS was responsible for about 60,000 deaths by the end of 1990. Within the next few years, AIDS is expected to become the major cause of death among both children and adults. It is anticipated that the spread of AIDS will reverse the reductions in the infant mortality rate (World Bank, 1992).

The burden that AIDS places on health care resources in Tanzania is massive. According to one estimate, the total per case lifetime treatment cost for AIDS patients in Tanzania is approximately US$290 for adults and US$195 for children. Currently, AIDS treatment may currently be absorbing as much as 40 to 50 percent of the government's recurrent budget for health (World Bank, 1992).

For policy purposes, it is useful to sketch the distribution of deaths by age and cause, even in the absence of reliable, nationally representative epidemiologic and demographic data[3]. From the available data, one can conclude that out of every 1,000 children born, 92 will die by the time they reach age 1, another 49 will die by the time they reach age 5, and an additional 70 will die by the time they reach age 15. That is, of 1,000 children born, only about 790 (or 4 out of 5) will survive to age 15. Between age 15 and 34, 200 additional deaths will occur in the cohort, so that 590 will be left of the original cohort by age 35.

Most of the 410 deaths will be caused by infectious diseases. About 120 of those deaths will be caused by malaria. Another 80 will result from respiratory infections, including pneumonia and tuberculosis. Water-borne disease will kill 25 (mostly infants), and AIDS will take the lives of 40 more (mostly young adults).

Utilization of the Health Care System

Accurate utilization and household expenditure data have been sorely lacking in Tanzania, a problem that makes planning, analysis of demand, and estimation of unit costs and productivity nearly impossible. In this section, we present data from the HRDS on household use of health services and health-related expenditures, from which we can better understand the components of demand for health care. In addition, we present information on respondents' views of the quality of the government health

---

[3] Readers are cautioned to interpret the figures that follow in the spirit in which they are presented, namely, as rough, illustrative estimates based on small-scale studies.

services available to them.

About 15 percent of Tanzanians reported being ill or injured during the month prior to the survey, and two-thirds of those sought care. Individuals in the poorest 20 percent of households were about one-half as likely as the richest 20 percent of households to report being sick, and were less likely to seek care if sick (see Table 5.3).

Table 5.3: Use of Selected Health Services, by Expenditure Level

Utilization Indicator	Lowest 20%	Highest 20%	All
% Ill/Injured in Past 4 Weeks	11	21	15
% of Ill/Injured Who Sought Care	57	74	66

Source: HRDS, 1993/94.

The pattern of greater incidence of reported illness and care-seeking in better-off households is seen throughout the world. This does not imply that richer individuals have more illnesses in an objective sense, but that better-off people are more likely to recognize and acknowledge signs of illness, label those signs as "being sick," and seek care.

Women are slightly more likely than men to report that they experienced an illness or injury in the past month. If they did, they are as likely as men to say that they sought care outside the home (see Table 5.4). As with the rich-poor comparison, this reflects only *reporting* of illness, and not necessarily incidence of illness or injury. In fact, there is reason to believe that women may experience even higher levels of morbidity. Empirical evidence from several African countries (McGuire and Popkin, 1990) suggests that women are more likely than men to be malnourished, because of women's higher energy requirements due to their heavier workload, the demands on their bodies of

Table 5.4: Population Sick and Seeking Care, by Sex

Self-Reported Condition	Male	Female
% Ill/Injured in Past 4 Weeks	13	16
% of Ill/Injured Who Sought Care	67	66

Source: HRDS, 1993/94.

frequent childbearing, and the preference given to men in intra-family food allocation. Anecdotal evidence seems to show that in some areas of Tanzania, traditions dictate that men eat before women and children. In addition, given the high fertility rates, women are exposed to health problems associated with pregnancy, labor, and delivery. All these factors may contribute to poor health among women. Given their specific role in providing for the health of other household members, the relatively higher level of morbidity of women certainly impacts more generally on family welfare than that of men.

Choice of Provider. About 58 percent of all those who were sick and sought care turned first to a government provider. Large variations in choice of provider are found in comparisons across welfare groups. Approximately 70 percent of sick individuals in the poorest 20 percent of households who sought care first went to a government facility. Better-off individuals sought care in the private sector. Still, nearly one-half (46 percent) of all ill or injured individuals from the richest households went to a government facility for curative care.

Government health centers or dispensaries were the most common source of outpatient care, used by 40 percent of those who sought care (see Table 5.5). Government hospitals were used by another 17 percent of the population. Surprisingly, given the recent legalization of private practice, private health centers and dispensaries accounted for about 14 percent of the visits, almost as high as government hospitals.

Government health centers are the main alternative for outpatient care for the poorest, while mission and private facilities are more common alternatives for those from the upper end of the distribution. Those in the poorest 20 percent of the households relied on government health centers and dispensaries twice as often as those in the richest 20 percent. The richest group split its visits among government clinics, private clinics, and pharmacies, and was more likely to use a government hospital than was the poorest group.

Table 5.5: First Source of Curative Outpatient Care, by Expenditure Level (%)

Source of Care	Lowest 20%	Highest 20%	All
Government Hospital	15	20	17
Voluntary Agency/ Private Hospital	5	9	6
Government Health Center or Dispensary	55	26	40
Voluntary Agency Health Center or Dispensary	10	9	10
Private Health Center or Dispensary	6	24	14
Other (traditional and pharmacy)	9	12	13

Source: HRDS, 1993/94.

Despite the fact that the government operates about one-half of the hospital beds in Tanzania, government hospitals are used by only about one-third of those who reported being admitted for at least one night. Better-off individuals are more likely than the poor to use government hospitals for inpatient services (see Table 5.6).

Because of the relative infrequency of inpatient care, the number of individuals for which health care utilization data are available is insufficient for stratification by both rural/urban residence and welfare group. However, the data suggest that much of the differences in choice of provider across the welfare distribution can be explained largely by rural-urban differences. On a national basis, the better-off households tend to be in urban areas, the poorest households tend to be in rural areas. Therefore, the observation that the wealthiest households tend to use government hospitals, which are in Dar es Salaam and a few other urban areas, reflects the relatively close proximity of the better-off population to those facilities.

Table 5.6: Use of Inpatient Services, by Expenditure Level (%)

Source of Care	Lowest 20%	Highest 20%	All
Government Hospital	35	44	35
Other	65	56	65

Source: HRDS, 1993/94.

Because individuals from wealthier households are more likely to report that they are ill and, if ill, to seek care, they tend to consume a larger relative share of all services than do the poor. Households in the top 40 percent of the welfare distribution consumed about 54 percent of all curative outpatient services in 1993/94, and about 54 percent of all inpatient admissions. They also consumed about 75 percent of the outpatient care provided by private facilities.

HOUSEHOLD EXPENDITURES ON HEALTH CARE

In 1994/95, the typical Tanzanian household spent about Tsh 15,139 (US$26.63) per year on health services, representing about 1.8 percent of total expenditures. Rural households spent about Tsh 11,532 (US$20.06) in 1994/95, while households in urban areas spent more than twice that amount. As shown in Table 5.7, health spending makes up a larger share of total expenditures in better-off

households than in poor households. There are no
differences between male- and female-headed households.

Tanzanians spent about Tsh 1,498 (US$2.61) per
short illness episode when health care was sought (see Table
5.8). Rural households spent more than urban ones for care
at a hospital, but substantially less for care at a health center
or dispensary. For example, individuals in rural areas spent
Tsh 4,332 (US$7.53) for a visit to a hospital, while patients
in urban areas other than Dar es Salaam spent only Tsh
1,404 (US$2.44), and Dar es Salaam patients spent Tsh
2,897 (US$5.04). A dispensary visit, in contrast, cost only
about Tsh 741 (US$1.29) to a rural patient, but more than double that amount to an urban one.

Table 5.7: Share of Total Household Expenditures on Health, by Residence and Expenditure Quintile (%)

	Lowest 20%	Highest 20%	All
Dar es Salaam	2.0	2.0	2.2
Other Urban	1.3	2.2	2.1
Rural	1.3	2.0	1.6
All	1.2	2.2	1.8

Source: HRDS, 1993/94.

The differences in expenditures (and
the distribution of expenditures) across the
welfare distribution show a distinctive
pattern. The poorest households, who also
tend to live in rural areas, spend relatively
little for the government services that are
nearest to them. However, they spend
substantial amounts for the more
sophisticated health services, even those
provided by the government, because of the
high transportation costs. Better-off
households tend to spend more per visit in
rural and urban areas, in part because they are
more likely to use non-governmental services.

Table 5.8: Total Expenditures per Illness Episode Among Those Seeking Care, by Residence in 1994/95(Tsh)

	Dar es Salaam	Other Urban	Rural	All
Hospital	2,897	1,404	4,332	2,751
Health Center	2,856	784	531	663
Dispensary	2,458	1,596	741	1,009
Other	1,337	2,291	1,395	1,715
All	2,641	1,495	1,361	1,498

Source: HRDS, 1993/94, inflated to 1994/95 levels.

Two additional tables illustrate the patterns
of expenditures on health services. Table 5.9 shows
that transportation costs are proportionately more
significant for the poor than for the better-off. For
visits to hospitals, the poorest group spent an average
of Tsh 1,396, about 17 percent of which was
expended on the visit, 35 percent on drugs, and 36
percent on transportation. The richest group spent
almost twice as much on a visit (Tsh 2,430), with 23
percent of that amount being spent on the visit, 56
percent for drugs, and 20 percent for transport.
Transport and drugs constitute two-thirds or more of
the costs of most visits.

Table 5.9: Distribution of Health Expenditures by Those Who Sought Care, by Expenditure Quintile (%age)

Type of Expenditure	Lowest 20%	Highest 20%	All
Visit	28	23	18
Drugs	35	56	54
Transport	36	20	28
Total	100	100	100

Source: HRDS, 1993/94.

The foregoing discussion covers *total* expenditures. The expenditures *per visit* (Table 5.10) for
government services at the dispensary level are lower for the poor than for the rich. For health centers

and hospitals, the poor pay *more* than the rich for the full cost of a visit, and this is influenced heavily by
higher transport costs.

DEMAND FOR HEALTH CARE

Perceptions of the Quality of Health Services

In the HRDS, respondents were asked for their opinions about various quality-related features of the government dispensaries or health centers nearest to them. The features included (a) drug availability, (b) qualifications and trustworthiness of doctors and nurses in attendance, (c) proximity of dispensary or health center, (d) pleasant and sanitary environment at the clinic, and (e) personnel who do not attend to the sick but help with community-wide health interventions.[4]

Above all, consumers are highly dissatisfied with the lack of availability of drugs (see Table 5.11). Out of every 100 respondents, about 63 stated that they believed that drug availability in government facilities was poor or very poor; while only about 10 said that availability was good or very good.

Not surprisingly, given the inclusion of both urban and rural residents, opinions were split on the acceptability of the facilities' proximity. About 45 percent of respondents thought that proximity was poor or very poor. In contrast, a full 28 percent said that proximity was good or very good.

The qualifications of health personnel and the availability of preventive services were viewed quite favorably by respondents. In each case, more than one-third said that these features were good or very good. There were no differences between the opinions of male and female respondents.

These findings closely parallel those of other studies. Gilson et al. (1993), for example, found that in a rural district in Morogoro, shortages of drugs were common and caused the greatest amount of dissatisfaction among consumers. End-of-month stock-outs caused (and were then exacerbated by)

Table 5.10: Expenditures per Visit, by Type of Provider and Expenditure Quintile 1994/95 (Tsh)

Source of Care	Poorest 20%	Richest 20%	All
Dispensary			
Government	107	322	229
Other	1,258	2,759	2,021
Health Center			
Government	804	531	257
Other	1,731	2,362	2,052
Hospital			
Government	1,611	1,522	1,276
Other	2,467	7,172	7,267
Total	878	2,399	1,572

Source: HRDS, 1993/94, inflated to 1994/95 levels.

Table 5.11: Ratings of Government Health Facility Quality (%)

Characteristics	Very Good or Good	Adequate	Poor or Very Poor	Total
Drug Availability	9.8	26.6	63.6	100
Personnel Qualifications	34.9	39.8	25.3	100
Distance	28.0	27.3	44.7	100
Preventive Services	36.9	37.8	25.4	100
Clean Toilet/Water	25.6	44.1	28.8	100

Source: HRDS, 1993/94.

---

[4] The question was worded: "...having personnel who do not care for the sick but who help the community control pests (like mosquitoes), improve sanitation, immunize children, and teach about good health practices–someone who helps keep people healthy."

consumers to feign illness and stock up on medications early in the month. Shortages of drugs were also seen to be a result of mismanagement and attempts on the part of health workers to supplement their wages through drug sales. This, in turn, created significant alienation between the health system and the community.

Willingness to Pay for Improved Health Services

Household survey respondents were asked a series of structured questions designed to determine how much they would be willing to pay to defray the full costs of one visit to a local health center or dispensary that matches the characteristics that the respondent thinks are important. The contingent valuation responses are influenced by the variables that economic theory implies should explain variations across households. Households with more educated heads and more educated respondents exhibited a greater willingness to pay on average than did those with less educated heads. Higher-income households also bid higher, and at increasing rates, than those living in less affluent households. Male respondents, older respondents, and married respondents were also willing to pay more. Having a large proportion of family members younger than 15 was associated with a greater willingness to pay for a visit to an health facility.

We also seek to determine how bids from households respond to the characteristics of the local health center or dispensary, as measured by a subjective index of quality, controlling for government expenditures. Like the education case, increases in the quality index have a positive impact on the willingness to pay for one visit to a health facility. However, unlike the education case, the impact is extremely small. The difference may reflect the fact that households face many more choices of where to seek health care, so they may not be willing to pay much for improvements in public sector services. However, in primary education, parents have no choice but to send their children to a public school, so they may be more interested in improving the quality of those schools.

SUPPLY OF HEALTH SERVICES

Since Independence, the Government of Tanzania has recognized that adequate health is integral to economic and social development on both individual and social levels. The path that the government pursued to improve health conditions was the creation of a publicly-funded health system that sought to be, in essence, as different as possible from the system that existed under colonial rule. That is, the government attempted to shift emphasis from limited urban, hospital-based care for the better-off populations to extensive rural, basic services for the subsistence-level majority. In the 1970s and 1980s, with donor assistance, the government adopted a primary health care approach, created an extensive referral pyramid, and rapidly expanded the number of facilities and staff at the base of that pyramid (dispensaries and health centers, staffed with paramedical personnel). Until the early 1990s, when financing pressures forced policy change, the government maintained universal and nominally free[5] access to government health services, and discouraged for-profit private-sector activities (see Box 5.1).

---

[5] Until recently, nearly all government-operated health services delivered care at no charge to the patient or his or her family. However, most patients have borne the burden of indirect costs such as transportation, and an unknown share have also paid unofficial access fees for treatment.

The supply-side orientation of the government health program succeeded in creating a network of 2,746 government health facilities and 21,973 health workers by 1991. It also succeeded in shortening the distance that rural residents have to travel to obtain basic curative care, and has distributed the benefits of health spending quite uniformly over the population.

What the government has not yet been able to achieve is to target public funds toward those health services that reduce the community-wide level of morbidity and mortality. While the major causes of death in Tanzania are malaria, respiratory infections, diarrheal disease and similar basic ailments, health resources are used more for treating than for preventing these diseases. The health of Tanzanian children and adults continues to be severely jeopardized by the high prevalence of preventable diseases.

Box 5.1: Features of the Tanzanian Health System

❑ The government took responsibility for meeting the population's health service needs. Much of the private medical sector was outlawed or nationalized. However, charitable organizations were allowed to continue operating, although with many constraints.

❑ The structure and staffing of government facilities was based on uniform, population-based standards.

❑ Government services were made available at no charge to all patients.

❑ Services were directed toward the rural areas and toward basic health needs as defined under primary health care. This included family planning services, integrated with maternal and child health. At the base of the referral pyramid and close to the village were rural dispensaries. Consultant hospitals in large cities were at the apex.

❑ The country invested in self-sufficiency in all types of medical and paramedical personnel.

Adapted from the *Social Sector Strategy*, November 1994.

Policy Framework

Historical Background. The Arusha Declaration of 1967 was reflected in health policy in three main ways. First, it was decided that the public sector would take responsibility for meeting the population's health service needs, and services would be available at no charge to patients. Second, services would be directed toward the rural areas, where the majority of the population live. Third, it was determined that the country would invest in being self-sufficient in all types of medical and paramedical personnel.

During the 1970s, the health sector, like much of the public sector in the country, grew dramatically. Most of the growth was seen in the peripheral, or rural, health system. The MOH developed a plan for 1972-80 in which the objective was to "limit the expansion of hospitals to the rate required to match population growth, to keep the bed-to-population ratio constant, and to push ahead as rapidly as possible with the construction and staffing by paramedical personnel of rural health centers and dispensaries" (Jonsson, 1986). The Third Five-Year Development Plan (1976-81) echoed these objectives and called for strengthening of preventive services and development of training programs for various health workers, particularly those who would serve in rural areas. Consistent with actions taken in other sectors, three mission hospitals were nationalized. Private for-profit medical practice was outlawed, though it continued informally.

The government network established during the expansionary period is impressive in size and clearly directed toward the rural areas. While the number of government-run hospitals changed little, the number of rural health centers increased from 22 to 267, and the number of dispensaries grew from 875 to 2,393.

Recent Policy. Since the beginning of the 1990s, the policy orientation has changed. Severe financial constraints, expanding demand for services, and declining service quality motivated the government to propose major reforms in the health sector[6]. It intends to redefine its role in health care service from that of a dominant provider to that of a facilitator. The government envisions that public health services will primarily be channeled through a decentralized system whereby authority and budgets are devolved to the district level. The government will focus on ensuring that an essential cost-effective package of services is financed, with full accountability to households as consumers, beneficiaries, and active participants. Various financing options to improve efficiency and equity are being explored. The cost-sharing program, first introduced in 1993, will be strengthened and expanded so that revenues are managed more efficiently, the fee structure will better reflect the cost of providing services, and efforts to exempt the poor are strengthened. Risk-sharing and -pooling mechanisms are under development, to include health insurance for civil servants and formal sector employees, and prepayment schemes for the population working in rural areas and for the urban informal sector. The government is also developing an appropriate public/private mix in health care provision whereby the private sector will take a larger role in providing curative health services, while the public sector will focus more on community and preventive interventions.

The Government has also initiated a pilot program that seeks to mobilize additional household resources for primary health care. The pilot modifies health management and incentive structures to augment local responsibility for, and management of, primary care facilities (see Box 5.2).

The Government adopted a nationwide cost-sharing initiative and, in January of 1993, introduced new and adjusted fees for Grade I and II services at referral, regional, and district hospitals. Similar charges for Grade III services were introduced in July of 1994. This incremental approach is intended to allow capacity building and improvement in implementation systems and to safeguard against any negative response to large changes that might jeopardize the sustainability of the policy change.

It is estimated that if all eligible patients and services are charged, a total of approximately Tsh 6.85 billion will be generated per year. This assumes, however, that price changes will not affect utilization. The extent to which user fees can form an effective source of revenues will depend on prices and price structures, the quality of services, exemption/waiver definition and implementation, and administrative ease for fee collection and use.

Organization and Structure of the Health Care System

At the central level, the MOH is responsible for policy formulation and development of guidelines to facilitate the implementation of the national health policy. The region interprets national policies and oversees their implementation in the districts. The MOH also runs the four main referral or consultant hospitals and the health-sector training schools.

The Regional Health Management Team (RHMT), headed by the Regional Medical Officer (RMO), is responsible for health services in the region. The RHMT's main task is to coordinate and

---

[6] The reform proposals are elaborated upon in several documents, including: *Proposals for Health Sector Reform* (December, 1994) approved by Cabinet in March 1996; *Strategic Health Plan: 1995-1998* (February, 1995); *Social Sector Strategy* (1995); and *Health Sector Reform Plan of Action 1996-1999* (May, 1996).

Box 5.2: Community Health Fund

The Government of Tanzania realizes that it is necessary to mobilize resources and change health management and incentive structures so that basic health services can be locally maintained and self-sustainable. To address these issues, the Government, assisted by the World Bank, began to test a Community Health Fund (CHF) in 1996.

The CHF, a prepayment health plan for rural communities, is a risk-sharing mechanism whereby basic health needs are funded by household contributions and a government matching grant. This program allows families to pay for a year of health services when they are most likely to have the money to do so. The program also increases local control over health services by decentralizing decision-making and directly involving communities in planning and management of local health services. By augmenting health care resources and fostering competition between public and non-governmental clinics, it encourages private service providers to expand their services in rural areas and to improve the quality of care.

Under the CHF, households make a voluntary contribution of Tsh. 5,000 (about US$9) to the fund that they earmark for a public or private health center or dispensary of their choice. Household contributions are matched one-to-one by a block grant from the Government. Contributions are collected during harvest season. Each participating household receives a "Health Card" that exempts household members from additional charges at the selected medical facility for one year. Non-members pay user fees for each facility visit. Currently funds are pooled only at the facility level. Due to the small size of pooling, benefit coverage is limited to basic health services at the primary level.

Normal government funding of health services is maintained during this pilot stage. Therefore, the CHF provides additional resources and can be used to cover the financial shortage that previously existed. Ten percent of contributions are set aside to finance public health activities agreed upon by the community (e.g., digging wells, buying mosquito nets, etc.).

The community funds are administered by the District Health Board (a newly created body comprising medical personnel) and representatives from local government and the community. Technical advice and regular supervision are provided by the District Health Management Team (DHMT). For each participating facility, a committee is set up composed of selected community members, health workers, and local government representatives. This committee is responsible for mobilizing community members, developing and implementing a Community Health Plan, and managing the fund.

The CHF "pre-test" was launched in Igunga District, a remote rural district in Tanzania. Each community has now established a CHF Committee and started sensitizing their local inhabitants. A District Health Board has been established as a legal entity. As of October 1996, about 2,000 households had joined the CHF and contributed over Tsh. 10 million (about $18,000). These funds were matched by a government grant. For households that did not contribute to the fund, user fees of Tsh. 500 per visit were introduced simultaneously at the participating government facilities.

The next steps in CHF pilot development include: (1) setting up a participatory planning process at each community for preparing Community Health Plans based on their own health needs and priorities; (2) establishing an adequate financial management and accounting system and providing necessary training; and (3) strengthening the District Health Board and the DHMT to provide adequate supervision, training, and guidance to facility workers and the community. The CHF will be rolled out in phases to other districts.

---

supervise district health services. In turn, the District Health Management team (DHMT), headed by the District Medical Officer (DMO), is responsible for health care services carried out in dispensaries, health centers, and the district hospital.

The Referral System. The referral system is comprised of three basic levels: dispensaries, rural health centers, and hospitals (district, regional, and consultant). A dispensary offers preventive, curative, and obstetrical services. In addition to these services, a health center has 25 to 50 inpatient beds. Hospitals provide both preventive and curative services of increasing sophistication, from the district and regional hospitals, to referral and specialty (or consultant) hospitals. Health centers and dispensaries are widely distributed in rural areas, whereas hospitals, and particularly consultant hospitals, are located in major towns and urban areas.

Vertical Programs. Programs for specific diseases such as tuberculosis, malaria, AIDS, as well as broader preventive services such as immunizations and MCH/FP, have been established[7]. Most are heavily donor-funded. The programs are characterized by their vertical organizational structure, which consists of a central unit in the MOH, coordinators at regional and district levels and, in most cases, specific implementing officers at health facilities.

Community-Based Health Care. Community-based healthcare activities take place in localities scattered unevenly in the country. These activities are undertaken to improve the living conditions of the community through, for example, the provision of clean water and pit latrines. Such activities usually are initiated by non-governmental organizations and donors and are not directly attached to the formal health facility network. Instead, they are managed independently by the community.

The Non-Profit Private Sector. Health facilities operated by religious missions have supplemented government services, both by design and by default, for decades, and the government has provided substantial subsidies to these private, non-profit organizations. The subsidies take the form of grants that cover all of the recurrent costs for hospitals that are designated as substitutes for government district hospitals (so called Designated District Hospitals), and smaller grants for other mission facilities, based on staff and bed size.[8]

Mission-run voluntary agencies provide a set of services similar to those offered in the public sector (basic curative care provided in outpatient and inpatient settings, and preventive services such as maternal and child health care). The organizational philosophy of the voluntary agencies, in general, is to provide low-cost services to those in need. Again, this is similar to the government's stated goals. However, the voluntary agencies charge for their services, recovering an estimated one-half of the costs of providing care.

As shown in Table 5.12, voluntary agencies run nearly one-half of Tanzania's hospitals, and provide almost one-half of all beds. The role of these non-profit providers is smaller, though not insignificant, in providing care in lower-level facilities (health centers and dispensaries). Regionally, the distribution of voluntary-agency facilities is remarkably similar to that of government facilities.

Table 5.12: Health Facilities, by Ownership, 1992

Indicator	Government (including parastatals) (%)	Voluntary Agencies (%)	Private For-Profit (%)	Total
Hospitals	49	48	2	174
Beds	52	47	<1	24,130
Health Centers	97	3	<1	276
Dispensaries	80	19	<1	3,014

Source: MOH, 1993.

There is no clear concentration of mission hospitals, despite varying economic and cultural conditions among the zones. The one observation that can be made is that mission facilities are less likely to be found in the Dar es Salaam area than in more remote areas. Clearly, the non-profit sector supplements (and in some ways substitutes for) the public sector.

---

[7] Among the major vertical programs are: Expanded Program on Immunizations, Village Health Worker Program, AIDS Prevention, TBA Training, Tuberculosis and Leprosy Control, and Iodine Deficiency Prevention.

[8] There is a debate about whether the total recurrent costs are, in fact, provided by the government. Managers of mission facilities frequently report that the government grants fall short of covering actual costs.

The For-Profit Private Sector. In contrast to the government and mission sectors, the for-profit private sector has had only a tiny, though increasing, role in the health sector, and geographic distribution is highly skewed toward a few areas of the country. Since re-legalization of private healthcare practice after a ban of about 10 years, approximately 500 organizations and individuals have registered with the Ministry of Health as private providers. The vast majority of these are small-scale dispensaries in Dar es Salaam, owned by a physician and staffed by one or more medical assistants (i.e., individuals who are permitted to prescribe most drugs). The growth of health units in Dar es Salaam has been extremely rapid, and the figures for the private sector shown in Table 5.12 are somewhat outdated as a result. In early January, 1992, there were 136 health units (primarily dispensaries) in the city, and by late September, 1993, there were 253 health units. Currently, about 30 applications for registration are received each month, and most applicants are seeking permission to establish outpatient units in Dar es Salaam and a few other areas.

The regional disparities are striking though not surprising, with private practitioners favoring the better-situated, more densely populated, higher-income areas. Since re-legalizing private practice, the Ministry of Health has registered 132 private doctors in Mwanza, while there are only 4 or fewer in Lindi and Mtwara. It is still too early to see how densely private practice will begin to cover the rest of the country.

Problems of Personnel, Drugs, Management, and Constraints on the Private Sector

Several problems have been highlighted in the numerous external and internal reviews of the health system in Tanzania. The most commonly cited are poorly trained and unmotivated personnel, lack of an efficient and effective drug distribution system, inadequate supervision and management, and severe constraints on the private medical sector.

Personnel. The large number of cadres (29 distinct cadres) represent a diverse group of workers with various levels of training from the 110 allied health training programs. Salaries for health personnel are widely considered to be inadequate. The "survival strategies" employed by both lower- and higher-paid workers has diminished the quality and effectiveness of the health system. As noted by Sandiford and Kanga (1994, p.2), ."..perhaps [the] most detrimental aspect of the system is the manner in which employees are remunerated. Wages are so abysmally low that even the most highly-paid member of the staff is obliged to engage in a variety of alternative income-generating activities in order to survive. There are several means of varying degrees of legality by which this is achieved [....] These 'extra-curricular activities' all distract staff attention from their "official" employment and undermine the influence that managers have over their staff in proportion to their importance as sources of income."

The current system for staff deployment is largely centralized. The MOH creates a list of newly trained health workers and then works with the Ministry of Regional Administration and Local Government to deploy staff from Dar es Salaam. The establishments for positions are national, and the bonding system ties graduates to the MOH at the national, not local, level. These features of the deployment system combine to create a centralized system that ."..prevents the development of creative, flexible and locally-oriented health services" (Ridley, 1993). MOH professionals can (and do) transfer among regions and have few incentives to remain in, and be responsive to, local communities.

Pharmaceuticals. For many years, the supply of drugs to rural health units through the government procurement and distribution system has been in a state of crisis or near-crisis. Drugs consume approximately 19 percent of the recurrent health budget. Yet the lack of drugs, particularly in the peripheral units, has been identified as a primary quality-related deficiency of the government health system, most recently in the marketing questions included in the HRDS.

Nearly all the drugs used in the peripheral units of the government health system (dispensaries and health centers) are imported through the Essential Drugs Program and distributed in pre-packaged EDP "kits," provided by DANIDA. Typically, according to field reports, the supply of drugs runs out within two weeks of the start of the month, when new kits are opened. The shortages are said to result from miscalculations about local drug needs, misappropriation and sale of drugs at both local and central levels, and over-consumption by patients early in the month.

Recent policy initiatives have attempted to address the deficiencies in drug procurement and distribution. In 1991, the government adopted a plan for the development of the pharmaceutical sector in the country (*Masterplan for the Pharmaceutical Sector 1992-2000*, September 1991). Its main components include:

- reorganization of central medical stores and the establishment of regional medical stores (this has been completed);

- changes in the drug distribution system from the present rigid kit system to a health facility inventory-based requisition system (this is pending);

- rational use of drugs through universal use of the National Essential Drug List and Standard Treatment Guidelines; and

- increased local production of pharmaceuticals.

From the perspective of the consumer, the lack of medicines has been the most critical problem. This has been experienced particularly in the peripheral units, so patients will typically bypass lower-level dispensaries in favor of health centers or outpatient departments of district hospitals.

Management. Serious criticisms have been leveled at the management training and authority structure within the government health system. For example, RMOs, who are responsible for all health-related activities at the regional level, typically are specialists in an area of clinical medicine but have little interest or knowledge of public health and community medicine. Similarly, DMOs tend to have little public health training and are unprepared to manage district health services.

Lack of a functioning health information system has long been cited as a fundamental weakness of the Tanzanian public health system. Only the donor-funded and -supervised vertical programs have had functioning systems in the past, and those typically operated in isolation from one another. However, a new Health Management Information System (HMIS) has been developed by the MOH and was implemented nationally over the period 1993-1995. The HMIS integrates the information requirements for existing vertical programs, and has built-in indicators and targets that can be used as tools to monitor service provision at facility, district, regional, and national levels.

District health planning, as a component of overall district planning, is constrained by lack of knowledge of available financial inputs both from government and other funded vertical programs. The

MOH, through the Primary Health Care Steering Committee, has initiated the development of National District Health Planning Guidelines which, when used with data input generated through the new HMIS, will form the basis for improved district health management.

Supervision and maintenance of standards of quality are weak in the extreme. The District Health Team's planning and coordination of transportation, management, supervision, and support to dispensaries and health centers is inadequate at best, and often nonexistent. Health centers are responsible for the supervision of satellite dispensaries, but even this function is absent in the rural areas due to a lack of transportation and motivation.

Maintenance of government health facilities is extremely poor. Budget allocations for both building and equipment maintenance are often small and/or used for other purposes. There also is a shortage of trained maintenance technicians. As a rule, maintenance personnel are provided by district or city public works units. However, bureaucratic procedures hamper an effective response to a repair request, even when funds exist. Such services are rarely procured from the private sector.

Budgeting in the health sector is done on a line-item, incremental basis, based on input costs. Each health facility or department in the MOH calculates their requirements for the coming year based on the previous year's expenditures, adjustments for previous underfunding, expectations for inflation, and plans for growth in activities. Budgets are aggregated at the regional and national levels. At the end of the day, however, budget requests are often cut somewhat arbitrarily by the central government.

The budgeting process is driven by accounting norms. Virtually no program-based budgeting or deliberate reallocation of resources across programs takes place. The recent increase in health centers' and dispensaries' share of total health sector spending was driven by sharp increases in employee salaries rather than by a deliberate decision to reallocate resources from hospitals to primary-care facilities.

Limitations on the Private Sector. Three major constraints affect the supply of private medical services in Tanzania. First, the existence of free public services and low-cost, subsidized, mission-run services may crowd out for-profit private sector activity to some extent. This problem will be reduced, though not eliminated, as cost sharing takes hold in the public sector.

Second, there are few insurance mechanisms, particularly in rural areas[9]. Therefore, both providers and consumers face considerable risk when treatment is offered. Out-of-pocket payment may be an adequate financing mechanism for most outpatient care, particularly if providers respond to a competitive market as they price their services. However, private inpatient care may be too costly for more than a very few consumers. The absence of a viable insurance mechanism is a serious constraint on the development of the private for-profit hospital sector. This is a particularly serious issue since the lack of an insurance mechanism inhibits the for-profit sector from mobilizing private resources for just the types of services that are placing the greatest burden on the public sector (i.e., hospital services).

---

[9] Some Tanzanians do already have experience with a form of insurance. In their study on health insurance in Tanzania, Abel-Smith and Rawal (1992) found that of 200 private and parastatal firms with more than 20 employees, 34 percent had contractual arrangements with private organizations to provide health care for their workers. This is mainly done on a fee-for-service basis, and tends to be used for outpatient services. Although this form of self-insurance does exist, it is limited to formal sector employees and is reported to be cost-ineffective and subject to considerable abuse by both patients and providers.

Third, available data suggest that there is in fact little, if any, quality improvement associated with existing voluntary agency facilities, or the recent development of the private sector. In several studies, comparisons between mission and government (district or regional) hospitals indicate that there is little difference in technical quality. While mission facilities may rank higher on amenities, interactions, and availability of some supplies, government facilities tend to have more highly trained workers (Gilson et al., 1993; Kanji et al., 1992).

In the for-profit sector, there is still less evidence that services are better quality than in the government units, and the reverse may be true. While no hard data have been reported, there are consistent reports that the private dispensaries are staffed by medical assistants, often with no direct supervision from a qualified medical doctor. The dispensaries may satisfy consumer demand by providing prescriptions, but there is reason to believe that the technical quality of services being delivered is very low. This is compounded by the difficulties in inspecting and monitoring private clinics. Market fragmentation reduces incentives to invest in inputs in order to enhance quality. In short, quality and efficiency problems in the health sector may be difficult to improve.

GOVERNMENT AND DONOR SPENDING ON HEALTH SERVICES

The Government of Tanzania spent approximately Tsh 57 billion, or an estimated Tsh 1,972 per capita, in 1994/95 on personnel, pharmaceuticals, and other recurrent costs of the healthcare system. Another Tsh 496 per capita was spent through the development budget, much of which came from donor contributions. In this section, we examine trends in spending on health care, and the allocation of spending among programs and inputs.

Recurrent Expenditures

Time Trends. The health sector's share of total government spending was virtually constant at 8 percent in the early 1990's. However, its share increased sharply in 1993/94 and 1994/95, increasing to 15 percent of spending. Similarly, government health sector expenditures increased from 1.2 percent of GDP in 1989/90, to 2.5 percent in 1994/95. However, it appears that this trend of increasing government focus on the health sector has recently been reversed. In the 1996/97 budget, the health sector is projected to receive 7 percent of government expenditures, equivalent to about 1.2 percent of GDP.

Spending per capita has kept pace with population growth and general inflation. Recurrent budget health care spending per capita has grown from Tsh 373 in 1989/90 to 1,972 in 1994/95. Real spending per capita was relatively constant from 1990/91 to 1992/93, then increased by approximately 16 percent in 1993/94, and by 30 percent in 1994/95. However, health spending per capita is projected to decline by 36 percent in real terms in 1995/96.

Expenditure by Program. Health resources are concentrated at the hospital level. An estimated 50 percent of the recurrent health budget was allocated to the MOH in 1994/95 (see Table 5.13). Most MOH funds were devoted to regional and district hospitals, whose share of total recurrent health sector spending is estimated to be 32 percent, equal to their average share over the course of the 1990s. Health centers and dispensaries account for 31 percent of health spending in 1994/95, markedly higher than its 1992/93 share. Referral hospitals account for 27 percent of total recurrent health sector expenditures, down from 33 percent in 1992/93.

Combined, so-called curative (or facility-based) health services comprise 90 percent, preventive services about 7 percent, and training and other expenditures (including MOH Administration and minor programs) approximately 4 percent of recurrent spending.

In addition to health-related expenditures under the recurrent budget, and in contrast to education, the Government of Tanzania funds health through the development budget. Donor spending is captured in the development budget, so accurate estimates of total public spending are possible only if the two are combined. While government-financed expenditures strongly favor curative services, donor expenditures are weighted more heavily toward preventive services.

Table 5.13: Distribution of Recurrent and Development Expenditures Among Health Sector Programs, 1994/95

| | Recurrent | | Development | | | | Total | |
| | Government | Share | Government | Share | Donor | Share | Government and Donor | Share |
Category	(Tsh million)	(%)	(Tsh million)	(%)	(Tsh million)	(%)	(Tsh million)	(%)
Total	56,968	100	1,610	100	8,382	100	66,960	100
Total Curative	51,027	90	1,127	70	2,539	30	54,693	82
Referral Hospitals	15,324	27	140	9	0	0	15,464	23
Reg/Dist. Hospitals	17,978	32	642	40	408	5	19,028	28
Disp/HC	17,725	31	345	21	2,132	25	20,202	30
Preventive Services	3,840	7	376	23	5,843	70	10,059	15
Ministry Administration	285	1	15	1	0	0	300	1
Training	1,787	2	83	5	0	0	1,870	3
Other	28	1	9	1	0	0	37	0

Source: Follmer and Kessy, 1996.

As shown in Table 5.13, 90 percent of recurrent, 70 percent of non-donor development, and 30 percent of donor expenditures are allocated to curative services, including the various levels in the referral hospital system (consultant, regional, and district) and the peripheral health units (health centers and dispensaries). Of total MOH and donor monies combined, the consultant hospitals consume 23 percent of financial resources, the regional and district hospitals use another 28 percent, and 30 percent of funds are allocated to health centers and dispensaries. Preventive services, primarily multiple vertical programs (e.g., AIDS, TB/leprosy), are budgeted to receive approximately 15 percent of non-household health expenditures. Nearly 58 percent of this, however, comes from donors. Thus, donors shift the overall budget in favor of dispensaries and preventive services because the donors favor these programs more than does the government.

Expenditure by Input (Table 5.14). Personnel costs account for 67 percent of the budgets for health centers and dispensaries. Drugs account for 26 percent of expenditures. Less than 1 percent of their budgets are allocated to facility operation and maintenance. It is difficult to estimate expenditures by input for hospitals because a large share of these facilities' budgets are provided to them as lump sum grants (internal subventions) for which expenditure by input information is not available. Referral hospitals receive almost one-half of their budgets in this form.

Table 5.14: Input Use in Health Sector Programs, 1994/95 (% shares of total program expenditures)

Input	Total Excluding Administration and Other	Referral Hospital	Regional, District Hospitals	Health Centers and Dispensaries
Total	100	100	100	100
Personal Emoluments	41	23	31	67
Traveling/Visits	0.1	0	2	0
Facility Operation/ Maintenance	0.4	6	4	1
Treatment Abroad	3	11	0	0
Total School Costs	0	0	0	0
Hospital Supplies	3	1	4	2
Food	3	2	4	1
Laboratory Services	0	0	0	0
Drugs	14	7	13	26
Non-Personnel Preventive Inputs	1	0	0	0
Internal Subventions	25	46	36	0
Other	5	4	6	3

Source: Follmer and Kessy, 1996.

Personnel costs account for about 23 percent of their budgets, treatment abroad, 11 percent, drugs, 7 percent, and operation and maintenance, 6 percent. Regional and district hospitals receive about one-third of their budgets as lump sum grants. Personnel expenses account for 31 percent of their budgets, drugs, 13 percent, and facility operation and maintenance, 4 percent. For the system as a whole, personnel expenses account for 41 percent of the budget, lump sum grants to hospitals, 25 percent, drugs, 14 percent, and food, hospital supplies, and treatment abroad each account for 3 percent.

Salaries have grown rapidly since 1991/92. Nevertheless, even with a substantial increase in personal emoluments' share of total spending, this division of spending by input is not out of line with generally accepted international standards.

Donor Spending. Donor agencies, which were budgeted to spend about Tsh 8.4 billion (13 percent of total non-household sector spending) in the Tanzanian health sector in 1994/95, emphasize preventive and primary health care. Donor funds account for 58 percent of total non-household preventive spending, 11 percent of non-household health center and dispensary expenditures, and 2 percent of non-household regional hospital expenditures. DANIDA is the largest donor in the health sector. Its Health Sector Program Support is budgeted at US$51 million from 1996 to 1999. Norway, Japan and Sweden are also significant bilateral donors. UNICEF operates health activities through local government and community-based organizations. The World Bank is a relatively small participant in the sector (the first health sector credit began in 1990). For a more detailed breakdown of donor activity in the health sector in the 1990s, see Box 5.3 at the end of this chapter.

Unit Costs

The absence of valid national utilization data, combined with the division of budgeting responsibilities between the MOH and the regional and district governments, precludes calculation of system-wide unit costs. However, the small-scale FAST study in 8 districts was undertaken to estimate illustrative unit costs per visit in government, mission, and for-profit private dispensaries. As shown in Table 5.15, in government facilities, the average cost per outpatient visit was about Tsh 150 (US$0.37) in 1993. For the mission facility visited, the unit cost was calculated to be over Tsh 2,000 (US$4.94), and for the private, for-profit dispensary, the estimated unit cost was slightly more than Tsh 1,000 (US$2.47). The main explanation for the striking differences in cost between governmental and other facilities is the availability of drugs. In private facilities, drugs were routinely provided as part of the visit, while in government facilities, care tended to be confined to diagnosis, advice, and prescription.

Table 5.15: Estimated Cost Per Outpatient Visit, 1993

Dispensary	*Cost per Outpatient Visit (Tsh)*
Government 1	131
Government 2	150
Government 3	177
Government 4	171
Government 5	180
Mission	2,239
Private for-profit	1,414

Note: This is a very limited sample of facilities, not randomly sampled, for the purpose of presenting a notional idea of costs.
Source: FAST, 1994.

Within the government system, the larger basic health facilities are more costly than the smaller ones, despite the fact that they currently provide equivalent levels of care in many cases. Compared to dispensaries, health centers have more staff and equipment and therefore consistently have higher unit costs for similar outpatient services. In a study in Morogoro, Gilson (1993, p.11) found that, ."..[the] health center median total cost was four times that of dispensaries and average per contact costs were greater across all services except immunization (e.g., fifteen times greater for delivery services)."

Summary of Spending Patterns

At first glance, the allocation of resources within the health budget may seem to run counter to the stated health sector objectives of providing primary health care services to the rural population. One might also conclude that donors place a higher priority on preventive and basic services than does the government. However, several additional observations are needed to supplement these interpretations.

First, it is true that many resources have remained at the consultant-hospital level, which primarily serve residents of urban areas and contribute relatively little to fighting the diseases affecting the majority of the population. There are ways, however, in which spending does reflect stated government priorities and policies. In any health system where the government takes the primary responsibility for providing health services *at all levels*, resources will be pulled toward the relatively more costly hospital-based curative services (just as they are to universities in education). Any efforts to push health services out to the rural areas, and to increase the capacity of the "feeder" system in the referral network, has the paradoxical effect of ultimately placing even heavier demands on the higher-level facilities. With the government and donors the sole financiers of the health system, the result is an unsustainable expansion of resource requirements, and a natural concentration of resources at the higher-level services that provide few community-level benefits.

Second, looking at the distribution of government and donor spending, donors typically will not fund recurrent costs. Therefore, by default the government is left expending many of its resources on the hospital and clinical side.

Third, there is no way to know what the government budgets would look like *in the absence of external assistance*. For decades, high levels of donor funding have affected the shape of the Tanzanian health system, apparently much more than the education system.

Fourth, and finally, it is not easy to separate spending for preventive from spending for curative services in the Tanzanian health system. Much of the infrastructure may appear to be primarily for curative services, though there is joint production of preventive services, especially at the dispensary level. Therefore, the figures should be interpreted somewhat loosely in the absence of more precise information about spending on curative and preventive activities.

TOTAL HEALTH SPENDING AND DISTRIBUTION OF BENEFITS

Estimate of Total Spending on Health

Any estimate of the total amount spent on health services in Tanzania necessarily depends on imprecise estimates. However, such an exercise is worth doing to discern, even in rough terms, the absolute and relative spending on critical investments to human capital.

In fiscal year 1995, the government and donors spent an estimated Tsh 2,317 per capita per year, and individuals spent an average of about Tsh 2,496 per capita per year. Employers added approximately Tsh 128 per capita in the form of insurance and reimbursement, and religious missions contributed approximately Tsh 79 per capita in the form of locally-generated and foreign subsidies[10]. Given these estimates, a total of about Tsh 5,020 (about US$8.73) per capita was spent on an annual basis, with households contributing approximately one-half of that amount.

Distribution of Public Subsidies

Do the funds spent in the Tanzanian government health system reach the poor? In many ways, the answer to that question is "yes." According to an analysis of the incidence of the benefits of public spending prepared for this report, the distribution of many types of health spending is equitable, or at least uniform across the welfare distribution. Funding for outpatient services delivered through health centers and dispensaries was found to benefit both rich and poor alike. For inpatient services and those outpatient services provided at hospital-based clinics, better-off households were more likely to obtain

---

[10] These estimates were derived as follows. Government and donor expenditures are from the total (recurrent and development) budgets, as reported in Follmer and Kessy (1996) for FY 1995. Per capita household expenditures are from the HRDS (aggregate annual spending on health divided by the average number of household members), and adjusted to 1995 Tanzanian shillings. Employer/insurance contributions are conservatively estimated from Abel-Smith and Rawal (1992), who found that the average annual insurance expenditures for each of the 255,000 was at most Tsh 4,172, or about Tsh 1.06 billion on a national basis in 1991. These figures were also adjusted to FY 1995 Tanzanian shillings. Mission contributions were estimated at a total of Tsh 1,360 million in FY 1994, based on the following assumptions and estimates: there were 8,160 beds in voluntary agency facilities (excluding designated district hospitals which are fully, or nearly fully, government-financed), and the facilities required approximately Tsh 320,000 per bed per year. This cost per bed is estimated from a review of several facilities. Thus, in the aggregate, the facilities must have generated about Tsh 3,023 million per year, of which about 90 percent came from private sources. These private sources were divided approximately equally between user fees and donations, and the user fees were already counted in the household expenditures. Per capita totals for mission contributions were adjusted to FY 1995 Tanzanian shillings.

the benefits than were the poor.

The benefits of government spending on health were distributed reasonably uniformly over the welfare distribution. The poorest 20 percent of households obtained benefits from about 18 percent of total health spending, and the best-off households benefitted from 28 percent of total health subsidies. The wealthiest 20 percent of the population received 29 percent of the benefits of the recurrent budget, while the poorest received 17 percent (see Table 5.16).

Table 5.16: Distribution of the Benefits of Public Spending on Health, by Expenditure Quintile

	Lowest 20% (1)	(2)	(3)	(4)	Highest 20% (5)	All
Hospital Inpatient						
Curative	20.0	13.3	12.5	18.4	35.9	100.0
Delivery	17.5	11.7	17.5	18.9	34.4	100.0
Hospital Outpatient						
Curative	11.3	14.1	14.9	22.9	36.8	100.0
Prenatal	17.7	21.6	15.2	25.0	20.6	100.0
Health Center or Dispensary Outpatient						
Curative	18.3	20.5	18.7	21.3	21.1	100.0
Prenatal	24.7	14.5	21.3	18.3	21.3	100.0

Source: HRDS, 1993/94; World Bank, 1994a.

Outpatient services available through health centers and dispensaries benefit the poor and the better-off households almost equally. For example, the poorest 20 percent of households obtain the benefits of about 18 percent of the government's health spending, while the richest households obtain the benefits of 21 percent of public spending.

Resources are skewed toward the better-off households in the relatively costly inpatient services[11]. Although they account for only a small share of total visits, they are much more costly to provide than the more uniformly distributed prenatal care or curative visits to dispensaries. For example, as shown in the table, while the poorest 20 percent of the households benefit from 20 percent of curative inpatient health sector spending, the richest 20 percent of households capture 36 percent of the benefits, or about 16 percent more than they would if spending were uniformly distributed. Similarly, for hospital-based curative outpatient services, the wealthiest obtain 37 percent of the benefits of spending, while the poorest households obtain only 11 percent.

There are two explanations for the benefit incidence patterns. First, most hospitals, and particularly the costly referral hospitals, are located in urban areas. Those urban areas are also more likely to have households with relatively high incomes. Although rural residents do travel long distances for inpatient care and thus receive some of the benefits of such spending, most of the inpatients and the vast majority of outpatients in urban hospitals come from in or around the city. Thus, the bias of spending toward hospitals in urban areas translates into a bias toward the better-off households.

---

[11] It should be noted that in this calculation the expenses for the tertiary hospitals were lumped together with those of the district hospitals. It seems likely that the benefits of the tertiary hospital probably are more confined to Dar es Salaam than are the benefits of the district hospitals. Since Dar es Salaam is relatively rich and since the consulting hospitals are more costly per patient seen, if we had assigned the budget of the consulting hospital only to hospital users in Dar or the urban areas, the overall distribution would be more regressive than shown here.

Second, the private (non-traditional) medical sector in Tanzania is small and, compared with the government sector, offers very few opportunities for patients to purchase inpatient services. Therefore, better-off households that otherwise would be likely to turn to the private sector for care use government-funded services instead.

CONCLUSION

Based on the preceding analysis, it appears that if little or nothing is done to alter the current course of the health sector, we can expect:

- minimal improvements in health status;
- declining quality at all levels of the health care system; and
- a persistent differential between the services available to the better-off and to the poor.

However, the Ministry of Health has developed a health sector reform strategy that addresses the issues of financing, liberalization, decentralization, and reallocation of funding towards public and preventive health services. If efficiently implemented, the policies advocated could significantly strengthen the sector. However, implementation of this strategy is not yet connected to the annual domestic budgetary process and is focused more on the role donors can play than on what the government can do. To correct these shortcomings, the Ministry of Health could develop a five-year implementation plan that identifies how the strategy could be financed, develops feasible reallocations, shows how such reallocations could be achieved, and proposes an outcome-oriented monitoring framework. In short, the implementation plan should outline the combination of central government funding, donor funding, user fees, insurance programs, and efficiency gains that would fully fund the strategy. Ideally, such a plan would address the following issues:

- *Allocative efficiency, equity, and government budget allocations.* The government could reduce spending on hospitals, training, and ministerial administration by 50 percent over the next few years and reallocate those resources to preventive health services and primary care (including family planning). The plan could also show how the government could gradually scale back expenditure on study and treatment abroad. This would imply that funding for acute services would have to depend much more on users' and employers' contributions, on risk sharing and prepayment schemes, and on charitable contributions.

- *Improving the efficacy of government funding.* Even with such reallocations, spending on primary and preventive services would only amount to about US\$2 per capita. To be effective, these limited government funds would have to be spent on only the most cost-effective, widely beneficial interventions, such as those to reduce communicable and infectious diseases (including malaria, water and airborne diseases, and sexually transmitted diseases) and to improve preventive services for mothers, infants, and small children. The implementation plan could identify these critical services.

- *District and facility level management.* It is important that district and community-based services be accountable to clients rather than to the central government, and that they have sufficient supplies and drugs to meet community needs. For these reasons, the health reform strategy proposes that the government decentralize public-health services to the district level and implement facility-based management of government-owned facilities. The strategy also emphasizes that households and communities should take a more active role in funding and supervising health services. Steps to achieve these objectives could be incorporated into the health strategy implementation plan. The plan could include provision for moving ownership of district hospitals, health centers, and dispensaries to the local authority most appropriate to the facility's catchment area, enabling each facility to manage itself, moving personnel and procurement decisions to the facility level, ensuring accountability of facilities to a local government entity, shifting government funding to a grant-making program, and providing central and district-level support for quality improvement. Although the health reform strategy supports such changes, there are now only a few donor-assisted pilots to implement elements of the decentralization program. The implementation plan could therefore propose ways to improve on, and expand nationwide, these pilots.

- *Hospital and training services.* The major result of the budgetary shifts and the decentralization initiative for referral hospitals and training facilities outlined in (a) above would be drastic cuts in government subsidies to these institutions. For these institutions to survive, they will have to be allowed to operate independently, with modest grant support from the central government, and be targeted to the poor. The government could facilitate this transition by encouraging the development of formal and informal risk-sharing and insurance programs to finance catastrophic care. Reducing subsidies to health facilities and training institutions, and promoting household-financed risk sharing, would also encourage the private provision of these services.

Box 5.3: Recent Donor Initiatives in the Health Sector

In 1996-1997, donors were budgeted to fund 21 percent of all non-private expenditures in the health sector. Eighty-two percent of donor funding will go to community and preventive care, and 18 percent to curative services. Most of the donors tie health initiatives in with education by promoting knowledge of basic health rights and risks. HIV/AIDS education and family planning centers are of major importance for many donors.

The Danish International Development Agency (**DANIDA**), the largest single donor in the health sector, launched a major health program in July 1996 to run through June 1999. The Health Sector Program Support (HSPS) is budgeted at approximately US$ 51 million and emphasizes close work with the government and other donors. On the district level, HSPS support is expected to help establish autonomous district health boards with uniform management and administrative systems. On the regional level, HSPS will support new regional health administrations that will have clear lines of authority and roles in helping to execute health reforms. At the Ministry of Health (MOH) level, HSPS will support the creation of a national health monitoring and evaluation system. This system will assess and record the impacts of investments in health reform. The HSPS program is targeted at improving health care for the lowest income groups.

The United Kingdom's Overseas Development Agency (**ODA**) funds smaller, more specific projects, such as the Adult Morbidity and Mortality Project (focused on Dar es Salaam, Morogoro Rural, and Hai districts). This project defines the causes of morbidity and mortality in adults and attempts to assist the MOH in establishing cost-effective priorities in the delivery of health care to adults. O.D.A. also funds the Health and Nutrition District Support Project (HANDS), devoted to four districts in the Mbeya Urban District. This project, funded at approximately US$ 1 million over 5 years, attempts to assist the Government of Tanzania (GOT) in prioritizing the use of resources allocated to the Mbeya district. ODA also contributes multi-lateral support to programs such as the National AIDS Control Program (NACP). ODA is expected to contribute US$ 2.6 million or more annually to the health sector.

The International Development Agency (**IDA**) has been supporting Tanzania's health sector through the Health and Nutrition Project Cr. 2098-TA. The project is IDA's first credit to the sector and aims at improving access, quality, and effectiveness of basic health services in urban and rural areas. The areas of support include: strengthening government's capacity in health planning, policy formulation, and human resources development; reforms in pharmaceutical procurement and management in the public sector; provision of pharmaceuticals and medical supplies; support to nutrition and the population policy; rehabilitation of hospitals, primary health facilities, and health infrastructure; and community mobilization and primary health care initiatives at the village level. In support of health sector reform initiatives by the government, the Credit has been restructured to assist various activities to help implement reforms, including design and pre-testing of the Community Health Fund — a pre-payment scheme for rural communities, planning of social health insurance for civil servants and formal-sector employees, and activities in the areas of public health and management. These activities will continue to be supported and expanded in the follow-up project which is currently under preparation.

The United States Agency for International Development (**USAID**) is sponsoring two programs in the health sector. The Tanzania AIDS Project (1993-1998) is a nation-wide effort channeled through the MOH. USAID will contribute US$ 20 million to this initiative over five years. The goal of the project is to reduce the impact of AIDS by reducing the transmission rate of HIV and by improving conditions for AIDS orphans. Family Planning Services Support (1990-1997) seeks to improve the health and economic status of women and children through increased of contraceptive usage and family planning awareness. This program also is to receive US$ 20 million in total funding.

The United Nations Family Planning Agency (**UNFPA**) is involved in various small programs geared towards population control and family planning. Only one program received more than US$ 1 million, that being the National Family Planning Programme (US$ 6.5 million from 1990-1993). The program worked through the Family Planning Unit at the MOH and provided equipment, transportation, training, and contraceptives. Altogether, UNFPA approved US$ 15 million in aid for the health sector from 1992 to 1996.

The Japan International Co-operation Agency (**JICA**) concentrates its funding on end-specific projects, such as the Malaria Control Programme that ran from 1986-1994. JICA funded the Strengthening Expanded Program on Immunization at approximately US$ 1.1 million from 1990 to 1995. It is currently supporting the Maternal and Child Health Care Service Project. Slated to run through 1998, the program focuses on increasing the quality and availability of health care to women and children throughout Tanzania. JICA's overall goal in funding to the health sector is to assist the GOT in its efforts at improving health and medical services in such a way that donor assistance can be successfully phased out in the future.

The Swedish International Development Agency (**SIDA**) helps fund the Tanzania Food and Nutrition Centre (TFNC), a nation-wide agency. SIDA's support is designed to strengthen the institutional capacity of the TFNC to improve women and children's diets. SIDA's support also strengthens the ability of the TFNC to obtain external supplies and equipment through international channels. SIDA's current plan runs from Fiscal 1994/95 to Fiscal 1998/99. It has allocated US$ 2.9 million to be spent over this period.

The Norwegian Agency for International Development (**NORAD**) focuses its support on AIDS and family planning.

For the past three years, the donors have attempted to work with the MOH to support a sector-wide strategy for health to put the MOH firmly in the leadership role in the sector and to reduce the geographic and programmatic problems of coordination among health sector donors. This effort has begun to show some success.

6
FAMILY PLANNING

Most Tanzanian households prefer large families. On average, women say that the "ideal" number of children is 6 (TDHS, 1991/92)[1]. This figure is close to the actual average family size, which has held steady at about 6 children for the last 20 years, and corresponds to low (though increasing) use of modern contraceptive methods.

High fertility has health costs, costs to the individual woman, costs to the household, and social costs. First, early childbearing, close spacing of births, and high parity are associated with maternal and child illness and mortality. Second, scarce household resources are stretched over many children, so that education, health, and other resources available per child are extremely limited in poor and even middle-income households in Tanzania. The same is true of the country as a whole. Finite resources are stretched over many children. Third, women who bear large numbers of children limit their chances of seeking opportunities for market employment. Typically this behavior is in response to few opportunities and can change quickly when women's opportunities in the economy improve.

Clearly, however, those costs are perceived to be outweighed by the value of children in a primarily agrarian economy with plenty of available land and low population density. There is persuasive evidence that fertility is high in Tanzania because demand for children is great in rural areas. There is potential for improving the provision of family planning services and increasing the understanding of modern contraception among women who may wish to delay the next birth or limit their family size. The clearest route to reducing fertility over the long term is through reducing the underlying demand for children. That, in turn, is most directly done through increasing female education, particularly girls' opportunities for secondary-school education.

OUTCOMES AND UTILIZATION

Between the 1978 and 1988 population censuses, the population on the Tanzanian mainland grew at an estimated annual rate of 2.8 percent, from 17.0 to 23.4 million[2]. At the current rate, the population will double in about 25 years.

---

[1] Because no one source has all the relevant variables, data for this chapter are derived from the Tanzania Demographic and Health Survey (TDHS) 1991/92, the Tanzania Knowledge, Attitudes and Practices Survey (TKAP) 1994, and the Human Resources Development Survey (HRDS) 1993/94. Readers should note that some changes in fertility preferences and behavior may have occurred between the TDHS 1991/92 and more recent surveys.

[2] There is some disagreement about this figure, and there are indications that the 1988 Census may have undercounted the population to a considerable degree. The growth rate of 2.8 is said to be on the low side (Bos, 1994)

The legacy of past high fertility rates, seen in the young age structure of Tanzania, implies a dramatic increase in the size of the population in the most highly reproductive age groups over the next decade. Approximately 18 percent of the population is younger than 5 years, and nearly one-half (46 percent) is under 15 years. Projecting the population under assumptions of moderate changes in fertility and mortality, the population of women in the 20- to 24-year age group is expected to increase from 1.1 million in 1990 to 2.5 million in the year 2000, and 3.1 million by 2010. Even with declines in fertility, the population momentum foreshadows a long period of continued high levels of population growth. Under the assumption that fertility and mortality will change as they have in the recent past, the population would continue to grow at more than 2 percent per year through at least the year 2020 (Bos, 1994).

Fertility

The total fertility rate, or TFR, is 6.3 children per woman[3] in Tanzania, which is about average for countries in the region (see Table 6.1). The TFR is now about three times the replacement-level rate. Comparing 1978 and 1988 censuses to the TDHS 1991/92 (the most recent and comprehensive source of information about fertility and contraception), fertility appears to be declining slowly. The TFR was estimated at 6.9 in 1978, 6.5 in 1988, and 6.3 in 1991/92. The gradual decline in fertility is also seen when comparing cohorts of older and younger women.

As one would expect, the level of childbearing in urban areas is somewhat lower than in rural areas. The TFR for women living in Dar es Salaam and other urban areas is 4.0 and 5.6, respectively; while that of rural women is about 6.59 children. Age-specific fertility rates in all regions show a peak in fertility during the span from 20-24 years, with higher fertility among rural women of all ages.

Reliable estimates of fertility by region are unavailable, but these can be estimated with confidence for the six zones of the country. Women living in the Lake and Central zones of the country have the highest fertility rate (about 7 children per woman), while the lowest fertility rates are found in the Southern and Coastal zones (see Table 6.2).

Health and Fertility

High fertility rates, young childbearing, and close birth spacing have distinct detrimental effects on the health of women and children in Tanzania.

Table 6.1: Total Fertility Rate in Sub-Saharan Africa, 1992

Country	Total Fertility Rate (per woman)
Ethiopia	7.5
Kenya	5.4
Tanzania	6.3
Uganda	7.1
Zambia	6.5
Zimbabwe	4.6
Sub-Saharan Africa	6.1

Source: World Bank, 1994c.

Table 6.2: Fertility by Zone of Residence, 1991

Zone	Total Fertility Rate (per woman)
Coastal	5.7
Northern Highlands	6.0
Lake	6.9
Central	7.1
Southern Highlands	6.3
South	5.1

Source: TDHS, 1991/92.

---

[3] The total fertility rate is the total number of children that a woman would be expected to bear during her lifetime, on average, if she lived until the end of her reproductive lifespan (age 49), and she experienced current age-specific fertility rates as she aged.

According to recent population surveys:

- about 26 percent of teenagers covered by the survey had already begun childbearing. Among those 15 years old, 7.5 percent had begun childbearing. Among those 19 years old, 53 percent had given birth or were pregnant (Weinstein et al., 1995).

- According to the TDHS 1991/92, about 18 percent of all births occurred less than 24 months after a previous birth.

- Among women aged 35 to 39 years, 7.4 percent had 10 or more children in 1994. Among those aged 40 to 44, 19 percent had 10 or more children. Among those ages 45 to 49, 27 percent had 10 or more children (Weinstein et al., 1995).[4]

The health consequences of childbearing patterns in Tanzania include fetal wastage, inferior anthropometric development of infants, and high rates of maternal morbidity and mortality. More than one-half of children born in the five years preceding the TDHS survey were at elevated risk of dying as a result of the mother's fertility pattern. Thirty-eight percent of children had a single high-risk characteristic, while 21 percent had more than one high-risk characteristic.

Unregulated fertility, combined with inadequate antenatal care visits, have major effects on maternal morbidity and mortality. About one-quarter of all deaths among women of reproductive age in developing countries are attributable to complications of pregnancy and delivery. Maternal mortality is currently estimated to be 342 per 100,000 live births in Tanzania, a level that could be decreased by 5 to 18 percent if all women who say they want no more children realized their desires.

Utilization of Family Planning, Antenatal, and Obstetric Services

Several types of behavior are relevant to family planning and reproductive health. These include use of contraceptives, family planning services, antenatal care, and delivery care.

Contraceptive Use. Almost 18 percent of women aged 15 to 49 used some form of contraception in 1994. About 11 percent of these women used modern contraceptives. A central reason that fertility has declined slowly in Tanzania, despite some improvements in contraceptive supply, female education, and other "modernizing" influences, is that traditional means of birth control, such as post-partum abstinence and breastfeeding, have not been replaced and surpassed by use of modern contraceptive methods. Use of modern contraception has increased in recent years, but remains low.

From 1991 to 1994, modern contraceptive use among women 15 to 49 almost doubled. Aboud, et al. (1996) attributes much of this increase to the success of Tanzania's National Family Planning

---

[4] In determining the effects of high-risk fertility behavior on child survival, a mother is classified as "too young" if she is less than 18 years of age, and "too old" if she is over 34 years of age at the time of delivery. A "short birth interval" is defined by a birth occurring less than 24 months after the previous birth, and a child is a "high birth order" if the mother had previously given birth to three or more living children.

(NFP) Program. The NFP
Program significantly augmented
family planning-related logistical
support to health facilities over
the early 1990's. Largely due to
this improved support, health
service facilities were able to
offer a better mix of family
planning services and were much
less likely to encounter shortages
of family planning supplies (see
Box 6.3).

According to the 1994
TKAP, almost one-third of
reproductive-age women in
Tanzania report that they have
used a method to delay or limit
births at some point during their
lives. About 13 percent of
women reported that they have
used the pill, 7 percent used
condoms, 3 percent used

> **Box 6.1: Changes in Modern Contraceptive Use in the Early 1990s**
>
> Contraceptive use among women aged 15 to 49 almost doubled in Tanzania from 9.5 percent in 1991 to 17.7 percent in 1994. Similarly, modern contraceptive use increased from 5.9 percent to 11.3 percent over the same period. Much of this growth may be attributable to the success of Tanzania's National Family Planning (NFP) Program.
>
> Survey results indicate that from 1991 to 1994, increased contraceptive use cannot be attributed to socioeconomic variables. Over this period, there was little change in the socioeconomic status of the households surveyed. Further, socioeconomic variables that were important determinants of contraceptive use in 1991 remained equally significant in 1994. Variables that were not important in 1991 remained insignificant.
>
> In contrast, access to family planning facilities had a significantly increased impact on contraceptive use in 1994. Aboud, et al. (1996), postulates that this phenomenon is due to the fact that the NFP Program significantly increased family planning-related logistical support to health facilities over the period. Largely because of this support, by 1994 health services offered a better mix of family planning services, including increased availability of injections, intra-uterine contraceptive devices, and foam. Furthermore, these facilities were much less likely to encounter shortages of Family Planning supplies. Survey results indicate that the NFP Program's information and education campaign also likely had a significant impact on modern contraceptive use. However, the NFP Program did not appear to have increased the number of facilities with staff trained in family planning.

injections, 2 percent used IUDs, and 2 percent resorted to female sterilization. Fourteen percent of
women stated that they used either the calendar rhythm method or withdrawal.

Though data are not available from the TKAP, the TDHS 1991/92 found that only 2 percent of
women used contraceptives before they gave birth to their first child. About 37 percent of the women
who have ever used birth control say that they began to use contraceptives when they had only one child,
which indicates an interest in delaying (rather than preventing) the next birth. Nearly one-quarter (22
percent) of married women who had ever used contraceptives did so for the first time after they had at
least four living children. It is likely that these women were seeking to limit their family size, rather than
simply delay the next birth.

Currently, about 11.3 percent of all women, and 13.1
percent of married women, use a contraceptive method.
Contraceptive use is highest among women ages 30 to 34 (see
Table 6.3). About 43 percent of the currently married women
who use a modern contraceptive method are taking the pill,
another 21 percent use injections, 15 percent have undergone
sterilization, and the remaining use condoms and IUDs.

The strongest correlate of contraceptive use in Tanzania,
as in most countries, is female education. Among women with no
education, 6 percent are using a modern contraceptive method.
This increases to 9.6 percent among women with incomplete
primary education, and about 13.6 percent among those who have

**Table 6.3: Current Use of
Contraception by Age, 1994 (% of all
women)**

Age	Contraceptive Prevalence
15-19	5.2
20-24	10.6
25-29	13.5
30-34	15.6
35-39	13.2
40-44	14.1
45-49	10.6
Total	11.3

Source: TKAP, 1994.

completed primary school. Most notably, a full
31.1 percent of the relatively few women with some
secondary schooling now use a modern
contraceptive method. In addition to being a
strong correlate of contraceptive use itself,
women's education is closely associated with
women's apparent ability to realize their
reproductive goals (see Box 6.2). Yet, between
1991 and 1994, modern contraceptive use
increased more rapidly among uneducated women
than among those with education.

Box 6.2: Women In Need of Family Planning Services
According to the TDHS, about 41 percent of currently married women wish to delay their next birth at least two years, and another 23 percent wish to have no more children. This means that a total of about 64 percent of married women are considered to be potentially in need of family planning for child spacing or fertility limiting purposes. While many of those women are using contraceptives, about 27 percent of all currently married women are not employing contraceptive methods, and are at risk of an unwanted or mistimed pregnancy. It is important to note that most of the women who are not using contraceptives and yet wish to delay or limit pregnancies have little education.

        Multivariate analysis has been undertaken
of demographic and health data in 10 other Sub-Saharan African countries, demonstrating surprisingly
consistent effects of secondary schooling of women on numbers of children born. On the basis of these
studies, the impact of completed primary school years (ages 7
to 10) is to reduce children born by 0.3 to 0.6 children, on
average, whereas the impact of 11 or more years of schooling
is to reduce children born by 0.9 to 1.4 children, on average
(Ainsworth and Nyamete, 1992). This generalization applies
almost equally to women residing in urban areas in Africa as
it does in rural areas.

        Regional differences in contraceptive use are striking
(see Table 6.4). The level of contraceptive use reaches
nearly 19 percent among married women in urban areas other
than Dar es Salaam. However, only slightly more than 4
percent of married women in rural areas use a modern
method to delay or limit births. By far the highest
contraceptive use occurs in Kilimanjaro region, where more
than one-quarter of all married women in the reproductive
years are currently using a modern family planning method.
The regions of Arusha, Lindi, Iringa and Singida also have
relatively high contraceptive prevalence (at least 9 percent).
The regions with the lowest contraceptive use are Mtwara,
Shinyanga and Mwanza.[5]

Table 6.4: Current Use of Contraceptives by Region, 1991 (% of currently married women)

Region	Contraceptive Prevalence
Arusha	12.3
Dodoma	9.6
Dar es Salaam	10.9
Iringa	9.0
Kagera	3.9
Kigoma	2.8
Kilimanjaro	25.3
Lindi	9.7
Mara	3.0
Mbeya	5.4
Morogoro	4.5
Mtwara	1.5
Mwanza	2.3
Pwani	3.3
Rukwa	4.4
Ruvuma	5.1
Shinyanga	1.2
Singida	10.7
Tabora	4.1
Tanga	7.5
Total	6.6

Source: TDHS, 1991/92.

Choice of Family Planning Service Provider.
According to the TKAP, 71 percent of modern contraceptive
users obtain methods from government facilities.
Dispensaries are the major providers for these clients (38
percent), followed by government hospitals (35 percent), and
health centers (25 percent). Village health workers hardly
figure in client use at all.

---

[5] Again, the regional estimates from the TDHS should be viewed cautiously, as they are based on relatively small samples.

On the other hand, a fledgling private medical sector serves about 19 percent of family planning clients, the majority of whom are served by mission facilities (52 percent), the rest by pharmacies (25 percent), and private doctors/clinics (19 percent). Mission facilities also receive public subsidies, and when they provide contraceptives, often do so for no charge. Again, the form of providing services that has proven to be effective and relatively inexpensive in many countries, that is, community-based distribution (CBD) agents, are not active in this market[6]. Only 0.7 percent of all clients report use of a CBD worker.

Use of Antenatal and Delivery Care. Most women in Tanzania have received antenatal care during recent pregnancies. According to mothers' responses in the TDHS, about 92 percent of all births received antenatal care from a medical professional. Most frequently, that care was provided by a trained nurse/midwife (56 percent) or a maternal and child health aide (30 percent). On opposite ends of the spectrum, doctors and traditional birth attendants provided only 7 and 4 percent of all antenatal care, respectively.

Educational attainment of the mother was closely related both to the likelihood of obtaining antenatal care, and to the source of that care. For example, about 7 percent of women with no education did not get antenatal care, compared to 1 percent among women with complete primary education, and 0.2 percent among those with secondary schooling. While, in general, very few women obtained services from doctors, one-quarter of those with at least some secondary schooling were under doctors' care (TDHS, 1991/92).

Despite the apparently high coverage of antenatal care, Tanzanian women tend to start their care later than is medically advised and thus have fewer than the recommended number of visits before delivery. On average, women start their antenatal care at 5.6 months gestational age (instead of the recommended 3 months). Thus, they obtain care only about 5 times before delivery, on average (instead of the recommended 12) (TDHS, 1991/92).

About one-half (53 percent) of births during the 5 years prior to the TDHS took place in health facilities, while the rest took place in the home. Place of delivery was strongly correlated with place of residence. Among urban women, about 85 percent of deliveries took place in health facilities, while among rural women, only 45 percent did. As would be expected, educated women were far more likely to deliver in health facilities than were uneducated women (81 percent of deliveries by women who had some secondary education, compared to 38 percent of deliveries by women with no education).

HOUSEHOLD EXPENDITURES ON FAMILY PLANNING, ANTENATAL AND OBSTETRIC SERVICES

The TDHS 1991/92 collected no information about household expenditures on family planning services. However, the HRDS 1993/94 did collect expenditure data and therefore provides clues about the direct and indirect costs of family planning and related reproductive health services.

The HRDS reveals that about one-third of women using family planning spend some money for contraception. Payments are made for consultations, commodities, and travel to and from family

---

[6] In community-based distribution, family planning workers visit women in their homes to provide information about family planning and to distribute oral contraceptives and condoms to interested women.

planning service centers. In rural areas, average expenditures for family planning were Tsh 843 per user in 1993, compared with Tsh 1,018 per user in Dar es Salaam, and Tsh 801 per user in other urban areas. An important component of these expenditures is travel costs. Per user, the travel costs amounted to Tsh 448 per user in rural areas, Tsh 306 in Dar es Salaam, and Tsh 223 in other urban areas. Since travel time also involves an opportunity cost (time that might have been devoted to household or farming activities), rural travel costs are likely to be even greater.

Among the one-quarter of those using antenatal care and delivery services in the past year who had any expenditures for those services, an average of Tsh 1,974 was spent on services related to the pregnancy. This figure varied from Tsh 2,619 per year in urban areas other than Dar es Salaam, to Tsh 4,247 in Dar es Salaam, and Tsh 1,374 per year in rural areas.

DEMAND FOR FAMILY PLANNING SERVICES

There are several components that allow a better understanding of reproductive behavior in Tanzania. First, we can look at the extent to which reproductive-age women are even aware of methods of regulating fertility, as well as couples' attitudes toward modern contraception. This information can identify the potential for increased contraceptive use through greater awareness of modern methods. Second, we can examine which women are likely to use modern contraception and how much of a role supply and demand factors play in that decision. By supply-side factors, we mean characteristics of the nearest potential source of family planning services (distance, the number of methods available, availability of other types of pharmaceuticals, and so forth). By demand-side factors, we mean individual and household characteristics that influence the underlying demand for children, or desired family size. Third, we can take a step back and examine the correlation between desired family size, contraception and fertility, and the determinants of desired family size.

Knowledge and Attitudes

<u>Knowledge</u>. Tanzanian women appear to have limited knowledge of modern contraception, and there is very little knowledge about methods other than those which are most common. About 80 percent of all reproductive-age women in Tanzania say that they know of at least one method to limit or space births, and most of those are familiar with modern contraceptive methods. Oral contraceptives are the best known method, and nearly all the women who are familiar with any family planning method say that they have heard of the pill. Most women (70 percent) have at least heard of condoms, and about 58 percent know of female sterilization (Weinstein, 1995).

Knowledge of methods and sources is greater among urban women than among the rural population. Women with no education are the least likely to be familiar with contraceptive methods. In contrast, nearly all of the women with at least a secondary education know about family planning. Knowledge of sources of family planning services parallels knowledge of the methods themselves.

<u>Attitudes</u>. The TDHS 1991/92 and the TKAP 1994 obtained indicative information about the attitudes that women and men have toward family planning. For example, women were asked whether they believed that it is acceptable to have messages about family planning on the radio or television. They were asked how frequently in the past year they had discussed family planning with their husbands. Among those who knew of at least one contraceptive method, each woman was asked whether she approves of family planning, and whether her husband does.

In general, most women thought that family planning messages on mass media were acceptable, and the percentage who found them acceptable increased in the early 1990's. In 1991, 80 percent of urban women and 67 percent of rural women held this view. By 1994, 89 percent of urban women and 71 percent of rural women approved of these messages. Women who had never been to school were somewhat less likely to approve of family planning messages than were women who had some primary education (58 versus 73 percent, respectively).

Husband-wife communication on the issue of family planning appears to be limited. Less than one-half (44 percent) of the married women of reproductive age said that they discussed family planning with their husbands during the year before the TDHS. Most of the women who had such conversations said that they had talked with their husbands about the topic only once or twice during the year.

About 85 percent of currently married, non-sterilized women said that they approve of family planning. This figure is lower in rural areas than in urban ones (83 percent and 92 percent, respectively). About one-quarter of the women said that they believe that their husband disapproves of family planning. Again, education is strongly correlated with approval of family planning, and with concordance between husbands' and wives' beliefs.

More than three-quarters of the married women with at least a secondary-school education said that they and their husbands agree that family planning is acceptable. About 11 percent are in disagreement with their husbands on this issue, and only about 9.5 percent of women who do or who do not approve of family planning say that they are unsure about their husbands' attitudes. In striking contrast, about 27 percent of women with no schooling say that they and their husbands agree that family planning is acceptable. In 18 percent of the cases, women with no schooling approve of family planning but believe that their husbands disapprove. A full 50 percent of women with no schooling (both those who approve and those who disapprove of family planning) are unsure what their husbands believe about the acceptability of contraception.

Determinants of Contraceptive Use

Access to family planning facilities appears to have had a significantly positive impact on contraceptive use over the early 1990's. In 1991, only the presence of a family planning hospital within 5 kilometers was found to be a statistically significant contributor to contraceptive use. However, by 1994, the presence of a hospital within 10 kilometers and a health center within 5 kilometers was also significant. Neither access to dispensaries nor facility quality measures contributed significantly to contraceptive use in either year. Aboud, et al. (1996), hypothesizes that the 1994 TKAP survey sample may not have been large enough to detect this effect. They also point out that in the 1994 survey, a health facility offering family planning had to meet minimum quality standards. This requirement may reduce the observable quality effect by eliminating the very low-quality facilities from the pool of considered locations.

On the other hand, individual characteristics, such as the woman's age, education, religious affiliation, residence and household assets, were strongly associated with the probability of using modern contraception. In particular, having a primary education of three years or more was the strongest independent predictor of current contraceptive use. Also important as determinants of contraceptive use were being a member of an organized religion (Catholic, Muslim or Protestant), residing in an urban area, and being in a household that had a wood, cement or tile floor, rather than a dirt floor[7]. As would be expected, women in the Northern and Southern Highlands were more likely to use contraception, all else being equal.

Demand for Children

Given the apparent importance of demand-side factors highlighted in the analysis by Beegle (1994), it is useful to examine women's reproductive goals. According to the TDHS and the TKAP, women in Tanzania wish to have about 6 children[8]. As is found for fertility itself, desired family size varies greatly by region and women's educational level. Women in urban areas wish to have about 5 children, for example, while those in rural areas state that they would prefer about 6 children. Women with no education reported that they would want 7 children, and those with complete primary schooling said that they would prefer 5 children. Women with at least some secondary education wished to have markedly fewer (4) children.

An analysis of the determinants of desired family size has shown that the same individual and household characteristics that were strong correlates of current use of contraceptives also are closely associated with desired family size. In particular, women's education over the first three years of primary school is strongly correlated with the desire to have few children, relative to the average. Women with three years of education, for example, wish to have about .5 fewer children than women with no education. Higher levels of educational attainment lead to more dramatic changes in reproductive goals. Women with 8 or more years of schooling wish to have 1.7 fewer children than do women with no education at all, controlling for factors such as residence, household assets, and age. Living in an urban area and being a member of an organized religion are also good independent predictors of wishing to have fewer children. Being part of an agricultural household is a predictor of wishing to have more children.

In short, individual and household characteristics that lead married women to want fewer (or more) children are the same ones that lead women to use (or not to use) modern family planning methods. Among those characteristics, female education is most important.

SUPPLY OF FAMILY PLANNING SERVICES

Policy Framework

Historical Background. The government's support for family planning can be traced to 1969, when the government advocated child spacing, advising that individuals have social responsibilities to raise their children to be responsible and productive adults. Official support strengthened the National Family Planning Association (UMATI) that had organized in 1967. In 1974, the MOH started providing

---

[7] In the absence of other data on the economic status of the household, type of flooring was used as a proxy for the economic well-being of a family in Tanzania.

[8] For the TDHS, information in this section refers to responses to the questions: (for women with living children) "If you could go back to the time you did not have any children and could choose exactly the number of children to have in your whole life, how many would that be?" and, for women without living children, "If you could choose exactly the number of children to have in your whole life, how many would that be?"

family planning services as an integral component of the Maternal and Child Health Program, with assistance from USAID. Four years later, Tanzania adopted the Alma Ata declaration, which recognized family planning as one of the essential elements of primary health care.

Current Policy. Recognizing the reproductive health benefits of family planning, as well as problems posed by rapid population growth, the Government of Tanzania adopted a national population policy in 1992 that aims to (a) reduce the country's population growth rate to 2 percent by the year 2007; (b) educate the public on benefits of family planning and reproductive health; and (c) foster conditions that will lead to greater accessibility to family planning services. A parallel endeavor, the National Family Planning Program Plan of Operations, was launched in 1987 with the explicit aim of increasing contraceptive use in the country from less than 6 percent in 1987/88 to 25 percent by 1993. A National AIDS Commission, responsible for combating the AIDS epidemic through a number of specific (and vertical) actions, has also been established.

A key concept underlying the country's National Family Planning Program is that bringing family planning services within easy physical and financial reach of potential clientele will lead to a significant and sustained increase in effective contraceptive use. The expansion of availability is being engineered primarily through the government's existing health infrastructure, that consists of the network of health centers and dispensaries found in each of 104 districts, as well as through district, regional, and consultant hospitals found in municipalities. In addition, some efforts have been made to institute community-based distribution through village health workers. Recently, the program has been giving increasing attention to a broader reproductive health agenda.

Organization and Structure of Family Planning Services

The major actors in the provision of family planning services in Tanzania are the MOH, through its maternal and child health program, and UMATI. Minor participants include the non-governmental Organization of Tanzania Trade Unions and the Tanzania Women's Organization. Over the years, the MOH and UMATI have developed a collaborative working relationship in the provision of family planning services, and are considered to be the primary institutions responsible for implementing the National Family Planning Program. MOH facilities function as the service delivery points. UMATI, in contrast, has been responsible for the procurement and distribution of contraceptives, providing training in basic family planning skills for service providers, and family planning advocacy. By April 1994, UMATI had eight clinics and funds to establish ten more. It was also operating a community-based distribution program, covering a total population of more than 500,000.

Family planning services do appear to be available throughout much of the country, in both government and private establishments. As shown in Table 6.5, of the nearly 4,000 government health centers and dispensaries in mainland Tanzania, the MOH reported that more than 3,100 (80 percent) were providing mother-child health (MCH) services and about 2,700 (69 percent) were providing family planning services in 1993.

There are some noteworthy regional differences. In the regions of Dar es Salaam, Pwani and Morogoro, relatively few of the government health centers and dispensaries offer family planning services, while in Ruvuma, Tabora, Kagera, Kilimanjaro, Mbeya, and Mwanza, more than 85 percent of the health facilities are reported to distribute contraceptives.

The widespread availability of family planning services was confirmed in a recent analysis of the TDHS 1991/92, which collected detailed data about a sample of 308 government and non-government health facilities in Tanzania. Beegle (1994) found differences in the availability of contraceptive methods by health facility ownership and level (hospital versus dispensary). The analysis showed that the greatest variety and level of family planning services could be found at government hospitals, closely followed by private hospitals and government dispensaries. Private dispensaries were least likely to be able to provide contraceptive services.

Table 6.5: Share of Health Facilities Providing Mother-and-Child Health and/or Family Planning Services, 1993

Region	Total Number of Facilities	Providing MCH Services (% of total)	Providing Family Planning Services (% of total)
Arusha	230	83	68
Dar es Salaam	315	32	25
Dodoma	201	68	76
Iringa	217	95	56
Kagera	167	99	86
Kigoma	142	89	71
Kilimanjaro	227	91	86
Lindi	128	83	76
Mara	163	88	87
Mbeya	251	86	65
Morogoro	258	74	53
Mtwara	142	95	95
Mwanza	244	95	86
Pwani	233	48	47
Rukwa	116	91	61
Ruvuma	147	95	95
Shinyanga	204	94	76
Singida	132	90	68
Tabora	158	89	87
Tanga	250	77	70
Total	3,925	80	69

Source: Beegle, 1994.

As shown in Table 6.6, all 54 government hospitals included in the TDHS sample offered family planning services. Nearly all hospitals (94 percent) had medical staff trained in IUD insertion, and a majority (61 percent) had a doctor on staff who was trained in sterilization procedures. At least 90 percent of the government hospitals in the sample offered condoms, oral contraceptives, IUDs, and injectable contraceptives. About 80 percent of the hospitals reported that they offered sterilization for the purpose of contraception[9]. The typical government hospital could give clients a choice among about five family planning methods. The 1994 TKAP indicated that contraceptive availability in government hospitals increased between 1991 and 1994.

About two-fifths of the 28 non-government hospitals in the sample reported that they offered at

---

[9] This is somewhat at odds with the statement that only 61 percent of the government hospitals had a doctor on staff who was trained in sterilization procedures.

least one family
planning method. A
large majority of the
private hospitals had
medical staff trained in
IUD insertion and
sterilization
procedures (79 and 70
percent, respectively).
As with government
facilities, private
hospitals were very
likely to offer
condoms, oral
contraceptives, IUDs
and contraceptive
sterilization. Unlike
public facilities, few
private hospitals
offered injectable
contraceptives. On
average, a private
hospital could offer about three contraceptive methods to clients.

Table 6.6: Availability of Family Planning Services in Government and Private Hospitals and Dispensaries

| Characteristic | Type of Facility | | | |
| | Hospital | | Dispensary | |
	Government (%)	Private (%)	Government (%)	Private (%)
Offer any family planning method	100	78.6	95.0	46.7
Have medical staff trained in ...				
IUD insertion	94.4	78.6	40.9	13.3
Sterilization	61.5	70.4	n/a	n/a
Methods Offered:				
Condoms	96.3	64.3	91.2	37.8
OC	92.6	71.4	83.4	28.9
IUD	90.7	67.9	8.3	11.1
Injections	90.7	39.3	15.5	4.4
Foaming tablet/foam/jelly	55.6	21.4	11.1	6.7
Contraceptive sterilization	79.6	70.4	n/a	n/a
Mean number of methods available	5.1	3.4	2.0	0.9

Note: Survey included data on 54 government hospitals, 28 private hospitals, 181 government dispensaries, and 45 private dispensaries.
Source: Beegle, 1994, based on TDHS 1991/92.

The TDHS found that government dispensaries were almost as likely as government hospitals to offer at least one form of contraception, but the range of choices was much narrower in dispensaries than in the higher-level facilities. By far the most commonly available methods in the 181 public dispensaries in the sample were condoms and oral contraceptives. While about 41 percent of government dispensaries had medical staff trained in IUD insertion, only about 8 percent of the facilities offered the method. The typical government dispensary could provide about two methods.

The TKAP study found that oral contraceptives and condoms were commonly available in dispensaries in 1994. Furthermore, injectable contraceptives, which were available in only about 20 percent of dispensaries in 1991, were found in 77 percent of these facilities by 1994. Similarly, the number of dispensaries offering IUD insertion increased to about 25 percent by 1994.

About one-half of the 45 private dispensaries in the 1991 sample offered family planning services, and few had medical staff trained in IUD insertion. About 38 percent offered condoms, 29 percent offered oral contraceptives, and 11 percent offered IUDs. On average, fewer than one method was available at private dispensaries.

Problems of Quality and Implementation

Quality and Access. A 1988 survey of services attributed poor program performance and low rate of acceptance of family planning methods to a lack of trained personnel, low worker morale, unsatisfactory and inadequate physical facilities, lack of basic equipment, frequent shortages, and non-availability and restricted choice of contraceptives. Above all, weak and poorly directed program support to information, education, and communication activities was blamed for the poor program performance.

There are major geographical disparities in the provision of family planning services throughout the country. For example, relatively few of the government health centers and dispensaries in Morogoro, Pwani, Rukwa, and Dar es Salaam offer family planning services, whereas more than 85 percent of the health facilities in Mara, Kagera, Mtwara, and Ruvuma are reported to be able to distribute contraceptives.

Logistic Support. The logistics component of the NFP was aimed at establishing viable commodity- procurement procedures, reliable transportation from the central stores to the distribution points, and good storage and record keeping practices at all levels. The program was to provide essential supplies and equipment to one-half of the dispensaries and health centers by 1991, and all of the facilities by 1993. Logistics systems were to be developed and/or improved. In addition, it aimed to provide transport for supervision to all facilities by 1993.

The 1992 National Family Planning Program Annual Report identified early difficulties with commodity distribution under the program. However, USAID and Aboud et al. (1996), state that since 1992, the program has significantly improved family planning-related logistical support to health facilities. Largely because of this support, by 1994 health service facilities offered a better mix of family planning services. Furthermore, these facilities were much less likely to encounter shortages of family planning supplies. However, the NFP Program did not appear to have increased the number of facilities that offered staff training in family planning.

Few improvements in the provision of transportation for the use of supervisors have been made. For example, the program was able to procure only two of the six trucks originally required, and only 20 of the planned 156 station wagons. None of the 5,700 bicycles that were anticipated have been distributed for use by supervisors at health centers, dispensaries, and villages.

PUBLIC EXPENDITURES ON AND UNIT COSTS OF FAMILY PLANNING

The Program's five-year budget was to be US$28 million for 1989 to 1994. Of this, the government was to contribute about US$1.8 million to institutional support, and donors would contribute the rest. At this level of funding, expenditures from all sources on family planning would average about US$0.20 per capita, per year. This compares with about US$0.22 per capita in Kenya in 1990, about US$0.53 in Lesotho in 1992, and more than US$1.40 per capita in Zimbabwe in 1989.

Arriving at a consolidated account of expenditures for the NFP Program is difficult because of the various means of accounting used by the major donor agencies, and the problem of disentangling the costs of delivering family planning services from the costs of other types of maternal and child health services in the public health system. However, it is possible to arrive at rough estimates of 1992 expenditures to illustrate the distribution of funds among program activities, and to arrive at rough estimates of some of the costs of the current level of service delivery.

Table 6.7 shows the estimated expenditures in 1992 by the two major donor agencies, UNFPA and USAID, and by the Government of Tanzania. This only covers items that are directly associated with family planning and population activities, such as contraceptive commodities and logistics, training of service providers and community leaders, international education and communication (IE&C)

campaigns, and population censuses and research. It excludes many of the direct costs of service delivery that cannot be separated from the overall government health budget, such as the cost of MCH staff time and multi-use equipment in health centers and hospitals. It also excludes any private expenditures for family planning, either on the part of private institutions or households.

Table 6.7: Illustrative Tally of Expenditures for the National Family Planning Program, by Source, 1992 (Tsh Millions)

Item	UNFPA	USAID	GOT	Total (% of total)
Training	65.41	73.04		138.45 (26%)
Logistics/Commodities	155.50	90.44		245.94 (46%)
IEC	2.05	n/a	7.60	9.65 (2%)
Research	1.48	n/a		1.48 (.3%)
Policy Development			10.97	10.97 (2%)
Population Census			11.20	11.20 (2%)
Other (including staff salaries not otherwise accounted for)	30.82	42.67	41.97	115.46 (22%)
Total	255.26	206.15	71.74	533.15 (100%)

Source: Mpangile, 1994.

An estimated Tsh 533 million were expended on the National Family Planning Program in 1992. About 85 percent of the total was donated by the major donors to the program, and the remainder was from the Government of Tanzania. Of the government's contribution, approximately 54 percent was in the form of tax exemptions. (It is important to reiterate that this estimate excludes the government's contributions in the form of staff support for Ministry of Health and local government personnel, which are likely to be substantial. It was not possible to arrive at plausible estimates of those contributions for this exercise.)

Several other donor agencies have provided smaller amounts of funding to the program. For example, the German development agency GTZ has family planning-related programs in the districts of Bagamoyo, Lushoto, Pangani, Rombo and Handeni. The UK's Overseas Development Agency started a five-year family health program in three districts of Kyela, Rungwe and Ileje in 1992, that eventually may be extended to include Makete and Njombe districts in Iringa.

Nearly one-half of the program funding was devoted to commodities and their distribution through a logistics system. This included purchase of vehicles and other supplies, as well as the contraceptive products themselves. Another 26 percent, or about Tsh 138 million, was spent on training of trainers and service providers, and on an orientation of local and national leaders.

Given the imprecision of the budget estimates, one can enter only cautiously into the calculation of unit costs. However, it is worth conducting the exercise for illustrative purposes, making conservative assumptions. There are two types of outputs for which unit costs can be very roughly estimated from the data at hand. The first is training outputs (or trainees), and the second is the cost of commodities. Lack of information about the effectiveness of contraception in the Tanzanian context precludes estimation of cost per birth averted, which is a standard type of unit cost often calculated in analyses of family planning programs.

Cost per Trainee. A total of 1,788 individuals were trained in the NFP Program. To be conservative in calculating unit costs, we can assume that all of these were trained during 1992. Under that assumption, and taking Tsh 138.45 million as a reasonable estimate of the total expenditures on training alone in 1992, the average cost per trainee is calculated to be Tsh 77,433. If the trainees were trained over several years, instead of just 1992, then the cost per trainee would be higher.

Cost of Commodities and Logistics per Contraceptive User. As noted earlier, the full costs of family planning service delivery are not captured in the expenditures for the NFP Program. Personnel costs at the service delivery point are excluded (for example, the salaries for the MCH workers). A reasonable alternative is to restrict the analysis to the cost of delivering commodities to contraceptive users exclusive of those personnel costs. This would cover the purchase and distribution of oral contraceptives, for example.

The total expenditures on commodities and associated logistics are estimated to be Tsh 246 million for 1992. According to the Demographic and Health Survey, 4.4 percent of women ages 15-49 were using a form of modern contraception in 1991[10]. That is, approximately 245,000 women were using a modern family planning method around 1992. Of those women, about 73 percent, or about 178,000 women, received services from a government facility. This implies that the commodity and logistical cost per user equaled Tsh 1,382 in 1992.

DISTRIBUTION OF PUBLIC SPENDING

This section suggests that at the low level of contraceptive prevalence that exists in Tanzania today, the benefits of the program are skewed toward higher income families who are mostly likely to use contraception. This is illustrated in Table 6.8. Among all users of hospital facilities for contraceptive services, 35 percent are from the wealthiest 20 percent of the population, whereas only 11 percent are from the poorest 20 percent[11]. This applies in both rural areas and urban areas (other than Dar es Salaam). Only in Dar es Salaam does this pattern vary, as members of higher-expenditure households have the option of using, and do indeed make greater use of, private providers, including pharmacies. Moreover, use of family planning is most likely to cut across expenditure groups in Dar es Salaam, where prevalence is highest. Charging fees is one way of remedying this distortion, but is unlikely to be adopted, since advocates of family planning would resist it as another barrier to universal availability.

Table 6.8: Share of Those Obtaining Family Planning Services and/or Supplies from Hospitals, by Expenditure Quintile (%)

Income Group	All Hospital Users	Rural Users	Other Urban Users	Dar es Salaam Users
Lowest 20%	10.5	21.4	15.0	22.9
Highest 20%	34.7	29.4	25.0	15.3

Source: HRDS, 1993/94.

---

[10] This figure does not correspond precisely to data presented earlier for two reasons. First, it refers to all reproductive-age women, rather than only those currently married. Second, it excludes women who have been sterilized, because they would not require any commodities.

[11] These data, which derive from the HRDS, are not disaggregated according to whether the hospital was a public, mission, or private-for-profit facility. It is reasonable to assume, however, that the general pattern of use by expenditure groups would prevail among purely public providers for two reasons. First, most hospitals in the country that provide family planning are government hospitals or are publicly subsidized mission hospitals. Second, use of curative health care (in hospitals) (see Table 6.6) follows an almost identical path among expenditure groups.

CONCLUSION

The Government of Tanzania, assisted by two strong donor agencies, has integrated family planning services into its vast rural health infrastructure. While there are opportunities for greater and more effective outreach and for correcting program weaknesses, services are reasonably accessible to women who seek them. As in health and education, Tanzania has done a remarkable job of making this service available to the public.

The main questions that remain are similar to those in the education and health sectors generally. Why so little impact? Why is contraceptive use still so rare and large families so common? The unambiguous answer lies in the preferences of households and individuals. In the predominantly small-scale agricultural economy with a very low stock of women educated beyond primary school, the demand for children is high and, consequently, the use of family planning services is low.

In Tanzania, as in virtually all other countries, the most significant influence on the demand for children is the education of women. Education alters the value of a woman's non-domestic and domestic time, widens her life horizons, improves her ability to space her children and to realize lower goals for family size, and induces rapid changes in fertility preferences and contraceptive use. This is not to say that the government should abandon its supply program, but that the impact of its current policies could be increased by focusing on increasing demand, particularly through improved education of girls. More than in other sectors, in the realm of population policy it appears that the most important step that the government can take is to increase education opportunities for girls and women. Education subsidies also lend themselves to much better targeting so that the incidence impact can be much more pro-poor than commodity-driven programs.

7
NUTRITION

High levels of maternal and child malnutrition in Tanzania are clear detriments to the well-being of individuals and households. Analyses of the nutritional status and food consumption patterns, however, indicate that Tanzania is in better shape than might be expected, given other health and social indicators. This implies that specific and targeted interventions, rather than national or universally available nutritional support programs, may have great potential to address the nutritional problems that exist.

OUTCOMES

Child Nutritional Status

Results from the 1991/92 TDHS show that, among children under five years of age, the percentages of moderately malnourished children are 29 percent for weight-for-age, 47 percent for height-for-age, and 6 percent for weight-for-height (see Table 7.1)[1]. Malnutrition rates are much lower in the first year of life, but increase sharply in the second year of life. These trends are similar to those found in malnourished children elsewhere.

Data suggest that urban children are better nourished than their rural counterparts. However, this appears to reflect the much lower incidence of malnutrition in Dar es Salaam. There is little variation in child malnutrition rates between the rural areas and the urban areas excluding Dar es Salaam.

Table 7.1: Nutritional Status by Demographic Characteristics (% of children under 5 years of age who are moderately malnourished)

Characteristic	Stunted (height-for-age)	Wasted (weight-for-height)	Underweight (weight-for-age)
Age (months)			
Less than 6	12.0	2.1	5.4
6-11	25.6	6.8	28.9
12-23	49.5	9.8	36.7
24-35	57.2	4.9	32.6
36-47	59.5	3.4	30.2
48-59	56.8	4.4	27.6
Sex			
Male	48.1	6.2	28.7
Female	45.3	5.1	28.9
All Children	46.7	5.6	28.8

Source: TDHS, 1991/92.

Tanzania's major child-nutrition problem appears to be stunting from longer-term, chronic undernutrition

---

[1] The reference that is used for malnutrition here (as in most other studies) is the United States National Center for Health Statistics (NCHS). The percentage of children whose anthropometric indicators are more than minus two standard deviations from the NCHS mean level are considered moderately malnourished. The percentage of children whose anthropometric indicators are more than minus three standard deviations from the NCHS mean level are considered severely malnourished.

rather than wasting from short-term, acute food deficits. Malnourishment for a significant proportion (about 17 to 19 percent) of children begins in the first year of life. Reasons for this may be low-birth weight, sustained by inadequate breast-feeding and complementary feeding practices.

For many children malnutrition sets in during weaning when breast milk intakes decline sharply. That problem may be further complicated by premature introduction of weaning foods. Perhaps more importantly, during weaning, children may be exposed to contaminated food and water, and thus contract diarrheal diseases that further deplete nutritional reserves.

International Comparisons. The levels of child malnutrition in Tanzania are not unusually high relative to other Sub-Saharan African countries or relative to other developing countries with comparable income levels. Indeed, the incidence of moderate wasting (i.e., the proportion of children with low weight-for-height) in Tanzania is only one-half of the level that would be predicted at its per capita income level. As shown in Table 7.2, while the incidence of moderate wasting in other Sub-Saharan African countries is in the range of 9 to 11 percent, that in Tanzania is less than 6 percent. Indicators of stunting and wasting, which are manifestations of longer-term nutritional deficiencies, show that Tanzania has about average conditions, compared to its neighbors.

Table 7.2: Indicators of Undernutrition in Sub-Saharan Africa, 1980-1992 (% of children under 5 moderately malnourished)

Country	Stunting	Wasting	Underweight
Tanzania	46.6	5.5	28.5
Zambia	59.4	10.0	24.7
Zaire[a]	46.0	9.6	33.4
Rwanda	34.0	11.4	36.6
Malawi	61.0	8.0	24.0
Kenya	41.0	10.0	17.0
Burundi	60.0	10.0	38.0
Uganda	25.0	4.0	23.0

a. Now Democratic Republic of the Congo
Sources: UNICEF, 1992; Government of the Republic of Zambia, 1990; Kenya Rural Nutrition Survey, 1987.

Time Trends. No nationally-representative estimates of child malnutrition were available until the TDHS 1991/92 was conducted, so it is not possible to analyze temporal changes in child malnutrition rates. The Tanzanian Food and Nutrition Center (TFNC) found no evidence of any trend since 1960 from the various spot surveys it conducted, except in areas where specific multi-sectoral nutrition intervention programs like the Iringa Joint Nutrition Support Program (JNSP) had been undertaken. TFNC spot surveys conducted in 1986-87 suggested an average moderate protein-energy malnutrition (PEM) rate of 40 percent and a severe PEM rate of 6 percent for children under 5 in the country. Corresponding rates obtained by the TDHS for 1991-92 were 29 percent and 7 percent, respectively. However, since the TFNC surveys were clinic-based spot surveys (not random household surveys of the population), no conclusions can be drawn from these sets of numbers about changes in malnutrition over time.

Micronutrient Deficiencies. The significant micronutrient deficiencies prevalent in Tanzania include nutritional anemia, iodine deficiency disorders, and vitamin A deficiency. While there are no nationally-representative data, spot surveys done by TFNC provide some insights about the prevalence of the deficiencies.

- Nutritional anemia. A 1991 TFNC study reviewed information related to anemia and gathered data from 15 hospitals in 14 regions. The study found that among hospitalized children under five years of age, anemia accounted for 20 to 80 percent of the admissions. Anemia accounted for 18 to 87 percent of admissions of pregnant women. Nationally, anemia has been estimated to affect about 7.2 million people (32 percent of the population), including 45 percent of children under five, and 80 percent of pregnant women (Kavishe, 1993).

- <u>Iodine deficiency disorders (IDD)</u>. TFNC estimates that nearly 40 percent of the population (10 million people) live in areas deficient in iodine and are at risk of IDD. Some 5 million people suffer from endemic goitre, and another 610,000 suffer from cretinism. The severity of IDD is highest in the highlands and mountains of the Western and Eastern arms of the Great Rift valley (Kavishe, 1993).

- <u>Vitamin A deficiency</u>. According to the WHO, there is a public health problem when more than 0.5 percent of children exhibit clinical signs of vitamin A deficiency. Virtually all geographical areas in Tanzania report clinical signs above 0.5 percent. It is estimated that vitamin A deficiency results in 2,000 to 4,000 new cases of childhood nutritional blindness each year (Kavishe, 1993).

<u>Regional Differences</u>. There are substantial regional differences in the proportions of children under 5 that are underweight, wasted, or stunted. Generally, Dar es Salaam and the Lake Zone (Tabora, Kigoma, Shinyanga, Kagera, Mwanza and Mara) have the smallest proportion of underweight children. On the other hand, the Central Zone (Dodoma and Singida) and Southern Zone (Mtwara, Lindi and Ruvuma) have among the highest proportion of underweight children. The regional differences are large. The moderate rate of protein-energy malnutrition (based on weight-for-age) in the region having the highest rate of child malnutrition (Mtwara) was over two-and-one-half times that in the region having the lowest rate (Mara). Thus there is scope for regional targeting of interventions.

<u>Gender Differences</u>. Few, if any, significant gender differences exist in the proportion of children under 5 who are malnourished by any indicator. If anything, the data suggest a slightly higher rate of wasting and stunting among boys relative to girls (although the differences are not statistically significant). The nutrition data are consistent with mortality data that show a small (about 10 percent) infant and child mortality advantage for girls. These results are in stark contrast to those from other parts of the world, such as South Asia, which show significantly higher rates of malnutrition for girls than for boys.

<u>Illness-Malnutrition Complex</u>. Critical for an understanding of the nutrient needs and problems in Tanzania is an acknowledgment of the relationship between poor health conditions and child malnutrition. The high prevalence of diarrheal disease, intestinal parasites, and measles all decrease children's ability to absorb essential nutrients and increase the total nutrient requirements. In turn, protein-energy malnutrition and vitamin deficiencies increase children's susceptibility to infectious disease.

A recent study of the burden of disease in Eastern Africa noted that malnutrition is a risk factor for many of the largest killers in the region (World Bank, 1995b). Using a calculation of Population Attributable Risk, the authors adjusted the estimates of the distribution across causes of deaths to children under 5. They found that up to 29 percent of all deaths to young children could be attributed to malnutrition, and that these were deaths for which the immediate cause was identified as either diarrhea or pneumonia.

Maternal Nutritional Status

Maternal malnutrition affects infant and child malnutrition. Child malnutrition, in turn, is a strong determinant of the nutritional status of the next generation of reproductive-age women.

A measure of maternal nutritional status is the prevalence of low birth weight, or the proportion of infants born with a weight under 2500 grams. The TDHS estimated the incidence of low birth-weight in Tanzania to be 18 percent. This is slightly higher than the average for Sub-Saharan Africa (15 percent) and may indicate that low birth weight is a public health problem in Tanzania. The high incidence of low birth weight may be the result of many factors, including the poor nutritional status of women, poor nutrition and prenatal care during pregnancy, and a high load of malarial and other infections during pregnancy. The TDHS also obtained information on the anthropometric indicators of mothers. These data show that about 4 percent of Tanzanian mothers are shorter than 145 centimeters (cm), and 10 percent have a mean body mass index (BMI) of less than 18.5 cm, indicating that they are likely to be malnourished. However, in some regions, such as Mtwara, as many as 12 percent and 21 percent of mothers have low height and BMI, respectively.

There is a strong association between low height and BMI on the one hand, and maternal education on the other. For example, only 4 percent of women with at least some secondary education had BMI less than 18.5, compared to 12 percent of women with no education.

HOUSEHOLD NUTRIENT INPUTS

With the exception of a few targeted interventions, there are no organized services providing nutritional support such as food supplements in Tanzania. Therefore, the main inputs that are associated with maternal and child nutrition are the foods that are prepared and eaten by the household on a daily basis. This section summarizes what is known about the level and type of nutrient inputs in Tanzanian households.

Food Consumption and Energy Intakes

Nutrient Intakes. Estimates of average calorie intake in Tanzania vary from 83 percent of requirements to over 100 percent (World Bank, 1984; FAO, 1984). Unfortunately, no national household survey has attempted to collect detailed data on individual food intake, so a precise estimate of average nutrient intake is simply not available. Average daily consumption of protein is estimated at around 42 grams, compared with the FAO recommended requirement of 50 grams (from vegetable sources). Approximately 62 percent of the protein intake is derived from cereals, 25 percent from meat, fish and dairy products, and 13 percent from pulses (World Bank, 1989). Oils and fats account for about 6 percent of calories in the Tanzanian diet, compared with the 15 percent recommended by WHO (although this recommended level is rarely achieved in developing countries). Not only are these mean values of nutrient intake imprecise and nationally *un*representative, they also probably mask substantial inter- and intra-household variations in food and nutrient intake.

Diet Composition. The Tanzanian diet is dominated by maize, in the form of maize meal, which is cooked into a stiff porridge or "ugali" and served with a sauce or relish of vegetables, pulses, fish, or meat. The next largest source of calories is cassava, which provides roughly 40 percent of the total calories derived from maize. Cassava, millet and sorghum are also cooked in the same form as maize meal. In some areas, such as Kilimanjaro, green bananas are the main staple, also cooked into a stiff porridge. Generally, maize, rice, and wheat are preferred over sorghum, millet, and cassava. However, rice and wheat are important only in the urban areas. The protein content of the porridge that is widely consumed in the country is around 11 to 13 percent for grains, but significantly lower for cassava and bananas.

The predominance of maize and cassava and the deficiency of oils and fats in the Tanzanian diet is of particular concern. This is especially true in the case of young children and pregnant and breastfeeding women, since the calorie density of the staple gruel and stiff porridge is low and these individuals may thus be unable to consume enough calories to meet their special energy needs. Additionally, since maize and cassava alone are deficient in several important nutrients such as iron, thiamine, Vitamin A, and fats (lipids), women and young children are especially susceptible to diseases associated with these deficiencies such as anemia and xerophthalmia (which can ultimately lead to blindness).

Micronutrient Intakes. Intakes of iron, iodine, and vitamin A are generally low throughout Tanzania. Iodine problems are mostly observed at high elevations where iodine-depleted soils prevail. Low iodine in the soil leads to poor iodine content in food and water, resulting in iodine deficiency disorders (IDD). This problem has been addressed by the Iodine Oil Capsule Supplementation Program, initiated in 1986. Spot evaluations undertaken after the program was implemented show that the IDD problem may have substantially declined after 1986. The country now plans on achieving universal salt iodation by 1997 as a permanent solution for the control of IDD.

The daily per capita intake of iron is very low, and much of it is in the non-absorbable form (non-heme iron). This is particularly problematic for pregnant women who need to absorb at least 6.3 mg/day in the last two trimesters of their pregnancies. The dietary deficiencies in iron, combined with malarial and hookworm infections, result in iron-deficiency anaemia, the most common form of anaemia in Tanzania.

Breastfeeding

Breastfeeding is almost universal in Tanzania, with about 98 percent of children under 5 being breastfed at least for a short period. Among last-born children, the percentage that were breastfed within one hour of birth varied from 40 percent in Dar es Salaam to 43 percent in rural Tanzania. On average, 44 percent of last-born children were breastfed within one hour of birth and 82 percent were breastfed within one day of birth (TDHS, 1991/92).

Since more than 50 percent of births in Tanzania take place at health facilities, hospital and institutional practices may be playing an important role in the promotion of breastfeeding. The fact that 56 percent of mothers wait for more than an hour, and 12 percent for more than a day after a baby is born to initiate breastfeeding suggests that there may be an incorrect perception that the first breast milk (colostrum) is an inferior food. In fact, colostrum is rich in antibodies and highly beneficial to the new-born infant.

As shown in Table 7.3, exclusive breastfeeding drops off sharply after the first month of life, and is rare after three months. In most cases, children are fed with a combination of breastmilk and supplements during their first year.

The mean duration of partial breastfeeding is 21.2 months, with rural mothers breastfeeding 1.6 months longer, on average, than mothers in Dar es Salaam. Mothers with no education or some (incomplete) primary education breastfeed approximately two months longer than mothers with secondary and higher education. The most common reasons for discontinuing breastfeeding tend to be both maternal perceptions about, and experience with, failure to produce milk, and the mother's return to work.

Table 7.3: Percent Distribution of Living Children by Breastfeeding Status, According to Child's Age in Months, 1991/92

Age in Months	Exclusively Breastfeeding	Breastfeeding and ...	
		Plain Water	Supplements
0-1	42.5	35.2	21.6
2-3	23.5	28.7	47.0
4-5	7.6	15.7	76.6
6-7	5.6	7.8	84.1
8-9	1.4	4.0	94.3
10-11	0.0	2.6	96.6
12-13	0.8	3.4	90.7
14-15	0.7	3.5	90.1

Source: TDHS, 1991/92.

Supplementary Feeding of Infants

Although there is universal breastfeeding, infants are rarely exclusively breastfed in Tanzania. The TDHS indicates that only about 43 percent of newborns aged 0 to 1 months are exclusively breastfed. The proportion of those exclusively breastfed drops to 24 percent for infants aged 2 to 3 months, and to a mere 8 percent for those aged 4 to 5 months. These are unusually low levels of exclusive breastfeeding, even for a low-income developing country.

As shown in Table 7.4, women in Dar es Salaam and other urban areas tend to feed their babies a breastmilk-only or breastmilk-and-water-only diet for shorter periods of time than do women in rural areas. Correspondingly, women with at least a completed primary education exclusively breastfeed their children for only about 2 months, on average, while those with no education are likely to exclusively breastfeed for three months.

One reason why mothers discontinue exclusive breastfeeding so early may be their perception that they are producing insufficient quantities of milk, in part because of their poor nutrition and heavy workload. Nutrition of the mother at this important stage is a key element in keeping the infant protected from environmental hazards. Premature introduction of supplemental foods greatly increases the risk of infection in the small infant.

Table 7.4: Duration of Breastfeeding by Residence and Mothers' Education

Characteristic	Median Duration of Full Breastfeeding
Residence	
Dar es Salaam	0.6
Other Urban	1.6
Rural	2.5
Mother's Education	
No Education	3.0
Primary Incomplete	2.3
Primary Complete	1.9
Secondary/Higher	1.9

Note: Full breastfeeding means either exclusive breastfeeding (breastmilk only), or breastfeeding in combination with plain water only

Source: TDHS, 1991/92.

Weaning diets are particularly inadequate in Tanzania. Supplementary feeding begins with a thin gruel (uji) of the local staple – maize, millet, potatoes, bananas, or cassava. A variety of vegetables or legumes is added as a relish depending on season and availability, but generally in very small quantities. From the age of 6 months or so, stiffer food (ugali) is given, and by the age of one year, children eat the same food as adults. The daily number of meals or snacks given to children is usually two or three.

In conclusion, breastfeeding in Tanzania is initiated late, solid supplements are introduced too early, and supplementary foods are low in energy and inappropriate. The reduced opportunities for suckling suppress breastmilk production, thereby promoting the cycle of inadequate infant-feeding. In addition, the early introduction of solids increases the risk of diarrheal infection in infants.

HOUSEHOLD EXPENDITURES ON FOOD

It is possible to analyze the share of the food budget devoted to various types of food, and to make comparisons across welfare groups, using the HRDS 1993/94. The results (shown in Table 7.5) are surprising. The shares of maize, other foodgrains (such as millet and sorghum), roots and tubers, and legumes and pulses in the total food budget decline with income. Rice is the only cereal that shows an increase in budget share with income. As would be expected, the shares of fruits and vegetables, meat, eggs, and dairy products, and other foods (including cooking oil) increase with income.

What is surprising from these results is the variety of foods that appear to be consumed by even the lowest expenditure group. In few low-income countries would one find the poorest 20 percent of households consuming nearly two-thirds of the value of consumption of a staple (maize) on a "luxury" commodity group like eggs, meat, and dairy products. The budget shares suggest one of two conclusions: (i) that the common assertions about the Tanzanian diet, especially among the poor, being monotonous and almost exclusively composed of maize or cassava are inaccurate; or (ii) that the prices per calorie of items like eggs, meat, and dairy products are so much higher than those of maize or cassava that the poor man's diet in Tanzania is still heavily staple-oriented in terms of calorie composition.

Table 7.5: Share of Individual Food Groups in Total Food Expenditure, by Expenditure Quintile (%)

Food Group	Expenditure Quintile (% of total food expenditure)		
	Lowest 20%	Highest 20%	All
Maize	24.9	11.2	15.6
Rice	5.4	9.6	9.0
Other Foodgrains	6.9	3.5	4.2
Roots and Tubers	11.9	7.7	9.4
Legumes and Pulses	16.8	12.2	13.8
Vegetables and Fruits	10.9	16.7	14.6
Meat, Eggs and Dairy	15.8	27.1	23.0
Other Foods (including cooking oils)	7.4	12.0	10.3
All Foods	100	100	100

Source: HRDS, 1993/94.

We have used the expenditure data to estimate the elasticity, or sensitivity, of demand for various types of foods to changes in income. In other words, we examined how household food consumption patterns would be likely to change if the total household income were to increase. The income (or expenditure per adult-equivalent) elasticity of maize is observed to decline from 0.86 for the poorest 20 percent of households to merely 0.26 for the richest 20 percent. With an income elasticity of 3.5, rice appears to be a highly favored commodity among the poorest. The only commodity whose income elasticity increases from poor to rich is "Other Foodgrains," which includes sorghum, millet and wheat. It is likely that this reflects a strong "distaste" for sorghum and millet among the poor, combined with a strong preference for wheat consumption among high-income urban households. There is almost no consumption of wheat by poor rural households.

The pattern of estimated expenditure elasticities is intriguing because it suggests that increases in household income, even among the poorest households, would be accompanied by substantial changes in their food expenditure patterns. The food budget would be reallocated from maize, sorghum, and millet to rice, meat, eggs, dairy products, fruits, and vegetables. Since the latter foods are expensive and inefficient sources of calories, this provides additional indirect evidence that the poor in Tanzania already are (or perceive themselves to be) consuming adequate amounts of calories. Otherwise, it would be difficult to explain such a strong taste for food quality and variety among the poor.

NUTRITION-RELATED GOVERNMENT ACTIONS

The range of policies, programs, and conditions that can be thought of as affecting the "supply" of nutrition is vast, ranging from specific nutrition interventions, such as micronutrient supplementation, to broad agricultural pricing policies. A comprehensive review is beyond the scope of this report. In this chapter, therefore, we first attempt to highlight the supply-side factors that are the most important determinants of the prevalence of malnutrition in Tanzania, namely food production and caloric availability. We then provide an overview of the policies and programs that are directly targeted toward preventing malnutrition.

Food Production and Availability

Food Production. During the 1960s and early 1970s, per capita food production in Tanzania increased steadily. Tanzania was the only independent African country achieving a growth rate of food production that was greater than that of its population. However, beginning with the economic crises of the late 1970s, food production growth slowed down and failed to keep up with population growth. There are some indications that in the last few years, due to good rainfall and price incentives resulting from structural reforms in agriculture, food production has been growing faster than during the 1978-88 period.

Caloric Availability. Food balance sheets prepared by the FAO show that average daily availability of calories and protein per capita, which fell dramatically during the 1970s, has been increasing - since the mid-1980s. At present, energy availability is estimated to be more than 2,250 calories per day. This amount is slightly higher than the recommended level of energy intake for a moderately active adult in Tanzania. Therefore, undernutrition in Tanzania is not a problem of inadequate food production, but instead one of distribution and demand. A poor procurement, storage, and transportation system continues to hinder the efficient distribution of food grains from the food-surplus to the food-deficit areas within the country. Indeed, talk of encouraging regional food self-sufficiency and security in the past may have prevented the development of storage, transportation, and distribution systems. In addition, sharp increases in the prices of staples in the face of stagnant incomes may have adversely affected the demand for food, and consequently nutritional outcomes, among the poor.

Nutrition Policy

Several policy initiatives have affected the nutrition sector since the early 1980s, including the Agricultural Policy, the National Food Strategy, and various versions of the National Health Policy. Most recent is the 1992 Food and Nutrition Policy, an elaborate statement that seeks to improve coordination among the many actors in the nutrition sector. The policy, which was strongly influenced by the conceptual underpinnings and experiences of the JNSP, placed its emphasis on the importance of government action in the nutrition sector, and sought to clarify the roles of each of the line ministries that influence nutrition.

As the leading ministry in the nutrition sector, the MOH is charged with developing and supervising the implementation of the nutrition policy through the Tanzania Food and Nutrition Center (TFNC). The TFNC, a semi-autonomous institution established in 1973 [2], is responsible for planning, initiating, and evaluating food and nutrition programs, carrying out and disseminating nutrition research, promoting good nutrition, and providing technical input to government on all nutrition-related matters. While the government supports the center's recurrent budget, most of TFNC's funding comes from donor agencies. SIDA and UNICEF have provided the largest shares of support in recent years, and an IDA credit has been provided for several micronutrient activities.

The nutrition policy assigned to all other ministries in the social sectors, and nearly all ministries in the economic and productive sectors, responsibilities for ensuring adequate food production, and mobilizing government and other nutrition-related actions.

Current Nutrition Interventions

Micronutrient Supplementation. The major micronutrient deficiency problems are being addressed through separate national efforts.

- Tanzania aims to achieve universal salt iodation as a permanent solution for the control of iodine deficiency disorder. Three salt iodation plants were installed in Bagamoyo, Dar es Salaam, and Uvinza (Kigoma) in 1990, and additional iodation plants are currently in the design phase. At the present time, approximately one-half of the salt consumed is iodized. Most of the funding for the IDD control effort comes from SIDA, UNICEF, the Government of the Netherlands, and WHO.

- A national control program for nutritional anemia has been put into place. The short-term strategy for control is to increase the distribution of iron and folate supplementation to women during pregnancy and early lactation through the Ministry of Health's Maternal and Child Health Services. The long-term strategy is to promote the production and consumption of vitamin-rich horticultural products. General public health measures to control malaria and other parasitic diseases are also essential to the control of anemia, and are to be carried out by the Ministry of Health. Funding for the national program comes from the World Bank, UNICEF, WHO, DANIDA, SIDA, and other organizations.

---

[2] TFNC was originally established under the Ministry of Agriculture, and then moved to the Prime Minister's Office.

- The national program for the control of vitamin A deficiency (VAD) consists of targeted supplementation of vitamin A capsules through the Essential Drugs Program, and promotion of foods containing vitamin A, including red palm oil and dark green leafy vegetables. Agencies supporting this program include the World Bank, UNICEF, WHO, FAO, DANIDA, SIDA, the Netherlands, and others.

The Child Survival, Protection, and Development (CSPD) Program. The most significant child nutrition activity in Tanzania has been the CSPD Program, a community-based program that was started in 1983 as the Joint Nutrition Support Program (JNSP) with funds and other assistance from UNICEF and WHO. The program, which started as a pilot activity in the Iringa region, has been widely viewed as successful in reducing child malnutrition and infant mortality levels, and has expanded to villages in 39 districts (12 regions) on the mainland and all of Zanzibar, with co-financing from other donor agencies.

The complement of interventions in the CSPD ranges from major civil works (piped water, the construction or rehabilitation of health and water facilities, and so forth), to support for supplies and logistics, training of village health workers, day-care workers, and others, and the promotion of income-generating activities. Two essential components of the program are community sensitization and mobilization for community-based growth monitoring (see Box 7.1).

A cost analysis of the Iringa JNSP concluded that the total cost of the project (in 1987 dollars) was US$17 to US$20 per child per year. Of the US$3.12 million expended, personnel represented about 39 percent of the total, with most of the personnel funds going for international technical support for program management. Putting aside the international management and local transportation costs for supervision, and taking into consideration the economies of scale achieved through expansion of the program, analyses of CSPD program costs concluded that US$2 to US$3 per child per year would support a cluster of activities to reduce child malnutrition. About one-quarter of that sum is for training, advocacy and information, and the remainder is for equipment, supplies, drugs, and local transportation.

The impact of the original JNSP in Iringa has been widely publicized. A 1988 evaluation found a significant decrease in severe malnutrition (from 6.3 to 1.8 percent) and a reduction in the prevalence of underweight children (from 60 to 38 percent) over the 5-year effort. The major improvements occurred during the first three years of the program, and were then maintained. As

---

Box 7.1: Child Support, Protection, and Development (CSPD): Structure and Implementation

The CSPD program emphasizes the local generation and use of information about the situation of women and children. The program uses children's nutrition status as an entry point for a multi-sector community-based program of interventions.

Structure of the Program. The overall policy and strategic planning for the program rests with the Regional Steering Committee composed of representatives from the line ministries. At the district level, the Chief Administrator designates a coordinator (usually the Planning Officer or the Community Development Officer). Implementation committees are formed and are often given the opportunity to visit districts that have greater experience in implementing the CSPD. Efforts are made to have strong representation from women at the committee and other levels.

Implementation. Male and female village health workers are selected following Ministry of Health guidelines. District and ward staff then promote the CSPD activities (such as growth monitoring) through social mobilization and discussion about whether a selected village wishes to participate in the program. If the response is positive, a health committee is elected. The local program is inaugurated by the showing of a film and a campaign day, during which all children are weighed and, if necessary, immunized. Other activities may be added over time, if the community chooses. These include feeding posts, informal day care for children of mothers working in the fields, vegetable gardens, introduction of grain mills, and so forth.

Kavishe (1993, p.152) stated, "The reductions in the malnutrition rates were attributed to the program, as marked differentials in the rates of severe underweight existed between the original 168 project villages as compared to 442 villages in the Iringa non-JNSP areas." While no comprehensive impact evaluation has been carried out for the larger CSPD program, the area reports indicate that comparable reductions in total and severe underweight has occurred between the initiation of the CSPD and the present.

CONCLUSION

The major conclusion that can be drawn from the above analysis is that Tanzania does not compare badly to many other countries in terms of the nutritional status of children. That said, however, it is clear that there are substantial human costs associated with the malnutrition that does exist. Targeted interventions, including several of those already underway, appear to be the most promising means of addressing the current nutrition problems among children and reproductive-age women.

8

WATER AND SANITATION

Starting in the late 1960s, the Government of Tanzania and many donors began a large, sustained effort to deliver safe, improved water supplies, and in some cases improved sanitation services, to the rural population of Tanzania. They accepted the proposition that the rural population was too poor to pay for the costs of improving their water supply, and that water should be provided free of charge. A variety of donor-financed master plans were drawn up for many regions of the country, and donors and the government attempted to provide free water for all.

To many sector professionals in both the government and the donor community, it is now clear that this supply-side master plan for the delivery of water services was a mistake. Thousands of schemes were built that are now no longer operating. There are many reasons for the high rate of project failure. One is that the government simply cannot afford the recurrent costs of past investments. Other explanations include a lack of participation of beneficiaries in project planning, a shortage of trained personnel, poor operation and maintenance, and inappropriate choice of technology.

UTILIZATION OF IMPROVED WATER SOURCES AND SANITATION FACILITIES

Household Water Supply

Only about 11 percent of households in Tanzania have a private water connection inside their home or yard (see Table 8.1). Even these households must sometimes collect water from other sources due to the unreliability of the municipal water supply system in most towns. One-half of the households of Dar es Salaam now have a private water connection in their dwelling or yard, but the other half collect water from outside their home (from a neighbor, public standpost, handpump, open well, or surface water source). About 3 percent of households purchase water at high prices from

Table 8.1: Primary Household Water Sources, by Residence (Percent)

Type of Water Source	Dar es Salaam	Other Urban	Rural	All
Private Connection (inside or outside dwelling unit)	50.0	28.6	1.8	11.3
Distributing Water Vendor	2.7	0.36	0.0	0.3
Tanker Truck Vendor	0.1	0.14	0.0	0.0
Neighbor	32.9	17.3	1.2	7.1
Public Standpost	8.7	26.1	19.7	20.6
Handpump	0.7	9.6	8.8	8.6
Open Well	3.9	10.6	27.8	22.2
Surface Water Source (river, stream, lake, pond)	0.4	7.2	41.0	29.9
Other	0.4	0.1	–	0.1
Total	100	100	100	100

Source: HRDS, 1993/94.

water vendors or tanker trucks that deliver water directly to their homes.

In other urban areas in Tanzania, private connections are far less common. Only about 29 percent of households have a private water connection in their home, and 17 percent obtain water from neighbors. The majority of households in these towns collect water from public taps and public wells. A small percentage rely on vendors or traditional surface water sources as their primary water source.

In the rural areas of Tanzania very few households have private water connections in their home or yard (only about 2 percent). The vast majority of households collect water from sources outside the home (98 percent). About 41 percent of rural households still rely on traditional surface water sources, such as rivers, springs, ponds, or lakes. About 28 percent of rural households obtain water from traditional open wells, almost all of which are located outside the home. Approximately 20 percent of rural households collect water from public standposts, and 9 percent from wells with handpumps. Both of these sources are often considerable distances from people's homes, and their use involves significant collection time, chiefly for the women and female children in the households. Many public tap systems and handpumps have proved to be unreliable, and, when they break down, households revert to using traditional sources.

Table 8.2 shows the percentages of households in different expenditure groups that obtain their water from different sources. As expected, households with higher expenditures are much more likely to have a private connection. The highest quintile has almost two-thirds of the private connections in Tanzania, and buys more than one-half the water sold by tanker trucks and water vendors[1].!!Similar data just for rural areas show that unimproved surface water sources are used by households in all income groups because households in many rural areas have no improved sources available. Very few households in rural areas purchase water from vendors, and all that do are high-income households. When improved water sources such as public standposts and handpumps are available in rural areas, they are used by all income groups.

Table 8.2: Household Water Sources, by Expenditure Quintile (%)

Water Source	Lowest 20%	Highest 20%	All
Private Connection	1.3	29.5	11.3
Neighbor	2.7	12.9	7.1
Public Tap	21.6	16.8	20.6
Handpump	11.7	7.8	8.6
Open Well	25.6	12.9	22.2
River, Spring, Lake	37.0	19.6	29.9
Water Vendor	0.0	1.1	0.3
Tanker Truck	0.0	0.1	0.0
Total	100	100	100

Source: HRDS, 1993/94.

Access versus use. Water policy discussions in Tanzania have often focused on the question of how many people have access to (or are "covered" by) an improved, safe water supply[2].!!At the time of

---

[1] This use of water vendors by high-income groups in Tanzania is different than in many parts of the world. In other countries it is typically the poor that must rely on vendors for their water, while urban households with middle and high incomes obtain water from their own private connections (often at subsidized rates).

[2] Estimates of coverage can be misleading in several important respects. First, they do not distinguish between the benefits to households of different levels of improved service (e.g., public taps or handpumps versus private connections). Second, they typically assume that, when improved water systems are installed, they continue to operate and that the intended beneficiaries of the project use the improved water source. Third, they are not based on measures of the quality of water households actually consume. Even the 2

Tanzanian independence, it was estimated that about 1.4 million people, or 12 percent of the rural population of Tanzania, had access to a clean water supply. A 1980 review of the results of rural water supply investments suggested that rural water coverage increased from 1.4 million to 7.4 million people during the 1970s (Mutalemwa, 1994). Government estimates put the portion of the rural population in Tanzania that now has access to an improved, safe water source at about 9.4 million or 46 percent of the total rural population (Mutalemwa, 1994).

The data from the HRDS indicate, however, that rural water coverage is probably less than one-third, or a total of about 6.0 million, of the rural population[3]. This *overestimates* coverage if one uses the government definition of coverage that households must be within 400 meters of an improved source, since this estimate assumes a household is covered if it uses an improved supply (private connection, handpump, public tap, or neighbor). These data suggest that the net result of the last three decades of investments and effort in the water sector has been to increase the percentage of the rural population covered from about 12 percent to 32 percent or, in terms of the absolute number of people served, from about 1.4 million to about 6.5 million. The capital costs of serving these additional 5 million people are difficult to estimate, but amount to at least several hundred million US dollars.

If the 1980 coverage estimates were correct and the HRDS results are accurate, then rural water coverage has actually declined since 1980 by about 1 million people. Apart from population growth, much of this problem is undoubtedly due to the large number of rural water schemes that were built but are now inoperative. Government figures indicate that of the 10,961 rural water supply schemes that existed in 1992, 30 percent were not operating at all (Mutalemwa, 1994)[4]. The reliability of the systems that were in "operation" varied widely.

In the urban areas, the percentage of the population now using an improved water source is much higher. The results of the HRDS indicate that in Dar es Salaam, 95 percent of the population now uses improved water sources. In other urban areas the comparable figure is 82 percent[5]. However, municipal water supply facilities are inadequate to provide the quantities demanded at the very low prices currently charged for water. Government estimates of the quantity of water that would be demanded in urban areas at current prices exceed the quantity supplied by 85 percent, and exceed installed capacity by 39 percent.

Sanitation

Throughout the world, households and communities go through three stages in their efforts to

---

percent of the population with piped water at their residence are at some risk of waterborne diseases because many piped systems are unreliable and subject to infiltration. The population using public taps and handpumps, or obtaining water from neighbors, should have high quality water and substantially reduced risk of waterborne diseases, but water contamination can still occur during transport and storage.

[3] This figure is based on the percentage of rural households that have private connections, obtain water from neighbors, purchase from vendors, and collect water from public standposts or handpumps.

[4] Shinyanga, Tabora, Singida, Mtwara, Dar es Salaam, and Dodoma regions have disproportionately high rates of inoperative projects.

[5] It is not possible to determine from the HRDS 1993/94 data the actual type of water system used to supply private connections and public standposts (e.g. gravity flow, diesel pump scheme) or the source of water (e.g. surface storage or groundwater).

obtain sanitary conditions: (1) safe, hygienic removal of human wastes from their immediate dwelling; (2) neighborhood collection of household wastewater and excreta, and (3) improved quality of surface water. The first stage involves the removal of excreta and waste water from the household's living space. This is typically a private responsibility of the household. Common technological solutions to this problem are traditional pit latrines and pour-flush toilets. Costs are generally paid by the household, and vary from minimal to US$5 per month. The principal benefits of such investments primarily accrue to the individual household in terms of convenience, amenities, and improved health.

However, in the course of solving their own individual sanitation problems, households often impose costs on their neighbors by discharging untreated human wastes and waste water from their property into streets or other public property. This is particularly true in urban areas and creates the setting for the second stage. A common technological solution here is for households with water-sealed toilets to discharge their waste water into underground sewer lines that remove the wastes from the neighborhood. Alternatively, desludging trucks may be used to empty pit latrines or septic tanks.

Removing the waste water from households improves neighborhood sanitary conditions and may improve public health conditions for everyone in the neighborhood. However, the quality of the surface water receiving the wastes will likely deteriorate. In some situations where a community discharges its waste water into a river, it may be the downstream communities that suffer the consequences of reduced water quality. In other cases, the costs of poor surface water quality may be borne by the residents of the city themselves. Costs for constructing a sewer distribution network and connecting individual households to the system vary depending on the terrain, urban spatial structure, and local costs of labor and materials, but are typically on the order of US$10-20 per month.

The third stage is to improve the quality of surface water. One of the first and most important steps toward meeting this objective is to treat the waste water collected by the sewer lines using primary and secondary treatment technologies. The benefits accrue to the broader community beyond the neighborhood, and government is typically involved in investment planning, financing, and perhaps operation and maintenance. Costs for primary and secondary treatment are approximately 50-100 percent of the costs of the sewer lines, or an additional US$10 per month.

<u>Sanitation Facilities Currently Used</u>. Given the very low per capita incomes in Tanzania, it should not be surprising that the majority of households in Tanzania have not completed even the first stage of this transition. In fact, as shown in Table 8.3, some Tanzanian households have not even started on the path to improved sanitation. Approximately 5 percent of the population have no sanitation facility at all. The most prevalent form of household sanitation in both urban and rural areas is a traditional pit latrine. Data from the HRDS show that between 90 and 95 percent of households in urban and rural areas use traditional pit latrines.

Table 8.3: Type of Sanitation Facility, by Residence (%)

Sanitation Facility	Dar es Salaam	Other Urban	Rural	All
Own or Shared Flush Toilet	8.1	4.9	1.1	2.5
Traditional or Improved Pit Latrine	90.2	92.4	92.3	92.2
No Facility, Bush/Pan, or Bucket	1.7	2.7	6.6	5.3
Total	100	100	100	100

Source: HRDS, 1993/94.

What these statistics do not show is the great variation in the quality of traditional pit latrine construction in Tanzania. There is a long tradition of pit latrine construction in Dar es Salaam and other areas of Tanzania dating back more than a hundred years, and many skilled artisans are constructing traditional pit latrines with large brick-lined pits, concrete slabs, and substantial superstructures. Such "traditional pit latrines" can provide reasonably good service, effectively removing most of the excreta from the household's living space. They can last for many years and cost a few hundred US dollars. At the other extreme, many pit latrines are simply small hand-dug pits covered by temporary wood planks or other materials, surrounded by brush or scrap metal, often without a roof.[6]

Over the last couple of decades several donor-funded projects have promoted the "Ventilated Pit Latrine" (also known by the brand name "VIP") in Tanzania as an alternative to the traditional pit latrine. This technology, which offers a safe, hygienic method of excreta disposal, is now used by about 1 percent of Tanzanian households. Households with VIP latrines have usually received them from donors at heavily subsidized prices. Although less expensive than some high-quality traditional pit latrines, VIP latrines typically cost on the order of US$200-300 (excluding labor) and are far too expensive for most Tanzanian households.[7]

In Dar es Salaam and other urban areas about 3 percent of the population have either a flush toilet for their own use or a flush toilet that is shared with other households. Eight towns on mainland Tanzania have small, limited sewerage systems. In these towns, some of the few households with flush toilets have connected to the sewer system, while others empty into septic tanks and drainage fields. Neither of the two surveys reveals the exact proportion of the flush toilets connected to sewer lines.

HOUSEHOLD EXPENDITURES ON WATER

Only a small percentage of Tanzanian households actually pay any significant amount of money for their drinking water. On average, households with private connections and those buying from neighbors spent about the same amount annually, slightly more than Tsh 8,000 per year in 1994/95 (see Table 8.4). A typical household in the richest 20 percent of the welfare distribution spends about twice as much as a typical household in the poorest 20 percent.

Table 8.4: Annual Household Expenditures for Water, by Expenditure Quintile (Tsh)

Type of Connection	Lowest 20%	Highest 20%	Average
Private Connection	5,083	10,018	8,446
Neighbor	4,685	9,368	8,252
Distributing Vendor	n/a	89,596	89,838

Source: HRDS, 1993/94, inflated to 1995 Tsh.

Very few households in Tanzania use vendors as their main source of drinking water, but those that do spend a lot of money for water. The average household purchasing water from vendors spends almost 10 times as much for water as a household with a private connection or a household purchasing from neighbors. Virtually no households

---

[6] The minimum standards set by the MOH calls for the provision of both a superstructure and a roof.

[7] In fact, many VIP latrines have been purchased by households that already use flush toilets. For them a VIP latrine serves as a back-up supplemental sanitation system in case the sewer line clogs or the flush toilet breaks down.

in the lower 40 percent of the welfare distribution choose to buy water from vendors.

Table 8.5: Share of Households Collecting Water Outside the Home and Estimates of the Time Spent Collecting Water

	Dar es Salaam	Other Urban	Rural	All
Share of Households Collecting Water from Outside the Home (%)	47.0	71.0	98.3	88.4
Average (one-way) Distance from Home to Water Source (kilometers)	0.25	1.10	1.6	1.5
Estimated Time Spent Daily Collecting Water (hours per day)	1.5	2.5	3.1	2.9
Annual Value of Time Spent Collecting Water (valued at US $0.06 per hour)	US $31	US$54	US$66	US$62
Annual Value of Time Spent Collecting Water as Share of Average Annual Household Income (%)	1	4	6	

Source: HRDS, 1993/94, inflated to 1994/95 levels.

The majority of Tanzanian households do not incur any monetary costs to obtain their domestic water supply. They pay instead with their labor. One of the implications of the current water supply situation is that the majority of Tanzanian households, predominantly women and children, commit a significant share of their human capital resources to the daily task of obtaining small amounts of water for domestic use. Table 8.5 presents estimates of the percentage of households collecting water from outside their dwelling, the average one-way distance from their home to the water source, and the average time spent collecting water per day.

It is in the rural areas, of course, where the burden of water collection is most severe. In rural areas of Tanzania the average household is 1.6 kilometers (one-way) away from its primary water source. Many households are located much farther from their water sources. Women and children from a typical household would make several round trips from their dwelling to the water source every day. An average rural household spends about 3 hours a day collecting water, or more than 1,000 hours per year. The market wage rate for unskilled labor varies significantly in rural Tanzania, from a low of about Tsh 335 per day to Tsh 670 per day in 1994/95. If the time spent collecting water were valued at Tsh 34 (US$0.06) per hour in 1994/95, it would have an annual value of Tsh 38,190 (US$66) per year. This is on the order of 6 percent of the rural household's imputed annual income and about 8 percent of annual cash income.

Interestingly, the collection times for households using public taps and handpumps (improved sources) and households using traditional sources (open wells and unimproved surface water sources) do not appear to be as different as one might expect. For example, the self-reported daily collection times for households using handpumps (3.0 hours per day) are about the same as the collection times for households using open wells (3.3 hours per day) or traditional surface water sources (3.2 hours per day). These data should be interpreted carefully, since households using public taps and handpumps are, on average, closer to their water source than households using traditional sources.

It might at first appear that the large public investments in rural water schemes based on public taps and handpumps had no effect on collection times in rural areas. Such an inference would be incorrect, since the household data refer only to a period of time following significant water-supply investments. We have no information on collection times for households before the improved water systems were installed, and we cannot assume that they would be equal to the collection times of households using traditional sources today[8]. Still, these results do raise an important, unanswered question, namely, have investments in rural water schemes significantly reduced water collection times in rural Tanzania? The data raise legitimate doubts as to whether the impact has been large.

Even in urban areas the amount of time spent collecting water is large. In Dar es Salaam members of a household collecting water from outside the home spend about 1.5 hours a day collecting water (about one-half as much as households in rural areas collecting water from open wells). Over a year, such a household spends over 500 hours collecting water. If this labor were valued at Tsh 34 per hour in 1994/95, the time spent collecting water would have an imputed value of only about Tsh 17,000 per year, or about 1 percent of household income. In other urban areas, more than 70 percent of households collect water from outside the home and the average distance from home to the water source is greater. These households probably spend on average about 2.5 hours per day collecting water. The annual value of time spent collecting water was about Tsh 31,490 (US$55) per household, or about 4 percent of imputed income in 1994/95.

In aggregate, households in Tanzania are spending almost 4 billion hours per year collecting water from outside the home. The current water supply arrangements thus require a large commitment of Tanzania's female labor force to extremely low-value work. Actually, this is somewhat of an underestimate because many households with private connections or buying from vendors must sometimes collect water from outside their home. Even in urban areas, it is estimated that about 750 million hours per year are spent collecting water. If the total time spent annually in Tanzania were valued at Tsh 34 per hour, it would be equal to about Tsh 136 billion (US$237 million), roughly 10 times the combined annual government and donor investment in the water and sanitation sector in 1994/95.

The current daily wages in rural Tanzania (US$0.50-$1.00) are very low by international standards. However, when agricultural wages are US$3-4 per day and water collection times are high, water vending often becomes quite common. These calculations suggest that if real incomes rise in Tanzania and the value of women's time were to increase to, say, US$2.50 per day, there would likely be a huge increase in effective demand for improved water services. Underpinning such cost-effectiveness analysis is the recognition of the health burden incurred by women and children from the weight-bearing activities required for transport of water.

DEMAND FOR IMPROVED WATER SOURCES AND SANITATION FACILITIES

Willingness to Pay for Improved Water Supplies

As is true in many developing countries, information about household demand for improved water services in Tanzania is quite limited. One study of household demand for improved water supplies has been carried out in Newala district in the Mtwara Region. The results indicated that households were willing to pay as much as 10 percent of their cash income for an improved water supply, but that the potential revenues would not be sufficient to pay for operation and maintenance costs of the system, much less capital costs (see Box 8.1). However, the region in which this study was conducted is one of the poorest in Tanzania, with one of the most difficult water supply situations, and is not typical of much

---

[8] Such an assumption would, for example, be unfounded if rural water investments were mostly made in places with the highest water collection times. However, donors have been working in the rural water sector throughout Tanzania, not just in the driest regions. Many donors gave priority within "their" region to villages with high collection times, but other criteria were also used.

of rural Tanzania.

Information from the HRDS offers an important insight into the likely magnitude of household willingness to pay for improved services. The survey shows low levels of water vending in both urban and rural areas, and the percentage of households reporting that they sometimes bought water from distributing vendors. In urban areas, over 10 percent of households report buying water occasionally, and in rural areas, only about 3 percent of households ever buy water.

Households whose primary source is vended water typically paid Tsh 3,350 to 6,700 per month for it in 1994/95. In numerous locations, some households paid as much as Tsh 13,400 per month for

---

Box 8.1: Households' Willingness to Pay for Water

In 1988 a research team from the Institute of Resource Assessment at the University of Dar es Salaam and the University of North Carolina at Chapel Hill conducted a study to determine how much households in one of the poorest areas of southern Tanzania were willing to pay for improved water service from a system of public taps. The study area was served by the Kitangari Water Scheme (also known as the Makonde Water Scheme), a project financed by FINNIDA, UNICEF, ODA, and the Government of Tanzania. When it was operating at capacity, the Kitangari Scheme served 106 villages and about 162,000 people living on the Makonde Plateau. Water for the scheme is obtained from six boreholes in the Kitangari Valley. Diesel fuel is trucked 150 miles over unpaved roads to a pumping station and water treatment plant where it is used to generate electricity to pump water from the valley up to the villages on the Makonde Plateau. The Ministry of Water was responsible for providing the diesel fuel, and when funds from the central treasury were not available, diesel could not be purchased, and the scheme did not operate. When the scheme was not functioning, households walked long distances to poor quality, traditional sources (typically 10 to 15 kilometers away) to obtain water.

The research team conducted 829 interviews in six villages in order to determine: (1) how much households served by the water scheme were willing to pay to keep the system running, and (2) what type of payment mechanism they would prefer. The survey results showed that households in the study area were willing to contribute what, for them, were substantial amounts of cash toward the operation and maintenance of the Kitangari scheme (about 10 percent of cash income). If a system of kiosks were established, and the price were set at Tsh 0.50 per 20-liter bucket (in 1988 US$1= Tsh 98), 89 percent of the respondents said that they would purchase at least some water from the kiosk. If a flat fee of Tsh 25 per household per month were charged for the right to collect water from the public taps, 79 percent of the households stated that they would pay it.

Based on these estimates, the maximum potential revenues from the water system would only be about one-third of the operating and maintenance costs of the Kitangeri scheme, without even accounting for the full costs including capital. The costs of operating and maintaining this water scheme were not particularly high by international standards (on the order of US$1.30 per month per household). The problem was simply that the population served was extremely poor. Almost every household was engaged in subsistence agriculture, and although annual cash household income was difficult to estimate, it was probably about US$50.

The full annual cost of the water scheme (including capital) was probably about US$2.50 per month, per household, or US$30 per year. With annual cash incomes of only US$50, paying US$30 per year for water was clearly unrealistic. However, an improved water system offered households in the study area an important development option: whether to spend approximately 6 months of a woman's time per year collecting water or to spend US$30 for water and apply these six months of labor to other activities that might pay for the costs of the improved water supply, and much more.

If economic development is to occur in this area of Tanzania, a water system that yields a return of six months of a woman's time for US$30 must become a fabulously attractive investment opportunity. From the perspective of an individual household, there are, however, three potentially important obstacles. First, the household may not have access to the credit to pay the initial US$30 to pay for water to get the process started. Second, some households may not perceive clearly the opportunities for using some of the six months of a woman's time savings to generate cash to pay for the water system—or such opportunities may not exist due, for example, to government polices in other sectors. Third, some level of government or institution must offer households the opportunity to make such a choice. In 1994 the Ministry of Water, Energy, and Minerals was actively exploring institutional options for transferring ownership of the Kitangeri Water Scheme to a private company so that households could actually make this choice.

vended water. Such payments provide compelling evidence that these households are willing and able to pay for the time savings and convenience obtained by having water delivered to their dwelling. Because the cost per cubic meter of providing households with water through private connections is much cheaper than service by water vendors, if extensive water vending exists, one can be fairly certain that households are willing to pay for the potentially superior service offered by a reliable piped water supply system. The fact that water vending appears to be so rare in most parts of rural Tanzania suggests that the vast majority of households without private connections in rural areas are not yet willing to make monetary payments of this magnitude for improved water services.

Such evidence on the absence of water vending must be interpreted carefully. The price of vended water sets an upper bound on potential household willingness to pay. We do not, however, know how much they would be willing to pay for a private connection or other levels of improved service. As noted, in urban areas many households are already paying US$1 per month for water from neighbors, and in numerous cities, a substantial minority of households are buying some water from vendors.

High water-collection times are another indicator of high household demand for improved services. The collection times in most parts of rural Tanzania are high by world standards. For many households, when employment opportunities are available in either the formal or informal sectors, the opportunity cost of time spent collecting water may approach the market wage for unskilled labor. Such opportunities for turning time savings into market wages typically translate into high willingness to pay for improved water services. The absence of extensive water vending in rural Tanzania suggests, however, that households' ability to convert time savings resulting from improved water services into financially productive activities is probably quite limited.

Household Demand for Improved Sanitation Services

At current income levels in Tanzania, demand for improved household sanitation is low and will remain so for some time. In a survey carried out in Kurasini, Dar es Salaam, respondents were asked whether they would like a loan to improve their latrines. Not surprisingly, many people asked that the money be made available to improve their houses instead (Mutalemwa, 1994). The rehabilitation or construction of sewerage systems would entail high costs and require large subsidies, the benefits of which would go largely to upper-income groups.

POLICY FRAMEWORK FOR THE SUPPLY OF WATER AND SANITATION SERVICES

Historical Background. In the 1950s, Tanzanian households obtained water at no charge from natural sources (surface water) or purchased it at kiosks, the charges for which were based on volume. The colonial government organized several water cooperatives with pumped and piped schemes in semi-arid regions, in which members paid a flat membership fee and an additional price for each container of water consumed. The best known of these cooperatives, the Makonde Water Development Corporation, sustained itself through these revenues (Mashauri and Katko, 1993).

A policy of "free" water was put into place at the time of Independence and became a hallmark of the ruling party's efforts to provide free social services in rural areas. Starting in 1965, the government was financing all water supply investments, and in 1970 it began to finance the costs of operation and maintenance as well. By 1970, rural water supply systems provided water at no charge to users. Urban water users, on the other hand, could pay vendors for water, or obtain water at no charge from public standposts (Mashauri and Katko, 1993).

It rapidly became apparent that the government would be unable to support the financial burden of constructing, operating, and maintaining the vast water systems required in the rural areas. As early as 1971, the advantages and disadvantages of the free water policy were being debated actively, and technical experts generally agreed that a sustainable policy would have to include some self-financing of water systems (Mashauri and Katko, 1993). However, the government of Tanzania remained committed to the policy and the promise of free water, and sought to obtain other sources of financing for the expansion of safe water supplies. In 1971, the government reinforced its policy of expanding availability of clean water with the launch of an ambitious 20-year water-supply program. The program had the objective of providing the entire rural population with clean, dependable water supplies within a reasonable distance (about 400 meters) from households. The program was followed in 1975 by a water-supply "crash" program intended to supply free, clean water for all by 1981.

From the early 1970s to the mid-1980s, water supply systems expanded rapidly, largely through the development of Regional Water Master Plans (RWMPs). The RWMPs were medium- to long-term sector plans for each region, typically projecting water system construction and the "optimal" domestic and agricultural use of all water resources over a 20-year time horizon. The RWMPs, which included "firm guidelines" for the supply of water, laid out the mix of pump and other technologies to be used (Therkildsen, 1988).

Foreign donors financed the implementation of the RWMPs in 12 regions, at an annual cost of US$0.5 to 1 million. According to Therkildsen (1988), donors provided about 60 percent of the total capital expenditure for rural water sector development from 1973 to 1988. Most of the plans were implemented by foreign firms, often with little involvement of the Regional Water Engineers who were to operate and maintain the systems, or of the communities which were to be served.

As the water sector developed, similar centrally-planned activities were initiated to expand access to sanitary facilities. In 1973, the government introduced the "latrinization" campaign under a program called "Mtu ni Afya." This campaign, which sought to ensure each household a latrine, was given additional impetus after a cholera outbreak in 1977.

While the latrinization campaign appeared to be relatively successful, with latrine coverage in rural areas increasing from 20 to 50 percent between 1973 and 1980, implementation of the RWMPs faltered. Over time, water delivery systems required regular maintenance, spare parts, and operational support. District and regional governments were unable to provide them. Within several years, a large share of the pumps, wells, and other schemes that had been installed were non-operational. In some regions, up to two-thirds of the schemes went out of service. Some systems were started and never completed, leaving communities with partially constructed wells and pumping systems, and no access to safe water.[9]

By the late 1980s (a few years before the end of the 20-year water-supply program), the government, donors, and the rural population itself had become disillusioned with the promise of safe

---

[9] Various sources of data provide conflicting estimates of latrine coverage. The estimate of 50 percent coverage in rural areas by 1980 is on the high side.

water supplies. Instead of launching new water projects, much of the effort in the water sector turned to trying to understand what had gone wrong.

> "The reality ... has been a high level of project failure, and very little impact. The majority of supplies installed are not in use, either because they do not work or they do not meet the real needs of the population. There are many factors involved in the poor success rate in the water sector. The economic crisis has reduced interest in the social sectors at planning levels, and increased difficulties in procuring fuel and spare parts. Other important factors include inappropriate technology choice; the neglect of operation and maintenance aspects; failure to include health education and sanitation improvements; the tendency to plan from above on a large scale with little or no consideration given to local social conditions; the dependency relationship caused by the nature and extent of donor involvement; and the almost complete lack of community involvement, in particular that of women, who are the managers of traditional water sources, and the collectors and users of water in the homes. A major overall problem has been that improvements to water supplies have been treated as purely technical problems, rather than as a process of social change necessarily requiring the full participation of the communities involved." (Andersson, 1989, p. 29)

It is crucial to add to this litany the problem of financing, and the market-distorting signals sent to the consumer by the policy of free water. Not only were members of the community generally excluded from participation in the design and construction of the water systems, except as hired labor or somewhat coerced "volunteers," but they were also asked to contribute little or nothing in cash or in kind to the operation and maintenance of the system. The effect of this policy was to perpetuate a lack of a sense of ownership on the part of system users, a lack of recurrent-cost financing to maintain the operation of the systems, and a continued dependence on external funds for implementation of new schemes.

Current Policy. In 1989, a comprehensive policy document was prepared to guide the water sector. That National Water Policy remains the central policy statement in the sector. The policy, passed by Parliament in 1991, is a very detailed document covering nearly all issues related to the water sector. These include water source protection, flood control and prevention, effective utilization of available water resources, formulation and implementation of water projects, rehabilitation, integration of water, sewage and sanitation projects, cost recovery and cost sharing, water pollution and environmental control, operation and maintenance issues, private sector participation, human resources development, and the creation of an urban water agency.

The policy sets out key elements in the sector, and reflects some of the lessons that were learned from past mistakes. For example, the document highlights the need for community participation in construction, plus cash and in-kind contributions toward operation and maintenance. It seeks to encourage the adoption of low-cost technologies to enhance water coverage.

The policy has been criticized for weaknesses in four main areas. First, there is little attention to the difficult issues of coordination among the many ministries and agencies that often have overlapping roles and responsibilities in the sector (see Box 8.2). Many projects are initiated by one agency and then turned over to Regional Water Engineers for operation and maintenance.

Box 8.2: Agencies Involved in the Water and Sanitation Sector

Several agencies are responsible for aspects of the construction and maintenance of water supplies and sanitation facilities in Tanzania. While the lead ministry is the Ministry of Water, Energy and Minerals, that ministry carries out much of its work in coordination with local government authorities, and with other ministries. The main responsibilities are outlined below.

The **Ministry of Water, Energy and Minerals** operates through regional and district water engineers at the local level. It is charged with policy formation, development of the rural and urban water supplies, construction of drainage works and facilities for safe disposal of waste water in urban areas, environmental hygiene and sanitation interventions in urban areas, development of river basins, water quality control and issuing of water rights, provision of consultancy services for water supplies and waste water disposal, and supervision of parastatals .

The **local government and regional administration under the Prime Minister's Office** is responsible for establishing, providing, maintaining and controlling public water supplies, preventing pollution of water in rivers, streams and water areas, and providing for, regulating, and where needed, prohibiting, the sinking of wells.

The **Ministry of Health** is responsible for rural sanitation and health education.

The **Ministry of Community Development, Women's Affairs and Children** is responsible for the implementation of the Health Through Sanitation and Water (HESAWA) program, funded by SIDA.

The **Ministry of Lands, Housing and Urban Development** implements water schemes under a special services program.

The **National Urban Water Authority** is charged with development, operation and maintenance of urban water supplies on mainland Tanzania. (To date, NUWA operates only in Dar es Salaam, Kibaha and Bagamoyo, though officially its jurisdiction extends to all towns on the mainland.)

Problems with the local government authorities are pronounced. Although the acts that established local governments indicate that many important roles and responsibilities have been delegated from the central to the local level, full delegation generally is lacking. To date, many of the functions thought to have been delegated are still being carried out by the central government. In addition, there are internal contradictions within the various acts that delegate responsibilities. For example, the act establishing that NUWA has the responsibility for operating and maintaining urban water supplies conflicts directly with the act passed in the same year (1982) establishing local governments and spelling out their responsibilities in the sector. Similarly, the Water Utilization Act, as amended in 1981, also contradicts some of the provisions of the Local Government Act.

Second, while the policy recognizes the importance of users' contributions to water systems, it does not lay out a clear and feasible plan for achieving sufficiently high levels of cost recovery for operation and maintenance. This is particularly problematic because the areas with the greatest water deficits are also those with the lowest per capita GDP.

Third, the plan implies large financial outlays from the public sector, with little attention to whether such outlays are possible given the current fiscal constraints facing Tanzania. For example, the 10-year water supply program (1993-2002), based on the National Water Policy, would require an estimated US$523 million (in 1993 prices). This implies that the government would have to devote about 50 percent of its annual development budget to capital outlays for water and sanitation systems during each of the next 10 years. Finally, the policy is silent on important issues such as the priority in allocating water in times of acute drought and the use of treated water for irrigation purposes.

EXPENDITURES IN THE WATER AND SANITATION SECTORS

Government Expenditures

In FY 1995, government expenditures on water and sanitation projects were Tsh 6.8 billion. This represented a decline of 58 percent in real terms from the previous year. Real declines in support to the water sector are projected to continue. Approved estimated water expenditures in FY 1996 declined by 33 percent from their FY 1995 level. Government water sector expenditures accounted for 0.3 percent of GDP, or about US$40 per capita, in FY 1995.

Donor Expenditures

Donors provide essentially all of the funding for capital investments in the water and sanitation sectors (Table 8.6). Many donor agencies have assisted with the implementation of water and sanitation projects since the government outlined its targets in 1971, including the various development agencies of Sweden, Finland, Denmark, Norway, Canada, Germany, Australia, Japan, and the Netherlands, plus ODA, the World Bank, UNICEF, UNDP, and ADB. Total external support to Tanzania increased from US$607 million in 1986 to US$1,059 million in 1991, an average annual increase of 9 percent. However, in recent years donor support for water and sanitation investments has decreased sharply. External funding for water and sanitation dropped from almost US$50 million in 1989 (5.4 percent of total foreign assistance), to US$2.6 million in fiscal year 1994 (0.3 percent of total foreign assistance). Foreign support for the sector rebounded to US$11 million in fiscal year 1995 (1 percent of total foreign assistance), and is projected to remain at this level through 1996/97.

Table 8.6: Foreign Assistance to Water and Sanitation, 1989-1995 (US$)

Year	Total Foreign Assistance (US$ million)	Foreign Assistance to Water and Sanitation (US$ million)	Water and Sanitation as Share of Total Foreign Assistance (%)
1989	924.0	49.6	5.4
1990	1147.0	30.3	2.6
1991	1081.0	18.5	1.7
FY 1994	972.0	2.6	0.3
FY 1995	984.0	11.0	1.1

Source: Mutalemwa, 1994; World Bank, 1997.

Unit Costs

The unit costs of both urban and rural water supply projects are difficult to estimate from the data available. Most published estimates of unit costs have been underestimated, in part because they have not included the real costs of donor, government administrative, and overhead costs. Table 8.7 presents an attempt by Katko (1987) to synthesize the unit costs of several donors in the rural water sector. Mutalemwa (1994) arrived at similar, very low unit-cost estimates. About the only thing that is clear from these estimates is that the pumped and piped schemes are much more expensive than gravity-fed systems or handpumps.

A recent study presents a much different, and probably more realistic, picture of the costs of providing improved water services in urban Tanzania. These studies indicate that costs per household in urban Tanzania are not cheap compared with other parts of the world and that per household costs vary

Table 8.7: Indicative Cost Data for Externally Supported Rural Water Supply Projects in Tanzania

Donor and Technology	Capital Cost per Capita (Tsh)	Annualized Capital Cost per Capita (Tsh)	Annual per Capita Operation and Maintenance Cost (Tsh)	Year
DANIDA				
Pumped scheme			150	1985
Gravity scheme			10-20	1985
Hand pump well (Iringa)	225			1985
Hand pump well (Ruvuma)	280			1985
Gravity scheme			25	
Hand pump scheme			25	
Gravity scheme	500			1987
FINNIDA				
Pumped pipe scheme (Kingari, Mtwara)	1730	155	50	1987
Pumped pipe scheme (no treatment)	1360	120	50	1987
Hand pump wells (hand dug)	210	15		
Hand pump wells (hand auger)	185	15	25	1987
Hand pump wells (DTH well)	740	55		
Hand pump wells (cable tool well)	360	27		
NORAD				
Gravity scheme			15	
Hand pump well			30-40	
TCRS				
Hand pump well	17.5			1987

Source: Mutalemwa, 1994

significantly from one town to another. Cost estimates for most towns appear to be on the order of US$10-15 per household per month. Costs in Mwanza are estimated at US$5 per household per month, while those in Morogoro would exceed US$20 per household per month.

Cost Recovery and Water and Sanitation Tariffs

Urban Water Supply. The central government retains its role as the financier of urban water supply projects through the development budget. Although the water policy calls for full cost recovery, in reality, the process of water tariff-setting and approval is lengthy, arduous, and painful. Until September 1992, for example, all proposals for increases in water tariffs had to be approved by the Ministry of Water, Energy and Minerals, after which the proposal was forwarded to the Cabinet for final approval.

In 1992, a slightly less cumbersome, but still centralized and standardized, process was developed. The National Urban Water Authority Board of Directors can revise water tariffs by a maximum of 15 percent every six months[10]. Larger increases require ministerial-level approval.

Tariffs have been revised only three times since 1980 (see Table 8.8). However, the revisions between 1992 and 1993 were very small. For example, the increase in charges per 1,000 gallons for domestic users was from Tsh 100 to 120 during that period. Not only is the tariff low, but many households never pay their water bills. Collections have consistently fallen far below actual recurrent costs.

Table 8.8: Charges for Water in Urban Areas, 1980-1993 (Tsh per 1,000 gallons)

Type of Customer	Water Charge (Tsh per 1,000 gallons)			
	1980	1988	1992	1993
Domestic	4.5	57.2	100	120
Institutional	–	–	160	190
Commercial	13.5	192	330	380
Industrial and Irrigation	–	248	420	485

Source: Mutalemwa, 1994.

The end result of the "tariff adjustment process" and "full cost recovery policy" is that the residents of Dar es Salaam and other urban areas enjoy some of the cheapest, most heavily subsidized water in the world.

Urban Sanitation. Before 1988, households connected to sewer lines did not pay for this service. In 1988, monthly household sewer fees were established (see Table 8.9), but there is widespread non-payment of these charges.

Table 8.9: Charges for Sewage Services in Urban Areas, 1994 (Tsh)

Type of Customer	Charges
Domestic	300 per Month
Commercial	1225 per Month
Major Commercial	14.6 per Cubic Meter
Institutions	14.6 per Cubic Meter
Industrial	114.6 per Cubic Meter

Source: Mutalemwa, 1994.

Rural Water Supply. According to the 1991 National Water Policy, the economic base of the rural population is weak, so cost-sharing (rather than cost-recovery) is the strategy that has been adopted. In concept, water consumers in rural areas contribute both to capital costs, and operation and maintenance of the water schemes.

To institutionalize community contributions, several donors and the central government have adopted a more participatory approach for new water supply projects. This approach supports the establishment of water and sanitation committees, and the creation of a special water account into which villagers make contributions. The primary objective is to enable villagers to use resources available to them to construct, operate, and maintain their own village water projects. Beneficiaries can make cash or in-kind contributions. Villagers are also asked to take part in the operation and maintenance of the systems. To date, there is insufficient experience with such efforts to know the extent to which cost-sharing in the rural areas will work.

---

[10] Typically, the costs of inputs to water systems have increased more rapidly than this. For example, electricity costs (accounting for about 70 percent of total NUWA expenditures) increased from Tsh 60 million per month in September 1992 to Tsh 103 million per month in March 1993, and then to Tsh 260 million per month in July 1993. This is an overall increase of 333 percent in a span of nine months.

DISTRIBUTION OF BENEFITS

As shown above, the water sector in Tanzania is characterized by full public (government and donor) financing of capital costs and little generation of revenues from users for operation and maintenance. The underlying assumption behind the water tariff structure has been that the rural poor would benefit from a free-water policy. We can examine whether this has, in fact, been the result by examining the distribution of benefits of public spending on capital and operational costs.

The distribution of government spending on water can be calculated using assumptions about the government subsidy for each type of service. Based on information about the current costs of existing systems, it can be estimated that households with a private connection to the public water system receive their water at about US$60 per year below the annual cost of providing service. Evidence indicates that households may be paying about US$1 per month for service that may cost about US$6 per month. Users of non-exclusive public water sources, such as public taps, wells, and neighbors' water connections, were estimated to be receiving a subsidy of about US$25 per year.

The distribution of households receiving these subsidies is shown in Table 8.10. About 60 percent of the expensive private-connection subsidy goes to the richest 20 percent of the population. The subsidy for publicly available water sources is much more evenly distributed. Overall, subsidies are distributed over the population of households in the following pattern: 52 percent of all households receive no subsidy; 36 percent receive an annual subsidy estimated at US$25; and about 12 percent receive an annual subsidy worth US$60.

Table 8.10: Distribution of Subsidies in the Water Sector, by Expenditure Quintile

Subsidy	Lowest 20%	Highest 20%	Total
Households Receiving No Subsidy			
Number of Households	421,026	347,303	2,174,375
Percent	19.36	15.97	100.00
Households Receiving Public Connection Subsidy			
Number of Households	257,827	379,223	1,512,259
Percent	17.05	25.08	100.00
Households Receiving Private Connection Subsidy			
Number of Households	10,420	291,575	484,981
Percent	2.15	60.12	100.00
Total	689,273	1,018,101	4,171,615

Source: HRDS, 1993/94.

Given this distribution, the incidence of government spending on water can be estimated. This is shown in Table 8.11. More than 40 percent of government (and donor) allocations for water services is used by the richest 20 percent of households, with an average subsidy of US$26.50 per household. The bottom 40 percent of households receive about 22 percent of government water spending, with an average subsidy of only about US$10 per year per household.

Table 8.11: Distribution of Public Subsidies by Expenditure Quintile, 1993

Subsidy	Poorest 20% (1)	(2)	(3)	(4)	Richest 20% (5)	Total
Per Household Subsidy (Tsh)	9.8	9.5	12.6	16.6	26.9	15.8
% of Total Subsidy	10.3	11.2	15.4	22.0	41.0	100.0

Source: HRDS 1993/94; World Bank, 1994a.

IMPLEMENTING A DEMAND-SIDE PLANNING STRATEGY: OPTIONS AND FIRST STEPS

The official government program to provide improved water and sanitation for all by the year 2002 is not consistent with the severe financial and other resource constraints facing the sector. In fact, at current government and donor funding levels, it is likely that the proportion of the Tanzanian households with improved water and sanitation coverage will continue to decline as population increases. In the urban areas, there is a wide gap between the current policy requiring full cost recovery from urban water users and the actual water tariffs.

The most important potential source of funds for water and sanitation investments is the Tanzanian household, but the magnitude of effective household monetary demand for improved services is probably low. There is little hope for real progress in the water and sanitation sector without economic pricing in both urban and rural areas. The alternative of heavily subsidized or free water and sanitation has already been tried, and is clearly no longer a feasible policy alternative. A few donors may continue to provide improved water services as a gift to very poor communities, with no prospect that they will be sustainable after donors withdraw. However, it must be recognized by all involved that neither urban nor rural water policy can be predicated on such gift giving or the assumption of large-scale donor funding.

A new "conventional wisdom" is emerging in Tanzania that a demand-side approach to the delivery of water and sanitation service is needed. This new paradigm holds that households should be provided with services that they want, and for which they are willing to pay. Beneficiaries need to be involved in decisions regarding choice of service level, and to understand the cost recovery implications of their choices. Communities need to assume responsibility for operation and maintenance of facilities, and have a sense of ownership in their water system.

Implementation of the new demand-side planning paradigm may mean that water and sanitation investments will not receive top priority. If given a choice, many rural communities in Tanzania could decide to delay investments in water and sanitation and tackle other problems first. Other communities would likely decide to make improved water supplies their top priority.

The World Bank Water Demand Research Team (1993) has proposed a classification scheme of four types of rural water situations in developing countries based on the levels of services that should be provided and how these services should be financed. In Type-I villages, there is high willingness to pay for private connections and low willingness to pay for public taps. In Type-II villages, a few households will pay the full costs of private connections, and the majority will pay the full costs of public taps. In Type-III communities, households are willing to pay for improved service, but the improvements are costly, and full cost recovery is not possible. Type-IV communities are characterized by low household willingness to pay and no possibility of cost recovery.

It is difficult to generalize, but there appear to be large numbers of Type-III and -IV communities in rural Tanzania, and probably some Type-II villages. It is important that the government and the donor community recognize the differences in these three types of communities and structure their limited investments and technical assistance accordingly. Type-II villages are likely to be located in rural areas with higher than average agricultural production and the ability to transport surplus production to regional markets at reasonable costs. On the water supply side, these villages will likely have opportunities to choose between either gravity-fed schemes or electricity-fueled pumping from boreholes. Since many systems have already been built by donors in Type-II communities, initial capital costs may

---

Box 8.3: The East Kilimanjaro Water Supply Project: Transferring Ownership and Control from Central Government to Community Ownership

The East Kilimanjaro Water Supply Project (EKWSP) serves approximately 250,000 people living on the eastern slope of Mt. Kilimanjaro. The 600-square kilometer service area has a cool, tropical climate and high annual rainfall. Many of the households served by the water system are engaged in agricultural activities such as coffee and banana cultivation. Three main water intakes capture high-quality surface water from the protected national forest, and pipes deliver the water to households on the slopes below via a gravity-fed system with over 500 kilometers of pipelines.

The planning and construction of the first phase of the water system began in the late 1950s and 1960s. The second phase was planned in the late 1970s, and construction was completed in 1980. Much of the distribution system is now over thirty years old and in need of repair and maintenance. The project is owned by the Ministry of Water, Energy, and Minerals. Because of the large project area, several district water engineers have been responsible for the operation and maintenance of different parts of the distribution system. As a result, no one was looking at the system from an overall management perspective, and crucial maintenance activities failed to take place. For a 12-year period spanning the late 1970s and 1980s, no one even visited the main water intake, and it suffered serious deterioration.

In 1991, with the help of GTZ, the local communities served by the project recognized that the system was only operating at 50 percent of design capacity. Most households were served by a system of free public taps, but about 2700 households are estimated to have tapped into the system and obtained private connections on their own initiative. Since water was provided free, there was no incentive for anyone to conserve, and lower-lying areas had less reliable water supplies, or no water at all. For many years, the two district water engineers and regional water engineer responsible for the system did not receive the financial resources from the central government to adequately maintain or operate the system, and it became increasingly clear that a new management approach was needed.

In 1991, GTZ began working with the Ministry to create a financially autonomous organization to which the Ministry could transfer ownership of the East Kilimanjaro Water Supply Project. A participatory workshop was organized to discuss the nature of the problems facing communities in the service area, what they wanted from a water system, and strategies for achieving their objectives. The plan that eventually emerged from these discussions and a series of committee meetings was to establish a new organization that would be chartered as a private company (but its charter would not allow it to make a profit). As of spring, 1994, the planning for this company ("Kiliwater") is now well along, but it has not yet been legally established, and final government approval for the transfer of the actual physical assets has not yet taken place.

The plan provides for a General Manager who would handle the management, planning, and administrative functions of the company. This individual would report to a Board of Directors that would consist of six representatives each from six zones, and two district water engineers. The plan is for the company to meter the water entering and leaving 58 separate user areas, and to bill the water committee responsible for each user area for the volume used. Each water committee is responsible for determining how water would be paid for in its user area, supervising tariff collections, paying its water bill, supervising caretakers of the distribution system and taps in its area, and liaising with zonal offices.

Households in the service area are offered the opportunity to purchase one "share" in the company for approximately US$2. This share is similar to a membership fee in a cooperative and allows the household to elect two delegates to represent their user area at the annual meeting. It is envisaged that the company will sell water to the water committees for approximately Tsh 150 per cubic meter. About Tsh 130 per cubic meter is needed to pay for operating and maintenance costs, and Tsh 20 per cubic meter is allocated for capital costs. It is anticipated that without any capacity expansion, the company should sell about 7000 cubic meters per day. This would imply total annual revenues on the order of Tsh 380 million (about US$750,000; or US$20 per household per year). To date, GTZ's financial contribution to the planning and preparation of this project to create Kiliwater has been on the order of 3 million DM.

---

be low, and the possibility exists for financially self-sufficient operations if an appropriate organizational structure can be adopted and good management found. The East Kilimanjaro Water Supply Project is one example of what appears to be a group of Type-II communities served by an existing gravity-fed scheme where financially self-sufficient operation of the water system is feasible (see Box 8.3).

In Type-III communities, there is still substantial revenue potential based on a system of public standposts, but the costs of providing improved water service are greater than the revenues that can be collected. This may be because gravity schemes are not possible, groundwater is beyond the reach of handpumps, and electricity is unavailable. Subsidies would be required to operate such water systems, at least until household incomes rise sufficiently to justify increased charges. Such communities are likely to be found in Mtwara, Shinyanga, and Mara regions. The Makonde Water Scheme in Mtwara is currently serving a population of about 150,000 people living in what would be considered Type-III communities.

It is important to recognize the water supply and development interactions in Type-III villages. Before an improved system is installed, women often walk several hours a day to collect water, and the household is unwilling to pay a sufficiently large portion of its limited cash resources to either purchase water from vendors or pay for the full costs of an improved water system. If a reliable, improved water system in a Type-III village is installed, it is likely to save substantial amounts of women's time. If some of these time savings can be converted to cash through increased labor inputs to agricultural production trading or other market activities, the household is likely to be able to pay for the full costs of the improved water system and still be better off than before the water system was installed.

It is crucial that other government or donor policies not distort the households' choices in Type-III communities so that this "virtuous cycle" of development is aborted. Donors and government must ensure that households in Type-III communities are fully aware that the initial water prices and charges are not sufficient for the long-term sustainability of the water system, and that water prices will have to rise over time as household incomes grow. Agricultural prices need to be high enough to provide strong incentives to households to increase production for market exchange.

In Type-IV communities, it is not feasible to recover the costs of public taps, handpumps, or private connections. In such communities, people are willing to pay very little for improved water supplies, either in absolute terms or as a proportion of income. In such communities, water is often available from nearby traditional sources. When water systems in such communities fail, households do not care much whether they are repaired or not. Tanzania probably has many of these Type-IV villages, especially in areas with high rainfall and plentiful surface-water sources such as in the Kagera, Kigoma, and Rukwa regions.

In the past, water planners have assumed that, if households in Type-IV communities were educated about the health benefits of clean water, they would switch from their traditional sources to an improved source, and they would be willing to pay for low-cost improved services such as handpumps. The experience of Tanzania over the last 25 years suggests that the decisions that households face in Type-IV communities are far more complex than this. When traditional sources are closer than a new improved source, households may go to the traditional source not only because it saves time, but because of the valued social interaction associated with the traditional water collection activities by women and children. Alternatively, the household may decide that the benefits from drugs, increased food supplies, or school fees may be greater than paying for water when traditional sources are already nearby. In such cases, financially viable water systems do not exist, and the appropriate strategy is to wait until such communities are able and willing to pay for improved services.

It is not always easy to distinguish Type-II, -III, and -IV communities from each other because outsiders may know little about the magnitude of household demand for improved water services or the other constraints facing households. Fortunately, the demand-side planning paradigm does not require that central planners or donors determine into which category communities fit. The role of the central government is rather to set up the proper incentives so that local government and the communities themselves can make resource allocation decisions with the full cost implications of all their choices clear to them. In this case, communities will identify themselves as Type-II, -III, or -IV by the decisions they make.

9
THE SOCIAL SECTORS IN ZANZIBAR

Tanzania is a union encompassing Zanzibar (the islands of Unguja and Pemba) and the Tanganyika mainland. The islands are comprised of 5 regions (North Unguja, South Unguja, Urban West, North Pemba and South Pemba), and 10 districts (North A, North B, Central, South, West, Urban, Wete, Michewani, Chake, and Mkoani). Most of Zanzibar's population (70 percent) live in rural areas. According to the 1988 census, the population density of Zanzibar is 275 inhabitants per square kilometer, while mainland Tanzania has only 19 people per square kilometer.

In matters such as defense, Zanzibar and Tanganyika act in concert and share a common central government. In other matters, including the financing and delivery of most social services, Zanzibar has a separate governance and implementation structure. For example, Zanzibar has its own Ministries of Education, Health and Water.

To complement the *Social Sector Review*, which focuses on the mainland, this chapter describes the key features of the health, education, water, and other sectors in Zanzibar. In addition, it presents analyses of the Zanzibar sample of the 1993/94 HRDS. We did not have adequate data to provide an analysis of public education and health expenditures[1]. The chapter is organized by sector, and covers outcomes and use of services, household expenditures, and government financing issues.

EDUCATION

Outcomes and Enrollment

Primary School. Most of the patterns of education participation, attainment, and expenditures seen on the mainland are also found in Zanzibar. Fifteen years following the declaration of universal primary education (UPE), only 68 percent of children age 7-13 are enrolled in school. According to the 1988 population census, the number of children attending primary school should have been 168,729, but only 114,710 were enrolled in the 131 primary schools.

Although there are low enrollment rates, Zanzibar's education system has experienced a rapid increase in both primary- and secondary-school enrollment due to an increased size of the cohorts. In 1990, the annual enrollment growth rate was 4.5 percent (Mosha and Sumra, 1992).

---

[1] We expect public expenditure patterns to be very similar to that of the mainland (with the exception of high-cost expenditures on universities and referral hospitals).

The gross enrollment rate for primary school is about 98 percent, while the net enrollment rate is 69 percent (HRDS, 1993/94). According to the 1992 statistics, the highest primary-school enrollment rate (82 percent) was in the South District, while the lowest rate (41 percent) was in Micheweni.

A pattern of late-start enrollments exists in Zanzibar as on the mainland. According to the HRDS, the most common reason given for late-starts was that 7- and 8-year olds are "too young" to attend school. The peak in attendance is in the very early teenage years. Between the ages of 7 and 9, about 53 percent of children are in school, but between ages 10 and 14, 83 percent are attending. Between ages 15 and 19, attendance falls to 54 percent (HRDS, 1993/94).

Gender Differences. Girls and boys tend to start school at approximately the same age (9.1 and 9.2 years, respectively). Sixty-three percent of females age 7 to 9 are enrolled, while 50 percent of males age 7 to 9 are in school. However, as boys and girls grow older, enrollment rates decrease, particularly among girls. About 56 percent of boys age 15-19 are in school, while only 50 percent of girls in the same age group are attending.

Economic Differences. Children from lower-income households are less likely to be enrolled than are children from better-off households. Among 10- to 14-year olds, 92 percent of children from the richest 20 percent of households are enrolled in school, while only 64 percent of the children from the poorest 20 percent of households attend school. Among 15 to 19 year olds, only 20 percent of children from the lowest-income households are enrolled, while 61 percent of children from the wealthiest households attend school.

Mainland Comparison. According to the HRDS, Zanzibar has higher enrollment rates than the mainland's enrollment rates. For example, of children age 7 to 9 on the mainland, 32 percent were enrolled in school, while in Zanzibar, for the same age group, 53 percent were attending school in 1993/94. A similar pattern exists for children between the ages of 15 and 19.

The self-reported illiteracy rate in Zanzibar is 40 percent (HRDS, 1993/94). Approximately 26 percent of women and 15 percent of men are illiterate. The illiteracy rates in Zanzibar are considerably higher than the mainland's rate of 25 percent.

Secondary School. Enrollment rates are much lower in secondary school than in primary school. The gross enrollment rate for secondary education is 50 percent, while the net enrollment rate is 21 percent (HRDS, 1993/94). Again, the South district had the highest enrollment rate (52 percent), while Micheweni had the lowest enrollment rate (13 percent).

The number of candidates for Form IV increased from 2,455 in 1986 to 3,598 in 1990, while the percent of students selected for Form IV decreased from 17.1 percent to 9.7 percent. In 1990, the transition rate from Form III to Form IV for boys (12.6 percent) was almost twice as high as the transition rate for girls (6.7 percent). Since schools must have a sufficient number of students in order to hold Form IV classes, only 5 of 12 schools were offering Form IV classes in 1991 (Mosha and Sumra, 1992).

Gender Differences. Within those households in the lowest 40 percent of household expenditures, girls make up 30 percent of the small number of students attending government schools. Among the richest 40 percent, girls comprise 62 percent of students attending government schools, but only 14 percent of students attending private secondary schools[2]. Overall, girls make up 49 percent of students attending school, while boys constitute 51 percent (HRDS, 1993/94).

Economic Differences. Better-off households send children to secondary school more often than do poor households. In the HRDS, the rate of current secondary-school attendance was found to be four times greater in the highest 20 percent of the expenditure distribution than in the lowest 20 percent.

Government secondary schools are the main source of secondary schooling, but they tend to serve the better-off households disproportionately. According to the results of the HRDS, of those attending secondary school in 1993/1994, 89 percent attend a government school and 11 percent are enrolled in a private school. Of those attending government secondary schools, only 10 percent come from the poorest 20 percent of the population, while 37 percent are from the richest 20 percent. Of those attending private secondary school, 89 percent come from the top 40 percent of the population, while only 11 percent are from the bottom 40 percent. In addition, almost two-thirds of students come from urban areas, while only one-third of students are from rural areas.

Mainland Comparison. More students attend government secondary schools in Zanzibar than on the mainland. In Zanzibar, a full 88 percent of students in secondary school attended government schools, while on the mainland only 39 percent were enrolled in government secondary schools in 1993/94. That is, 61 percent of secondary students on the mainland attended either private, church-affiliated or community schools. Given the high demand for education and the government's financial constraints, non-governmental schools could play an instrumental role in Zanzibar, as they do on the mainland.

Box 9.1: School Drop-Outs Compared to Parents' Education and Occupation

According to "Absenteeism in Schools in Zanzibar," parents without any formal education were most likely to have children who drop out from school. Almost two-thirds of drop-outs were children of parents with no education. Not surprisingly, as parents' education level increased to Standard VII, the proportion of school drop-outs decreased to 25.4 percent. The proportion declines further to 2.3 percent when one parent's level of education was at least Form IV.

Mothers' education appeared to have more influence on children remaining in school. For example, among households with mothers with no formal education and fathers with at least some formal education, the proportion of school drop-outs was 12 percent. However, when mothers had some primary education and fathers had no formal education, the proportion of drop-out children declined further to 7.3 percent.

The proportion of school drop-outs also varied by parents' occupation. Farmers' children were more likely to drop out of school (at the rate of 63%) than children whose parents worked in the public sector(at the rate of 15%), and fishermen's children (at the rate of 8%). Parents working in the private sector had the lowest proportion of school drop-outs.

Reasons for dropping out included marriage, employment, and the belief that attending school does not guarantee employment. Respondents mentioned that they knew of Forms-III, -IV and -VI leavers who did not have jobs.

---

[2] The estimates presented are based on a small absolute number of girls attending secondary school.

Household Expenditures on Education

Households across Zanzibar spend from 0.4 to 1.4 percent of their total expenditures on education. Nationwide, wealthier households spend a greater percentage of their total expenditures on education than poorer households (0.8 versus 0.6 percent, respectively). However, poorer households in rural areas spend a slightly larger share than do richer households (0.5 and 0.4 percent, respectively). Rural households spend a larger percentage (of smaller household budgets) than urban households.

On average, households spent a total of Tsh 11,786 on children's education in 1993. There is great variation in total expenditures on education across the welfare distribution. Households in the lowest 20 percent of the expenditure distribution spent a total of Tsh 3,363 on education, while those in the highest 20 percent spent almost six times as much, or Tsh 19,915. Households living in urban areas paid considerably more than households living in rural areas in 1993/94 (Tsh 18,179 and 5,535, respectively).

Primary School. In 1993, households spent approximately Tsh 3,391 per pupil in primary school. Rural households spent Tsh 1,792, while urban households spent Tsh 4,976. Not surprisingly, per-pupil expenditures vary across the welfare distribution, with the wealthiest households paying more than 3 times as much per student as the poorest households (Tsh 5,233 and 1,446, respectively)

The three largest expense categories for primary school were uniforms, books and supplies, and contributions and fees, which made up 58, 19, and 10 percent of expenditures, respectively. For the poorest 20 percent, these three categories accounted for 100 percent of spending, but for the richest 20 percent, they accounted for only 85 percent.

Secondary School. Households with children in secondary school spent an average of Tsh 12,324 per student in 1993. Households in the lowest 20 percent of the expenditure distribution spent about Tsh 3,226, while those in the highest 20 percent paid more than five times as much, or Tsh 16,984. Households in rural areas spent about Tsh 6,105, while households in urban areas paid Tsh 16,390. Households with children in private secondary school spent almost twice as much as households with students in government secondary school (Tsh 21,669 versus 12,026)[3]. When comparing expenditures on primary versus secondary education, households spent, on average, three times as much on secondary education than primary.

Mainland Comparison. Zanzibari households with children in school spend substantially less on education than mainland households do. On average, Zanzibari households only spent Tsh 12,324 per secondary student in 1993/94, while mainland households spent Tsh 41,877 per student. This is

> **Box 9.2: How Do Zanzibari Parents Perceive the Quality of Education?**
>
> In the HRDS, respondents were asked for their opinions about various quality-related features of the nearest government primary school. The features included (a) quality of teaching staff, (b) quality of headmaster, (c) adequacy of supplies, (d) state of physical infrastructure, and (e) amount of self-reliance work. Overall, respondents are dissatisfied with several aspects of the educational services. The most obvious shortcoming is in supplies and infrastructure. Three-quarters of respondents stated that the supplies were "poor" or "very poor," and about one-third said that the infrastructure and self-reliance work was "poor" or "very poor." In contrast, almost 90 percent of respondents thought teachers and headmasters were adequate or better. These results mimic those from the mainland survey.

---

[3] There are very few students attending private secondary school. Thus, these figures are presented for illustrative purposes.

primarily due to high boarding costs on the mainland. Very few students in Zanzibar attend boarding schools. Although the differential is smaller, Zanzibari households also spent less on primary school than mainland households did in 1993 (Tsh 3,391 and 3,842 per primary student, respectively). Mainland households spend twice as much on contributions, fees, books, supplies, and tutoring than Zanzibari households do on these same items (HRDS, 1993/94). Households in Zanzibar pay slightly less on uniforms than do mainland families (Tsh 1,220 and 1,544 per student, respectively). Expenditures on uniforms make up the largest share of total primary-school expenditures.

Structure of the Education System

Management and Organization. Zanzibar has a separate Ministry of Education (MOE) and different educational system from the mainland. The MOE is responsible for the development and management of the educational services in the islands. It is divided into seven directorates by levels of education and functions, and has offices in all of the islands' districts.

The provision of education is managed, organized, and administered by the MOE. Until recently, formal primary-school education lasted 8 years. Zanzibar currently provides 7 years of primary education (Standards I-VII) and three years in the first cycle of secondary school (Forms 1-3), which together make up the basic primary-education cycle. For those who qualify, there are a variety of higher secondary and further education opportunities.

The Department of Research and Curriculum Development is responsible for the curriculum at all levels of education. The department is also in charge of in-service training of teachers as well as monitoring and evaluation of the education system. The primary-school curriculum includes arithmetic, Kiswahili, English (from Standard III onward), religious studies, and environmental study. Lower-secondary education (O level) streams include science bias, arts bias, technology bias, and Islam. In 1994, a commercial stream was introduced.

Examinations and Types of Schools. In many schools, primary and lower-secondary classes are provided in the same school, and some teachers conduct both primary- and secondary-level classes. Of 165 education institutions in Zanzibar, there are 62 exclusively primary schools (Standards I-VII), 69 schools with both primary and lower-secondary levels (Standard I through Form III), 1 primary/secondary school, 10 secondary schools, and 5 post-secondary schools.

At the end of Standard III and VI, students are required to take an examination. Students performing below standard must repeat the year. However, after repeating the year, they are automatically promoted. Recognizing that many students drop out instead of repeating, the Ministry has subsequently decided to discontinue the practice of asking students to repeat the year, and now allows them to continue. Students who perform well in primary school are selected to pursue specialized subjects in biased secondary schools.

At the conclusion of Form III, students sit for an examination, and those who pass are admitted to Form IV. At the end of Form IV students sit for the Tanzania National Examinations. Successful candidates may continue to higher-secondary education (Forms V and VI) institutions, either Lumumba School in Zanzibar, or Fidel Castro in Pemba. Those who pass Form IV examinations also may attend the technical education institutions, including Mikunguni Technical Secondary School and the Karume Technical College. Graduates from Mikunguni continue with their course work at Karume and earn full

Technician Certificates in civil engineering, mechanical engineering, electrical engineering, automotive engineering, or telecommunications. The total enrollment at Karume College in 1993 was 126 students. Alternatively, students who successfully complete Form IV may enroll at the Nkrumah Teacher Training College, The Institute of Kiswahili and Foreign Languages, or in the certificate teachers' course at the Islamic School.

Those who successfully finish Form VI and pass their A-level examination continue their further education at universities on the mainland, outside the country, or in the diploma course at the Nkrumah Teacher Training College. Only 108 students completed Form VI in 1990.

<u>Teachers and Other Education Inputs</u>. Teachers in Zanzibar are employed under normal government procedures. Apart from a salary differential, the conditions and benefits of employment adhere to standard government regulations. In 1993/94, there were 4,372 teachers, 2,084 of which were female and 2,288 male.

Teacher education is offered in three institutions. These institutions accommodate 3 grades of teachers: (a) diploma teachers, who have a Form VI education level and two years training; (b) Grade A teachers, who have a Form IV education level with two years training; and (c) Grade B teachers, who have a Form III education level with one year of training.

To cope with the massive enrollment increase in the late 1960s and early 1970s, the MOE had to overlook most quality-related teacher employment criteria. A number of failed Form III and Form IV school leavers were employed and deployed to schools without teacher training or a briefing course. By 1978, there were more untrained teachers than trained ones. However, a concerted training effort decreased the number of untrained teachers from 59 percent in 1978 to 28 percent in 1993.

More than one-half of the students at Nkrumah College are in-service students, and there are several indications that in-service training will remain the main mode of teacher training in Zanzibar. There are more than 20 categories of teachers with various academic backgrounds. According to one study, only 36 percent of the teaching force has both the education and skills to teach effectively (Mosha and Sumra, 1992).

The demand for lower-secondary teachers has deprived the primary level of an adequate number of trained teachers. Due to remuneration benefits, primary-school teachers tend to upgrade themselves by earning a diploma, which results in a transfer to a secondary school. There are few incentives to remain teaching at the primary level. The present system of withdrawing teachers for 1-2 years of in-service training further decreases the current supply of teachers.

In the past, many teachers left due to poor working conditions and low monthly wage (which ranged from Tsh 3,790 to Tsh 9,655 in 1993/94). The government, in turn, recruited unqualified individuals to teach. In order to prevent this practice, it is necessary to improve teachers' working and living conditions and to increase their wages.

Many schools were built in rural areas after the 1964 revolution, and further expansion occurred in 1978 when UPE was declared. In order to achieve UPE, communities erected temporary buildings, and these continue to be used today. These buildings have not been properly constructed and maintained. Most schools, especially in the rural areas, lack basic amenities, like water, lavatories, electricity, and furniture. According to the 1992 statistics, only one-quarter of school classrooms had furniture. In 1990, most classrooms were overcrowded, with an average class size of 40 children (Mosha and Sumra, 1992).

Zanzibar's rapid increase in primary- and secondary-school enrollment has not been met by a corresponding expansion in school facilities. Increased enrollment has been accommodated by having double and, in some cases, triple sessions. The average annual growth rate of classrooms was 0.29, while the average annual growth rate of class streams was 3.44. The number of streams per classroom has increased from 1.52 in 1986 to 1.72 in 1991 (Mosha and Sumra, 1992).

School committees have been established in all schools. In some schools where the committees have been active and have supported the head of the school, a number of minor changes have occurred, such as repairs of the building and involvement in academic activities.

Cost-Sharing in the Education System

Education in Zanzibar is financed partly by the government, external donors, and as we know from the HRDS, by households. Recently, cost-sharing mechanisms to supplement Ministry funds have been introduced. All newly registered students, as well as those registering for Zanzibar examinations, pay a fee of Tsh 200. Parents also contribute by purchasing uniforms, text books, and other school supplies, and by providing free labor to construct classrooms. In addition, the Ministry used to provide (free of charge) school supplies, such as rulers, to students at some schools. Currently, they charge a lower-than-market price for such supplies. Furthermore, teachers who are selected for in-service training are required to pay for their transportation costs to the college.

Textbooks and other reference materials, especially for secondary schools, are scarce. Donor financing from SIDA, ODA, and DANIDA is improving the situation. Nevertheless, there is demand for 5.3 million books, while the government, with SIDA's assistance, provided only approximately 1.5 million textbooks in 1993/94.

Changes in the economic situation, coupled with the great expansion of the education system, have financially strained the education budget. In 1988, 11.9 percent of the total budget was spent on education. In 1993, this figure decreased to 10 percent. In an effort to improve the quality of education, the government decided that the education budget should be raised from 10 percent to 20 percent in 1995/96.

HEALTH

Outcomes

Infant and Child/Maternal Mortality. Despite considerable efforts made by several health initiatives, the infant mortality rate (IMR) and the mortality rate for children under five are still quite high. In 1988/89, infant mortality rates were estimated to be 130 per 1000 live births. However, in 1992 the IMR decreased to 100 per 1,000 live births. Over the period of 1985 to 1989, the mortality for children under five decreased from 210 to 165 per 1,000.

Infant and child mortality in Zanzibar is higher than in mainland Tanzania (see Table 9.1).

The overall maternal mortality ratio is 314 deaths per 100,000 live births. The overall risk of dying from delivery is high. On average, the risk of death from maternal causes during the reproductive life-span is 1 in 40 (Garssen, 1992).

Table 9.1: Infant and Child Mortality Rates, 1994

	Infant Mortality per 1000 live Births, 1992	Child Mortality
Mainland	92	141
Zanzibar	100	165

Source: World Bank, 1994c; Garssen, 1992.

Infectious Diseases. Several studies indicate that most of the major health problems of infants, young children, and other vulnerable groups in Zanzibar are preventable. Major diseases affecting the population include malaria, schistosomiasis, intestinal parasites, and diarrhoeal diseases. According to the Household Survey on Diarrhoeal Diseases, Acute Respiratory Infections and Breastfeeding, malaria accounted for 38 percent of all hospital deaths, pneumonia accounted for approximately 10 percent, and diarrhoea accounted for about 4 percent (Jansen, 1992). Furthermore, malaria comprised 35 percent of all hospital diagnoses, pneumonia 7 percent, anaemia 6 percent, and diarrhoea and dysentery 4 percent. In 1991, 356 cases of HIV had been identified, of whom 228 had AIDS.

Utilization[4]

Twenty-eight percent of Zanzibaris indicated that they experienced an illness or injury during the month before the 1993/94 HRDS survey. Forty percent of the wealthiest households reported being ill, while only 13 percent of the poorest households reported being ill. Furthermore, those in the wealthiest 20 percent of households were about 40 percent more likely to seek care than those in the poorest 20 percent.

As in mainland Tanzania, women were slightly more likely than men to report that they had been sick (29 versus 26 percent, respectively). Sixty percent of both women and men who reported being ill sought care and used health services. However, only reporting of illness is shown, and not necessarily incidence of illness or injury. There is reason to believe that women have higher levels of morbidity due to malnutrition. Women are more likely than men to suffer from malnutrition because they have higher energy requirements as a result of heavy workloads. One study showed that many women in rural areas work 14 hours a day, 7 days a week. Their tasks included collection of firewood and water, agricultural production, and home and child care. In urban areas, women worked in the informal sector in order to contribute to household income. In the main, they performed labor-intensive activities requiring high levels of energy.

The high malnutrition rates in Zanzibar and on the mainland are compounded by high fertility. This leaves women particularly vulnerable to health problems associated with pregnancy, labor, and delivery.

Choice of Provider. Overall, three-quarters of those who sought care in Zanzibar went first to a government provider. All of those in the poorest 20 percent of households and 69 percent of those in the

---

[4] The information in this and the next section on expenditures come from the HRDS conducted in Zanzibar in June, 1994. Most of the results are quite close to the overall average from the mainland survey.

richest 20 percent of households sought care at a government facility. Thirty-one percent of sick individuals in the richest 20 percent of households sought care at a private health facility.

For in- and outpatient care[5], individuals in the poorest 20 percent of households only used government facilities, primarily dispensaries. Those in the richest 20 percent of households sought care at government dispensaries and hospitals, and private dispensaries. Those in the richest group were one-half as likely to seek care at a government dispensary as those in the poorest group (32 percent and 62 percent, respectively). Those in the richest 20 percent of households were slightly more likely than those in the poorest group to seek care at a government hospital (22 versus 19 percent), while those in the poorest group were more likely than those in the richest group to seek care at a government health center (19 and 15 percent, respectively).

The wealthier households consume a larger relative share of all services than do the poor. Overall, households in the top 40 percent of the welfare distribution used health services twice as often as those in the bottom 40 percent (52 and 25 percent, respectively). The services of the for-profit private sector were used solely by the richest 20 percent of households.

Mainland Comparison. According to the HRDS, a higher percentage of Zanzibaris reported being ill or injured in the last month than mainland individuals in 1993. Furthermore, sick people in Zanzibar used government health facilities more than sick people on the mainland. Of those who reported being ill or injured in Zanzibar, 78 percent sought care at government health facilities, while of mainland individuals who sought care, only 59 percent went to a government facility. Higher use of government facilities is due to the small number of NGO and private health facilities in Zanzibar.

Household Expenditures on Health Care

Households in Zanzibar spent about Tsh 10,787 per year on health services in 1993, comprising 1.2 percent of total expenditures. Rural households spent approximately Tsh 4,917 annually, while households in urban areas paid almost four times that amount (Tsh 18,189). Health spending comprised over three times as much of total expenditures in better-off households than in poor households (1.6 versus 0.5 percent, respectively).

On average, Zanzibaris spent Tsh 730 per short illness episode when health care was sought in 1993. Overall, urban households spent more for care than rural households (Tsh 1,118 and 378, respectively). Urban households paid considerably more for care at a dispensary than rural households (Tsh 1,493 and 484, respectively). Rural households were more likely to seek care at health centers, while only a tiny number of urban households sought care at health centers and did not incur any expenditures. Urban households were more likely to seek care at a hospital, while very few rural households sought care at hospitals.

Only sick individuals in the top 40 percent of the expenditure distribution sought care at nongovernmental dispensaries. These individuals paid almost fifteen times as much as those in the same

---

[5] Due to the small number of sick individuals who received inpatient care, our analysis combines in- and out-patient services.

income group who sought care at government dispensaries.[6]

As on the mainland, the poorest households, who also tend to be in rural areas, spent relatively little for the government services nearest to them. Better-off households spent more per visit, in part because they were more likely to use non-governmental services. For the poorest households, the only costs incurred were transportation costs (Tsh 52). For the richest households, transportation costs only accounted for 10 percent of expenditures, while visit costs accounted for 23 percent, and drug costs accounted for 64 percent.

Mainland Comparison. Sick individuals in Zanzibar spent one-third less per illness episode than did mainland individuals. Zanzibaris spent almost one-half to two-thirds less on facility visits and transportation costs as those on the mainland (see Table 9.2).

Table 9.2: Expenditures per Illness Episode, 1993 (Tsh)

	Visits	Transportation	Drugs	Total Expenditures
Zanzibar	120	135	474	730
Mainland	209	331	578	1,118

Source: HRDS, 1993/94.

Structure of the Health Care System

The organization of Zanzibar's health care system is similar to that of the mainland. There are four types of medical facilities serving the islands in a pyramidal organizational structure. At the first level there were 116 primary health care units/dispensaries (PHCU) in 1994. PHCUs are similar to dispensaries on the mainland, and provide services at the community level. The average population per dispensary is about 5,000. Approximately ninety percent of all Zanzibari live within 5 km of a health unit. Four to five health workers, headed by a nurse or a medical assistant, provide a comprehensive package of preventive and curative services. Outreach activities, such as MCH and EPI, are also provided at this level. Unfortunately, about 60 percent of the dispensaries are in poor condition, and others are approaching a stage of irreparable damage. Many lack water, transport services, electricity and telephones. Box 9.3 reviews clients' perceptions of these facilities.

At the intermediate level in 1994 there were four 30-bed Primary Health Care Centers (PHCC or cottage hospitals), which are similar to health centers on the mainland. There are two in each of the rural areas of Unguja and Pemba. They provide more extensive medical treatment than is available at dispensaries. These centers provide an intermediate level for referral cases from PHCUs, particularly in areas far from the main town. However, due to their well-stocked drug supply, and the presence of medical assistants, people travel considerable distances to receive their first consultations at these facilities.

There are four general hospitals and five specialist hospitals that deal with leprosy, maternity, mental health, and TB. The hospital in Zanzibar Town acts as the referral hospital for specialized care for the two islands.

According to the HRDS, in 1993/94 the government provided approximately 78 percent of all

---

[6] Expenditure estimates for the private health facilities are based on a small number of observations. The data are presented for illustrative purposes.

health services, while the private sector provided only 21 percent. Non-governmental organizations in Zanzibar do not play the important role they do on the mainland. Only five NGO facilities, which charge user fees, are known to exist. In addition, there are no village health workers in Zanzibar.

While health services in the public sector are currently provided primarily free of charge, as on the mainland, some user fees for certain services have been incorporated. The restriction of the right to private practice has recently been liberalized. However, there is strict government regulation of private and voluntary medical services on the islands.

FAMILY PLANNING

In the past there have been high fertility rates, as shown in the young age structure in Zanzibar.[7] This suggests a dramatic increase in the size of the population in the most highly reproductive age groups over the next decade. According to the HRDS, 18.3 percent of the population were below age 5, and 29 percent of the population between the ages of 5 and 15 years old in 1993/94. Thus, 47 percent of the population was less than 15 years old at that time. If the total population continues to grow at the current rate of 3 percent per year, the population will double by the year 2017.

> **Box 9.3: How Do Zanzibaris Perceive the Quality of the Health System?**
>
> In the HRDS, respondents were asked about the quality of the government dispensaries or health centers located nearest to their dwelling. They were asked about the drug availability, the trustworthiness and qualifications of doctors and nurses, the distance from their home to the facility, the cleanliness of the health clinic, and the personnel who help with community-wide interventions.
>
> Respondents were most dissatisfied with the lack of availability of drugs, just as on the mainland. About 56 percent indicated that the drug availability in the government facilities was "very poor" or "poor," while only 10 percent thought the availability was "good" or "very good."
>
> Over forty percent of consumers were satisfied with the proximity of the facility to home, the qualifications of the doctors and nurses, and the cleanliness of the facility.

Total fertility rates in Zanzibar have declined slowly. Comparing the 1978 census and UNICEF and UNFPA 1988 and 1992 surveys, fertility appears to have declined at a rate of 0.5 percent per year (Garssen, 1992). The TFR was estimated at 8.6 in 1978, 8.2 in 1988, and 8.0 in 1992[8].

High fertility rates, young childbearing, and close birth spacing have detrimental effects on the health of women and children in Zanzibar. According to a study in Pemba, about 6 percent of women age 14, and 19 percent of women age 16, experienced their first pregnancy (TKAP, 1991)[9]. In addition, among women aged 31 to 40 years, 15.1 percent had 10-12 deliveries, while among women aged 40 and over, 26 percent experienced 10-12 deliveries. In addition, approximately 26.5 percent of all births occurred less than 24 months after the previous birth (TDHS, 1991/92).

Utilization. In April 1993, 98 MCH/FP clinics were in operation (MOH, 1993). According to

---

[7] In the family planning section, we used the 1991/1992 TDHS where possible. However, due to the small number of observations in the Zanzibar sample of the TDHS, we could not always reference it. Thus, other sources were included, such as the HRDS 1993/94, and the 1992 UNICEF survey.

[8] According to the TDHS 1991/92, the total fertility rate was 6.4 children per woman. However, this rate should not be compared to the rates from the 1978 census and the UNICEF and UNFPA surveys.

[9] All estimates from the TKAP study should not be compared to the TDHS 1991/92 data. They are presented for illustrative purposes.

the TDHS 1991/92, health workers were available to provide family planning services to 69 percent of the women in Zanzibar. Over 83 percent of women lived within 5 km of a facility providing family planning services.

As on the mainland, use of modern contraception is very low in Zanzibar and is increasing slowly. Only 17 percent of reproductive-age women in Zanzibar reported that they have used any method of birth control at some time (MOH, 1993).

However, according to the TDHS, only 7 percent of currently married reproductive-age women are currently using a modern method of birth control. Forty-one percent of those use birth control pills, 21 percent avail themselves of sterilization, and 15 percent receive injections. The remaining women are using IUDs and condoms (TDHS, 1991/92).

According to one study, urban and rural differences are striking. Only three percent of reproductive-age women in rural Unguja, and 3.6 percent of reproductive-age women in rural Pemba, are currently using family planning (Garssen, 1992). In Zanzibar Town, the rate of family planning users is 15.5 percent of reproductive-age women.

According to the TDHS 1991/92, almost one-third of currently married women wish to delay their next birth by one or two years, and another 15 percent wish to have no more children. In other words, a total of 45 percent of married women are considered to be potentially "in need" of family planning. Of these women, about 16 percent use a modern contraceptive method, leaving 84 percent of the "women in need" (or 38 percent of all currently married women), at potential risk of having an unwanted or mistimed pregnancy.

Choice of Provider. According to the HRDS, 95 percent of modern contraceptive users obtained birth control supplies from government facilities in 1993/94. Government hospitals and health clinics were the main providers of these services (37 and 41 percent, respectively). Nurses supplied methods and provided counseling to three-quarters of the women using modern methods.

Use of Antenatal Care. Approximately 99 percent of all pregnancies received antenatal care from a medical professional (TDHS, 1991/92). Care was provided most often by a trained nurse/midwife (64 percent) or a maternal and child health care aide (33 percent), while doctors only provided a small proportion of all antenatal care services (2 percent).

Place of Delivery. Approximately one-quarter of the births taking place in 1992/93 took place in government hospitals, 2 percent occurred in government health centers, and the rest were delivered in the home. Place of residence and education were correlated with place of delivery. Among urban women, 51 percent of deliveries took place in hospitals, while among rural women, only 14 percent did. Among women with at least some secondary education, 34 percent of deliveries occurred in a hospital, while among women with no education, only 12 percent did (HRDS, 1993/94).

Expenditures. The majority of women using contraceptives and receiving antenatal care did not incur expenditures. Of the very few who had expenditures, transportation made up 100 percent of total expenditures for family planning, and 90 percent of total expenditures for antenatal care (HRDS, 1993/94).

One-half of the women incurred expenditures for delivery services. Women spent, on average, Tsh 800 for delivery services in 1993. Transportation costs constituted 38 percent of total expenditures, while visits made up 38 percent and drugs comprised 23 percent.

Knowledge and Attitudes. About 96 percent of all reproductive-age women in Zanzibar indicated that they knew of at least one modern method to limit or space births. According to the TKAP study in Pemba, oral contraceptives (used by 69 percent of reproductive-age women) were the best known method, while injections were the next most commonly known method (37 percent). Approximately 16 percent of women knew about the IUD, and 16 percent were familiar with condoms. Only 3 percent of women were familiar with female sterilization. Knowledge about contraceptive sources was also high. About 93 percent of reproductive-age women knew where they could obtain a modern contraceptive method (TDHS, 1991/92).

Almost three-quarters of women thought that family planning messages on mass media were acceptable, and about the same figure (70 percent) of currently married, non-sterilized women said that they approved of family planning. A full fifty-one percent of the women believed that their husband disapproved of family planning.

Women's desired family size was clearly correlated with their education. Women between the ages of 15 and 29 with no formal education said that they wanted an average of 7.4 children. Women in the same age group with a primary education reported that they preferred an average of 6.1 children, while women with at least some secondary education wished to have an average of 5.5 children (Garssen, 1992). Since 1988, there has been a general decrease in the number of desired children borne by women who had at least some secondary education.

Mainland Comparison. The differential in desired family size with respect to education is much smaller in Zanzibar than on the mainland. Women on the mainland with no education reported that they preferred an average of 7.3 children, while women with at least some secondary education wished to have only an average of 4.3 children.

The effects of female education on contraceptive use, IMR, and place of birth delivery are more striking on the mainland. For example, according to the HRDS, among Zanzibari women with no education, only 1 percent currently use a modern method of birth control. Among those women with at least some secondary education, 13 percent were using a modern method[10]. On the mainland, only 6 percent of women with no education were using a modern contraceptive method. However, 31 percent of women with at least some secondary schooling were using a modern method (TDHS, 1991/92).

Overall, there is greater contraceptive use on the mainland than in Zanzibar. About 13 percent of currently married reproductive-age women on the mainland use a modern method of birth control, while only 7 percent of currently married reproductive-age women do in Zanzibar. Both men and women in Zanzibar are more likely to disapprove of family planning than their counterparts on the mainland (18 and 7 percent, respectively) (TDHS, 1991/92).

---

[10] Due to the small number of women in Zanzibar using modern methods of contraception, the data is presented for illustrative purposes only.

NUTRITION

Child Nutritional Status. According to the TDHS 1991/92, among children under five years of age, 40 percent of children were moderately malnourished weight-for-age (also referred to as "under-weight"), 48 percent height-for-age (also known as "stunted"), and 11 percent weight-for-height (also referred to as "wasted"). The prevalence of under-weight children has decreased from 51 percent in 1990 to approximately 40 percent in 1993 (Khatib, 1994). Thus, there is some indication of improvement in the nutritional status of children. As on the mainland, Zanzibar's main child-nutrition problem appears to be stunting from longer-term, chronic undernutrition rather than wasting from short-term acute food deficits.

Child malnutrition indicators show that the health status of children in Zanzibar is worse than that of their counterparts on the mainland. There is a higher percentage of underweight children in Zanzibar than on the mainland (40 and 29 percent, respectively). The incidence of moderate wasting in Zanzibar is almost twice as high as the incidence on the mainland. Furthermore, only the incidence of underweight children in Mtwara region (48 percent) is higher than in Zanzibar.

Table 9.3: Indicators of Undernutrition, 1991/92 (figures refer to % of children under 5 years of age who are moderately malnourished)

	Stunting	*Wasting*	*Underweight*
Zanzibar	47.9	11.0	39.9
Mainland	46.7	5.6	28.8

Source: TDHS, 1991/92.

Maternal Nutritional Status. A measure of maternal nutritional status is the prevalence of low birth weights, or the proportion of infants born with a weight under 2500 grams. High incidence of low birth weight babies was most common among women less than 20 years of age (9.8 percent). Overall, the incidence of low birth weight babies was 6.9 percent (MOH, Nutrition Unit 1993).[11]

The TDHS obtained information on the anthropometric indicators of mothers. These data showed that 6 percent of Zanzibari mothers were shorter than 145 cm and 12 percent had a mean BMI of less than 18.5 percent, indicating that they were likely to be malnourished.

The underlying causes of undernourishment in Zanzibar and on the mainland are heavy workloads, inadequate food consumption, low levels of education, short intervals of birth spacing, and nutrient depletion due to nurturing.

Breastfeeding. Breastfeeding is almost universal in Zanzibar, with about 99 percent of children under 5 being breastfed at least for a short period. Among last-born children, only 61 percent were breastfed within one hour of birth, and 97 percent were breastfed within one day of birth. The mean duration of breastfeeding is 21.2 months.

Although there is almost universal breastfeeding, infants are rarely exclusively breastfed in Zanzibar. However, the average duration of full breastfeeding is only 0.4 months (TDHS 1991/92). According to one study, the rate of exclusive breastfeeding was only 5 percent of children age 0 to 3 months, and another 38 percent of children in this age group were predominately breastfed (Jansen,

---

[11] The low birth weight figures are not comparable to the mainland birth weight estimates from the TDHS 1991/92.

1992). Another study conducted in North A and Micheweni districts indicated that one-half of infants aged 2 to 3 months were receiving supplementary foods (Khatib, 1994). This is dangerous because receiving these foods at such an early age carries considerable risk of infection, particularly diarrhea. In short, breastfeeding practices in Zanzibar share the same problems as on the mainland. Solid supplements are introduced too early, and supplementary foods are low in energy and inappropriate.

WATER AND SANITATION

Utilization of Improved Water Sources and Sanitation Facilities

Over one-half of households in Zanzibar use an improved source of water (i.e. a private water connection inside their home or yard, or a well with a pump or a public tap). There are large variations by urban and rural areas. The majority (86 percent) of households living in urban areas use an improved source of water, while only 30 percent of households in rural areas do (see Table 9.4). Approximately 9 percent of households living in urban areas of Zanzibar collect water from neighboring households, while only 4 percent collect water from open wells[12]. For households living in rural areas, a full 70 percent collect water from open wells. Virtually no households rely on water vendors, tanker trucks, or surface water as their primary source.

Table 9.4: Household Water Source by Residence (%)

Type of Water Source	Urban	Rural	All
Improved Source of Water	86.0	30.3	55.1
Open Well	4.1	69.7	40.5
Neighbor	8.9	0.0	4.0
Water Vendor, Tanker Truck, Surface Water	0.0	0.0	0.0
Total	100	100	100

Source: HRDS, 1993/94.

Table 9.5 shows where households from different expenditure groups obtain their water. As expected, households in the highest expenditure quintile are much more likely to use an improved source of water, while those in the lowest expenditure quintile are more likely to depend on open wells as their primary source.

Table 9.5: Household Water Source, by Expenditure Quintile (%)

Water Source	Lowest 20%	Highest 20%	All
Improved Source of Water	28.0	75.0	55.1
Open Well	69.6	18.1	40.5
Neighbor	2.4	5.3	3.9
Water Vendor, Tanker Truck, Surface Water	0.0	0.0	0.0
Total	100	100	100

Source: HRDS, 1993/94.

Zanzibari households used private connections more than mainland households did in 1993/94 (42 versus 11 percent). Furthermore, approximately 50 percent of mainland households, as compared to about 40 percent of Zanzibari households, relied primarily on unimproved sources of water (open wells and surface water) (HRDS, 1993/94).

---

[12] Estimates on households collecting water from neighboring households and wells without pumps in urban areas are based on a small number of observations.

Sanitation Facilities.
According to the HRDS, approximately 30 percent of the Zanzibari population (primarily in rural areas) has no sanitation facility. The traditional pit latrine is the most common form of sanitation system in both urban and rural areas. About 61 percent of urban households, and 50 percent of rural households, use a pit latrine. A full 35 percent of urban households use flush toilets, while no households in rural areas do (see Table 9.6). Ninety-two percent of mainland households rely on pit latrines, and only 5.3 percent do not have a sanitation facility.

Table 9.6: Type of Sanitation Facility, by Residence (%)

Sanitation Facility	Urban	Rural	All
Own or Shared Flush Facility	34.8	0.0	15.7
Traditional Pit Latrine	60.8	49.5	54.5
No Facility, Bush, Pan, Bucket	4.4[a]	50.5	29.8
Total	100	100	100

[a] estimate based on very few observations.
Source: HRDS, 93/94.

Water Tariffs

Prior to independence, and for nearly two decades after independence, water charges of Tsh 3 to 4.5 were collected in Zanzibar. Rates charged in the years just following independence were adequate to cover all recurrent costs. In 1980, the Government of Zanzibar abolished domestic charges and took full responsibility for provision of water. The deterioration of water services occurred recently and coincided with the removal of water charges.

If user fees had been charged, the unit price should have been approximately Tsh 200 per cubic meter in 1990 (FINNIDA, 1991). At present, water charges are collected only from private and state-owned enterprises, restaurants, hotels, guest houses, and cafes. Approximately, Tsh 2.5 million was collected per year in 1990, which constitutes 10 percent of the DWD recurrent budget (FINNIDA, 1991). Due to inaccurate recordings in the customer register, the amount of uncollected revenue cannot be determined. However, it is clear that the current level of revenue is not sufficient for any cost recovery-based operation.

Willingness to Pay for Improved Water Supplies. According to one household survey in urban Zanzibar, the majority of people were willing to pay for reliable water supply services (FINNIDA, 1991). Urban residents in Pemba were more willing to pay, and willing to pay more, than those in Zanzibar Town. This is most likely due to greater water supply problems in Pemba. On average, households in Pemba were willing to pay Tsh 76 per month in 1990, while households in Unguja were willing to pay Tsh 87 per month. It is clear that households value improved water service and are willing to contribute substantial amounts of cash to improve the operation and maintenance of the urban water supply.

CONCLUSION

The mainland and Zanzibar share many problems in the social sectors. These include:

- low primary- and secondary-school enrollment rates, and high illiteracy rates;
- high IMR, child mortality, and malnutrition rates;
- low use of modern methods of birth control; and
- little access to, and use of, improved sources of water, and poor sanitation facilities.

Primary- and secondary-school enrollment rates are considerably higher in Zanzibar than on the mainland. Although enrollment rates are higher in Zanzibar, the illiteracy rates in Zanzibar are more than one-third higher than the illiteracy rates on the mainland.

The IMR, child mortality, and under-nutrition rates are also higher in Zanzibar than on the mainland. In addition, almost twice as many Zanzibari reported being ill or injured in the last month than on the mainland.

Although the knowledge of at least one modern method of birth control, and the knowledge of contraceptive sources among reproductive-age women, are both high in Zanzibar and on the mainland, the use of modern methods is quite low. Twice as many reproductive-age women on the mainland use a modern method of birth control as in Zanzibar.

The private sector and NGO facilities do not play as significant of a role in the provision of health and education services in Zanzibar as they do on the mainland. In view of the government's financial situation, they could play an instrumental role in the provision of these services in Zanzibar.

Almost one-half of the households on the mainland and in Zanzibar use unimproved sources of water. The use of unimproved water sources is slightly higher on the mainland than in Zanzibar. The quality of the water supply could be greatly improved in Zanzibar with the restoration of user fees. Studies have shown that households are willing to pay for improved water services. Finally, almost five times as many households in Zanzibar as on the mainland do not have a sanitation facility.

BIBLIOGRAPHY

Abel-Smith, B. and P. Rawal, 1992, "Report on the Potentiality for Cost-Sharing: National Health Insurance," Second Report, for Overseas Development Agency (ODA), Dar es Salaam.

Aboud, S., G. Angeles, P. Bardsley, et al., 1996, "The Impact of Family planning on Contraceptive Use in Tanzania: An Exploration of Change Between 1991 and 1994," The EVALUATION Project, Tanzania.

Ainsworth, M. and A. Nyamete, 1992, "The Impact of Women's Human Capital on Fertility and Contraceptive Use in Sub-Saharan Africa: A study of 10 Sub-Saharan Countries, " Paper presented at the annual meeting of the Population Association of America.

Andersson, I., "Rural Water Supply Development in the Context of Economic Crisis and Structural Adjustment" (parts 1 and 2), *Waterlines* 8:28-30.

Babyegeya, E.B., 1993, "Efficiency and Cost-Effectiveness Indicators in Private and Public Secondary School," MA Dissertation, University of Dar es Salaam.

Batageki, W.B. and F.W. Magambo, 1994, "The Tanzania Nutrition Sector Overview," background paper prepared for the *Social Sector Review*, The World Bank Resident Mission, Dar es Salaam.

Beegle, K., 1994, "The Quality and Availability of Family Planning Services and Contraceptive Use in Tanzania," The World Bank, Washington, D.C.

Bloom, G., G. Singleton and J. Toye, 1992, "Public Expenditure in the Tanzanian Health Sector During Structural Adjustment," European Community, Dar es Salaam.

Boerma, P., 1993, "Tanzania: Water Resources and Urban Pollution – A Situation Analysis," Unpublished paper.

Bos, E., 1994, "Population Projections for Tanzania," background paper prepared for the *Social Sector Review*, The World Bank, Washington, D.C.

Cooksey, B., 1993, *Parents Attitudes Toward Education in Rural Tanzania*, TADREG, Dar es Salaam.

Cooksey, B. and A. Ishumi, 1986, *A Critical Review of Policy and Practice in Tanzanian Secondary Education Since 1967*, Rockefeller Foundation, New York.

DANIDA, 1994a, *Donor and Government Financing of Primary Education in Tanzania.* Royal Danish Embassy, Dar es Salaam.

DANIDA, 1994b, *Donor Assistance to the Education Sector in Tanzania.* Royal Danish Embassy, Dar es Salaam.

DANIDA, 1995, *Donor Assistance to the Health and Population Sector in Tanzania.* Royal Danish Embassy, Dar es Salaam.

DANIDA, 1996, *Sector Programme Support Document.* Royal Danish Embassy, Dar es Salaam.

Dar, A. and R. Levine, 1996, "Higher and Technical Education in Tanzania: Investments, Returns and Future Opportunities," Green Cover, World Bank, Washington, D.C.

European Union, 1996, *Proposal for a Pilot Programme of Decentralised Teacher Management,* European Union, Brussels.

Ferreira, Luisa, 1994, "Poverty and Inequality During Structural Adjustment in Rural Tanzania," Research Paper Series, Paper No. 8, Transition Economics Division, Policy Research Department, The World Bank, Washington, DC

FINNIDA, 1991, *Zanzibar Urban Water Supply Development Plan. 1991-2015,* Dar es Salaam.

Follmer, A. and N. Kessy, 1996, "Tanzania Social Sector Expenditures Review 1997," The World Bank, Washington, D.C.

Food and Agriculture Organization, 1984, *State of Food and Agriculture,* Rome.

Galabawa, J.C.J., 1994, "Characteristics, Financing, Unit Costs and Selection Issues of Non-Government Secondary-school Provision in Tanzania," background paper prepared for the *Social Sector Review,* World Bank Resident Mission, Dar es Salaam.

Garssen, J., 1992, "Recent Demographic Trends in Zanzibar," UNICEF, Dar es Salaam.

Garssen, J., 1988, "Mortality, Fertility, and Contraception in Zanzibar," UNICEF and UNFPA.

Gilson, L., M. Alilio and K. Heggenhougen, 1993, "A Tanzanian Evaluation of Community Satisfaction with Primary Care," Unpublished paper.

Gilson, L., 1991, "Value for Money?: The Efficiency of Primary Health Care Units in Tanzania Final Summary Report," ODA Research Project No. R4519.

Government of Tanzania Ministry of Education and Culture, 1992b, "Report of the Task Force on the Education System for the 21st Century," Ministry of Education and Culture, Dar es Salaam.

Government of Tanzania Ministry of Education and Culture, various years, *Basic Education Statistics of Tanzania,* Ministry of Education, Dar es Salaam

Government of Tanzania Ministry of Health, 1994, "Burden of Disease and Cost-Effectiveness in Tanzania," Ministry of Health.

Government of Tanzania Ministry of Health, 1993, *Tanzania Health Statistics Abstract*, Ministry of Health, Dar es Salaam.

Government of Tanzania Ministry of Water, Energy and Minerals, *Water and Sanitation Sector Review*, Ministry of Water, Energy and Minerals, Dar es Salaam.

Government of Tanzania Ministry of Health, 1991, *Masterplan for the Pharmaceutical Sector 1992-2000*, Ministry of Health, Dar es Salaam.

Government of Tanzania Planning Commission, 1992, *Review of Critical Issues: The Primary and Secondary Education Subsectors*, Planning Commission, Dar es Salaam, Tanzania

Government of Tanzania Planning Commission, 1994, "Social Sector Strategy," paper prepared for the Consultative Group, Planning Commission, Dar es Salaam.

Government of Zanzibar Ministry of Health, Nutrition Unit, 1993, Study on Mortality and Low Birth Weight in Zanzibar Hospital, Ministry of Health

Government of Zanzibar Ministry of Health, Department of Preventive Services, 1993. Family Planning Programme Service Statistics.

Hedkvist, F., 1996, "Final Report on Baseline Study on Teaching Learning Material Availability in Primary Schools in Tanzania," SIDA.

Ishumi, A.G.M., 1994. "Participation of the Non-Governmental Sector in the Provision of Education in Tanzania," background paper prepared for the *Social Sector Review*, World Bank Resident Mission, Dar es Salaam.

Irish AID, 1996, "Project Support for Education in Tanzania, 1997-2000," memo to World Bank, Dublin International Institute for Educational Planning, 1994, *A Statistical Profile of Education in Sub-Saharan Africa in the 1980s*, Donors to African Education, Paris..

Jansen, H., 1992, "Household Survey on Diarrhoeal Diseases, Acute Respiratory Infections and Breast-Feeding," WHO, Geneva.

Jimenez, E., M. Lockheed and V. Paqueo, 1991, "Relative Efficiency of Private and Public Schools in Developing Countries," *World Bank Research Observer* 6:205-218.

Jonsson, U., 1986, "Ideological Framework and Health Development in Tanzania 1961-2000," *Social Science Medicine*, 22(7): 745-753.

Kanji, N., P. Kilima and G. Munishi, 1992, "Quality of Primary Curative Care in Dar es Salaam," Urban Health Project and ODA, Dar es Salaam, Tanzania.

Kavishe, F.P., 1993, *Nutrition-Relevant Actions in Tanzania,* Tanzania Food and Nutrition Center, Dar es Salaam.

Khatib, M., 1994, Assessment of Nutritional Situation of Women and Children in Zanzibar. February. Ministry of State Planning.

Lawson, A., 1993, "Strengthening of Budgeting and Planning in Health and Education: Draft Inception Report and Indicative Work Program," Budget Commission, Ministry of Finance, Dar es Salaam.

Leach, V., 1990. "Women and Children in Tanzania: A Situation Analysis." UNICEF, Dar es Salaam.

Malekela, G., D. Ndabi and B. Cooksey, 1990, *Educational Opportunities and Performance in Tanzania,* TADREG, Dar es Salaam.

Mashauri, D. and T. Katko, 1993, "Water Supply Development and Tariffs in Tanzania: From Free Water Policy Towards Cost Recovery," *Environmental Management* 17:31-39.

Mason, A. and S. Khandker, 1996, "Household Schooling Decisions in Tanzania," The World Bank, Washington, D.C.

McGuire, J. and B. Popkin, 1990. "Helping Women Improve Nutrition in the Developing World: Beating the Zero Sum Game." World Bank Technical Report No. 114, Washington, D.C.

Meena, R., 1994, "Gender Issues in the Educational Process in Tanzania," background paper prepared for the *Social Sector Review*, The World Bank Resident Mission, Dar es Salaam.

Mnyika, K. S., 1991, "Anaemia in Tanzania: A Situational Analysis," TFNC Report No. 1436.

Mosha, H.J., 1990, "Twenty Years After Education for Self-Reliance: A Critical Review," *International Journal of Educational Development* 10(1):59-67.

Mosha, H.J. and S. Sumra, 1992, "Zanzibar Educational Policies Affecting the Teacher Quality Supply and Demand," DANIDA/Ministry of Education.

Mpangile, G., 1994, "Review of the 1989-93 Plan of Operations of the National Family Planning Program: Achievements and Constraints," background paper prepared for the *Social Sector Review*, The World Bank Resident Mission, Dar es Salaam.

Mukyanuzi, F., 1994, "Health Sector Overview Paper," background paper prepared for the *Social Sector Review*, The World Bank Resident Mission, Dar es Salaam.

Mutalemwa, A., 1994, "Water and Sanitation Sector Overview," background paper prepared for the *Social Sector Review*, The World Bank Resident Mission, Dar es Salaam.

Mzee, O., 1993, "Absenteeism in Schools of Zanzibar," Ministry of State (Planning).

Ndabi, D.M., 1994, "School Examinations in Tanzania: Review and Critique," background paper prepared for the *Social Sector Review*, The World Bank Resident Mission, Dar es Salaam.

Nditi, N., 1994, "Report on the Legal Context of the Non-Governmental Sector in Education in Tanzania," background paper prepared for the *Social Sector Review*, The World Bank Resident Mission, Dar es Salaam.

Ngallaba, S.H., I. Kapiga, I. Ruyobya and J.T. Boerma, 1993, *Tanzania Demographic and Health Survey 1991/92*, Bureau of Statistics, Dar es Salaam and Macro International, Columbia, Maryland.

ODA, 1994, *Policy Implications of Adult Morbidity and Mortality*, ODA, Dar es Salaam.

ODA, 1996, *Tanzania Education Strategy Review*, ODA, Dar es Salaam.

Omari, I.M., 1994, "Review of Critical Issues in Tanzanian Education," background paper prepared for the *Social Sector Review*, The World Bank Resident Mission, Dar es Salaam.

Omari, I.M. and H.J. Mosha, 1987, *The Quality of Primary Education in Tanzania*, Man Graphics.

Omari, C.K., 1994, "Tanzania Household and Community Structures and Dynamics," background paper prepared for the *Social Sector Review*, The World Bank Resident Mission, Dar es Salaam.

Omari, I.M., S. Sumra and R.E. Levine, 1994, "Availability, Quality and Utilization of Social Services: Preliminary Results from Focused Area Studies Techniques," background paper prepared for the *Social Sector Review*, The World Bank Resident Mission, Dar es Salaam.

Psacharopoulos, G., 1993. "Returns to Investment in Education: A Global Update." *WPS* 1967, The World Bank, Washington, D.C.

Ravicz, M., C. Griffin, A. Follmer, and T. Fox, 1996, "Health Policy in Eastern Africa: A Structured Approach to Resource Allocation, Volume I: Main Report," The World Bank, Washington, D.C.

Ridley, A., 1993, "Assessment of Human Resources Management in the City Medical Office of Health," City Council, Urban Health Project, Dar es Salaam.

Samoff, J., 1991, "The Facade of Precision in Education Data and Statistics: A Troubling Example from Tanzania," *Journal of Modern African Studies* 29(4):669:689.

Sandiford, P., G. Kanga, 1994, "A Discussion Paper on the Need for Health Sector Reform Based on Findings From the Kisarawe Health Information Project," Unpublished paper.

Semboja, J. and O. Therkildsen, 1991, *Handbook on District Level Administration in Tanzania*. Educational Publishers and Distributors, Ltd., Dar es Salaam.

Shirima, L.L., 1994, "Tanzania: Structure of Local Government Implementation Overview," background paper prepared for the *Social Sector Review*, The World Bank Resident Mission, Dar es Salaam.

Sivalon, J.C., 1993, "Quality and Equity in Tanzania Religious Affiliated Secondary Schools," paper presented at TADREG Seminar.

Therkildsen, O., 1988, *Watering White Elephants? Lessons from Donor-Funded Planning and Implementation of Rural Water Supplies in Tanzania.*, Uppsala: Scandinavian Institute of African Studies.

UNESCO, 1989, *Education in Tanzania: Sector Review, Volume II Technical Chapters: Key Issues and Proposals for Remedial Action*, UNESCO, Education Financing Division, Paris.

UNICEF, 1992, *State of the World's Children*, UNICEF, New York.

UNICEF, 1995, "Child Survival, Protection and Development: Joint Programme of the United Republic of Tanzania and UNICEF," UNICEF presentation to World Bank Donor Consultative Workshop, Dar es Salaam.

Walter, I., 1990, "Engineering and Management Studies," Zanzibar and Pemba Rural Water Supply, Zanzibar.

Weinstein, K., S. Ngallaba, A. Cross and F.M. Mburu, 1995, *Knowledge, Attitudes and Practices Survey 1994*, Bureau of Statistics Planning Commission, Dar es Salaam and Macro International, Calverton, Maryland.

World Bank, 1984, Tanzania Country Economic Memorandum, Country Data Sheet, Report No. 5019-TA.

World Bank, 1989, Tanzania: Population, Health and Nutrition Sector Review, Report No. 7495-TA.

World Bank, 1991a, "Teachers and the Financing of Education," The World Bank, Washington, D.C.

World Bank, 1991b, *World Development Report 1991*, Oxford University Press, New York.

World Bank, 1992, *AIDS Assessment and Planning Study: Tanzania*, World Bank Country Study, World Bank, Washington, D.C.

World Bank, 1993, Water Demand Research Team, The World Bank, Washington, DC

World Bank, 1994a, *Tanzania Public Expenditure Review: The Role of Government*, The World Bank, Washington, D.C.

World Bank, 1994b, *Tanzania: A Poverty Profile*, The World Bank, Washington, D.C.

World Bank, 1994c, *World Development Report: Infrastructure for Development*, Oxford University Press, New York.

World Bank, 1995a, *World Development Report: Workers in an Integrating World*, Oxford University Press, New York.

World Bank, 1995b, "Health Policy in Eastern Africa: A Structured Approach to Resource Allocation," Report No. 14040, AFR Region.

World Bank, 1996, *World Development Report: From Plan to Market*, Oxford University Press, New York.

World Bank, 1997a, *1996 Public Expenditure Review*, The World Bank, Washington, D.C.

World Bank, 1997, *Africa Development Indicators, 1996*, The World Bank, Washington, D.C.

World Bank and Government of Tanzania Planning Commission, 1994, *Tanzania Human Resources Development Survey 1993/94*, The World Bank, Washington, D.C.

Zayumba, J., 1994, "Textbook Production and Distribution in Tanzania," SDA Project, Planning Commission, Dar es Salaam.

Distributors of World Bank Group Publications

Prices and credit terms vary from country to country. Consult your local distributor before placing an order.

ARGENTINA
World Publications SA
Av. Cordoba 1877
1120 Ciudad de Buenos Aires
Tel: (54 11) 4815-8156
Fax: (54 11) 4815-8156
E-mail: wpbooks@infovia.com.ar

AUSTRALIA, FIJI, PAPUA NEW GUINEA, SOLOMON ISLANDS, VANUATU, AND SAMOA
D.A. Information Services
648 Whitehorse Road
Mitcham 3132, Victoria
Tel: (61) 3 9210 7777
Fax: (61) 3 9210 7788
E-mail: service@dadirect.com.au
URL: http://www.dadirect.com.au

AUSTRIA
Gerold and Co.
Weihburggasse 26
A-1011 Wien
Tel: (43 1) 512-47-31-0
Fax: (43 1) 512-47-31-29
URL: http://www.gerold.co/at.online

BANGLADESH
Micro Industries Development Assistance Society (MIDAS)
House 5, Road 16
Dhanmondi R/Area
Dhaka 1209
Tel: (880 2) 326427
Fax: (880 2) 811188

BELGIUM
Jean De Lannoy
Av. du Roi 202
1060 Brussels
Tel: (32 2) 538-5169
Fax: (32 2) 538-0841

BRAZIL
Publicaçôes Tecnicas Internacionais Ltda.
Rua Peixoto Gomide, 209
01409 Sao Paulo, SP.
Tel: (55 11) 259-6644
Fax: (55 11) 258-6990
E-mail: postmaster@pti.uol.br
URL: http://www.uol.br

CANADA
Renouf Publishing Co. Ltd.
5369 Canotek Road
Ottawa, Ontario K1J 9J3
Tel: (613) 745-2665
Fax: (613) 745-7660
E-mail: order.dept@renoufbooks.com
URL: http:// www.renoufbooks.com

CHINA
China Financial & Economic Publishing House
8, Da Fo Si Dong Jie
Beijing
Tel: (86 10) 6401-7365
Fax: (86 10) 6401-7365

China Book Import Centre
P.O. Box 2825
Beijing

Chinese Corporation for Promotion of Humanities
52, You Fang Hu Tong,
Xuan Nei Da Jie
Beijing
Tel: (86 10) 660 72 494
Fax: (86 10) 660 72 494

COLOMBIA
Infoenlace Ltda.
Carrera 6 No. 51-21
Apartado Aereo 34270
Santafé de Bogotá, D.C.
Tel: (57 1) 285-2798
Fax: (57 1) 285-2798

COTE D'IVOIRE
Center d'Edition et de Diffusion Africaines (CEDA)
04 B.P. 541
Abidjan 04
Tel: (225) 24 6510; 24 6511
Fax: (225) 25 0567

CYPRUS
Center for Applied Research
Cyprus College
6, Diogenes Street, Engomi
P.O. Box 2006
Nicosia
Tel: (357 2) 59-0730
Fax: (357 2) 66-2051

CZECH REPUBLIC
USIS, NIS Prodejna
Havelkova 22
130 00 Prague 3
Tel: (420 2) 2423 1486
Fax: (420 2) 2423 1114
URL: http://www.nis.cz/

DENMARK
SamfundsLitteratur
Rosenoerns Allé 11
DK-1970 Frederiksberg C
Tel: (45 35) 351942
Fax: (45 35) 357822
URL: http://www.sl.cbs.dk

ECUADOR
Libri Mundi
Libreria Internacional
P.O. Box 17-01-3029
Juan Leon Mera 851
Quito
Tel: (593 2) 521-606; (593 2) 544-185
Fax: (593 2) 504-209
E-mail: librimu1@librimundi.com.ec
E-mail: librimu2@librimundi.com.ec

CODEU
Ruiz de Castilla 763, Edif. Expocolor
Primer piso, Of. #2
Quito
Tel/Fax: (593 2) 507-383; 253-091
E-mail: codeu@impsat.net.ec

EGYPT, ARAB REPUBLIC OF
Al Ahram Distribution Agency
Al Galaa Street
Cairo
Tel: (20 2) 578-6083
Fax: (20 2) 578-6833

The Middle East Observer
41, Sherif Street
Cairo
Tel: (20 2) 393-9732
Fax: (20 2) 393-9732

FINLAND
Akateeminen Kirjakauppa
P.O. Box 128
FIN-00101 Helsinki
Tel: (358 0) 121 4418
Fax: (358 0) 121-4435
E-mail: akatilaus@stockmann.fi
URL: http://www.akateeminen.com

FRANCE
Editions Eska; DBJ
48, rue Gay Lussac
75005 Paris
Tel: (33-1) 55-42-73-08
Fax: (33-1) 43-29-91-67

GERMANY
UNO-Verlag
Poppelsdorfer Allee 55
53115 Bonn
Tel: (49 228) 949020
Fax: (49 228) 217492
URL: http://www.uno-verlag.de
E-mail: unoverlag@aol.com

GHANA
Epp Books Services
P.O. Box 44
TUC
Accra
Tel: 223 21 778843
Fax: 223 21 779099

GREECE
Papasotiriou S.A.
35, Stournara Str.
106 82 Athens
Tel: (30 1) 364-1826
Fax: (30 1) 364-8254

HAITI
Culture Diffusion
5, Rue Capois
C.P. 257
Port-au-Prince
Tel: (509) 23 9260
Fax: (509) 23 4858

HONG KONG, CHINA; MACAO
Asia 2000 Ltd.
Sales & Circulation Department
302 Seabird House
22-28 Wyndham Street, Central
Hong Kong, China
Tel: (852) 2530-1409
Fax: (852) 2526-1107
E-mail: sales@asia2000.com.hk
URL: http://www.asia2000.com.hk

HUNGARY
Euro Info Service
Margitszgeti Europa Haz
H-1138 Budapest
Tel: (36 1) 350 80 24, 350 80 25
Fax: (36 1) 350 90 32
E-mail: euroinfo@mail.matav.hu

INDIA
Allied Publishers Ltd.
751 Mount Road
Madras - 600 002
Tel: (91 44) 852-3938
Fax: (91 44) 852-0649

INDONESIA
Pt. Indira Limited
Jalan Borobudur 20
P.O. Box 181
Jakarta 10320
Tel: (62 21) 390-4290
Fax: (62 21) 390-4289

IRAN
Ketab Sara Co. Publishers
Khaled Eslamboli Ave., 6th Street
Delafrooz Alley No. 8
P.O. Box 15745-733
Tehran 15117
Tel: (98 21) 8717819; 8716104
Fax: (98 21) 8712479
E-mail: ketab-sara@neda.net.ir

Kowkab Publishers
P.O. Box 19575-511
Tehran
Tel: (98 21) 258-3723
Fax: (98 21) 258-3723

IRELAND
Government Supplies Agency
Oifig an tSoláthair
4-5 Harcourt Road
Dublin 2
Tel: (353 1) 661-3111
Fax: (353 1) 475-2670

ISRAEL
Yozmot Literature Ltd.
P.O. Box 56055
3 Yohanan Hasandlar Street
Tel Aviv 61560
Tel: (972 3) 5285-397
Fax: (972 3) 5285-397

R.O.Y. International
PO Box 13056
Tel Aviv 61130
Tel: (972 3) 649 9469
Fax: (972 3) 648 6039
E-mail: royil@netvision.net.il
URL: http://www.royint.co.il

Palestinian Authority/Middle East
Index Information Services
P.O.B. 19502 Jerusalem
Tel: (972 2) 6271219
Fax: (972 2) 6271634

ITALY, LIBERIA
Licosa Commissionaria Sansoni SPA
Via Duca Di Calabria, 1/1
Casella Postale 552
50125 Firenze
Tel: (39 55) 645-415
Fax: (39 55) 641-257
E-mail: licosa@ftbcc.it
URL: http://www.ftbcc.it/licosa

JAMAICA
Ian Randle Publishers Ltd.
206 Old Hope Road, Kingston 6
Tel: 876-927-2085
Fax: 876-977-0243
E-mail: irpl@colis.com

JAPAN
Eastern Book Service
3-13 Hongo 3-chome, Bunkyo-ku
Tokyo 113
Tel: (81 3) 3818-0861
Fax: (81 3) 3818-0864
E-mail: orders@svt-ebs.co.jp
URL: http://www.bekkoame.or.jp/~svt-ebs

KENYA
Africa Book Service (E.A.) Ltd.
Quaran House, Mfangano Street
P.O. Box 45245
Nairobi
Tel: (254 2) 223 641
Fax: (254 2) 330 272

Legacy Books
Loita House
Mezzanine 1
P.O. Box 68077
Nairobi
Tel: (254) 2-330853, 221426
Fax: (254) 2-330854, 561654
E-mail: Legacy@form-net.com

KOREA, REPUBLIC OF
Dayang Books Trading Co.
International Division
783-20, Pangba Bon-Dong,
Socho-ku
Seoul
Tel: (82 2) 536-9555
Fax: (82 2) 536-0025
E-mail: seamap@chollian.net

Eulyoo Publishing Co., Ltd.
46-1, Susong-Dong
Jongro-Gu
Seoul
Tel: (82 2) 734-3515
Fax: (82 2) 732-9154

LEBANON
Librairie du Liban
P.O. Box 11-9232
Beirut
Tel: (961 9) 217 944
Fax: (961 9) 217 434
E-mail: hsayegh@librairie-du-liban.com.lb
URL: http://www.librairie-du-liban.com.lb

MALAYSIA
University of Malaya Cooperative Bookshop, Limited
P.O. Box 1127
Jalan Pantai Baru
59700 Kuala Lumpur
Tel: (60 3) 756-5000
Fax: (60 3) 755-4424
E-mail: umkoop@tm.net.my

MEXICO
INFOTEC
Av. San Fernando No. 37
Col. Toriello Guerra
14050 Mexico, D.F.
Tel: (52 5) 624-2800
Fax: (52 5) 624-2822
E-mail: infotec@rtn.net.mx
URL: http://rtn.net.mx

Mundi-Prensa Mexico S.A. de C.V.
c/Rio Panuco, 141-Colonia Cuauhtemoc
06500 Mexico, D.F.
Tel: (52 5) 533-5658
Fax: (52 5) 514-6799

NEPAL
Everest Media International Services (P.) Ltd.
GPO Box 5443
Kathmandu
Tel: (977 1) 416 026
Fax: (977 1) 224 431

NETHERLANDS
De Lindeboom/Internationale Publicaties b.v.-
P.O. Box 202, 7480 AE Haaksbergen
Tel: (31 53) 574-0004
Fax: (31 53) 572-9296
E-mail: lindeboo@worldonline.nl
URL: http://www.worldonline.nl/~lindeboo

NEW ZEALAND
EBSCO NZ Ltd.
Private Mail Bag 99914
New Market
Auckland
Tel: (64 9) 524-8119
Fax: (64 9) 524-8067

Oasis Official
P.O. Box 3627
Wellington
Tel: (64 4) 499 1551
Fax: (64 4) 499 1972
E-mail: oasis@actrix.gen.nz
URL: http://www.oasisbooks.co.nz/

NIGERIA
University Press Limited
Three Crowns Building Jericho
Private Mail Bag 5095
Ibadan
Tel: (234 22) 41-1356
Fax: (234 22) 41-2056

PAKISTAN
Mirza Book Agency
65, Shahrah-e-Quaid-e-Azam
Lahore 54000
Tel: (92 42) 735 3601
Fax: (92 42) 576 3714

Oxford University Press
5 Bangalore Town
Sharae Faisal
PO Box 13033
Karachi-75350
Tel: (92 21) 446307
Fax: (92 21) 4547640
E-mail: ouppak@TheOffice.net

Pak Book Corporation
Aziz Chambers 21, Queen's Road
Lahore
Tel: (92 42) 636 3222; 636 0885
Fax: (92 42) 636 2328
E-mail: pbc@brain.net.pk

PERU
Editorial Desarrollo SA
Apartado 3824, Ica 242 OF. 106
Lima 1
Tel: (51 14) 285380
Fax: (51 14) 286628

PHILIPPINES
International Booksource Center Inc.
1127-A Antipolo St, Barangay, Venezuela
Makati City
Tel: (63 2) 896 6501; 6505; 6507
Fax: (63 2) 896 1741

POLAND
International Publishing Service
Ul. Piekna 31/37
00-677 Warzawa
Tel: (48 2) 628-6089
Fax: (48 2) 621-7255
E-mail: books%ips@ikp.atm.com.pl
URL: http://www.ipscg.waw.pl/ips/export

PORTUGAL
Livraria Portugal
Apartado 2681, Rua Do Carmo 70-74
1200 Lisbon
Tel: (1) 347-4982
Fax: (1) 347-0264

ROMANIA
Compani De Librarii Bucuresti S.A.
Str. Lipscani no. 26, sector 3
Bucharest
Tel: (40 1) 313 9645
Fax: (40 1) 312 4000

RUSSIAN FEDERATION
Isdatelstvo <Ves Mir>
9a, Kolpachniy Pereulok
Moscow 101831
Tel: (7 095) 917 87 49
Fax: (7 095) 917 92 59
ozimarin@glasnet.ru

SINGAPORE; TAIWAN, CHINA MYANMAR; BRUNEI
Hemisphere Publication Services
41 Kallang Pudding Road #04-03
Golden Wheel Building
Singapore 349316
Tel: (65) 741-5166
Fax: (65) 742-9356
E-mail: ashgate@asianconnect.com

SLOVENIA
Gospodarski vestnik Publishing Group
Dunajska cesta 5
1000 Ljubljana
Tel: (386 61) 133 83 47; 132 12 30
Fax: (386 61) 133 80 30
E-mail: repansekj@gvestnik.si

SOUTH AFRICA, BOTSWANA
For single titles:
Oxford University Press Southern Africa
Vasco Boulevard, Goodwood
P.O. Box 12119, N1 City 7463
Cape Town
Tel: (27 21) 595 4400
Fax: (27 21) 595 4430
E-mail: oxford@oup.co.za

For subscription orders:
International Subscription Service
P.O. Box 41095
Craighall
Johannesburg 2024
Tel: (27 11) 880-1448
Fax: (27 11) 880-6248
E-mail: iss@is.co.za

SPAIN
Mundi-Prensa Libros, S.A.
Castello 37
28001 Madrid
Tel: (34 91) 4 363700
Fax: (34 91) 5 753998
E-mail: libreria@mundiprensa.es
URL: http://www.mundiprensa.com/

Mundi-Prensa Barcelona
Consell de Cent, 391
08009 Barcelona
Tel: (34 3) 488-3492
Fax: (34 3) 487-7659
E-mail: barcelona@mundiprensa.es

SRI LANKA, THE MALDIVES
Lake House Bookshop
100, Sir Chittampalam Gardiner Mawatha
Colombo 2
Tel: (94 1) 32105
Fax: (94 1) 432104
E-mail: LHL@sri.lanka.net

SWEDEN
Wennergren-Williams AB
P. O. Box 1305
S-171 25 Solna
Tel: (46 8) 705-97-50
Fax: (46 8) 27-00-71
E-mail: mail@wwi.se

SWITZERLAND
Librairie Payot Service Institutionnel
C(tm)tes-de-Montbenon 30
1002 Lausanne
Tel: (41 21) 341-3229
Fax: (41 21) 341-3235

ADECO Van Diermen EditionsTechniques
Ch. de Lacuez 41
CH1807 Blonay
Tel: (41 21) 943 2673
Fax: (41 21) 943 3605

THAILAND
Central Books Distribution
306 Silom Road
Bangkok 10500
Tel: (66 2) 2336930-9
Fax: (66 2) 237-8321

TRINIDAD & TOBAGO AND THE CARRIBBEAN
Systematics Studies Ltd.
St. Augustine Shopping Center
Eastern Main Road, St. Augustine
Trinidad & Tobago, West Indies
Tel: (868) 645-8466
Fax: (868) 645-8467
E-mail: tobe@trinidad.net

UGANDA
Gustro Ltd.
PO Box 9997, Madhvani Building
Plot 16/4 Jinja Rd.
Kampala
Tel: (256 41) 251 467
Fax: (256 41) 251 468
E-mail: gus@swiftuganda.com

UNITED KINGDOM
Microinfo Ltd.
P.O. Box 3, Omega Park, Alton,
Hampshire GU34 2PG
England
Tel: (44 1420) 86848
Fax: (44 1420) 89889
E-mail: wbank@microinfo.co.uk
URL: http://www.microinfo.co.uk

The Stationery Office
51 Nine Elms Lane
London SW8 5DR
Tel: (44 171) 873-8400
Fax: (44 171) 873-8242
URL: http://www.the-stationery-office.co.uk

VENEZUELA
Tecni-Ciencia Libros, S.A.
Centro Cuidad Comercial Tamanco
Nivel C2, Caracas
Tel: (58 2) 959 5547; 5035; 0016
Fax: (58 2) 959 5636

ZAMBIA
University Bookshop, University of Zambia
Great East Road Campus
P.O. Box 32379
Lusaka
Tel: (260 1) 252 576
Fax: (260 1) 253 952

ZIMBABWE
Academic and Baobab Books (Pvt.) Ltd.
4 Conald Road, Graniteside
P.O. Box 567
Harare
Tel: 263 4 755035
Fax: 263 4 781913

Your Complete Guide to Sexual Health

Elizabeth Thompson Ortiz

for

PLANNED PARENTHOOD
of San Diego and Riverside Counties

PRENTICE HALL
Englewood Cliffs, New Jersey 07632

Library of Congress Cataloging-in-Publication Data

Ortiz, Elizabeth Thompson.
    Your complete guide to sexual health / Elizabeth Thompson Ortiz
for Planned Parenthood of San Diego and Riverside Counties.
        p.   cm.
    Bibliography: p. 334
    Includes index.
    ISBN 0-13-679580-3.   ISBN 0-13-679572-2 (pbk.)
    1. Hygiene, Sexual.   I. Planned Parenthood of San Diego and
Riverside Counties.   II. Title.
RA788.077   1989
612'.6—dc19
                                                        89-3768
                                                           CIP

Editorial/production supervision: *Serena Hoffman*
Interior design and page layout: *Lorraine Mullaney*
Cover design: *Lundgren Graphics, Ltd.*
Photo editor: *Lorinda Morris-Nantz*
Photo research: *Ilene Cherna*
Cover photo: *Ron Chapple / FPG International* (1987)

 © 1989 by Prentice-Hall, Inc.
A Division of Simon & Schuster
Englewood Cliffs, New Jersey 07632

Printed in the United States of America
10 9 8 7 6 5 4 3 2 1

ISBN 0-13-679580-3
ISBN 0-13-679572-2 PBK

Prentice-Hall International (UK) Limited, *London*
Prentice-Hall of Australia Pty. Limited, *Sydney*
Prentice-Hall Canada Inc., *Toronto*
Prentice-Hall Hispanoamericana, S. A., *Mexico*
Prentice-Hall of India Private Limited, *New Delhi*
Prentice-Hall of Japan, Inc., *Tokyo*
Simon & Schuster Asia Pte. Ltd., *Singapore*
Editora Prentice-Hall do Brasil, Ltda., *Rio de Janeiro*

Overview

Contents

PART II Reproduction and Fertility Control

PART III   Reproductive Health Problems

Preface

The purpose of this book is to provide a comprehensive family reference book on reproductive health and sexuality, written in simple, nontechnical language. Our aim was to produce a book that all members of the family would find easy to read, and that would answer most questions about the human reproductive system, how it works, and the health problems related to it. Recognition of the need for such a book came from the large demand by Planned Parenthood clients for educational materials on various aspects of reproductive health. Although there are many books available on specific problems, particularly those related to women's health, we felt that there was a need for a single volume that would provide basic information covering the broad area of reproductive health. We also felt it was particularly important to cover certain areas in which it is difficult to find readable information, such as men's reproductive health problems, sexually transmitted diseases, and sexual victimization, including rape and child molestation.

An additional goal of this book is to present needed information in a way that is acceptable and usable for *all* readers, regardless of their religion or values regarding sexuality. We hope that this book will be helpful to people regardless of their individual beliefs and values about premarital sex, contraception, abortion, homosexuality, *in vitro* fertilization, and so on. If we offend at any point in the book, we hope our readers will let us know.

As a Planned Parenthood sponsored project, this book *does* promote some specific values, namely:

1. *Information and education:* We believe in the right of all people to have the most complete and up-to-date information possible to guide them in the choices they make regarding sexuality, fertility, and health care.

2. *Choice:* We believe in the right of each individual to make his or her own choices about sexuality and related matters.

3. *Responsible sexuality:* We believe in the importance of responsible sexual behavior, which means taking care that sexual choices and behaviors are not harmful to oneself or others.

Because it takes about a year from the time a book is written until it is printed and available to the public, some of the facts and figures in this book (such as statistics on AIDS and information on the latest developments in contraceptive technology) may be out of date by the time the reader sees them. This is unavoidable in the rapidly changing field of reproductive health. We urge readers to keep up with the latest developments in areas of special interest to them through newspapers, magazines, and television.

The book is organized into three parts: (I) *Human Sexuality*, which includes chapters on the human body, conception, sexual behavior, talking to children about sex, and sex and the law; (II) *Reproduction and Fertility Control*, which includes chapters on pregnancy and childbirth, unwanted pregnancy, infertility, contraception, sterilization, and abortion; and (III) *Reproductive Health Problems*, which includes chapters on women's and men's health problems, sexually transmitted diseases, and AIDS.

Both a summary table of contents and a detailed table of contents are provided at the beginning of the book. Suggested readings and community resources and organizations that may be helpful are listed at the end of each chapter. A complete bibliography and an index are included at the back of the book.

We invite feedback and advice from readers for use in future editions, so feel free to write to the author in care of the publisher.

ACKNOWLEDGMENTS

The development of this book has taken seven years from the initial explorations and planning to the completion of the manuscript. It could not have been completed without the assistance and expert review of numerous people. Because of the comprehensive nature of the material covered, we decided that in addition to a core group who reviewed drafts of all chapters of the book, experts with specialized knowledge or experience in specific subjects would also be asked to assist. Enthusiasm about the project was high, and I am very thankful to all the people who volunteered many hours of their time to meet with me, to read multiple drafts of chapters, and to record and share their reactions and suggestions. A number of other people, too numerous to name here, were most generous with ideas and suggestions for the book. However, any errors or misstatements that remain in the manuscript are solely my responsibility.

The first group of people who deserve recognition are the personnel at Planned Parenthood of San Diego and Riverside Counties, California. Mark Salo, Executive Director, first recognized the need for the book and commissioned me to develop the concept and draft an outline. He reviewed each chapter as it was written, and provided wise and supportive guidance at each turn. Katherine Sheehan, M.D., Medical Director of the organization, was also involved in the initial planning and scrupulously reviewed all chapters for medical accuracy up until 1987, when other responsibilities prevented her from working on the last few drafts. The book owes much to her medical expertise and her clear and logical approach to communication of complex material. Ava Torre-Bueno, M.S.W., former Director of Counseling Services (now at Sharp Rehabilitation Center, San Diego) read every word (and some sections twice). Her knowledge of the family planning, reproductive health, and counseling fields was invaluable, as was her rapid and forthright reviewing style and her sensitivity to cross-cultural issues. Marilyn Fowler, M.P.A., Executive Director, World Affairs Council of San Diego, also reviewed drafts and provided helpful liaison during her time as Education Director. Bob Coles and Janet Stanley, M.A., Director of Education and Training, each reviewed several chapters. Additional expert reviewers included:

Estela Andujo, Ph.D., Assistant Professor, Department of Social Work, California State University, Long Beach

Katherine Brubaker, M.D., F.A.C.O.G., obstetrician/gynecologist, Kaiser Permanente (Kaiser Foundation Health Plan, Inc.)

Dr. Stuart Chalfin, M.D., F.A.C.S., Diplomate, American Board of Urology; private practice, Long Beach, California

Howard Fradkin, Ph.D., Professor, Sociology Department, California State University, Long Beach

Lin Fujitsubo, Police Crisis Assistance Program, Irvine, California

Mindy Halperin, M.S.W., L.C.S.W.

Myrna Hamid, M.S.W., M.P.H., Lecturer, Department of Social Work, California State University, Long Beach

Jim Kelly, Ph.D., L.C.S.W., Professor, Department of Social Work, California State University, Long Beach

Ray Kincade, R.N., Coordinator, Long Beach AIDS Project, Long Beach Health Department, Long Beach, California

Paul Kirchgraber, M.S.W., L.C.S.W., Lecturer, Department of Social Work, California State University, Long Beach

Vickie Polusky, C.N.M. (Certified Nurse Midwife), Kaiser Permanente (Kaiser Foundation Health Plan, Inc.)

Beverly Willie, Child Abuse Prevention Service, Orange, California

In my attempt to get the consumer point of view, I had the good fortune to find a number of men, women, and teenagers who were willing to give me feedback. Special thanks go to my daughter, Cici Ortiz, and to her friends for providing the teenage perspective. Thanks also to Sarah Adams, Sherrie Simerman, and Nancy Manriquez-Dowell, school counselor, as recent mothers as well as expert editors, and to Phil Presser, Ellen Presser, and Grace Orpilla for giving me feedback on several chapters.

My greatest appreciation also goes to my family (especially Cici and Phil) and friends for their extraordinary patience, tolerance, and understanding as I somewhat singlemindedly pursued this project through days, nights, weekends, holidays, and vacations over the last few years.

Finally, I would like to thank John Isely, Gordon Johnson, Susan Finnemore, Susan Willig, and Serena Hoffman, all of Prentice Hall, for their foresight, faith, support, and skill in helping bring this project to completion.

Elizabeth Thompson Ortiz, D.S.W.
Department of Social Work
California State University, Long Beach

1

The Human Body

This chapter describes the reproductive systems of both women and men and how hormones guide their development and functioning. Information on human sexual behavior and the physical changes in the sex organs during sexual activity is contained in Chapter 3. The external (outside the body) and internal (inside the body) reproductive organs of women and men are described first, and then the ways in which hormones affect the reproductive system are presented.

WHY DO YOU NEED TO KNOW?

Understanding This Book

You will need basic information about the reproductive system to understand some of the information given in later chapters of this book. The book is written as a reference, with the idea that

you will use it to look up answers to specific questions. We don't expect you to read it cover to cover, or to read this chapter before any of the others, but we do want to make sure this basic information about the body and the reproductive system is part of the book, so that you can turn to it as needed.

Understanding Our Own Bodies

Most people's understanding of the sexual organs and their functioning is limited. You may be very familiar with your own external sex organs, but have no idea about the parts of your system that are hidden inside the body. You may be unsure about the sexual organs of the other sex and how they work.

Even if you are familiar with your own sexual organs and those of a partner of the opposite sex, you may wonder if other men and women are different. One of the purposes of this chapter

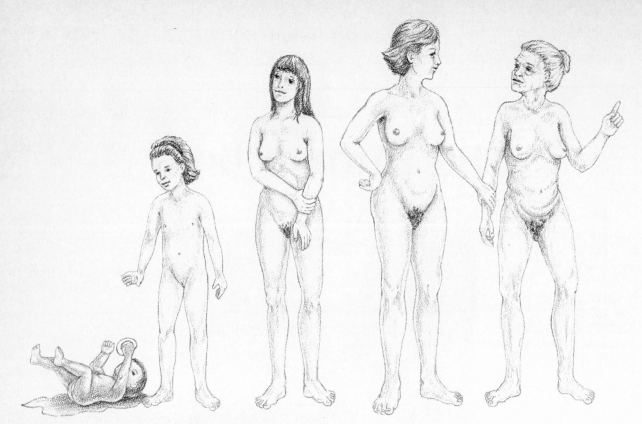

FIGURE 1–1A. *Women's bodies at different ages.*

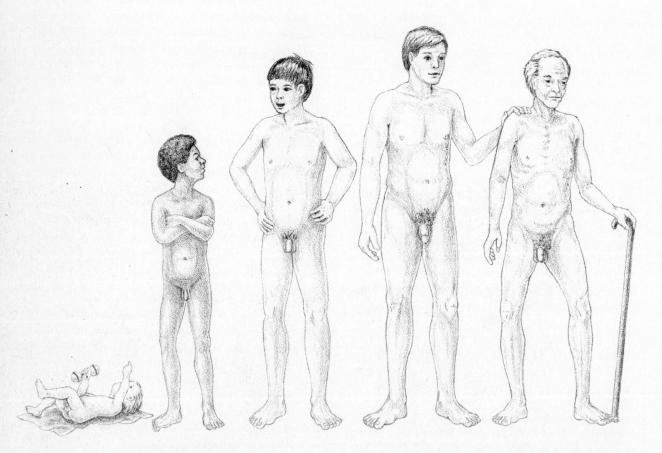

FIGURE 1–1B. *Men's bodies at different ages.*

is to give you the information you need to gain a clearer understanding of your own sexual organs and reproductive system and those of the opposite sex.

Understanding Health and Sex

A clear understanding of the sexual organs and reproductive systems of both sexes is an important foundation of knowledge for good health and for satisfying sexual adjustment. The reproductive organs and hormones are an important part of health and functioning throughout most of our lives. Further, many of the health problems of men and women involve the reproductive system. Reproductive system–related problems are by far the most common reasons that women of childbearing age seek medical care. And the most commonly performed surgical operations in the United States are on the reproductive system.

DIFFERENCES IN SIZE AND SHAPE

The question of how individuals differ in the size and shape of their external (outside the body) sexual organs and in secondary sex characteristics (such as pubic hair, breasts, and beards) is a subject of great interest and curiosity for both girls and boys during puberty. This is understandable, as their own sexual organs are growing and changing, and the question of what they will look like as sexually mature adults is soon to be answered (see Figure 1–1). What adolescents (or adults) discover when they compare bodies is that just as there are differences between people in height and weight and in the shapes of

faces, ears, and noses, there are also considerable individual differences in the size, shape, and appearance of the sexual organs and secondary sex characteristics. In women, breasts and vaginas come in many sizes and shapes. In men, there are differences in the length and the thickness of the penis and in the size and shape of the scrotum. In addition, there may be changes in the sexual organs over time. For example, pregnancy and childbirth cause changes in women's pelvic organs.

Regardless of size and shape, sex organs all have the same functions. There are no "perfect" or "best" sex organs or characteristics. What is viewed as beautiful or attractive is a matter of personal taste. Different people have different ideas about what is most appealing, and usually the people we care most about seem most attractive to us.

THE FEMALE SEXUAL ORGANS

External Sex Organs

A woman's genital area is called the **vulva** and is shown in Figure 1–2. In adult women, coarse, curly **pubic hair** covers the area. Pubic hair varies in amount and color, but usually forms an upside down triangle over the **mons pubis,** which is the fat-padded area covering the pubic bone. The parts of the vulva are the **labia majora** (also called the major lips or outer lips), which are plump folds of tissue that form a protective cover over the other organs. Inside the labia majora are another smaller set of tissue flaps called the **labia minora** (also called the minor lips or inner lips) that shield the entrance to the vagina. In Figure 1–2B, the major and minor lips partially cover the other genital or-

Human bodies vary a great deal in size and shape.

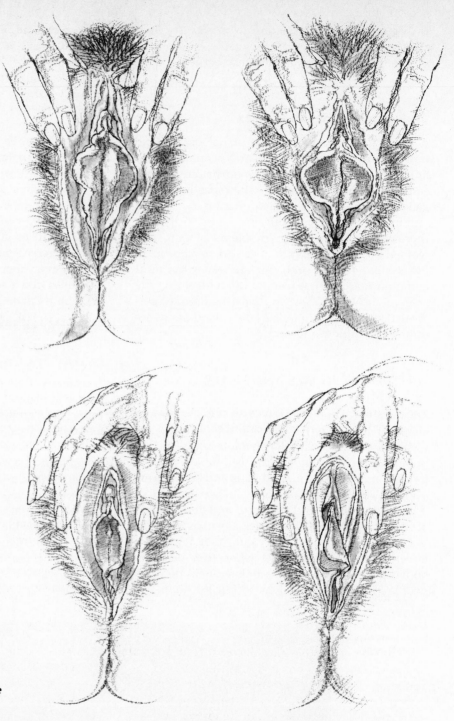

FIGURE 1–2A. *Four examples of female external sex organs.*

gans. During sexual intercourse they are parted, but the rest of the time—sitting, standing, or lying down—the lips are closed over the area, protecting the sensitive tissues.

Just below the mons pubis is a small, highly sensitive little knob or button of tissue partially covered by a flap of skin, which forms the top of the labia minora. This little bump is the **clitoris**, which is the part of the woman's anatomy that is most sensitive to sexual stimulation. The little hood of tissue over it is called the **prepuce** or clitoral hood. The clitoris develops from the same tissue that be-comes the penis in men and becomes erect with sexual stimulation. The clitoral hood is similar to the male prepuce or foreskin.

Above the clitoris is a small ridge of tissue called the **clitoral shaft**, which is about one inch long and attaches to the **crura**, which are fixed to the pelvic bone. Like the clitoris, both these areas are made of erectile tissue, which means they fill with blood and become enlarged and sensitive un-der sexual stimulation. The **vestibular bulbs**, which are located just within the labia minora, are also made of this erectile tissue.

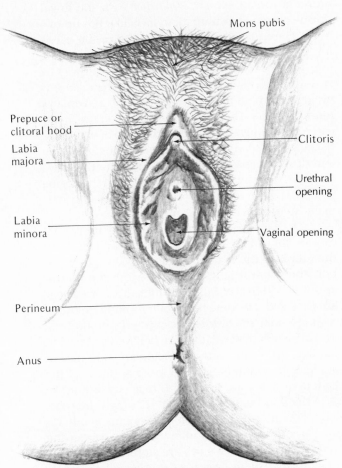

Mons pubis

Prepuce or
clitoral hood

Clitoris

Labia
majora

Urethral
opening

Labia
minora

Vaginal opening

Perineum

Anus

FIGURE 1–2B. *The anatomy of the female sex organs.*

Below the clitoris, women have a small opening, the **urethral opening**, through which they urinate. Just below the urinary opening is the **vaginal opening**. The **hymen** is a thin membrane that may partially cover the vaginal opening. In many young girls, the hymen covers most of the vaginal opening, but it can be stretched or torn easily by physical exercise. In most adolescent girls who are virgins, the natural opening is large enough to insert a tampon or a finger. The first time sexual intercourse takes place, the hymen may be painfully stretched or may tear and bleed a little if the opening is small. In rare cases a young girl may have a completely closed hymen, which means that menstrual blood cannot drain naturally. This can cause health problems, but is solved easily by having a physician create a small opening in the hymen.

The **Bartholin's glands** are tiny glands located

just below the vaginal opening within the labia minora. They are not normally noticeable, but they do release a small amount of fluid when the woman is sexually stimulated. Between the vaginal opening and the **anus** (opening of the rectum) is a short space of skin about 1 to 1½ inches wide called the **perineum**.

All the tissue in the vulva and perineal area is richly supplied with blood vessels and nerves and is highly sensitive to sexual stimulation and to pain. The labia majora are made up in large part of fatty tissue and are covered with skin. The labia minora and other inner surfaces of the vulva are highly sensitive and covered with **mucous membrane**, the delicate, moist type of surface also found inside the mouth, nose, and eyelids.

Under the surface tissues, the **pubococcygeus (PC) muscle**, or pelvic diaphragm, stretches from the pelvic bone in front to the coccyx in the back and connects to the lower pelvis on the sides (see Figure 1–3). This is a voluntary muscle, which can be controlled by the woman herself and which supports the openings in the woman's vulva. It is the muscle women use to start and stop urination, and tensing the muscle to stop urination also tightens the vaginal opening. The PC muscle controls tightness or looseness of the outer third of the vagina. After childbirth and aging, the muscle tends to become weaker, but it can be strengthened through exercise (see the discussion of Kegel's exercises on page 273). A strong PC muscle and a tight vaginal opening seem to increase sexual sensation and enjoyment during intercourse for some women and their male partners. Many mild cases of urinary incontinence (inability to control urine) can also be cured by strengthening the PC muscle.

Internal Sex Organs

The internal reproductive organs of the female are located within the lower abdomen surrounded by the pelvic bones. They are attached to the pelvis by various ligaments and muscles. The **vagina** (the part of the woman's body that is entered by the man's penis during sexual intercourse) extends from the vaginal opening to the uterus. The vagina is about three inches long most of the time, but increases in length when the woman is sexually aroused. The first one-third to one-half of the vagina is controlled by the pubococcygeous muscle, described earlier, but the inner part of the vagina is lined with smooth muscle, which is controlled by a different part of the nervous system. Under certain conditions it can contract, but the muscles of the inner part of the vagina are not under a woman's conscious control. The inner surface of the vagina is covered with

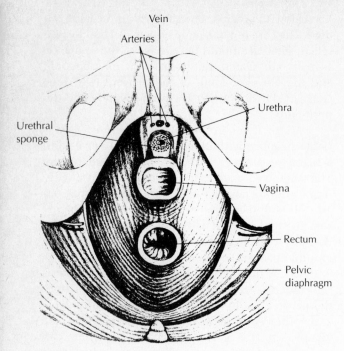

Vein

Arteries

Urethral sponge

Urethra

Vagina

Rectum

Pelvic diaphragm

FIGURE 1–3. *The pubococcygeus (PC) muscle (pelvic diaphragm).*

mucous membrane, which remains wet and smooth like the interior of the mouth. It lies flat, like an empty balloon, with many folds in the surface, so that it can expand to accept a penis of any size. Within the vagina is a small area called the Grafenberg spot, or G spot, which seems to be especially sensitive to sexual stimulation in some women. Details about the G spot are given on page 52.

Above the vagina is the **uterus,** which is the organ in which the fetus develops during pregnancy. As Figure 1–4 shows, it is located behind the bladder and in front of the lower intestine just above the rectum. The uterus is loosely suspended from the pelvis by ligaments, and its location shifts slightly depending on pressures from the bladder and rectum, which expand and contract depending on fullness. The uterus is a muscular organ shaped like an upside-down pear, and is about three inches long and two inches wide in a woman who has not had children. After a pregnancy, the uterus shrinks back to a small size, but remains a little larger than before. The uterus is made up of three layers of tissue: the **perimetrium,** which is the outer surface; the **myometrium,** a thick wall of muscle that provides the strength for contractions of the uterus during childbirth; and the **endometrium,** the soft inner layer of cells that is shed each month during menstrual bleeding. The endometrium is renewed each month and provides the environment for the fertilized **ovum** (egg) if the woman becomes pregnant during that cycle.

At the bottom of the uterus is the **cervix** or

neck of the uterus, which extends into the top of the vagina. The cervix provides the opening between the uterus and the vagina through which sperm can enter to fertilize the woman's ovum. It is also the opening through which menstrual blood is expelled each month, and through which the infant passes during childbirth. It is a small, smooth, muscular organ, which, when felt with the finger during a vaginal examination, feels like the tip of a nose. The **internal os** is the opening of the cervix into the uterus, and the **external os** is the opening into the vagina. The channel between the vagina and the uterus is normally quite small, and is plugged with mucus during most of a woman's monthly cycle. The mucus thins out so that sperm can pass through the cervix at the time of ovulation. Because the cervix is not plugged during ovulation and during menstrual bleeding, these are the times it is easiest for an infection to travel from the vagina (which is host to many organisms) into the normally sterile environment of the uterus.

The **Fallopian tubes** are muscular tubes that extend about four inches out on either side from the uterus to the ovaries. Their purpose is to transport the ovum (egg) from the ovary to the uterus, and it is within the Fallopian tubes that ova (eggs) are fertilized. The outer ends of the Fallopian tubes, resting next to the ovaries, are covered with **fimbria,** fringelike bits of tissue that are believed to assist in guiding the ovum into the Fallopian tube after it emerges from the ovary. The inner surfaces of the Fallopian tubes are lined with cilia, small hairlike growths that help to move the ova down the tube.

The **ovaries** are egg-shaped organs about 1½ inches in length and ¾ inch in width. It is in the ovaries that a woman's ova are stored and develop to maturity. The ovaries are also the major producers of the female hormones estrogen and progesterone. In addition, they produce small amounts of some male hormones. There are two parts to the ovary: the **medulla,** which is made up of blood, lymph vessels, and connective tissue, and the **cortex** (in which the ova are stored in **follicles**) (see page 18 for details on ovulation). After ovulation, the follicle is transformed into the **corpus luteum,** which has a temporary function of providing hormones needed for early pregnancy. If fertilization does not take place, the corpus luteum disappears at the next menstrual period.

Breasts

The breasts are considered to be secondary sex characteristics; that is, like pubic hair and other body changes, they develop during puberty. Breasts vary a great deal in size, shape, texture, and appearance. Like height and body type, the size and shape

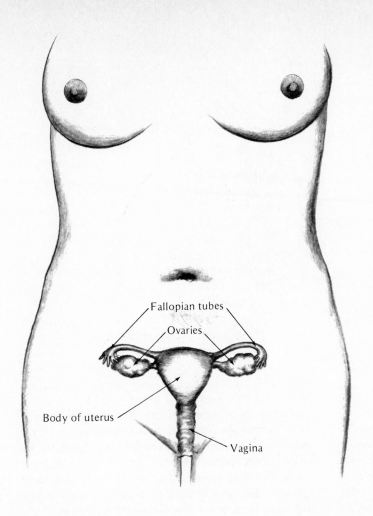

Fallopian tubes

Ovaries

Body of uterus

Vagina

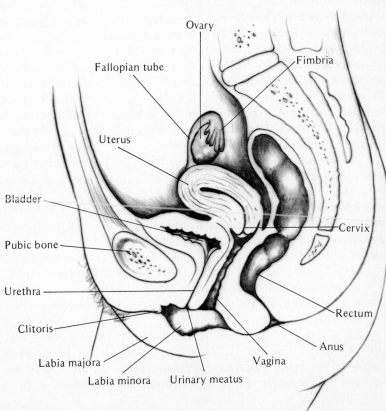

Ovary

Fimbria

Fallopian tube

Uterus

Bladder

Cervix

Pubic bone

Urethra

Rectum

Clitoris

Anus

Labia majora

Vagina

Labia minora

Urinary meatus

FIGURE 1–4. *Front and side views of the female internal sex organs.*

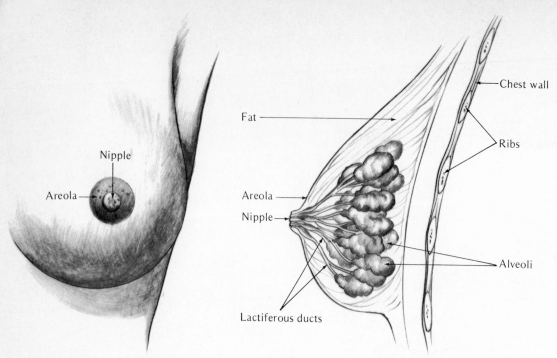

FIGURE 1–5. *External and internal views of the female breast.*

of breasts a particular woman will develop is partly determined by inheritance. Most of the breast is made up of fatty tissue (as many women discover when they gain or lose weight). All breasts, however, function the same way; they are capable of producing milk to nurse an infant. The size of the breast or the nipple does not affect the amount or quality of a mother's milk.

The parts of the breast are the **nipple**, through which milk leaves the breast of the nursing mother; the **areola**, which is the dark circle of skin around the nipple; and the **mammary glands** (or alveoli), which are capable of producing milk (see Figure 1–5). There are also small bumps on the areola that release an oily substance that keeps the skin of the nipple from drying out. Milk travels from the mammary glands through the **lactiferous ducts** to the nipple.

There are small muscles underlying the nipple that can tighten, causing the nipple to become erect in response to touch, cold, or sexual stimulation. The nipples and breasts (in addition to their function in milk production) are for many women a highly sensitive area for sexual stimulation and are viewed as an important part of female beauty.

THE MALE SEX ORGANS

External Sex Organs

The **penis** is the major external sex organ in the male. It has the reproductive function of placing sperm in the woman's vagina. It is also the organ of urination in men. As with female anatomy, the size and shape of the penis varies among men. In the adult, most penises in the limp or flaccid state measure from 3.3 to 4.5 inches. When erect, most penises measure between 4.7 and 9.2 inches. The average diameter of the penis is 1.25 inches in the limp state, and 1.5 inches when erect. The size of a man's penis does not seem to be related to his height or to the size of other parts of his body, and there is no way to guess the size of a man's penis on the basis of other physical characteristics. Just as breast size does not indicate a woman's ability to produce milk for nursing, penis size does not indicate a man's fertility or his sexual ability.

As Figures 1–6 and 1–7 indicate, the penis is a very complicated organ. At the base the **crura** are attached to the pelvic bones. The middle portion of the penis, which extends out from the body, is called the **shaft**. It is made up of two sections of the **corpus cavernosum**, which lie along the top of the penis, and the **corpus spongiosum**, which extends up the bottom of the shaft and widens to become the **glans** at the tip. The corpus cavernosa is tissue with many hollow spaces that expand and fill with blood during sexual excitement, causing an erection. The corpus spongiosum does the same, but to a lesser degree. The **glans** is rounded at the end and has a ridge called the **corona** at the point where it joins the shaft of the penis. The **urethra**, through which both urine and sperm travel out of the

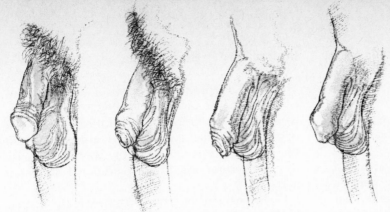

FIGURE 1–6. *Four examples of male external sex organs.*

FIGURE 1–7. *The internal structures of the male sex organs.*

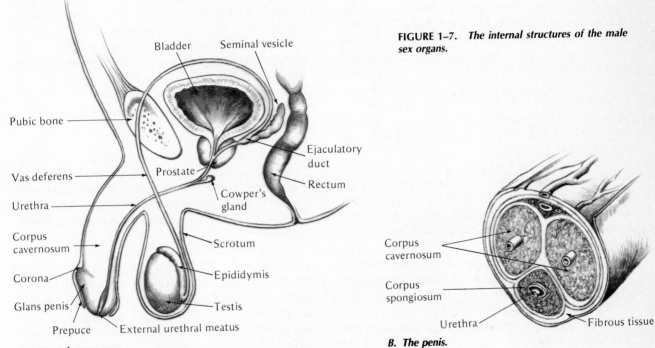

Bladder
Seminal vesicle
Pubic bone
Vas deferens
Urethra
Corpus cavernosum
Corona
Glans penis
Prepuce
Prostate
Cowper's gland
Ejaculatory duct
Rectum
Scrotum
Epididymis
Testis
External urethral meatus

A. Internal sex organs.

Corpus cavernosum
Corpus spongiosum
Urethra
Fibrous tissue

B. The penis.

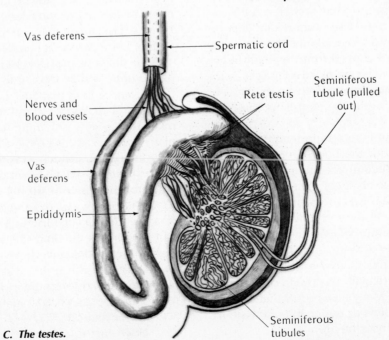

Vas deferens
Spermatic cord
Nerves and blood vessels
Rete testis
Seminiferous tubule (pulled out)
Vas deferens
Epididymis
Seminiferous tubules

C. The testes.

body, goes up the center of the corpus spongiosum to the **urinary opening** (external urethral meatus) in the glans. The three major sections are each enclosed in tough fibrous tissue, so that when the sections are filled with blood and the penis is erect, it has a rigid strength, like a garden hose under pressure.

The surface of the penis is covered with thin, loose skin, which is wrinkled when the penis is limp and smooths out when it is larger and erect. In men who are not circumcised, a flap of loose skin called the **foreskin** (or **prepuce**) covers the glans when the penis is limp, and slides back to bare the glans when the penis is erect. When this skin has been removed by circumcision, the glans remains uncovered both when the penis is limp and when it is erect (see pages 291–292 for details about circumcision).

The penis has many nerve endings and is extremely sensitive both to sexual stimulation and to pain. Most men report that the glans is the most sensitive part, followed by the underside of the penis. The upper surface is less sensitive.

The other external sex organ in men is the **scrotum,** which contains the **testes** (or **testicles**), the **epididymis,** and the **spermatic cord.** The scrotum is a sac of tissue covered by loose, wrinkled skin with a little hair and many sweat glands. It contains the testicles, which are the sperm-producing organs and which evolved from the same tissue that becomes the ovaries in women. The scrotum changes in size and shape in response to heat and cold and in response to sexual stimulation.

The **cremaster muscle,** which surrounds the testicles, pulls the testicles closer to the body in response to cold or extreme sexual stimulation, creating a smaller, tighter scrotum resting just behind the penis. In warm conditions the cremaster muscle relaxes, and the scrotum appears larger, hangs lower, and is less wrinkled. Changes in the scrotum are handled automatically by the nervous system and are not under the conscious control of the man.

The changes in response to temperature are thought to be part of the body's mechanism for stabilizing the temperature of the testicles. Excessive heat reduces the ability of the testicles to produce high-quality sperm. In most men the left testicle hangs lower in the scrotum than the right, for reasons that are not known (the penis is also often bent slightly to the left).

The scrotum has many nerve endings and, like the penis, is extremely sensitive to sexual stimulation and to pain. Many men report that it is less sensitive than the glans or underside of the penis, but more sensitive than the top.

Internal Sex Organs

The internal reproductive system of males provides a complex path for sperm leading from the testes (where they are formed) up into the pelvis to just below the bladder, and then down the urethra to the end of the penis. Along the way sperm pass through several organs, and additional fluids are added.

To begin at the beginning, sperm are created in the testes, which are the male counterpart to the ovaries in women. The testes are smooth, firm, egg-shaped organs averaging about 1¾ inches in length and 1 inch in width. In addition to creating sperm, the testes produce testosterone, the most important male hormone. The sperm are created in the **seminiferous tubules,** small compartments within the testes made up of coiled tubing (approximately one to three feet within each tubule). It is estimated that altogether each testicle contains half a mile of these tiny tubes. The seminiferous tubules all empty into a series of ducts at the top of the testes that carry the sperm to the **epididymis,** a small organ about two inches long attached to the back side of each testicle. The sperm spend about two weeks in the epididymis, traveling through ten to twenty feet of coiled tubing and developing to maturity.

The next step is from the epididymis to the **vas deferens,** a muscular tube that carries the sperm from the scrotum outside the body into the pelvis. The vas deferens, along with blood and lymph vessels, nerves, and the cremaster muscle, are all contained in the **spermatic cord,** which exits from the top of each side of the scrotum and passes through the pelvic muscles into the lower abdomen. If the small hole in the pelvic muscles is strained or enlarged, a hernia often develops there. The vas deferens passes behind the bladder, where the **seminal vesicle** feeds into it. The seminal vesicle secretes a fluid that supports the survival of the sperm and makes up about 60 percent of the **semen,** the sperm-containing fluid that a man ejaculates. The vas deferens then feeds into the **ejaculatory duct,** which runs through the center of the **prostate gland.** The prostate contributes more fluid to the sperm-carrying semen, making up about 30 percent of the total volume. Within the prostate, the ejaculatory duct performs an important function at the time of ejaculation. It closes off the bladder opening so that the ejaculate is forced down through the urethra. It is this duct that is often damaged during surgery for an enlarged prostate, causing retrograde ejaculation (see pages 309–310 for details).

Once in the urethra, the semen is expelled

through the urinary opening at the tip of the penis. Just below the prostate gland are two tiny organs called Cowper's glands that secrete a small amount of fluid in the early stages of sexual excitement. This fluid seems to neutralize the acid environment of the urethra, making the survival of sperm more likely. It makes up the small amount of fluid that sometimes comes out of the penis early in sexual arousal. It may contain sperm, and thus a pregnancy can be caused even if the man does not ejaculate.

MALFORMATIONS OF THE REPRODUCTIVE SYSTEM

A few babies are born with sexual organs that have not developed properly. This section presents basic information about some of the more common malformations of the reproductive system. Most of these malformations are minor and can be treated with surgery, so that the infant grows up to be capable of normal sexual functioning. In rare cases, however, an infant may be born without a complete set of reproductive organs or with organs that have both male and female characteristics. This may be caused by genetic (inherited) problems or by chemical or hormone problems of the mother that affect the baby while it is still developing in the uterus.

Two of the best-known genetic conditions are Klinefelter's Syndrome (in men) and Turner's Syndrome (in women). Men and women who have these conditions are sterile, since the men do not have testes and the women do not have ovaries. Although people with these syndromes or other similar conditions are sterile and often have other health problems, they can usually have normal sexual functioning, but they may need to stay on hormone treatment throughout their lifetimes.

Undescended Testes

Undescended testes (testicles) is a condition in which the testes, which are normally located in the scrotum of a boy or a man, are not found there. During the development of the fetus, the testes are located in the abdomen. In most cases they descend into the scrotum before the baby is born, but approximately 3 percent of baby boys are born with no testes in the scrotum. For most of these babies the testes descend during the first few weeks after birth, but in a small percentage of cases (less than 1 percent) surgery will be needed. In rare cases a baby may be found to have no testicles in the abdomen either, or there may be only one. One tes-

ticle is enough to produce the needed hormones and fertility for a man, but the boy born with no testicles will be sterile and will need hormone treatment all his life.

Hypospadias

Hypospadias is a condition in which the development of the penis is not complete at the time a male infant is born. The baby urinates through a small opening along the underside of his penis, rather than at the end. This problem is quite common and can be corrected early in life by surgery. It is not likely to affect the little boy's appearance or capacity for sexual functioning in adulthood. Adult men with untreated hypospadias may have difficulty starting a pregnancy, since the semen comes out of an opening on the underside rather than at the end of the penis. In severe cases of hypospadias, which are very rare, the penis may be curled forward and not straighten out when the child gets an erection. The genitals of the newborn boy may look more like those of a girl. These cases can also be treated by surgery.

It is rare for babies to be born with serious malformations of the reproductive system.

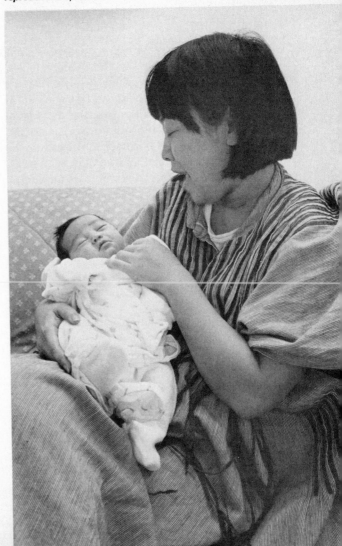

Congenital Absence of a Vagina

In rare cases a baby girl may be born with genitals that appear to make her a boy. The cause is usually an excess of male hormones during fetal development. The vagina is sealed off, and instead the infant appears to have a scrotum. The clitoris is large and appears to be a small penis. Usually the internal parts of the reproductive system, the uterus and ovaries, are normal. The treatment of this condition is surgery to reduce the size of the clitoris and to open the sealed vagina. Female hormones are also given if needed.

Imperforate Hymen

The hymen is a thin membrane that partially covers the entrance to the vagina. Occasionally a baby girl is born with an **imperforate hymen,** that is, a hymen that has no opening. Normally the hymen has one or more small openings and is stretched or torn into a larger opening when the woman begins to have sexual intercourse. An imperforate hymen may not create a problem for a young girl, but when her periods begin, an opening is necessary in order for the menstrual blood to flow. Treatment for an imperforate hymen is minor surgery to create the necessary opening.

Hermaphroditism

A **hermaphrodite** is a person born with the characteristics of both the male sex and the female sex. This is a rare condition in when a newborn baby may appear to have both a penis and a vagina, or in which an infant may have the external genitals of one sex and the internal reproductive organs of the other sex. The causes of hermaphroditism may be either genetic or hormonal. Fortunately, with modern medical techniques, the correct sex for such a baby can be determined. With surgery and later hormone treatment if needed, the infant can develop into a male or a female and live a normal life.

The correct sex for such babies is determined by chromosome tests, hormone tests, and examination of the external and internal reproductive system. The external genitalia of newborns can be confusing, even in infants who will develop into perfectly normal males and females (see Figure 1–10 on page 15).

Hermaphroditism, or any confusion about the sex of their child, is naturally very upsetting for the parents. Fortunately, such problems are rare and can usually be resolved. It is extremely important that any child born with this problem be raised with the correct sex, as a boy or a girl, from the earliest months. The psychological and emotional development of the child could be harmed by changing the sex in which the child is being raised after the first few months of life, or by confusion about the sex in which to raise the child.

HORMONES AND THEIR EFFECTS ON THE REPRODUCTIVE SYSTEM

What Are Hormones and How Do They Work?

Hormones are the secretions of the endocrine glands. The endocrine glands are organs such as the pituitary, thyroid, and adrenal glands, which produce chemicals (hormones) that influence body processes. The hormones that affect the development and functioning of the sexual and reproductive organs are discussed here. Hormones guide the development of the reproductive system at two important points—before birth and at puberty (sexual maturation). They control development of the secondary sex characteristics, such as pubic hair and breasts. The menstrual cycle and fertility in both men and women are controlled by hormones as well.

The **sex hormones** are those produced by the **gonads** (ovaries and testicles). Both men's and women's gonads produce all three of the sex hormones, but in women the amounts of **estrogen** and **progesterone,** the female sex hormones, are higher, and in men the level of **testosterone** produced is higher. Two other hormones that are produced in the adrenal glands of both sexes (*aldosterone* and *androsterone*), together with testosterone, form a group known as **androgens,** or masculinizing hormones.

The production of sex hormones and the other functions of the gonads are regulated by the **pituitary gland** (located in the brain), which in turn is guided by the **hypothalamus** (a part of the brain), which sends substances called **releasing factors** to the pituitary. The relationship between the hypothalamus, the pituitary, the gonads, the adrenal glands, and the breasts in women is seen in Figure 1–8.

Two of the pituitary hormones, FSH (follicle-stimulating hormone) and LH (luteinizing hormone) are called **gonadotrophins** because they directly affect the gonads. FSH stimulates the ovaries to produce ova and estrogen, and stimulates the testes to develop sperm. LH, also known as ICSH (interstitial-cell-stimulating hormone) in males, promotes ovulation (release of the ova from the ovary) in women and the production of testosterone in men.

The release of hormones in men is a relatively stable pattern, but in women the levels of hormones

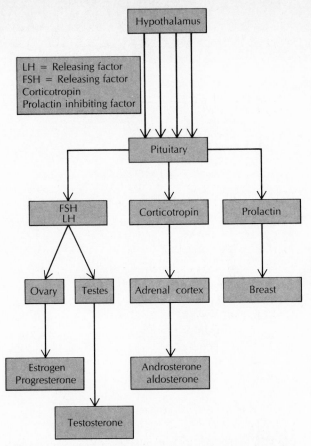

FIGURE 1–8. *The production of sex hormones by the endocrine glands.*

shift throughout the monthly cycle, with higher levels of FSH released in the first half of the cycle, and higher levels of LH just before ovulation. This means that women have higher levels of estrogen in the first half of the cycle, and higher levels of progesterone in the second half. The way hormones operate in the menstrual cycle is described in more detail on pages 16–19.

Corticotropin stimulates the adrenal cortex to produce aldosterone and androsterone. Prolactin stimulates the breasts to produce milk. Prolactin-inhibiting factor, from the hypothalamus, prevents the pituitary from releasing prolactin, except in pregnant women and nursing mothers.

The hormones interact in a complex cycle with the hypothalamus and pituitary. The hypothalamus picks up its cues as to what hormones should be released from the state of the body metabolism, and promotes the right balance of the different hormones for the person's sex and age. Various aspects of the person's health and life-style, including nutrition, exercise, alcohol consumption, and medications, affect the way in which the sex hormones are metabolized (used) by the body. In addition, all the sex hormones are similar in chemical structure, and the body can convert them from one to another. For example, certain chemical conditions in the body may cause testosterone to be converted to estrogen. The hypothalamus stands watch over the situation and responds with signals to the pituitary to keep the hormones in correct balance.

A Girl or a Boy? Developments before Birth

The sex of a human being is determined at the time of conception by the fertilization of the woman's egg with a sperm carrying either an X (female) or a Y (male) chromosome. During the first 40 days of development, however, the organs of male and female embryos are not different from each other. Each has a ridge of tissue from which the sexual organs will develop, but it has not yet begun to differentiate. At 40 days, a male embryo begins to develop testes from the same tissue that will become ovaries in the female. At this point sexual differentiation begins.

The gonads of the unborn fetus produce hormones that guide the body in developing either a male or a female sexual system. The two different sets of organs evolve out of the same tissues, and males and females have corresponding organs. A male child can be produced only if the testes begin to develop and produce testosterone at this time. If there is a problem and the embryo does not develop either testicles or ovaries, a physically female child will be produced.

Internal Sex Organs

Figure 1–9 on page 14 shows the primitive internal sexual organs in the embryo at six weeks and the way they develop differently in the male and the female fetus.

The embryo in the first few weeks of life develops two sets of ducts, the **Mullerian** and the **Wolffian**, which serve as primitive kidneys until the more sophisticated kidney system develops. The internal reproductive organs of men and women are developed from these early ducts. In females the Mullerian duct becomes the Fallopian tubes, the uterus, and the upper part of the vagina. The Wolffian duct does not continue to develop, and little is left of it in the adult female. A small bit of the tissue that becomes the prostate in males is found at the opening of the bladder in women (for more on this, see details about the G spot, page 52).

In the male, the Wolffian duct develops into the vas deferens, the epididymis, the seminal vesicles, and the ejaculatory duct. The Mullerian duct does not develop, and few traces of it are left in the adult male, other than a small bit of tissue called the *verumontanum* or *prostatic utricle*.

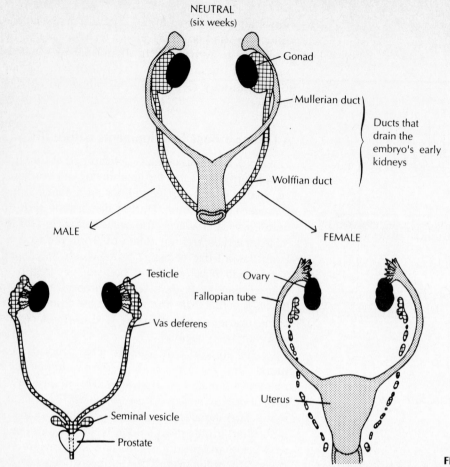

NEUTRAL
(six weeks)

Gonad

Mullerian duct

Ducts that
drain the
embryo's early
kidneys

Wolffian duct

MALE

FEMALE

Testicle

Vas deferens

Ovary

Fallopian tube

Seminal vesicle

Prostate

Uterus

FIGURE 1–9. *Formation of the male and female internal sex organs.*

In the male fetus the testes develop in the abdomen. Then, during the last few weeks before birth, the testes move out of the abdomen into the scrotum. In a few cases (especially in premature babies) this process is not complete at the time of birth, and the testes descend during the first few weeks after birth. **Undescended testicles,** which can be a health problem, are discussed on page 11.

External Sex Organs

Although the reproductive organs of adult men and women appear to be very different from each other, in fact they develop from the same embryonic tissues, as Figure 1–10 show. The genital tubercle grows to become the glans of the penis in men and the glans of the clitoris in women. The genital fold becomes the labia minora and the entrance to the vagina in women. In men it forms the underside of the penis, closing off and creating a channel so that urination is from the tip of the penis. Figure 1–11 shows how the penis develops in the male embryo.

The skin that forms the two labia majora in females fuses together in males and forms the skin covering the scrotum.

Puberty: Gaining Sexual Maturity

Hormones guide and control the physical changes of adolescence, when girls and boys mature into women and men over a period of several years. The age at which puberty begins and the amount of height and weight gained are also influenced by inheritance and by the environment. Throughout this century in the United States, the average age of puberty has progressively become younger, and the overall height and weight gain has become greater. This change is thought to be due to improved nutrition and general health.

Puberty begins with an increase in LH and FSH production in the pituitary, which triggers an increase in the hormones produced by the gonads. This increase usually begins between the ages of 9 and 11 for both boys and girls, but girls mature faster, and at age 12 or 13 they may be as much as two years ahead of boys in development. The period of greatest growth and weight gain for girls comes around age 12, and for boys around age 14. Because of inherited timetables for development and environmental influences, some boys and girls will mature years earlier than others. The age at which a girl or boy goes through puberty may be

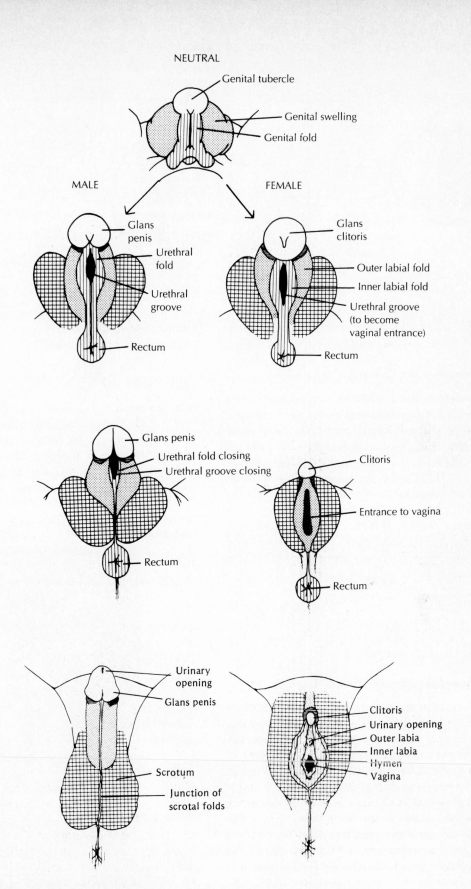

FIGURE 1–10. *Formation of the male and female external sex organs.*

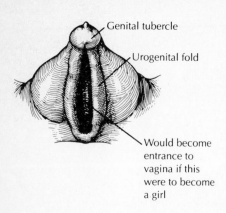

Genital tubercle

Urogenital fold

Would become entrance to vagina if this were to become a girl

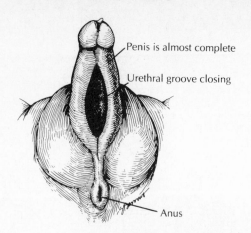

Penis is almost complete

Urethral groove closing

Anus

FIGURE 1–11. *Formation of the penis in the early embryonic stages.*

very important to her or him socially, but it has no effect on future health, fertility, or appearance.

Secondary Sex Characteristics

Puberty is the process of sexual maturation, after which both females and males are fertile and able to reproduce. Puberty also brings about many other changes in size and appearance that are not directly related to the sex organs or to the ability to reproduce. These are called **secondary sex characteristics** and include such things as facial and pubic hair. In infancy and childhood, male and female children are similar in body size and appearance. At puberty, the secondary sex characteristics begin to develop, creating those differences that distinguish adult females and males from each other.

On average, adult males are taller and heavier than adult females, although individual females are larger than some males. As Figure 1–12 shows, there are many other changes in body shape and characteristics that develop at puberty.

Psychological and Emotional Changes

In addition to tremendous physical changes, adolescents undergo great emotional and psychological changes as well. Adolescence is known as a time of stormy, rapidly changing emotions and attempts to establish oneself as a separate individual, different from parents and family members. Rapid physical growth and changes in levels of hormones probably contribute to the emotional climate. But other social and environmental influences are probably just as important. Social roles and expectations change rapidly as the girl or boy matures, creating pressure to behave differently and to take on adult responsibilities. Further, the arrival of sexual maturity and fertility creates new opportunities and new ways of relating to others. Few adults

remember adolescence as an easy time, but fortunately most of us survive it.

The Menstrual Cycle

The **menstrual cycle** refers to the monthly changes in an adult woman's reproductive system that makes her fertile (capable of becoming pregnant) and that bring on monthly bleeding from the vagina. The cycle is controlled by the hypothalamus releasing factors and by hormones produced by the

Going through puberty is no joke, but the teenage years can also be a lot of fun.

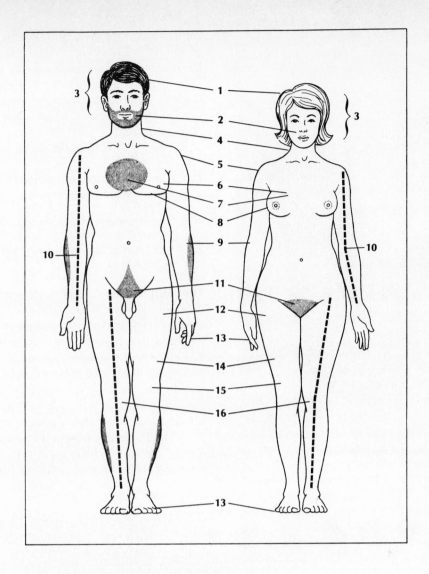

THE SECONDARY SEXUAL CHARACTERISTICS

The Male: On the average, taller and heavier than the female.
1. *Head hair:* may fall out with age. **2.** *Facial hair:* grows throughout adult life.
3. *Features:* more pronounced, face longer, head (front to back) longer. **4.** *Neck:* thicker, longer, larynx one-third larger. **5.** *Shoulders:* broader, squarer. **6.** *Chest:* larger in every dimension. **7.** *Body hair:* more evident, especially on chest and arms. **8.** *Breasts:* rudimentary in size. **9.** *Muscles:* bigger, more obvious. **10.** *Arms:* longer, thicker, "carrying angle" straight. **11.** *Pubic hair:* growing up to a point, forming triangle. **12.** *Hips:* narrower. **13.** *Hands and feet:* larger, fingers and toes stronger and blunter. **14.** *Thighs:* more cylindrical with bulge of muscles. **15.** *Legs:* longer, bulging calves. **16.** *Angle of thigh and leg:* as with "carrying angle" of arm, forming straight line, thigh to ankle.

The Female: On the average, shorter and lighter than the male.
1. *Head hair:* more lasting. **2.** *Facial hair:* very faint, usually noticeable only in later years. **3.** *Features:* more delicate, face rounder, head smaller, rounder (from top). **4.** *Neck:* shorter, more rounded, larynx smaller. **5.** *Shoulders:* more rounded, sloping. **6.** *Chest:* smaller, narrower. **7.** *Body Hair:* very light and faint. **8.** *Breasts:* prominent, also well-developed nipples with large surrounding rings. **9.** *Muscles:* largely hidden under layers of fat. **10.** *Arms:* "carrying angle" bent. **11.** *Pubic hair:* forming straight line across at top. **12.** *Hips:* wider, more rounded. **13.** *Hands and feet:* smaller and narrower. **14.** *Thighs:* wider at top and shorter in length. **15.** *Legs:* shorter with smoother contours. **16.** *Angle of thigh and leg:* as with "carrying angle" of arm, slightly bent, forming an angle at the knee.

Teenage bodies grow and mature at different rates.

pituitary and the ovaries. It begins on the first day of menstrual bleeding and averages 28 days until the next cycle begins. Women's cycles vary, but over 90 percent of cycles are between 25 and 35 days in length. Menstrual bleeding usually continues for 3 to 5 days, and amounts to a few tablespoons of fluid.

The cycle can be divided into three parts:

1. The **follicular phase**, during which the egg follicle is maturing in the ovary and the uterine lining is preparing to receive the egg
2. The **ovulatory phase**, during which the ovum is released from the ovary
3. The **luteal phase**, during which the **corpus luteum** is present in the ovary

The corpus luteum is a temporary hormone-producing body (progesterone and estrogen) that is created each cycle in the ovary. It develops from the cells that line the egg follicle after the follicle has burst and the ovum has been released. At the end of the menstrual cycle the corpus luteum dies, unless the ovum is fertilized, in which case the corpus luteum continues to provide hormones for the first three months of pregnancy (Figure 1–13).

The cycle begins when low levels of estrogen during menstrual bleeding cause the pituitary to release FSH (follicle-stimulating hormone), which

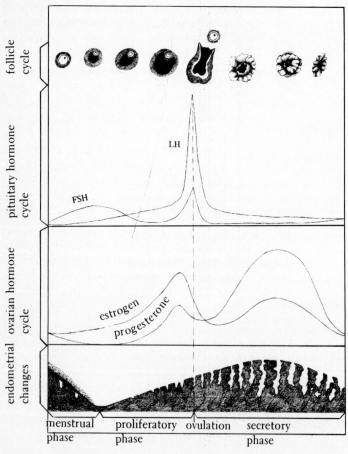

FIGURE 1–13. *The menstrual cycle.*

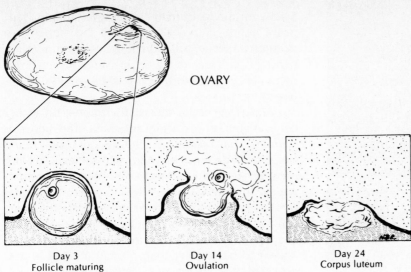

OVARY

Day 3
Follicle maturing

Day 14
Ovulation

Day 24
Corpus luteum

FIGURE 1–14. *Changes in the ovary during the menstrual cycle.*

in turn causes several follicles in the ovaries to begin to mature. The maturing follicles produce estrogen, causing an increase in the level of the hormone circulating in the body. Eventually, one or two follicles continue to grow to maturity, producing more estrogen as they do so, and the remaining follicles become inactive. At the midpoint in the cycle, just before ovulation, the estrogen levels are at their highest and cause the pituitary to release a burst of LH (luteinizing hormone), which triggers ovulation. Following release of the ovum, the cells lining the follicle continue to produce estrogen, and, under the influence of LH, begin to produce progesterone as well. This little group of cells takes on a yellowish color at this point and is known as the corpus luteum. During the second half of the cycle, the levels of LH slowly drop, and eventually the corpus luteum ceases to produce hormones and begins to die. At the low point of both estrogen and progesterone production, menstrual bleeding begins (see Figure 1–14).

Fertilization can take place only in the 24 hours following ovulation. It occurs in the Fallopian tube as the ovum journeys toward the uterus. If the ovum is fertilized, a whole new set of hormonal changes begins to prepare the body to support the growing embryo. This information is covered in Chapter 2.

There is a great deal of variation among women in menstrual cycles, and many factors such as general health, nutrition, exercise, and stress can affect the cycle. For details on menstrual problems, see Chapter 12 (pages 248–251).

Menopause

Menopause refers to the end of menstruation in women, which usually occurs between the ages of 45 and 55. It is the major sign of a set of changes in women called the **climacteric.** When the cycle ends, the woman no longer has monthly bleeding, and she is not fertile. Menopause is brought on by hormonal changes, primarily reduced estrogen production by the ovaries. The hormonal changes that bring about menopause begin years before the menstrual cycle stops. In the early forties most women experience a decline in fertility, as fewer eggs mature and the level of estrogen produced in the ovaries is lower. The exact reasons that this change takes place are not clear, but it seems to be a normal part of aging. The ovaries put out less estrogen each year and become insensitive to stimulation of FSH and LH from the pituitary. Eventually, ovulation ceases and menstrual bleeding ends.

Menopause is a process that may be spread out over several years or may take place within a single year. Its first signs are usually irregular periods due to lack of ovulation, and over time the menstrual bleeding becomes less and less frequent until it stops altogether. Estrogen production by the ovaries drops very low, but estrogen begins to be manufactured in other parts of the body, mainly by converting other hormones into estrogen. These alternative sources of estrogen keep producing the hormone throughout the woman's life, although at much lower levels than during the fertile years.

The changes in hormone balance that take place during menopause create temporary physical and emotional problems for some women. Common symptoms are hot flashes and vaginal dryness. Fortunately, over half of all women have mild symptoms that do not cause problems, and some claim no symptoms at all.

The lower levels of estrogen after menopause have effects on other parts of the body as well as the reproductive system. The body's ability to absorb calcium is reduced, and women need more

Women's and men's bodies change with age, but feelings stay the same.

calcium in their diets after menopause in order to avoid the development of osteoporosis, or brittle bones. Women with osteoporosis are at high risk of bone fractures. Details on the health problems associated with menopause are given in Chapter 12 (pages 251–252).

Male Climacteric

Both men's and women's bodies change as they age, but men do not have a dramatic change in their reproductive abilities similar to menopause in women. Men remain capable of reproducing throughout their lives, but their fertility (number and quality of sperm) and their sexual responsiveness begins to decrease slowly while they are still in their twenties. Over time, there are gradual shifts in the amounts and balance of sex hormones in the body. By the time men reach their fifties, they usually notice some mild changes, such as taking longer or needing more stimulation to get an erection, or being slower to reach orgasm. These changes can be psychologically and emotionally upsetting for men in the same way that menopause can be troubling to women. Reduced fertility is not likely to be noticed unless the man wants to get a woman pregnant, in which case it may take longer than it would have when he was younger. For details on fertility and age, see Chapter 8. For more on the changes in sexual responsiveness associated with age, see Chapter 3.

Hormones and Sexual Behavior

The relationship between hormones and sexual behavior in human beings is not well understood. In lower animals, hormones seem to cause mating

behavior, but in human beings the situation appears more complex. Although hormones are needed for sexual function, it appears that learned behavior, culture, relationships, and the environment are more important influences on sexual behavior in humans.

Evidence of the effects of hormones on sexual behavior includes certain automatic and nonconscious sexual responses, such as nocturnal emissions (wet dreams) in men, which begin during puberty. In addition, most adult men and women appear to develop some conscious form of sexual release, either in a relationship with another person or through self-stimulation (masturbation). People with severe sex hormone deficiencies often appear to have lower than normal interest in sex, especially if the deficiency develops before puberty. On the other hand, sexually experienced adult men who lose the function of their testicles (and are not producing testosterone) often report near normal levels of sexual interest and ability for several years, although their interest does appear to decline slowly over time.

No single hormone has been identified as the cause of sexual interest or desire, although it appears that testosterone is related to sexual desire and sensation in both men and women. Testosterone supplements can maintain sexual interest and ability (as well as masculine appearance) in men whose gonads do not produce the hormone for them. However, additional testosterone given to a man who already has normal levels of the hormone does not seem to increase his sexual desire or abil-

Hormones appear to influence sexual behavior, especially in young people.

ity. Small amounts of testosterone are added to some estrogen replacement programs for post-menopausal women, because the testosterone supplement appears to increase sexual desire and enjoyment for women as well (if they are not producing sufficient testosterone in their own bodies).

In youth, sex hormones are necessary to bring on puberty and sexual maturation. They may also be a necessary (but not sufficient) condition to cause development of sexual behavior. In adulthood, however, the sexually experienced person may continue to show high interest in sex even if the sex hormone levels are low, as a result of behavioral conditioning. In other words, the person has learned that sexual activity is pleasurable and therefore has the desire to continue it, without needing the support of high hormone levels.

In both men and women, sex hormones reach a peak in adolescence and early adulthood, followed by a gradual decline into old age for men, and a sharper drop for women at the time of menopause. Fertility levels follow a similar pattern: a peak in early adulthood followed by gradual decline. Men remain fertile throughout their lives, however, whereas women can reproduce only until menopause. Patterns of sexual activity over a lifetime differ for each individual and do not follow the same pattern as hormones and fertility, although sexual activity is generally greater in youth, when both hormones and fertility are high. However, depending on culture, the environment, and relationships, sexual activity may follow any number of patterns, including being low in youth and higher in old age.

THE SEXUAL ORGANS AND THE NERVOUS SYSTEM

The nervous system plays a central role in the functioning of the sexual and reproductive organs of women and men. It is responsible both for the sensations and feelings of which we are aware, and for our ability to respond physically to sexual stimulation. The sexual and reproductive systems of women and men have very different and very complex "wiring," involving two branches of the nervous system. The part of the system that feeds back sensations to the brain, and also controls conscious responses, is called the **somatic** branch. But most of sexual response is not under the conscious control of the individual woman or man. Instead, it is controlled by the **autonomic** branch, which is the part that automatically regulates things like heart rate and blood pressure. Thus, we cannot decide to have an erection, vaginal lubrication, or an orgasm simply and directly (the way we decide to pick up a pencil or wiggle our toes). Sexual response is a more indirect process, depending on stimulation through the physical senses such as touch and sight, and on thoughts and emotions. These stimuli are processed by the brain, which uses the autonomic system to prepare the sex organs for sexual activity. Considering this roundabout process, it is not surprising that developing satisfying sexual relationships is a complicated business, and takes time to learn.

Within the autonomic system, two divisions, the **sympathetic** and the **parasympathetic**, control different parts of sexual response. Response in women seems to be mainly under the sympathetic system, but the complete cycle of sexual response in men seems to require both systems. For example, erection in men appears to be controlled by the parasympathetic system, and ejaculation by the sympathetic system. Thus, men with serious damage to the nervous system sometimes lose the ability to ejaculate but still have erections, or the opposite.

The details of how the nervous system affects sexual response in men and women are not yet fully understood, although knowledge on the subject is increasing rapidly. Psychological and hormonal factors, as well as messages from the neurological system, are all processed by the brain, and the three together contribute to the body's response to sexual stimulation.

FOR FURTHER READING

Federation of Feminist Women's Health Centers. *A New View of a Woman's Body*. New York: Simon & Schuster, 1981.

GEER, JAMES, JULIA HEIMAN, AND HAROLD LEITENBERG. *Human Sexuality*. Englewood Cliffs, N.J.: Prentice-Hall, 1984.

HOLE, JOHN W., JR. *Human Anatomy and Physiology*, 4th ed. Dubuque, Iowa: Wm. C. Brown, 1987.

2
Conception:
How Human Life Begins

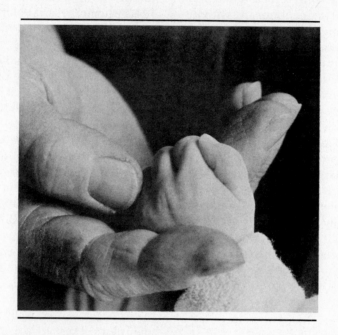

This chapter describes the process of conception and gives information about how the fertilized egg develops into an embryo and then a fetus during the nine months of pregnancy. Information about pregnancy, about changes in the mother's body, and about labor and delivery is provided later in the book, in Chapter 6.

CONCEPTION

This section describes how pregnancy is started. For details on women's and men's bodies and how the reproductive system works, see Chapter 1, "The Human Body."

Pregnancy begins when a single male sex cell (a sperm) joins with a single female sex cell (an egg or ovum) to create a new and unique cell (known as a **zygote**). Eggs and sperm are different from every other cell in the human body because they carry only half as much genetic information as other cells do. Most cells have thousands of genes, which are arranged on strands of tissue called **chromosomes.** In most cells there are 23 pairs, or a total of 46 chromosomes. But there are only 23 chromosomes in each normal egg and sperm. When the egg and sperm unite, the full 46 chromosomes needed to form a new human cell are present. Since half of the chromosomes come from the mother and half from the father, the new person will be similar to both of them but will not be exactly like either one of them. Furthermore, the genes carried on the chromosomes vary somewhat from one egg to another and from sperm to sperm. This is why brothers and sisters often look and act so different from each other. But before we can understand how genetics makes each baby unique, we must know more about the egg and the sperm and how they come to be united.

The Egg

The egg has three roles in pregnancy:

1. It contains the genetic information that the mother contributes to the baby.
2. It holds the "master plan" for pregnancy. This master plan determines the sequence and timing of the baby's development during pregnancy.
3. It provides the nutrition the zygote needs during the first few days after conception.

Later, the fetus will get nutrition through the umbilical cord and the placenta (to be discussed). In the first few days, however, neither the cord nor the placenta is available.

The eggs are contained in a woman's ovaries (see Chapter 1). A baby girl is born with all the eggs she will ever have. No one knows exactly how many eggs an average newborn girl has, but the number has been estimated at around 400,000. These eggs are immature at birth and simply lie in the ovaries. It is not until puberty that the ovaries begin to release the eggs.

The average woman will produce 400 to 500 mature eggs during her lifetime. Usually, one or the other of a woman's ovaries will release one egg every month. This process is called **ovulation** (see Figure 2–1). The egg is typically released about halfway through the menstrual cycle. If a woman is on a regular 28-day cycle, then ovulation should occur around the 14th day. But since most women do not have such a regular cycle, simply counting days is not a reliable indicator of ovulation (see Chapter 9).

Once an egg has been released from the ovaries, it does not live very long. In fact, it will disintegrate within about 48 hours. So, if pregnancy is to occur, the sperm and the egg must join together within the first 12 to 24 hours following ovulation.

The Sperm

Sperm are some of the smallest cells in the human body. Each one is only about 0.002 (two one-thousandths) of an inch long. A normal sperm has three sections. The uppermost section is the head, which contains the 23 chromosomes that the father will contribute to the zygote. The middle section provides the energy that the sperm needs to move. The bottommost section is the tail. This tail whips back and forth very rapidly and moves the sperm forward (see Figure 2–2).

Sperm are produced in the seminiferous tubules of the testes (see Chapter 1, "The Human Body," for details about the male reproductive system). It takes about 70 to 74 days for newly produced sperm to mature. For about 60 of these days, they are stored in the seminiferous tubules. For the last 12 or so days, sperm are stored in the epididymis. Although sperm may survive in the epididymis for several weeks, they must eventually be released (through ejaculation) or they will die, be reabsorbed by the man's body, and be replaced by new sperm.

After puberty, men produce sperm constantly. It would be difficult to estimate how many sperm the average man produces in his lifetime, but the number is clearly in the billions. In a typical ejaculation, 300 million sperm leave the man's body.

Different men produce different numbers of sperm, and a low sperm count is a common cause of male infertility (see Chapter 8). Even in a healthy man (that is, a man who is capable of producing "normal" amounts of sperm), the number of sperm may be affected by various circumstances. For example, sperm die if the temperature in the testes gets too high. This can happen if a man has a fever, takes frequent long hot baths, spends time each day in a hot tub or Jacuzzi, or wears clothes that keep the testes too close to the body.

The sperm carries with it the father's genetic contribution. It also determines the sex of the baby. One pair (of the normal 23 pairs) of chromosomes

FIGURE 2–1. *Ovulation.*

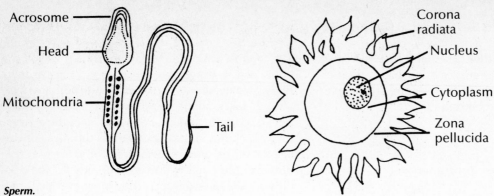

Sperm.

Egg.

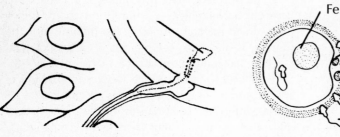

Sperm penetrates the egg.

Other sperm cannot penetrate.

FIGURE 2–2. *The union of sperm and egg.*

determines an individual's gender. An individual sperm carries either an X (female) or a Y (male) chromosome. An individual egg always carries an X chromosome. If the sperm that joins the egg is also carrying an X, then the newly formed cell will have two X chromosomes and will become a girl. If the sperm carries a Y, then the new cell will have an X from the mother and a Y from the father and will become a boy.

Intercourse

Conception involves the joining of an egg and a sperm, and of course this most commonly occurs through sexual intercourse (see Chapter 3 for details about intercourse). For pregnancy to occur, the man must ejaculate semen, which contains the sperm, into or near the woman's vagina (Figure 2–3). This occurs when the man reaches orgasm ("climaxes" or "comes") (see Chapters 1 and 3). It does not matter what position the couple is in when ejaculation occurs. For example, having intercourse while standing up does not reduce the chances of pregnancy. The sperm are strong swimmers, and some of them may overcome the force of gravity and make the journey up to the egg.

Although the man must reach orgasm in order for pregnancy to occur, it is not necessary for the woman to do so. Women's orgasms are not related to conception or pregnancy. A man can

produce the sperm necessary to cause pregnancy at any time, but a woman only produces the egg that is needed once a month. Sperm stay alive inside a woman's body for about 48 hours, and the egg is intact for about 24 hours after ovulation. So pregnancy is most likely to occur if the couple has intercourse a day or two before ovulation, or on the day that the woman ovulates.

The father's role is as important as the mother's in creating a new life.

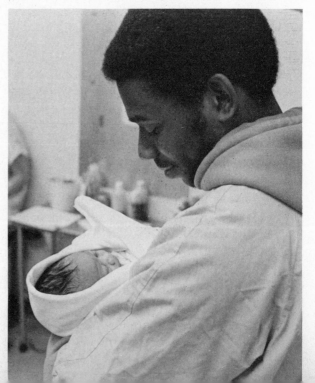

24

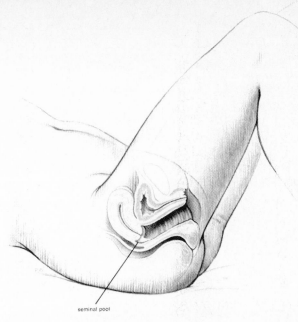

FIGURE 2–3. *During intercourse a pool of semen is deposited at the opening of the woman's cervix.*

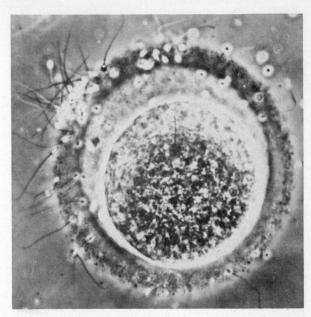

A human ovum (egg) at the moment of conception.

Fertilization

The process of the egg and sperm joining together to form a zygote is called **fertilization** or **conception**. Fertilization occurs when the sperm penetrates the outer covering of the egg, allowing the 23 chromosomes in the egg and the 23 chromosomes in the sperm to unite. This process takes place in the Fallopian tubes (usually in the outer one-third). However, conception cannot occur until the sperm has made a long and hazardous journey from the vagina to the Fallopian tube. The difficulty of the sperm's journey is pointed out by the fact that only one of the 300 million sperm contained in the average ejaculation actually fertilizes the egg. Some of the sperm cannot make the journey because of defects, but at least 60 percent of the sperm in each ejaculation are capable of making the journey.

What happens to all these sperm to prevent them from becoming the fertilizing cell? Some of them are lost in semen that flows out of the vagina because of the force of gravity. Furthermore, in the long trip from the vagina to the egg, the sperm must swim a distance that is 3,000 times its own length, similar to a person swimming three miles. The fastest sperm can make the trip in about 1½ hours. But others get lost and swim in the wrong direction, or simply die of "old age" during the journey.

The woman's body also creates obstacles. For example, the vaginal environment is highly acidic, and this kills some of the sperm. The sperm may find difficulty in entering the cervix if the texture of the cervical mucus is not correct. Other sperm may be attacked by the woman's antibodies (of the same type produced to fight an infection). About half of those sperm that reach the Fallopian tubes swim into the wrong tube, that is, into the tube that does not contain an egg. And even reaching the "correct" Fallopian tube does not ensure success. The same force that moves the egg down the Fallopian tube makes it necessary for the sperm to swim upstream. Sperm can also become trapped in the cilia (tiny, hairlike projections) that create this current. Finally, once fertilization occurs, a protective coating forms around the zygote, preventing another sperm from entering. Thus, any other sperm in the Fallopian tube will simply die there.

The Chances of Twins or Triplets

The chance of having twins is around 1 in 90, and triplets make up around 1 in every 7,000 or 8,000 births. Births of more than three infants are extremely rare, and in the United States are often the result of the mother's having taken fertility drugs (see page 179 in Chapter 8 on infertility). Twins are more common among older mothers and women who have given birth several times.

There are two ways in which twins or triplets can develop. In the first case, the fertilized zygote splits into two or three parts, and two or three fetuses develop, each of which has exactly the same genetic makeup. These fetuses will develop into infants of the same sex and will look almost exactly alike because they developed from the same genetic blueprint. They are called **identical twins** or **identical triplets**. Identical twins or triplets often share a single placenta.

A woman's chances of giving birth to twins is about 1 in 90.

The second way that a woman can have a multiple birth is if more than one egg is fertilized. In this case the twins or triplets develop from separate eggs, which are separately fertilized. This means that, genetically, they are as similar or as different as any two children the couple would produce, and they may be of different sexes. They will not look exactly alike. They are called **fraternal twins** or **triplets,** and each has its own placenta. It is possible for a multiple birth to combine both identical and fraternal twins. For example, triplets might be made up of two identical twins and one fraternal twin.

Implantation and Early Development

Once fertilization has taken place, it is the zygote's turn to make a journey. The zygote must travel through the Fallopian tube down into the uterus, where most of its development will occur. This trip takes several days (see Figure 2–4). But by about the seventh to the ninth day after fertilization, the zygote will have made it into the uterus and will have implanted itself in the **endometrium** (lining of the uterus; see pages 16–19). The endometrium will provide nourishment to the developing zygote until the placenta and the umbilical cord are formed.

By the time the zygote implants in the uterine lining, it has already undergone considerable growth. About 30 hours after fertilization, the zygote divides to form two connected but separate cells. It keeps dividing so that, by about the fifth day of pregnancy, there are about 100 cells joined together in the shape of a hollow ball called a blas-

tocyst. The outer layer of the blastocyst will become the placenta and the umbilical cord. The innermost mass of cells will grow into the fetus.

Development of the Placenta

When the blastocyst reaches the uterus, its outer layer begins to burrow into the endometrium (see Figure 2–5). Because the blastocyst contains genes from the father, the mother's body treats it as an unwanted invader (much as it would a virus or bacteria). This reaction causes there to be an increased amount of blood in the tissue near the blastocyst. The blastocyst immediately begins to take advantage of the increased blood supply, using it as a source of nourishment. It does this by beginning to form a **placenta** (see Figure 2–6). The placenta is a mass of spongy tissue that, in mature form, resembles a large piece of raw beef liver. It contains blood vessels that connect the fetus to the mother through the umbilical cord. This system allows the fetus to get nutrition and oxygen from the mother, and to dispose of its bodily wastes through the mother's body. Thus, the placenta actually functions as the fetus's respiratory and digestive systems.

The placenta also serves two other functions. First, it produces several hormones that are important to maintain pregnancy. In fact, some of these hormones, first produced by the outer layer of the blastocyst, stop the mother's body from treating the blastocyst as an invader. Pregnancy tests are based on the presence of one of these hormones. Second,

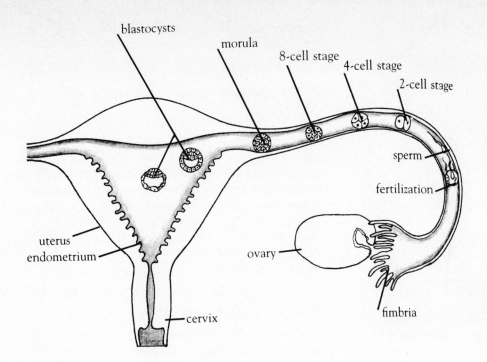

blastocysts

morula

8-cell stage

4-cell stage

2-cell stage

sperm

fertilization

uterus
endometrium

ovary

cervix

fimbria

FIGURE 2–4. *A five-day trip for the egg from the ovary to the uterus, with many changes along the way.*

FIGURE 2–5. *The cells on the blastocyst's surface form the trophoblast, which will become the placenta.*

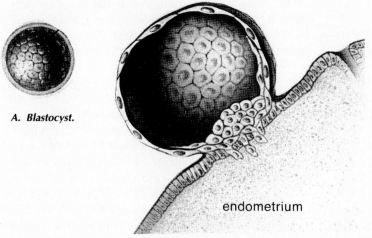

A. *Blastocyst.*

endometrium

B. *Implanting blastocyst.*

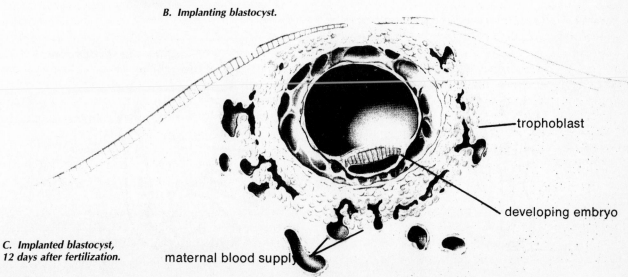

trophoblast

developing embryo

C. *Implanted blastocyst, 12 days after fertilization.*

maternal blood supply

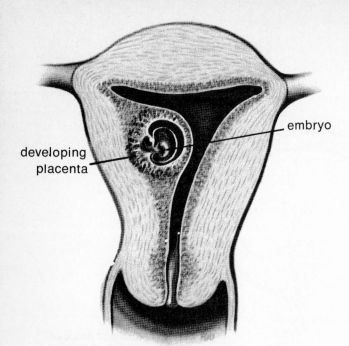

FIGURE 2–6. *The human embryo at 6 weeks of pregnancy* (*actual size*).

the placenta serves as a barrier, filtering out harmful substances and organisms (such as certain viruses, bacteria, and drugs).

Correcting Mistakes: Early Miscarriages

With so many things happening at once, there is a sizable possibility that something will go wrong. So it is not surprising that a substantial number of pregnancies are miscarried during the first few days or weeks after conception. It is impossible to know exactly what percentage of pregnancies are miscarried because many women do not even know they are pregnant when they miscarry. But estimates suggest that the rate may be anywhere from 10 to 50 percent, with a rate of around 20 percent the most commonly accepted. Such miscarriages may be viewed as nature's way of dealing with its own

mistakes, since the vast majority of blastocysts that are miscarried are probably developing abnormally.

DEVELOPMENT OF THE EMBRYO AND FETUS

Pregnancy can be divided into three periods. The period we have just discussed is known as the **germinal period** and lasts for roughly the first 2 weeks of pregnancy. From 2 to 8 weeks (2 months) of pregnancy, the developing baby is referred to as an **embryo.** This is known as the **embryonic period.** The rest of the pregnancy (from week 9 to delivery) is called the **fetal period,** and the developing organism is known as a **fetus.**

The Embryonic Period (Week 2 to Week 8)

Prenatal development (development before birth) occurs in stages (Figure 2–7). For example, the brain and heart start their development before the digestive tract, skeleton, or muscles start to form. Such "details" as hair and eyelashes appear much later. If anything (such as drugs or radiation) interferes with a particular stage of development, the damage will be permanent. For example, fingers and toes are formed from the sixth to the eighth week of pregnancy. If anything interferes with their development at this stage, there is no way it can be corrected later in pregnancy.

Most of the critical periods for organ development occur within the first 12 weeks of pregnancy, so the developing embryo is most likely to be seriously damaged by drugs or disease during this time. Once the organs and organ systems are in place, they are much less susceptible to injury. This is why contracting German measles during the first 12 weeks of pregnancy can result in serious abnor-

FIGURE 2–7. *The embryonic period of development between week 3 and week 7.*

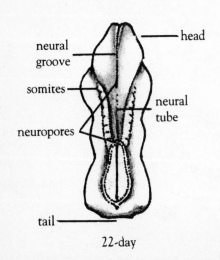

22-day

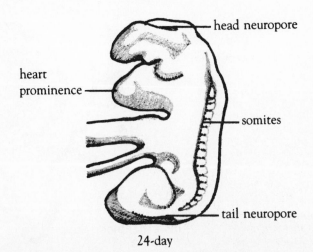

24-day

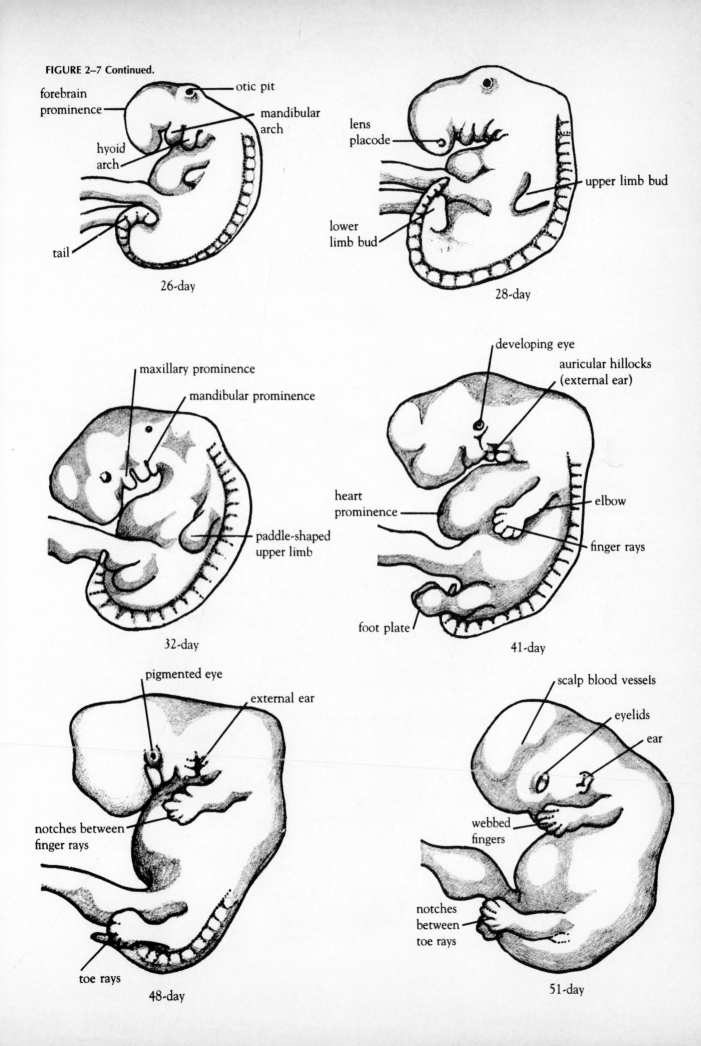

FIGURE 2–7 Continued.

26-day

forebrain prominence
otic pit
mandibular arch
hyoid arch
tail

28-day

lens placode
upper limb bud
lower limb bud

32-day

maxillary prominence
mandibular prominence
paddle-shaped upper limb

41-day

developing eye
auricular hillocks (external ear)
heart prominence
elbow
finger rays
foot plate

48-day

pigmented eye
external ear
notches between finger rays
toe rays

51-day

scalp blood vessels
eyelids
ear
webbed fingers
notches between toe rays

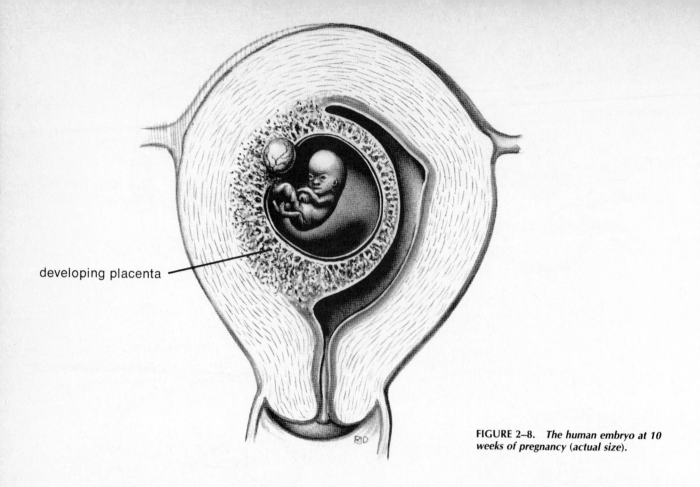

developing placenta

FIGURE 2–8. *The human embryo at 10 weeks of pregnancy (actual size).*

FIGURE 2–9. *The fetus at 14 weeks (actual size).*

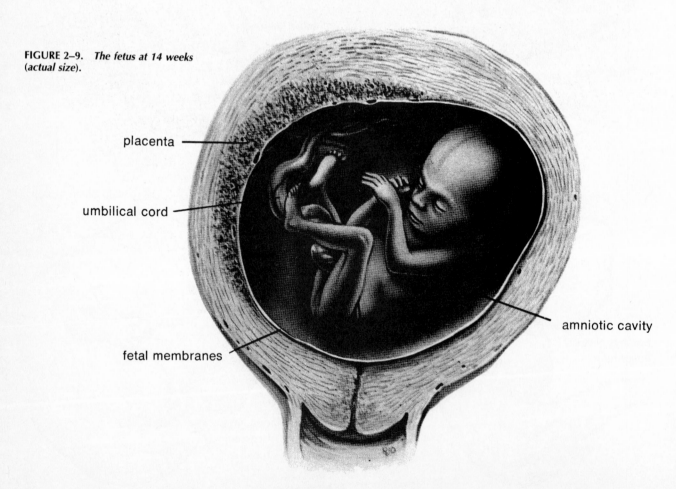

placenta

umbilical cord

amniotic cavity

fetal membranes

FIGURE 2–10. *The fetus at 24 weeks (actual size).*

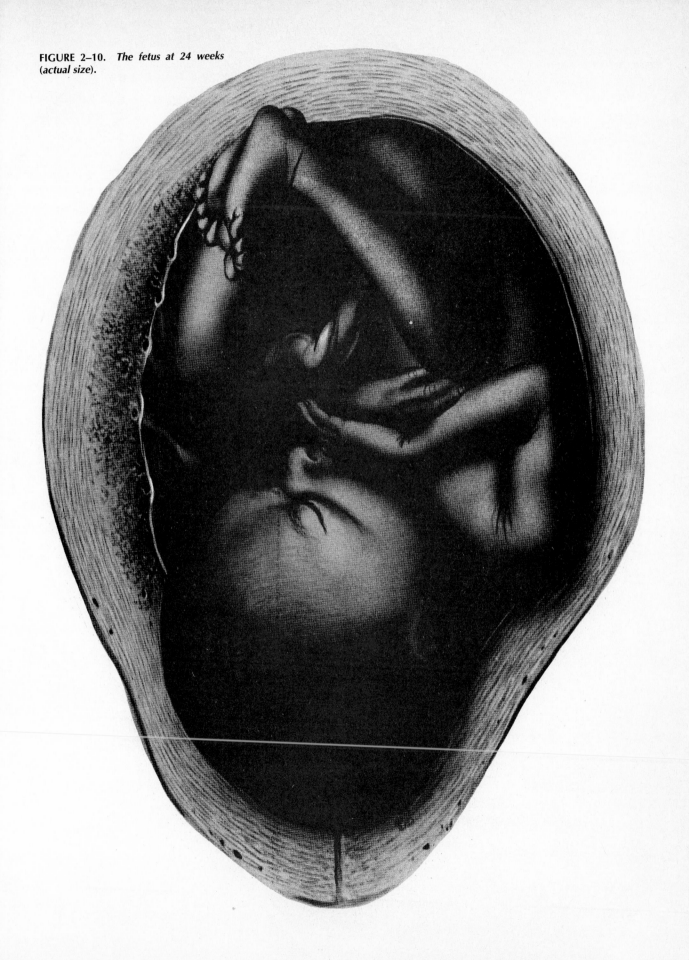

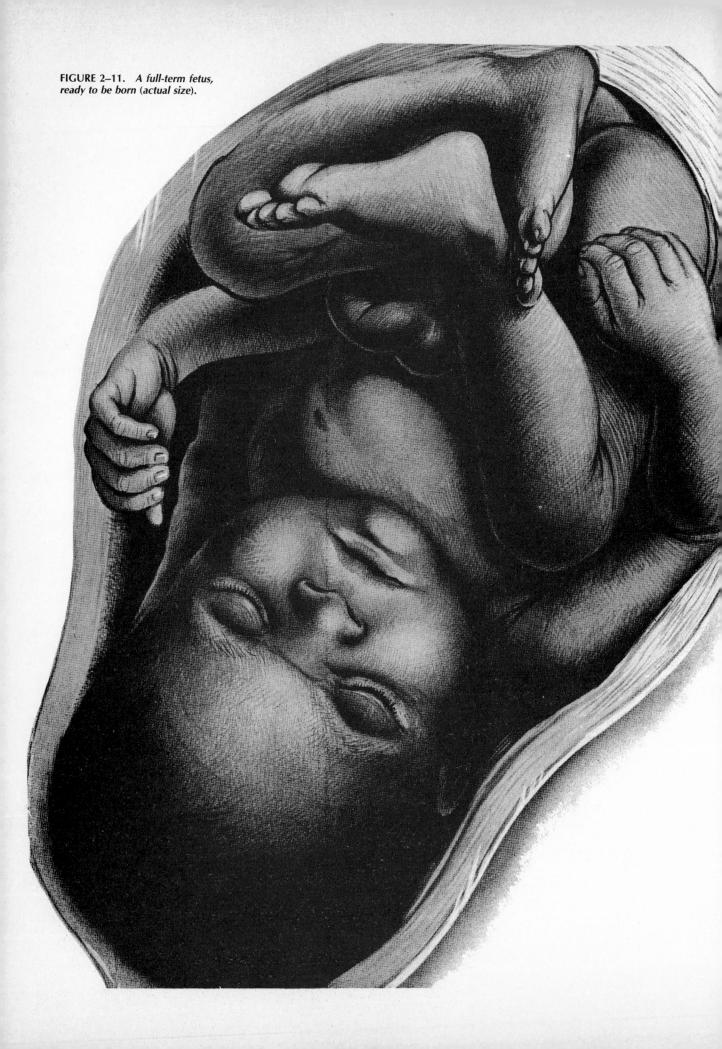

FIGURE 2–11. *A full-term fetus, ready to be born (actual size).*

malities, but infection with the same disease at the end of pregnancy usually does not harm the fetus.

By eight weeks of pregnancy the embryo begins to look human, although it is still very small (about 1½ inches long and about one-thirtieth of an ounce in weight). There are arms and legs with fingers and toes, and the eyes and ears have started to form (Figure 2–8).

Even though the embryo looks human, it is important to note that it is not yet *viable*. This means that it cannot survive outside the uterine environment.

The Fetal Period (Week 9 to Delivery)

During the third month of pregnancy, we start to refer to the developing organism as a *fetus*. Since most of the organs are already formed, the fetal period is primarily devoted to the growth and refinement of the organs. The fetus becomes viable (has the capacity to survive outside the uterus) at around 24 to 26 weeks (180 days after fertilization). Although it is technically possible for a fetus born this early to survive, a great deal of highly specialized medical care is needed to make survival possible, and most infants born this early die. The chances of healthy survival improve with every day that a fetus remains in the uterus until it is due.

The fetus grows quite rapidly, especially during the last 3 months of pregnancy. At 6 months, the average fetus is 10 to 12 inches long and weighs between 1 and 1½ pounds. The fetus gains about 2 pounds per month from then on, so that the average full-term newborn weighs 6 to 7 pounds and is about 21 inches long. Of course, birth weights and lengths vary considerably, and any weight over 5½ pounds is considered normal (see Figures 2–9, 2–10, and 2–11).

Development of the Sex Organs

The sex organs develop during the early fetal period. Until this happens, all embryos have the same physical appearance. They all have sexual organs called gonads, which will later become testes in the male and ovaries in the female (see Chapter 1 for more details about this).

If the fetus has an XY (male) chromosome pair (discussed earlier), a substance called HY antigen will begin to be produced during the seventh week of pregnancy. The HY antigen causes the previously neutral gonads to become testes. The testes then begin to produce the male hormone testosterone (see Chapter 1). It is the testosterone, rather than the XY chromosomes themselves, that causes the male reproductive system to develop. Testosterone also causes the development of the external geni-

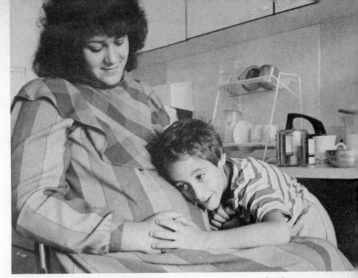

During the fifth through eighth months of pregnancy the fetus kicks and moves frequently within the uterus.

tals, with the penis becoming visible by about 12 weeks of pregnancy. If these male hormonal influences are not present at this point, the child will develop the physical characteristics of a girl even though it has the XY pair of chromosomes.

If the fetus has the XX (female) pair, the undifferentiated gonads develop into ovaries. By 14 weeks of pregnancy, the fetus's external genitalia will look like a girl's. As far as is known, no substances similar to the HY antigen or testosterone are involved. It appears that, in the absence of testosterone, a female child develops. See Chapter 1 (pages 13–15) for illustrations of sexual differentiation.

Feeling the Fetus Move (Quickening)

There is one event that occurs during the fetal period that is usually of great interest to parents. Sometime around 4½ months of pregnancy, the mother will feel the fetus move. At first, there is simply a fluttering sensation known as **quickening.** Soon, however, the fetus will move so vigorously that there are kicks and punches. Some of these even create visible movements of the mother's abdomen. It is normal for the movement to be quite noticeable during the fifth through the eighth months as the fetus not only moves its arms and legs but also turns over and around. Toward the end of pregnancy, however, the movements become less noticeable (although they are still evident) because the fetus runs out of room for such large movements.

FOR FURTHER READING

HOLE, JOHN W., JR. *Human Anatomy and Physiology,* 4th ed. Dubuque, Iowa: Wm. C. Brown, 1987.

MASTERS, WILLIAM H., VIRGINIA E. JOHNSON, AND ROBERT C. KOLODNY. *Human Sexuality,* 2nd ed. Boston: Little, Brown, 1985.

3

Human Sexual Behavior

THE DEVELOPMENT OF SEXUAL BEHAVIOR

The first section of this chapter describes how sexual behavior develops in human beings from infancy through adolescence and old age. Special sections on sexuality and aging, homosexuality, and disabilities are also included.

Infancy and Childhood

Sensual and Sexual Response in Infants

People often think of baby girls and boys as asexual, or as too young to have sexual responses of any kind. In fact, the sexual organs of babies are capable of automatic responses from the moment of birth (and probably even before birth). For example, baby boys are capable of erections from the time they are born, and baby girls discharge fluid from the vagina. These responses do

not mean that the infant is aware of sexuality in any adult sense, but only that their small bodies are capable of the beginnings of what will eventually become adult sexual response.

As everyone knows, babies are very responsive to touch. They enjoy being cuddled, stroked, kissed, and fondled, and the adults who care for them usually enjoy touching them. Physical touching, holding, and caressing are a very important way in which love and caring are communicated to the baby. This contact is not only enjoyable for babies, it is now known to be necessary for their normal development. Studies of babies in orphanages or other situations where they are not picked up, held, and touched show that such neglected babies become depressed, learn more slowly, do not grow as much, and have more health problems than other babies. The baby's early experiences of love expressed through touching are likely also to have an effect on his or her sexual responsiveness in adult life.

Babies love to be touched.

Masturbation

All infants explore their bodies with their hands, discovering ears, mouths, toes, and so on. They also discover their sex organs and find that touching them is pleasurable. Many babies form the habit of touching themselves, which may continue into childhood. This is masturbation, although in most infants and small children it does not seem to end in orgasm. Masturbation by infants and small children is found throughout the world and is harmless. Parents or other caregivers, however, may be concerned or embarrassed by such touching. According to present knowledge, it is best not to punish or discourage the infant from touching herself or himself. As soon as the child is old enough to understand, however, parents can teach the child that this is an activity done in private. Self-stimulation is the first way in which people learn about their own sexuality, and it is believed to be a natural building-block of adult sexual responsiveness.

Many children continue to masturbate when they become toddlers, and may continue to do so throughout childhood. Masturbation is also a common practice among both males and females in the adolescent years, in adulthood, and in old age.

Forming Sexual Identity

Infancy and early childhood are the years in which children learn to identify themselves as female or male, as girls or boys. Surprisingly, most of this learning takes place in the first two years of life, before a child even learns to talk well.

Children form a sense of themselves as male or female by the way they are treated by those who care for them, and by observing the people around them. Adults treat male and female babies differently from the moment they are born, shaping the infants' behavior and responses to match the expectations for their sex. In addition, clothing, toys, and activities are different for girls than for boys. In a few rare cases where children have been mistakenly raised as boys when they really were girls, or vice versa, it has been found that by age 2 it is very difficult for a child to change his or her sexual identity, and that after age 5 it is nearly impossible.

Childhood Sexual Exploration

Almost all children carry out some kind of sexual exploration, often as a part of playing house or acting out what they understand to be adult roles and behaviors. Playing doctor is another favorite game that allows children to satisfy their curiosity by examining other children's sex organs. These games may be played with children of the same sex, but they often are convenient vehicles for children to find out more about the opposite sex. There is no reason to fear that sexual exploration with others of the same sex will cause homosexuality.

Most sex play among children is a harmless and understandable effort to learn more about each other's bodies. Parents and other caregivers need to be able to communicate clearly to children the family rules and standards about what is acceptable and what is not. It is also very important not to frighten or shame children about sex play while setting limits to what is allowed. For more on this subject, see Chapter 4, "Talking to Your Child about Sex."

There are some risks to sex play, including the possibility that children may harm each other by

A baby discovers her fascinating feet and toes.

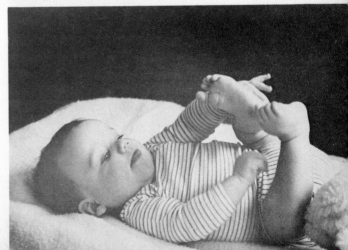

inserting objects into the body (for example, by "taking a temperature" rectally, using a pencil). It is also possible for older children to have intercourse as a part of sex play. Probably the greatest risk of childhood sex play is that older children or bullies may force younger children into activities that they do not want.

If an adult or much older child involves a young child in sex games or explorations, or if a child is forced into such activities against his or her will, this is not the harmless exploration that we are calling sex play, and the child must be protected from it (see Chapter 5, pages 98–100, on child molestation and learning to say no).

Adolescence

The physical changes of puberty, which is the period of sexual maturation occurring during the teenage years, are described in Chapter 1. The next section describes the social and behavioral changes that accompany this physical maturation.

Socialization into Sex Roles

During the teen years, adolescents in this society are not yet treated as adults, even though they may be physically mature. Teens are in the process of learning to become adults; they are testing out various activities and values to see what will suit them as adults. They take their cues for adult behavior from their parents and other adults, and also from other teens. It is typical that their attitudes, values, and beliefs change rapidly as they develop. This is also the time when children separate themselves from their family and develop a separate identity.

A large part of the learning of the teen years

During the teen years boys and girls practice adult roles.

has to do with sex roles—with what it means to be a man or woman. In addition, teenagers practice behaving like adults with peers and family. The large amount of time that teens spend socializing with their peers provides opportunities for practice at being a socially adult man or woman, and at relating to the opposite sex.

The rapid changes in recent years in the roles of men and women, especially changes in women's status, create a confusing environment for today's teens. There are many new choices open to both women and men as to how to conduct their lives, and few clear messages as to "best" or "right" ways to live as adult men and women. For many teens, these are years of painful conflict with the family. Teens from immigrant families or subcultures within the United States may have a particularly difficult time, since the values of their families may be very different from those of their peers and the larger community.

Sexual Activity during Adolescence

Fantasy and self-stimulation Despite what the movies and television show, the most common forms of sexual activity for most American teens are probably fantasy and self-stimulation (masturbation). Fantasizing about sex seems to be a common activity for both boys and girls. It may or may not be accompanied by masturbation. By the late teens almost all boys have masturbated. The average frequency is just under twice a week, and boys almost always have an orgasm. At the same age, about three-quarters of teenage women

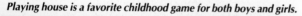

Playing house is a favorite childhood game for both boys and girls.

report having masturbated, but only about half of them have had orgasms during masturbation. These women report masturbating about once every two weeks.

It is not surprising that masturbation plays such an important role in the sex lives of teenagers. There are many reasons for teens not to have sexual intercourse even though they have strong sexual urges, and masturbation allows a natural outlet for their sexual energy. Some reason for not having intercourse are:

Not feeling ready for a sexual relationship
Wanting to avoid the risk of pregnancy and/or sexually transmitted disease
Not having a partner
Choosing not to have intercourse before marriage

Masturbation is an enjoyable sexual experience, and many teenagers who do have a sexual relationship with a partner also masturbate. It is also perfectly normal for a teenager to choose not to masturbate.

Dating and sexual relationships   Dating and exploring sexual relationships are important activities of the teen years, preparing adolescents for adult sexual and family roles. Patterns of dating are different in different communities around the United States. In general, however, boys and girls in the early teens tend to socialize in groups, pairing off into couples as they get older. Teens may date several people at one time or may "go steady," focusing on just one person.

Sexual exploration usually takes place during

A happy teenage couple.

dating and usually follows a pattern of slowly increasing intimacy. In general, both teens and adults divide sexual activities into four levels of intimacy. However, the exact meaning of the following terms varies from one community to another and from one age group to another. For example, parents and children may not mean exactly the same thing when they say "necking."

1. *Kissing and hugging:* This involves embracing and kissing on the face or mouth, similar to the embraces given in nonsexual relationships (greeting friends and relatives, etc.). Kissing evolves over time into open-mouthed kissing (also called French kissing).

2. *Necking:* Necking includes everything described under kissing and hugging, but may continue for a long time, become very intense, and include kissing and fondling any part of the body from the neck up.

3. *Petting:* Petting includes everything described above under kissing and hugging, and necking, as well as kissing and fondling the breasts and sexual organs. It is the same thing as foreplay (see pages 54–57 for information about foreplay and the different forms of sexual intercourse). Some people also consider manual and oral intercourse to be petting, because they believe genital intercourse to be the only "real" sexual intercourse (especially if their main concern is avoiding pregnancy). It is common for both men and women to have orgasms during petting.

4. *Intercourse, or "going all the way":* When people talk about "going all the way," they usually mean genital intercourse.

Risks and responsibilities   When teens begin to have sexual intercourse, they take on adult risks and adult responsibilities for their behavior. This book contains many chapters, such as those on contraception, unplanned pregnancy, and sexually transmitted diseases, that can help teens to understand these risks and responsibilities, but we want to highlight some important issues here as well.

Sexual intercourse involves another person. When we become sexually involved with someone, it is important to consider that person's feelings, thoughts, and beliefs, which are as important as our own. Sexual partners can be hurt easily, both emotionally and physically, and they share in the risks of unwanted pregnancy and sexually transmitted diseases. All decisions about what to do sexually should be agreed to by both partners, and both should be comfortable with what is decided. Both men and women should share equal responsibility in decisions about sex, including contraception. Any couple who are having sexual intercourse also need to be able to *talk* about sex with each other. It may be difficult at first, but the ability to communicate is the key, not just to good sex, but also to a good relationship.

Sexual intercourse can mean making babies.

Over 90 percent of all couples in their teens and early twenties will start a pregnancy if they have regular intercourse over a year and do not use any method of birth control. Many women get pregnant the first time they ever have intercourse. Teens are extremely fertile, and most teenagers in this country do not use birth control when they first have intercourse. For this reason, it is estimated that 1 out of every 3 girls in the United States will get pregnant before finishing high school! In Europe and Canada the rates of teenage pregnancy are much lower, although teens are just as sexually active. The reason for the difference is thought to be that the European countries advertise and promote birth control for teenagers, as well as supporting more open discussion of sexual matters. In addition, European teens can get birth control services more easily.

Over a million teenage girls get pregnant in the United States every year, and most of these pregnancies are unwanted. Teens who become parents are more likely to drop out of school and more likely to be poor all their lives than teenagers who delay childbearing. (See Chapter 7 for more information about unplanned and unwanted pregnancy.)

Fortunately, many effective methods of birth control are available, so that teenage couples *can* avoid unwanted pregnancy if they choose to. Some contraceptive methods, such as condoms and foam, can be purchased in a drugstore or even a supermarket without prescription. (See Chapter 9 for details about contraceptive methods.)

Sexual intercourse means new health risks. When men and women begin to have sexual intercourse, they expose themselves to a whole new world of diseases that attack the reproductive system, and which are transmitted by sexual contact, including AIDS. In addition, women are exposed to a new set of health risks related to pregnancy and childbirth. Most of the health problems of women in the childbearing years are related to the reproductive system.

When teens take on adult sexual relationships, they should be aware of the health risks and should know how to keep these risks to a minimum for themselves and their partners. Teens should read Chapters 12 and 13 in this book on men's and women's health problems and Chapters 14 and 15 on sexually transmitted diseases and AIDS for more information on this.

Avoiding unwanted sex No man or woman, boy or girl should have sexual intercourse unless he or she chooses to. No one should pressure a partner to have intercourse if she or he does not want to, or allow himself or herself to be pressured

into it. No one "owes" sex to another person because they were asked on a date or because money was spent on them. Sometimes misunderstandings can develop about whether or not a girl really wants intercourse. Some boys and men believe that when a woman says "no," she sometimes means "yes." *Boys and men are responsible to accept a woman's word when she says "no." Women are responsible to say what they mean, and not to expect men to read their minds.*

Some ways for teens to avoid unwanted sex are:

1. Be very clear with dates/partners about your expectations. Don't "play games" about what you want or don't want sexually.
2. Socialize in groups and/or with people you know well. Avoid dates where you are alone with a stranger.
3. Alcohol and drug consumption limits judgment. Be aware of what you and your date/partner are consuming. A lot of unwanted sex happens when teens are drinking heavily or using drugs.
4. Avoid socializing with people who are likely to make sexual demands that you are not prepared to meet.
5. Be aware that all sexual activity does not have to end with intercourse, and couples can enjoy a great deal of sexual intimacy without actually having intercourse.

For information about rape and other serious sex crimes, see Chapter 5, "Sex and the Law."

Homosexual experiences Sexual contact with someone of the same sex is not uncommon for teenagers, particularly males, and it does not automatically mean that the teen will grow up to be an adult homosexual. Most teens have already developed a clear preference for the opposite sex, which does not change because of a few homosexual experiences. Since much of our sexual behavior is learned behavior, however, teenagers who focus exclusively on homosexual relationships and have few or no contacts with the opposite sex could develop a preference for homosexuality. For more on homosexuality, see pages 42 to 44.

Adulthood

Adult Sexual Relationships

In adulthood most men and women settle into a long-term sexual relationship with a partner of the opposite sex. In most (but not all) cases they marry. These relationships usually involve much more than sex; they include love, companionship, commitment, and often children. Although most people hope for a relationship that will last a lifetime, it can be very difficult for couples to maintain a satisfying relationship for 50 or 60 years; about half of all marriages in the United States end in divorce. Most divorced men and women remarry, committing themselves to another long-term relationship.

Although a long-term committed relationship with a single partner (including both married and unmarried relationships), is the most common form of adult sexual relationship, there are many other patterns of adult sexual behavior that are frequently seen. They are described in the next few pages.

Sex and Love and Values

Sex is an important issue in the lives of most adults, but different individuals handle it very differently. Our sexual behavior is strongly affected by our values and beliefs. The attitudes and values of family, community, and religion usually shape our views about what is acceptable and desirable sexual behavior. But there are tremendous variations in people's attitudes toward sex. At one extreme, some people believe that sexual intercourse should take place only between married partners of the opposite sex, and then only for the purpose of creating children. At the other extreme are people who view intercourse as a recreational activity to be enjoyed with anyone, anytime.

Most people fall somewhere between these extremes, and most have a strong preference for a long term sexual relationship that includes love, caring, and commitment. The desire for sex is strong in many people, however, and it is not un-common for men and women to enter into a sexual relationship that is in conflict with their own values. Such relationships are less likely to be long-lasting, even if there is a great deal of love and caring. Most couples seem to need common values about sexuality, family life, and commitment in order to maintain long-term relationships.

Marriage and the Family

Most children in the United States are raised in a family with married parents, although almost half will see their parents divorce before they are grown. Children's attitudes and beliefs about love, sex, caring, respect, commitment, and responsibility are shaped by the example of their parents and other family members. They will carry these attitudes with them into adulthood, and their own relationships will be strongly affected by them. Destructive family behaviors such as child or spouse abuse, incest, and alcoholism also tend to be repeated by children when they are grown. So parents bear a heavy responsibility in the examples they set for their children. In addition, with the current high rates of separation, divorce, and remarriage, many couples may be concerned about the messages about relationships that they are passing on to their children.

Fortunately, most children turn out fine, and parents can be role models of loving, caring relationships with others even if they do have problems and do go through divorces. Parents who are concerned about the environment they are creating for their children can often find helpful information in parenting classes, available in many communities.

A young couple with their attendants on their wedding day.

Most communities also have family counseling services to deal with just these kinds of concerns.

Single Adult Relationships

In the United States today, there are very large numbers of single adult men and women in all age groups. There are several reasons for this. Couples are marrying later, leaving many young people single into their thirties. Divorce rates are high for all age groups, but many men and women in their middle years, particularly, are separated or divorced. And many older people become single when a spouse dies. Most single adults, like most married adults, want a long-term committed relationship. However, it may take them time to find such a partner, or there may be barriers connected to work, children, finances, health, or age that make remarriage unlikely.

Single adults develop various kinds of sexual relationships. Dating or going steady (which may include sleeping over at each other's homes) and living together are two common arrangements. Many new social institutions have sprung up to provide ways for adult singles to meet. Singles clubs, bars, health clubs, and personal advertisements in magazines and newspapers are popular. In addition, matchmaking services such as video dating organizations are in great demand.

The sexually active single man or woman faces many health risks that are not encountered by people who are in a monogamous relationship (having sex with only one person). The more sexual partners a man or woman has, the greater the chances of infection with a sexually transmitted disease. Although most sexually transmitted diseases can be cured, some can be life-threatening or even fatal (see Chapter 14, "Sexually Transmitted Diseases," and Chapter 15, "AIDS: Acquired Immune Deficiency Syndrome"). In addition, men and women who wish to have children in the future run an increased risk of becoming sterile as the result of scarring caused by sexually transmitted diseases like gonorrhea and chlamydia (see pages 313–314). For this reason, many single people avoid sex with multiple partners, and try to get to know a new partner well before having intercourse. Because of the serious danger of AIDS infection, the use of condoms is now recommended for *all* sexual intercourse with new partners.

Although newly single adults who did not enjoy the teenage dating years may find it difficult to fit in at first, most single adults in the cities and suburbs can choose from a plentiful array of organizations and activities through which they can meet other singles with similar interests. In rural areas, being a single adult may be more difficult, and older women may face problems finding a partner because of the smaller number of older men. Both older women and older men often consider younger partners as a way of increasing their choices.

Extramarital Sex

Extramarital sex means sexual intercourse between a married person and another person to whom he or she is not married. According to surveys, most men and women in the United States believe it is wrong to have intercourse with someone other than your spouse, and view extramarital sex as much more serious than intercourse between unmarried persons. In spite of these beliefs, however, extramarital sex is quite common, and an estimated half of all married men and a quarter of all married women have had intercourse with someone other than their spouse. It is too early to tell whether the serious risk of AIDS infection that has developed in recent years will affect this pattern. *Because of AIDS, involvement in extramarital sex these days is potentially a very serious act. There is the potential of infecting oneself and one's spouse with a fatal disease. All sexually active adults should know how to practice "safe sex"* (see Chapter 15 on AIDS).

Extramarital affairs may involve a single incident with a near stranger, a long-term love relationship, or some other pattern. Married couples who are unhappy or dissatisfied in their relationship seem to be more likely to have extramarital affairs, but many people who report affairs also say that they are happy in their marriages. Although extramarital affairs have reportedly caused many divorces, in some cases an affair may be a symptom of a couple's unhappiness rather than the cause of the breakup.

Outside the United States, many cultures support extramarital intercourse, particularly for men, and some societies permit the practice of having more than one wife or husband. On the other hand, some cultures view extramarital intercourse as extremely serious, and in some nations punishment (for women) can even include the death penalty. Most cultures are more concerned about controlling the sexual behavior of women than in regulating men's sexuality.

Most extramarital relationships are conducted in secret and are hidden from the spouse. Some married couples, however, agree to a relationship that includes sex with others. In addition to affairs in which either the husband or the wife has another sexual partner, a few couples engage in extramarital sex together, as will be described next.

1. *Open Marriage:* An open marriage is one in which the couple agrees that both can have other lovers, although it is usually part of the agreement that they are not to become seriously involved with them. The couple may agree to tell each other about their involvements or not, and may have rules about whom they can become involved with and under what conditions. The purpose of open marriage seems to be to allow the couple the freedom to explore other sexual relationships without damaging or losing the marriage relationship. Little is known about how successful these arrangements are or how long they are likely to last.

2. *Swinging:* "Swinging" is a general term used to describe married couples who, together, have sexual intercourse with a third person, with another couple, or a part of a group. In one approach, known as *wife swapping* or *mate swapping,* two couples agree to have intercourse with each other's spouses. A couple may also invite a third person (male or female) to join them, or may attend a swinging club or party where they are free to have sex with other members individually or in groups. Swinging couples and swingers' clubs often locate each other through personal advertisements. From a health point of view, swinging is very risky. There is a good chance of being exposed to sexually transmitted diseases, including AIDS.

3. *Group Marriage:* Group marriage refers to situations in which more than two people consider themselves married to each other. It is an informal arrangement, which cannot be a legal marriage in the United States. It is not known how common this type of arrangement is between small groups, or how well it works. Experiments with large groups practicing group marriage and communal living have been attempted many times in U.S. history. Although some communes have lasted successfully for long periods of time, it appears that the group marriage aspect of the arrangement has usually not worked well over the long run and has been given up.

4. *Polygyny and polyandry.* Polygyny, the custom in which men have more than one wife, is accepted in many parts of the world today and was practiced by Mormons in the United States during the early days of the church. It was given up before 1900 and was never legal according to U.S. law. Polyandry, which is the custom of women having more than one husband, is quite rare, but has been found in a few parts of the world.

Casual Sex and Promiscuity

Another sexual life-style chosen by some men and women in this society is casual sex, which means sexual relationships with partners with whom there is no emotional relationship or commitment. It includes sex with strangers, "one-night stands," and so on. Many men and women go through a temporary period, often as young adults, in which they engage in casual sex.

Promiscuous is the term used to describe women who have frequent casual sex with more than one partner. The fact that men are not called promiscuous reflects a double standard in our society, which, until recently, viewed casual sex as an acceptable and normal choice for men but not for women.

Over the last twenty years patterns of sexual relationships have changed a great deal in the United States. Casual sex has become an accepted life-style for single young adults in many communities. This trend may reverse itself in the near future because we are now learning that those who choose casual sex as a life-style are at higher risk of sexually transmitted diseases such as gonorrhea, chlamydia, herpes, and AIDS. The risk of loss of fertility due to disease is also a concern for many. See Chapters 14 and 15 for details about sexually transmitted diseases and Chapter 8 for information about infertility.

Celibacy

The term **celibate** has been used in recent years to refer to men and women who live without sexual relationships with others (although, according to the dictionary, *celibate* means "unmarried"). Most people are celibate during some periods of their lives, either by choice or because they do not have a sexual partner. For example, a young person may be celibate because he or she does not yet feel ready to become sexually active. A person of any age may choose celibacy for a time after the breakup of a marriage or other relationship. Some people, particularly the elderly and the disabled, may be

Choosing celibacy doesn't mean dropping out of life.

celibate because of health problems or difficulties in finding a partner.

Although most people have periods of celibacy in their lives, relatively few are celibate over a lifetime. Men and women who take vows of chastity to enter religious life make up part of this permanently celibate group. Other people may make a personal choice to lead a celibate life. The reasons that some people choose celibacy over a lifetime have not been studied, but there are clearly many factors that can affect this choice.

Celibacy as a life-style is not harmful to the health; in fact, celibate women such as nuns have lower rates of uterine and breast cancer, and of some other reproductive system problems, than other women. Celibate men may be more likely to develop inflammation of the prostate gland than others, but this is not usually a serious problem (see pages 296–297).

Aging

Sexual interest and ability continue throughout a lifetime for most people, although sexual intercourse usually becomes somewhat less frequent in the later years. Health problems and loss of partners can contribute to a decrease in sexual activity for the elderly. Problems related to menopause can make intercourse uncomfortable for older women, but these difficulties can be quite successfully treated (see Chapter 12, pages 275–276).

Older people who wish to remain sexually active may encounter some barriers to doing so. Friends and relatives may assume the older man or woman is no longer interested in sex. Some may ridicule any expression of continued interest. The lack of privacy in nursing homes and some retirement homes is evidence that the residents are not expected to be sexually active.

Despite the barriers to sexual activity, most older people do attempt to maintain the sexual and

Interest in sex and romance continues in aging women and men.

relationship patterns established in earlier years. Old relationships are maintained and new sexual relationships, including marriages, divorces, extramarital affairs, dating, and living together, continue to develop right up until the end of life.

Homosexuality and Bisexuality

Homosexuality

What is it? Homosexuality refers to sexual attraction or activity between persons of the same sex. It is contrasted to **heterosexuality**, which refers to the same between males and females. Homosexual men and women are often called **gays,** and homosexual women are called **lesbians.** There are several component parts of homosexuality: homosexual attraction (being attracted to others of the same sex), homosexual behavior (sexual activity with a same-sex partner), and homosexual identity (awareness of preference for sexual partners of the same sex). These three elements are not all present in all homosexuals. For example, a man might be attracted to other men and be aware of his preference for sex with men, but avoid homosexual behavior.

The term **bisexual** (meaning sexually attracted to and/or active with both sexes) is probably more accurate in describing many people whom we call homosexuals. It appears that people who are exclusively homosexual over a lifetime make up only a small proportion of the total group of people having homosexual experiences. It is more common for men and women to have both homosexual and heterosexual experiences over a lifetime. For example, in surveys of self-reported homosexuals, around 50 percent of men and 75 percent of women reported that they had also had heterosexual intercourse.

Is it common? Homosexuality is quite common, not just in the United States but throughout the world, and it has been known to exist since the beginning of recorded history. Although it is estimated that around 10 percent of people are homosexual, surveys get somewhat lower reports. For example, around 4 percent of American men and 2 percent of women identify themselves as primarily or exclusively homosexual. On the other hand, approximately 25 percent of all Americans report having engaged in homosexual behavior at some point in their lives. Homosexual experiences in adolescence are very common and do not necessarily mean that the teenager will grow up to be a homosexual.

A minority of men and women will be homosexual regardless of their environment. In addition, men and women who consider themselves heterosexual, but are under special environmental conditions—for example, in prison—are likely to enter into temporary homosexual relationships because no partners of the opposite sex are available. It is believed that most of these people resume heterosexual relationships when it becomes possible. An estimated 30 to 45 percent of male prisoners and 50 to 75 percent of female prisoners become involved in homosexual behavior.

Male homosexuality has received much more attention in the past than female homosexual behavior, and the result is that much less is known about women homosexuals than about men. The information that follows reflects this gap.

What causes it? The causes of homosexuality are not known, and it is believed that there are many routes to becoming homosexual. Three past theories about the causes of homosexuality (which are not considered valid today) are:

1. *Inheritance:* There is no proof that homosexuality can be inherited.
2. *Mental illness:* Homosexuality is not a sign of mental illness or maladjustment, and homosexuals' scores are similar to those of heterosexuals on tests of psychological well-being.
3. *Parents:* In the past, psychiatric theory blamed parents, particularly overly possessive mothers and weak, passive fathers, for creating homosexual males, but there is no evidence to support this theory.

Early experiences of love and caring during infancy, and early sexual experiences, shape future sexual behavior for all human beings, but it is not known how, or even if, these experiences contribute to creating a homosexual adult in some cases and a heterosexual in others.

Is it acceptable? Although homosexuality is found in all human societies, it is treated very differently from one culture to another. U.S. society is less tolerant of homosexuality than many others. Although many homosexuals find acceptance and live comfortable and successful lives in the United States, it is never easy. Opinion surveys show that the majority of Americans feel that homosexuals should be prevented from holding certain jobs, such as teaching. Around 70 to 75 percent of Americans view homosexual sex as always morally wrong.

In this environment, homosexuality is a socially undesirable life-style. This causes many people to hide their homosexual feelings and activities. The risks of "coming out of the closet" or publicly identifying oneself as a homosexual male are very serious, including possible job loss and job dis-

A gay pride march in New York City.

crimination as well as the danger of upsetting and/or alienating family and friends. Female homosexuality is taken slightly less seriously, and seems to be less risky to reveal.

There are many laws and traditions that prohibit and punish homosexuality, although recent efforts to reduce discrimination against homosexuals have changed laws and attitudes in some areas. Homosexual activity is still illegal in most states of the United States, although these laws are rarely enforced. Homosexual behavior is also sufficient cause for dismissal from the armed forces.

Are homosexuals different? As a defense against stigma and discrimination, many homosexuals choose to socialize almost exclusively with other gays. Certain city neighborhoods, restaurants, and bars become places where gays can live, work, and play surrounded by other homosexuals and protected from the hostility of the larger society. Some homosexuals live double lives, presenting a heterosexual or "straight" image on the job, and living as a homosexual on weekends and evenings. Homosexuals living in rural areas and small towns have a much harder time socially, and some move to large cities in order to find a more accepting and positive environment.

Homosexual patterns of sexual behavior are somewhat different from heterosexual patterns. Homosexual men report less frequent sex than heterosexuals, but tend to have many more partners. A pattern of casual sex with many partners is common among homosexual men, with one survey reporting that 84 percent of the men interviewed had had sexual relations with more than fifty partners. Homosexual men who pursue this life-style are at the highest risk for sexually transmitted diseases. Long-term relationships seem to be less common for homosexual men than for heterosexual couples, and more difficult to maintain. Gay men tend not to be sexually exclusive, whereas homosexual women tend to develop long-term, exclusive relationships that are more stable.

Many bisexuals and homosexuals, particularly males, hide their attraction for others of the same sex and make their sexual contacts secretly and anonymously. In bars, clubs, restrooms, and parks where anonymous homosexual sex is available, some estimate that as many as half of the patrons are married. Leading a double life is stressful for these homosexuals, who risk public exposure and embarrassment if they are found out. These hidden or "closet" homosexuals, because they fear being exposed, may be very hostile to others who are openly gay.

Can homosexuals change? Most homosexuals do not wish to change to heterosexuality, but some do seek psychiatric treatment or psychological counseling because they are unhappy with their sexual orientation. Others, who are satisfied with their sexual orientation, feel that their energy is better spent trying to educate the public toward a more positive and accepting attitude toward homosexuality.

Sexual preference is believed to be strongly embedded in a person's mental and emotional identity and very difficult to change. Sexual choices and behaviors, however, may be easier to change. Counseling can help homosexuals who feel conflicted and unhappy about their sexual relationships to change to a more comfortable and positive homosexual life-style. Some therapists also report success in helping homosexual patients reshape their sexual behavior patterns to heterosexuality (although their sexual preference may remain homosexual).

Some homosexuals really are bisexual—attracted to both sexes. They may be able to choose to live exclusively as a heterosexual or a homosexual, depending on the life-style they prefer. For example, a bisexual man may choose marriage, children, and a conventional family life, and may give up his homosexual activities. Some bisexuals seem to be able to do this without apparent difficulty; others cannot.

Many men and women whose adolescent sexual explorations included homosexuality, and others who have had homosexual relationships while in prison or in another environment where they had no access to the opposite sex, are not really homosexual. Their first choice for sexual relations is a person of the opposite sex, and they have no problem giving up homosexual sex when they have the opportunity.

Bisexuality

Bisexuals are persons who are attracted to and/or sexually active with both men and women. It appears that most people are primarily either heterosexual or homosexual, but that many are attracted to both sexes (though not equally so). A person may be bisexual over the course of a lifetime but always in an exclusive relationship, or sexually involved with both men and women at the same time. Sometimes bisexuals are considered homosexuals because they have homosexual as well as heterosexual relationships. The information given previously about homosexuality applies to their relationships with people of the same sex.

Sex and People with Limitations

Most disabled men and women have the same desires for sex and for relationships as others their age. But disabilities can limit sexual behavior and cause special problems with sexual relationships. Disabled people often have difficulty finding a sexual partner and in some cases may be limited in what sexual activities they can perform. There are several kinds of difficulties for the disabled:

1. *Appearance:* The disabled person, who may have an unusual appearance or may be in a wheelchair, may have more difficulty attracting a partner than the nondisabled.

Disabled people enjoy the same kinds of activities as the nondisabled do.

2. *Self-image:* Disabled people may feel unattractive or unacceptable as sexual partners because of their limitations. When someone is sexually attracted to them, they may not recognize or be able to accept the situation.

3. *Opportunity:* Many disabled people are limited in their mobility and have difficulty getting out to socialize and meet other people.

4. *Sexual ability:* some disabilities, such as those caused by damage to the central nervous system, can cause impotence (inability to have an erection) in men and lack of physical responsiveness in women. In rare cases the reproductive organs may be damaged or missing.

5. *Strength and flexibility:* Disabled people may lack the strength for certain sexual activities, and may be limited in the positions in which they can comfortably have intercourse.

6. *Society's attitudes:* The society makes it clear in a number of ways that disabled people are not expected to have normal sexual relationships. For example, disabled people who live in institutions usually find that the living arrangements do not provide the opportunities or privacy needed for sexual relationships. These kinds of signals from society can be very discouraging for the disabled person.

In recent years many self-help groups and clubs for the disabled have developed (as well as many new social services and programs). These new opportunities for disabled men and women to get together for social and other activities are often helpful to the self-image of the disabled person who participates. They can also be an excellent place to meet other people who share similar problems and may be potential friends or lovers.

HUMAN SEXUAL RESPONSE

This section describes the ways in which female and male bodies respond to sexual stimulation. The psychological, emotional, and social aspects of sexual response were presented earlier in the chapter in the section on development of sexual behavior.

During sexual arousal, the sexual organs of both men and women undergo important changes in size, shape, coloring, and position. The most obvious and well-known is the erection of the penis in the man, but a number of other changes also take place in men's and women's bodies, as Figures 3–1 and 3–2 show. Many of the changes caused by sexual response in women cannot be easily seen since most of women's organs are internal, but they are just as important as the more obvious changes in men (Figure 3–3). Sexual intercourse cannot take place without the physical changes that occur in men, and it is difficult if the woman does not also respond.

If you start to read this section and find it confusing, go back and look at Chapter 1, "The Human Body."

The Four Stages

Excitement

Sexual response begins as a result of stimulation of some kind. In addition to the touch, sight, or voice of a partner, certain sights, sounds, or smells may set off sexual excitement. Memories or fantasy may also cause sexual response. In the past it was thought that women were slower to respond to sexual stimulation than men, but it is now believed that women can respond as quickly as men and in a very similar way.

The first sign of sexual response in men is erection of the penis, and in women lubrication of the vagina. Both sexes experience an increase in the heart rate, a rise in blood pressure, and increased muscular tension. The nipples may become erect, and the "sex flush," a reddening of the skin which is more common in women, may develop on the chest, neck, and face. Other physical changes for both men and women are listed in Table 3-1.

During the excitement phase, distractions such as an unexpected noise, a ringing telephone, or upsetting thoughts can interrupt the response cycle. If this happens, the body will begin to return to the preexcitement state, and the sexual excitement will be lost if the distraction is prolonged.

In men As blood fills the tissue of the penis, causing erection, the penis increases dramatically in size. Other changes take place as well, including an increase of about 50 percent in the size of the testicles, and the thickening of the skin of the scrotum as the cremaster muscle (see page 10) pulls the testicles up close to the body.

In women During the excitement phase, the woman's vagina begins to lubricate and also changes in size and shape, becoming longer and wider. If you looked inside the vagina, you would see that it also becomes darker in color as the tissues fill with blood. The clitoris, the outer lips, and the inner lips also increase in size as they become congested with blood, and the labia minora become darker in color. The uterus is pulled up into the abdomen, away from the vagina, creating space in the inner third of the vagina and adding to its length. The breasts increase in size, becoming up to 25 percent larger.

Plateau

The plateau stage is basically a continuation of the excitement phase, during which excitement continues to increase, the penis continues to en-

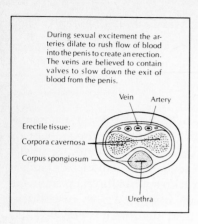

During sexual excitement the arteries dilate to rush flow of blood into the penis to create an erection. The veins are believed to contain valves to slow down the exit of blood from the penis.

Vein   Artery

Erectile tissue:
Corpora cavernosa
Corpus spongiosum

Urethra

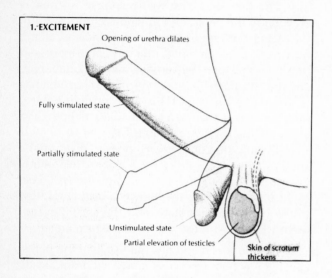

1. EXCITEMENT

Opening of urethra dilates

Fully stimulated state

Partially stimulated state

Unstimulated state

Partial elevation of testicles

Skin of scrotum thickens

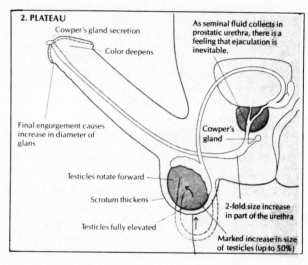

2. PLATEAU

Cowper's gland secretion

Color deepens

As seminal fluid collects in prostatic urethra, there is a feeling that ejaculation is inevitable.

Final engorgement causes increase in diameter of glans

Cowper's gland

Testicles rotate forward

Scrotum thickens

Testicles fully elevated

2-fold size increase in part of the urethra

Marked increase in size of testicles (up to 50%)

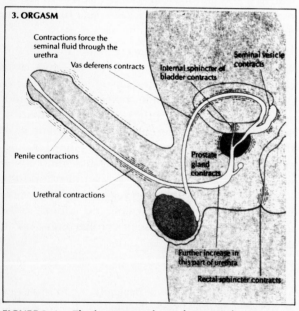

3. ORGASM

Contractions force the seminal fluid through the urethra

Vas deferens contracts

Internal sphincter of bladder contracts

Seminal vesicle contracts

Penile contractions

Prostate gland contracts

Urethral contractions

Further increase in this part of urethra

Rectal sphincter contracts

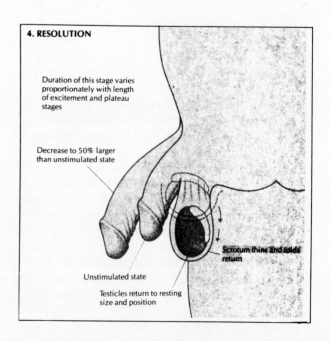

4. RESOLUTION

Duration of this stage varies proportionately with length of excitement and plateau stages

Decrease to 50% larger than unstimulated state

Unstimulated state

Testicles return to resting size and position

Scrotum thins and folds return

FIGURE 3–1. *The four stages of sexual response in men.*

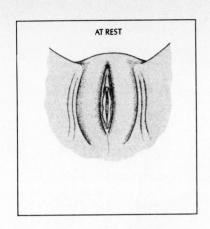
AT REST

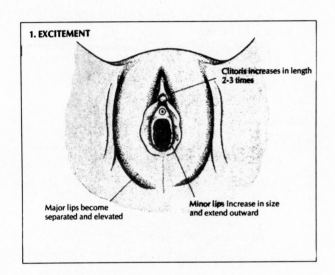

1. EXCITEMENT

Clitoris increases in length 2-3 times

Major lips become separated and elevated

Minor lips increase in size and extend outward

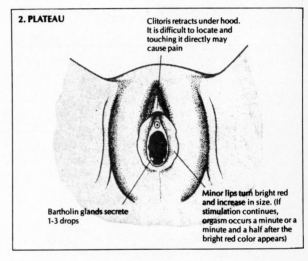

2. PLATEAU

Clitoris retracts under hood. It is difficult to locate and touching it directly may cause pain

Bartholin glands secrete 1-3 drops

Minor lips turn bright red and increase in size. (If stimulation continues, orgasm occurs a minute or a minute and a half after the bright red color appears)

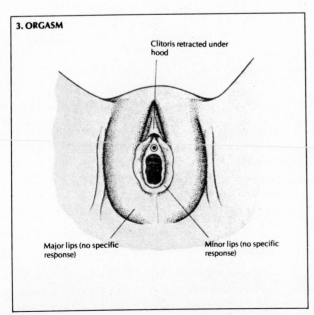

3. ORGASM

Clitoris retracted under hood

Major lips (no specific response)

Minor lips (no specific response)

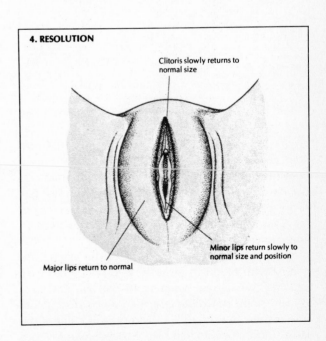

4. RESOLUTION

Clitoris slowly returns to normal size

Minor lips return slowly to normal size and position

Major lips return to normal

FIGURE 3–2. *The four stages of sexual response in women.*

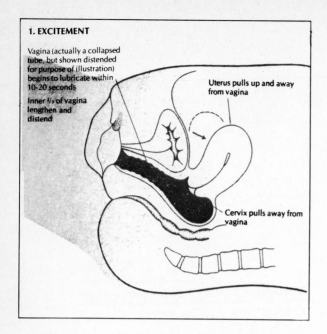

1. EXCITEMENT

Vagina (actually a collapsed tube, but shown distended for purpose of illustration) begins to lubricate within 10-20 seconds

Inner ⅔ of vagina lengthen and distend

Uterus pulls up and away from vagina

Cervix pulls away from vagina

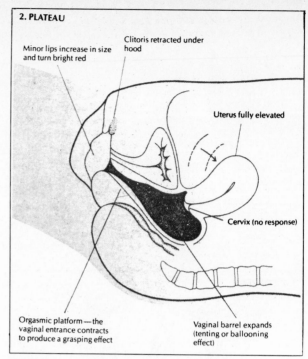

2. PLATEAU

Minor lips increase in size and turn bright red

Clitoris retracted under hood

Uterus fully elevated

Cervix (no response)

Orgasmic platform—the vaginal entrance contracts to produce a grasping effect

Vaginal barrel expands (tenting or ballooning effect)

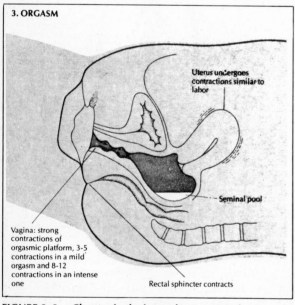

3. ORGASM

Uterus undergoes contractions similar to labor

Seminal pool

Vagina: strong contractions of orgasmic platform, 3-5 contractions in a mild orgasm and 8-12 contractions in an intense one

Rectal sphincter contracts

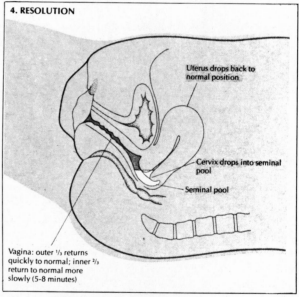

4. RESOLUTION

Uterus drops back to normal position

Cervix drops into seminal pool

Seminal pool

Vagina: outer ⅓ returns quickly to normal; inner ⅔ return to normal more slowly (5-8 minutes)

FIGURE 3–3. *Changes in the internal sex organs of women during sex.*

large, vaginal lubrication continues, muscular tension increases, and the other signs of excitement continue to grow. The Cowper's glands in men and the Bartholin's glands in women may secrete a few drops of fluid at this time. *Note: Fluid released from the Cowper's glands at this stage may contain sperm and can cause pregnancy.*

In women, the outer third of the vagina engorges with blood to form the **orgasmic platform,** causing the vaginal opening to narrow, and at a certain point of excitement the clitoris disappears under the clitoral hood. A darkening in color of the labia minora occurs just before the woman reaches orgasm.

The plateau stage can last as little as a minute or two or can be prolonged for hours. During this time men and women are less easily distracted than earlier, and gradually become totally focused on sexual sensations and unaware of the surrounding environment.

Orgasm

Orgasm, also known as climax or "coming," is the release of all the physical and nervous tension built up in the body during the excitement and plateau phases. An orgasm lasts only a few seconds. There are a number of measurable physical

TABLE 3-1   The Human Sexual Response: The Excitement Phase

GENITAL CHANGES

Females	Males
Clitoris: Increases in size early in phase and appears to withdraw under clitorial hood as arousal increases.	*Penis:* Rapid beginning of erection; size increases throughout most of this phase.
Vagina: Begins lubricating rapidly, becomes longer and wider, and color changes to a darker purple. The outer one-third (called the *orgasmic platform*) fills with blood.	*Scrotum:* Becomes thicker and pulls up toward body.
	Testes: Pulled up toward body wall and increase in size as much as 50 percent.
Uterus: Starts rising and, by the end of the phase, is pulled up from vagina, providing a "tenting," or open area, at the inner one-third of the vagina.	*Cowper's gland:* May secrete two or three drops of fluid, which may contain viable sperm.
Labia majora: Become increasingly filled with blood, move somewhat away from midline where they normally touch.	
Labia minora: Become somewhat larger; become much more deeply colored due to increased blood congestion.	
Bartholin's glands: May secrete a few drops of fluid late in this phase.	

EXTRAGENITAL CHANGES

Females	Males
Breasts: Nipples erect and breasts increase in size, up to 25 percent larger.	*Breasts:* Nipples erect in some males.
Sex flush: A reddening of the skin may develop over the upper abdomen and spread over the body.	*Sex flush:* Typically develops later and less frequently than in females.
Breathing: May become rapid late in this phase.	*Rectum:* Some voluntary contractions late in the phase.
Heart rate: Slows early, then begins to increase up to as high as 175 beats per minute.	*Breathing:* May become more rapid late in phase.
Blood pressure: Rises as phase progresses.	*Heart rate:* Slows early, then begins to increase as phase develops, as high as 180 beats per minute.
Muscle tension: Both voluntary and involuntary muscle activity increases as phase progresses.	*Blood pressure:* Rises as the phase progresses.
	Muscle tension: Both voluntary and involuntary muscle activity increases as phase progresses.

SOURCE: Adapted from *Human Sexuality* by James Geer, Julia Heiman, and Harold Leitenberg, p. 40. © 1984. Reprinted by permission of Prentice-Hall, Englewood Cliffs, N.J.

reactions that usually accompany orgasm in both men and women, mostly contractions of involuntary muscles of the reproductive organs. But orgasm involves more than just genital contractions (and ejaculations in men); muscular and nervous tension in the entire body is released during orgasm (see Table 3–2). The contractions of the sexual organs are shown for both men and women in Figures 3–1 and 3–3. The exact locations and the number of contractions experienced vary in different men and women, and from one orgasm to another in the same person.

Orgasms are reported by both men and women to be highly pleasurable, and many people consider an intense orgasm to be the greatest physical pleasure of which humans are capable. The reported sensations of orgasm differ somewhat between people and also may change over time for an individual. The same person may have very intense orgasms some of the time and milder ones at other times. The longer and the more intense the sexual stimulation, the more intense the orgasm generally will be. A mild orgasm has been described as giving the same kind of release of tension as a badly needed sneeze. Very intense orgasms have been described as so pleasurable as to almost cause a loss of consciousness.

In men   Men report two stages to orgasm. The first is a feeling that orgasm and ejaculation are about to begin and cannot be avoided. The second is the ejaculation and orgasm itself. The force of ejaculation can be so strong that semen may be carried one to two feet from the body. Following ejaculation there are a series of involuntary contractions of the genitals, about eight-tenths of a second apart. The first contractions are intense, and they gradually become weaker. In general, the greater the number of contractions, the more intense the orgasm is reported to be. The anal sphincter (muscles around the rectal opening) usually also contracts at this time.

Ejaculation and orgasm usually occur together in men, but in some cases (particularly when there is nerve or muscle damage) a man may have an orgasm without ejaculating. Also, young boys

TABLE 3-2 The Human Sexual Response: The Orgasm Phase

GENITAL CHANGES	
Females	Males
Vagina: Orgasmic platform contracts from 5 to 12 times; the contractions occur slightly faster than one per second, with the time between contractions becoming longer and the strength of the contractions decreasing.	*Penis:* Contractions of the penile urethra occurring slightly faster than one per second, but fewer in number than in women.
Uterus: Contractions of the uterus, similar to those that accompany labor.	*Prostate and seminal vessels:* Contractions occur, moving semen to the exterior.

EXTRAGENITAL CHANGES	
Females	Males
Sex flush: Its intensity is related to the psychological intensity of the experience and is more widespread than in other phases.	*Sex flush:* In those men where it occurs (25 percent), maximum development.
Rectum: Contractions linked in time to vaginal contractions, but usually fewer.	*Rectum:* Contractions linked to genital contractions.
Breathing: Maximum change; some women also make sounds.	*Breathing:* Maximum change; some men make sounds.
Heart rate: Maximum change, with rate of up to 180 beats per minute recorded.	*Heart rate:* Maximum change, with rate of up to 180 beats per minute recorded.
Blood pressure: Greatest elevation.	*Blood pressure:* Greatest elevation, generally somewhat greater than in women.
Muscle tension: Some loss of voluntary control, with spasms and contractions of many muscle groups.	*Muscle tension:* Some loss of voluntary control, with spasms and contractions of many muscle groups.

SOURCE: Adapted from *Human Sexuality* by James Geer, Julia Heiman, and Harold Leitenberg, p. 44. © 1984. Reprinted by permission of Prentice-Hall, Inc., Englewood Cliffs, N.J.

who have not yet developed the capacity to ejaculate may have orgasms. Ejaculation without orgasm is also possible, but rare.

In women   Like men, women report a feeling of inevitability just before orgasm, and also a spreading warm feeling in the genital area. During orgasm itself, the outer third of the vagina, called the orgasmic platform, contracts (anywhere from 3 to 15 times), strongly at first with contractions less than a second apart, and then more mildly with contractions further apart. The anal sphincter (muscles around the rectal opening) may also contract a few times in the same rhythm. The uterus also contracts during orgasm, but the contractions are irregular and are not related to the vaginal contractions.

Unlike men, women commonly are able to have more than one orgasm (often several) during a single act of intercourse. Why women can do this and men generally cannot is not known. When women have multiple orgasms, they often describe them as increasing in intensity.

Resolution

The resolution phase takes place after orgasm and involves the return of the body to its nonexcited state. This can take as long as 30 minutes, but most of the changes take place within the first 5 to 10 minutes. Heart, blood pressure, and breathing rates return to resting levels, and the genitals of both sexes return to the unexcited state.

It appears that the longer the excitement and plateau phases, and the more intense the sexual excitement, the longer the resolution phase will take. If sexual activity ends before having an orgasm, the resolution phase will also take longer.

In men   The penis loses about half of the erection almost immediately after ejaculation, and the remainder over the next few minutes. The testicles decrease in size, the cremaster muscle relaxes, and the scrotum is lowered. Within half an hour the genitals have returned to the unexcited state, and the other signs of excitement, such as erect nipples, have disappeared.

Once a man has had an orgasm, he is generally not able to get another erection and to have another orgasm for a period of time called the refractory period. This time period can be as little as a few minutes or as much as several hours, depending on many factors including the man's age and health. In rare cases (mainly involving young men), men have reported being able to have several orgasms in quick succession with no refractory period. In these cases the orgasms were generally described as decreasing in intensity. The length of the refractory period varies for individual men, but in general it is shortest for young men and becomes longer as a man ages.

In women During the resolution phase the woman's body gradually returns to the unexcited state. The vagina and the uterus return to their normal size and positions; the labia majora, labia minora, and clitoris decrease in size and return to normal coloration and position, the breasts decrease in size, and the nipples are no longer erect. Many women are capable of having several orgasms within a short period of time without going through the resolution phase.

Sexual Response in Older People

Both men and women continue to be interested in sex and capable of sexual activity throughout their lives. Sexual desire, feelings, and abilities do not end for either men or women at a certain age, and there is no reason that men and women cannot enjoy sexual activity throughout their lives. In the past some people believed that older men and women naturally lose interest in sex. Others believed that sexual activity was not dignified or proper for older persons. In the case of women, some thought that after menopause women have no interest in sex. These beliefs have no basis in fact. See Table 3–3 for a list of changes in sexual response with age.

Older married couples continue to have intercourse, with couples age 55 and older reporting intercourse approximately once a week in one survey (in comparison to 2.5 times per week for couples aged 25 to 34). Certain circumstances, such as not having a partner or being ill, may keep an older person (or a person of any age) from being sexually active.

There are some physical changes in sexual response in older men and women. The whole response cycle slows down a bit, so that they are slower to respond during the excitement phase, they are slower to reach orgasm, and men have a longer refractory period. The sex organs appear to become somewhat less sensitive with age, and both men and women report the sensations of excitement and orgasm to be less intense but still highly pleasurable.

Older women often have less vaginal lubrication, and the walls of the vagina may become thinner and less elastic. The "tenting" or ballooning effect in the upper vagina is less because there is less uterine elevation. Older men are usually slower to get an erection, may require direct stimulation of the penis. The erection may not be as complete as before. Men generally reach orgasm more slowly, which can be an advantage because they have time to satisfy their partner completely before their own orgasm.

Men and women who have been sexually active all their lives seem to be more sexually responsive in old age than those who have not been. It appears that the key to maintaining sexual ability

TABLE 3-3   Changes in the Sexual Response with Age

Females	Males
Breasts: The response of the nipple is not affected except that loss of erection takes longer. Increases in breast size occur less frequently.	*Breasts:* Nipple erection reaction happens less often, but when it occurs it lasts longer after orgasm.
Sex flush: Occurs less frequently and spreads less widely when it occurs.	*Sex flush:* Becomes less common and less intense.
Muscle tension: Decreases with age, but much less so in women who continue regular sexual activity.	*Muscle tension:* Decreases with age, but much less so in males who experience regular sexual activity.
Clitoris: Response is quite similar at all ages, with somewhat less swelling in the glans.	*Penis:* Getting an erection is slower, but it is maintained for longer periods. More difficulty in renewing an erection if it is lost before orgasm, the refractory period is longer, and loss of erection after orgasm is more rapid. The force of ejaculation and intensity of contractions is less.
Labia majora: This structure loses its ability to move away from the vagina.	
Labia minora: No longer become enlarged, and the color change becomes less pronounced.	*Scrotum:* Less blood congestion and less frequent lifting toward the body wall.
Bartholin's glands: Secretion gradually becomes less.	*Testes:* Less elevation of the testes, and increase in size is not as evident. Return to prestimulation levels after orgasm is very rapid.
Vagina: Lubrication occurs at a slower rate (but can be extensive in sexually active older women). The vagina's ability to increase in width and depth becomes less, and the return to prestimulation levels occurs rapidly.	*Prostate and ejaculatory ducts:* Appear to respond less.
	Ejaculation: Volume and force are less intense, and sensations are different for the older male. Less of a phase of inevitability and less feeling of expulsion of semen, so that experience is more like a single stage.
Uterus: Elevation less pronounced, and contractions may be uncomfortable.	
The intensity of the subjective experience of orgasm decreases.	The intensity of the subjective experience of orgasm decreases.

SOURCE: Adapted from *Human Sexuality* by James Geer, Julia Heiman, and Harold Leitenberg, p. 48. © 1984. Reprinted by permission of Prentice-Hall, Inc., Englewood Cliffs, N.J.

into old age is a pattern of continuing sexual activity over a lifetime. Older people who have maintained a pattern of regular sexual activity may be more responsive than some young people.

The Grafenberg Spot

The Grafenberg spot (G spot) is a small area inside the vagina that is especially sensitive to sexual stimulation in some women. In a few women, it also appears to be the source of a small amount of fluid ejaculated at orgasm. The G spot is a somewhat controversial concept, as not all experts are sure that it really exists and most agree that we do not know much about it yet. It appears that the G spot may be a small amount of tissue similar to the prostate in men (called the Skenes glands in women). The tissue has no reproductive function in women but may provide an extra area of sexual stimulation.

Since the concept of the G spot helps to explain some previously unexplainable symptoms and sensations that many women report, it is presented here even though the existence and characteristics of the G spot are not yet established as scientific fact. Women reading this will be able to judge for themselves whether or not they have experienced the sensations or the fluid production ascribed to the G spot.

The G spot is a small patch of tissue (about the size of a dime or a quarter) on the front wall of the vagina (where it is closest to the bladder and urethra). It is located midway between the pelvic bone and the cervix and is not too far inside the

FIGURE 3–4. *The Grafenberg spot.*

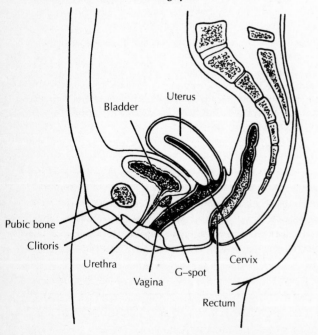

Uterus
Bladder
Pubic bone
Clitoris
Urethra
Vagina
G–spot
Cervix
Rectum

vagina for a woman to reach with her own fingers (see Figure 3–4). If touched or rubbed, whether by fingers or by a penis during intercourse, the area is more sensitive than the surrounding tissue, and swells (becomes engorged with blood) when stimulated. Stimulation of the area may at first cause a feeling of needing to urinate, but this usually passes and is replaced by pleasurable sexual stimulation. Some women report that they can reach orgasm by stimulating this spot, which for many is more directly approached by a rear-entry position in intercourse (when the penis enters the vagina from the back). In some women a little fluid is expelled from the G spot through the vagina (or, in a few cases, from the urinary opening) at orgasm. In the past, when women reported this fluid, it was thought to be urine, vaginal lubrication, or semen.

The G spot has no known function for women except as a source of sexual stimulation. After intercourse in which the G spot has been stimulated, some women report difficulty urinating. This may be because the swelling of the tissue creates temporary pressure on the urethra until the swelling subsides, usually within a few minutes.

INTERCOURSE AND OTHER SEXUAL ACTIVITY

This section describes the most common types of sexual activity, starting with self-stimulation (sex in which no other person is involved) and then describing heterosexual intercourse (sex between men and women) and homosexual intercourse (sex between two men or two women).

Self-stimulation

Orgasm during Sleep

By the age of 40, the majority of men (80 percent and many women (40 percent) have experienced orgasm during sleep, often during sexual dreams. In men these orgasms are called **nocturnal emissions** or **wet dreams** because semen is ejaculated and when the man awakes, he will know he had an orgasm during sleep, even if he doesn't remember it. Women and girls, and young boys who have not yet passed puberty, do not ejaculate any fluid, and may not be aware of or remember an orgasm that takes place during sleep. Orgasms during sleep may occur quite often or only occasionally.

Sexual arousal and orgasm during sleep may not always be accompanied by a sexual dream. All males, including male infants and small boys, have erections during certain phases of sleep (REM or *rapid eye movement* sleep, which is believed to be the period when dreams occur). REM sleep occurs several times each night. Most of these dreams are probably not sexual, but erection takes place regardless. These erections usually subside without an orgasm or ejaculation. Women also develop the physical signs of sexual arousal (increased blood flow to the genitals and increased vaginal lubrication) during REM sleep.

The reasons for sexual arousal and orgasms during sleep are not understood. Nocturnal emissions in men may have the function of helping to empty the prostate gland. In the past it was thought that orgasms during sleep might be a way for the body to release sexual tension for the person who does not have a sexual partner and/or does not masturbate. This appears to be false, for women at least, since they report having orgasms during sleep as frequently when they are sexually active as when they are not.

A nocturnal emission is a natural human function, but it can be surprising and embarrassing the first time it happens to a young boy if he does not know what it is.

Masturbation

What is it? Masturbation refers to sexual stimulation and gratification that an individual provides for him or herself. It takes place without a partner and does not involve another person (unless it is part of sex play and the partner is watching). To masturbate, a person stimulates his or her own genitals to orgasm (or may stop before reaching that point).

Who does it? Over 90 percent of men and over 60 percent of women report having masturbated at some point during their lives. The fact that touching and rubbing the sex organs feels good is something babies discover within the first year of life, and small children often must be taught that touching their genitals is something they should do only in private. Small children know that masturbation feels good, but they do not know that it has anything to do with sex. Infants and small children do not usually have orgasms, but a few people report being able to masturbate to orgasm from a very early age.

Most men and women report the first experience with masturbation that they remember as taking place around puberty (sexual masturbation) or later. Some masturbate regularly throughout their entire lives; others masturbate rarely. Although masturbation is often thought of as an outlet used by men and women who do not have a sexual partner, many married and unmarried people mas-

turbate in addition to having sexual intercourse with the partner. Since sexual desire and interest continue into old age, masturbation also continues over the lifetime.

How is it done? Masturbation is a learned behavior, and most men and women develop a particular way of masturbating that they repeat, although the pattern may change over time. The most common way for both men and women to masturbate is by rubbing the sexual organs (penis or vulva) with their fingers; but there are many other ways to masturbate as well, for example by rubbing against a pillow, or running water over the genitals. Some women also insert the fingers (or other objects) in the vagina. Tissues in the genital area are very sensitive and it is important that nothing sharp, pointed, or rough on the surface be inserted into the vagina, urethra, or anus during masturbation.

Why is it done? People masturbate for many different reasons, but mainly for pleasure and enjoyment—because it feels good. For infants and very small children it is probably a general sense of pleasure and comfort. For older children, masturbation may be for exploration and experimentation. After puberty it may be used for relief of sexual tension. Some men and women also masturbate for relief of general tension and anxiety, or when they are bored.

Masturbation is used as a sexual outlet by people who are temporarily separated from their partners, and by people who do not have a sexual partner. Sometimes couples masturbate together or stimulate each other as a substitute for sexual intercourse. Since masturbation does not cause pregnancy, it can be useful when a couple does not have access to birth control. It also a way for a couple to enjoy sex together if one or both is still a virgin or is not ready for sexual intercourse. Masturbation is also often recommended as a part of sex therapy for both men and women, as a way of becoming familiar with one's own body and sensations, and as part of training to improve responsiveness during sex with another person.

Can it do any harm? Masturbation is an almost universal human practice which has been known since prehistoric times. It is also seen in animals and appears to be a natural response. Masturbation does no harm to the health of males or females at any age. To the extent that it relieves tension, it probably has a good effect. Like anything else, masturbation could be used harmfully, in that a person could injure himself or herself by using dangerous objects to masturbate, or could focus on masturbation so strongly that he or she becomes socially isolated and does not seek out relationships with other people.

In the past, many have believed that masturbation was harmful, and it has been blamed for causing all kinds of physical and mental illnesses and for causing general physical and mental weakness. Psychiatrists in the 1800s considered masturbation a cause of insanity. Orgasm during sleep was also thought to cause health problems, and devices to prevent both masturbation and orgasm during sleep were used in England and in the United States in the 1800s to prevent erections in boys and men. Another common belief has been that boys and men are weakened by losing semen through ejaculation, and that they can best preserve their health and strength by losing as little semen as possible. There is no evidence at all that this is true.

Is it wrong? The question of whether masturbation is wrong or not can only be answered by each person for himself or herself. Since masturbation does not harm the individual and does not involve anyone else, any decision about whether or not it is acceptable is based on the values and beliefs of the person. Some religions and cultures forbid masturbation. Both the Christian and Jewish faiths have in the past viewed masturbation as sinful, but most religious denominations are more accepting of the practice today. Even so, because of the history of viewing masturbation as forbidden, sinful, and a cause of illness and insanity, many Americans still feel guilty and secretive about masturbation, although the majority (around 75 percent) also believe it is a healthy practice.

Sexual Intercourse

What Is It?

The word *intercourse* means "exchange" or "communication," and **sexual intercourse** refers to sexual activity between two persons. Often it is used to mean only **coitus,** or **genital intercourse,** which is sexual activity between a male and a female in which the penis penetrates the vagina. This is the only kind of sexual intercourse that can cause pregnancy. (It is said that there is an exception to every rule. For the exception to this one, see page 214 of Chapter 9, "Contraception"—the part about how you don't have to have intercourse to get pregnant!) Other times the word *intercourse* is used more generally to mean a variety of kinds of sexual activity in which two people are involved. These include **oral intercourse,** in which the genitals of one partner are in contact with the mouth of the other; **manual intercourse,** in which partners use the

hands to stimulate each other's genitals; and **anal intercourse,** in which the anus (rectal opening) of one partner is in contact with the genitals of the other. All forms of intercourse can be practiced by a man and a woman, in which case they are called **heterosexual intercourse.** Since coitus is the only kind of intercourse that can result in pregnancy, the other forms of intercourse are sometimes used as contraception. Same-sex couples can practice all forms of intercourse except coitus; sexual activity in these couples is called **homosexual intercourse.**

During intercourse the bodies of the partners go through the four stages of sexual response described on pages 45–51. Intercourse usually ends with an orgasm and ejaculation for men, and frequently (but not always) with an orgasm for women.

This section describes the basic ways in which both heterosexual and homosexual couples have intercourse. The variety of ways in which couples can have intercourse is almost endless, but the most common, basic patterns are described. Although genital, oral, manual, and anal intercourse are described separately, it is important to know that many heterosexual couples combine the first three of these activities in one lovemaking session. Anal intercourse is less common. Male homosexual couples also may combine all the approaches (except coitus), and are more likely to have anal intercourse. Female homosexuals are limited to oral and manual intercourse unless they use a dildo or other substitute for a penis.

Foreplay

Before sexual intercourse begins, couples almost always engage in **foreplay,** affectionate physical contact such as kissing, hugging, caressing, and stroking the partner's body (including the genitals). Foreplay may continue for just a few minutes, or may go on for hours. Its purpose is to express and enjoy physical and emotional closeness, and to stimulate the sex organs so that they become prepared for intercourse (see page 49 for details about the excitement phase in sexual response). Only after the man has an erection and the woman's vagina is lubricated are both partners ready for intercourse.

Foreplay is highly enjoyable for its own sake, and does not always lead to intercourse. The same kinds of touching and contact usually continue during intercourse and sometimes after it is completed. Caressing and touching after intercourse is called **afterplay.**

What is called foreplay when describing sexual intercourse is the same thing as necking and petting for couples who do not have intercourse.

Necking generally refers to kissing from the neck up and hugging. **Petting** generally means kissing and touching the body below the neck as well, particularly the breasts and sexual organs. Both teenagers and adults enjoy necking and petting as a way of getting to know new partners before they are ready to have sexual intercourse, and as a way of being close to partners if they do not plan to have intercourse. It is also the way most young people learn about being sexual with another person, slowly increasing the intimacy of contact from necking to petting until they feel ready for intercourse.

Oral or manual intercourse to the point of orgasm is sometimes called **heavy petting,** to set it apart from coitus or genital intercourse, which could cause pregnancy (and which causes a girl or women to lose her virginity).

The Importance of Communication

Satisfying and enjoyable sexual intercourse depends on excellent communication. Foreplay and intercourse are very powerful means of nonverbal communication between people, and many satisfying sexual encounters do not involve much talking. To have a successful sexual relationship over time, however, couples also must be able to talk about their feelings, responses, and preferences in order to develop a relationship that gives the maximum enjoyment to both partners. For human beings, sexual intercourse is mostly a learned behavior rather than an instinctive one, and learning requires time and practice as well. However close we may feel to our partners, we are still separate beings, and no one can know exactly what the partner is thinking or feeling unless he or she shares that information. To use an example other than sex, when we tickle another person, we can see some of the person's response (laughing, wriggling, and so on), but we don't know until the person tells us whether he or she is enjoying it or being made miserable. We don't know whether to continue or to stop, or how to make the experience more enjoyable.

Communication is also important because sexuality is just one part of a relationship and is strongly affected by other dimensions of the relationship. It is not surprising that happily married couples report more frequent and more satisfying sex than those whose marriages are less happy. In order to maintain a good sexual relationship, couples must also maintain positive feelings and trust in the rest of the relationship, and this requires a lot of communication.

Heterosexual Intercourse

Genital Intercourse

There are a great number of positions in which a man and a woman can have genital intercourse or coitus. The four most commonly used are described here. Why are they the most common? Probably because they are comfortable and satisfying for many people. But each couple develops their own choice of positions that are most satisfying, because body shapes and sizes are different, and so are people's preferences for sensation. Over time most couples choose one or more favorite positions and develop a stable pattern of how they have intercourse. Most of the information available about preferred positions for sexual intercourse has been learned from surveys of married couples. It is assumed that the patterns are similar for unmarried couples, but there may be differences.

Man-on-top, or missionary position The man-on-top position is the most popular in the United States and Europe, but is not the most commonly used throughout the world. It was named the *missionary position* by Pacific Islanders (for whom the woman-on-top was the standard position) when they learned that the missionaries who came to convert them had intercourse differently.

In the man-on-top position, the woman lies on her back, and the man lies between her legs, supporting some of his weight on his knees and elbows and hands. The woman's legs may be extended, slightly bent, pulled up toward her chest, or wrapped around the man. Each of these positions will affect the angle and depth of penetration of the man's penis in her vagina. The man controls the pace, rhythm, pauses, and depths of thrusting with the penis. These vary between couples, depending on what they find enjoyable.

Woman-on-top position The woman-on-top position is also very popular. One survey found that about 75 percent of American couples used it sometimes. It consists of the man lying on his back and the woman sitting astride him. There are many possible variations, with the woman leaning forward for more contact, or extending her legs back toward the man's feet. In this position the woman controls the pace and rhythm of thrusting, and her clitoris and breasts can easily be stimulated by her partner.

Side-by-side position The side-by-side position, used sometimes by 50 percent of Americans, is also popular. It consists of the couple lying face to face, side by side, with the upper legs flexed and across each other's bodies. There are many possible variations of this position, which leaves both partners free to caress each other with their hands, and to share equally in controlling movement.

Rear-entry position   This position is the least popular of the four most common positions for Americans (around 40 percent reported having tried it). The woman kneels or lies on her stomach or side, and the man's penis enters the vagina from the back. This leaves the man's hands free to caress the woman's body, but has the disadvantage that the couple are not face to face, so that some couples find it less intimate. Some women report that this is the best position for stimulating the G spot. Rear entry is the most common way for most mammals, including apes and other primates, to copulate.

Oral Intercourse

Oral intercourse involves using the mouth to stimulate the partner's sexual organs to orgasm. Many couples also use oral intercourse at some point during foreplay or lovemaking but change to genital intercourse before orgasm. Two terms are used for oral intercourse: **cunnilingus,** which refers to the man using his lips and tongue to caress and stimulate the woman's vulva, and **fellatio,** which refers to the woman using her mouth to stimulate her partner's penis and scrotum.

Oral intercourse has apparently become common among couples in the United States over the last 40 years, and a survey of married couples show that the 50 to 90 percent have had oral sex, and around 40 percent practice it often. Some people, however, find oral–genital contact unpleasant, feeling that it is abnormal or unclean, and some women dislike the idea of a man ejaculating in their mouths. Whether or not a couple has oral intercourse, and exactly how they do it, is a matter of personal preference. There is no right or wrong way, or normal or abnormal way, to do it.

Cunnilingus   In cunnilingus, the man uses his lips and tongue to kiss, stroke, suck, and nibble the inner and outer lips of the vagina and the area around the clitoris. Often this brings the woman to orgasm. Some women reach orgasm more easily through cunnilingus than through genital intercourse. Air should never be blown into the vagina during cunnilingus, as this can (in rare cases), cause an air bubble to enter the bloodstream. Such a bubble can create a fatal blockage of a blood vessel; the risk is higher for pregnant women.

Fellatio   In fellatio, the woman uses her mouth to stimulate the man's genitals, often to orgasm. She may lick the glans of the penis with her tongue and may lick and nibble the scrotum as well. She may take the glans of the penis in her mouth and suck it while stroking the shaft with her fingers, or she may take as much of the penis in her mouth as possible, sliding it in and out between her lips. A gagging reflex is normal if the penis presses the back of the throat. Some women keep the penis in the mouth when the man ejaculates, and some like to swallow the semen. Others have the men ejaculate outside the mouth, continuing to stimulate the penis with their fingers.

Taking turns or together?   A couple having oral intercourse can take turns stimulating each other, or having cunnilingus and fellatio simultaneously. The slang term for simultaneous oral sex is "sixty-nine." Simultaneous oral intercourse can result in quite an overwhelming array of sensations, and probably takes more practice for most couples than taking turns.

Manual Intercourse

Manual intercourse consists of stimulating the partner's genitals to orgasm with the hands. It is similar in technique to masturbation, except that the touching is done by the partner. A couple can take turns with stimulating each other or can do it simultaneously. Manual intercourse is sometimes called heavy petting and can be used by couples when one partner wants intercourse but the other doesn't or is not able to for some reason (such as a health problem).

For the woman   For the female, manual intercourse involves stroking the vulva, especially the area around the clitoris, with a stroke, pressure, and rhythm that the woman finds arousing. In addition, one or two fingers may be used to penetrate the vagina, if the woman enjoys this. Stimulation of the breasts may take place at the same time.

For the man   Manual intercourse for the man involves stroking and caressing the penis and scrotum, according to a pressure and rhythm that the man finds stimulating. The glans and corona (ridge around the glans,) along with the underside of the penis, are reported to be the most sensitive areas of the penis.

Anal Intercourse

Anal intercourse refers to penetration of the anus (rectal opening) by the penis. It is much less common for heterosexual couples than the other forms of intercourse described, but it has been tried at least once by a substantial number of couples. Anal intercourse can take place in any of the four basic positions for genital intercourse, but it must be approached with care to avoid pain for the woman, since the anal muscles are usually tight, and the anus does not provide its own lubrication as the vagina does.

Warning: *Men should wear condoms (rubbers) during anal intercourse. Rectal tissues are easily scratched and torn creating a risk of transmission of disease, including AIDS, hepatitis B, and other infections. In addition, the organisms that normally live in the rectum and in feces can cause infection in the genitals of both men and women. Women are most susceptible to infection. For this reason, a man should never move his penis from the anus to the vagina without washing it first, and should wash his penis when anal intercourse is completed in any case.*

Homosexual Intercourse

Homosexual intercourse involves two partners of the same sex, either two men or two women. Obviously, a homosexual couple cannot start a pregnancy or engage in coitus. Other than these differences, homosexual intercourse is much like heterosexual intercourse. This section will describe the basic ways in which homosexual intercourse takes place. For more details about homosexual lifestyles, see pages 42–44.

Genital intercourse between same-sex partners involves closely embracing so that the genitals are touching, and then moving rhythmically. Homosexual women can also stimulate each other by inserting the fingers in the vagina or by the use of a dildo or other penis-shaped object. Oral and manual intercourse for same-sex partners follows the same pattern described for heterosexuals.

Many male homosexuals use anal intercourse, often with a technique similar to that described for heterosexuals. Some also enjoy placing other objects in the rectum. Needless to say, the inserting of very large objects in the rectum can be very dangerous and damaging to the body.

Warning: *Homosexual men should wear condoms (rubbers) during anal intercourse for the reasons given above under "Anal Intercourse"* (see also Chapter 14, page 323, for information on the special risks of anal intercourse).

Frequency of Intercourse (How Often?)

Information about how often heterosexual couples have sexual intercourse is mainly obtained from surveys of married couples. The frequency of intercourse seems to be highest among young couples and then to drop gradually with age, so that the average figure seems to be around 3 to 3½ times a week for couples under 24 and around once a week for couples 55 and older. The length of time people have been married also appears to be a factor, with recently married couples likely to have more frequent sex than those who have been married longer. It should be noted that these figures are averages, and that the range of sexual behavior is very great; some couples have intercourse several times a day, and some once a month or less often. There is less information about frequency of intercourse for unmarried couples, but it can probably be assumed that they are similar for couples who are living together. For those who are not, the availability of time together and privacy may limit their frequency of intercourse.

Duration of Intercourse (How Long?)

As with frequency, there is a tremendous range in the amount of time couples spend in sexual intercourse. There is also more difficulty getting accurate information, as people are so focused on sexual sensations during intercourse that they have difficulty calculating time. In addition, a person's feelings or beliefs about what is desirable in intercourse may affect his or her reporting. One survey of married couples done in the 1970s estimated that the average time of penis-in-vagina intercourse (not counting foreplay) was 10 minutes, but more and better information is needed before we can be confident that we know.

Intensity of Intercourse

The intensity with which people experience sexual intercourse also appears to vary a great deal, both between people and also within one person over time. When two people are having intercourse with each other, the level of intensity may be different for each of them. Intercourse and orgasm can sometimes be an extremely intense experience, totally absorbing, very emotional, and almost unbearable in the amount of pleasure experienced (as described in romantic novels). Men and women have reported a feeling of almost losing consciousness during orgasm. At other times intercourse can be comfortable, relaxing, and not terribly exciting. A middle range of intensity is probably experienced most often, with extremes of high or low intensity occurring less frequently. Little is known about the factors that affect how intense a sexual experience will be. Certainly attraction, feelings about the partner, and the environment or situation in which intercourse takes place are important. Beyond that, the specifics of what is arousing or exciting may be different for each person.

Intercourse during Menstruation

Intercourse during menstruation is not harmful to either the woman or the man, but around 50 percent of couples apparently do not have intercourse during the woman's menstrual period. Some cultures and religious groups forbid intercourse at this time, but for most people it is a matter of personal choice whether they have intercourse during menstruation.

The Role of Fantasy

A large proportion of men and women, perhaps 50 to 60 percent, report that they fantasize about other sexual activity during sexual intercourse. Fantasies typically include such things as imagining oneself with another partner (real or imaginary), imagining having intercourse with more than one person, or imagining a different location or environment for sex. Fantasies may include things that the man or woman finds exciting to think about but would not consider doing in real life. Some men and women report that they feel guilty about having these fantasies, and worry that they are in some way disloyal or not sufficiently aroused by their partners. It appears, however, that fantasies are a natural and common way for people to increase sexual arousal and enjoyment, and that they do not do any harm.

Sexual Satisfaction

Satisfaction with one's sex life involves much more than just orgasm. It is also related to general happiness in the relationship and to frequency of sex. For many people, however, the physical satisfaction and release of tension that comes with orgasm is an important part of sexual satisfaction. Sexual intercourse almost always ends with orgasm for the man, but only sometimes for the woman. In surveys of married couples, over 60 percent of women reported always having an orgasm during sexual intercourse, or having one most of the time. The likelihood that a woman will experience orgasm in intercourse increases as she grows older and as she has been married more years, probably because of increased sexual practice. Some women report that orgasm is not necessary for them to feel sexually satisfied, but to many others it is important. Occasional problems of sexual functioning, such as difficulty getting excited or premature ejaculation, do not seem to affect satisfaction in married couples.

SEXUAL PROBLEMS

Sexual problems most commonly arise from cultural, psychological, and relationship problems. In some instances, however, sexual problems are caused by health factors, such as the effects of disease, injuries, and medications.

Sexual response and enjoyment depend on a very complicated set of conditions, involving a person's physical, psychological, and emotional aspects. Certain social and environmental conditions are also required. This means that when individuals or couples have a sexual problem, there may be any number of causes. Fortunately, a great deal has been learned about human sexual behavior in recent years, and most sexual problems can be helped.

In the next section basic information about some of the diseases, drugs, and health problems that can affect sexual functioning is presented. Following this, information about cultural, psychological, and relationship causes is provided. Common types of sexual problems are also described, along with the kinds of treatment available.

Causes

Health Problems

The next pages deal with sexual problems that can be produced by physical disorders and diseases or by drugs. It should be noted that most of the information that follows relates to the effects of these problems on the sexual functioning of men. Little is known about the effects of these conditions on women.

Alcoholism   Alcoholism is a common cause of impotence in men and of other problems in sexual functioning. Heavy drinking of alcohol, which is a central nervous system depressant, has a negative effect on sexuality while the person is under the influence. Although alcohol may help a person relax and feel free from inhibitions about sex, it also decreases a man's ability to perform sexual intercourse.

Heavy alcohol consumption by men affects the hormone system in two ways: First, it decreases the body's production of the male hormone testosterone; second, long-term alcoholism causes liver damage, which results in abnormally high levels of the female hormone estrogen. These hormone changes reduce a man's sex drive and, if severe, can cause **impotence** (inability to get an erection). Damage to the nervous system caused by long-term alcoholism is also a cause of impotence.

Little is known about the effects of alcoholism on women's sexuality, but it can be assumed to be as serious a problem as for men.

Diabetes   Diabetes is a major cause of impotence in men, with an estimated 50 percent of long-

Heavy drinking is a common cause of sexual problems.

term diabetic men eventually developing the condition because of deterioration of the blood vessels and the nervous system. Treatment of impotence caused by diabetes involves surgery. An inflatable prosthesis can be implanted in the penis, allowing the man to produce an erection when desired and to have sexual intercourse (see page 308 for more on surgery for impotence). The damage to the circulatory and nervous systems caused by diabetes causes a great number of health problems for both men and women, and can be assumed to affect the sexual experience and sexual functioning of women as well as men.

High blood pressure   High blood pressure (hypertension) is associated with problems in sexual functioning for men for two reasons. First, most of the medications prescribed to control high blood pressure have a negative effect on sexual function and can cause impotence. More details about this are given in the section on medications for high blood pressure later in this chapter. Second, the atherosclerosis (clogging of blood vessels with fat deposits) found in people with high blood pressure appears to damage the ability to produce an erection in some men.

Heart and respiratory diseases   Both heart and respiratory disease can have a negative effect on sexual activity because of problems such as difficulty in breathing and/or pain that comes with exertion. Persons with chronic conditions such as angina pectoris or emphysema may be afraid to have sexual intercourse for fear of worsening their condition or bringing on a crisis. In most cases they can resume sexual activity if they are careful. Under a doctor's guidance, the timing of their medications may be adjusted so that the extra physical exertion of sexual intercourse is less stressful.

Infection, surgery, and injury   Sexual activity can be made difficult or impossible by infections and by recent surgery or injury to the genital area. In most cases these problems are resolved as soon as recovery from the infection or wound takes place. Occasionally, however, pain or fear of pain may continue long after the original problem is solved. Treatment in this situation involves a thorough examination to look for causes of discomfort (see Chapter 12, "Women's Health Problems," for more on pain during intercourse for women). If no physical causes are found, the possibility that there are psychological or emotional aftereffects of the illness or injury should be considered.

In rare cases, surgery to remove the sexual organs may be necessary as a result of cancer or another life-threatening problem. In these cases the person's sexual abilities will be permanently affected. Surgery of this kind is extremely stressful and disturbing for the man or woman involved and for his or her sexual partner. For some people, sexual function may be at least partially restored by further surgery. But in most cases the people affected will have to learn new ways to express their sexuality and to give and receive sexual satisfaction.

Mental illness   Serious mental illnesses such as schizophrenia and organic brain syndrome are likely to affect sexuality, but the kinds of changes or problems that may develop are not predictable. Loss of interest in sex is a common symptom of severe depression; when this is the case, sexual life usually returns to normal after treatment.

Illness, surgery, or injuries can create sexual diffculties.

Circulatory system diseases Diseases of the arteries and veins such as atherosclerosis can cause sexual problems by limiting or cutting off the blood supply to the genital area.

Central nervous system disorders Damage to the central nervous system affects the body's ability to move and to control bodily functions. The pathways for sensation or feeling in various parts of the body are also affected. Obviously, such changes are likely to affect sexual abilities in both men and women. The specific problems or limitations for an individual will depend on the exact nature of the damage to his or her central nervous system. There is great variability between persons with similar injuries or illnesses. Understanding of how these injuries affect sexual functioning and sexual enjoyment is not yet well developed, but it is an area in which great progress is being made.

Hormone disorders Disorders of the pituitary gland, the thyroid gland, and of course the ovaries and testes can cause problems with sexual functioning. Depending on the type of problem, treatment may be medical, including hormone replacement therapy, or may be surgical.

Effects of Drugs

Hormones Hormones are crucially important to sexual growth and development as well as to sexual function. Normally the body manufactures the right balance of hormones needed for sexual functioning. Both men and women manufacture the male hormone (testosterone) and female hormones (estrogen and progesterone), but in different amounts. Although estrogen and progesterone are necessary for normal sexual functioning in women, testosterone appears to be the hormone most responsible for sexual desire in both men and women.

Supplementary hormones are given as medications under many different conditions, ranging from genetic abnormalities such as Turner's syndrome (in which the body does not produce its own sex hormones) to the estrogen replacement therapy frequently given to women after menopause. Sexual function can often be improved or restored by treatment with hormones (if a hormone imbalance or deficiency is the problem), but hormone treatment can also have negative effects on sexuality. For example, certain hormones used to treat disease may have a "masculinizing" effect on women's appearance and others a "feminizing" effect on a man's body. And some drugs (which are not hormones themselves) have undesirable side effects that can cause the body to create hormonal imbalances.

Testosterone, although it is the hormone that is believed to stimulate sexual desire, does not necessarily increase sexual desire when it is taken as a supplement, and it is not often a cure for impotence in men. Most impotent men already have normal levels of testosterone; the cause of impotence lies elsewhere, in psychological or other physical problems.

Prolactin, a pituitary hormone that governs milk production in women, also has important effects on sexual functioning. High levels of this hormone can cause a form of impotence in men and reduce sexual desire in both sexes. Excessive amounts of this hormone may be produced when there is a disorder of the pituitary, during pregnancy, after childbirth, under stress, or as a side effect of certain drugs.

Tranquillizers and other mood-altering drugs Tranquillizers of the phenothiazine group (such as Thorazine, Stelazine, and Mellaril), when given at high dosages, often depress sexual functioning. If a man or woman suffered from anxiety over sexual functioning, the use of these drugs could actually add to the problem rather than helping to resolve it.

Antidepressants of the tricyclic group (such as Elavil, Endep, and Tofranil) or the monoamine-oxidase (MAO) inhibitor groups (such as Marplan, Parnate, and Nardil) may also depress sexual functioning when given at high doses.

Amphetamines may cause a temporary aphrodisiac effect (increase in sexual desire) when first taken, but later act to suppress sexual interest.

Marijuana, LSD, and other illegal "recreational drugs," have inconsistent effects, sometimes enhancing sexual functioning and sometimes depressing it. The expectation of the drug user about what the drug will do, and the situation in which the drug is taken, are probably more powerful factors than the real effects of these drugs on sexual function. Alcohol, the most widely used psychotropic drug in the United States, was discussed earlier.

Medications for high blood pressure Almost all types of medication used to control high blood pressure have a negative effect on sexual functioning for some people, primarily by causing impotence in men. Drugs containing methyldopa (such as Aldomet), thiazide diuretics (such as Hydro-DIURIL and others), beta blockers (such as Inderal), and spironolactone (such as Aldactone or Aldactazide) are all known to cause problems. Persons who need to take medication for hypertension should discuss this common side effect with their doctors.

A Victorian drawing warned women about the dangers of sexual relationships.

Anticholinergic drugs Anticholinergic drugs are smooth-muscle relaxants used for problems of the digestive tract, particularly the intestines. Drugs such as propantheline bromide (Pro-Banthine) have a negative effect on sexual functioning because of the way they affect the nervous system and muscle tone.

Cultural Standards (What Is Normal?)

Our social and cultural environment shapes our beliefs and expectations about sexuality. The decisions we make about whether or not we have a sexual problem are based on our understanding of what is considered normal. Our ideas about what is normal are based on what our culture or society finds acceptable and unacceptable.

Today in the United States a very high value is placed on having frequent and satisfying sexual relations. The ideals of sexual activity presented in literature and the media probably cannot be met by many people, who may feel that their sex lives are inadequate in comparison, or that they have sexual problems. The large sales of self-help books on sexuality point to the interest people have in getting the most out of their sex lives, and to the belief that there is more to be gained.

Cultural norms for sexual behavior have changed rapidly over the last hundred years in this country. Thus, in the 1980s a woman who enjoys satisfying sex but does not have orgasms during intercourse is likely to view herself as having a sexual problem. One hundred years ago, in Victorian times, her great-grandmother was not expected to desire or enjoy sex, and was certainly not expected to have orgasms. Women living at that time were sometimes seen as having a sexual problem if they showed "too much" interest in sex.

There is a great deal of variation across cultures in what is considered acceptable and desirable sexual behavior. But there are also some universals that are found in almost every culture. For example, the expectation that most adults will join in a long-term sexual relationship with a partner of the opposite sex (which will include childbearing and rearing children) is found in almost all cultures. Behaviors such as sexual experimentation among children, masturbation, and homosexuality are known in all cultures, although attitudes toward these behaviors vary.

An example of the importance of the social and cultural environment can be seen in the change in the way masturbation was viewed in the past and in the way it is viewed today in this country. In the late 1800s and early 1900s in Europe and the United States, masturbation was believed to be an important cause of illness and insanity, and strong measures were taken to discourage children and young people from masturbating. Today masturbation is viewed as a harmless activity that may have some benefits in releasing sexual tension and in preparing young people for future sexual relations with a partner.

Psychological Problems

Mental status Some sexual problems are caused by the mental state of the individual man or woman. For example, a person who is depressed or preoccupied with problems often loses interest in sex temporarily. Exhaustion, anger, fear, worry, and other mental states can interfere with sexual interest, desire, and ability. Continued over a long period of time, these feelings can be the cause of sexual problems.

Values and moral beliefs Persons with strong moral or religious beliefs that forbid or strictly limit sexual behavior and enjoyment may have problems of sexual adjustment. Men and women who were raised with strict beliefs but have since given them up may find that their sexual adjustment is still affected by the teaching they received in childhood.

Reactions to past experiences Past sexual experiences, especially those of a frightening or painful nature, can greatly affect a person's sexual adjustment in the present. Thus, men and women who were molested as children (or assaulted or raped at any age) often need counseling to help them deal with these experiences before they are able to develop satisfying sexual relationships. An unpleasant experience the first time a woman or man has intercourse can have long-lasting effects. Even people who have had positive sexual relationships may find that after a traumatic experience they are no longer able to respond in the same way; they may need time (and sometimes professional help) to recover.

Learned behavior Behavior learned during past sexual experiences can be the cause of problems. A man or woman may carry forward sexual habits or expectations learned during a previous sexual experience which may keep him or her from developing a positive relationship in the present. It is important to know that no matter how sexually experienced or skilled a man or woman is, it is usually necessary to relearn what is satisfying to each new partner.

Relationship Problems

Poor communication Poor communication is probably the single most important cause of sexual problems in relationships, affecting both young couples and partners who have been together for many years. It is most important for partners to learn to talk with each other openly and frankly about sex, and about their likes and dislikes. It is not safe to assume that your partner wants sex at the same time you do, enjoys the same things you do, or knows by your reactions what you enjoy.

Lack of trust If there is a lack of trust between the partners, sexual problems are likely. Women in particular report that trust in their partner is necessary for them to relax and be fully sexually responsive. Partners who do not know each other well may have difficulties because there has not been enough time for trust to develop. If either partner fears violence or dishonesty, there is likely to be a lack of trust.

Different needs and styles Differences in sexual needs can also cause problems. In most couples one member wants intercourse more frequently than the other. If one partner needs more time to be satisfied than the other, the length of

Traumatic past experiences with sex can cause difficulties in the present.

Poor communication is an important cause of sexual problems.

time spent on foreplay or intercourse can also be a problem. In addition, there may be differences between partners in their basic approach to sex. For example, one partner may take a very energetic, athletic approach, while the other prefers a slow, relaxed kind of intercourse. Or one partner may like to talk a lot during intercourse, while the other may prefer not to. The partners may also differ as to the amount of romance that is important.

Fortunately, most couples can adapt to these kinds of differences in needs and desires, and compromises can be made. Partners should be willing to try new and unfamiliar sexual activities to please each other, but they should not agree to things that are painful or frightening.

Boredom Most couples who have been together for several years slip into a routine for how often they have intercourse and how they do it. Over time this can become boring, and the partners can lose interest. One or both partners may then have the problem of lack of desire for sex. If this is the case, planning some changes in how often, or where, or how the couple has sex can often renew interest. For example, weekends away from home, special private evenings planned ahead, erotic videotapes or books, and experimenting with new approaches to intercourse may add interest.

Neglect Problems can also develop from neglect of the sexual relationship. Many people assume that a sexual relationship, especially a satisfying one, takes care of itself. In fact, it is more like a garden that needs care and cultivation. It is common for a couple, particularly if they are very busy or tired, to neglect their sexual relationship. Events like the birth of a new baby or changes in working hours may disrupt the household routine

so greatly that time and energy for sexual communication is lost. Once the problem is recognized, it can usually be solved. Some busy couples have to schedule dates or appointments to be alone together and make love.

Stress Stress from other areas of life often affects sexual relationships. If either or both partners are worried about a sick relative or whether there will be enough money to pay the bills, they may not be able to focus on sex and may appear to lose interest. We are all under various kinds of stress all our lives, but at particularly stressful times we may temporarily lose interest in sex. Since stress is always with us, and there is always something to worry about, it is important to learn to manage stresses so that we still have energy for other aspects of our lives, including our sexual relationships.

Lack of privacy Lack of privacy is not as common a problem as it was years ago when families were larger and elderly parents often lived with their grown children. Still, sexual problems can develop for a couple who do not have enough private time together. The biggest loss of privacy for couples today probably comes when children are born. Basically, a couple needs a private bedroom where they can be free from interruptions, or private time when they are alone together in the house. Some feel more comfortable having a lock on the bedroom door so the children can't enter. Some people can't relax if they fear that sounds carry through the walls, or if there is a squeaky bed. The partners should try to create an environment for lovemaking that feels private and relaxing to both.

Other problems in the relationship Sexual problems can be an expression of other problems

Financial worries and other stresses can cause a loss of interest in sex.

in the relationship. For example, anger at the partner over something unrelated to sex, such as a disagreement over money or the disciplining of children, may be expressed in the sexual relationship. This means that sometimes sexual problems are just a symptom of other relationship problems. When the other problems are resolved, the sexual relationship usually will return to normal.

Types of Problems

Lack of Desire or Interest

Lack of desire or interest in sex is a common complaint, and there are a great many reasons that a person may experience it. If an adult has never been interested in sex, there may be some hormonal or other physical problems, or the adult may not have had enough sexual experience to be fully awakened to sexual desire or the pleasures associated with a sexual relationship. More commonly, adults report that they have been interested in sex in the past but have lost the feeling. There are innumerable possible reasons for this, including reasons within the individual (such as illness, exhaustion, worry, the effects of drugs, or the fear of intimacy), reasons in the relationship (such as a lack of trust in or anger at the partner), and reasons in the environment (such as not having access to a comfortable, private place for sexual activity).

The loss of desire or interest in sex is usually temporary, and goes away when the cause is discovered and the problem is solved. In some cases, however, the problem may persist unsolved for

years. In other situations, a woman or man may know the reason (such as a poor relationship with the spouse) but not be willing or able to make the needed changes in the relationship.

Pain and Discomfort

Sexual intercourse does not normally cause pain or discomfort. As with other parts of the body, pain in the sexual organs is usually a sign that something is wrong, and it is important to seek medical care when such a problem develops. Of course, there are times in everyone's life when sexual intercourse can be painful because of infection, injury, or surgery on the reproductive organs. Simple skin irritations, including those caused by very frequent or prolonged intercourse, can also make sex temporarily painful.

Women are more likely than men to have problems of painful intercourse because of differences in their anatomy, because they have more medical problems with the sexual organs, and because of the changes that occur with pregnancy and childbirth. Medical care providers usually recommend that genital intercourse be avoided at times when there is infection or disease, and when the body is healing after childbirth or surgery. Couples who desire sex at these times can substitute oral or manual intercourse.

There are some chronic (long-lasting) medical conditions that can cause pain during sexual activity for years. For example, in men Peyronie's disease (see Chapter 13, "Men's Health Problems") can cause pain when the penis becomes erect or when the vagina is entered, and in women endometriosis (see Chapter 12, "Women's Health Problems") can cause pain when the penis thrusts deep into the pelvis. Pain deep in the pelvis can also be caused by the aftereffects of surgery or severe infection. When long-lasting problems exist, the couple may need to adjust their sexual practices (for example, positions and depth of thrusting) to achieve intercourse without pain.

Pain and discomfort in sexual intercourse can also be caused by ignorance and lack of understanding of sexual response. For example, it can be painful for both men and women if the man tries to force his penis into the woman's vagina when it is not sufficiently lubricated (see pages 45–49 for information about women's sexual response and lubrication). Discomfort can also be caused by positions for intercourse that are awkward or painful for one or both partners. There are differences in the size and length of both penises and vaginas that affect comfort and the types of positions that are most enjoyable.

Pain from these sources is usually easily eliminated as the couple learns about sexual response in general and about each other's bodies in particular. No two bodies are exactly the same, and sexual positions that worked well with one partner may be uncomfortable or painful with another.

Can pain and discomfort in intercourse be psychologically caused? Is it all in your head? Yes, sometimes. A person who has deep fears of sex or of becoming intimate with the partner may unconsciously (without being aware of it) express these feelings by finding sexual contact with the partner painful. It is often difficult to distinguish "real," physically caused pain from psychologically caused pain. The first step is a medical checkup to see if there is a physical cause. If none is found, the second step is for the couple to talk about their relationship and sexual practices. They need to explore whether there is some psychological discomfort that is being expressed as physical pain. Sex therapy (see pages 69–70) may be helpful in such situations.

Women's Problems

Lack of arousal Relatively little is known about problems of lack of arousal in women, for two reasons. First, unlike men, who must have an erection before they can have intercourse, women are able to have intercourse when they are not at all aroused. Second, it is harder to tell when a woman is aroused because most of her sexual organs are internal. The most obvious sign of a woman's sexual arousal is vaginal lubrication, and even this may be absent under certain conditions. Additional signs of arousal in women are swelling of the tissues in the vulva and vagina (see page 49 for details).

Because the signs of arousal are subtle, some women may have difficulty knowing when they are aroused. Learning to identify the body sensations that signal arousal is important. Women who have

difficulty with this may find that practice with masturbation helps them get in touch with their own sensations without the distraction of the partner's responses.

Even though lack of arousal is not obvious and does not prevent intercourse, it is still an important problem for some women. Full enjoyment of sex and the release of orgasm both depend on the woman becoming aroused. If the couple's foreplay does not arouse the woman, she may not begin to become aroused until genital intercourse is underway. In this case, she may not have enough time to be satisfied or to reach orgasm.

Lack of orgasm The lack of orgasm (*orgasm* is defined and described on pages 48–49) is very common in women. Only 60 percent of married women and only 30 percent of unmarried women report that they have orgasms regularly during sexual intercourse. A large proportion of those who do have orgasms during intercourse with a partner require additional stimulation (usually oral intercourse or manual stimulation of the clitoris). Around 15 percent of women report that they never (or almost never) have orgasms under any conditions. A large number of women are orgasmic in masturbation but not with a partner. Some women report that they find sexual intercourse satisfying without orgasms and do not feel the need for them, but many others are frustrated and would prefer to have an orgasm with each act of intercourse. It also appears that some women have difficulty recognizing orgasms and may have them without being aware.

The ability to have and to recognize orgasms seems to be in part a learned behavior. A woman may need time with a new partner for both of them to learn how best to stimulate her. Oral intercourse (where the man uses his lips and tongue to stimulate the clitoris and vagina) and manual stimulation

Lack of sexual satisfaction can cause tension and difficulty for some couples.

(use of the hands and fingers to stimulate the area) are common techniques to help women reach orgasm. In masturbation, women use their fingers or other objects to stimulate the clitoris and vagina. Some also use electric vibrators to help them reach orgasm. These may be either applied directly to the vulva or used to vibrate the fingers, which are placed in the area. Vibrators can be used both during intercourse with a partner and during masturbation.

Since men usually have an orgasm without difficulty with each act of intercourse, it is not surprising that some have trouble understanding women who do not. Some women "fake" orgasms so that their partner will feel good about his sexual ability. Faking orgasms can be harmful to progress toward real orgasms, since the man is getting false messages about what excites the woman.

A male partner may feel that he should be able to bring the woman to orgasm using his penis alone; he may resist the idea of oral or manual stimulation. This attitude is based on an inaccurate understanding of women's sexuality, since only a minority of women can have orgasms by this method. It is also possible for a couple to be unaware of the existence of female orgasm, if the woman has never had one and if the man has never had a sexual partner who was orgasmic.

Very high success rates have been reported by sex therapists who treat women who do not have orgasms. One group treatment program reported that 93 percent of women treated were able to have orgasms consistently (usually through masturbation) after five weeks of treatment. Three months after the training was over, half of these women were able to have orgasms with their partner. Nonorgasmic women may be treated individually, with a partner, or in a group of women with the same problem. Excellent books describing the therapy are also available so that women can help themselves without involving a therapist (see the resource listing at the end of this chapter).

Treatment is based on a behavioral model where the woman can practice and "learn" to have orgasms the way a child practices and learns to ride a bicycle. About an hour of practice a day is usually assigned. Both women who have never had an orgasm and women who are not orgasmic with their partner are usually assigned "homework," which is masturbation, to familiarize themselves with their own sensations and to achieve a first orgasm if they have never had one. Once a woman is orgasmic in masturbation, she masturbates in the presence of her partner so they can share information about what stimulates her and so she can become accustomed to having an orgasm in the partner's presence. The third stage is for the couple to attempt to stimulate the woman to orgasm during intercourse.

Vaginismus Vaginismus is a rare problem in which the muscles surrounding the vagina involuntarily tighten so that, in severe cases, the penis cannot enter and intercourse is impossible. It is most often found among women who have had a very painful or frightening sexual experience in the past (such as rape or molestation as a child), who fear pregnancy, or who have very negative feelings about sex. This fear is expressed through the tensing of involuntary muscles, making intercourse difficult or impossible. When vaginismus prevents intercourse or makes it unpleasant, the couple should not attempt intercourse, but should stop and examine their relationship and their feelings for each other.

If a trusting relationship has been established, both partners desire intercourse, and vaginismus is still a problem, treatment by a sex therapist may be needed. As with treatment for lack of orgasm, the usual treatment for vaginismus is behavioral learning. The woman practices masturbating while inserting small objects (for example, her own fingers) into her vagina until she is comfortable with this. She then proceeds to use larger objects until the size and shape of an erect penis is reached. The partner's fingers can also be used. Other possibilities are special dilators, which can be lent by a sex therapist, or other objects that women sometimes use to masturbate. Once the woman has learned to tolerate other objects in her vagina, in most cases she should be able to begin to have intercourse without discomfort.

Men's Problems

Impotence Impotence is a condition in which a man is not able to get a sufficiently hard erection to allow the penis to penetrate the vagina, making genital intercourse (and starting a pregnancy) impossible. Impotence can be caused by psychological or emotional conditions (including lack of attraction to the partner) or by physical problems. This section of the book talks about impotence that is caused by psychological or emotional factors. Impotence caused by physical problems is discussed on pages 307–309 in Chapter 13, "Men's Health Problems." A simple way to figure out whether impotence is physically or psychologically caused is also described in that section.

Around 50 percent of men report that they have occasional difficulty with getting erections, which is considered normal. Common causes of occasional erectile problems are fatigue (tiredness);

Most impotence in young men has psychological or emotional causes.

stress, anxiety, or worry; the effects of alcohol consumption; and lack of attraction to a particular partner, or boredom.

Psychological and emotional causes are also blamed for half to two-thirds of all chronic or long-term impotence in men. Until about fifteen years ago, almost all long-term impotence in men was thought to be psychologically caused. Recent progress in techniques for diagnosing the problem, however, have meant that physical problems are being identified in more and more cases.

Most men who have never had an erection in their lives, and a high percentage of those who have never been able to complete an act of intercourse, have a physical problem. Men who have been sexually active in the past but have lost the ability are more likely to have psychologically caused problems. Impotence in younger men is more likely to be emotionally caused; in older men the chances of a physical problem or of one caused by medication are greater. In some cases both physical and psychological factors may be at work. For example, a man who is a heavy drinker of alcohol may frequently attempt intercourse when he has been drinking, and may be impotent because of the physical effects of the alcohol. Not understanding the cause, he may assume that something else is wrong, and may become so worried and anxious about the situation that he becomes impotent when he is sober as well.

Treatment for the man who is impotent for psychological reasons can take many forms. Education may be needed to help him become aware of the conditions that make it difficult for him to become aroused (tiredness, drinking, and so on) and to help him develop reasonable expectations for himself. Some men feel that they should be able to have intercourse with any woman at any time, regardless of their feelings toward the woman or the situation. *This attitude may not be realistic* for many men, who require a partner whom they know and care for and an environment that is private and relaxed. When a man learns to be aware of his own needs and limits, he will know which sexual situations are likely to work well for him.

Other kinds of treatment for men with psychologically caused impotence include sex therapy for the man and his partner together, in which they are assigned "homework"—practicing touching and caressing each other but stopping short of intercourse. The idea behind this type of treatment is to reduce the couple's anxiety about whether the man will be able to have an erection by reducing the emphasis on intercourse and orgasm and focusing on the pleasures of touching. Another technique is for the couple to practice repeatedly stimulating the man to erection and then letting the erection subside without intercourse. The idea here is for the couple to learn not to get anxious when the man loses an erection and to realize that an erection can be regained. After practicing for a few weeks, the couple are allowed to begin to have intercourse again. This type of treatment is reported to succeed with around 75 percent of men who have been potent in the past. The success rate is even better (80 percent) for men who are in stable relationships.

Treatment for men who do not have partners may involve self-help and a support group of men who have similar problems. There has also been some experimentation in providing a "sexual surrogate" (a paid, experienced female partner) to work with men in treatment on their "homework." This appears to have been effective in many cases but

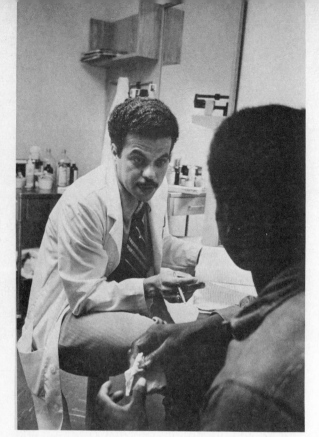

Premature ejaculation is often related to lack of sexual experience.

has been considered controversial. Reputable sex therapists today do not get involved in providing sexual partners for their patients.

Problems with ejaculation   There are several kinds of problems men may have with ejaculation. One, called **premature ejaculation,** is very common. Another, called **retarded ejaculation,** is less frequent. Both these conditions are usually caused by psychological or emotional factors or by a lack of sexual experience. Other problems with ejaculation, such as having no ejaculation at all or ejaculating into the bladder (retrograde ejaculation), are usually caused by physical factors and are discussed in Chapter 13, "Men's Health Problems."

Premature ejaculation   Premature ejaculation means that the man has an orgasm and ejaculates before he is able to have intercourse for long enough to satisfy himself and his partner. The problem is the man's lack of ability to control and delay when he will have an orgasm. This can be frustrating for the man, as it may mean that intercourse ends almost immediately after his penis enters the woman's vagina. It can also be a problem, because it may make bringing the partner to orgasm through intercourse difficult or impossible. Premature ejaculation is more common in younger and less experienced men; it is less frequent among older men.

Treatment is built around exercises to help the man learn to recognize the sensations of impending orgasm and to control his responses in order to delay orgasm. The man can learn to enjoy several peaks during which orgasm is almost inevitable before he allows himself to ejaculate. To avoid ejaculation in the earlier peaks, he stops the stimulation of the penis temporarily until the sensations subside.

Treatment for men with premature ejaculation usually involves "homework" exercises. Success rates as high as 85 to 95 percent have been reported. The "Semans technique" calls for the man's partner to stimulate him manually almost to orgasm, and then to stop the stimulation until the feelings of impending orgasm subside. The partner then resumes stimulating the penis to another peak. This is done three or four times before the man is allowed to ejaculate. The "squeeze technique" operates in the same way, except that, at the peak, the woman gently squeezes the penis between thumb and forefinger, just below the glans, for about 20 seconds. This causes the feeling of impending orgasm to diminish and also causes partial loss of the erection. Practice with either of these techniques allows the man to develop his awareness of the sensations that come just before orgasm and to learn to control whether he has an orgasm at that time. Practicing these techniques does not necessarily require a partner, since it is also possible to do the exercises while masturbating. Most cases of premature ejaculation are cured with patience and practice.

If premature ejaculation develops in a previously satisfactory sexual relationship, it may be a sign of other problems. The couple will need to talk frankly about their relationship and any problems they have. Counseling or psychotherapy may be desirable if the couple are unable to solve the problems on their own.

Retarded ejaculation   Retarded ejaculation is a condition in which a man is able to ejaculate under some conditions, but is not able to or has difficulty ejaculating under other conditions. Retarded ejaculation usually has psychological or emotional causes rather than physical ones.

Around 1 to 2 percent of men complain of difficulty ejaculating during intercourse. Often they have no difficulty reaching orgasm and ejaculating during masturbation or foreplay. During intercourse, however, they are able to maintain an erection for 30 minutes to an hour or more without ejaculating. Intercourse ends when they become tired or lose the erection, as no orgasm or ejaculation takes place.

It is not clear what causes this problem, but men who suffer from retarded ejaculation seem to be more likely than others to have had a strict religious upbringing or to have fear, anxiety, guilt, or negative feelings associated with sexual intercourse. Fear of making the woman pregnant or negative feelings about the partner could also cause the problem. These are similar to the kinds of factors that are often present in women who have difficulty having orgasms. There is little information about what kinds of treatment are successful, since relatively few men have been treated for retarded ejaculation. In the cases reported, around half of the men treated for retarded ejaculation improved. It appears that the same kinds of homework assignments described earlier for various sexual difficulties can be effective. The goals are to reduce anxiety and negative feelings about sex and ejaculation, to learn to ejaculate pleasurably through masturbation or manipulation by the partner, and then to transfer that ability over to intercourse.

Treatment for Sex Problems

What Is Sex Therapy?

Sex therapy is the treatment of problems of sexual functioning. It is similar to psychotherapy (treatment for emotional and mental problems) in that it usually involves talking about the problem during regular visits to a specially trained counselor. Sex therapy may be provided to an individual, to a couple, or through group sessions of people who share the same problem. Sex therapists must have special training for their work, but their original training is likely to be as psychologists, social workers, or physicians, and they may do other kinds of therapy as well. *Reputable sex therapists do not have sex with their clients.*

Modern sex therapy is a recent invention, with most of the new techniques of treatment developed within the last thirty years. Previously, individuals and couples with difficulties in sexual functioning had to try to solve their problems by themselves or turn to a limited supply of marriage manuals and sex books, many of which were inaccurate and of low quality. Psychiatrists, psychologists, and social workers treated people with sexual problems, and family doctors often saw them in their practices. Until recently, however, knowledge of how to treat the problems was very limited.

How Effective Is It?

Sex therapy appears to be very effective with certain kinds of sexual problems that have psychological or emotional causes, and less effective with others. It does not work for sexual problems that have a physical cause; they must be treated medically. It is hard to measure the effectiveness of sex therapy, and there are few follow-up studies of people who have received such treatment. It appears, however, that problems that require information and education, improved communication between partners, and learning through practice have a very high rate of cure (80 to 90 percent) in sex therapy. Treatment of long-standing sexual difficulties that are related to deeper personality or relationship problems is less successful.

When Is Treatment Needed?

People who seek sex therapy usually have difficulties with sexuality that they have not been able to solve for themselves and that are creating serious problems for them or making them unhappy. Some people, however, who feel quite content with their lives and their sexual relationships, seek sex therapy because they want to learn more about their sexuality and to try to make it even better. Problems with sexual functioning are very common, but most people who have them do not receive sex therapy. Seeking treatment for sex problems is a choice that is available today, but not everyone is interested or can afford the cost.

It is sometimes difficult to know whether sex therapy or some other kind of treatment is needed. For example, if a couple, married fifteen years and with a previously good sexual relationship, begin to have problems with sex, are the sexual problems a reflection of other difficulties or pressures in the relationship, or of medical problems, or are they primarily sexual problems? The couple's evaluation of the situation will determine whether they seek help from a doctor, a marital therapist (marriage counselor), a social worker, or a sex therapist.

When there are sexual problems and it is not clear where to turn first, the following self-help steps should be followed:

1. Talk it over with your partner.
2. Give it some time if you think you and your partner can solve it.
3. Talk with a trusted and experienced friend about the problem.
4. Go to the library or bookstore and read up on the problem.

If you think you need professional help, follow these steps:

1. See your health care provider to check on the possibility of a physical or medical problem.

Many good self-help books are available to men and women who want to improve their sexual functioning and relationships.

2. See a psychotherapist or counselor if there are other problems in your life or relationships that could be affecting the sexual relationship.
3. See a sex therapist.

There are many high-quality self-help books available both on solving sexual problems and on improving sexual relationships. Both individuals and couples can often solve problems using these materials. This approach has the advantage of being less expensive and more private than professional help. Some useful books are listed at the end of this chapter.

What Kinds of Treatment Are Available?

Sex therapy is available to individuals, to couples, and as group treatment. Often a male–female team will work as co-therapists so that both a woman's and a man's point of view are represented. Therapists are usually psychologists or social workers, but psychiatrists, other physicians, and other people trained as counselors also practice sex therapy. Sex therapy is usually only part of their practice, so they may have other specialties as well.

Most sex therapy involves the following areas:

Information and education about sexuality
Training in communication skills (for use with partner)
Exercises for reducing anxiety about sexuality
Exercises for learning to be more aware of sensual and sexual sensations
Exercises for practicing sensual and sexual stimulation and orgasm

Sex therapy sessions usually involve talking with the therapist about feelings and experiences. There is no sexual activity during the session and none with the therapist. The exercises to learn more about sexual sensations and to practice stimulation are carried out as "homework," which the client reports on at the next session.

What has just been described is the mainstream of sex therapy. It is a well-known and respected specialty, and clients are often referred for treatment by physicians, ministers, and others. There are also a number of practitioners who call themselves sex therapists who use other techniques, ranging from psychotherapy that looks at all problems in the client's life, not just the sexual area, to hypnosis, biofeedback, and the like. Some people are helped by these other approaches, but the greatest evidence of effectiveness so far has come from mainstream sex therapy.

Sexual surrogates were used in sex therapy during the 1970s to provide a paid, experienced female partner for men in treatment. However, male sexual surrogates were rarely used with women. The use of surrogates was stopped because of a number of problems, and reputable sex therapy today does not get involved in providing sexual partners.

How Do You Choose?

A trusted doctor or minister or psychotherapist is a good source of a referral for sex therapy in your local area. Look for someone who has training in this specialty and who has had experience treating others with similar problems. The only way to know if you will like a particular therapist is to make an appointment to discuss his or her qualifications, experience, and approach to treatment. Since in some parts of the country there are few qualified sex therapists, you may have to travel a distance to find one.

Be sure to explore the cost and expected length of treatment, and whether medical insurance will cover any of it. If the treatment costs more than you can afford, ask about scaled fees or payment over time. If you want to find free or very low-cost treatment, check with universities that offer graduate programs in psychology or social work, and with medical schools. There may be low-cost clinics (where students are trained) or research programs that could meet your needs.

COMMON AND UNCOMMON VARIATIONS IN SEXUAL BEHAVIOR

This section describes a number of variations in sexual behavior, some common and some quite rare. Many of these activities are socially disapproved and/or illegal. Some, however, are commonly practiced, and many people fantasize about these behaviors. We are free to think and fantasize about whatever we please, and we do not have to act on our fantasies (or even tell anyone else about them). But when behaviors are actually carried out, it is important to be aware of the possible consequences.

Several kinds of illegal sexual behavior that are very harmful to their victims—incest, child molestation, rape, and sexual harassment—are covered in detail in Chapter 5, "Sex and the Law."

Nudity

Nudity refers to being unclothed or naked. **Nudists** are people who believe in the healthful effects of living without clothing as much as possible. All societies have rules about proper clothing and about which parts of the body should not be shown in public, but there is tremendous variation from one culture to another. Most communities in the United States have laws requiring that the genitals of adult men and women and the breasts of adult women be covered in public. Unless there is a complaint, however, these laws are often not enforced. Nudity is practiced in many parts of the United States at certain beaches, at health clubs with separate facilities for men and women, and at nudist organizations, without interference from the police.

In general, the practice of nudity within the home or within private organizations is not challenged by the law unless other members of the public complain.

Prostitution

What Is It?

Prostitution refers to the business of selling sex for money. Most prostitutes are women who sell sex to men, but there are also males who also sell sex to other men, male and female child prostitutes, and men who provide sexual services to women for a price. There does not seem to be a demand for female prostitutes to provide sex to female customers. Prostitution exists in most but not all societies in the world, and has been known to exist for thousands of years.

Prostitutes do business in several ways. The best known type of prostitute is the **streetwalker,** who uses the street to seek customers and then has sex with them in a car or nearby hotel. Other prostitutes work in houses of prostitution, or **brothels. Call girls** make appointments by telephone to meet customers, and **B-girls,** or bar girls, meet their clients in bars. Many but not all prostitutes work for a man called a **pimp,** who provides protection and helps to locate customers. The pimp collects a percentage of the woman's earnings, and usually manages several women.

Is It Illegal?

Prostitution is illegal in all of the United States except for parts of Nevada. It exists in almost all

Some people feel comfortable about nudity.

areas, however, and is common in large cities. The laws related to prostitution are different in each state, and there are local differences in how the laws are enforced. In many nations of the world, prostitution is not a criminal offense. In those countries where prostitution is legal, there are public health programs to help to prevent the spread of sexually transmitted diseases by prostitutes and their customers.

Who Becomes a Prostitute?

Most women who become prostitutes do so for economic reasons; they are not kidnapped or otherwise forced into the occupation. There are prostitutes of all racial and religious groups. Some come from poor families and have little education. For these women, prostitution may offer a better living than they could earn in another job. Others discover that prostitution can be an easy way to support themselves with little work while they are young. An additional group of women get into prostitution to support a drug habit or other expenses. Many prostitutes have other jobs as well, and some are in school. Most prostitutes are young women, and they generally quit or retire before reaching their middle years.

It appears that prostitutes are more likely than other women to have experienced incest or molestation (see Chapter 5, "Sex and the Law") as children, and are likely to have begun to have intercourse at an early age. It is not known if these early experiences influenced their decisions to become prostitutes.

Who Uses Prostitutes?

Men of all ages, races, religions, and occupations use prostitutes. There are many reasons for using a prostitute, including:

1. Separation from the usual partner by travel or military service
2. Inability to attract an unpaid sexual partner
3. Desire for special sexual services that other partners might refuse
4. Preference for prostitutes, and lack of interest in developing another kind of sexual relationship

Research done in the late 1940s showed that almost 70 percent of men in the United States had visited a prostitute at least once, and almost 20 percent used one several times a year. It is believed that fewer men use prostitutes today because attitudes toward sex have changed, and sex is more easily available from other women.

Is Prostitution Dangerous?

Prostitution can be dangerous for both the prostitute and the customer, for several reasons. The most important one is the risk of becoming infected with a sexually transmitted disease, including AIDS (see Chapters 14 and 15). The second set of risks is related to the fact that prostitution is illegal and is frequently connected to other illegal activities, such as drug dealing and robbery. The violence and danger of other illegal activities often spill over and affect the prostitute and/or her customer. A third area of risk is related to the sexual services performed. Prostitutes have been kidnapped, seriously injured, and even murdered while helping to fulfill the fantasies of violent and/or sadomasochistic customers.

Pornography and Erotica

Pornography is literature or artwork that depicts sexual activity in a way that is offensive to most people in a community. It includes sexually explicit movies, videotapes, books, comic books, and pictures. Sexually explicit materials that are not offensive to most people are called **erotica**. Erotica is considered to be sexually stimulating material that men and women enjoy reading or viewing for recreation or to enhance their own sexual activities. Sexually explicit art and writings have existed throughout the world since the beginning of history.

The kinds of materials that are considered pornographic vary from one culture to another around the world, and there are different views about what is offensive in different regions of the United States as well. Sexually explicit videotapes showing men and women having sexual intercourse may be viewed as harmless erotica in one community and as offensive and illegal pornography in another. Laws relating to the control of pornography in the United States are left up to local communities in recognition of these differences in attitudes.

An important concern about pornography is whether it is harmful. There are a number of theories about the effects of pornography, including the idea that if pornography is available sex crimes will be reduced because the potential criminal will have an alternative to meet his sexual needs. Another theory is that exposure to pornography may increase sex crime because people will model their behavior after what they've been exposed to. Pornography is also criticized by some for promoting a demeaning view of women as sex objects who exist only for the pleasure of men. The actual effects of pornography on human behavior are not yet known.

There is a great deal of pornographic material available in the United States. Much of it describes sexual activities between consenting men and women, and some of it is geared to a homosexual audience. Unfortunately, there are also materials depicting sex with children and showing sadomasochistic sex including violence, rape, torture, and even murder as part of sexual gratification. Such materials are extremely offensive to most people, and are feared to be linked to real-life violence and victimization.

Sexual Products and Devices

Sexual products and devices are items used to enhance enjoyment of sexuality. Contraceptives to prevent pregnancy are not included in this category; they are described in Chapter 9. There are numerous sexual products for sale, such as:

> See-through and suggestive sleepwear and undergarments
> Perfumed and flavored massage oils and lotions
> Battery powered and electric vibrators
> Reproductions of erect penises (dildoes) made out of plastic or other material

Pornographic movies and books are readily available in most parts of the United States.

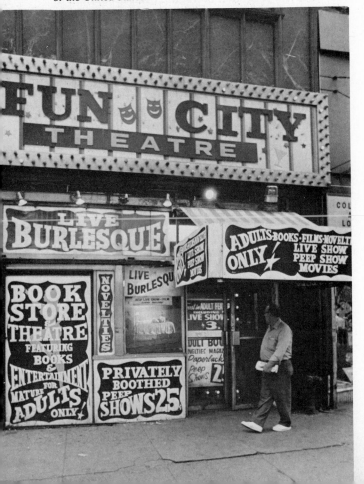

Plastic or inflatable reproductions of the female body, including the vagina
Sex-related toys and jewelry

The demand for these products seems to be growing in the United States in recent years, and the number of companies selling such items is increasing. Sexual aids are available from stores specializing in sex-related products and through mail order companies that advertise in magazines.

Use of Aphrodisiacs

Throughout history, certain foods, substances, and drugs have been regarded as **aphrodisiacs**—as having the effect of increasing desire or ability to function sexually. For example, some cultures regard powdered rhinoceros horn as a cure for impotence, and in our own culture eating oysters is thought by some to increase a man's potency. In most cases the benefits of these substances are psychological rather than physical, and some of the drugs used to enhance potency can actually be toxic or dangerous as well as ineffective. It is often the belief or expectation that a certain drug or food will increase sexual feeling that actually causes the person to feel sexy.

As far as is known, there are no universally effective aphrodisiacs, but very little serious research has been done to document the claims made for various substances. Not much is really known about use of chemicals for this purpose.

Sexual desire and functioning are very complicated matters, involving physical, psychological, emotional, and situational factors. A person who uses a certain drug or food frequently when he or she has sex may, over time, learn to associate the substance with good sex, and come to believe that it makes sex more enjoyable. For someone who believes this, it is true. For example, many people have learned to look forward to drinking alcohol before having sex, yet in reality drinking alcohol has a negative physical effect on sexual functioning. In some people's minds, smoking marijuana is tied to good sexual experience, and yet there is no scientific evidence that the drug enhances sexual experience, and it may even have a negative effect.

Certain drugs used as aphrodisiacs, such as cantharides (Spanish fly) and amyl nitrate, work by causing irritation to the urinary tract and the genital area. They can also cause *priapism* (a painful, long-lasting erection in a man, which is not accompanied by sexual desire). Priapism can cause damage to a man's sexual organs, and anyone who develops it should get medical treatment as quickly as possible (see Chapter 13, page 305).

Group Sex

An unknown number of men and women in the United States, both married and single, are involved in group sex of some kind. This means sexual activity involving more than two people. Married couples who participate in group sex are sometimes called *swingers*. The purpose is usually to obtain greater sexual excitement and variety. Group sex may develop informally, between friends or at a party, or it may be an organized event through a club or organization formed for that purpose. Organizations of people interested in group sex sometimes advertise in magazines. The opportunity to participate in or observe group sex can also be purchased through people who provide prostitutes. Group sex is more likely to be an unusual event, in which people participate rarely, than the main source of sexual activity. Group sex involves a very high risk of exposure to sexually transmitted diseases, including AIDS.

Transvestitism

A **transvestite** is a man who enjoys dressing as a woman. Female transvestites are extremely rare. Transvestites are often confused with homosexuals, some of whom also dress as women. Most male transvestites, however, are heterosexual, are married, and report that they have enjoyed dressing in women's clothing since they were children. The cause of the behavior is not known. Since society does not approve of such behavior, most transves-

A transvestite ballet dancer dresses for a performance.

tites keep it secret and practice it only at home. Often their sex partners are not aware of their interest. Some men become sexually aroused while wearing women's clothes, while others simply enjoy trying to pass as women.

Transvestitism can create marital problems if a man's wife discovers it and does not accept it. Otherwise, if it is kept private, it is not likely to create difficulties. Some men who wish to change their behavior seek psychotherapy or sex therapy, but there is little information as yet concerning what treatments are used or how successful they are.

Transsexualism

Transsexuals are men and women who think of themselves as members of the opposite sex, trapped in the wrong body. It is estimated that around 1 in 35,000 men and 1 in 100,000 women are transsexuals. Transsexuals generally report that they have known since they were small children that they were meant to be members of the other sex. Many have reported extreme unhappiness and frustration with living in the "wrong" body. Some have sought sex-change surgery, which has been available in the United States since the 1960s but is less widely available today. Around 4,000 sex-change operations have been done in the United States to date, mostly to change men to women.

Sex-change surgery for men involves castration and the creation of a vagina from the tissues of the penis and scrotum. It is reported that a usable vagina, capable of intercourse and orgasm, can be created. The man must also take hormones for the rest of his life to develop and maintain a feminine appearance. Other treatment, such as hair removal and surgery on the Adam's apple and the nose, may also be desired to make the man look more like a woman. Sex-change surgery for women involves a double mastectomy, often a hysterectomy, and the creation of a penis and scrotum by plastic surgery. The penis will not be capable of normal sensations or a normal erection, but it can be constructed so that it is capable of an erection sufficient for intercourse. The woman will need to take masculinizing hormones all her life.

In recent years the numbers of requests for sex-change surgery has dropped off and the operation has become less available. It is believed that, as society becomes more accepting of a variety of life-styles, transsexuals may be able to find comfortable ways to live and develop relationships without having to go through the extensive (and expensive) surgery and treatment involved in a sex change.

Jan Morris, a British journalist and author, is a transsexual who was formerly known as James Morris. The photo on the left was taken in 1960; the photo on the right, in 1974.

Fetishism

Fetishism is a condition in which a man experiences intense sexual arousal by looking at or touching an inanimate object. Little is known about fetishism in women. Common items to which fetishists are attracted are women's (or men's) underclothing or shoes, but almost any kind of object could be involved. The man usually masturbates while touching, smelling, or fondling the fetish object. If the object is clothing, the man may wear it while he masturbates. Some men may have intercourse with a woman while using their fetish object, but most masturbate.

The cause of this obsession is not known, but it may be related to early childhood experiences or memories where a certain item or article of clothing becomes associated in the mind with a sexually attractive woman (or man).

Fetishists sometimes get into trouble for stealing the items that attract them from homes, laundries, or stores. They have been known to follow women and to steal items of clothing directly from them, but fetishists are rarely violent or dangerous.

Exhibitionism

Exhibitionism or "flashing," as it is sometimes called, is the exposure of the genitals to strangers in public places for the purpose of sexual gratification. Almost all exhibitionists are male, and they tend to be young men under 30 rather than older men. Some exhibitionists expose themselves to adult women, others to female teenagers or children of either sex. Some have erections and masturbate while exposing themselves, and others masturbate later when they are alone. Exhibitionism is illegal throughout the United States and is the most common sexual offense in terms of the number of arrests. It must be remembered, however, that since it is carried out in public places, exhibitionists are likely to be caught. Apparently, the fear of being caught is part of the thrill for some exhibitionists. Exhibitionism is a minor offense in most states, but in some places exposing oneself to children can carry a long prison sentence.

The causes of exhibitionism are not known, but it seems to be most common among shy, passive, insecure men who do not have satisfactory sexual relations with a partner. Although most exhibitionists are married, their sexual relationships with their wives are usually reported to be infrequent and unsatisfying. Exhibitionists are generally of average or better intelligence, are employed, and are not mentally ill. Various kinds of treatment have been tried with this group; the most successful appear to be behavioral therapies in which the man learns to avoid exhibitionism and to substitute other more appropriate (and legal) sexual behavior.

Exhibitionists almost never expect any direct sexual contact with the women they "flash." They usually remain at a distance from their victims and do not attempt to touch them. For them, the thrill is to see the woman (or child) register shock or fear at the sight of their exposed genitals, although they often also hope for a positive reaction. Exhibitionists are disappointed if they are ignored or if the woman does not react. Exhibitionists are not usually considered dangerous or violent and they are unlikely to attempt to rape or otherwise harm those to whom they expose themselves.

Voyeurism

Voyeurism is the act of observing another person or people for the purpose of sexual gratification. Voyeurs carry to an extreme the normal interest both men and women have in observing and appreciating the bodies of others; they substitute looking for other forms of sexual activity. Little is known about the extent of voyeurism in the private lives of adults. Most of the information about voyeurism available is obtained when people are arrested or get into trouble. Almost all known voyeurs are men. In most cases voyeurs seek opportunities to observe women dressing or undressing, bathing or otherwise nude, or engaged in sexual activities.

"Peepers" or "peeping Toms" are also sometimes young boys who may simply be expressing curiosity. Most men arrested for voyeurism are young, and this is not a behavior that seems to lead to other, more serious sex crimes. Voyeurism may be less of a problem today than it was in the past because of the many socially acceptable opportunities to view unclothed bodies at the beach and through movies (and, in the case of R- or X-rated movies, to see simulated or real sexual intercourse).

Obscene Phone Calls

Obscene phone calls are anonymous phone calls usually made by men to women for the purpose of sexual gratification. Such callers are not uncommon, and most women who live alone have had such calls. The caller may not speak but may be heard breathing heavily into the telephone, or he may talk about sex and use obscene language. Some callers pretend to be carrying out a survey or have some other justification for the call. The caller often knows the woman he calls slightly, but some obscene phone callers look for listings for single women in the telephone book or make random calls.

Obscene phone callers are similar to exhibitionists in that their aim is to shock women and to obtain sexual gratification without direct contact with a woman. Many masturbate while they are on the phone. Those who are identified have similar personality characteristics to exhibitionists. They

are rarely dangerous and do not normally attempt to meet the women they call in person.

Although obscene phone calls are illegal, the callers are hard to catch, and the telephone company is not usually able to help. In general, listening to them or talking with them encourages them. Hanging up the phone as soon as it is clear that the call is obscene, blowing a loud whistle into the phone, and leaving the phone off the hook after repeated calls are three ways to discourage callers.

Frottage

Frottage, or groping, is the practice of secretly touching or rubbing another person (usually a stranger) for the purpose of sexual gratification. Gropers are usually men, and their victims are usually women. Frottage is commonly practiced in crowded buses, trains, or public areas, but it can also be carried out in situations where men normally come into contact with a woman's body. In some cases the crowding may be so great, and the touching may be so subtle, that the woman may not realize she has been groped. Little is known about how common groping is or about the characteristics of men who practice it, but it seems to exist throughout the world in crowded public areas. It is a nuisance that can be very upsetting to women, but it is rarely dangerous or seriously harmful. Some women who ride crowded subways or trains strike back by stepping on toes and using elbows, pins, umbrellas, or other sharp objects to discourage gropers.

Sadomasochism

Sadomasochism refers to sexual practices in which arousal and satisfaction are gained by inflicting pain (verbal or physical) on the partner or by receiving painful treatment from the partner. Sadist is the term used for those who gain pleasure from inflicting pain, and masochist is the term for those who like to experience pain. A couple may enjoy taking turns with the sadistic and masochistic roles.

Around 5 percent of men and women report having received sexual pleasure from inflicting or receiving pain. Fantasy about sadomasochistic sex seems to be quite common, with women more likely to have masochistic fantasies involving being punished or imprisoned, and men more likely to have sadistic fantasies of domination and control. The fact that men and women fantasize about these behaviors does not mean that they would actually enjoy carrying them out in real life. Sadomasochistic sex seems to be somewhat more common between male homosexuals than between male–female couples or two female homosexuals.

Couples who do carry out sadomasochistic sex may plan a "script" about punishment and domination, which they can act out. The dominant or sadistic partner has to be very careful to make sure the masochistic partner is not really injured or made to experience pain beyond what he or she actually wants. Sadomasochistic practices include bondage, which involves tying up the partner, whippings, spanking, verbal abuse, and so on—all with the goal of furthering sexual excitement for the partners. Many kinds of equipment and clothing are sold for sadomasochists, including leather clothing, masks, whips, and handcuffs.

It is not known why some people find that pain or inflicting pain on others increases sexual enjoyment. It appears that mild pain (such as from love bites or scratches) increases the physical arousal level, but "real" pain is a turnoff for most people. Those who link pain with sexual enjoyment may have had early childhood experiences where love or sexual stimulation was linked with pain, or they may feel a great deal of anger, which they express through sadistic sex. Another theory is that some people who feel that sex is dirty or disgusting may only be able to enjoy it if it is accompanied by punishment.

Mild sadomasochistic behavior can be a harmless game played by loving partners. But sadomasochism carried out with strangers or under the influence of drugs or alcohol can get out of control and be a very dangerous, life-threatening practice. Real injury or even death can happen unintentionally during sadomasochistic sex. Some rapists and murderers have sadistic sex fantasies, which they carry out through these crimes.

Bestiality

Sex with animals, called **bestiality**, has been known throughout recorded history. It is illegal, but the laws are rarely enforced since the public is usually unaware of it. Sex with animals cannot produce a pregnancy for the animal or the human. It is more common for men than women to have experienced it, and men raised on farms or in rural areas are most likely to have had this experience. A survey conducted in the 1950s showed that around 8 percent of all men (and 3 percent of women) had had at least one sexual experience with an animal, and 17 percent of men living in rural areas had had such an experience.

It is not known what causes men and women to be interested in having sexual relations with an-imals, but lack of a human sexual partner and the desire to experiment are probably two reasons.

Necrophilia

Sex with dead bodies is called **necrophilia**. It is illegal and is considered something that only a very disturbed person would do. Male necrophilia has been known throughout recorded history, but it is considered very rare and is not accepted by any society.

FOR FURTHER READING

AYRAULT, EVELYN WEST. *Sex, Love, and the Physically Handicapped.* New York: Continuum, 1981.

BARBACH, LONNIE. *For Yourself: The Fulfillment of Female Sexuality.* New York: Doubleday, 1975.

———. *For Each Other: Sharing Sexual Intimacy.* New York: Doubleday, 1982.

Boston Women's Health Collective. *The New Our Bodies, Ourselves: A Book by and for Women.* New York: Simon & Schuster, 1984.

COMFORT, ALEX. *The Joy of Sex: A Gourmet Guide to Lovemaking.* New York: Simon & Schuster, 1972.

GEER, JAMES, JULIA HEIMAN, AND HAROLD LEITENBERG. *Human Sexuality.* Englewood Cliffs, N.J.: Prentice-Hall, 1984.

MASTERS, WILLIAM H., VIRGINIA E. JOHNSON, AND ROBERT C. KOLODNY. *Human Sexuality* (2nd ed.). Boston: Little, Brown, 1985.

STARR, BERNARD D., AND MARCELLA BAKUR WEINER. *The Starr-Weiner Report on Sex and Sexuality in the Mature Years.* New York: Stein and Day, 1981.

RESOURCES

Information and referral services are available in your local community through the United Way Agency, county or state department of social services, and in the telephone book (the Yellow Pages usually have sections listing social services). In addition, the following national resources can be contacted:

American Association of Sex Educators, Counselors and Therapists
11 Dupont Circle, Suite 220
Washington, DC 20036
(202)462-1171

A nonprofit organization that provides information and referral to sex experts in your local area.

The Fund for Human Dignity
The Educational Foundation of the Lesbian and Gay Community
666 Broadway
New York, NY 10012
(800)221-7044
(212) 529-1600

A nonprofit organization that provides a national crisis line for gay and lesbian information and AIDS counseling, and provides referral to services in your local area.

4
Talking to Your Child about Sex

HOW IMPORTANT IS IT?

Education about sex and sexuality is of tremendous importance for children. After all, our sexuality is what makes us women or men, and what defines our sexual and reproductive roles in life. There is no part of human life that is not affected in some way by sexuality, and trying to muddle our way through life without a good understanding of it can cause needless emotional pain as well as social and medical problems.

Teenagers (and adults) who are ignorant about sex have a much higher risk of developing sex-related problems such as unwanted pregnancies and sexually transmitted diseases. The growing epidemic of AIDS (see Chapter 15 for details), which is a fatal sexually transmitted disease, makes it even more important to educate children early about the risks and responsibilities of sexual behavior.

Children must learn about sex in order to grow up and function as adults, and they will learn about it somehow. The only questions are:

> *What will they learn?*
> *How will they learn?*
> *From whom will they learn?*

Parents are by far the most important teachers about sex and sexuality for their children —even if they never say a word on the subject to them. There is simply no getting around it. If you are raising a child, you will be a sexuality educator, and so will the other people who live in your home.

How do parents teach children about sex without talking about it?

1. By the way they show love and caring for their children and for each other
2. By the way they care for their own bodies and the bodies of their children
3. By the examples they set of how to live as a man or a woman
4. By how they treat members of the opposite sex
5. By the sexual topics they discuss openly and the ones that are considered secrets (such as extramarital affairs, unwanted pregnancies, miscarriages)
6. By how they react to their children's sexual questions and behavior (for example, masturbating or "playing doctor")
7. By how they react to the sexual matters in the family and community (for example, marriage, pregnancies, births)
8. By how they react to sexual material on television or in the newspapers (for example, explicit sex on television or rapes reported in the newspapers)

Many parents choose to take an active role in the sex education of their children, in the hope that they can reach their children with accurate and appropriate information early, before their children learn from their peers or from other adults.

WHAT ARE THE GOALS OF SEX EDUCATION?

There are a number of goals that parents may set for their children's sexual education. The goals are likely to be different for children of different ages. Here is a list of some important goals:

1. Understanding one's own body and how it works
2. Understanding one's own sexual feelings and behavior
3. Understanding what it means to be a boy or girl, a man or woman
4. Understanding how life begins and how families are formed
5. Understanding the consequences of various kinds of sexual behavior—for example, how pregnancies are started
6. Understanding the family's values and standards for sexual behavior—for example, values about sexual intercourse before or outside of marriage
7. Understanding community standards for acceptable sexual behavior
8. Understanding the health risks of sexual behavior, such as the risks of sexually transmitted diseases, including AIDS (acquired immune deficiency syndrome)
9. Understanding about sex crimes such as rape or child molestation, and knowing how to protect oneself
10. Understanding the methods of contraception

WHY IS IT SO DIFFICULT TO TALK TO CHILDREN ABOUT SEX?

Most parents do not look forward to their role as sex educators. They find the topic embarrassing and difficult to discuss with children. Many feel they do not have enough knowledge to do the job. Others fear that educating children about sex will make them more likely to experiment with sex at an

Parents are the most important teachers about sex and sexuality.

The goals of teaching about sexuality are different for children at different ages.

earlier age. Some have had the experience of a small child explaining some new piece of information about sex in public or to strangers in an embarrassing way. Many adults were never able to talk with their own parents about sexual matters, so they have no examples to follow.

Most of us have some discomfort to overcome. But once we get started, the experience can be rewarding and even enjoyable, bringing us closer to our children than before, and improving communication with them. In fact, those who put off and avoid discussing sex with their children out of fear of embarrassment are likely to find watching television (with its explicit sexual content) with their teenager even more uncomfortable!

WHEN SHOULD IT BE DONE?

Talking to children about sex does not mean a single lecture or discussion, or even a series, which

It is important for children to feel free to bring up sexual topics and questions with either parent.

should take place when the child is a certain age. The most effective approach is to begin to talk about sexual topics (appropriate to the child's age) as early as possible. What is important is to *communicate the acceptability of bringing up such topics*, so that your child will feel free to ask questions.

Sexual behavior in children begins in infancy (see pages 34–35 in Chapter 3), and sex-related questions begin as soon as a child can talk. Answering those first questions about the sex organs and where babies come from can be the beginning of open communication on the subject.

It is also helpful to encourage small children to notice sex-related events that they can understand—a pregnant friend, a new baby, a nursing mother, a pet that has given birth. This provides an opportunity to teach the child in a natural, easy way.

WHO SHOULD DO IT?

There are no set rules for which parent should talk to children about sex. Ideally, both parents would be comfortable talking with children, and either one could answer questions as they came up. There is no reason to think that mothers are better at this kind of thing than fathers.

Traditionally, the sex education of small children of both sexes has fallen to mothers, because they have been the main caretakers. But when the children are teenagers, some parents change their approach: mothers now talk to daughters and fathers to sons. In fact, it is a good idea for teenagers to hear the point of view of both sexes, if possible, and there is no reason that talks with teenagers must be only by the same-sex parent. In some families only one parent may be interested or feel the topic is important to discuss. And in the many single-parent households, there is only one parent available.

Parents should not depend on sex education in the schools to do the job for them. Many schools do not have sex education at all, and in some it is offered only in high school—too late for many children. In addition, the content of such courses varies from one community to another and is rarely complete. Many sex education classes do not cover subjects like birth control or the details of intercourse. Further, parents cannot depend on their children's friends to educate them, as the information shared by children and teenagers is frequently inaccurate and incomplete.

Neither friends nor classes at school can teach the child the family's values and beliefs about sexuality. Even if the child gets the facts, he or she may remain confused about what they mean, without the added dimension of family values.

SHOULD BOYS AND GIRLS BE TREATED DIFFERENTLY?

The basic needs to learn about sex and sexuality are the same for boys and girls. Obviously, the specifics about their bodies and the changes of puberty are different for boys and girls, but the general

When a pet gives birth, parents have a great opportunity to teach about sex.

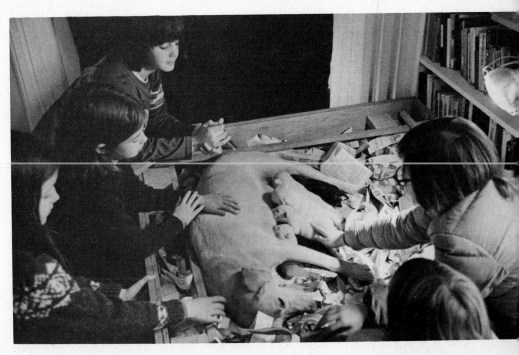

experience of growing up and facing new feelings, sensations, and situations is very similar.

Although parents should view the sexual education of their sons and daughters as equally important, they tend to be more likely to talk with their daughters about sex. This is thought to be because daughters can become pregnant, and because of the double standard (the belief that women should not be sexually experienced, but men should be). Many teenage boys report that neither parent has discussed sex with them, and they have very little information about sexuality.

WILL SEX EDUCATION MAKE CHILDREN MORE CURIOUS AND MORE SEXUALLY ACTIVE?

Some parents fear that information about sexuality presented at home or at school may increase children's interest in and curiosity about sex. They fear that it may lead to early sexual experimentation and intercourse. In fact, it appears that sex education has the opposite effect, partly because it decreases curiosity by bringing information about sex out into the open. Further, frank discussion between parents and children about what is considered appropriate behavior and the meaning and consequences of sexual activity gives children clear guidelines and standards for behavior.

Children who receive accurate and complete answers from parents about sexual matters, and who feel confident that they can take their questions and concerns to their parents, seem to be much less at risk of early and irresponsible sexual activity. Another advantage is that parents who have good communication with their children on the subject of sex are more likely to be told if the child is ever abused or molested.

LEARNING TO TALK ABOUT IT

This section provides some basic pointers for parents who want to be able to talk with their children about sex. Any parent can learn to communicate with children on this subject, but it may be difficult to get started. And the subject usually provides a few embarrassing moments for both parents and children, even under the best of conditions. If you are uncomfortable, it often helps to acknowledge it and then to keep on with the discussion.

Start Early

Talking about sex with children can begin as soon as children are able to talk. Small children give you plenty of opportunities to get started—they ask questions about everything. It is important not to ignore or refuse to answer those early questions. Questions from a 3-year-old girl, such as, "Why is Michael's wee-wee different from mine?" or "Why is that lady's stomach so big?" provide a perfect opportunity to give a simple answer that the child can understand. Here is a possible answer to the first question: "Because he is a little boy and has a penis; you are a little girl and you have a vagina. This means when he grows up he can be a daddy and you can be a mommy." In answer to the second question, you might say: "That lady's stomach is big because a new baby is growing inside her. When a baby is growing inside we say a lady is 'pregnant.' Soon she will have a new baby boy or girl."

Simple answers like these, given casually, will

Talking about sexual matters works best when parents start as early as possible.

make the child feel that sexual matters are a normal part of life, and will allow him or her to feel free to ask more. As the child grows, the questions get more detailed (and potentially more embarrassing to parents), but if a pattern of openness has been established, it should be able to be continued into the teen years.

Teach Correct Terms

Teaching correct terms for body parts as early as possible—such as *penis* and *vulva* or *vagina* instead of "wee-wee"—is also a good idea. It is more accurate and accustoms you and your child to clear communication on the subject. Correct names for body parts are also important in situations where there is concern about whether a small child has been molested. If the child has no names for his or her sexual organs or anus, it is difficult to learn what actually happened.

Listen to Your Child

Many times when your child is thinking about or has questions about sex, he or she may not ask you directly. But you may pick up on the questions from the child's conversation—for example: "When I become a mommy I'm not going to be fat and pregnant like Lisa's mommy. I'm going to buy my baby." The games your child plays or the pictures he or she draws may also give you clues. When this happens, it's a good time to ask the child about his or her ideas, clear up any misunderstandings, and share new information.

Don't Wait for Questions

Some parents of older children would like to talk to them about sex, but the children never ask. In these situations it is a good idea for the parents to try to anticipate possible questions and to bring up the subject themselves. Family events such as engagements, marriages, and divorces provide plenty of opportunity for parents to bring up subjects they feel need discussing. For example, a parent saying, "I wonder if Joe and Lisa will have a baby right away?" about soon-to-be married relatives can kick off a discussion about the basics of birth control and family values about birth control.

At the junior high and high school levels, the experiences of peers or newspaper stories about teens provide plenty of material to start a discussion. If a classmate has become pregnant and left school, a parent might ask, "What do the kids think about what happened to Joanne?" to start a discussion about unplanned pregnancy.

Parents' behavior teaches more about respect and love than any words can.

When You Don't Know, Admit It

One fear many parents have is that they do not know enough about some aspects of sex to discuss them with their children. They are afraid of showing their ignorance. But not having all the information is no reason to avoid discussing sexual matters with your children. In fact, admitting to a teenager that you don't know exactly what *sodomy* is in discussing a newspaper article about a rape, or admitting that you aren't sure exactly what your church's stand on abortion or birth control is, gives you an opportunity to work with your child to find the answers. This sets a good example of family honesty and problem solving for your child.

What You Do Is as Important as What You Say

As we mentioned earlier, your actions and nonverbal behavior speak louder than words to your children. Pay attention to the nonverbal messages your children are getting from you. For example, parents who teach that respect and love are an important part of a sexual relationship, but who constantly argue and treat each other disrespectfully at home, are giving two conflicting messages. Divorced parents who oppose sexual relations for teenagers before marriage but who have their own dates sleep over at their homes have a similar problem. Sometimes these conflicting messages are unavoidable. It is important, however, to acknowledge the conflict to your child. Let him or her know what you believe is right and, to the extent it is possible, why your behavior or the situation they observed is different.

Be Clear about Family Values

Sex education is much more than just facts. The facts don't make much sense outside of a set of values for how people should behave and how they should treat each other. This is where family values come in. Most families have beliefs about whether virginity is important, whether sexual intercourse should be restricted to married couples, whether birth control should be used, whether an abortion or a divorce is acceptable, and so on. These may be ideals (which cannot always be lived up to), or they may be strict rules for behavior. There may be different values for the boys in the family than for the girls.

Because our society is changing all the time, and because many of us were raised in a very different environment from our children, we may find that our older children and teens disagree with family values. They may argue for a different set of standards—one that they feel is more like those of their peers. Parents can strengthen their position by being willing to listen to conflicting views and to discuss differences with their children. They may not convince the child, but their willingness to discuss the matter shows respect for the child and the independent person he or she will soon be. When parents and children disagree about standards, the parents have the right to insist that the children respect their values while living in their home.

Avoid Teaching Shame and Fear about Sex

Our ability to have healthy and positive sexual relationships as adults is strongly affected by our upbringing. The way parents treat sexual matters in the family in general (but especially the way they handle masturbation and toilet training) seems to affect children's later attitudes toward sex. When a child is treated harshly, punished, shamed, frightened, or treated with disgust as part of toilet training, he or she develops negative feelings about the sexual organs and organs of elimination. As the child grows into an adult, these negative feelings often become attached to feelings about sexuality. Adults who view sexuality and the sexual organs with disgust and shame are likely to have difficulty establishing comfortable and rewarding sexual relationships. And these negative feelings, once developed, are not easy to change.

In addition, preschool-age children are not able to understand sexual intercourse. If they accidentally see their parents or others having intercourse, they often conclude that the couple are fighting or hurting each other. Parents should take care that their young children not see them having intercourse. If a child does see intercourse, the parents should explain and make sure the child is not left with lingering fears or misunderstanding about what happened.

Respect Your Child

Sex education is one area of child rearing that is particularly frightening to some parents because it calls attention to the child's future separateness and independence. We raise children with hopes that they will turn out to be people who will share our beliefs and values about what is important. But once they become teenagers and adults, they are quite independent and can choose to be like us or to be different. This is especially true in the area of sexual values and behavior. Parents have very little power to control the sexual behavior of their older children and teenagers directly. They have to depend on the values and good judgment instilled in the child in earlier years.

For this reason, the task of sex education of our children also includes more general kinds of education in preparation for future independence. This section describes three important areas that will affect how your child handles sexual matters as a teenager and an adult: self-esteem, privacy, and decision making.

Self-Esteem

Self-esteem is defined as a positive view of oneself, a respect and liking for oneself. It includes the concept of self-respect. Good self-esteem is a very important part of good mental health, and it seems to be necessary for people to live happy lives. Good self-esteem is created in children from the moment they are born: first by the undemanding love, care, and acceptance they receive when they are helpless babies, and later by the love, accep-

Praise and support for children's efforts builds self-esteem.

tance, and respect they are shown as they begin to learn to do for themselves. Praise and support for children (or people of any age) build self-esteem; undeserved criticism and negative expectations tear it down. Parents seem to know naturally about building self-esteem. You see it in their praise of a baby's first attempts to speak or walk, and in their encouragement of their baby's first attempts to use the toilet. The need to support growing confidence and self-esteem continues throughout childhood and adolescence.

There is strong evidence that teenagers who have good self-esteem, who feel good about themselves, and who feel that they are worthy of respect have far fewer problems related to sexuality than others do. Teens with good self-esteem seem to be more likely to delay beginning sexual activity until they are older, seem to be more likely to use contraception when they do become sexually active, and seem to have less risk of being raped or sexually abused by others. For all these reasons, a focus on building healthy self-esteem in your child is an important part of preparing him or her to be a sexual adult.

Privacy

The concept of privacy is one that goes along with education about sexuality from the earliest years. A toddler gets some of his or her first rejections when he or she is told that certain things are private. The genitals are often called *private parts*, meaning that others do not have the right to see or touch them without our permission. Small children are quickly taught that you do not touch the genitals of others, and that masturbation is something that is done in private. They also learn that their parents want some private time together, and that they are not always welcome to visit their parents in their bedroom.

When teaching small children about adult needs for privacy, it is important to accord them the right to privacy as well. This means respecting their wishes for privacy as much as possible when they are little, and completely when they are older. It means not searching their rooms when they are at school, not reading their diaries or letters, and not spying on them. It also means allowing children the privacy of their own thoughts and experiences.

Except where there is a concern for safety, children should not be pressured to tell more than they want to about their sexual experiences. Particularly with teenagers, parents should not expect to hear the details of sexual activities, and should not share such details of their own lives with their children. Parents who wonder what stage of sexual

It is important to respect a child's wishes for privacy.

exploration their 14-year-old is at will learn more by having a general discussion or by asking about peers than by asking their child directly about his or her experiences. For example, asking "If Sandy and Bob are going steady and he gave her a ring, what does that mean in your school? Can they go out with other people? Does it mean they are having sex?" will usually bring out a lot more information than a direct question to your own child. It also allows your child to voice his or her concerns about sex ("Sandy says she doesn't need birth control because she is too young") without having to give up privacy about his or her own activities.

Many parents find that sharing what things were like when they were teenagers also helps to open up honest discussion. Obviously, in such discussions, parents need to remain calm and not be too judgmental about what they hear. When a teenager says, "I can talk to my Mom or Dad about anything," it is because the parents are willing to listen and not to judge. These parents can still make their own values and standards clear to their children, but they are willing to hear that not everyone has the same views.

Decision Making

The development of children's skill in decision making and confidence in their own judgment is also a very important part of sex education. Most of the decisions our children make about sex (even when they are young) will be made privately, when we are not there to guide them. From the earliest decisions to say yes or no to sex play with another small child, or to report inappropriate touching by an adult, the child is likely to be on his or her own. So besides a pattern of openness and trust in the parents that allows a child to report something bad, the child also needs enough confidence to make a decision when the incident happens. This is part of the focus of the programs that teach small children to report sexual abuse.

As children get older, situations and decisions become more complex, but still parents will not hear directly about many of the decisions their children make. They need to have confidence that their child has been given the information, the values, and the self-confidence to do what is best.

The way to build a child's decision-making skills is to allow him or her some independent decisions from the earliest years and slowly to increase the child's responsibilities as he or she grows. It is important to talk over the decision in advance with the child, discussing the different elements that must be weighed and the possible consequences of various decisions. It is also important to support the child in the decision made and to respect his or her choice.

Through independent decision making the child learns that every decision has consequences, an important concept in dealing with sex. The earliest decisions may be which doll to take on a trip to the supermarket, which sweater to wear, or whether to leave the light on or off at bedtime. But this prepares the child for more important responsibilities later on, including responsibilities for pets, for staying home alone for brief periods, and for scheduling schoolwork.

During the preteen and teenage years most children will be faced with numerous sexual situations about which they will have to make decisions. They will definitely be offered opportunities for sexual exploration by peers, and they may be propositioned by adult strangers as well. They may be offered the chance to sell sex for money, or to trade it for drugs. They will need to know how to judge a safe date or social outing from one that has the potential for rape or abuse. How well they handle these and other decision-making situations will depend in part on the skills and confidence they have developed since early childhood.

LOCATING AND SHARING INFORMATION

Many parents will find that they need more information to support them in talking with their chil-

dren about sex. Unfortunately, there are not many community organizations that provide training for parents or children on this important topic. Nor can parents count on their schools, the health care system, the media, or community agencies to do the job for them. However, there are many resources, starting with this book, that parents can use to teach themselves and their children.

Using This Book

This book is intended as a family reference on sexual and reproductive health. It should provide basic information in answer to most questions. It is written as simply and nontechnically as possible so that all members of the family, including older children and teenagers, can read it for themselves. Suggestions for further reading are offered at the end of each chapter.

Other Books and Pamphlets

There are good books on this subject at the local library, and most family planning clinics such as Planned Parenthood have books and pamphlets on sexual health matters for sale. If you are looking for in-depth reading on a specific issue, try a local college library. (There is usually no problem in using a college library for reading even if you are not a student, but if you want to take a book home, you may have to pay for a special membership.) If you want information about a medical problem, try a library on a campus that has a medical or nursing school. For information on specific problems, such as AIDS or birth defects, contact a social service agency that deals with the problem; they usually have materials to give away or to sell. Your local bookstore also is likely to have good materials, but check the book carefully before buying it to make sure it answers your questions.

There are also books about sexuality written especially for children, which you may find at the library or bookstore. They range from very simple picture books for young children showing how a baby develops inside its mother to sophisticated discussions on the choices that face teenagers.

TV and Movies

There is not yet much sex education on educational TV channels or in the videotape rental business. Occasionally television offers responsible coverage on specific sex-related problems such as teenage pregnancy or AIDS, which parents may want to watch with their children. Commercial TV programs such as soap operas, situation comedies, and movies present a lot of material about sex and

A new baby in the family of a friend or relative provides a good chance for children to learn more about sex.

sexual problems that can lead to family discussions. Unfortunately, much of this material is not realistic or accurate, and parents need to point out where this is the case.

Other People

People other than parents may be able to help with sex education. Local experts such as a family doctor or school hygiene teacher may be able to talk with children. Friends or relatives may be especially knowledgeable (a relative who is an obstetrical nurse, for example) or may have special expertise because of their own experiences. For example, children may be able to talk with relatives who have recently been pregnant and given birth, who have adopted a child because of infertility, or who have given a child up for adoption.

Classes and Organizations

Parents may find a variety of supports for child rearing in the local community, including parenting classes offered by hospitals, schools, social service agencies, and community colleges. But these classes do not usually spend much time on talking with children about sex.

Family planning clinics such as Planned Parenthood are dependable places to make an appointment for a teenager if parents want to make sure that all the facts and choices about birth con-

trol are presented. Teenagers can be seen with or without a parent. A child does not have to be sexually active to be seen and given information. Such clinics may also have an education and/or counseling department that specializes in counseling and educating teenagers (and their families) for responsible sexuality. It may present programs in the community as well as services to individuals.

Parents who want the specifics of natural family planning (fertility awareness) explained to their teenager can locate such training through a local Roman Catholic parish or Catholic hospital. It is not necessary to be Catholic to obtain this information; non-Catholics are welcomed.

WHAT CAN YOU EXPECT?

How Children's Ability to Understand Grows

The kinds of questions a child will have about sex depend on his or her age, and the kinds of answers the child can understand will be different at different ages as well. A child's capacity to think and to understand increases as the child grows. There are often noticeable changes in a child's behavior when a new level of mental ability develops. For example, very young babies do not enjoy the game of peek-a-boo (in which a toy or an adult's face is repeatedly hidden and then displayed), because they do not yet have the capacity to understand that an object that is out of sight still exists. When a baby's mental development has progressed enough so that he or she is beginning to understand this idea, the game of peek-a-boo becomes fascinating.

Similarly, small babies do not have an awareness of whether they are male or female. This comes later, when they are toddlers and begin to notice that not all children and adults are the same. At this point they begin to identify with their own sex. Only the simplest answers to questions about the sexual organs and about where babies come from can be understood at this age. Answers that are too complicated for the child to understand will go over his or her head or be misunderstood. For example, when a 2-year-old boy wants to know why he has a penis and his sister doesn't, he is not asking for (and cannot understand) a lecture on male and female sexuality and how human beings have intercourse. He will lose interest fast if parents attempt such a lecture. What he is interested in finding out is that there are two kinds of children, little girls and little boys, and that they will grow up to be women and men, like Mommy and Daddy.

Understanding the stages of children's mental development will help parents to keep their discussions about sex at a level that their child can un-

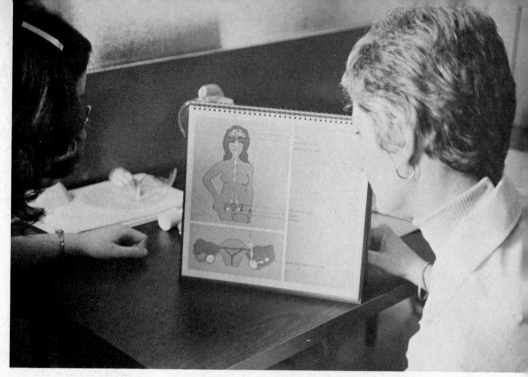

Parents may wish to supplement their teenager's sex education with a special class or counseling session with an expert.

derstand. It is often helpful to ask the child to explain his or her understanding about a specific issue before launching into an answer. As the child gets older, his or her ability to understand (and to ask questions about) the same set of facts, for example how a pregnancy is started, becomes more complex.

Concerns of Different Ages

Ages 0–2

In the first months of life, a new baby learns about love and caring, and about trust and security, from the way the parents care for him or her. Awareness of sensual pleasures also begins and can be seen especially in the way most babies love to be cuddled, stroked, and kissed. These early experiences provide a base for attitudes toward sensual experiences later in life. When the baby is a few months old and begins to explore his or her own body, he or she often is especially fascinated by fingers and toes. The baby also discovers the sex organs and learns that touching them feels good. After that, the baby may reach for the sex organs whenever diapers are changed.

At around 2 years of age most babies are ready for toilet training (although some, usually girls, may be ready earlier). Toilet training focuses attention on the organs of elimination and on the sex organs, and at this point the child becomes much more aware of them. Questions about why some children have penises and some don't, and about why adults' organs look different from children's, are likely to come up at this time, especially if the child

has the chance to see others in the bathroom. This awareness of physical differences is the beginning of the child's development of sexual identity as a male or female. These questions signify curiosity, not about sexual behavior or how babies are made, but rather about why our bodies are the way they are—what makes us girls or boys. More questions

Toilet training is a child's first major challenge in life, and it is important to instill a sense of success and pride in the accomplishment.

may follow about which hairstyles, clothing, and activities are for boys and which are for girls.

The way the child's toilet training is carried out may affect his or her future feelings about sexuality, so it is important to be careful not to communicate shame, disgust, and anger, even when the inevitable mistakes are made. The emphasis should be on the good qualities of the child's body, how well it works for him or her, and how well the child is learning to control himself or herself. Praise should be given for successful attempts to control urination or bowel movements, and mistakes should be handled with understanding. Parents who are not sure how to go about toilet training a child can find very helpful information in the many how-to books on parenting and the care of infants and young children. Such books are available at the local library or from bookstores.

Toilet training is a child's first major challenge in life, and it is important to instill a general feeling of success and pride in the accomplishment. Toilet training involves a complex set of skills that the child must learn to master, and it sets the tone for how the parents and the child will work together on skills in the future. For some children toilet training comes easily, for others not. Boys often have a more difficult time learning the self-control needed than girls.

Ages 3–5

From age 3 to 5 children work hard on developing their sexual identities as boys or girls. They imitate the same-sex parent and want to include all that they know about sex roles in their play. "You be the Mommy and I'll be the Daddy" is frequently heard in play. When the parent, wondering if this game is going to involve sexual exploration, looks over, usually the Mommy and Daddy roles involve who goes to work, who shops, who cooks, who drives the car, and so on. On the other hand, curiosity about one's own body and the bodies of others continues, and games such as "playing doctor," which allow children to examine each other's bodies, are common.

This is the age at which little girls hope to grow up and marry their fathers, and little boys hope to marry Mom. This is a sign of the extent to which they identify with and are imitating their same-sex parent. It is also the first experience with romantic longing and other feelings similar to adult feelings of love.

At this age correct terms (*penis, vagina,* etc.) for the body parts can be taught. The parents' basic standards for nudity and privacy can be learned at this time, and the child can be taught that his or

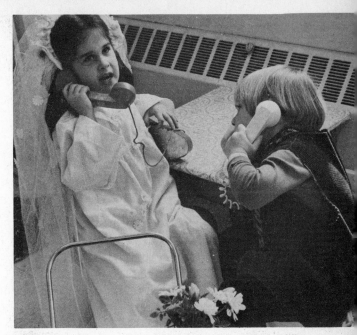

Between the ages of 3 and 5, children imitate their parent of the same sex.

her sexual organs are private and are not to be touched by others. The concepts of "good touch" and "bad touch" can be taught to help children learn to identify and reject situations where they may be molested (see Chapter 5 for details on preventing child molestation).

At around age 5 children are also able to understand a simple explanation of where babies come from. The fact that babies grow in a special place inside the mother and come out of a special opening can usually be understood with no problem. The father's role in starting the pregnancy may still seem vague to children at this age, even after it is explained.

Ages 6–9

During this period children become much more intellectually developed and, for the first time, are able to grasp all the basic facts about intercourse, conception, pregnancy, and the birth process. They may also be curious about such things as how inheritance works, how twins come about, birth defects, and so on. At this age children still do not understand the emotional and erotic feelings that are part of sexuality. They may understand sexual intercourse and conception very well, but may assume that their parents have only had intercourse once or twice, for the purpose of producing children.

In addition, children at this age continue to develop their conception of what it means to be a girl or a boy, and to develop a more complex sense of sex roles outside the family. Children this age continue to identify with their same-sex parent and tend to socialize mainly with peers of the same sex.

As the influence of school friends and other peers becomes stronger, children begin to hear conflicting stories about sex and reproduction, which may cause them to have questions. They may also try out sexual slang and swear words at home that they hear at school. Talking about what these words really mean and when they should or should not be used can open doors for parents to discuss sex with their children and get a sense of their child's level of understanding.

Children this age have more freedom and independence, and training to recognize and avoid potential child molesters should be reinforced. Although children cannot understand all the motivations and feelings that are involved with these crimes, they can become very competent at protecting themselves. This kind of training should be presented as a way of making the child more powerful, more independent, and more capable than he or she already is. It should not be presented in such a way that the child learns to see himself or herself as a likely victim in a dangerous world, or learns to view all adult strangers as dangerous. Basic information about AIDS and how it is spread should be shared at this time (see Chapter 15 for details about AIDS).

Questions about puberty may come up at this age. If not, it is a good idea for parents to start discussions on this subject. The changes of puberty may start as early as age 9 for some children. And it is much easier to talk about these changes before they actually occur. Furthermore, children can be frightened of sudden changes, such as the begin-

As children become more independent, they need training to recognize and avoid potential dangers.

ning of menstruation or the first nocturnal emission, if they do not know what is happening to their bodies.

Ages 9–12

During the years from 9 to 12 many children will start to go through the changes of puberty. Parents should have talked about these changes with their children before they happen. Both boys and girls need detailed information on menstruation, nocturnal emissions, fertility, and the possibility of pregnancy. Parents will probably want to have reading material available to supplement discussions and to help answer questions. This book is one good source that can be read by both parents and children, and there are many other materials available in local libraries and book stores. The basic facts about birth control, sexually transmitted diseases (including AIDS), and sexual exploitation should be shared with children at this age. It should be pointed out to the child that others will soon begin to respond to him or her not as a child but as a "teenager" and as a potential sex partner (regardless of how the child sees himself or herself).

There is a great deal of variation in the level of maturity of children in this age group. Parents need to listen to each child in order to understand how he or she sees sexuality at this point.

Some children will be beginning to have "boyfriends" and "girlfriends" and to go to parties with their peers of both sexes. Children in this age group do not have the maturity to handle unsupervised parties and dates. The social life of preteenagers should be well supervised, and parents should know where their children are and with whom. Parents can be helpful to their children by providing enough structure to make sure they are protected from unwanted sexual pressure and possible exploitation.

At this age children are beginning to understand the social and emotional meaning and the consequences of sexual relationships. They may know teenagers who are already sexually active. At the same time, children aged 9 to 12 have not yet started to reject family values (as many will when they are teenagers). Therefore, this is a good time to talk about family values and standards and to listen to the way the child sees the world and relationships at this point.

Teenagers

Teenagers are usually more difficult for parents to talk to than younger children. They are often in the process of challenging family values and focusing on the standards of their peers. If a

Teenagers are usually more interested in the opinions and beliefs of their peers than those of their parents.

pattern of openness has not been established in earlier years, it is likely to be quite difficult for parents to start talking with their children about sex at this point.

The teenage years, however, are the time when children will actually experience the continued changes of puberty, and will begin to develop adult social and sexual relationships. As those of us who are older can remember, the teenage years can be very difficult, even under the best of conditions. The changes in body size and shape, the emotional ups and downs, and the rapid shifts in social roles and expectations can be very confusing and upsetting. Some teenagers seem to sail gracefully through these years without noticeable difficulties. But we can be sure that all teenagers have many questions and concerns about their changing lives and bodies, whether or not they talk to their parents about them.

Sex educators find that there are several topics that always head the list of subjects that teenage boys and girls want to discuss. They are:

Menstruation
Wet dreams
Masturbation
Intercourse and pregnancy
Birth control
Sexually transmitted diseases
Homosexuality

Parents should try to make sure that each of these topics comes up for discussion with their teenagers at some point. Detailed information about these subjects is contained in other chapters of this book; both parents and teens may want to read the appropriate sections for themselves, and then talk.

In many cases, parents may feel confident that their children know all the important facts about sex by the time they reach the teenage years. But the same topics may need to be discussed again and again, as the teenager's experience broadens and he or she begins to put some of this knowledge into practice. Sex education can be compared to driver education. Knowledge and training about how a car operates and how to control it that is obtained in a classroom or by reading or observing others cannot prepare a person for the actual experience of driving. In the same way, reading or talking about sexual arousal, necking, and petting

Teenagers may need help with specific sexual problems, such as menstrual pain or the need for birth control.

does not prepare a person for the emotional and erotic power of the experience.

Parents also need to be prepared for the fact that their teenagers may need help with specific problems related to sexuality. There may be menstrual pain or other difficulties with the reproductive system. A teenager may want help in obtaining birth control, or may request advice for a friend who is at risk of pregnancy. If the parents are seen as easier to talk to than some others, their teenager's friends may also ask for advice. Teens may want to share their experiences with relationships and sexuality, and to ask questions.

Parents who are open to discussing these topics, who make time to talk with teenagers, and who show respect for their views, are the ones who are most likely to be approached for discussions about sexuality. *Being willing to talk and really listening to your teenager is more important than having all the answers.* Parents need not fear that expressing their own values will drive teenagers away, as long as the teenager's views are also respected and taken seriously.

FOR FURTHER READING

CALDERONE, MARY S., AND ERIC W. JOHNSON. *The Family Book about Sexuality.* New York: Harper and Row, 1981.

JOHNSON, ERIC W. *Love and Sex in Plain Language* (4th rev. ed.). New York: Harper and Row, 1985.

Planned Parenthood Federation of America (Faye Wattleton with Elisabeth Kieffer). *How to Talk with Your Child about Sexuality.* New York: Doubleday, 1986.

POMEROY, WARDELL B. *Boys and Sex.* New York: Delacorte Press, 1968.

RESOURCES

Information and referral services are always available in your local community through the United Way Agency, county or state department of social services, the local public library, and the school district. In addition, the following national resources can be contacted:

American Association of Sex Educators, Counselors and Therapists
11 Dupont Circle, Suite 220
Washington, D.C. 20036
(202) 462-1171

A nonprofit organization that provides information and referral to sex experts in your local area.

Sex Information and Education Council of the United States
32 Washington Place
New York, N.Y. 10003
(212) 673-3850

A nonprofit information and education clearinghouse on all aspects of sexuality.

5

Sex and the Law

LAWS REGULATING SEXUAL BEHAVIOR

There are many laws concerning sexual behavior in the United States. They reflect our society's views about what is acceptable and unacceptable sexual behavior. As society has changed over time, some of these laws have become outdated and are rarely enforced (but they still are in effect and *can* be enforced until they are officially revoked). Laws regarding sexual behavior can be found at the federal, state, and local (county, city, township, village) levels. Most are state or local statutes.

This chapter has two purposes: to give basic information about some of the most common kinds of laws regulating sexual activity, and to give detailed information about four serious sex crimes: incest, child molestation, rape, and sexual harassment. Some other sex crimes that are victimless or are considered less serious are described in Chapter 3.

Sex with Children

It is illegal in all states for adults to involve children in sexual intercourse and other kinds of sexual activity, although the exact laws vary from one state to another. Sexual acts between children may also be considered criminal. In most cases it does not matter whether the child participated in the sexual acts willingly, because children are considered too young to give their consent for sexual activity. The age at which a young person is considered an adult in matters of sex is called the **age of consent**. It varies between states and is often different for boys and girls. For girls, the age of consent is 18 in many states. It is important to be aware that the legal age of consent is not the same as the legal age for driving a car or buying alcoholic beverages. There are also legal minimum ages for marriage, both with and without the parents' permission, which also may be different for girls and boys.

The following paragraph defines the most important types of sexual offenses against children, using the best known names for them. The laws of different states may use different names for these crimes, but every state has laws that forbid these behaviors.

Sexual relations (not necessarily intercourse) between a child and a member of the family are called **incest**. Incest is considered a serious crime if an adult is involved, but is viewed more leniently if the sexual relationship is between two children of nearly the same age. Sexual contact with a child by a person outside the immediate family is called **child molestation**. Sexual intercourse with a girl under the age of consent is **statutory rape** if the man is not married to her, even if she wants sexual relations. The use of children for other sexual purposes, such as child pornography or child prostitution, is also illegal.

The intent of these laws is to protect children from sexual exploitation and harmful experiences. Although these crimes are surprisingly common (for example, it is estimated that between 9 and 28 percent of American women have had an incestuous experience during childhood), most cases of incest, child molestation, and statutory rape are never reported to the police. When they are reported, there is a great variation from one locality to the next in how they are handled. Reporting of suspected incest and child molestation cases has increased a great deal in recent years because of new laws requiring teachers, doctors, social workers, and others to report all suspected child abuse. Statutory rape laws are rarely enforced today in cases involving teenagers who agree to have sexual relations, but if the sex takes place against the girl's (or boy's) will, forcible rape laws (to be discussed) are enforced.

Sex between Adults

There are thousands of different state and local laws in the United States regulating sexual activity between adults, but most are rarely enforced. **Rape**, which is forced sexual intercourse with another person, is illegal everywhere and is considered a serious crime, but the laws are different in different states. All states have laws restricting **prostitution**, which is the selling of sexual intercourse or other sexual acts by women or men. The laws in each state are different, some focusing on the prostitute and some on the customer. **Homosexual intercourse** is illegal in many areas, but the laws are not usually enforced. Most states and localities also have laws against specific sexual activities, such as:

Fornication: Sexual intercourse between an adult man and woman who are not married to each other
Adultery: Sexual intercourse by a married person with someone to whom he or she is not married
Sodomy: Anal intercourse
Oral copulation: Oral intercourse
Bestiality: Sexual intercourse with an animal

More details about these behaviors were given in Chapter 3. Laws against these activities are rarely enforced unless another crime, such as rape, has also taken place. The authorities in many localities believe that when these sexual acts take place between consenting adults, enforcing the law serves no useful purpose. Some states and localities have revoked these laws on the basis that they are out of date and not enforceable.

When all the laws against fornication, oral sex, adultery, prostitution, and homosexuality are considered, most Americans are guilty of one or more sex crimes! However, very few are ever prosecuted.

Marriage and Divorce

Laws related to marriage and divorce are primarily passed by the states. The states have different requirements concerning the minimum age for marriage, the waiting time after applying for a marriage license, the cost of the license, the need for blood tests, and so on. **Bigamy**, which is marriage to two people at one time, is illegal in all states. If a man or woman marries a second time without getting a divorce from the first spouse, the second marriage is not legal. Some states have laws regarding **common law marriage**, in which a man and a woman who have lived together for a certain number of years are legally considered to be married.

The divorce (and annulment) laws of each state are very different and complex. There are differences in the allowable grounds for divorce, the procedure for filing for and obtaining divorce, the waiting time, and the laws on property division, alimony, child support, and the custody of children. The differences between states are so great that people sometimes move from one state to another seeking more favorable divorce laws.

SERIOUS SEX CRIMES

The next pages describe four serious sexual offenses affecting children and adults, and what can be done to prevent or avoid them. But before reading about them, if there is a chance that you have been a victim of a sex crime in the past, please read the next section.

If You Have Been a Victim

As you will see from reading this section, the crimes of incest, child molestation, rape, and sexual harassment are surprisingly common. This means that many readers of this book may have been victims of one or more of these experiences at some time. In one way it is a comfort to know that you are not alone, and that many others have had similar experiences. But at the same time, reading about these situations can bring back unpleasant feelings and memories. In addition, because people have the ability to "forget" very unpleasant or upsetting things that have happened to them (especially things that happened during childhood), a few readers of this chapter may suddenly "remember" an experience that they did not know they had had. This can be very upsetting and can cause a person to look at family, childhood, or relationships in a whole new light.

If you have been a victim of one of crimes described here, please keep the following in mind:

1. It is quite possible and normal that reading about these experiences will bring back upsetting feelings and thoughts (but this does not happen to everyone).
2. You are not alone; many others have shared similar experiences.
3. If you do feel upset, talking with someone about your feelings will usually help you feel better. This is especially true if you have never talked to anyone about the experience before.

Reading about rape, incest, and molestation can bring back unpleasant feelings and memories to those who have been victims.

4. There are many choices if you want to talk to someone:
    Trusted friends or family members
    Self-help groups of people who have shared the same experience
    Counselors who specialize in working with victims of these experiences
5. Self-help groups and counselors in your community can be located through community social service agencies that work with the victims of these crimes. You do not have to report the crime to the police in order to get help, and it does not matter if the incident happened a long time ago.

Incest

What is it? Incest is sexual activity between people who are related to each other in a way that would prohibit marriage—for example, brothers and sisters, fathers and daughters, or mothers and sons. Sexual relations with grandparents, cousins, stepparents, and other close relatives is usually also considered to be incestuous. *Incest is illegal everywhere in the United States and is considered to be morally very wrong.* The term *incest* refers to any sexual activity, such as touching or fondling the genitals; it does not necessarily mean sexual intercourse.

Incest has been known throughout recorded history, and appears to exist in all societies, although it is unacceptable everywhere. The focus of this section is on incest involving children, although incest may also occur between adults who are closely related.

How common is it? It is difficult to know how common incest is because most cases are never reported. Surveys of American men and women have produced estimates of 9 to 28 percent of women reporting some kind of incestuous experience in childhood, and 14 to 23 percent of men. Most of these experiences were with brothers, sisters, or cousins. Father–daughter incest is the kind that is most commonly reported to authorities; reports of mother–son incest are much less common, and father–son and mother–daughter incest reports are very rare. Reported incest cases may not reflect the true picture, however, since father–daughter incest may be viewed as more serious and therefore reported more often. In the past, early sexual experiences for boys have not been viewed as harmful, and it is possible that boys' experiences with incest may be far more common than is realized, but not as likely to be reported.

How serious is it? Incest is considered a serious crime because of the severe and long-lasting psychological and emotional damage it causes the victim. Although physical injury is less common, there can also be damage to the reproductive system or anus, especially when very young children are involved. Some children are infected with sexually transmitted diseases, and girls past puberty may become pregnant as a result of incest. In fact, a pregnancy or a sexually transmitted disease is sometimes the crisis that causes incest to be discovered. In spite of this, authorities such as the police and medical doctors have been reluctant to believe reports of incest until recent years.

Information about the effects of incest on victims is not as complete as it should be. It does appear, however, that incest causes severe and long-lasting psychological and emotional damage, particularly in cases involving parents and children. Studies of adult women who were victims of incest as children indicate that incestuous relationships often cause severe problems. These women report difficulties in trusting others, in self-esteem, and in forming adult sexual relationships. The effects of incest are also seen in teenage runaways and prostitutes, many of whom left home because of sexual abuse.

Incest affects the whole family, not just the people directly involved. The attempts to hide the incest create an atmosphere of secrecy, lies, and fear. The sexual abuse of a child may continue for years, and in some cases several members of the family may be involved. When incest is discovered, it usually creates a very serious crisis for the family, but at least it provides the opportunity for the family members to get help and make changes that create a healthier environment in which the children can grow up.

When parents or grandparents are involved in incest, they usually obtain the child's cooperation by using the child's desire to please, but they may use bribery or threats of punishment if necessary. Most incest is kept secret from the other family members and from people outside the family. In the case of father–daughter incest, both the father and the daughter usually make great efforts to hide the incest from the mother. Daughters report remaining silent for several reasons: threats by the father to harm the daughter or another family member, fear of not being believed by the mother or by authorities, and fear of destroying the family. Father–daughter relationships often continue for years, ending only when the girl leaves home, resists the father, or reports the relationship to her mother or to someone outside the family.

Any child who has been the victim of incest should receive counseling in order to understand what has happened and to resolve the feelings about the experience. Counseling for the child as soon as possible after the incest is discovered may help to reduce the chances of long-term problems. Among other things, children need to know they are not to blame for the incest, and that the adult involved is a sick person who did something that is not right.

Both parents are also likely to need help to resolve their guilt and feelings about the incest, to understand the home conditions under which incest developed, and to learn how to prevent sexual abuse of their children in the future.

Many adults involved in incest as children have never told anyone about it, but others have found that talking about the problem with family and friends has helped them to resolve their anger and hurt. Talking with a trained counselor is another way to resolve feelings, and there are counselors who specialize in working with victims of sexual abuse. In addition, in many cities there are self-help groups for adults who were victims of incest as children. In these groups both women and men have a chance to talk with others who have shared a similar experience and can understand their feelings.

Who is at risk of incest? Incest is a problem that exists at all levels of society. Families of all races, religions, and economic levels are affected. Incest affects families that are otherwise considered normal and successful. The most commonly reported incest, which is between fathers and daughters, is most likely to begin after the daughter begins to go through the changes of puberty.

Incest is more likely to develop in some homes than in others. The following is a list of some of the characteristics that are often found in reported incestuous families (primarily father–daughter incest):

1. Father views family members as his "property," to use as he wishes.
2. Alcoholism or other drug abuse is present, particularly in the father.
3. A stepfather is present (it is estimated to be five to six times more likely for a stepfather to develop an incestuous relationship with a daughter than for a biological father).
4. There is a poor marital and sexual relationship between the parents.
5. The mother is absent or ill, and/or the daughter is taking on the mother's role.
6. There is a poor relationship between mother and daughter.
7. One or both parents were deserted or abandoned by their own parents.
8. One or both parents have unresolved psychological or emotional problems.

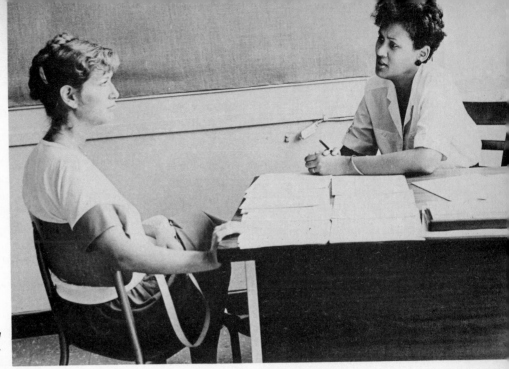

When incest is reported, a social worker usually investigates and interviews all family members.

Contrary to popular belief, however, incestuous parents are not usually mentally ill or retarded. *Incestuous fathers are usually "normal" men who hold jobs and are devoted to their families.* When confronted about the incest, they tend to deny that it happened or to blame the child or others. They are different from child molesters, because molesters are sexually attracted to children. Most incestuous fathers are primarily attracted to adult women, and are most likely to begin an incestuous relationship with a daughter after she reaches puberty.

Some fathers may feel sexually attracted to their daughters as they grow to adulthood, but most would not become involved in incest under any circumstances. There have been cases in which the father has claimed that the daughter is responsible for seducing him into a sexual relationship. Blaming the daughter is not valid, however, since the father is the adult and the daughter is the child. It is his responsibility not to exploit a child to meet his own sexual needs. It is also the responsibility of both parents to see that their own and the children's habits regarding nudity, dress, and behavior do not provide unwanted sexual stimulation.

What happens when incest is reported? When incest is reported to police or a child welfare agency, it is usually handled by the child protective services, which also investigate other forms of child abuse. Incest is considered a form of sexual abuse, and doctors, nurses, teachers, social workers, and others who work with children are required by law to report suspected cases to the local child protection agency or child abuse hotline. A social worker investigates the situation and interviews the child,

parents, brothers and sisters, and others. Medical examinations are required, and in some cases psychological evaluation as well. In many cases the child is separated from the incestuous adult. To accomplish this, the adult may be arrested or ordered by the court to move out of the home. The child (and the brothers and sisters) may be temporarily removed to foster care if it is felt they are at risk of further incest or other abuse.

Once the investigation is completed, the child protection authorities work with the family to make a plan that ensures that the child is protected from future incest. Counseling for the child and the parents is usually recommended, and may be required. If it is believed that the child will be safe, the whole family may be reunited, but many couples separate and divorce.

Little is known as yet about treatment of the incestuous parent, and it is not clear how likely such parents are to repeat the offense with the same child or with another.

How can incest be prevented? There are many things parents can do to reduce the chances of incest occurring in the family. Some of them are the same as the precautions that help to prevent child molestation. For example, it is important to teach children that:

1. No one has a right to touch their private parts.
2. They should tell parents or teachers if someone touches their private parts or does something that makes them uncomfortable.
3. They should trust their inner feelings if they sense that "something is not right" about the way an adult acts toward them.
4. It is all right for children to say no to adults and to

refuse to cooperate if they are told to do something they don't think is right.

Since incest occurs within the home, there are other ways parents can work to prevent incest as well:

1. Discuss how to protect the children and what risks could occur.
2. Share opinions and any past experiences with incest and child molestation with each other.
3. Share the information if there are any relatives who have ever been involved in incest or child molestation.
4. If either partner feels the marriage is not working or the sexual relationship is not good, discuss it and get marriage counseling if needed.
5. If either parent is an alcohol abuser, get treatment.
6. Keep family communications open; don't keep secrets from each other.
7. Believe the children if they report sexual advances by family members.

Divorced parents (especially women with daughters) considering remarriage should remember that they are not just choosing a new partner for themselves, but a new parent for their children as well!

Child Molestation (Pedophilia)

What is it? Child molestation refers to sexual activity between an adult and a child who are not related to each other (if they are related it is called incest). Adults who prefer children as sex partners are called **pedophiles.** Sexual activity with children has been known throughout history and seems to exist in all parts of the world. Child prostitution exists in many countries, including the United States. However, all sexual relationships with children are illegal in the United States, and the penalties for child molestation are severe in some states.

Molestation usually occurs in the home of the pedophile or in the child's home. Normally (around 80 percent of cases) it does not involve intercourse; but the older the child is, the more likely it is that intercourse will take place. The use of force or violence to obtain the child's cooperation is rare, but there may be bribes, gifts, and threats. The sexual activity usually involves fondling and caressing the genitals and other parts of the body, and having the child look at and/or touch the molester's genitals. The molester may or may not have an orgasm and ejaculate.

How common is it? Child molestation seems to be common; between 11 and 16 percent of all women report having been either molested or exposed to an exhibitionist when they were children. Only a tiny percentage of all molestation cases are ever reported to the police, and often children do not even tell their parents of the incident.

How serious is it? Child molestation is a serious crime because of the serious and long-lasting damage it can do to the emotional and psychological well-being of the victim. When child molestation involves force, violence, threats, and repeated incidents, the child is very likely to suffer long-term psychological and emotional effects. There can also be damage to the reproductive system or anus, infection with sexually transmitted diseases, and possibly pregnancy for girls past puberty. It should be noted, however, that in the case of a single incident in which the child is not harmed by the molester, overreaction by the parents may frighten the child more than the incident itself.

Most child molesters are men who are known to the child, often friends or relatives.

If a child is molested, it is important that the parents prevent further harm by:

1. Handling the incident in a calm, rational way
2. Reassuring the child that he or she is not to blame
3. Making sure that any reporting, court appearances, and so on are handled in a way that does not frighten the child or cause the child to dwell on the incident
4. Keeping the incident confidential from those who do not need to know
5. Getting counseling help for themselves and/or the child if the child remains upset or develops problems after the incident

Counseling for children who have been molested and for their parents is definitely recommended if the child has been harmed, if there were several incidents, or if the child develops problems after the molestation. Such counseling is available in most communities, and counselors who specialize in working with sexually abused children can be found through local social service agencies or child abuse programs.

Who is at risk of child molestation? Almost all known child molesters are men, and girls are more likely than boys to be the victims. *Children of all ages are at risk of molestation.* Most child molesters are men under 40 years of age, and in over 80 percent of cases they are friends or acquaintances of the child's family. *The greatest risk of child molestation is from men the parents already know, not from strangers.*

The men who have become known to police for molestation are generally of normal intelligence, often married, and not mentally ill. Most child molesters view themselves as heterosexual, even when their preferred child partners are boys. They seem to belong to three types:

1. *Fixated pedophiles:* Men whose sexual interests and fantasies have never progressed beyond childhood. They like and enjoy children, and prefer them as sexual partners. These men have never been interested in or attempted a sexual relationship with an adult woman.
2. *Regressed pedophiles:* Men who have had a sexual relationship with an adult woman, but because of a poor relationship with the adult partner, loss of the partner, stress, alcoholism, or other factors, now turn to children to meet their sexual needs.
3. *Mentally retarded persons:* People who do not realize that the child is not an appropriate sex partner.

Most fixated pedophiles are very fond of children and do not want to hurt them or make them unhappy. They are often interested in the well-being of the child and want to maintain a relation-

It is important to teach children not to talk to or get into a car with strangers.

ship over time. Some do not believe that they have done anything wrong or harmful to the child. A small proportion (estimated at 5 to 10 percent) of child molesters are violent and sadistic. These are the persons who may kidnap, assault, or kill a child for sexual reasons. Fortunately, they are not the typical child molester.

What happens when child molesting is reported? Since most cases of molestation are never reported, and it is rare for molesters to seek help on their own, most molesters are never punished or treated. Molestation is illegal throughout the United States. When a case is reported to the police, if the molester is convicted, he may receive a prison sentence or probation. He may also be ordered to attend psychological counseling or a behavior modification program, but it is not known how effective this is. Little research has been devoted to the treatment of the child molester. In a few cases, convicted child molesters have been surgically castrated or treated with hormones to reduce their sex drive in order to prevent future molestation. These approaches to treatment are very controversial and are not supported by most experts who work with child molesters. The effectiveness of this type of treatment is not known.

A very small minority of people in the United States believe that sex with children is natural and that it should not be a criminal offense. This point of view is unacceptable in the United States and is viewed as a harmful exploitation of children. These people have formed organizations that promote sex with children and lobby for changes in the law. These organizations do not favor the use of violence or force with children, but they promote the idea of adults introducing children to sex at an early age.

How can child molesting be prevented? There are many things parents can do to reduce the chances that their child will be molested. The following list shows some of the important things to do:

1. Know where children are at all times.
2. Choose babysitters carefully.
3. Never leave small children with strangers or casual acquaintances.
4. Teach children not to talk to or go with strangers.
5. Be aware that children sometimes molest other children.
6. Teach children that no one has a right to touch their private parts.
7. Teach children to tell parents or teachers if someone touches their private parts or does something that makes them uncomfortable.
8. Teach children that it is all right to say "no" to adults and to refuse to cooperate if they are told to do something they don't think is right.
9. Report child molesters, to reduce the chances that they will molest again.

The local public schools and child welfare agencies are likely to have books and other materials that parents can use to teach children how to avoid molestation.

Rape

What is it? Rape is sexual intercourse forced on a woman against her will or when she is not in a condition to give her consent. The exact legal definitions of rape vary from state to state, and sexual acts other than penis-in-vagina intercourse may not be considered rape according to the law.

Rape is generally divided into two categories, **forcible rape** (with which this section is concerned), which is intercourse with a woman against her will, and **statutory rape,** which is intercourse with a woman who is under the age of consent (16 or 18 in most states).

A man can be charged with statutory rape even if the girl had intercourse with him willingly (or invited the contact). Statutory rape laws are rarely enforced unless there is a complaint, such as from the girl's parents, but a conviction on this charge carries a long prison sentence in some states.

Rape exists in all countries of the world and has been known throughout recorded history. Rape is commonplace during wars, causing injury and death to many women and girls. Through much of world history women have been regarded as the property of men, and the laws about rape have reflected this, punishing the victim as often as the rapist. In recent years, as women in the United States have gained legal status more equal to that of men, the handling of rape has changed. Women now receive better protection, although the issue is still problematic.

Outside of the legal definition, the term *rape* is often used to refer to forcible sexual attacks on women that involve sexual acts (such as oral or anal intercourse) other than genital intercourse. It is also used to describe sexual attacks on men in which they are forced by other men to have anal intercourse. Rape of men by women seems to be extremely rare, but a few men have reported being forced by one or more women to have intercourse. This section deals primarily with forcible rapes of women.

How common is it? *Rape is very common and is listed by the Federal Bureau of Investigation (FBI) as the fastest rising violent crime in the United States.* An estimated 1 in 5 women will experience an attempted rape in her lifetime (and 1 in 24 will be the victim of a completed rape). Since only 1 in 10 (or fewer) rapes are ever reported, it is hard to get a clear picture of the true number of rapes, but it is estimated that there may be as many as half a million a year. It is not known whether more rapes are actually being committed each year, or whether an increase in the numbers of women reporting them accounts for the rising rates listed by the FBI.

How serious is it? Rape is a serious crime because of the severe and long-standing damage it does to the lives of those who are raped. Severe physical injury and sometimes death can be the result. Some women suffer permanent damage to their reproductive and sexual organs from rape, particulary gang rape. In addition, women can contract sexually transmitted diseases, including AIDS, and can become pregnant as a result of rape. Even in rapes where physical injuries are minor, rape has very negative effects on most women, causing them to go into shock and having long-lasting effects on personality and self-confidence. However, not every woman experiences negative aftereffects.

Interviews with women who have been raped indicate that, for many, the aftereffects of rape last for years and affect many areas of life. The following are more common long-term reactions to rape:

1. Moving and changing one's phone number out of fear the rapist may return

2. Having nightmares and fears (fear of crowds, fear of being alone, etc.)

3. Suffering depression and decreased pleasure from life

4. Experiencing loss of confidence and loss of a sense of control over one's life

5. Having sexual problems. Many women report long-term loss of the ability to enjoy intercourse after rape.

Although less is known about male victims of rape, they are also severely traumatized and probably experience similar aftereffects. Rape victims' reactions are similar to those of posttraumatic stress syndrome, which affects veterans of combat, survivors of disasters, and former hostages. Although most women wish to avoid sex for a time after rape, a few attempt to deal with their feelings by becoming prostitutes or by becoming indiscriminately sexually active.

Fortunately, the psychological and emotional reactions of the rape victim are becoming better understood, and there are excellent counseling programs to help both female and male victims and their partners resolve feelings about the assault. Counseling can be very effective in helping a woman (or man) to regain confidence and the ability to enjoy life, and in helping her to sort out her feelings about the rape and about sex so that relations can return to normal with her partner (or with future partners).

Who is at risk of rape? Rape victims are most commonly young women (in their teens and twenties), but girls and women of all ages are raped, from toddlers to senior citizens. Disabled, retarded, and homeless women are at especially high risk for rape because they are less able to protect themselves.

Over half of all rapes occur within the woman's home. Automobiles and other enclosed spaces are other common locations. Weekend evenings are the most common time, although rapes take place at every time of day or night. *Around 75 percent of rapes are planned in advance by the rapist.* Most attacks involve a single rapist, but a pair or a group of men may also commit rape (known as gang rape). Although almost all rapes are violent and dangerous, gang attacks frequently cause serious injury or death.

Around half of all rapists are strangers to the women they attack, but 30 percent are acquaintances and 10 percent are family members. Besides forcible rape by a stranger or casual acquaintance, two additional types of rape, **date rape** (also called *acquaintance rape*) and **mate rape** (also called *marital* or *spousal rape*), have recently been identified. Date rape refers to a rape that takes place while a woman is on a date or in a similar social situation. In one survey of 300 women between the ages of 18 and 30, 1 woman in 25 had been raped on a date or at a party. Most women do not report this type of rape, because it can be very difficult to prove unless there are serious injuries or witnesses. The risk of date rape is a strong argument for caution in dating, particularly for not going out with strangers.

Mate rape refers to the rape of a woman by her husband. The concept is controversial because access to sex with the partner is assumed in marriage. In one study, however, 1 woman in 8 reported that she had been forcibly raped by her husband at least once. Mate rape is a form of family violence, like wife beating or child abuse, but it is not illegal in most states.

According to crime statistics, rapes are most likely to take place in low-income urban areas, and to involve low-income (frequently minority) men and women. These figures, however, may not present an accurate profile of rape in the United States, since rapes in more affluent areas or involving wealthier people may be less likely to be reported. On the other hand, the crowding, stress, and poverty of some areas may create pressures and opportunities for rape that make it more common.

Rape victims are most commonly young women, but women of all ages, as well as boys and men, are also raped.

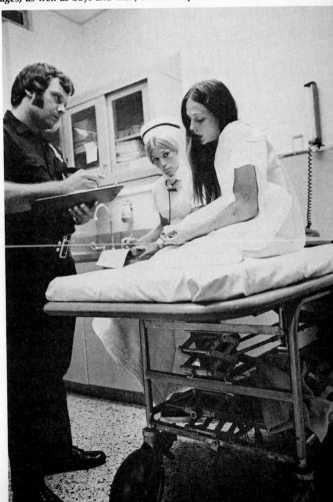

Why do men commit rape? It appears that rapes are committed for many different reasons. According to crime statistics, a convicted rapist is most likely to be a young (in his teens or twenties) minority man with a history of previous rapes and other crimes. Unfortunately, these statistics probably tell us more about who is likely to be *convicted* of a crime than who is likely to *commit* one. It is safer to assume that a rapist may come from any racial or ethnic group, may have no criminal record, and may be from any economic or educational level. Many rapists are repeaters, and some have committed hundreds of assaults.

Rape is considered to be an act of aggression carried out through sexual means. The primary purpose in many cases appears to be not sexual gratification but, rather, assertion of power over a woman, to punish or hurt her. Many men have problems of impotence or lack of ability to ejaculate during rape.

Before going further, it should be pointed out that *in a small number of cases rapes may be the result of serious misunderstandings.* Some date rapes, in particular, may take place because the man misunderstands the woman's desires and intentions. *A misunderstanding does not excuse the serious crime of rape*, but it is important to understand that it can occur. For more on this, see the section on preventing rape later in this chapter. Following are some of the reasons that misunderstandings may develop:

1. The man has been drinking or taking drugs, and his judgment is impaired.
2. The man knows little about women or about social relationships.
    He thinks that when women say *no* they may mean *yes*.
    He thinks a woman's resistance is a normal part of lovemaking.
    He thinks the woman owes him sex if he paid for the costs of a date with her.
3. The man is from a foreign country where women do not have much freedom, and he misinterprets the meaning of being alone with a woman.

Studies of rapists show that most have other sexual outlets, and that rapes are primarily an expression of aggressive rather than sexual energy. The motivations of rapists can be divided into four groups—anger rape, power rape, exploitive rape, and sadistic rape—each of which is thought to have a different motivation.

1. *Anger rape* is thought to be carried out by an angry, depressed man on impulse rather than by planning ahead. The man is likely to be unnecessarily violent with the victim, may beat her, and is likely to show anger and use abusive language.

2. *Power rape* is thought to be carried out by an insecure man with feelings of inadequacy. He preplans rape and is likely to repeat the crime many times. He uses force and threats to keep control over the woman, but usually does not intend to harm her physically. He may keep her captive for a period of time, and he is likely to talk with her or ask her questions. He may believe that the woman should like or love him and should enjoy the rape.

3. *Exploitive rape* is thought to be carried out by a man whose life pattern is to exploit others to meet his own needs. He is likely to be involved in other crimes and antisocial behavior, and is frequently in trouble with the law. Typically he does not see rape as serious, he may repeat it often, and his behavior may be supported by other people he associates with.

4. *Sadistic rape* is the most dangerous type. The rape is preplanned, and the woman is kidnapped, raped, and then let go or disposed of. Bizarre rituals, torture, and bondage may be involved. The sexual organs may be mutilated, and the woman may be murdered.

What happens when rape is reported? Most rapes are never reported to the police. Those cases that are reported, however, begin with a police report and a visit to a hospital emergency room or other treatment center where the woman can be treated and evidence for a court case can be collected. The medical examination should take place as soon as possible after the attack, even if the woman is not sure she will press charges against the rapist. It is best for the victim not to shower or clean up before going for treatment, as this may destroy evidence that will be needed. She should take a change of clothes to the hospital because the clothes worn before or during the attack may be kept for evidence.

The woman may also wish to contact a rape crisis center for advice. The center may be able to send a counselor to accompany her through the reporting and medical examinations. Many hospitals use specially trained staff who understand and provide a supportive environment to care for rape victims. Similarly, many police departments have specially trained officers to work on rape cases.

The woman will have a choice as to whether to press charges against the rapist. When rape victims do press charges, over 50 percent of rapists are located, but only a minority are ever convicted. The woman does not have to make a final decision about whether to pursue the case immediately. She can wait for a few days, until she feels better and has a chance to learn more about what pressing charges will mean for her.

Many women are afraid of publicity and embarrassment if they press charges, afraid of retaliation by the rapist, or afraid that they will be treated disrespectfully by the police and the courts. These

Rape crisis counseling is available in many areas and can be very helpful.

fears are based on real possibilities, and each woman must make her own decision about how to handle the case. On the other hand, some women seem to recover faster and feel better about themselves if they do take action against the rapist.

Some communities are much more supportive of rape victims than others, and it is important for the woman to talk to a rape crisis center, the police, an attorney, and others involved in rape cases to find out what she can expect if she pursues the case, and how good the chances of conviction of the rapist are. A woman can withdraw the case at any time if she changes her mind, although this may waste considerable work done by the police and the courts.

How can rape be prevented? There is a great deal women can do to prevent rape and, if a rape is attempted, to avoid it. It is important, however, to strike a balance—to use good sense while not becoming a prisoner of fear.

Some basic safety habits can reduce a woman's chances of being raped. Since more than half of rapes occur in the woman's home and many others in cars, these are two areas to be especially careful about. The following are some precautions women can take to prevent rape. They are also basic safety rules for women of all ages to follow. Most of these precautions apply to men as well.

1. Do not open the door to strangers without identification. Use a peephole if possible. Do not count on the strength of chain locks; they are easily broken.

2. If you are a woman living alone, do not advertise that fact. Use only first initials on mailboxes, telephone listings, and so on.

3. Have keys ready in your hand when approaching your front door or your car, so you will not be delayed.

4. Keep car doors locked both when driving and when leaving the car parked. Check the back seat before getting into the car.

5. Keep your car gassed up and in working order, so you won't be stuck on the highway.

6. Don't be a hitchhiker or pick up one; don't take rides from strangers or give rides to strangers.

7. Avoid traveling alone in deserted or high-crime areas in cities, especially at night. Travel with a friend when you go places that could be risky.

8. Use your intuition if you think you are being followed. Do not go home if you will be alone there. Go into the nearest open store, restaurant, or other place where there are people.

9. Women in good physical condition are less likely to be attacked. When walking alone, show your strength by moving purposefully and confidently.

10. If you must walk alone in risky areas, show that you will not be an easy victim by wearing low-heeled shoes, loose clothing, and a purse with a shoulder strap. Do not load yourself down with bundles.

11. Don't count on chemical Mace, whistles, or weapons like hatpins or umbrellas. Most women forget they have them or don't have time to use them. Carrying a gun is illegal in many communities and is not recommended because of the high risk of accidental injuries.

What if you are attacked? There are many different opinions about the most effective way to avoid rape if you are attacked. Since most rapes and attempted rapes are never reported, there is no way of knowing what percentage of attempts are actually carried out, but it appears that in a high percentage of cases, women who are attacked are able to avoid rapes. Often women avoid men who are following them or strangers who come to the door without ever knowing for sure what the man's purpose was (rape, robbery, etc.). It is important to trust your instincts. When you feel a situation could be dangerous, avoid it. It is better to be too cautious than not cautious enough, even though some women are able to escape from men who physically seize them and make their intention to rape very clear.

There are basically two approaches when confronted by a rapist. In the **passive approach,** the woman passively goes along with the rapist's demands. This is a good idea if the man is armed and seems prepared to do serious injury or to kill the woman if she resists. In the **active approach,** the woman actively tries to escape, and (if she can't escape) to fight off her attacker. Many women use this approach when the rapist is not armed.

One study of women who were attacked ranked the different strategies the women used by their effectiveness in avoiding the rape. In general, fleeing or escaping seemed to be most effective if it was possible. Fighting back and screaming also scared off many rapists. Talking and pleading with the rapist seemed to be less effective.

It is not possible to recommend one approach over another, because each rape situation is different, and each woman handles this kind of crisis differently. Clearly, the first goal is to escape if possible, and the second is to avoid serious injury or death if escape is not possible. Women should not be embarrassed to choose the passive approach if necessary for their safety or survival.

Sexual Harassment

What is it? Sexual harassment is any unwanted sexual advance (verbal or physical) in which a man or woman is threatened with not being hired, loss of employment, loss of a promotion, or other negative employment-related action if she or he does not comply with the harasser's sexual demands. The legal definition of sexual harassment is restricted to harassment related to employment, but the same problem is commonly found in educational institutions, where students are threatened with failing grades, poor evaluations, refusal of letters of reference, or other punishment if they do not comply with the harasser's demands. Sexual harassment can be anything from mildly suggestive behavior, to talk that is not repeated, to continued threats and actions that can cost a job, career, reputation, or college degree if the victim does not cooperate.

How common is it? Sexual harassment is a problem that has received attention only in the last twenty years, and there is relatively little information about it. It is clear, however, that it is a very serious and a very common problem for women, and that it also affects a minority of men. In some occupations the majority of women have been sexually harassed, and most working women will probably experience harassment at some point. For example, in a survey of nurses, 60 percent reported sexual harassment within the past year, and a survey of 20,000 federal employees showed that 42 percent of women and 15 percent of men had been sexually harassed within the previous two years. In a survey of several thousand working women conducted by a women's magazine, 9 out of 10 reported that they had been sexually harassed at work. Sexual harassment by a person of the same sex (homosexual harassment) also occurs.

The problem is also extremely common in colleges and universities, where it is estimated that 1 out of 5 female students is subjected to sexual harassment. In a survey done at a large Ivy League university, one-third of undergraduate females and 41 percent of graduate women students reported that they had been sexually harassed.

How serious is it? Sexual harassment is a very serious offense because a person's employment, career, and reputation may be ruined if she (or he) does not comply with the harasser's demands. At present there is little legal protection against sexual harassment, and the majority of victims are women. Since most women receive low salaries (around 60 cents for each dollar men are paid), and many are single parents with responsibilities to support others, sexual harassment can cause severe financial hardship and great distress.

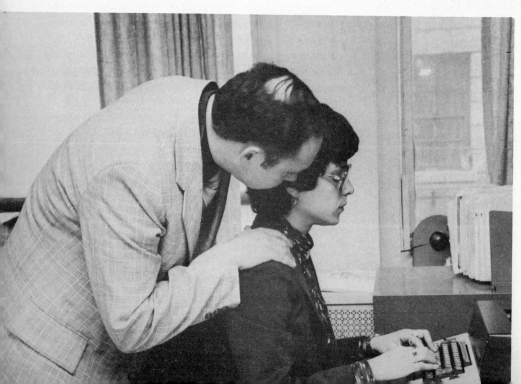

Sexual harassment is surprisingly common.

Little is known about psychological and emotional reactions to sexual harassment, but women who have been victims report that it is a very frightening experience in which they feel powerless to protect themselves. Some have compared it to the feelings of assault and violation brought on by rape. There is little information about the reactions of men who have been sexually harassed, but they are probably similar.

Who is at risk of sexual harassment? Sexual harassment usually involves a situation where a boss, personnel worker, or teacher (usually male) uses his superior position and power to try to force an employee or student (usually female) into a sexual relationship. Other people in a position of power may also use their authority to sexually harass those for whom they are responsible. The disabled, retarded, mentally ill, and others who live in institutions are also very much at risk of sexual harassment.

The threats may be direct and verbal, such as a male personnel worker telling a woman that she will have to sleep with him in order to get or keep a job. Or they may be indirect and subtle, leaving the threat of what will happen up to the worker's imagination. Harassment can also be physical, ranging from inappropriate touching or unwanted hugs or kisses, to assault and rape.

When sexual harassment is subtle, women may not be sure what is happening, and may find themselves increasingly uncomfortable and anxious at work without knowing why. They may feel that the sexual overtures are intended as compliments or that they have unintentionally communicated sexual interest. They may blame themselves for the problem. Many women (and men) give in to (or put up with) sexual harassment because they are afraid of losing their employment when they are under financial obligation to care for a family. Fortunately, there are ways to protect yourself and to avoid harassment, which will be explained in the next section.

What happens when sexual harassment is reported? Most states do not have laws against sexual harassment in the workplace. But sexual harassment cases have been filed with departments of the federal government concerned with discrimination in employment. *So far it has been very difficult to win sexual harassment cases, even when the evidence has been strong.* Sometimes criminal and civil suits against sexual harassers can be filed if there has been a rape, assault, threats, or other illegal behavior. Many large companies, universities, and unions have policies that forbid sexual

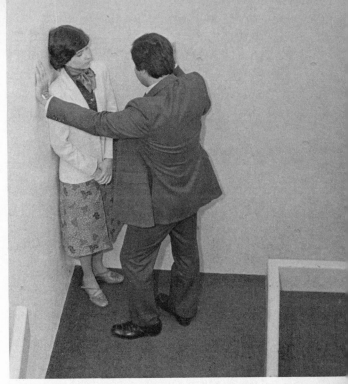

Don't be a passive victim. Speak up when someone behaves inappropriately.

harassment, but it may be difficult to get them to enforce these policies.

How can sexual harassment be prevented or avoided? Since sexual harassment is very common in the workplace and in colleges and universities, and since there are few legal means to protect oneself from it at this time, we can assume that most women and some men will experience sexual harassment at some point in their careers. Prevention of the problem would require much stricter laws and regulations than exist at present. In most cases, however, it should be possible to avoid or neutralize sexual harassers. No one should have to submit to unwanted sexual intercourse or other activity out of fear for work or school status. Following are several steps to prevent or avoid sexual harassment.

PREVENTION

1. Sexual harassers will choose the easiest prey, so show confidence on the job or at school. Avoid looking and acting helpless.

2. Set limits early and clearly with anyone who tries inappropriate sexual talk or touching. These people need to hear a loud and clear message that their behavior is offensive.

3. Listen to other workers or students who can tell you if certain people have a history of sexual harassment. Some of them are well known and have been harassing for years.

4. Avoid situations where you will be alone with or under the direct supervision of a potential harasser.

AVOIDANCE

1. If you are sure you are being harassed, start to keep a detailed log of what the harasser says and does, your meetings with the person, and so on.

2. Start investigating sources of advice and help in the organization. Personnel, a union, a dean of students, and others can tell you what the policies are and what kinds of support you can get. You may also find out if your harasser has a history of this behavior.

3. Investigate sources of help and advice outside the organization. Government equal opportunity offices and programs, and feminist (women's rights) organizations are the best sources (for men also!). Feminist organizations can often recommend attorneys who have experience with this type of problem.

4. Consider confronting the harasser directly, with a letter asking him to stop the behavior, with a letter from an attorney, or with a grievance. Be cautious, plan carefully, and be aware of all the possible consequences of confrontation.

5. If you can't see a way to confront the harasser or solve the problem, or if the cost to your career will be too great, consider transferring to another job, class, or location to get away.

6. As a last resort, consider a lawsuit, but it is likely to take years, and so far few sexual harassment cases have been won. However, since lawsuits are expensive and bad publicity, many organizations will try to resolve the problem to avoid one. They may be willing to give back an unfairly lost job, or to review a failing grade or bad evaluation.

RESOURCES

Information and referral services are available in your local community through the United Way agency, county or state department of social services, and local child protective services organizations. The police department is a source of information, and there may be local rape hotlines and crime victim programs as well. In addition, the following national resources can be contacted:

CHILDHELP National Child Abuse Hotline
(800) 422-4453

A 24-hour hotline run by a private nonprofit organization providing crisis intervention, information, and referral to local area services to those who wish to report abuse, victims, and abusers.

Children's Defense Fund
122 C Street, N.W.
Washington, D.C. 20001
(202) 628-8787

A nonprofit organization that provides information about child abuse prevention, teenage pregnancy, foster care, health and welfare programs, and other matters concerning the well-being of children.

National Clearinghouse on Marital Rape
2325 Oak Street
Berkeley, CA 94708
(415) 548-1770

A nonprofit organization that provides information and education on the subject of marital rape.

National Center for Missing and Exploited Children
1835 K Street, N.W., Suite 600
Washington, D.C. 20006
(800) 843-5678
(202) 634-9836

A nonprofit organization that provides information about the problem of missing and exploited children free to the public and is a clearinghouse for parents who wish to report missing children, citizens who have information about missing children, and the police.

Parents Anonymous National Headquarters
6733 South Sepulveda
Los Angeles, CA 90045
(800) 421-0353 except in California
(800) 352-0386 in California
(213) 410-9732

A nonprofit organization that provides information and referrals to parents at risk of abusing their children and to adults who were abused as children.

6
Pregnancy and Childbirth

This chapter provides information about pregnancy, about changes in the mother's body during pregnancy, and about the experience of labor and delivery. (Information about how babies are conceived and the stages of development of the embryo and fetus is found in Chapter 2.) This chapter also covers the details of what to expect from prenatal care and the different choices for delivery of the baby. Health problems and complications of pregnancy and delivery are discussed, along with treatments available.

PREGNANCY

Signs and Symptoms

How can a woman tell if she's pregnant? The only way to be certain is through a pregnancy test or a pelvic (gynecological) examination. Most women first suspect pregnancy when they miss a menstrual period. However, there are many reasons other than pregnancy that a period might be missed (see Chapter 12, "Women's Health Problems"), and a few women continue to have monthly bleeding during the first few months of pregnancy. So, although a missed menstrual period is a good indicator of possible pregnancy, it is far from 100 percent reliable.

The following are other early signs of pregnancy that may develop during the first 6 to 12 weeks. These changes are likely to begin to appear when the woman is about 3 weeks pregnant (that is, 1 week after her period should have started, and 5 weeks after her last monthly period began). They are caused by changes in hormone levels that are part of the new pregnancy.

A woman may develop some of these symptoms, or none at all. It is unlikely that she will have all of them.

1. Enlarged and tender breasts
2. Morning sickness (nausea and vomiting, not necessarily in the morning)
3. Frequent urination
4. Tiredness; need for extra sleep
5. Slight weight gain
6. Bloated feeling in abdomen
7. Slightly elevated temperature (noticeable if you have been taking your basal body temperature; see Chapter 9, page 90)
8. Moodiness
9. Changes in sex drive
10. Food cravings
11. Increased appetite

Some women claim that they know right away when they become pregnant, that they feel different. A woman who has experienced several pregnancies may, in fact, be so familiar with the changes in her body that she can recognize pregnancy fairly reliably. But most women have no recognizable signs or symptoms except missing a menstrual period. For all women, a pregnancy test and a pelvic examination are the only ways to be certain, other than waiting for the pregnancy to develop.

Pregnancy Tests

There are several kinds of pregnancy tests, including some that women can purchase at the pharmacy and use in the privacy of their homes. Pregnancy tests are based on the detection of a pregnancy hormone, HCG (human chorionic gonadotropin), in the woman's body. The most frequently used tests (including the home pregnancy testing kits) check for the presence of this hormone in the woman's urine. There are also more expensive tests that check for the hormone in a blood sample. These must be ordered by your doctor or health care provider. There are both urine and blood tests now available that can detect a pregnancy well before the woman's period is due.

Urine tests are 97 to 98 percent accurate in cases where they show a woman to be pregnant but somewhat less reliable when they show a negative result (no pregnancy). Home pregnancy test results are less reliable than those done at the doctor's office or clinic; false negative results (showing no pregnancy when the woman is pregnant) can be as high as 20 percent.

All women who suspect they are pregnant should have the pregnancy confirmed by their health care provider, even if they have used a home

pregnancy test. The visit to the doctor's office or clinic will include a urine test for pregnancy and a pelvic exam. You will probably be asked to bring along a sample from the first urination of the morning and your records of the dates of the most recent monthly periods. In the pelvic exam, your provider is looking for a slightly enlarged and softened uterus and a change in color of the cervix (a bluish color). He or she needs the dates of your most recent periods to calculate how many weeks you may be pregnant. If it cannot be determined for certain whether you are pregnant or not, a more expensive but more accurate blood test may be performed, or you may be asked to return in a week or so for another urine test.

Calculating a Due Date

If you are pregnant, your health care provider will calculate your **due date** (the date the baby is expected to be born) using Nagele's rule. This is done by taking the date of the first day of your last period, subtracting three months, and adding seven days. For example, if your last period started on January first, your baby is expected on October 8th of the coming year.

Learning your due date is very important for planning for the baby. This is only an estimated date for the baby's arrival, however, since a normal pregnancy can be anywhere from 38 to 42 weeks in length. It is considered normal for birth to take place as much as two weeks before or after the due date. In fact, fewer than 10 percent of women actually deliver on their due date, and almost half of all babies are born more than 10 days before or 10 days after their expected date of arrival!

Starting Prenatal Care

Once pregnancy is confirmed, a regular program of prenatal health care should be started, using the health care provider(s) who will deliver the baby. This means you need to make your choice early about where to give birth and about who will provide your prenatal care and delivery. Details about the choices for delivery are given on pages 129–136 of this chapter. It is a good idea to read that section before making a decision about who will provide your prenatal care. You may need to make some telephone calls and perhaps visit a few providers to find out which ones offer the approach to pregnancy and delivery that you want. Good communication and a trusting relationship with your health care provider is extremely important, so be picky. If you do not feel comfortable with a particular provider, look for another one.

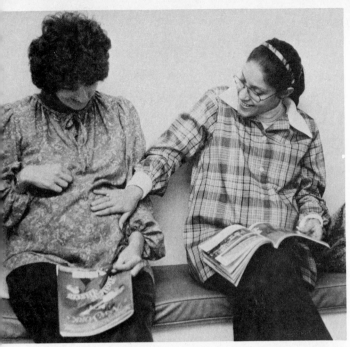

Regular prenatal care is very important for both mother and baby.

Once you have selected a doctor, group practice, health maintenance organization (HMO), clinic, midwife, or other provider, you will schedule your first prenatal visit. During this visit you will get a thorough physical examination, including a pelvic exam and Pap smear (see Chapter 12 for details on these exams). The baby's due date will also be calculated. A detailed history of your health (and of health problems in your family and your husband's or partner's family) will be taken as well. A blood sample will be drawn to test for anemia, blood type, and immunity to certain infections. If you are 35 or older (or if certain birth defects run in the family), a prenatal test for birth defects called *amniocentesis* (see page 119 for details) may be recommended for later in pregnancy.

After the first prenatal visit, you will probably be scheduled for monthly checkups until the seventh month, and for visits every two weeks after that until the last month of pregnancy, when your provider will examine you every week. These visits usually involve weight and blood pressure checks, a urine test, measurement of the size of the uterus, and checks of the fetal heartbeat and position. A pelvic exam is usually not done at each visit. If you have a *high-risk* pregnancy (a pregnancy in which there is a greater chance of complications or illness than normal), you may be seen more often, and different kinds of tests may be done.

At the first prenatal visit you will probably also be provided with information about pregnancy and self-care. This typically includes nutritional information (some providers have pamphlets about this with sample diets, or see pages 115–116 in this chapter) and self-care information (about smoking, drinking, and so on). A prescription for special vitamins may also be provided. Pregnancy is a drain on the mother's body, and most women take iron and vitamin supplements in order to maintain a healthy pregnancy. Vitamin supplements appear to be needed even if you eat a well-balanced diet, and most prenatal care providers recommend them in order to be certain that you and the developing fetus get the proper nutrients.

High-Risk Pregnancies

Some pregnancies are riskier than others for the mother and/or the fetus.

1. Pregnant women over age 35 and those under the age of 18 seem to have higher rates of complications than others.
2. Health problems such as diabetes, high blood pressure, or heart disease can make pregnancy potentially dangerous for the mother and can have negative effects on the fetus as well.
3. Certain drugs, such as those used to control epilepsy, can be harmful to the fetus.
4. Women with a history of miscarriages, stillbirths (baby born dead), or babies with birth defects have a higher risk of problems with later pregnancies.
5. Carrying more than one fetus (twins or triplets) creates a higher-risk pregnancy.
6. Accidents, infections (especially sexually transmitted diseases), surgery, and illnesses during pregnancy also create high-risk situations.

Once a pregnancy is identified as high-risk, the expectant mother will be seen more often by her health care provider, and may also have more limitations placed on her activities and her diet. She may be referred to a **perinatologist,** an obstetrician specially trained in working with high-risk pregnancies. The woman's cooperation with the recommendations of her care provider can often make the difference between a successful, healthy pregnancy and serious problems. This means that if a woman does not agree with what is recommended, or for some reason cannot follow the instructions given (for example, to quit work, not to lift heavy objects, or to follow a certain diet), she should speak up and let her care providers know. There may be some other way to solve the problem.

In most high-risk situations, a successful pregnancy is possible if the woman receives the proper prenatal care. But in the most serious high-risk situations (if the future mother's life or future health may be endangered, or if the fetus is unlikely to survive), the woman's health care provider is likely to suggest abortion.

Genetic Concerns

Couples who are planning to have a baby should give some thought to their genetic backgrounds. They should check whether they or any relatives (especially brothers and sisters, parents, and grandparents) have any inherited defects or health problems.

New babies have a 5 percent chance of being born with a genetically caused (inherited) defect. In most cases the parents were not aware that they could transmit such a defect to their children. Genetically caused defects can affect any part of the body, including the brain, and can range from a very minor problem to a defect so serious that it will be fatal to the fetus. An example of a genetic defect is Down's syndrome ("mongolism"), which causes mental retardation and health problems. People from various ethnic backgrounds—for example, British, Jewish, and Afro-American—have different rates of risk for carrying certain genetic disorders. Other defects are found equally often among all groups in the United States. The age of the parents can also affect the chances of giving birth to a child with a genetic defect.

If there is the possibility of an inherited defect in the family, the couple would be wise to seek genetic counseling to find out what their chances are of passing it on to a new baby. Couples who have already had one child with an inherited defect should definitely seek counseling. Rapid progress is being made in understanding how to predict, diagnose, and prevent birth defects, so couples who are at risk (and their future children) may benefit greatly from expert evaluation and advice. Basic information about genetic risks can often be provided by your own doctor or clinic. If specialized tests and evaluation are needed, however, you will probably be referred to a genetic counseling service at a research or teaching hospital.

Changes during Pregnancy

Physical Changes

A normal pregnancy lasts 38 to 42 weeks, or about nine months. For the purposes of discussion, pregnancy is typically divided into three-month periods called **trimesters.**

First trimester The most dramatic effects of pregnancy (aside from the weight gain) occur dur-

Morning sickness is common during the first trimester of pregnancy. Eating crackers sometimes helps.

ing the first trimester. During these first three months, there are substantial changes in hormonal levels, especially levels of estrogen and progesterone. These changes cause the breasts to swell and the nipples and the surrounding areola to darken (the latter is particularly noticeable to first-time pregnant women). The pregnant woman may need to urinate more frequently than usual and may experience constipation. Should constipation become a problem, laxatives are not recommended, as these can endanger the pregnancy. Instead, the woman should increase liquids and fiber in her diet by drinking more fluids and eating raw vegetables, bran, oatmeal, or other high-fiber foods.

Fatigue and sleepiness, probably due to the high levels of progesterone, are also common. A pregnant woman typically needs 8 to 10 hours of sleep per day. If possible, some of this sleep may be taken as an afternoon nap. Particularly during the first trimester, a woman may need naps in order to maintain her sense of well-being.

About half of all pregnant women experience nausea or vomiting. Although this is commonly called "morning sickness," it can occur at any time of the day or night. For example, some women get nauseous at the sight or smell of particular foods, or if they smell food cooking. Others wake up with an upset stomach. Eating frequent small snacks (such as crackers) every two to three hours may help to relieve nausea. Avoiding fried, greasy, and heavily spiced foods often helps as well.

Morning sickness almost always passes and is usually gone by the beginning of the fourth month. It is important not to take any medications such as antacids to treat an upset stomach unless you have cleared them with your care provider. Any time morning sickness becomes so severe that you are not able to eat or drink anything at all, you should contact your prenatal care provider.

If a miscarriage, also known as a spontaneous abortion (see details later in this chapter), is going to occur, it is most likely to happen during the first trimester. *Miscarriages usually occur because of natural causes, not because of anything that the woman or her doctor did.* In fact, the cause of most miscarriages is never pinpointed. Any vaginal bleeding at this early stage can be a sign of impending miscarriage and should be reported to the prenatal care provider. For more details on the common complaints and health problems of pregnancy, see pages 121–123.

Second trimester Most of the first-trimester problems subside during the second trimester. Now there is rapid growth of the abdomen (see Figure 6–1). Most women will need to start wearing maternity clothes by the time they are five months pregnant.

By the fifth month, the woman will feel some fetal movement ("quickening"; see page 33), which is usually a very exciting and pleasurable experience, since it is evidence that the fetus is developing well. Also around this time, the fetal heartbeat can first be heard through a stethoscope.

Some problems do continue during the second trimester. Constipation is common and this, in conjunction with the pressure of the pelvic organs on the rectal blood vessels, may cause the development of hemorrhoids. Consult your doctor before using medications for hemorrhoids. Some women may also experience edema (swelling) due to water retention, particularly in the hands, feet, and ankles. Since edema can be an indicator of toxemia (see pages 127–128), it is

FIGURE 6–1. *The development of the fetus by weeks.*

Woman in 6th week of pregnancy

Woman in 12th week of pregnancy

Woman in 16th week of pregnancy

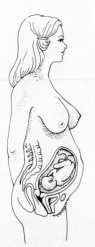
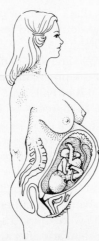

Woman in 24th week of pregnancy

Woman in 36th week of pregnancy

Woman in 40th week of pregnancy

During the last months of pregnancy the uterus becomes noticeably larger.

wise to point out any swelling to your prenatal care provider.

Around the nineteenth week of pregnancy (or later), the breasts may begin to produce colostrum. Colostrum is a sticky, yellowish fluid that is produced before breast milk (which will not begin until about three days after the baby is born). Women do not produce a lot of this fluid, but it is enough to be noticeable.

Third trimester During the third trimester, the uterus (and therefore the abdomen) becomes very large, and the considerable weight gained becomes very noticeable. The recommended weight gain during pregnancy is about 22 to 27 pounds (although some women gain considerably more). Most of this occurs during the second and third trimesters, when the woman gains around a pound a week.

Late in pregnancy (two or three weeks before delivery for first-time mothers, and later for others) the fetus drops to a lower position in the abdomen,

as the bottom of the uterus stretches in preparation for delivery. This change in the baby's position is called **lightening** (probably because it reduces uncomfortable pressure on the lungs and stomach), and is a sign that labor will begin soon (Figure 6–2). Lightening increases pressure in the lower abdomen, which can cause a new set of discomforts, including frequent urination, constipation, and swollen ankles.

The body changes of pregnancy, which are most noticeable in the third trimester, produce a number of side effects that can cause discomfort (see the section on common complaints, pages 121–123). Fortunately, these problems are only temporary, and usually disappear once the baby is born. Most women will probably develop at least one or two of these side effects, but (happily) no woman is likely to have all of them.

Psychological and Emotional Changes

The mother-to-be The physical changes associated with pregnancy are similar for all women, but emotional reactions to pregnancy are another story. There are as many different reactions to pregnancy as there are pregnant women. A wanted and planned baby, a healthy and comfortable pregnancy, freedom from financial worries, and a good relationship between the future father and mother are some of the factors that contribute to a woman feeling positive about her pregnancy. But even under the best of conditions a woman (and a man) may have very mixed feelings about a pregnancy. If the pregnancy is not wanted, a woman may experience tremendous stress and emotional discomfort (see Chapter 7 for details about unplanned and unwanted pregnancies). Each pregnancy is different and takes place under different conditions, so a woman should not expect to have the same feelings each time she is pregnant.

The first few weeks of pregnancy are often a time of particularly mixed emotions. The woman may be thrilled to be pregnant, but she may also have many doubts and fears, especially if it is her first pregnancy. Some women are so concerned that they become superstitious and may refuse to talk about the pregnancy or to tell anyone about it for fear that they will "jinx" the pregnancy. Since an estimated 20 percent of known pregnancies are miscarried, it is a good idea to wait until around the twelfth week of pregnancy before making a public announcement. The woman may also have doubts about her ability to be a good mother. In fact, she may not yet be able to picture herself as a mother, or her husband as a father.

As the woman moves into the second trimester, and particularly after she feels movement, some of these concerns lessen. She usually feels better physically, and women often report they have much more energy during the second trimester and the beginning of the third trimester.

Many women find that pregnancy affects their relationship with their own mother. The pregnant woman may develop a new level of respect for her own mother. Both women may feel that they have more in common now, and they may become closer. Or the pregnancy may reawaken old uncomfortable feelings between the pregnant woman and her mother.

The last few weeks of pregnancy can be difficult for the woman. She may be tired of being pregnant and may find it difficult to get around. She may have begun her maternity leave from work, and this may leave her feeling isolated and bored. She may feel more tired, and her back may ache at times. Furthermore, she will have completed any childbirth classes she enrolled in and will have made arrangements for the birth. In other words, she is psychologically and physically ready to deliver. Yet all she can do is wait.

It is important to note that different women have different reactions at every phase of pregnancy. A certain amount of doubt and anxiety are to be expected. But there is also a substantial amount of excitement, joy, anticipation, and enthu-siasm. Pregnancy, then, is often a time of mixed emotions. After all, becoming a mother is one of the biggest life transitions a woman ever makes.

The father-to-be   Like women, men usually have both positive and negative feelings about the pregnancy. Since expectant fathers do not go through the physical changes of pregnancy, the pregnancy itself may not seem very real to them at first. The mother-to-be may be very involved in finding out all she can about pregnancy and child-birth, but the father-to-be may not feel very interested at first. During the second trimester, however, once he can hear the fetal heartbeat and feel the baby-to-be kicking, the pregnancy usually seems more real.

Expectant fathers often worry about what is expected of them at the time of birth. They may fear that they might not be able to handle staying with the mother through labor and delivery, or that they might faint at the sight of blood. The best way to combat these feelings is with information. Talking with other fathers about their experiences at the time of labor and delivery will help. Accompanying the mother-to-be on a prenatal care visit and meeting the provider who will deliver the baby is also a good idea. Childbirth preparation courses and movies that show labor and delivery are also excel-

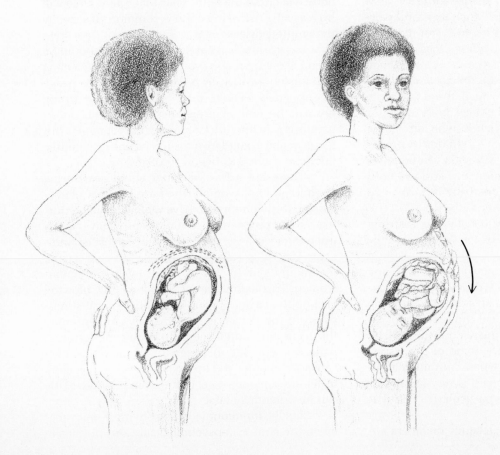

FIGURE 6–2. *In late pregnancy the fetus drops to a lower position in the uterus. This is called "lightening."*

lent sources of information that can help the father-to-be decide what role he wants to play during labor and delivery.

Most men find that the positives of being able to share the childbirth experience with the mother far outweigh the negatives. But it is also true that not every man is cut out for assisting with labor and delivery (and some men may have to be away from home at the time the baby is due). In such cases, a close relative or friend of the mother-to-be can substitute for the father and train to be the labor coach and companion during childbirth.

Men also tend to worry more than women do about what life will be like after the baby is born. Women are likely to be so focused on the pregnancy itself that they don't think as much about what it will be like actually to live with the baby after it is born. Men who will be the sole support of the family tend to be particularly worried about financial issues. And most men become more concerned about such things as life insurance and having a will.

Men wonder how the new baby will affect the couple's social life, since they will have less freedom than in the past. They may also worry about the effects on the couple's sexual relationship (which has already been affected by the pregnant woman's changing shape).

All these feelings may be intensified if the man has no one to talk to about them. Not every man has the kind of friendships in which fears and worries are easily discussed, and some men may feel that they should not share such feelings with the mother-to-be. A man's own father or brothers may be easier to talk to about these things, and friends who have recently been through the experience themselves are often a good choice. Both men and women often make new friends who are going through the same experience in childbirth preparation classes, and these new friends can be a tremendous source of information and support both during pregnancy and after the baby is born.

The family Pregnancy usually has a strong impact on the relationship of the future parents. The couple may become much closer as a result of the pregnancy, but pregnancy also adds many stresses to the relationship. Worries about the future, concern about the woman's changed appearance and limitations in physical and sexual activity, and uncertainty about what the relationship will be like after the baby arrives are some of the issues that come up for couples. Open communication about feelings, fears, and worries is very important to a good relationship and is particularly helpful at this time.

Children and other close family members are also affected by the pregnancy. They may respond with joy and support or with fear that they may lose attention or love to the new baby. Often, reactions are a combination of happiness and fear of change.

It is especially important to prepare older brothers and sisters of the baby-to-be for the new arrival. This can help to keep negative feelings and jealousy to a minimum. Children under age 6 especially need preparation, since they may have difficulty understanding where the baby came from, why their mother has to be absent, and so on. Children should be informed about the baby-to-be by the time the pregnancy starts to show, or even earlier if the pregnancy has been publicly announced. Using a picture book (or this book) to show the child how the baby-to-be is developing inside the mother is an excellent idea for children of all ages.

Sex during Pregnancy

Most women continue to have sexual intercourse throughout pregnancy, but many couples have questions and concerns about sex during this time. Some women don't feel attractive or sexy during the later months of pregnancy; others fear that the thrusting of the penis or the weight of their lover's body will crush the fetus. Fear that intercourse will increase the risk of infection is common. (If sexually transmitted disease is a possibility, both partners should seek medical care, and condoms should be used.) Some men and women have a vague feeling that it is not proper for pregnant women to engage in sex. Such feelings may be particularly strong toward the end of pregnancy. In general, intercourse is safe into the last month of pregnancy. But it is probably a good idea to stop having intercourse once the cervix has begun to dilate.

There are a few warnings about sex during pregnancy. First, women who have a history of miscarriages or women who have vaginal bleeding during the pregnancy should probably avoid intercourse unless their prenatal specialist indicates that it is safe. Second, at least one sexual technique should be avoided by all pregnant women. This technique involves forcefully blowing air into the vagina during cunnilingus (oral stimulation of the female genitals). Some women enjoy this technique, and it seems to be safe for nonpregnant women. But in pregnant women this may cause air to enter the uterus and, via the placenta, to get into a blood vessel in the woman's body. This can be potentially fatal.

Finally, intercourse is usually most enjoyable when the couple is psychologically and physically comfortable. As pregnancy progresses, it becomes increasingly difficult for the woman to be comfortable. The missionary position (man on top, woman on the bottom) becomes difficult, but the side-by-side and rear-entry positions usually remain comfortable and satisfying for pregnant couples. By the end of pregnancy, however, some women and men may find that almost any position for intercourse is uncomfortable or awkward. Other forms of sexual activity, such as manual or oral stimulation of the genitals (see Chapter 3), are still available without any problems.

Working during Pregnancy

Most women today work outside of the home for pay, and about 85 percent of these women will become pregnant at least once during their work lives. Many working women wonder how long they should work when they are pregnant. There is no simple answer to this question, since it depends on the woman's health and the nature of her job. In most cases, it is safe to keep working right up until the end of pregnancy.

There are some situations, however, when women should or must stop working. First, some employers require that women stop working at a certain point in pregnancy. Check with your employer about such regulations. In many (but not all) of these cases, the employer is legally obligated to hold your job for you until you return. Under federal law, pregnancy must be treated the same way as any other physical disability; if your company offers disability leave, it must also offer pregnancy leave. If you think you are being treated unfairly, contact your state or federal labor department.

Second, women who have a history of miscarriage or are experiencing difficult pregnancies may need extra bed rest. This usually means taking a leave of absence or quitting your job. Your health care professional can advise you about how long you will need to be absent from work.

Third, certain types of jobs create health risks for the developing fetus and/or the mother. For example, radiation exposure is dangerous to a developing fetus, so dental hygienists and assistants, X-ray technicians, and some nurses and doctors need to take extra precautions during pregnancy to eliminate this worry. Exposure to anesthesia gases used in operating rooms has also been shown to be a cause of miscarriage and pregnancy problems. There are many other toxic substances that may be encountered on the job (or in the home or the community) that can affect pregnancy. Toxic chemicals can also cause problems for pregnant women if a husband or another member of the household

Many women continue to work throughout pregnancy.

works with them and brings home contaminated clothing, tools, or other items.

Health during Pregnancy

Nutrition

Pregnant women need more protein, vitamins, minerals, and total calories than do nonpregnant women. Recommended diets vary in the total number of calories recommended (2,000 to 2,400 calories), but experts are in agreement about the importance of including adequate amounts of all the basic food groups. A woman's height, weight, body type, and level of physical activity will affect her total need for calories. In addition, health problems such as diabetes must be taken into account in planning a diet for pregnancy. Your prenatal care provider is the best source of advice about your specific dietary needs during pregnancy.

A diet of 2,000 to 2,400 calories a day (more on physically active days) includes the following:

Milk
Meat group
Vegetables
Fruit
Bread and other starches
Fats and oils

Unlimited amounts of very low calorie foods (free foods) such as salad greens, radishes, and sprouts are allowed, along with herbal teas, water, and other noncaloric drinks. It should be noted that diet soft drinks contain chemicals (including caffeine) which may be undesirable for pregnant women. Check with your prenatal care provider regarding limitations on these beverages.

A sample menu pattern is given in Table 6-1. Women who do not need to watch their weight can eat more, but is important to make sure that servings from all the basic food groups are included. Avoiding unnecessary and low-nutrition foods such as sweets and snack foods is also a good idea, since these foods cannot provide the substances needed for healthy pregnancy.

Various minerals, such as iron and calcium, are also especially important during pregnancy. They help ward off fatigue, muscle cramps, anemia, and nerve pains. A vitamin and mineral supplement may be needed to make sure that the nutritional demands of both the growing fetus and the mother's body are met. Your health care provider can recommend the right ones. Pregnant women should be careful about taking extra vitamins and minerals that are not prescribed by their health care provider, because it is possible for certain vi

Good nutrition is extremely important during pregnancy.

TABLE 6–1 Sample Menu Pattern

BREAKFAST
Orange juice
Soft cooked egg
Whole wheat toast
Oatmeal
Margarine
Milk

LUNCH
Roast turkey
Tomato slices
Lettuce salad with salad dressing
Whole wheat bread
Vegetable soup
Mayonnaise
Apple
Milk

DINNER
Broiled fish
Green beans
Lettuce salad
Potatoes
Roll
Margarine
French dressing
Pineapple
Milk

BEDTIME
Whole wheat bread
Lean roast beef
Mayonnaise
Milk

tamins to build up in the body and become toxic if they are taken in very large quantities.

Weight

Because many women are concerned about their weight, they may worry that pregnancy will cause them to become permanently fat. It is possible to gain so much weight during pregnancy that it is difficult to get back to prepregnancy weight, but if a woman stays within the recommended weight gain of 25 to 30 pounds, she will not have much more than 10 pounds to lose after the baby is born. It is also possible to gain *too little* weight, thereby endangering the fetus's health. The woman who gains far less or more than the recommended 25 to 30 pounds has a higher risk of complications for herself and/or the fetus.

Exercise

Exercise can help to keep weight to a manageable level, can be enjoyable, and contributes to general health and feelings of well-being. If you already exercise regularly, there is usually no reason to stop during pregnancy. Most women can even start a new exercise program during pregnancy, but if this is your plan, check with your prenatal care provider first. Many communities offer special exercise, dance, or aerobics classes for pregnant women (check, for example, with your local YM/YWCA or recreation center). Swimming is also good exercise and has the added advantage of making you temporarily "weightless." And, of course, there's always walking.

You may find that, as your pregnancy progresses, you have to modify your exercise program. Your abdomen may actually get in your way, and the increased weight can increase the risk of injury from high-impact exercises like aerobics. Also, as your abdomen grows, your center of gravity shifts; it may become difficult to maintain your balance during certain forms of exercise. In addition, the pressure of the uterus on the diaphragm can cause shortness of breath. If exercising causes you to ache, feel tired, or experience any abdominal pain, stop until you check with your prenatal care provider.

Drugs

When we hear the word *drugs*, many of us automatically think of illegal drugs such as marijuana, cocaine, or heroin. But there are many kinds of drugs. Some, like aspirin, antacids, decongestants, or laxatives, are used so commonly that we may not think of them as potentially dangerous. Others are prescribed by doctors, so we feel safe using them under medical supervision. Still others, especially alcohol and nicotine, are a part of everyday social life. We may think of them as potentially harmful, but we often don't think of them as "drugs." Yet all of these substances are drugs, and all of them can be dangerous to a developing fetus.

It is tempting to think that nature "protects" a fetus from drugs that the mother takes. Indeed, the placenta does provide some protection by filtering some dangerous substances out of the mother's blood before it reaches the fetus. But this placental barrier is limited. Many drugs cross it and reach the fetus. This is dangerous because as the fetus develops, its organs (especially the brain) are particularly vulnerable to damage from drugs. Drugs that seem harmless to an adult can be very dangerous to a fetus.

Alcohol Many cities and states have recently passed laws that require bar owners to post signs warning that drinking alcohol can be dangerous if you are pregnant. There is good reason for this.

Since 1977, the federal Food and Drug Administration (FDA) has warned that there is scientific evidence linking alcohol to fetal deformities. It is estimated that between 78 and 690 babies out of each 1,000 babies born to women who are alcoholics suffer from defects or health problems caused by the mother's alcohol intake. And a woman does not need to be an alcoholic to drink enough to cause problems for the fetus.

The effects of alcohol are dose-related: the more a pregnant woman drinks, the greater the risk to her baby. No safe level of alcohol consumption has been established, and it is not clear whether small amounts of alcohol can cause problems. The best advice for pregnant women is not to drink at all during pregnancy.

If you are pregnant and have been drinking, stopping now reduces the risk. Some of the problems associated with alcohol are much less likely to appear if the mother does not drink during the last three months of pregnancy.

Smoking Many of us recognize that women should not use drugs extensively during pregnancy. But most of us do not think of cigarettes as a drug (although they do contain an addictive drug—*nicotine*). We realize they present a health risk—but to our lungs, not to a developing fetus.

In fact, cigarette smoking during pregnancy is dangerous. The clearest negative effect is on the fetus's growth. Babies born to smoking women

WHY START A LIFE UNDER A CLOUD?

Smoking is harmful to your baby's health. Quit for both of you. For help call your American Cancer Society.

weigh an average of half a pound less than those born to women who don't smoke! They are also shorter and have smaller heads. These effects may be long-term and perhaps even permanent. Cigarette smoking is also suspected of causing learning disorders and possibly mental retardation.

Cigarette smoking also seems to increase the likelihood of miscarriage and of fetal and infant death. This is particularly true in the cases of women whose pregnancies are already high-risk because of other factors (such as high blood pressure).

Little is known about the effects of using other forms of tobacco, such as chewing tobacco. Since the same substances are involved, however, we can assume that other forms of tobacco may also harm the fetus.

Caffeine   Many different foods and medications contain caffeine, and many Americans consume substantial amounts of caffeine daily. Coffee, of course, is a major source of caffeine. So are many soft drinks, especially colas. Chocolate and tea contain caffeine. Some pain-killing medications also contain caffeine, as do nonprescription drugs that help one stay awake. There are also prescription drugs, such as Cafergot, which is used to treat migraine headaches, that contain caffeine.

In 1980 the FDA issued a warning stating that pregnant women should avoid high levels of caffeine because it might cause fetal deformities. More recent studies suggest that caffeine may actually be relatively safe for pregnant women unless they are also smokers. Until we have more information, it is probably best to avoid large amounts of caffeine. An occasional chocolate bar, cup of tea, or cola drink is probably all right, but drinking several cups of coffee a day is probably not a good idea.

Medicines   A wide variety of medicines can have negative effects if taken during pregnancy. Aspirin may cause a lack of blood-clotting ability for both the baby and the mother during the delivery. This is particularly true if it is taken in large doses during the last trimester. Some antihistamines may cause deformities. Streptomycin, a commonly prescribed antibiotic, may cause hearing loss. Another common antibiotic, tetracycline, is associated with permanent discoloration of the teeth (both the baby teeth and the permanent teeth are formed before birth). Often, the problems of babies born to diabetics are more the result of the drugs the mother must take than of the diabetes itself. Medications for epilepsy also can cause serious damage to the fetus (although the problems caused by *not* taking the drugs could be even more harmful to the pregnancy).

This is only a partial list of the medicines that can harm the developing fetus. The point is: *a pregnant woman should not take any medicines at all unless they are prescribed or recommended by a health care provider who knows she is pregnant.* Drugs that seem harmless can lead to tragic consequences.

Certain medical treatments can also cause damage. One that deserves special mention is X-rays. X-rays, particularly of the back or abdomen, can cause miscarriage and fetal deformities. They are particularly dangerous during the first six weeks of pregnancy, when all the major organ systems are forming. Do not submit to any type of X-rays if you suspect or know you are pregnant, unless you have told the doctor and have discussed the risks. If X-rays are necessary, always be sure the technician provides you with a lead apron to cover the abdomen. (Ultrasound tests do not use radiation and do not cause the same risks.)

Illegal drugs   Little is known about the effects of most illegal drugs on a developing fetus. Both heroin and methadone addictions are known to be extremely dangerous and sometimes fatal to the baby. Like alcohol, these drugs are associated with growth problems. Babies born to addicts are themselves addicted to drugs and must go through withdrawal from the drug, just as an adult must do. This is very stressful and unpleasant, and can be dangerous. The effects of marijuana, cocaine, PCP, and other street drugs on pregnancy and on the developing fetus are not known. It is generally accepted, however, that these drugs are probably dangerous to the fetus and should be avoided by pregnant women.

In addition to the effects of illegal drugs themselves, it is important to note that women who use needles to take drugs and who share the needles with others run the risk of becoming infected with the AIDS virus, which can be fatal to both mother and baby. Women who have sexual relations with men who share needles are also likely to be exposed to the infection. (For more on AIDS, see Chapter 15.)

Other Risk Factors

It is important to be aware of the risks of coming in contact with toxic chemicals in the environment. Some substances, such as lead, have long been known to have negative effects on the reproductive process, but there are also thousands of chemicals in common use in the home, in the workplace, and in agriculture that we know little about. Many have been shown to be harmful to animals and are suspected of being harmful to human reproduction as well. Most chemicals cross the placenta, and some can cause minor or major damage to the fetus. Women who work in certain occupations, such as laboratory work, anesthesia, and soldering, are known to have higher rates of miscarriage and malformed babies than other women.

The following are a few basic precautions that pregnant women can take to reduce the risk of contact with toxic chemicals:

AT HOME

1. Avoid using or having contact with strong chemicals in the home (such as pesticides and solvents).
2. Wash all fruits and vegetables carefully.
3. Avoid contact with the clothing of other family members who work with chemicals.
4. Drink bottled water during pregnancy if the local tap water is known to contain harmful chemicals.
5. Avoid outdoor areas where pesticides have recently been used.

AT WORK

1. Ask supervisors about substances you may be exposed to on the job.
2. Be aware of the high-risk occupations (for example, hair dressing and cosmetology, health care, laundry and dry cleaning, in addition to the occupations mentioned above).
3. Consider trying to transfer temporarily to work that does not involve chemicals.
4. Consider taking maternity leave as early as possible if you are in a high-risk job.

Large companies usually have a health worker who can provide helpful information. If there is a union, this may also be a good source. Local public health departments can also give guidance about toxic substances in the environment.

Prenatal Tests

Until a few years ago, parents had to wait until their child was born to find out whether the baby was healthy. For those parents who knew they were carriers of genetic disorders, this meant a difficult nine months of waiting. Many such couples chose not to have children. Older women also had cause for worry, since women over 40 have a much greater chance of giving birth to a child with Down's syndrome or other problems.

In recent years, however, several methods have been developed that enable physicians to diagnose genetic defects and some health problems in the developing fetus before birth. These methods include amniocentesis, fetoscopy, the alphafetal

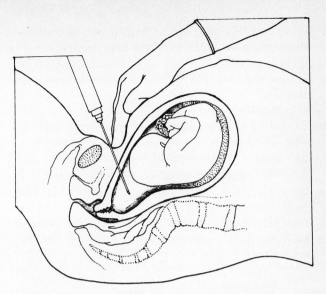

FIGURE 6–3. *The amniocentesis procedure.*

protein (AFP) test, the sonogram, and chorionic villus sampling.

Amniocentesis

In amniocentesis, a needle is inserted through the woman's abdomen into the amniotic sac, the "bag of waters," surrounding the fetus (Figure 6–3). The placement of the needle is guided by a sonogram (ultrasound picture) so that there is little risk of the needle injuring the fetus. A small amount of amniotic fluid is withdrawn. This fluid contains some cells shed by the fetus, and these cells contain information about the genetic makeup of the fetus, as well as the sex. The cells are then examined through a process called *karotyping*, which allows evaluation of the individual chromosome pairs. Doing this permits the identification of chromosomal abnormalities (such as Down's syndrome, which causes mental retardation and certain physical health problems). The biochemical composition of the fluid can also be analyzed. This allows the diagnosis of various metabolic disorders such as Tay-Sachs (a fatal genetic disorder most commonly found in people of eastern European Jewish descent). In all, nearly 100 genetic disorders can be diagnosed through amniocentesis. However, there are many other birth defects, such as cerebral palsy, which are not genetically caused and cannot be diagnosed by anmiocentesis.

Amniocentesis can be done at a hospital on an outpatient basis or in the doctor's office, and takes only about 15 to 30 minutes to perform. It is nearly painless. However, it takes 10 days to a month for the results of the tests to be ready. Since amniocentesis cannot be performed until the woman is at least 14 weeks pregnant, this means the woman may be four and a half months pregnant, and may have felt the fetus move, by the time the results are available. If the test results show a serious problem, the fact that the pregnancy is so advanced can make it difficult for women to choose abortion.

Amniocentesis carries a small risk of complications, and in 1 in 200 cases may cause miscarriage or infection. There is also a small risk of injury to the fetus. Amniocentesis seems to be quite safe for both expectant mother and fetus when it is performed by trained and experienced doctors and technicians. However, it is not recommended except for medical reasons (that is, it is not recommended just for the purpose of finding out the baby's sex).

Sonogram

Sonograms (ultrasound) create a "picture" of the fetus. Sound waves, transmitted through the woman's abdomen, are "bounced off" the fetus (Figure 6–4). Medically, sonograms are useful in exploring the fetus's position just before birth. Sonograms are also used to gauge the size of the fetus. The availability of such information allows the physician to decide the safest way and time to deliver the baby. Sonograms can also be used to diagnose many neurological, cardiac, and limb deformities. Depending on the age and position of the fetus, sonograms are sometimes detailed enough to show the fetus's sex. Sonograms are painless and appear to be harmless, but information on the long-term effects on the mother-to-be and the fetus is not yet available (although no negative effects have been seen in children born to mothers who had several sonograms during pregnancy).

Fetoscopy

A less commonly used technique for prenatal diagnosis is **fetoscopy.** In this method, an instrument called a *fetoscope* (or *endoscope*) is inserted through the abdomen and the wall of the uterus into the amniotic sac. It can then be used to look directly at portions of the developing fetus, to obtain fetal blood or tissue samples, or to administer medication. Fetoscopy enables the physician to confirm the presence of malformations such as spina bifida and to diagnose sickle-cell anemia and other blood disorders.

Fetoscopy creates some risk to the pregnancy, and can be the cause of complications. It is used only when the importance of the information to be gained or the treatment to be given is thought to be greater than the risk of complications. As with amniocentesis, it should be performed only by trained and experienced specialists.

AFP Testing

AFP (alphafetal protein) testing is another prenatal diagnostic technique. This is a simple test of the mother's blood used to identify the possible presence of *anencephaly* (a birth defect involving the lack of a developed brain) and *spina bifida* (a defect in which bone and tissue do not close over the base of the spine). The test is usually performed at 16 to 19 weeks of pregnancy and is routinely offered to pregnant women. Some states require that the test be offered to all pregnant women. The test carries no physical risk to either the mother or the fetus. However, it is associated with a relatively

FIGURE 6–4. *The sonogram (ultrasound) procedure.*

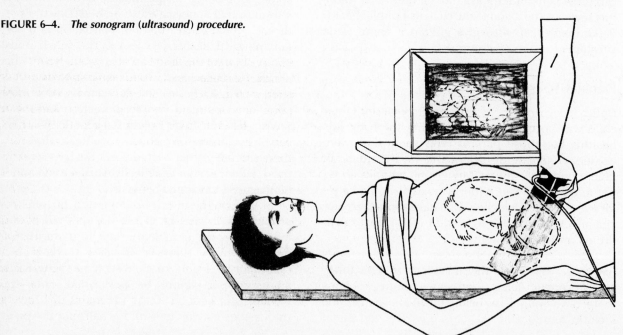

high rate of false positives. This means that the AFP level registers high for reasons other than the presence of anencephaly or spina bifida. The AFP level may be high, for example, because the fetus is older than the doctor thought or because there is more than one fetus in the uterus. Additional tests such as amniocentesis and sonogram can help to pinpoint the cause of a high AFP reading.

Chorionic Villus Sampling

A test that is still in the experimental stage but is being used at some university medical centers is chorionic villus sampling. It provides genetic information about the baby (similar to amniocentesis) by taking a small sample of the surface of the placenta. The sample is obtained by inserting a thin catheter through the cervix or through the abdomen (using ultrasound). The big advantage of chorionic villus sampling is that it can be done early enough in the pregnancy that an abortion can be done quite easily if the fetus is found to have serious defects. This test is not yet widely available, however, and it has a higher risk of complications than amniocentesis.

When Defects Are Found

What can the parents do if prenatal tests indicate the fetus is not healthy? In most cases, choices are limited to continuing the pregnancy or ending it by therapeutic abortion. For this reason, future parents who feel they could not consider abortion under any circumstances sometimes choose not to do prenatal testing for inherited defects. Others like to have the information so they can plan ahead for a healthy or a handicapped child. Deciding on abortion for a defective fetus is difficult, especially if the woman is quite far along in pregnancy when the tests are completed. In making such a decision, parents need to consider the severity of the problem, how treatable the problem is, and how they would cope with a handicapped child. (For more information on abortion, see Chapter 11.)

In some cases, the defect may be treatable and may simply require specialized care after birth. Prenatal diagnosis makes planning for such care easier. Prenatal treatment (treatment before birth) is also sometimes possible. For example, doctors have successfully performed surgery on hydrocephalic fetuses (fetuses that have excess fluid in the brain area, potentially a cause of severe brain injury) while they were in the uterus. In the future, prenatal treatment is expected to become more common and may be extended to include many disorders.

Major and Minor Health Problems during Pregnancy

Common Complaints

Morning sickness A large number (but fewer than half) of all pregnant women experience nausea and vomiting at some point during pregnancy. This is called morning sickness, although it may occur at any time of the day or night. Morning sickness is most common during the first three months of pregnancy, but some women have problems with it in the second and third trimesters as well. The causes of morning sickness are unknown, but many experts believe that pregnancy-related changes in hormone levels are often to blame. For most women, morning sickness is only a minor inconvenience, but for a few it can be so severe that hospitalization is needed.

Morning sickness is best treated by natural remedies such as changes in diet, particularly since medications should be avoided whenever possible during pregnancy. Eating frequent small meals, having a snack before getting out of bed in the morning, and avoiding heavy, greasy, and spicy foods are all popular ways to reduce the symptoms. Some herb teas are said to be helpful. Rest, fresh air, and proper nutrition are also important. Each woman has to find the techniques that work best for her, but she should also seek the advice of her prenatal caregiver, particularly if she is considering using herbal teas or special vitamin supplements to combat the problem. No medications, either prescription or over-the-counter, should be used without consultation with the care provider.

Tiredness Fatigue is often a problem during the first few months of pregnancy, and again toward the end. Pregnancy does put extra stress on

Women tire easily during pregnancy and need extra rest.

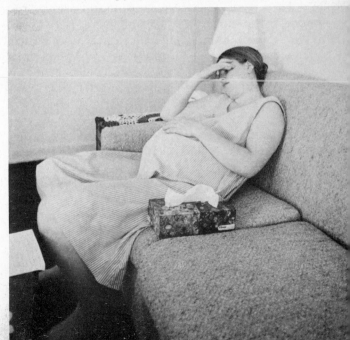

the body, and in the final months the bulk of extra weight can be tiring. In addition, some women have difficulty sleeping during the final weeks. Mothers-to-be need to allow themselves extra hours of sleep and a nap or rest period during the day as a normal part of good self-care during pregnancy.

Stretch marks The increased size of the abdomen stretches the skin, and many women develop stretch marks—vertical reddish lines along the abdomen and sometimes on the breasts and hips. The chances of getting stretch marks seem to be partly inherited, but many women believe the number and size of stretch marks can be reduced by keeping the skin moist with hand or body lotion. Fortunately, stretch marks shrink, fade, and become much less noticeable after the baby is born.

Frequent urination Most women find they need to urinate much more frequently when they are pregnant, and the frequent visits to the bathroom can be inconvenient. A combination of body changes is responsible. The most obvious is the pressure of the uterus on the bladder late in pregnancy, which leaves little room for urine to collect. But earlier in pregnancy, hormonal changes cause the body to retain more fluid and to process fluids more quickly, so the volume of urine produced is larger.

Reducing fluids such as water and juice to cut down on urination is not wise, and could lead to health problems such as urinary tract infection. It is better to plan on frequent bathroom stops as a normal part of pregnancy. Kegel's exercises (see Chapter 12, page 273) can help strengthen muscles around the urethra if leakage or partial loss of bladder control develops toward the end of pregnancy.

Constipation Constipation is a very common complaint of pregnancy. High levels of the hormone progesterone during pregnancy cause increased absorption of fluids out of the intestines, relaxation of the intestinal walls (creating more space in the intestines), and reduction in the automatic muscle contractions that normally push waste along through the system. These changes, combined with the pressure of the expanding uterus in the lower abdomen, often make it difficult for the bowels to move normally. In addition, if the pregnancy has caused the woman to stop exercising or change her diet, these shifts may also contribute to constipation.

The best remedies for constipation are to increase fluid intake (water or fruit juice) and to exercise more. Changes in diet to increase the amount of high-fiber foods and cooked fruit such as prunes are also helpful. No laxatives should be taken without the advice of your prenatal care provider, as some can cause problems for pregnant women.

Varicose veins Varicose veins (protruding, swollen veins) frequently develop and cause aching in the legs during the third trimester. They appear to develop partly because of the action of hormones, and partly because of the pressure of the uterus on veins in the pelvis that drain blood from the legs. Overweight women are more likely to have a problem, and the tendency for varicose veins can also be inherited.

Keeping the feet propped up higher than the heart whenever possible, exercising the legs, avoiding clothing such as girdles or garters that fit tightly around the legs, and wearing support hose can reduce the symptoms. If support hose are put on in the morning before getting out of bed, the pooling of blood in the legs can be kept to a minimum.

Hemorrhoids Hemorrhoids are varicose veins located in and around the anus. They are caused by the hormonal changes of pregnancy, which relax the walls of the blood vessels and intestines, and by pressure. The weight of the uterus creates pressure in the area, as does straining to have a bowel movement when constipated. It is important to try to avoid constipation and straining, which make hemorrhoids worse. In addition, reducing pressure and blood congestion in the area by lying down and propping up the legs and hips will help. Ask your health care provider for advice before using hemorrhoid ointments or other remedies.

Leg cramps Some women experience leg cramps, which are sharp pains in the calf muscle. This problem is frequently caused by a deficiency of potassium, calcium, or salt in the body and can be resolved by eating foods that provide enough of these substances. If cramps develop, standing with your foot flat against the floor, straightening the leg and pulling the toes toward you, or using a heating pad wrapped around the leg may help.

Sleeping problems Some women have difficulty sleeping, particularly late in pregnancy when it can be difficult to get comfortable. If a woman gives herself enough hours rest, sleeping or awake, occasional sleeplessness should not be a problem. Sleeping on your side is usually most comfortable, and the left side is particularly recommended because that position allows greatest blood flow to the uterus and fetus. Placing a pillow under the uterus while in this position helps provide support. Lying on your back decreases the blood flow to the uterus and may make breathing more difficult because of pressure on the lungs.

Resting or sleeping on the left side is considered best for the fetus.

The usual techniques for avoiding insomnia may help, such as drinking warm milk at bedtime, taking a warm bath, and avoiding TV shows or bedtime reading that is exciting or upsetting. Sleeping pills (including nonprescription sleep aids) should be avoided; talk with your prenatal care provider before taking any medication.

Dental problems   The teeth and gums are affected by pregnancy in several ways. First, the developing fetus absorbs a great deal of calcium. If the woman's diet does not include enough calcium, the mineral will be absorbed from her teeth, leaving them brittle and at risk of decay. Second, the changes in hormone levels due to pregnancy can cause the gums to swell, so that they bleed easily. The swelling may also create tiny gaps between the gums and teeth, increasing the chances of gum infection and tooth decay.

Breathing difficulties   The uterus is so large toward the end of pregnancy that it may take up space needed for comfortable breathing. There may be pressure on the lungs and diaphragm (the muscle that pushes air in and out), making breathing difficult. Exercise may have to be limited, and sleep may be affected. The best way to rest or sleep may be propped up on pillows to reduce the pressure of the uterus on the lungs and diaphragm.

Indigestion   The combination of hormonal effects and pressure of the enlarged uterus may create frequent heartburn and indigestion. Avoiding smoking, coffee, and foods that cause problems may help. Drinking carbonated beverages may also bring relief. If antacids are needed, ask your health care provider for a recommendation.

Miscarriage

What is it?   **Miscarriages,** also known as **spontaneous abortions,** are the natural termination of a pregnancy before the fetus could have survived outside the uterus. About 20 percent of all pregnancies are commonly believed to be miscarried (although estimates range from 10 to 50 percent of all

pregnancies). Most miscarriages (85 percent) occur within the first three months of the pregnancy, and they are most likely to occur during the second month. Miscarriages are thought to be nature's way of ending seriously defective pregnancies, which could not have produced a normal, living baby. But miscarriages can also be caused by certain health problems of the mother. Miscarriages are not commonly caused by emotional shock or physical trauma such as accidents or injuries (unless the trauma is sufficient to cause internal bleeding).

What are the signs and symptoms?   The symptoms of miscarriage are spotting or bleeding and abdominal pain and/or cramping. It is not uncommon to have these symptoms early in pregnancy, and many times a miscarriage does not occur. The longer the bleeding and pain persists, however, the more likely a miscarriage becomes. During a miscarriage the embryo, the placenta, and other material related to the pregnancy will be expelled through the cervix (the opening of the uterus into the vagina) and the vagina. If this happens early in the pregnancy, the material will look like large blood clots, but in a late miscarriage a fully formed fetus may be expelled.

What is the treatment?   If a woman starts to miscarry early in the pregnancy (the first four months or so), medical personnel usually do not try to prevent the miscarriage.

It is important to note that spotting or bleeding does not always mean that a miscarriage will occur. Sometimes bed rest for a day or two stops the bleeding. In some cases the bleeding is due to an irritation of the cervix, which does not affect the pregnancy.

Any bleeding during pregnancy should be checked by your prenatal care provider in order to determine whether or not a miscarriage is in progress. A miscarriage is not definite until the cervix opens so that the fetus can be expelled.

Once the cervix opens, there will be considerable bleeding and cramping, similar to labor pains but milder. The fetus and its support systems may be expelled intact, or they may be destroyed during the miscarriage. After the miscarriage, a **D & C (dilation and curettage;** see Chapter 12, pages 277–279) procedure may be performed. This involves scraping the uterine wall to ensure that the miscarriage is complete. It is usually done in an operating room and may be done under general anesthesia (the woman is not awake). If a D & C is not done, parts of the placenta or other material may remain in the uterus, and this can cause prolonged bleeding or infection.

If a woman is about to have a miscarriage (if she is experiencing bleeding and cramping), it is probably wise for her to go to a hospital, for several reasons. First, once the miscarriage is underway, she can be given pain medication. Second, a D & C can be performed afterwards if necessary. Third, a major way of determining the cause of the miscarriage (in pregnancies of 12 weeks or more) is to examine the miscarried fetus. If the woman miscarries at home, she must collect the fetus and take it to her physician to have the appropriate tests done. Needless to say, this can be very upsetting. If a woman miscarries at home, she should see her doctor immediately afterward to make sure she is all right. If she continues to bleed, she may need a D & C.

What are the aftereffects? In most cases miscarriage has no physical aftereffects, and there is no reason to believe that a woman who has miscarried will have an increased chance of problems with future pregnancies. Many people, however, are not aware that miscarriages can be psychologically stressful to the couple. In fact, miscarriages often produce the same feeling of helplessness, grief, and confusion that any death brings. The parents may blame themselves or each other. They may be afraid to "try again." These feelings should be discussed and resolved, and some couples may wish to seek outside help to deal with them. Some communities have support groups for couples who have miscarried. Check with your local hospital or United Way to see if your community has one. If not, counseling help for both individuals and couples can be found through local mental health or social service organizations.

Ectopic Pregnancy

What is it? In most pregnancies, the fertilized egg moves down the Fallopian tube into the uterus and implants itself into the endometrium (lining of the uterus; see Chapter 2, page 26). In rare cases, however, the fertilized egg implants itself somewhere else. Such pregnancies are called **ectopic pregnancies.** Other names for these pregnancies are based on the place of implantation: **tubal pregnancy** (Fallopian tube implantation), **abdominal pregnancy** (abdominal cavity implantation), **cervical pregnancy** (cervix implantation), and **ovarian pregnancy** (ovary implantation).

Ectopic pregnancies occur in about 1 of every 200 pregnancies. They are located in the Fallopian tubes 95 percent of the time. Ectopic pregnancies are fatal to the embryo, which cannot develop outside the uterus, and are very dangerous for the mother. *Ectopic pregnancies are always dangerous. Left untreated, they may cause rupturing of blood vessels, internal bleeding, and possibly death to the pregnant woman.* Tubal pregnancies cannot be carried to term. Either the embryo will be miscarried and expelled, or it will grow until the Fallopian tube bursts, endangering the life of the mother.

Ectopic pregnancies have become more common in the United States in recent years. This is thought to be related to higher rates of sexually transmitted diseases and other pelvic infections. These infections cause scar tissue to form in the tubes, which may interfere with the passage of the embryo into the uterus.

What are the signs and symptoms? If the Fallopian tube bursts, the woman will experience considerable abdominal pain, and possibly vaginal bleeding as well. She may also develop severe internal bleeding, but may not be aware of it. *Severe abdominal pain early in pregnancy is the major symptom of ectopic pregnancy. If a woman develops this symptom, she should seek medical help immediately.* All vaginal bleeding early in pregnancy should also be reported, since it could be a symptom of ectopic pregnancy as well. The major danger of a ruptured tube is the internal bleeding.

What is the treatment? A ruptured Fallopian tube or other complications of ectopic pregnancy require emergency hospitalization and surgery. The pregnancy is lost, and the Fallopian tube may be so damaged that it cannot be saved.

Ectopic pregnancy is dangerous, partly because it is so difficult to diagnose. The symptoms are hard to recognize, and it is easily confused with other disorders such as appendicitis. There is a high rate of error in diagnosis; in about 25 percent of cases where a woman is operated on for ectopic pregnancy, this turns out not to be the problem.

Occasionally a tubal pregnancy will be diagnosed prior to either a miscarriage or the tube bursting. In such cases, an abortion or surgery can decrease the risk to the woman.

What are the aftereffects? If the woman requires surgery, there will be several weeks of recovery time. In addition, the couple may experience the same feelings of grief and loss that can develop with miscarriage. Further, if the Fallopian tube is destroyed, the woman may find it more difficult to get pregnant again (she may be infertile, if her other Fallopian tube is not functioning properly).

Premature Labor

What is it? Painless contractions of abdominal muscles that occur before the thirty-seventh week of pregnancy may be a sign of the beginning of premature labor. Around 6 to 8 percent of all babies are born prematurely (before 37 weeks), but

Premature labor brings some couples to the hospital early.

probably around 15 percent of all women experience premature labor. In about half of these cases the labor stops if the woman rests and avoids physical activity. Prompt medical treatment can stop premature labor in many other cases. Premature birth puts the infant at higher risk for a number of health problems. So, unless there are problems with the pregnancy, it is desirable to stop premature labor if possible. Poor diet, stress, and other complications of pregnancy seem to increase the chances of premature labor.

What are the signs and symptoms? The contractions of premature labor are often described as similar to a tightening or hardening of abdominal muscles. If they are irregular and go away with rest, they are probably harmless Braxton-Hicks contractions (which seem to be a preparation for future labor). But if they are regular and do not go away when resting, it is important to seek advice from your prenatal caregiver. Additional symptoms of premature labor are low abdominal pain, a backache similar to menstrual cramps, and a mucous-like vaginal discharge.

What is the treatment? Bed rest is effective in about half of all cases. If this does not work, hospitalization and treatment with drugs can often stop the labor. If the labor is stopped, however, there may be health risks to the mother and to the fetus, so the risks and benefits must be weighed. In certain situations, physicians do not try to stop the premature labor but, instead, prepare for the birth of a premature infant. These cases include situations (such as severe high blood pressure, heart disease, or kidney failure) where continuing the pregnancy would be more harmful to the mother or the fetus than the birth of the baby prematurely.

If the mother is going to give birth prematurely, she may need to be admitted to a hospital that has special facilities to care for premature babies. If she delivers at a hospital that does not have these facilities, there is a chance that the baby might need to be moved shortly after birth to a facility that offers neonatal intensive care.

What are the aftereffects? If premature labor is stopped, and the birth is delayed until the fetus is fully developed, there should be no aftereffects. The use of drugs to stop the labor may create a small risk of future complications for the mother and/or the infant.

If the infant is born prematurely, there is a higher risk of a number of health problems, and the infant is likely to need special medical care. (More details on premature births are given later in this chapter.) In general, the closer to the delivery date the baby is born, the better the chances of survival and good health.

Blood Incompatibility (Rh Factor)

What is it? Rh factor incompatibility is a complication that develops when the mother is one of the 15 percent of the population (only 5 percent of the black population) who have Rh negative blood. Such people are missing the Rh factor, a protein-like substance in the red blood cells. This is a normal condition and does not cause any health problems except for certain pregnant women and their fetuses.

If the fetus is Rh positive (has the Rh factor) and the mother is Rh negative, the mother's body may develop an immune system reaction to the substance in the fetus's blood. Her system attacks the fetus and can cause severe anemia and other problems. If this situation develops and is not treated, the infant born will have only a 70 percent chance of survival. (A similar, but far less serious, type of problem can develop in mothers who have type O blood and are carrying a fetus with another blood type.) Damage to infants caused by Rh incompatibility is much less common in the United States than it used to be, because an injection is now available that can prevent problems from developing.

What are the signs and symptoms? Rh incompatibility does not produce noticeable signs or symptoms in the pregnant woman or the fetus. The potential for a problem is identified when a pregnant woman is found to have Rh negative blood. Prenatal caregivers routinely check women for this. When a woman is found to be Rh negative, information about the father's blood is also needed. If

A doctor explains how RH factor incompatibility can cause problems for the expected baby.

the father is also Rh negative, there is no risk of an Rh incompatibility problem.

Prenatal blood tests can also show if the woman already has antibodies to Rh positive blood (developed during an earlier pregnancy). Rh incompatibility is less likely to be harmful during the first pregnancy, since the woman does not usually develop antibodies until she is exposed to fetal blood during delivery. In a second pregnancy, the antibodies may be present from the outset and can cause serious damage.

If not treated early, Rh incompatibility can be fatal to the infant or cause severe brain damage in the worst cases. More commonly, the infant may suffer from anemia and/or jaundice and may require blood transfusions.

What is the treatment? The best treatment for Rh incompatibility is preventive. This is one reason that early prenatal care is so important. A drug called RhoGam is available, which, if given to the woman during pregnancy and after delivery, can prevent her system from developing the harmful antibodies. Thus, she will not harm the fetus she is carrying, and will not develop the antibodies that would be harmful to a future fetus. RhoGam treatment may also be needed after miscarriage, abortion, or ectopic pregnancy for the same reason.

Once a woman develops the antibodies, they are permanent, and all future pregnancies will be at risk. The most effective treatments in these cases

are blood transfusions for the fetus while it is still in the uterus, and early (premature) delivery.

What are the aftereffects? If the woman is treated preventively and never develops the antibodies to the Rh factor, there should be no aftereffects for her or the infant. But she will need to be treated again during each additional pregnancy.

If the woman has developed the antibodies, all future pregnancies will be risky and will require special medical care.

Anemia

What is it? Anemia means either a lower number of red blood cells in the blood than is needed, or a lack of hemoglobin in the cells, or both. Pregnant women are especially at risk of anemia because of the rapid increase of blood volume to supply the fetus, and the increased burden on their systems caused by the nutritional needs of the fetus. Other causes of anemia include an unbalanced diet, loss of a large amount of blood, infections, or inherited blood diseases such as sickle-cell anemia.

What are the signs and symptoms? The symptoms of anemia are pale skin, a feeling of exhaustion, and a tendency to catch infections. Shortness of breath and a fluttering sensation of the heart after exercise are also signs of the condition.

What is the treatment? The treatment depends on the cause. In most cases, iron supplements and special diets are used to build up the blood. If the anemia is due to blood loss, transfusions may be needed in severe cases. If the problem is an inherited blood disease, the treatment is more complicated.

What are the aftereffects? If the anemia is not severe, there should be no negative aftereffects for mother or infant. In general, the fetus is not affected by the mother's anemia, but the increased demands the fetus puts on the mother's body may leave an anemic mother in a weakened condition. She may be more likely to get infections and have other health problems during pregnancy and after birth.

Diabetes

What is it? Diabetes is a chronic disease in which the body is unable to process sugar properly, creating chemical imbalances in the blood and other systems. For most people, it can be managed by special diets and by injections of the drug *insulin*. But it is a lifelong disease, one that requires the diabetic to manage diet, exercise, and medication carefully to keep the body system in balance. If diabetes is not treated, or if the diabetic is not careful to keep her or his system in balance, there can be serious damage to health.

Pregnant women with diabetes have a higher risk of complications for themselves and for the baby than other women. Fortunately, if the condition is under control before the pregnancy begins, and if they receive good prenatal care, many problems can be avoided. But a diabetic woman who is pregnant can expect to have frequent visits to the doctor or clinic, many blood tests, and possibly a few days of hospitalization during her pregnancy.

Diabetes can develop at any time in childhood or adulthood. In addition, some women become diabetic during pregnancy. Diabetes is a problem in pregnancy because if the body chemistry is out of balance, it can create serious defects in the developing embryo or fetus. The most serious damage can be done in the first three months of pregnancy, when the major organ systems are developing. Diabetes also can also create problems for the pregnant woman and the fetus in the final weeks of pregnancy. Fortunately, with modern medical care, 95 percent of diabetic women deliver a healthy baby.

What are the signs and symptoms? Most pregnant women with diabetes are already aware that they have the disease and are under treatment. In a few cases, however, diabetes develops during pregnancy as a result of stress on the body created by the growing fetus. This is more likely to happen in the second or third trimester than in the first, and most prenatal care providers test all women for diabetes at 28 weeks of pregnancy. Women with high-risk pregnancies may be tested earlier. Prevention of possible birth defects and health problems caused by diabetes is another important reason for women to get early prenatal care.

Women with untreated diabetes are less likely to get pregnant than others. If they do get pregnant, they have a much higher risk than normal of serious problems for themselves and the fetus.

What is the treatment? The treatment of diabetes in pregnancy is focused on keeping the woman's body chemistry in balance so that it does not interfere with normal development of the fetus. Frequent checkups and blood tests (which are more sensitive than urine tests) are usually needed. If the woman is not able to keep her blood sugar stable, she may require hospitalization for a few days so her diet and medication can be carefully controlled, and additional tests can be done. She

may be referred to a perinatologist (an obstetrician specializing in high-risk pregnancies).

The final month of pregnancy has special risks for diabetic women, as the placenta may stop functioning prematurely. In this case the fetus must be delivered prematurely to save its life. Diabetic women are also more likely to have a very large baby, which may require a caesarean section. Hospitalization during the final weeks to watch for problems is not uncommon.

What are the aftereffects? In 95 percent of cases diabetic women in the United States give birth to healthy babies. But those who are untreated or have difficulty keeping their body chemistry in balance have increased risks of miscarriage, stillbirth (baby born dead), birth defects, and health problems for themselves.

Most of the women who develop diabetes during the pregnancy (women who were not previously diabetic) will not have the disease after they give birth. Approximately 3 percent will continue to be diabetic or will become diabetic later in life.

Toxemia (Preeclampsia)

What is it? Toxemia (also known as **preeclampsia** or **pregnancy-induced hypertension**) is a dangerous and potentially fatal complication of pregnancy involving high blood pressure and other problems. Women with a history of high blood pressure before pregnancy are at higher risk of toxemia than others, but any woman can develop it. The cause is unknown, but the condition develops in the second half of about 5 to 10 percent of all pregnancies, and is more common in first pregnancies. Toxemia is a reaction of the woman's body to her pregnancy, and it disappears as soon as she gives birth. If toxemia (preeclampsia) is not recognized or treated, it may progress (in about 1 in 200 cases) into *eclampsia*, which is a severe, life-threatening state involving convulsions and possible death.

What are the signs and symptoms? The symptoms of toxemia in pregnancy are high blood pressure, rapid weight gain due to retaining excess fluid in the body, and protein in the urine. Headaches and blurred vision may also develop. The symptoms are often not noticeable to the woman, and she may not be aware that a problem is developing. Fortunately, the blood pressure, urine, and weight gain checks given at each prenatal visit will identify toxemia.

In addition to women with a history of high blood pressure, certain other groups of women are more likely to develop toxemia than others. They

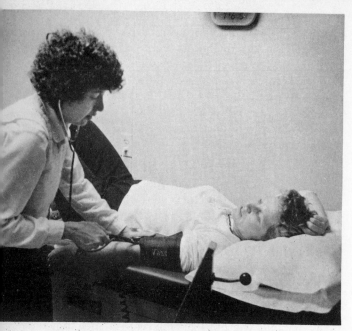

High blood pressure is the major sign of toxemia.

include women with first pregnancies; women who are over 30 or under 18; women who are pregnant with twins, triplets (or more); and women with diabetes or chronic kidney disease.

What is the treatment? There is no known way to prevent toxemia from developing. Diagnosis of the condition at the earliest possible date can usually prevent it from harming the pregnant woman or the fetus. The only cure for toxemia is to end the pregnancy. But in most cases frequent checkups, bed rest, and reducing stress will help to ensure that the blood pressure remains at a level that is not dangerous, so that the pregnancy can be continued until close to the due date. Hospitalization may be needed so that the woman's condition can be closely supervised, and if necessary sedatives or other medications can be given. If the blood pressure remains dangerously high, premature delivery of the fetus may be necessary. In addition, delivery by caesarean section may be necessary.

What are the aftereffects? In most cases, both the woman and her new baby suffer no permanent damage from toxemia. For women who do not receive prenatal care, however, toxemia can be life-threatening for both the mother-to-be and the fetus. Death is a possibility for both, as is a disabling stroke for the mother and other permanent damage to health.

Women who have toxemia with the first pregnancy are no more likely to have it with the second than are other women.

Twins and Other Multiple Pregnancies

About half of the time, multiple births are a surprise to the parents and the medical care providers. In the other cases they are suspected because of the woman's rapid weight gain or other signs. They are confirmed by hearing two (or more) heartbeats or by sonogram showing the two (or more) distinct fetuses.

Women carrying more than one fetus (usually twins, but in rare cases more) have a higher risk of several problems during pregnancy. This is probably because of the extra demands and stress placed on the body by the additional fetus. Women carrying twins are four times more likely to lose the pregnancy than are women with only one fetus. The risks become higher with each additional fetus in the uterus. The most common complications are first trimester bleeding, anemia, miscarriage, premature delivery, and low birth weight infants.

Carrying more than one fetus increases the woman's nutritional needs, her total weight gain, and her chances of developing anemia and toxemia. Her general discomfort may be greater as well because of the larger bulk and weight of the uterus.

For all these reasons, any woman carrying more than one fetus needs to be watched closely by her prenatal care provider to avoid developing problems that could be harmful to her or to the fetuses.

Infections and Viruses

There are a number of infections and viruses that can cause serious problems in pregnancy. **Cytomegalovirus** and **herpes** are two viruses that can be harmful to a fetus if the mother carries them in her body. Special arrangements such as a caesarean section may be needed to avoid infecting the fetus during passage through the vagina. These infections are described in Chapter 12, "Women's Health Problems."

Other infections such as rubella and toxoplasmosis can cause severe damage to the fetus if the mother contracts them during her pregnancy.

Rubella (German measles) Rubella is usually a mild infection, but if a pregnant woman becomes infected during the first three months of pregnancy, it causes severe deformities or defects in the fetus (for example, mental retardation, heart disease, and blindness) in 50 percent of cases. Some women consider abortion if they are certain they have had this infection early in pregnancy.

Rubella can be prevented through immunization, and around 80 percent of women of childbearing age have received the vaccine or are naturally immunized because they have had the disease in the past. Those who are not immune should get the vaccine at least three months before starting a pregnancy. To avoid problems for your own children in the future, it is important to make sure they are immunized against German measles while they are small.

Toxoplasmosis Toxoplasmosis is a mild infection caused by a microorganism found in raw meat and cat feces. If a woman becomes infected with toxoplasmosis during pregnancy, the organism will cross the placenta to the fetus and may cause birth defects. Around 25 percent of women of childbearing age have immunity to this disease because they have been exposed in the past, but the remainder are at risk of catching the infection during pregnancy. There is no vaccine to provide immunity from this disease. A pregnant woman can avoid exposure to this infection during pregnancy by avoiding contact with cat feces (by not cleaning a litter box and by wearing gloves when gardening) and by making sure that all the meat she eats is thoroughly cooked. A woman who handles raw meat should wash her hands (and the kitchen utensils and surfaces used to prepare the meat) carefully.

BIRTH

Birth Choices

Choosing a doctor or midwife who will provide prenatal care and deliver the baby, and choosing the type of place in which the baby will be born, are very important decisions. These choices will determine the type of care, the cost, and how satisfied

Choosing prenatal and delivery care providers early and carefully can make a big difference when it is time for the baby to be born.

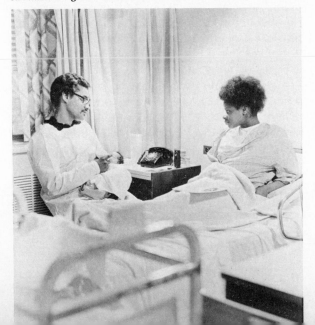

the future parents will be with the care that is given. These choices need to be made early in pregnancy (or even before a pregnancy is started) because the same caregiver should follow the woman through the pregnancy and birth.

Some couples may find their choices are limited by the kinds of facilities available in their area, by costs, or by the type of insurance coverage they have. Women with high-risk pregnancies may be limited in their choices by the need to deliver in a hospital that has special services available (such as doctors who specialize in the care of high-risk newborns and a special care nursery). Still, it is important for all couples to find out about the different types of medical practitioners who deliver babies, and about the different approaches to delivery.

Successful delivery of a baby is measured by a number of things. Of course, the health of the new mother and the baby is most important. But in addition, the ease or difficulty of the labor and delivery for the woman is important. The less stressful the labor and delivery are, and the fewer drugs used, the better for both mother and infant. Although high-quality medical attention is important, there are other issues that also affect the success of the delivery.

It appears that a woman who is relaxed, comfortable, and unafraid is likely to have a shorter, less painful labor (and is less likely to develop complications) than a tense, fearful woman. On the other hand, problems and complications can develop in any delivery, no matter how prepared or relaxed the woman is.

The following things seem to help women to handle the stresses of labor and delivery more easily:

1. Good communication and a trusting relationship with the obstetrician or midwife
2. The companionship and support of the father, another family member, or a friend throughout the labor
3. Training in preparation for childbirth (see details later in this chapter).
4. A relaxed and supportive environment to labor in, where the woman can move about, talk with her partner, read, watch television, etc.

These are all things to keep in mind when selecting a caregiver and a place to give birth.

Almost all babies born in the United States today (99 percent) are born in hospitals, and doctors deliver most of them. Certified nurse midwives deliver around 1.4 percent of all babies born in hospitals and a high percentage of those born at birthing centers or at home. Despite these figures, birth outside the hospital and the use of nurse midwives are trends that are growing in popularity, and for this reason details about these choices are given.

There are three decisions to be made, and they are linked together.

1. *Choice of a caregiver.* This is usually an **obstetrician** (doctor specializing in prenatal care and delivery) or a **certified nurse midwife** (nurse with special training in prenatal care and delivery).

2. *Choice of the type of health care delivery organization.* For example, obstetricians and midwives can be found in **private practice, group practice, HMOs** (health maintenance organizations), and **clinics.** These different delivery structures vary in important ways, especially with regard to cost and the type of care you can expect.

3. *Choice of where to give birth.* The choices here are mainly between different **hospitals,** although some parents-to-be are also interested in exploring **birthing centers** (medical settings that specialize in labor and delivery, but are not attached to a hospital) and **home births.**

The following section begins with information about choosing a caregiver and delivery structure, followed by details about choices in where to give birth.

Choosing a Caregiver

There are a number of things to consider when choosing your caregiver for pregnancy. The following are a few basic considerations:

1. COST

How much will you be charged for prenatal care and delivery?
Will your insurance cover this caregiver?
How much will your insurance pay?

Obstetricians and certified nurse midwives specialize in providing prenatal care and delivering babies.

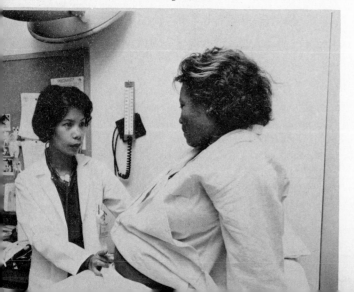

2. CONVENIENCE

Can you get to appointments easily?
Are the hours for appointments convenient?
Can you reach your caregiver easily by telephone?
How far away is the place where you will deliver?
How long does it take to get there?

3. CARE

Will you always see the same caregiver?
Will your prenatal caregiver be the same person who delivers the baby?
Will your caregiver stay with you through all of labor and delivery? If not, who will?
Can the father and/or other family or friends stay with you through the labor and delivery?

4. COMFORT

Do you feel comfortable with this caregiver?
Do you feel free to ask all your questions?
Do you feel that you can trust this caregiver?
Do you feel that this caregiver will listen to you?
Do you feel that this caregiver will respect your wishes?

Things to Ask About

The following are some other important issues you may want to discuss when talking with potential caregivers.

Drugs You will want to know the caregiver's philosophy and beliefs about administering drugs during labor and delivery. If the obstetrician does administer drugs, you will want to know what types are used, when they are used, and what the possible side effects are. Drugs given to the mother during labor and delivery usually enter the baby's bloodstream, so the risks and benefits to both the mother and the baby have to be considered when drugs are used.

The most common kinds of anesthesia used for childbirth are regional pain-blocking drugs that numb the woman's lower body so she does not feel pain, but leave her awake and alert. There are a number of different drugs that may be used for this purpose. General anesthesia (in which the woman is not awake) is rarely used for childbirth today except in emergencies.

In addition to anesthesia, there are many other drugs that may be used during labor and delivery, including analgesics (pain-killers), tranquillizers, sedatives, and/or uterine stimulants (to speed up labor) during labor (see pages 140–141 for more details on drugs used in childbirth).

Episiotomy Episiotomy is a medical procedure performed just before the baby is born. It involves cutting the perineal tissue, which is the tissue between the vagina and the anus (see Figure 6–5). The procedure makes the birth quicker by increasing the size of the vaginal opening, and also prevents the tissue from tearing as the baby's head is pushed out. Although episiotomy is quite painless at the time it is done because of a natural anesthesia in the vaginal area at the time of birth, your caregiver may inject a local anesthetic (like novocaine) as well. Once the baby is delivered, a local anesthetic is given (if it was not done before), and the episiotomy is sutured closed. It is uncomfortable for several days, but heals completely within a few weeks.

Although an episiotomy is not harmful, it can be uncomfortable, and it is not clear that it is a necessary procedure. Episiotomy is a common practice with obstetricians in the United States, but most midwives (and European doctors) do not perform them routinely. Those who do not do episiotomies believe that, given enough time, the tissue will stretch on its own, particularly if warm compresses are applied during labor. Tearing may occur, however, if the baby is very large or comes very suddenly. A perineal tear can be sutured closed, like an episiotomy, although it may be more time-consuming to suture (because it is not a clean cut) and also may be more uncomfortable.

Care during labor   Most nurse midwives and some obstetricians remain with their patients throughout the labor and delivery process, although they may not be at the bedside for the entire time. Parents-to-be generally find the presence of their caregiver during labor to be very reassuring and supportive. This is one reason that nurse midwives are gaining such popularity as caregivers. Many obstetricians leave the supervision of their patients during labor to the hospital staff, and come to the hospital only for the delivery. Others stop in to visit the patient during labor, but may not stay.

In the rare cases in which the caregiver does not arrive in time for the delivery, the hospital staff may try to slow down the labor process (which doesn't usually work). If necessary, they deliver the baby in the absence of the caregiver. Medically speaking, this is not usually a serious problem, but the parents-to-be may have strong feelings about it.

Obstetrician or Other Doctor

Most women choose a doctor to provide their care, and this doctor is most likely to be an **obstetrician/gynecologist** (OB-GYN), a specialist in pregnancy and childbirth. An obstetrician/gynecologist has a medical degree, plus three years residency training in a hospital, which includes a year and a half each of obstetrics and gynecology. Surgery re-

mediolateral incision   midline incision

FIGURE 6–5. *An episiotomy is performed just before birth. Two kinds of incisions are shown.*

lated to the female reproductive system is emphasized, and obstetricians are experts in the complications and problems of pregnancy and delivery. A *board-certified* obstetrician (certified by the American College of Obstetrics and Gynecology) has passed additional specific tests and requirements. A **perinatologist** is a board-certified obstetrician/gynecologist who has received two additional years of training in high-risk pregnancies and is also certified in maternal–fetal medicine.

In some parts of the country (particularly rural areas) an obstetrician may not be available, and a **family practice** or **general practice** doctor may be the best choice to provide care. These physicians do not have the specialized training in obstetrics, but they may have years of experience delivering babies.

Certified Nurse Midwife

A **certified nurse midwife** is a specialist in normal prenatal care and delivery. Nurse midwives are RNs (registered nurses) who have completed at least one year of specialized training in prenatal care and delivery. Such programs are approved by the American College of Nurse Midwives.

Nurse midwives tend to be less medically oriented than physicians. They usually emphasize nutrition and health, prepared childbirth, and allowing time for the baby to be born naturally. They tend to allow their patients freedom to move about, to drink fluids, and to take whatever positions they find most comfortable during labor and delivery. At prenatal visits, they usually spend more time with their patients than physicians do, and

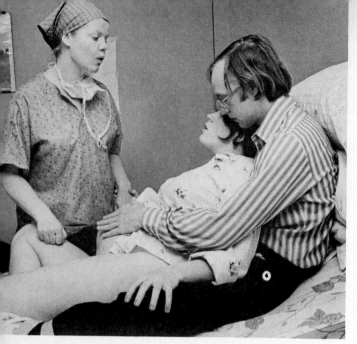
A nurse midwife assists a couple in labor.

they often stay with the mother-to-be throughout labor and delivery. Nurse midwives cannot perform surgery such as caesarean sections or certain other procedures, so if a birth becomes complicated or an emergency develops, care by a physician is necessary. Complications develop in 10 to 20 percent of deliveries.

Nurse midwives usually work closely with obstetricians. Their patients may be seen by an obstetrician at least once during pregnancy, and an obstetrician will be readily available should an emergency develop. Otherwise, the nurse midwife provides all of the care, including delivery of the baby. Some nurse midwives deliver babies only in hospitals or birthing centers. Others are available for home births.

Care from a midwife can be much less expensive than an obstetrician's care, but it is less likely to be covered by health insurance, so it is important to figure out the actual cost after insurance payments are subtracted.

A **certified nurse midwife** should not be confused with a **lay midwife,** who is a person who provides prenatal care and delivery but does not have formal training (although she or he may have years of experience). Only a few states allow lay midwives to practice, but some work illegally in other states.

Choosing a Health Care Organization

Solo Private Practice

Solo private practice refers to a single care provider, an obstetrician (rarely a midwife) who

works alone and independently. Such a doctor has attending privileges (is authorized to admit and treat patients) at one or more local hospitals, so when you choose a doctor, you also choose the hospitals available to you for labor and delivery. A large number of physicians are in solo practice.

Some of the possible advantages of using an obstetrician in solo practice include being sure you will always see the same provider and getting to know the provider a little better. Disadvantages include the possibility that the doctor may be unavailable (on vacation, out of town, delivering another baby) at the time of delivery. Caregivers try to avoid this, but it can happen.

Most obstetricians in solo practice charge a flat rate for normal prenatal care and delivery, and accept insurance. The charges may be higher if there are complications such as a caesarean section or if extra care is needed. In an area where there are a number of obstetricians to choose from, there may be big differences in how much they charge.

Group Practice

Group practice is a common form of organization for obstetricians, in which several physicians share a set of offices and facilities (and sometimes patients). A group may commonly include several obstetricians, an obstetrician and several doctors in other specialties (such as general surgery or pediatrics), or (rarely) obstetricians and midwives. Like physicians in solo practice, doctors in group practices have attending privileges only at certain hospitals.

Group practice has many advantages for care providers, including the fact that it allows them to provide good care for patients and still get some nights, weekends, and vacations free without worrying about who will care for their patients.

Advantages for patients include the fact that someone from the group will always be available if needed. Possible disadvantages include receiving care from several different providers and/or being delivered by an unfamiliar caregiver. Different group practices have different policies about whether a specific doctor will commit himself or herself to be present for a patient's delivery, so it is important to ask. The costs of care are likely to be similar to those of obstetricians in solo private practice.

HMO

An **HMO** (health maintenance organization) is a large organization that provides for all the basic medical care needs of an individual or family (including prenatal care, laboratory tests, and labor and delivery). HMO members (patients) usually pay a flat monthly fee that covers any care needed. This is frequently a big savings over the cost of paying for private practice doctors and hospital care. HMO members do not usually need health insurance in addition to HMO coverage, and many employers offer a choice between the HMO or private health insurance as a fringe benefit.

Some of the advantages of HMOs are their low cost and the convenience of receiving all care from one organization. For those interested in receiving care from a nurse midwife, these specialists are more likely to be found in an HMO than in private practice. Possible disadvantages are that the service may be impersonal, and it may not be possible to see the same caregiver at each visit. Different HMOs have different policies on this, so it is important to ask.

Prenatal Clinic

Some communities, especially large cities, offer free or reduced-rate **prenatal clinics.** These clinics are often run by a hospital but may be located in separate offices in the community. Clinics that are not hospital-operated usually have a cooperative arrangement with a local hospital for low-cost delivery for their patients. The quality of care offered by these clinics varies somewhat, but is usually adequate and sometimes excellent.

The staff typically includes obstetricians or obstetrical residents (doctors who are training to specialize in obstetrics) and nurses. In addition, there may be nutritionists, child care experts, social workers, and other staff members available to consult with and assist the pregnant woman.

The main advantage of such clinics is their low cost, and many couples who have no health insurance choose clinics for this reason. In addition, clinics often have a team of specialists including social workers, nutritionists, and others who can provide extra care, information, and support to the parents-to-be. One disadvantage is that there is rarely any guarantee of seeing the same caregiver for prenatal visits and delivery. In addition, many clinics have long waiting times after you arrive for an appointment and an impersonal atmosphere. There may be no one nurse or doctor whom you see often enough to develop a relationship, and it may be difficult to get answers to questions if you telephone between appointments.

If low-cost care is important to you, it is a good idea to check out any clinics in your area. You may find one that meets your needs, and you may save a lot of money.

Where to Give Birth

The next choice to be made is where to have the baby. There are several choices. First, you can have the baby in a **hospital,** as 99 percent of women do. Second, in some communities a **birthing center** may be available. Third, you can have the baby at home. Giving birth in a hospital is considered to be the safest choice for all women; most health care providers do not recommend giving birth at home.

Women who know from the beginning that their pregnancy will be at high risk of complications need to choose hospital care so that the experts and the equipment that may be needed for them or the baby will be available. Some women develop high-risk symptoms during pregnancy, and if an out-of-hospital birth was planned, they may have to change plans and go to a hospital for delivery instead.

Hospital Births

The availability of medical care for both mother and baby is the greatest advantage of giving birth in a hospital. Should a problem develop during labor or delivery, the needed personnel and equipment are available to deal with it.

Many hospitals offer a choice of care for labor and delivery, including special rooms where women can go through both labor and delivery (rather than being moved to a different room for delivery), and *rooming-in* arrangements where the baby can stay with the mother rather than in a nursery. These choices allow the parents-to-be to select the kind of birthing environment that is most comfortable for them. The combination of choice

Most births take place in hospitals.

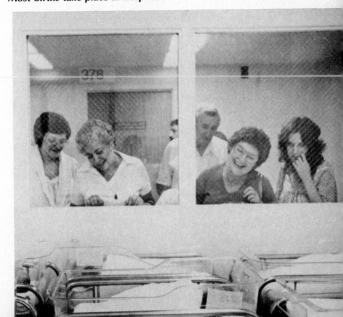

plus safety can make hospital birth a very attractive option.

In addition, the hospital will often take care of such tasks as registering the birth and sending a birth announcement to the local newspaper. Most hospitals also provide information about caring for the baby (and for yourself) after discharge from the hospital.

The disadvantages of hospital births have to do with the "medicalized" approach to labor and birth, which some couples do not want. There are a number of preparations for delivery and medical procedures that are commonly used but do not seem to be necessary (in most cases), and these can be avoided in home births or births at birthing centers. Separation of the laboring woman from her family and separation of the mother and child after birth, which are worrisome to some couples, are also more likely to occur in a hospital. Some people wish to avoid the impersonal and highly regulated environment of the hospital if possible.

Home Births

Some couples like to think of birth as a natural family event, and they would prefer to have their baby at home if possible. However, there are serious risks and disadvantages to home birth. Years ago, home birth might have been almost as safe as hospital birth because medical science was not as advanced and childbirth was more risky for babies and mothers under all conditions. But today most of the life-saving treatment that a mother and baby might need in an emergency cannot be administered at home (or in an ambulance en route to the hospital). *Couples who choose home birth should be aware that that they are choosing a higher risk of death or permanent damage for both the baby-to-be and the mother.*

It is usually difficult to find a professional who is willing to do a home delivery. Most physicians and nurse midwives are not willing to participate in them because of the high risk to mother and infant due to lack of a medical support system. In some areas nurse midwives may be restricted by law to deliveries in hospitals or under a physician's supervision.

In some communities there are lay midwives, who are usually women without formal training who have had experience delivering babies. Some lay midwives have had training in other countries. Lay midwifery is illegal in many areas, and is not covered by health insurance.

Lack of money to pay for care is not a good reason to plan a home birth. The risks are too high. Most communities have a prenatal clinic and a hospital that will not turn away people who do not have health insurance or money. It is important to find out about these programs early in pregnancy, and to make plans for a safe and affordable delivery.

Of course, in emergencies babies are still delivered at home, in ambulances, and even in the family car—and most of them do fine. But few people today choose such conditions for childbirth.

Birthing Centers

A birthing center can be an attractive choice for couples who do not like the medical orientation of hospital birth but feel that home birth is too risky. Unfortunately, many communities do not have birthing centers, so this option is not available to everyone.

A birthing center is intended to provide both a homelike atmosphere and professional care. As with home births, the family can usually be together, and delivery takes place in a bed. Usually, there is considerably less medical intervention and routine than in a hospital, and the mother and baby stay only about 2 to 24 hours. These are two reasons that birthing centers can be considerably less expensive than hospitals.

On the other hand, there is less medical care available than in a hospital. An emergency will mean that the mother or baby must be transported to a hospital. Birthing centers are not recommended for high-risk pregnancies or when there is a good chance of complications during delivery.

Birthing centers do offer more medical advantages than a home birth. Some have obstetricians on staff; others are staffed by midwives. Still others are supervised by obstetricians, but the actual care is provided by nurses. It is important to make sure you know what you are getting. There is usually a system for transporting women and babies to a hospital if an emergency develops.

Policies and procedures vary considerably from one birthing center to another, so prospective parents should ask the same types of questions they would ask of a hospital. It is especially important to make sure of the type of emergency care that is available. Also, it is important to check whether or not your health insurance policy will cover the costs of a birthing center.

Making a Choice

How can a couple decide which hospital is best for them, or whether they should consider birth outside a hospital? The best approach is to be well informed. (If an obstetrician or nurse midwife has already been selected, talk to him or her first. He or she only does deliveries at certain hospitals, and may not consider deliveries outside of a hospital.) Most hospitals and birthing centers offer tours of their delivery areas and are happy to answer questions. It is an excellent idea to take advantage of these tours in order to become familiar with the labor and delivery rooms and the hospital procedures. It is also wise to ask friends and relatives about their experiences with local hospitals. But a word of warning is in order. Many hospitals have dramatically changed their birth policies during the last few years to be more responsive to the wishes of parents-to-be. So unless your friend has delivered recently, be certain to double-check the information you receive.

The following are some of the hospital policies and procedures you may want to ask about. In the past, these procedures were often required, but in recent years most hospitals have become more flexible.

Enemas Hospitals may have a policy that laboring women are routinely given enemas. An enema is the passing of fluid into the rectum. It causes the bowels to contract and the woman to expel any feces in the lower bowel. The bowels often do their own "cleaning out" naturally a day or two before labor begins. If the bowels are empty, the chances of passing stools during delivery are reduced. The disadvantages of enemas are that they are uncomfortable, especially for a woman in labor, and do not seem to be necessary. Passing feces during labor or delivery is a bit messy, but not harmful to the woman or the fetus.

Shaving A hospital may require that the pubic hair be shaved or trimmed. The purpose of this is to reduce the number of bacteria in the area in order to prevent infection, and to ensure better visibility for the obstetrician. There is no evidence that shaving helps prevent infection, but it is understandable that long pubic hair may need to be trimmed short so the obstetrician can see the area clearly. Many women dislike shaving because of the problem of itching as the hair grows back.

Intravenous drip A hospital may require that every laboring woman be put on an IV (intravenous drip). This is a tube attached at one end to a needle, which is inserted in a vein, usually in the arm or hand. The other end is attached to a bottle of sterile fluid, which is hung from a pole and kept higher than the woman's body. The intravenous needle and tube are taped securely to the skin so that they do not move and are left in place throughout labor and delivery. The advantages are that this permits a rapid delivery of drugs should a problem develop and is a means of providing fluid to the woman, who may not eat or drink for many hours during labor. The disadvantages are that it restricts the woman's ability to move around during labor, and it can be distracting and uncomfortable.

Fetal monitors Most hospitals use fetal monitors, which are devices that provide information about the condition of the fetus during labor. These monitors can be very helpful in detecting fetal distress and avoiding harm to the fetus during the birth process. Like the IV, however, if they are used throughout labor, they severely restrict the woman's ability to move around, and this may add to her discomfort. Although such monitors are important with problem deliveries, it is not clear that they are needed in uncomplicated births.

There are two types of fetal monitors. External fetal monitors consist of two straps, which are placed around the woman's abdomen. One strap monitors the fetal heart rate. The other records the duration and frequency of contractions. An internal fetal monitor, involving the attachment of a small electrode to the fetal scalp while it is still in the uterus, may also be used. This type of monitor has been used for many years and seems to be quite safe for the baby. It does not leave a scar.

Mobility Aside from the equipment just described, which may prevent movement, there is another reason a woman may be unable to walk around. Some hospitals have a policy requiring that laboring women stay in bed. This can be a disadvantage, since some women like to be able to get up and walk around when they are in labor. They may

A nurse adjusts an external fetal monitor.

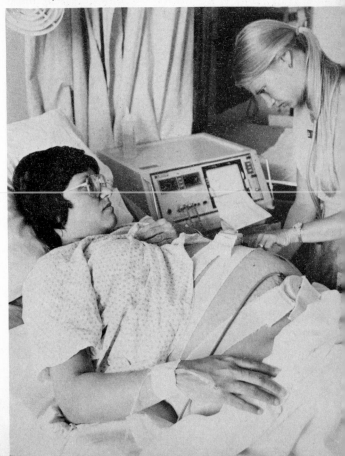

also prefer to use the toilet normally rather than using a bedpan, and may be more comfortable during labor if they can stand up part of the time.

Delivery position Most deliveries in the United States take place with the woman reclining on her back. Some hospitals require that the woman's legs be placed in stirrups (similar to those on the table on which pelvic exams are given) to give birth. Others allow the woman to give birth in a special bed that allows her more freedom to move around. At some hospitals and birthing centers, birthing chairs and stools are available. These allow the woman to deliver in a sitting position, which is preferred in many parts of the world. There are advantages and disadvantages to all the different possible positions for giving birth. *Unless a woman is sure what she prefers, an environment that allows her the most freedom to choose the most comfortable positions during both labor and delivery is the best choice.*

Family presence Almost all hospitals now allow fathers to stay with the woman during labor and to be in the delivery room for normal vaginal deliveries. Some require that the father go through a childbirth preparation class if he is to be present. Many hospitals also allow the father to be present during caesarean sections. At some places, other family members may also be allowed in the delivery room. The hospital also may have policies concerning photographing or videotaping the delivery.

Care of newborns Hospitals also have routine policies about the care of newborns immediately after birth. Some may encourage the new parents to spend a few minutes with the baby before anything else is done. In other hospitals the baby may be separated from the parents for several minutes immediately after birth while certain care

Hospitals differ in their policies concerning family visits.

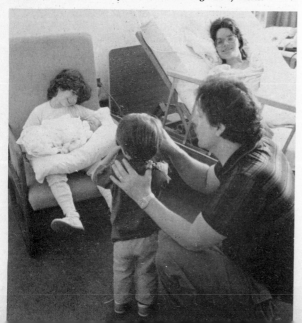

is provided. The procedures that are done immediately include cutting the umbilical cord, administering eye drops, injecting vitamin K (to help blood clotting), weighing, cleaning, footprinting, and possibly other care.

Rooming in Many hospitals offer a rooming-in option. This means that the baby stays in the same room as the mother, rather than in a separate nursery for newborns. This has the advantage of allowing mother and child to get to know each other, and letting the mother learn how to care for her baby with the help of the nursing staff. Rooming in makes breastfeeding easier and more convenient. Some women may not want it, however, because they feel they need rest for a day or two after the delivery and do not want to start taking 24-hour responsibility for the baby yet. In a few cases the baby's medical needs or the mother's may mean that rooming in is not possible.

Preparing for Delivery

Some form of childbirth education is available in most communities. Even small towns may offer a variety of programs. The Red Cross, YM/YWCA, local hospitals, and social service organizations are likely sponsors. Some programs focus on preparation for childbirth, and others on childcare and parenting, so it is important to know what you will be getting in a particular program. Some of these programs are free; others may charge a fee.

There are several different approaches to childbirth preparation, but they all share certain basic principles:

1. Birth does not have to be a very painful process that requires drugs and anesthesia.
2. The fewer drugs used by the mother during birth, the better for the baby.
3. The better the mother understands the birth process, the less fear and discomfort she will experience.
4. There are specific physical and psychological techniques that can be taught which will help the woman relax and will minimize pain.
5. The more relaxed and confident the woman, the faster the labor and the fewer complications of birth.

Some of the best known approaches to training for childbirth are described briefly in this section.

Lamaze Method

The **Lamaze method** is the best known and most popular form of childbirth preparation in the

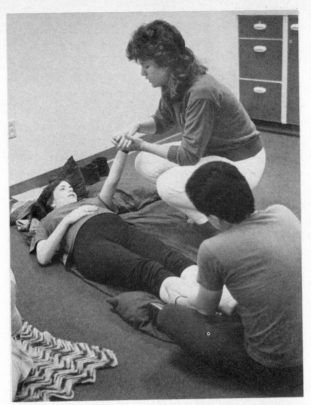
Expectant parents find Lamaze classes reassuring and helpful.

United States. Because it emphasizes giving birth "naturally," without drugs or anesthesia, it is sometimes called *natural childbirth*. Most courses include around six weekly meetings in which the details of labor and the birth process are explained and the pregnant woman and her partner are taught exercises, breathing, and relaxation techniques to help the woman cope with labor and delivery. With techniques similar to those taught in yoga classes, women learn to identify and relax specific muscles. They also learn to use specific breathing patterns to distract themselves from discomfort during contractions, and to assure that the muscles receive enough oxygen. Homework and practice exercises are given.

Although the Lamaze method can be used by a woman who does not have a partner to coach her and keep her company during labor and delivery, the technique is more effective with a partner. The partner does not have to be a husband or the baby's father. Many women use their mother or sister, or a close female friend. A good partner will have a close and trusting relationship with the mother-to-be, will participate in the training, and will be available when labor begins.

The positive effects of preparation for childbirth through Lamaze training are that women are likely to have a shorter labor, with less discomfort and fewer complications. Many are able to give birth without any drugs or pain-killers, which is very beneficial to the baby.

Bradley, Kitzinger, and Dick-Read Methods

Besides Lamaze, there are several other approaches to childbirth preparation that are well known in the United States, including the Bradley, Kitzinger, and Dick-Read approaches. These methods have many similarities to the Lamaze, but focus more on education and understanding of the labor and delivery process. Each has a specific emphasis. In the Bradley method the importance of the husband or other coach is emphasized. The Kitzinger method stresses imagery (using mental pictures to relax and guide the mind and body). The basic idea is that much of the difficulty and pain of childbirth is related to the woman's fear and lack of understanding of what is happening. Education before birth, along with an understanding and supportive birthing staff who explain everything as it happens, are basic ingredients of these approaches. As with Lamaze, a partner or coach is also present, and concentration and relaxation techniques are used to ease the discomfort of labor and delivery.

Other Childbirth Preparation Approaches

Yoga, exercise, and hypnosis classes are also available in some areas to provide preparation for childbirth. Yoga classes focus on relaxation, flexibility, and strength, and may also teach meditation and visualization approaches to relaxing and minimizing pain during labor and delivery.

Exercise classes usually focus on general fitness, strength, and flexibility. Hypnosis training provides the woman with a self-help technique to reduce fear and discomfort during childbirth. For some people, hypnosis can substitute for pain-killing drugs.

Leboyer Method

The Leboyer method is not a preparation for childbirth for the mother, but it is included here because it is part of the delivery. It is an approach to handling the infant during and after delivery that is based on the idea that birth is very traumatic (upsetting and frightening) to the infant, who moves from the relative silence, warmth, darkness, and protection of the uterus to a cold, noisy, brightly lit environment where he or she must breathe independently. It is thought that this experience may have long-lasting effects on the infant. The Leboyer approach calls for a darkened, quiet delivery room, for placing the baby on the mother's stomach (where her heartbeat may be heard) immediately

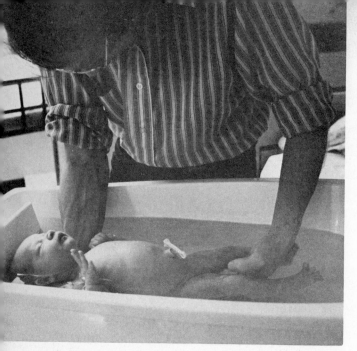

A newborn infant is bathed in a darkened room after a Leboyer method delivery.

after birth, and for massaging the infant's back. The umbilical cord is not cut immediately. The infant is handled gently and is given a warm bath.

It is not known if the Leboyer approach to birth has long-lasting effects, but babies born this way appear to be calmer and more alert than others while they are in the hospital. There are no known ill effects of the Leboyer method.

Planning Ahead

Parenting classes Many communities also offer parenting courses to expectant parents (and to new parents). Such classes usually cover the basics of child care (such as nutrition and identifying illness), offer advice about how to deal with problems (often related to crying and sleeping patterns),

and provide information about infant development. These classes are very important for new parents having their first baby, especially if they are not familiar with the care of infants and young children. Many new parents have no close friends or relatives living nearby who are experienced in infant care, so without parenting classes they would have few sources of advice and help. Although the mother's and the child's health care providers can answer many questions, they seldom have the time to talk with new parents about all their questions.

There are also many good books available on parenting and child care, both at the library and at the bookstore. *Most parents will probably want to own at least one basic book about infant and child care.* Your doctor or parenting class may recommend one of the many inexpensive paperbacks available at the bookstore. If not, look at several, checking the table of contents and reading a few pages to make sure you choose a book that covers the things you have questions about.

Along with childbirth preparation classes, parenting classes are a good place to meet other new parents to share ideas and problems. Sometimes supportive friendships develop that last beyond the class. Parents having a second or third child probably won't feel a parenting class is quite so important, but they may want to attend one if they never have before.

Breast or bottle feeding It is a good idea to make a decision about whether to breast or bottle feed before the baby is born, so that you will be prepared with information and any equipment (such as bottles and formula) you may need. Most mothers today breastfeed at least for a short time. Many women enjoy breastfeeding a great deal, and feel a special closeness to their babies while they are nursing them. There are also important health benefits for the baby.

Childbirth preparation classes and parenting classes are good places to meet other parents and share ideas and problems.

FIGURE 6–6. *Breastfeeding has many advantages for both mother and baby.*

Successful breastfeeding is not something that a new mother knows how to do "naturally"; she usually needs education and advice from an expert. Your prenatal care specialist will be able to give you some information about breastfeeding, and your childbirth preparation class may cover it as well. In most communities there are also organizations such as the LaLeche League, which provide education and support for breastfeeding mothers.

Breastfeeding has many important advantages for the baby:

1. Breast milk contains more of the nutrients needed by the baby than prepared formula or cows' milk, as well as antibodies that protect the infant from disease.

2. Breast-fed babies do not become allergic to their mother's milk, and are much less likely to develop colic or other digestive problems.

3. Breast milk cannot spoil or become contaminated and make the baby sick.

4. Breast milk is always available and does not require special preparation.

5. Breast milk is free (unless you count the extra food and liquid the mother must consume).

6. Many mothers enjoy the sensations of breastfeeding and the closeness with the baby.

Given these advantages, why would anyone choose *not* to breastfeed? There are disadvantages also:

1. The mother must be available to feed the baby every few hours throughout the day and night.

2. The mother must watch her diet and avoid drugs to make sure her milk is adequate and safe for the baby.

3. In a few cases, because of illness, medications, or not producing enough milk, the mother is unable to breastfeed.

4. Breastfeeding can become uncomfortable if the nipples become dry, cracked, or infected.

5. Breastfeeding can cause inconvenience, such as leaking breasts or difficulty finding a private place to feed the baby when traveling.

6. With breastfeeding, it's impossible to know exactly how much milk the baby is getting.

7. Some women may not enjoy the sensations of breastfeeding, or may find it embarrassing.

Working mothers in particular may find breastfeeding difficult. However, it is very beneficial for the baby, so even if the mother will only be able to breastfeed for the first few weeks, it is still worthwhile. If the mother has to be away from the baby at times, it is possible to express milk from the breasts in advance, by hand or with a breast pump. The milk can be stored in a bottle in the refrigerator for up to 48 hours (or even frozen) to feed the baby when the mother is not home. Another possibility is to have the baby fed formula when the mother cannot be at home.

A common worry for new mothers is that they will not have enough milk to feed the baby. It is difficult to measure how much the baby is getting. If the baby is well, is gaining weight, and seems satisfied, this is probably not a problem. In general, the more a woman nurses (but not more than every two hours), the more milk is produced. Breast size (before pregnancy and while breastfeeding) does not affect the amount of milk a woman can produce.

Breastfeeding mothers need to be particularly careful about their diet, rest, drug use, and stress levels. Tiredness can affect milk production. Stress on the mother (and the hormonal changes that go with it) may make the baby more irritable. Breastfeeding mothers also need to drink extra liquids in order to maintain their milk supply, and many women find that they also need to avoid certain foods, such as garlic and chocolate, which may

Some mothers choose to bottle-feed their babies rather than nurse them.

upset the baby's stomach. Breastfeeding mothers should not use any drug, even over-the-counter medications, without consulting their health care provider.

Most health professionals recommend breastfeeding, mainly because of the benefits to the baby. If a couple decides against breastfeeding, however, they should not worry that they are doing harm to their baby. Bottle-feeding mothers can be just as close to their babies as breastfeeding mothers. And most babies will thrive on formula just as they would on breast milk. If you choose bottle feeding, commercial baby formula is the next best thing to breast milk. Cows' milk or goats' milk is less desirable and should be avoided until the baby is a year old.

Even if you decide to bottle feed, you will produce milk. Many physicians will recommend medication to "dry up" your milk. The milk will also dry up on its own, although this will take longer. In either case, you will probably experience

some leaking and discomfort until your breasts stop producing milk.

Details about Delivery

There are basically two types of childbirth. The natural form is a **vaginal delivery,** when the baby exits the womb through the birth canal and the vagina. The other type is the **caesarean section,** in which an incision is made in the woman's abdomen, allowing the physician to remove the baby directly from the uterus. Caesarean deliveries have become much more common in the United States in recent years, and in some areas as many as 1 out of every 4 babies is born by this method. Both kinds of deliveries are described in detail on the following pages.

Use of Drugs/Medications

One purpose of childbirth education classes such as Lamaze is to reduce the need for drugs during labor and delivery, which is why such classes are sometimes called natural childbirth training. Although most childbirth educators feel that the fewer drugs used, the better for the baby, they also recommend that the mother-to-be accept drugs when they are needed. In fact, over 90 percent of all American women use some form of medication during labor or delivery. Fortunately, only a minority require the heavy anesthesia that was common years ago, when women would wake up after the delivery with no memory of having given birth! Labor and delivery can be very painful, particularly if the woman has no childbirth training, if she is delivering lying on her back, or if the baby is not in the correct position.

Types of drugs used   There are several categories of drugs that may be administered during labor and delivery.

1. **Uterine stimulants** (such as oxytocin) may be given to bring on or strengthen labor.
2. **Pain-killing drugs** (such as the narcotic Demerol) may be used to reduce the pain of contractions.
3. **Anesthesia** (general, regional, or local) may be used to put part (or all) of the body to "sleep" so that pain is not felt.

Less commonly, other kinds of drugs such as **sedatives** (like phenobarbital) and **tranquillizers** (for example, Librium) may be used. These drugs are given during labor rather than during the delivery itself. Within each of these categories, a wide variety of drugs may be used.

The third category of obstetrical drugs, **anesthesia,** is used during the latter part of labor and during delivery. Anesthesia is less commonly used during vaginal deliveries today than it was years ago, but it is still used in some situations. Several types of anesthesia are available. There are **general anesthetics,** which put the woman to sleep. These are rarely used today for vaginal deliveries, but are occasionally still used in caesarean sections. (In an emergency, general anesthesia is faster to administer than local anesthesia.)

Then there are **regional anesthetics,** which are used to numb the back, abdomen, and upper legs. These are called **epidural, spinal,** and **caudal blocks,** depending on where in the spinal area they are injected. Epidural blocks are used during prolonged or difficult labor or when labor is induced with drugs. Spinal and caudal blocks are used for delivery only and are administered shortly before birth. Regional anesthetics given during labor and delivery must provide relief from pain without interfering with labor contractions or the woman's ability to push. When given at the time of delivery, they may also help to relax certain muscles so that delivery is easier.

Finally, there are **local anesthetics** (like the novocaine the dentist uses), used to numb a very small region. A local anesthetic is most commonly used to numb the vaginal area in order to suture an episiotomy (see pages 130–131) after the baby is born.

Effects of drugs on newborns Almost all medications given by injection or by intravenous drip during labor and delivery cross the placental barrier, reaching the about-to-be-born baby. This can be a problem for several reasons. First, the drug may have a negative effect on the baby's vital functions, such as breathing and heart rate. Second, heavy doses of drugs can potentially cause damage to the infant's brain or vital organs. Third, since the baby's liver and kidneys are immature, the drug may be slow to clear from the system.

General anesthesia has the most extreme effects on newborns. In fact, some research has indicated that these effects may be evident for several *years* after birth. For example, there is research indicating that school-age children born under general anesthesia showed slightly lower intelligence test scores than those who were not.

General anesthesia also has other effects (which may also occur with regional anesthesia to a lesser degree). These include lowered physical functioning and increased irritability in newborns. In addition, anesthesia can reduce the mother's ability to participate actively in the delivery process, which can mean increased risk of a forceps delivery (described later in this chapter).

The indirect effects of drugs given during labor and delivery may be important as well. The first hours after birth can be especially important in establishing a good mother–infant relationship. Medications can leave the mother sleepy and sometimes disoriented. This, in combinatiion with the effects of the drugs on the newborn, can make it difficult for mother and baby to respond to each other at first.

Birthing Positions

A large variety of birthing positions are used successfully in different cultures around the world. Many women deliver in a squatting position or sitting, as well as reclining on pillows or lying on their sides. In the past, most American women giving birth in hospitals did so lying flat on their backs with their legs raised (in stirrups), in a position very similar to that used in a routine gynecological examination. This position is no longer widely used because it is now believed to make labor and delivery more difficult than is necessary for both mother and baby.

Recently a new position, called the **dorsal position,** has become common in hospitals. In this position, the woman leans back slightly from a sitting position, so her back is supported and her vagina is exposed (Figure 6–7). This position allows both the mother and the caregiver to see what is going on, and does not have the negative effects on circulation and ability to push that are found when the woman lies on her back.

How much does position during labor and delivery matter? The answer to this question is not known. It is clear, however, that lying flat on your back is not a good position for giving birth. Lying

FIGURE 6–7. *The dorsal position is often used for delivery.*

flat on the back lowers a woman's blood pressure because the uterus presses on the large abdominal blood vessels returning blood to the heart. This drop in blood pressure may reduce the flow of blood, and thereby oxygen, to the baby.

Lying flat on your back is also believed to decrease the strength of contractions and the rate of cervical dilation, resulting in longer labor. You are also working against gravity when you are in a horizontal position. For these reasons, many women seem to prefer a sitting or squatting position while giving birth.

It is important to discuss what birth position choices will be available to you with your prenatal specialist and birthing setting before the baby is due. It should help you to relax during labor and delivery if you know what to expect at each point.

Breech Presentation

A **breech presentation** occurs when a baby is not emerging from the uterus in the normal head-first position, but rather with the feet or buttocks presenting first (Figure 6–8). This can be dangerous because the head is the largest part of the baby, and may become trapped if the rest of the body is born first. A breech delivery can deprive the baby of oxygen during the birth process, resulting in possible

brain injury or death. There are four times as many stillborns and newborn deaths among breech babies, compared to normal (head-first) presentations.

There are two types of breech presentations. In a **footling breech**, the baby is emerging feet first. This is considered the more dangerous form of breech presentation and is always treated with a caesarean section. In a **complete** or **frank breech**, the baby is emerging buttocks first. This presentation, too, is dangerous and will most often be resolved through a caesarean section. Some specialists, however, will attempt to deliver frank breeches vaginally, particularly if it is not the woman's first baby, if the baby is average in size (as opposed to premature or very large), and if the labor progresses normally.

If a breech presentation is diagnosed during the seventh or eighth month of pregnancy, a breech birth may be avoidable. The pregnant woman can do exercises that may turn the baby into the appropriate position, or the doctor may be able to turn the baby into position by massaging and pushing on the abdomen. At some hospitals ultrasound is used to view the baby as the doctor attempts to turn it. This is done several weeks before labor begins. There comes a point, however, where there is not enough room in the uterus to turn the baby

FIGURE 6–8. *In a normal birth the baby is delivered head first (top). In a breech birth the lower body is delivered first (bottom).*

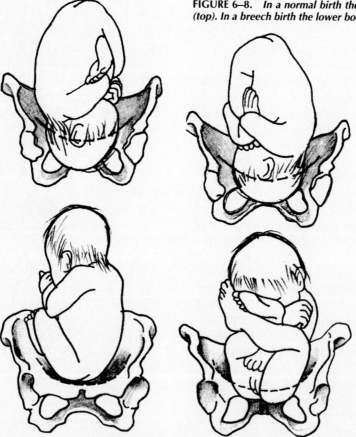

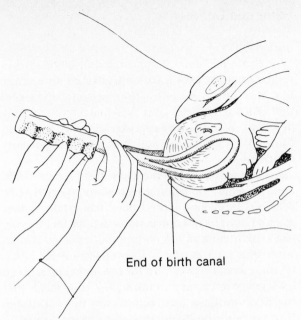

FIGURE 6–9. *The use of forceps for delivery.*

safely and easily. If the baby is still in the wrong position at that point, it will almost definitely be a breech birth.

Use of Forceps

Forceps are an instrument that resembles tongs. They are used to assist with certain difficult deliveries. The "blades" of the forceps are used to grasp the baby's head and gently pull him or her out of the birth canal (see Figure 6–9).

A forceps delivery can become necessary if the baby's well-being is endangered by the continuation of labor. This may occur if the umbilical cord is wrapped around the baby's neck, if the child is in a breech presentation, or if anesthesia or birthing position is preventing the mother from pushing. Forceps are probably not necessary when labor is simply long but there is no fetal distress. They are not always needed in breech presentations. In some cases, a woman may have a choice between forceps and caesarean delivery as a means of resolving the delivery complication.

When forceps are used, there is some increased risk of injury to the baby, although it is not clear whether the risk comes from the forceps themselves or from the problems that sometimes lead to forceps delivery. The risks are small, but forceps should be used only when absolutely necessary.

Caesarean Section

What is it? In a caesarean section (C-section), the baby is delivered through an incision in the mother's abdomen. Actually, there are two

incisions. The first is through the skin, muscle, and other tissue of the abdomen, and the second is through the uterus itself. There are two types of incisions in the abdominal skin and muscle (Figure 6–10). One is the midline or vertical incision, which runs from just below the mother's navel down her abdomen to just above the pubic bone. The other is the horizontal (Pfannenstiel) incision (sometimes called a **bikini cut**). This incision is made just above the pubic bone and therefore leaves a less visible scar. It also requires more time than the midline cut, however, and may not be used in an emergency situation.

The second incision is in the uterus itself. It is usually a horizontal incision across the lower part of the uterus. The use of this incision (as opposed to an incision in the upper part of the uterus) reduces the need for C-sections in later births.

Today, C-sections are usually performed under regional rather than general anesthesia. This means that the mother is awake and may be able to watch the procedure either directly or through a mirror.

How common is it? The rate of C-sections has been rising dramatically in the United States during the last twenty years. Today a woman has a 1 in 5 chance of having her baby delivered by C-section. Some people see this as a sign of progress, indicative of our increased ability to diagnose and treat complications and to deliver healthier babies. Others view the increase in C-sections as reflecting the desire of physicians to end labors quickly and deliver babies at their own convenience. They also claim that physicians use C-sections to reduce the likelihood of malpractice suits.

FIGURE 6–10. *Two types of incisions used in caesarean sections.*

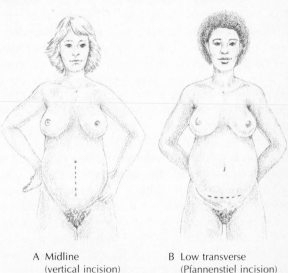

A Midline
(vertical incision)

B Low transverse
(Pfannenstiel incision)

There certainly are reasons to avoid C-sections, including the following:

1. Since a C-section is major surgery, the recovery period is longer (about six weeks) and more painful than with a vaginal delivery.
2. Anesthesia is necessary, and this creates an increased risk to the newborn and the mother.
3. A C-section can be a disappointment to the parents if they were looking forward to participating in a normal labor and vaginal delivery.
4. A C-section can have an effect on how the woman's future babies will be delivered.
5. A C-section is more expensive.

When is it necessary? In general, a C-section should be used when the mother or baby's life is endangered. Women with diabetes, active herpes lesions, and severe preeclampsia (see descriptions of these conditions earlier in this chapter) are usually delivered by C-section. In addition, certain complications at the time of delivery, such as placenta previa (when the placenta is in front of the cervix instead of high in the uterus), certain breech presentations, and a prolapsed cord (when the umbilical cord drops into the birth canal in front of the baby) also call for a C-section.

There are two other situations in which C-sections are commonly performed. One is delayed or prolonged labor. Different women take different amounts of time to complete labor. Long labor is more common for first-time mothers, women who are anxious and fearful, those who have weak contractions, and those who have a small pelvis and a large fetus. As long as the fetus does not appear to be in distress (as indicated by the fetal monitor), the mother's condition is normal, and labor is progressing (even if slowly), it is not usually necessary to shorten a labor by doing a C-section.

The second circumstance is if the woman has had previous C-sections. In some cases, the problems that led to the first C-section (for example, if the mother has severe diabetes) may also necessitate later C-sections. But if the circumstance requiring the first C-section, such as a breech presentation, is not present during a later delivery, then a vaginal delivery is possible. This depends on the original uterine incision. If the incision is vertical on the uterus, there is a high risk that it will rupture during normal labor. But if the more common low, transverse incision was used, the chance of rupture is quite low. Perhaps as many as 75 percent of all women who deliver a baby by C-section can later have a vaginal delivery. In the future it is likely that vaginal delivery for women after a C-section will become even more common than it is today.

Labor and Delivery

Labor

Signs of labor In the movies, labor always seems to begin with a sudden, strong contraction. In reality, however, contractions are only one signal that labor is starting, and these contractions may be relatively mild and irregular. Many women continue with their normal activities during these early contractions.

The early contractions are not always a reliable indicator of labor. Most women experience Braxton-Hicks contractions (**false labor**) late in their pregnancy. These contractions, which feel mainly like a tightening of the abdominal muscles, are an "exercise" for the uterus in preparation for labor. Women who are pregnant for the first time (and so have never felt a labor contraction) may think that the Braxton-Hicks contractions are the real thing. How can they be distinguished from real labor?

If you think you are in labor, start timing the contractions. There are two elements to be timed. One is the amount of time from the beginning of one contraction to the beginning of the next. The other is how long each contraction lasts. Braxton-Hicks contractions will tend to be irregularly spaced and will be relatively short in duration. They will get weaker and further apart as time goes on and are usually gone within an hour or so. Labor contractions, on the other hand, get stronger and, often, more regular. If your contractions become regularly spaced and are no more than 10 minutes apart, or if your contractions are lasting more than 30 seconds each, it is time to contact the caregiver who will deliver your baby. Do not wait for the contractions to be regularly spaced if they are lasting for at least 30 seconds. Not all women have regularly spaced labor pains. If in doubt, call your caregiver and ask for advice.

Contractions are just one way labor may begin; another way is with a **bloody show,** a vaginal discharge of blood-streaked mucus. This means the mucous plug that has been blocking the entrance to the uterus has come out. If the bleeding is heavy, as with a menstrual period, call your practitioner immediately. Otherwise, you can wait for the contractions to begin.

The third way that labor can begin is with the rupturing of the amniotic sac. In other words, your **water breaks** (the "water" is actually amniotic fluid). The fluid may come out of your vagina in a sudden gush or in a steady trickle. In any case, labor contractions should begin within about 24 hours.

Contact your caregiver if your water breaks, even if you aren't having contractions. The amniotic sac serves to protect the fetus from infection

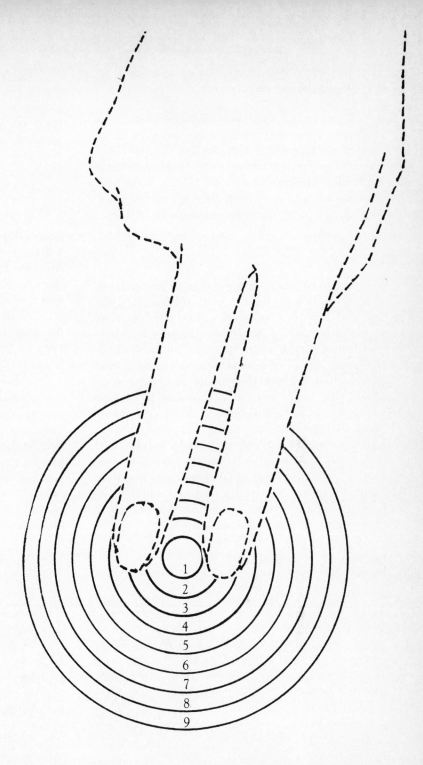

FIGURE 6–11. *Dilation of the cervix during labor (actual size) measured in centimeters.*

and trauma. Therefore, if your labor does not begin spontaneously within about 24 hours, your caregiver may want to induce labor.

What to do when labor begins When you suspect you are in labor, the first thing to do is to stay calm. Although the baby is about to arrive, it could still be many hours until the actual delivery, especially if this is your first baby. First-time labors often last 14 to 16 hours or longer.

Call the doctor or midwife who will deliver your baby. He or she may ask you to come into the office or go to the hospital to be checked. Your caregiver will check to see how much your cervix has dilated (see Figure 6–11). If it has not dilated or is less than two centimeters dilated, you may be sent home for a while. Your caregiver will also check the fetus's position and condition to make sure that everything is normal.

Contact the people who need to know you are in labor, including:

1. The person who is going to drive you to the hospital

2. Your labor coach (if you are using one)

3. The person who will stay with your other child-(ren) while you are in labor

Chances are that you will have a little time while you are waiting to see your specialist or for your coach to arrive home. Use this time to check the suitcase you are taking to the hospital or birthing center; this should already be at least partially packed, but you may wish to add toiletries and something to read. If all this is done, use the time to try to relax. When you reach your caregiver, ask whether you need to avoid eating while you're waiting.

Stages of labor A normal labor and delivery progresses through three stages: (1) **labor**, (2) **delivery**, and (3) **delivery of the placenta**. The first stage is the labor itself. This is when the cervix flattens and begins to dilate. In first-time mothers, these two steps occur separately. In women who have already had a child, they occur simultaneously. This is the major reason that second labors are usually only half as long as first labors. The cervix needs to dilate to about 10 centimeters (roughly the size of an adult's fist) before the baby can be born (Figure 6–12). This takes some time. For first-time mothers, the first stage of labor averages about 13 hours; for others, the average is about 8 hours. Labor can be subdivided into three phases: **early phase, active phase,** and **transition**.

Early phase In the **early phase** the cervix is dilating to three to four centimeters. Contractions will be mild to moderate in strength during this time. If you are in a hospital, hospital staff will probably monitor the strength of your contractions. Wherever you are, the specialist will periodically check your level of dilation. In addition, your blood pressure and the fetus's heart rate will be monitored.

If you are in a hospital, any needed preparations, such as trimming or shaving the pubic hair, will be done at this time. You may also be asked to urinate frequently. This helps to prevent the bladder being full during the delivery. As noted earlier, you can read, talk to your coach, or walk around (if your birth setting and specialist allow it) during this phase. You may be encouraged to drink fluids, but you will need to avoid solid foods.

Active phase The second subdivision of labor is the **active phase,** during which you will dilate to about seven centimeters. The contractions will intensify, and you will need to use any breathing and relaxation techniques you have learned (if you haven't already begun to use them). You may need a pain-killing drug or even anesthesia during this phase. There is a chance you will vomit from the strain of the labor. Your coach becomes extremely important now as he or she helps you to concen-

FIGURE 6–12. *How labor contractions affect the uterus.*

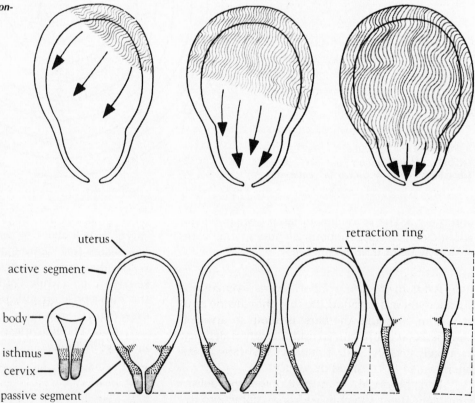

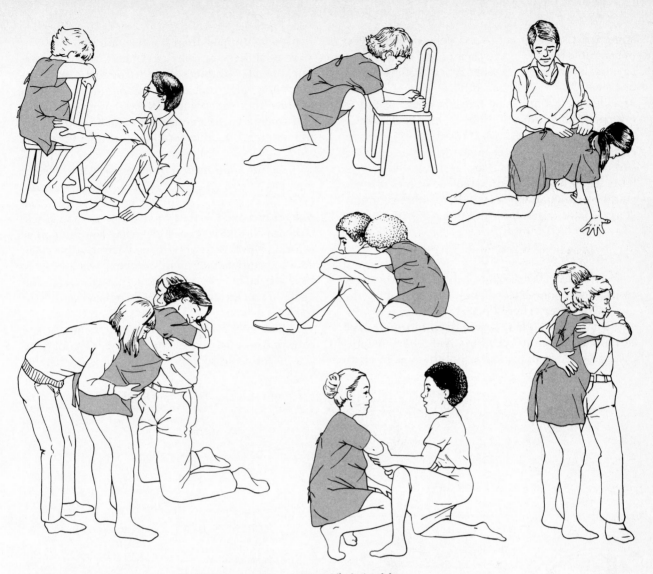

FIGURE 6–13. *Different women find different positions comfortable during labor.*

trate on the breathing and relaxation techniques you learned in childbirth training. If your water has not broken, your specialist may break it now. If so, you will experience some increased discomfort and, possibly, intensified contractions. Your condition and the condition of your baby will continue to be watched closely by hospital staff. If you are using an obstetrician and he or she has not stayed at the hospital with you, he or she will probably arrive toward the end of this phase.

Transition　The final subdivision of labor itself is **transition**. During transition, dilation to 10 centimeters is completed. This is probably the most intense part of labor in terms of the pain you feel. Contractions are very strong. The good news here is that you are almost finished. Transition is usually relatively short. You may feel an urge to "push" or "bear down" toward the end of transition. Various specialists have differing opinions on when you

should start to push. Pushing before you are completely dilated can lead to tearing of tissues and/or swelling, which will slow labor, so it is best to follow your caregiver's instructions about when you may begin to push.

Your labor coach is now of critical importance. Many women become frightened, disoriented, or ill-tempered at this point and need their coach to calm and reassure them. They will need help in maintaining their concentration and the use of their breathing techniques. The coach, too, may feel distressed, especially if he is a first-time father watching his wife go through labor.

If you are in a hospital with separate labor and delivery rooms (these are becoming less common, as most hospitals now have combination labor–delivery–recovery rooms), you will be taken to a delivery room at the end of transition, often just a few contractions before the baby will be born. This usually means a ride on a rolling labor bed or stretcher. Once you get to the delivery room, you may be able to remain in the labor bed or may have to move to the delivery table, where your legs will be placed into the stirrups and may be strapped in. The moving around may be disconcerting but is not particularly uncomfortable. Your coach will be permitted to stay with you throughout this period except for the time he or she spends putting on a surgical gown (if this is required). You will always have someone with you (usually a nurse) to help you through contractions, so there is no reason to worry if your coach is absent briefly.

Delivery

The next stage is the birth of the baby. The cervix is now completely dilated, and the baby is on the way. Delivery should occur within one to two hours if this is your first baby, and within about half an hour to an hour if you have had a baby before. Contractions are now intense, but the urge to push

is usually stronger than the discomfort. Once you start pushing you will feel better, because each push usually reduces the discomfort. Use your breathing and relaxation techniques between pushes. Your coach will be there to help you sit up and to count while you push (usually you will be trained to push while your coach counts to at least 10).

By now you have now assumed your delivery position (whether that is reclining, sitting, or squatting). Many places, including hospitals, will have mirrors arranged so that you can see as soon as the baby appears. (If you need glasses to see, remember to bring them with you.) If you are in a hospital, your obstetrician or family doctor will probably have arrived by now and will be ready to "catch the baby." If you are going to have an episiotomy, it will be done now.

The first few pushes rarely actually get the baby out. You may have to push longer if your baby is a posterior presentation. This means the baby is

FIGURE 6–14. *Typical passage of an infant through the birth canal. Note how the head turns to get through the small space.*

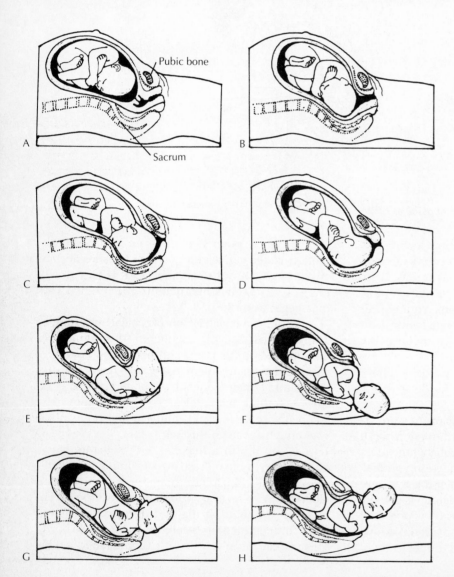

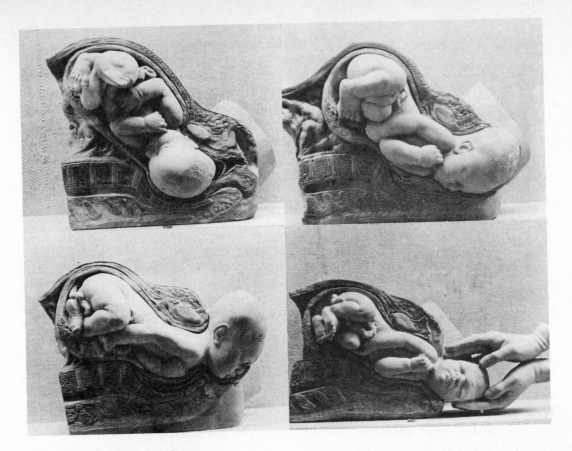

FIGURE 6–15. *The stages of childbirth.*

emerging face up rather than in the normal face-down position. But sooner or later, during one of the pushes, whoever is positioned to catch the baby will say something like, "Here it comes." What they have seen is the crown of the baby's head entering the vaginal opening. It is normal to feel an intense burning or stretching sensation at this point. You may be able to watch in the mirror if it doesn't interfere with your pushing.

The baby's head and shoulders are the most difficult to deliver because the baby's head is large relative to the rest of his or her body. After the birth of the head, mucus will be suctioned from the baby's nose and mouth. You may or may not be asked to push for delivery of the shoulders. Then the remainder of the body is birthed quickly, without much effort.

In most cases your baby will start to breathe

A woman delivers in the dorsal position.

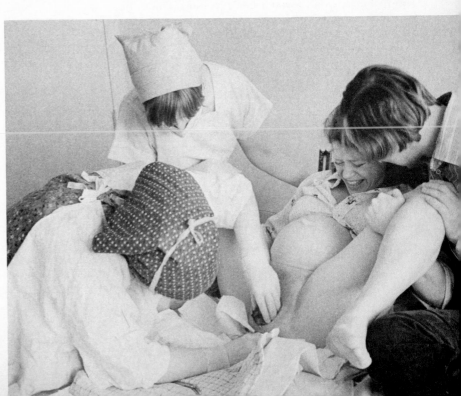

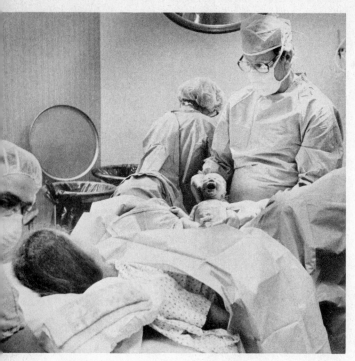

A newborn baby thirty seconds after delivery.

as soon as he or she is born. Some babies cry; others do not. Contrary to popular belief, doctors do not slap babies to make them breathe. If the baby is slow to breathe, the doctor or midwife will "stimulate" the baby by massaging the back and feet; oxygen may be necessary also. It is very important to keep the baby warm and to dry the baby right away. This can be done on the mother's abdomen or in a special baby warmer.

After the baby is born, the umbilical cord is clamped and cut. The umbilical cord carried oxygen and nutrients to the baby from the mother's body, and carried away waste products. Once the baby is born, it is no longer needed. At some hospitals the father may be allowed to cut the cord. Cutting the cord does not hurt the baby, and the way it is cut does not affect the type of "belly button" the child will have.

Immediately after the birth of the baby, the parents—especially the mother—experience an intense feeling of relief. They may express this feeling by crying, by talking, by just looking at the baby, or even by closing their eyes and feeling exhausted.

Delivery of the Placenta

The third phase of labor and delivery, the delivery of the placenta, takes place within half an hour after the baby is delivered (Figure 6–16). Often the new parents hardly notice it is happening because they are so busy looking at and getting to know their new baby. Within three to five minutes after delivery of the baby, the uterus begins to contract again, but these contractions do not feel strong or very uncomfortable to the new mother. As the uterus contracts it shrinks in size, and the placenta becomes detached from the wall of the uterus. The placenta, which looks like a large piece of beef liver and weighs about one and a half pounds, is pushed out easily and is accompanied by one to two cups of blood. This is blood from the vessels that connected the uterine wall and the placenta. When the placenta detaches, these vessels are torn, but the contractions of the uterus squeeze them closed, so that bleeding is limited. The blood lost during a normal delivery of the placenta does not endanger the mother, as she has created extra blood volume during the pregnancy to support the placenta and the fetus.

Finishing Up

Once the placenta is delivered, your episiotomy (if you have one) will be stitched up. You will not feel this if you have had a local anesthetic in the area. After this, you will be permitted to put your

FIGURE 6–16. *Uterine contractions cause the placenta to detach from the wall of the uterus and be pushed out.*

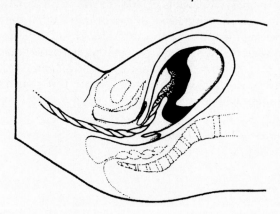

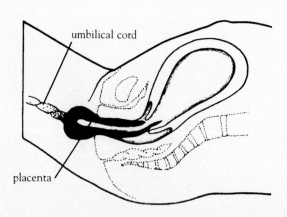

umbilical cord

placenta

legs down. You will not be able to stand up for a while (at least half an hour, and considerably longer in most hospitals). This is to allow your blood pressure to return to normal and to avoid fainting. Usually you can eat whatever you want at this point and are encouraged to do so. If you and the baby are all right, the staff will usually leave the new family alone for a while.

The Newborn

The baby may be placed on your abdomen immediately after delivery. The umbilical cord may be cut immediately, or the caregivers may wait for a few minutes until any additional blood that was in the placenta has been passed to the baby. In some hospitals, hospital staff wash the baby (who will be covered with mucus, amniotic fluid, and some blood) before presenting him or her to the mother.

The staff may also weigh the baby and perform an APGAR test. The APGAR test is a ten-point scale that is used to assess the baby's general well-being, with 10 being the highest possible score. It measures breathing, muscle tone, heart rate, color (babies who are getting enough oxygen will have a pinkish skin tone, those who are not will be grayish), and reflexes. Most hospitals do this one minute and again five minutes after birth.

The staff may eventually take the baby briefly for footprinting (for identification) and a more thorough checkup. This checkup will include drawing blood samples to test for anemia and jaundice.

You should be prepared for the appearance of your newborn. As noted before, a newborn baby is covered with mucus, some blood, and so on. The head is the largest part of the baby, and the baby's brain is already at about 25 percent of its adult weight (while the body is only about 5 percent of its adult weight). The average newborn weighs six to seven pounds and is about 21 inches long.

In addition to appearing large, the newborn's head may appear to be misshapen. This is because the baby's head is temporarily molded by the pressure of passage through the birth canal during delivery. The head regains its normal shape within the first 24 hours after birth. These changes in head shape are possible because the baby's skull is made up of several bony plates, which can move under pressure. There is a soft spot called the **fontanel** on top of the skull, and another on the back of the head, where the skull bones have not yet joined. All babies are born with these soft spots, which close naturally at different ages in different babies (somewhere between 9 and 24 months). Until it closes, this part of the baby's head is somewhat more vulnerable than the portion covered with skull. But

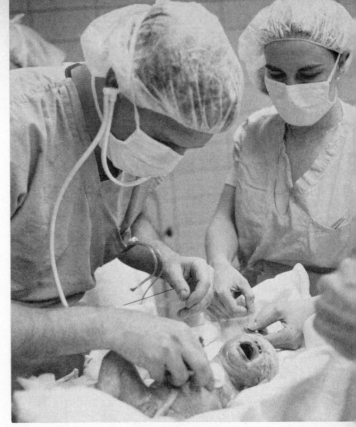

A newborn baby gets her first medical check-up.

normal touching and activities such as shampooing the baby's hair will do no harm.

Beyond these characteristics, there is tremendous variability in the appearance of newborn babies. Newborns have different amounts and colors of hair (this hair often falls out and may reappear in a different color). Most babies are born with blue eyes, which darken within a few months. Some babies are covered with fetal hair (**lanugo**), and many have some skin peeling. A few even have teeth ("milk teeth"), which will fall out and be replaced by the real primary or "baby" teeth. Whatever your baby's appearance, chances are that you will think he or she is beautiful.

The Experience of Delivery

Reading through the description of labor and delivery, you may think that everyone—mother, father, and baby—will be totally exhausted when the birth is over. Actually, the baby is very alert (especially if the mother used no medication for the delivery) and ready to interact with people.

The parents are usually so excited and elated that neither of them can sleep. They too are ready to spend time with the new baby. Some babies will even begin breastfeeding within a few minutes after being born.

If the labor and birth have gone well, with no complications, the parents are likely to have two major reactions to the birth of a healthy baby. One is sheer elation. After waiting nine months and go-

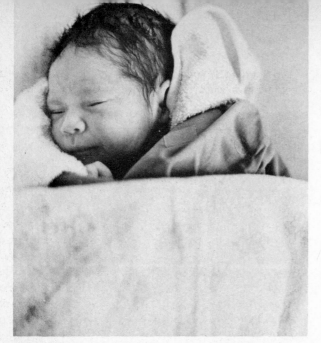

Newborn babies always look beautiful to their parents.

ing through labor, the baby is finally here. Mother and baby are safe and healthy. The mother and father are now joined in a special way.

The other major feeling for the new parents is fascination with their newborn as they count fingers and toes, discuss whom the baby resembles, wonder at the baby's abilities, and so on. Both the mother and the father will react this way, especially if the father was present at the birth. The parents, especially the father, will soon get to share these happy feelings by calling the new grandparents and siblings (if they did not attend the birth). In an hour or two, everyone will be tired. But for the moment, no one wants to sleep.

For women who deliver by caesarean section, and those who have required heavy sedation or anesthesia, these experiences may be delayed for several hours, until the drugs wear off. If the father was present, he is able to enjoy the new baby immediately, but the couple cannot share the experience until the mother is also awake and comfortable enough to enjoy the baby.

Around 1 in 10 babies is born with a minor health problem or defect (and around 1 in 100 has a serious problem). Most new parents are so pleased that the baby has arrived that the presence of a minor health problem or defect does not bother them at all. If there is a serious problem, however, they may be uncertain of how to react to the baby until they know more about his or her condition.

Birth Complications

Late Births and Induced Labor

Most babies are born within the period from two weeks before to two weeks after the due date. If you do not spontaneously begin labor within two weeks after your due date, your physician or specialist may run tests, such as sonograms, to determine the condition of the baby and its support system. If the baby is mature but, for some unknown reason, labor does not start, this can be risky. The baby's support systems (such as the placenta, umbilical cord, and amniotic fluid) are not designed to work indefinitely.

If the baby is at risk, labor may be induced using uterine stimulants such as **oxytocin**. Oxytocin is administered through an intravenous tube and is carefully monitored, starting out with a low dose and increasing until labor is well established. There are some risks connected with the use of oxytocin, including the chance that the labor will feel more intense than a normal labor. The laboring woman may then need more pain-killing drugs, and if contractions are too strong or too close together, they can decrease the baby's supply of oxygen.

Premature Births

Premature labor is a relatively common pregnancy complication, occurring in about 8 of every 100 pregnancies. It is more common in younger women (under 17), in older women (over 35), in women with an obstetrical history of premature labor or twins, and in women who use drugs, are poor, or have high blood pressure.

Not every woman who goes into premature labor actually gives birth prematurely. Sometimes the labor can be stopped (at least temporarily) by a combination of bed rest and drug treatment. Such treatments can be effective only if the labor has not progressed too far. Therefore, it is crucial that you seek help immediately if you think you are starting labor prematurely. Every day that the baby can be

FIGURE 6–17. *After delivery, the new mother usually wants to relax and get to know her baby.*

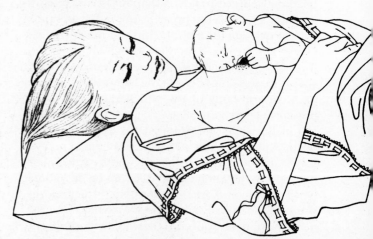

kept in the womb increases the chances of survival and good health at birth.

A **premature** baby is one who weighs under 5.5 pounds and is carried for less than 38 weeks. If the baby is full term (a 38 to 42 week pregnancy) and weighs less than 5.5 pounds, the baby is considered small-for-date rather than premature. Although such babies may have problems, they tend to be physically more developed than premature infants, so their chances for a good outcome are better. The earlier (in terms of weeks carried) and smaller a premature baby, the less positive the outlook is. Infants born weighing under 1,500 grams (around 3.3 pounds) are particularly at risk for developing problems.

Premature babies have higher rates of death, neurological disorders, learning disabilities, and developmental delays than full-term babies do. For example, probably about 2 percent of all full-term babies have neurological disorders, but about 20 percent of all premature babies do. But not all premature babies develop problems. Today we have better treatment and technology to ensure their survival and health than ever before.

If you do have a premature baby, you may find your baby unattractive at first. Premature babies, especially very early ones, do not look like full-term babies. They have less body fat, may appear thin and drawn, and may have a grayish or mottled skin color. Their eyes may be partly closed and surrounded by dark circles. Fortunately, the baby's appearance will improve soon. Also, once you get to know the baby a little, the appearance will not matter so much.

A premature baby will probably be placed in a neonatal intensive care unit (NICU). If the hospital where you give birth does not have one, the baby may be transferred to another hospital. An NICU can be a frightening place for new parents at first. The baby will be in a special bed, and there may be wires and tubes attached to his or her body. The medical staff will be busy caring for the baby, and the parents may feel helpless and left out.

The parents play an important role in the care of premature babies, however, even while they are still in intensive care. The touching, talking, and affection that parents provide is very important to the baby's development. In addition, this early time with the baby forms the basis for your relationship when you eventually take the baby home.

A premature birth catches the parents by surprise, and the special care needed can be frightening and confusing. There may be long-term medical decisions to be made, and the specialized hospital care can be extremely expensive. All these things may contribute to feelings of guilt, doubt, and fear

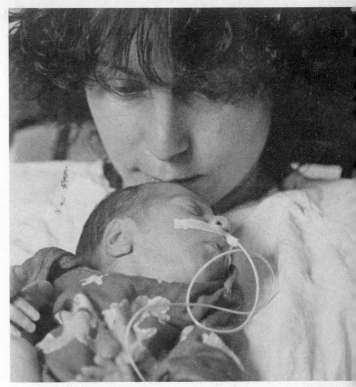

A mother holds her premature baby.

for the parents. If your premature baby is to have the best chance of normal development, it is important to resolve these feelings. Talking with the hospital social worker about your feelings can be very helpful at this time.

Birth Defects

About 95 percent of all American babies (live births) are born relatively healthy. They may have a mild condition such as **tachycardia** (a heartbeat that is too fast, mainly from the stress of labor) or **jaundice,** a yellowing of the skin indicating that the body is not eliminating bile as quickly as it should. But such conditions are easily treated and rarely have any long-term effects.

About 2.5 percent of babies, however, (about 250,000 babies born in the United States every year), have some major birth defect. These include spina bifida, cleft palate, Down's syndrome, or any number of other physical or mental defects. Another 2.5 percent will have a problem that will not affect the baby until later, such as cystic fibrosis, sickle-cell anemia, or Tay-Sachs disease.

Many, but not all, birth defects are preventable through genetic counseling or through proper prenatal care. In addition, prenatal diagnostic techniques (see details earlier in this chapter) can identify many of these problems during pregnancy. These tests, however, will be done only if a possible problem is suspected. Particularly in first pregnancies, there is often little reason to suspect a problem. Furthermore, not all birth defects can be detected during pregnancy.

If your baby has a birth defect, you will need to consult doctors (possibly specialists such as pediatric cardiologists or neurologists) in order to understand fully the treatment and prognosis of your baby's problem. Even if your baby's problem is a relatively rare one, up-to-date information is available from such sources as the March of Dimes and from the many organizations formed for specific diseases (such as the Cystic Fibrosis Foundation or the Tay-Sachs Foundation). Your library may also be able to provide additional information about the disorder.

Parents of babies born with birth defects often feel a great deal of grief, anger, and guilt. This is a normal reaction. Information alone may not help you get through these feelings. Counseling and support may also be needed. The hospital where your baby is being treated probably has a social worker who can help. If you are religious, a member of the clergy may be a good source of support. Your friends and relatives may also be helpful.

Death of a Baby

In a small number of cases, babies are born dead, or do not survive the first few days or weeks of life. These are often terribly difficult situations for the expectant mother and father. The sense of loss can be as great as it would be if an adult or an older child had died, even though the parents never had a chance to get to know the baby. Different families handle the death of a new baby differently. Some name the baby, have him or her baptized, and hold a funeral or memorial service. Others choose not to do any of these things. Some states have laws requiring burial, and the parents are financially responsible for the costs.

Most couples want to see their baby, even if he or she is not alive.

Sometimes it takes a few days before families know what they want to do. Families may want to seek the advice of their religious adviser if they have one. Hospital chaplains and social work departments can also help a family sort out their feelings.

The loss of a baby, like any death in the family, takes time to get over and may affect a couple's feelings about having another baby. The couple may be afraid to try, or they may want to try again as soon as possible. It is important to resolve the feelings connected with the lost baby before the next child is born, so that the new baby is not burdened with the parents' sadness and fears related to the dead infant.

RECOVERY AFTER CHILDBIRTH

Physical Recovery

How quickly you regain your strength and energy after childbirth depends very much on how the birth process has gone. Expect to be tired for at least several weeks (longer if you have had a C-section). Many new mothers claim it takes as long as a year until they feel completely "like themselves" again. Temporary help with housework, shopping, and baby care can reduce stress for the new parents and speed the mother's recovery. Family or friends may be able to provide support, or a paid helper may be needed. Friends and relatives will want to meet the new baby, but the new parents need to be careful not to overtire themselves with extra entertaining. Fathers can help by being actively involved in housework, infant care, and the care of the other children.

For the new mother, there are several after-

After childbirth it takes time to recover full strength and energy.

effects of childbirth during the early postpartum period (the first few weeks after giving birth).

Vaginal Bleeding and Cramps

You will be bleeding from the vagina as the uterus recovers from the pregnancy and returns to its normal nonpregnant state. Sanitary pads should be used rather than tampons, since the cervix has not completely closed, and there is a risk of uterine infection. The bleeding may last as long as six weeks.

Some women experience some cramping (**afterpains**) along with the bleeding, especially the first few times they breastfeed. These pains are sometimes quite strong but should go away in about a week. The pains and bleeding should not limit your physical activity. In other words, you need not avoid walking, carrying the baby, and so on because of the bleeding. It is important to keep the vaginal area clean in order to avoid infection.

Recovery from Episiotomy

If you had an episiotomy, you will have stitches, and there may be some bruising of the perineal area. All this causes discomfort, which can be considerable in some cases. You may be particularly uncomfortable when you try to walk. Warm baths and wearing a premoistened gauze pad may help relieve the pain.

The stitches can also cause some concern about the first bowel movement after delivery. Usually your bowels will not move for several days after giving birth. Many women with stitches are worried about how much pain there will be when a bowel movement finally does occur. The fear is often worse than the actual event. If you are very concerned, you might request a stool softener or laxative (many doctors give these routinely anyway). It is also important to remember the importance of using the toilet paper to wipe toward your back (rather than toward the perineal area and vagina) in order to reduce the chances of infection. Using a spray bottle filled with warm water to rinse off the area after each urination or bowel movement also helps to prevent problems.

Recovery from Anesthesia

If you were given anesthesia, you may experience some additional problems. General anesthesia, of course, will leave you disoriented for up to 24 hours and tired for several days. With a regional anesthetic, this effect is much less pronounced but may still occur. In addition, some women experience headaches (which can last for days) if they have had spinal anesthesia.

Recovery from Caesarean Section

If you have had a C-section, your recovery will take longer than for a vaginal delivery and will be somewhat more involved, since you have had major surgery. After the surgery, you will probably have an IV, and possibly a catheter for urination. Although you may feel weak and your incision will be sore, it is usually recommended that you get out of bed within 24 to 48 hours. This helps to prevent the formation of blood clots in the legs, aids digestion, and decreases gas pains and constipation.

As with all major surgeries, a C-section normally requires a hospital stay of several days and an at-home recovery period of roughly six weeks. Recovery time can vary considerably, depending on your overall health, age, help available at home, and so on. It is very important to have help at home during this time. Trying to do too much will only make the recovery period longer and cause an increased risk of infection or injury.

Emotional Recovery

The first reaction to a new baby is usually one of tremendous excitement and joy (often mixed with exhaustion). As the responsibilities of parenthood become more real, however, these initial feelings may fade. This seems to be especially true for women. Babies need constant care, and it is an exhausting job for someone who is already tired. Furthermore, it means a loss of privacy and time.

Postpartum Depression in Mothers

A short period of mild depression after giving birth seems to be quite normal for many women. About 60 percent of all women experience the "baby blues." This usually lasts two to three days, beginning two to four days after the birth. The new mother feels teary, sad, and anxious. She may find herself easily frustrated, worried, or upset. In addition, about 10 to 20 percent of women experience a more severe temporary depression within six months of giving birth. Another 10 to 20 percent experience no depression or even mild blues.

Postpartum blues and depression may be caused in part by the physical and hormonal changes of pregnancy and delivery. But strong support from the husband, friends, and relatives can help reduce the severity of depression and the length of time it lasts. A new baby can cause a mother to feel socially isolated because it is much harder to get out and do things than it was before the baby was born. This sense of social isolation can cause negative feelings toward the baby as well as depression.

Fortunately, most women come through these

temporary depressions without problems. If the woman or her family becomes worried about her condition, she should see her health care provider.

Depression in Fathers

Fathers may also suffer from baby blues. For example, two-thirds of the fathers in one study reported mild to moderate postpartum blues, but none suffered from long-lasting or severe depression. About one-third of the men in the previously mentioned study had the blues for more than eight days. The men who reported the more extended blues seemed to be less certain of what to do or how to help their wives.

Fathers' reactions to and involvement in parenthood seem to depend heavily on the mother. Men who have a good relationship with their wives and whose wives react well to pregnancy seem to be more satisfied and involved fathers. Thus, men, too, seem to need support and encouragement in order to adjust well.

Sex

It is usually recommended that women avoid sexual intercourse for three to six weeks after giving birth. This is to prevent infection, since the cervix is open, making infection of the uterus a higher risk than usual. Of course, the couple can substitute sexual activity other than intercourse during this time (see Chapter 3 for alternatives). Some women feel sexy soon after giving birth, and others do not for many weeks. Fatigue, both from the birth pro-

Fathers as well as mothers need time to recover from the birth and adjust to the new baby.

cess and from caring for a new baby, may contribute to a woman not feeling sexy. A little reassurance (including nonsexual affection) from the partner can be very helpful in rekindling a woman's sexual feelings.

A common worry is that the vagina may have been stretched out of shape by the birth, so that sex will not be as satisfying as before. Although there is stretching at the time of delivery, the vagina regains its shape, and the permanent changes should not be so great that sex becomes unsatisfying. If there are difficulties with intercourse when the couple does resume (several weeks after delivery), the woman should see her care provider.

Contraception

Once you resume intercourse, you should also resume contraception unless you want to get pregnant again immediately. If you are not breastfeeding, your menstrual cycle will start within about two months after birth. If you do breastfeed, it could be six months to a year before you menstruate. Many people mistakenly believe that this means that you cannot get pregnant if you are nursing. *Although breastfeeding does reduce the chances that you will get pregnant, it is far from 100 percent effective.* You have no way of knowing when your menstrual cycle (and ovulation) will begin. So if you don't want to be pregnant again right away, it is best to use contraception. The Pill is not recommended for breastfeeding women because the hormones may be passed to the infant. (See Chapter 9 for details on the various contraceptive choices.)

Weight and Body Shape

Immediately after your baby is born, you will still look more or less pregnant, even though you will have lost 10 to 15 pounds (roughly twice the baby's body weight) at the time of delivery. Indeed, you may find yourself still wearing maternity clothes for at least a couple of weeks after the baby is born. This is because it takes the uterus about 10 days to shrink down to a nonpregnant size. The afterpains experienced by some women are caused by the uterus contracting back to its normal size. Breastfeeding helps to speed up this process.

Most women have extra weight left over from the pregnancy. This weight may slowly come off on its own. If it does not, the nursing mother may have to put up with the extra weight for a while, as dieting is not recommended for women who are breastfeeding. New mothers who are not breastfeeding should also be careful about starting a new diet or exercise program, since they are still recovering from the pregnancy and delivery and may be tired from caring for the new baby.

When you return to your prepregnancy weight, you may find that some of your clothes do not fit properly. This is especially true if you have had your first baby. Your hips may be a little wider because of the spreading of the pelvis to accommodate the baby, and your breasts may be larger. Your breasts are likely to return to prepregnancy size eventually, whether you breastfeed or not.

FOR FURTHER READING

ASHFORD, JANET ISAACS (ed.). *The Whole Birth Catalog: A Sourcebook for Choices in Childbirth.* Trumansburg, N.Y.: The Crossing Press, 1983.

BEREZIN, NANCY. *After a Loss in Pregnancy: Help for Families Affected by a Miscarriage, a Still Birth, or the Loss of a Newborn.* New York: Simon & Schuster, 1982.

GUTTMACHER, ALAN F. *Pregnancy, Birth, and Family Planning.* New York: New American Library, 1987.

KITZINGER, SHEILA. *The Complete Book of Pregnancy and Childbirth.* New York: Knopf, 1980.

LESKO, WENDY, AND MATTHEW LESKO. *The Maternity Sourcebook.* New York: Warner Books, 1984.

MESSENGER, MARIE. *The Breastfeeding Book.* New York: Van Nostrand Reinhold, 1983.

NANCE, SHERRI. *Premature Babies: A Handbook for Parents.* New York: Arbor House, 1982.

SMOLAK, LINDA. *Infancy.* Englewood Cliffs, N.J.: Prentice-Hall, 1986.

WILSON, CRISTINE COLEMAN, AND WENDY ROE HOVEY. *Caesarean Childbirth: A Handbook for Parents.* New York: Dolphin/Doubleday, 1980.

RESOURCES

Information and referral services are available in your local community through the health department, community hospitals, the United Way agency, and the county or state Department of Social Services. In addition, the following national resources can be contacted:

American College of Nurse-Midwives
1522 K Street, N.W., Suite 1120
Washington,DC 20005
(202) 347-5445
A nonprofit organization that provides information about nurse midwifery as a profession and as a choice, and provides referrals to services in your local area.

La Leche League
9616 Minneapolis
Franklin Park, IL 60131
(312) 455-7730
A nonprofit organization that provides breastfeeding information hotline, education about breastfeeding, and referral to local chapters and support groups.

March of Dimes Birth Defects Foundation
1275 Mamaroneck Avenue
White Plains, NY 10605
(914) 428-7100
A nonprofit organization that provides information on inherited disorders and birth defects and referral to genetic counseling and services in your local area (or call the March of Dimes in your local area).

7

Unplanned and Unwanted Pregnancy

This chapter is for women and girls who have an unwanted pregnancy, and for their families and friends. It explains what you can do about the situation and what your choices are. It also provides information about all the different things you need to take into consideration in this situation. The chapter is especially written for teenage girls, but women of all ages and men as well may find it useful.

The first part of the chapter provides information about how to deal with the problem. The last part contains some general information about the seriousness of this problem in the United States and what some of the causes are.

SIGNS OF PREGNANCY AND PREGNANCY TESTS

There are pregnancy tests available that can tell if a woman is pregnant within a few days after she has intercourse, long before her period is due. Women do not need to wait until they have missed a period or developed other signs of pregnancy to find out. (For details on the signs of pregnancy and the kind of tests available see Chapter 6, "Pregnancy and Childbirth.")

There are emergency treatments (called morning-after birth control) for women who have had intercourse and fear they may be pregnant. These can be done before tests show the woman is pregnant (to make sure a pregnancy does not get started). This treatment with hormones must be started within 72 hours after intercourse. (For more details, see Chapter 9, "Contraception.")

It is not difficult to get a pregnancy test. Doctors, HMOs, hospitals, and clinics all perform these tests, and many clinics offer free pregnancy testing. Women who are under 18 years of age may need their parents' permission to be tested by a private doctor or a hospital. Family planning clinics will usually provide the service to a minor without contacting the parents. Do-it-yourself kits to test for pregnancy can be bought at a pharmacy by women and girls of any age. If a kit is used, an examination by a health care provider is also needed to confirm pregnancy.

Any girl or woman who has had intercourse since her last menstrual period and is two weeks (or more) late for the next one should get a pregnancy test. There is a good chance she is pregnant.

WHAT TO DO IF YOU ARE PREGNANT

When a girl or woman finds out that she is pregnant—and the pregnancy was not planned—it often creates a crisis in her life. She may feel helpless and overwhelmed. She may be angry—at herself, her partner, or the world in general. Or she may be happy to learn of the pregnancy, even though it is unexpected. She may look forward to having a baby.

It is normal to have strong emotional feelings at this time. And it is important to sort through all your feelings and reactions, and to develop a plan for the pregnancy—a plan that fits in with the rest of your life.

Taking Control of Your Life

Sometimes it is tempting to sit back and wait—to let time make decisions for us. This is especially true when we are dealing with a confusing and frightening problem like an unwanted pregnancy. But pregnancy is too important to leave to time and fate. Too many lives are affected—the mother, the father, and the family, as well as the child that could be born.

Many women feel powerless to control their own lives and futures. Sometimes that is how they got pregnant! None of us has complete control over everything that happens in our lives. But we can all have more power over our lives if we try.

Whatever happens, the woman who chooses her own future feels better about it than the person who just lets things happen. Even if your past pattern of handling problems has been *not* to handle them, an unwanted pregnancy is a good time to start to take control of your life!

Looking at All the Choices

Being pregnant is a fact. Pregnancy does not go away if you ignore it or pretend it is not there. But there are many choices about how to deal with the situation. For some people, the solution to the problem may be clear from the beginning. But for most people, it is not.

This section of the book is written to help women and their partners and families to explore and understand what the choices are, and how to go about making a decision. The first point is this: *Look at all the choices.* A woman with an unplanned pregnancy can consider **marriage**, **single parenthood**, or **adoption** for the baby. She can also end the pregnancy by choosing **abortion**. There are many community services and programs that support women with counseling, with medical help, and with children's services. Even if you are single, pregnant, and expecting no help from the father or from your family, you are not alone.

Projecting into the Future

Each of the possible choices must be looked at not just as a short-term solution to an unplanned pregnancy, but also for what it would mean over the long run. What will each choice mean two years—five years—ten years—twenty years from

Getting a pregnancy test is the first step.

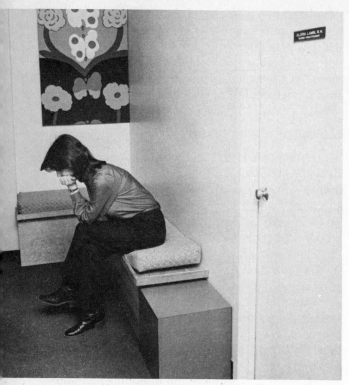

Thinking through all the choices is not easy, but it is important when the problem is an unwanted pregnancy.

now? What will it mean for the mother? For the child? For other family members?

Time Limits on Decision Making

The earlier in the pregnancy decisions are made, the more choices are available, and the more protection against health problems for both the mother and the baby. Early prenatal care is important for the woman who plans to have the baby. If a decision is made to have an abortion, it also should be done as early as possible.

Besides the importance of early prenatal care, early planning is also important for the woman who plans to have her baby because of the many changes that will take place over the nine months of pregnancy. The woman needs to prepare for changes in her appearance and for the fact that she may not be able to be as active as before. Her school or job attendance may be affected. Her health care and nutritional needs will change. And after the baby is born (if she plans to keep it), there will be drastic changes in her life-style.

MAKING A DECISION YOU CAN LIVE WITH

The decision about an unplanned pregnancy belongs to the woman who is pregnant. She may take into consideration the wishes of others—of her partner and her family—but the choice is really hers. It is her health and her future that are most directly affected. This is true even for the very young teenager. The woman's future mental and emotional health will be affected by the way this decision is made. It is important that she make a decision that she personally can live with.

What Is Best for You?

The first thing for a woman to consider is what is best for herself. People must take care of their own basic needs before they are able to take care of others, so it is not selfish for her to think of herself first in this situation.

One way to look at the situation is to take both a short-term and a long-term view. The question of how the pregnancy and birth of a child will affect the woman's life over the next year or two is important. But it is also important to ask how a child will fit into her long-range plans.

If a pregnant woman is young and single, how will a baby affect her plans for education, career, and marriage? How good is her physical and emotional health? What kinds of support will she need to help her to be a good mother? What are the rights and responsibilities of mothers? There are many legal protections of a mother's right to keep and care for her child. There are also legal responsibilities.

Children must be fed and cared for. They must receive necessary medical care and live in a safe environment. Children must attend school. Parents are responsible for making sure that children have and do all these things. Beyond these basic responsibilities, a baby has many more needs for care, love, and attention from parents that must be met.

What Is Best for the Baby?

The second person to think about is the baby. When babies are brought into the world, the parents take on twenty years of responsibility for care—and a lifetime of concern and involvement.

The following things should be considered when thinking about the needs of a baby:

1. *Basic needs:* A baby must have food, clothing, a place to live, and someone to take care of him or her 24 hours a day.
2. *Health and safety:* A baby must have checkups, inoculations, medical care, supervision at home, and safe home conditions.
3. *Love and care:* To develop into a normal adult, a baby must have love. A baby who is not loved may not learn how to love others, and may not grow and develop normally.

4. *Education and opportunity:* To have a happy and productive life when he or she is grown up, a baby will need at least 12 years of education, as well as opportunities to learn about different jobs and careers.

How Does the Father Feel?

The father's feelings and wishes about the pregnancy are important. In situations where the couple is very close, the man may be as involved as the woman in making plans. But sometimes an unplanned pregnancy is the result of intercourse with a man whom the woman hardly knows. In these cases, women often do not tell the man about the pregnancy. However, in most situations, men would like to know if they have made a woman pregnant.

It is important to find out how the man feels about the pregnancy. What would he like the woman to do? This does not mean that the final decision is his. It means that his ideas should be considered in making plans. Some men have no interest in becoming fathers. Others care very much about the baby and want to be as involved as possible.

There are really three questions for the man.

1. How does he feel about the pregnancy?
2. How does he feel about the relationship with the pregnant woman?
3. What role does he want to play with the baby? With the mother?

The news of an unplanned pregnancy is likely to be as much of a shock to the man as it is to the woman. He may need some time to get used to the idea before he knows what his feelings are.

Some families consider anyone who gets involved in a pregnancy outside of marriage to be evil or no good. This kind of attitude can keep the man and woman from understanding and helping each other at this time. There are many ways besides marriage that the father can participate in the life of the child.

Like the mother, the father has legal rights and responsibilities toward the child. If the couple is married, the father's rights and responsibilities are equal to the mother's. If the couple is not married, he still has some rights to participate in plans made for the child after it is born. He also has responsibilities to help to support the child financially until it is 18 years old.

Legally, the decision to end a pregnancy by abortion belongs to the woman alone. She may want to include her partner in making the decision, but his permission is not required (even if the couple is married).

How Does the Family Feel?

In some cases a woman may plan an early abortion and may not even discuss the pregnancy with family members. It is up to her how much she chooses to involve the family in the decision making.

If she plans to have the baby, the woman needs to consider her own family's feelings about the pregnancy. If she lives with her parents, they will certainly know about the pregnancy. They will have strong feelings about it—but not always the

Not every family is in a position to make room for another baby.

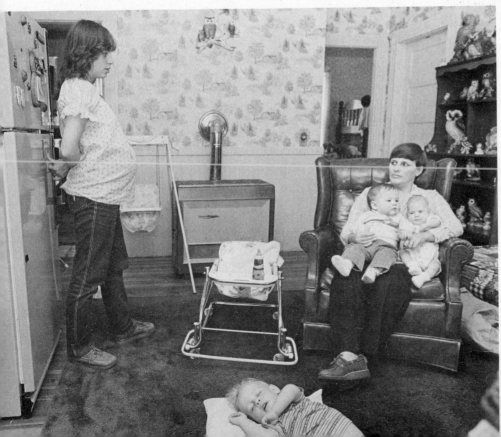

feelings that the woman expects. There is no way to know how her parents will react without telling them. Parents who might be expected to be angry and judgmental often surprise their daughters by accepting the pregnancy and the baby. Parents whom the daughter may expect to support her may surprise her by not wanting any involvement with the baby, or with her as an unmarried mother.

One thing is clear. After her partner, the woman's parents and other close family members are the most important people to consult, as they will be the baby's family too, if she continues the pregnancy.

After finding out the family's feelings about the pregnancy, the next questions are:

1. Do they support the idea of keeping the baby?
2. Do they want to accept the baby as a family member?
3. What involvement in the pregnancy would they like to have?

The mother's parents have few legal rights to the child. But they do have a lot of influence on what plans are made if the mother is young (under 18) and lives at home. If something should happen to the mother and there were no father involved, the mother's parents (as the child's closest relatives) would be expected to make plans for the child. Years ago financial responsibility for support included grandparents, but this is no longer the case in most states.

Getting Help in Deciding

Coming to a decision about how to handle an unplanned pregnancy is difficult for most women. They may need help to sort through all their different ideas and feelings. Usually a woman turns to her family and friends, but those who are closest can't always be objective. They may push her in one direction or another because of their own needs or wishes.

Sometimes a woman needs an objective counselor, someone who is not involved in the situation. This could be someone the woman already knows and trusts, such as a minister, teacher, or doctor. Or it could be a trained counselor at a family-planning clinic, family services agency, or child welfare service. To find this kind of help, you can call one of these agencies in your local community (or in a nearby city, if you live in a small town and are worried about privacy). If the organization you call doesn't offer the service, they will be able to refer you to one that does. The yellow pages and the white pages of the telephone book both list social service agencies.

It is important to choose a counselor who will be objective and help you to make your own decision. Some agencies that advertise in newspapers that they will advise pregnant women support only one solution to unplanned pregnancy, and oppose other choices.

Coming to a Decision

In the following pages, information about each of the possible choices—keeping the baby, adoption, and abortion—is given. In reading about the choices, keep in mind the following three points:

1. *Consider all the facts and all the choices:* Don't jump to a decision without thinking. Don't assume that there's only one way for you. You do have choices, and those choices are legally yours to make.
2. *Remember to consider emotions and feelings:* Feelings aren't always logical. They don't always make sense, but they are real. Making a decision you can live with means understanding your feelings and accepting them. After that you can make a decision that respects your feelings as well as what is practical.
3. *A chance to be proud of yourself:* An unplanned pregnancy can be a frightening crisis in life. But it is also a chance to learn, to grow, and to make the best possible decision. Making choices can be painful, but this crisis can also be an opportunity to gain pride and self-respect.

ALTERNATIVE CHOICES

Keeping the Baby

Marriage

Marriage is often the first thing that occurs to a single woman faced with an unplanned pregnancy. For a couple with a strong relationship, the pregnancy may seem like a sign that it is time to make a permanent commitment and get married. But many other unplanned pregnancies happen to partners who are not deeply involved.

Under what conditions should the couple consider marriage?

1. If they feel that they would like to get married even if there were no baby
2. If both parents want the baby, even though it was unplanned

A marriage in which these two conditions are not met is not likely to succeed. And a marriage that ends in divorce in a year or two will probably cause more problems and heartache than it prevents.

Many of the old reasons for pregnant women getting married to someone (anyone!) are no longer valid. For example:

1. *To give the child a name:* In most states today, the child's last name is chosen by the parents. A couple does not have to be married to give the child the father's last name.

2. *To keep the child from being illegitimate:* In most states today, the child's birth certificate will not show whether his or her parents were married or not. Birth records no longer label children as legitimate or illegitimate.

3. *To give the child a father:* Fathers can acknowledge their children and give them the rights of support and inheritance without being married. In most states this can be done by signing as the child's father at the time of birth.

Making It on Your Own

Many women who have an unplanned pregnancy discover that they very much want the baby, even though they are not in a position to get married. Then they may decide to have the baby, keep it, and try to make it on their own. It is quite common in the United States today for women to give birth outside of marriage, and to raise the child themselves. Years ago such women were under a lot of pressure to hide their pregnancy and then to give the child up for adoption. But in the 1980s most single women who give birth choose to keep their own child rather than give it up for adoption. Most communities accept these women and children, although prejudice and discrimination still exist. But there are so many single-parent families headed by divorced mothers today that single-parent families where the mother was never married are not very noticeable.

Under what conditions should a woman consider trying to make it on her own with the baby?

1. If she wants the baby, even though it was unplanned
2. If she can support herself and the baby financially
3. If she is mature enough to take on full-time responsibility for the baby

Unfortunately, many women want to raise their own child but can't make enough money to support a family. A high percentage of single mothers, both never married and divorced or separated, live in poverty. There are welfare programs for women who can't work or can't find a job, but in most cases they don't provide enough money to allow the woman and her child to live with dignity and self-respect.

A woman who is planning to make it on her own should plan very carefully to see what her expenses and her income would be if she kept the child. Women who have not finished high school and who have never held a job usually have a very hard time supporting themselves, even without a child.

Help from the Father

The father of the baby can be a tremendous help, even if the couple does not get married. Many men want to be involved with their babies, and are willing to help. There are legal obligations for unmarried fathers to support their babies financially, but it can be very difficult and expensive to force a father to pay if he doesn't want to. On the other hand, many fathers are willing to support their child and also want to be involved in raising the

It is not easy to make it on your own as a young single mother.

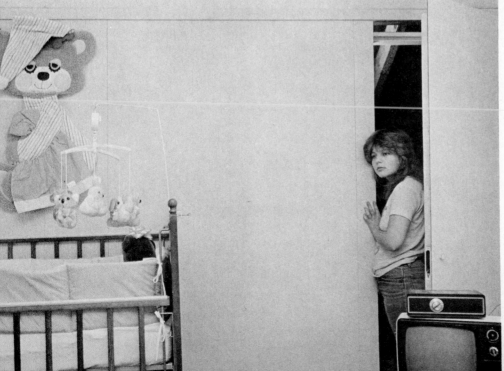

child. The father's parents also may want to be involved as grandparents.

In an unmarried situation, it is up to the woman to decide what is best for herself and the baby. Each situation is different. Some fathers would be helpful and a good influence on the baby's life; others would not be. The mother should think carefully about what kind of help she wants from the father, and about how involved he should be in raising the baby.

Help from Your Family

The people who are most likely to help a single woman with an unplanned pregnancy are her own family, especially her parents. When the parents are willing to help, a woman often can keep her baby when otherwise she would not be able to. The only way to find out if a woman's parents are willing to help is to talk to them.

Sometimes the pregnant woman is still living at home with her parents. She may be very young and still in school. In these situations the parents have a lot of influence over what plans she makes, but the final decisions still belong to her.

When a woman has an unplanned pregnancy and doesn't know what she wants to do about it, sometimes it is tempting to wait and do nothing. If she is young and still lives at home, she may hide the pregnancy from her parents and friends and try to forget about it. This is not a good idea. The earlier she talks to her parents, the more choices she has about the pregnancy, and the more time she and her parents have to get used to the idea.

Not everyone has a good relationship with their parents and family. Living with parents, or accepting a lot of help from them, is not a good solution for all women. And some parents don't want to be involved. *Some women have to make it on their own, without help from the baby's father or from their own family.* How do they do it?

Help from the Community

Money problems One of the most serious problems for most single (or divorced) women with children is lack of money. Most families with young children headed by women are poor. Fortunately, most communities have free or low-cost programs that can help these women to make it on their own.

Finding help Finding out about these resources can start early in the woman's pregnancy. Social workers are the people most likely to have this information. They can be found at the hospital or clinic where the woman gets prenatal care, at social service agencies (which can be found in the Yellow Pages, or by calling the United Way), or at the city or county Department of Social Services (sometimes called Human Resources or Public Welfare).

Even if a woman is not poor enough to qualify for welfare such as Aid to Families with Dependent Children (AFDC), she might want to visit the local welfare office, because these offices have information about all kinds of other programs, including medical coverage, Food Stamps, low-cost day care, parenting education, job training, and other things that the woman might need.

Teenage mothers often have little money or free time to enjoy being a teenager.

There are many resources to help a woman make it on her own with her baby, but it takes a lot of research to find them. It is useful to join a club or group that includes other women in the same situation, because they can share information about programs that can help. Others in the same situation can also provide support and friendship, because they understand what the woman is going through.

Teenage mothers Some communities have special programs for pregnant teenagers, including special high school classes, training in how to be a parent, and counseling. These programs can be found by calling the guidance counselor at a local high school.

Preventing child abuse Women trying to make it on their own with a baby have a tough time. There are more cases of child abuse and neglect reported for families of this kind than for others. There are several reasons for this, including:

1. Lack of other family members to help out
2. Lack of knowledge about parenting
3. The stress of living in poverty

Since everyone has the potential to be a child abuser or a person who neglects his or her child, it is important to find ways to make sure this does not happen to you and your child. One of the best ways to prevent problems is to learn as much as possible about child development and effective parenting. There are courses in most communities through social agencies, schools, and churches. There are also organizations like Parents Anonymous, which abusive parents (or parents who fear they might become abusers) can join.

Temporary foster care Every community has foster care services, offered through the county or state Department of Social Services. Foster care services are provided for children whose parents cannot care for them because of illness or other problems. The children are cared for in private homes by foster parents, or in group homes, until the parents are able to take them home again. In some communities this service is available for the woman who wants to keep her baby, but will not be able to care for it by herself for the first few weeks or months.

If a child is placed in foster care, the mother needs to visit often and bring the child home as quickly as possible. The baby's psychological and emotional development can be damaged if the person providing the care is changed too often. Babies need one person whom they can depend on to care

Under difficult circumstances, everyone has the potential to become a child abuser.

for them every day. Moving them from one home to another can create serious problems.

Adoption

Adoption is a legal process by which a baby's natural or biological parents release their rights to the child and give them to another couple, who then become the legal parents.

Adoptions are provided in three different ways, each of which is described below.

Agency Adoptions

Agency adoptions are provided through non-profit social service organizations that specialize in adoptions. They may be religious-based, nonreligious, or run by the county or state. Some specialize in adoptions of a particular kind, such as refugee children from other countries or disabled children. Adoption agencies do not usually charge any fees to the pregnant woman, but they may charge the adopting parents for such expenses as legal and medical costs. They may be able to help the pregnant woman with some of her expenses. Adoption agencies are run as a public service and try to offer high-quality services to the families who use them. Their main focus is the welfare of the child.

Adoption agencies can be located by asking a social worker in a hospital or health clinic, or by calling the United Way or the county Department of Social Services for information. They may also be listed in the Yellow Pages under "Social Services."

Adoption agencies are run by social workers who carefully investigate the parents seeking to adopt to make sure that they can offer a good home for a child. They also provide counseling to the birth parents (biological parents) to help them make a plan for their baby with which they are comfortable. The agency also makes the match between a particular baby and the adoptive parents, and supervises the home for the first few months after the baby is placed to make sure things are going well. The agency takes care of all the legal arrangements for both the birth parents and the adopting parents. Adoption agencies provide confidentiality and privacy for both sets of parents.

Independent Adoptions

Independent adoptions are those that are arranged without the help of an agency, using a lawyer to make the legal arrangements. There are two kinds, known as **private adoptions** and **black-market adoptions.** The difference between the two is that in private adoptions the only money paid or received is for expenses related to the adoption. In black-market adoptions, money is charged above the actual expenses, so that someone is making a profit on the adoption. This is illegal in the United States; it is considered "baby selling."

Private adoptions are legal in all states except Connecticut and Delaware, but the regulations are different in each state. In private adoptions there is often no investigation of the adoptive parents (like the one done by adoption agencies), and the natural mother may have no way of knowing what kind of home her baby is going to. Private adoptions are usually arranged by lawyers, who get referrals of pregnant women from doctors, ministers, and health care workers.

Adoption is one option to consider.

Informal Adoptions

Informal adoptions are adoptions that are never formalized in court; for example, if a woman gives birth to a baby she cannot care for, and gives it to her sister to raise as her own child. If the two sisters never go to court to change the baby's birth certificate and name officially, this would be an informal adoption. All legal documents would show the baby as the child of his or her birth mother. There would be no written evidence of the adoption, and the child's rights of inheritance would be affected. Informal adoptions are more common between family members than between unrelated families. Sometimes they are formalized in court after many years.

An informal adoption can work out well if it is within a family, but it is better to formalize it in court for protection of the child and other family members. It is also important for the child to know the truth about his or her birth. Any adoption outside the immediate family should definitely go through the courts.

Taking an informal adoption to court to be formalized should not be an expensive process. If a lawyer's fees seem high, check directly with the family court or with a local adoption agency for more information about what is needed.

Making Choices about Adoption

There are so few babies available for adoption today in the United States, and so many families who want these babies, that most pregnant women can be sure of getting an excellent home for their baby if adoption is chosen. Both adoption agencies and lawyers who do private adoptions have waiting lists of couples, many of whom have been waiting for years. Unfortunately, some children of color and children born with physical or mental handicaps are not as easy to place as others. Some are at risk of not being adopted and spending their lives in foster care if the mother gives them up. A local adoption agency is the best source of information about a baby's potential chances for adoption.

If a woman tells her doctor or personnel at her health clinic that she is considering adoption, they will be able to refer her to the adoption agencies in the area and possibly to reputable attorneys who handle private adoptions as well. If it becomes known that a woman is considering adoption, she may also be contacted by someone from the black market offering money for her baby.

It is recommended that a woman considering adoption for her baby work only with an adoption agency. Adoption agencies have been around for a long time, and they do a large percentage of the adoptions that take place in the United States.

In this family the younger child is adopted.

Agency adoption offers the most protection for the baby and the mother. Agencies carefully investigate the adopting parents and maintain privacy for both sides. The legal arrangements made by agencies are also completely reliable, so there won't be problems about the adoption later on. Another advantage of agency adoption is that the agency will honor the mother's legal right to change her mind and keep her baby if she has not yet signed final adoption papers (which happens several weeks after the baby is born). In an independent adoption, the mother may be pressured into releasing her baby, even if she decides she wants to keep it after it is born.

Why would a woman choose an independent adoption? Many doctors and attorneys handle independent adoptions, so a woman may be offered this service before she is aware of the agencies that also exist. She may be told that her medical and other expenses during pregnancy will be paid and that she will be able to choose the couple who will adopt her baby, perhaps meet them in person. If a woman receives an offer like this, she should also check with an adoption agency in her area. An agency may be able to help with medical and other expenses as well, and will have expert social workers who will try to match the mother's choice of the kind of family she wants for the baby with the list of qualified parents who are waiting. She may also be able to help choose the adoptive parents. Some of the families waiting for independent adoptions are people who did not pass the investigation of the adoption agency.

Stay away from black-market adoptions!! Being involved in baby selling is a crime. Adoptions arrranged in this way will not be legal. One reason for using an agency is that sometimes it is hard to tell the difference between an independent adoption and a black-market adoption. *If a woman is offered more money than just her expenses of pregnancy for the baby, then it is probably a black-market adoption.* It can be tempting, especially if you have no money, but *don't do it! It is illegal and unfair to your baby, who will have no protection as to the kind of people who adopt him or her or the kind of care that he or she will receive.*

An adoptive family goes through the final legal steps while the baby looks on.

Ending the Pregnancy: Abortion

Abortion is another choice for the woman with an unplanned and unwanted pregnancy. **Abortion is the ending of the pregnancy before the fetus has fully developed, and before natural birth would occur. It is a medical procedure in which the fetus is removed from the uterus by one of several methods.** Over 90 percent of abortions are done within the first three months of pregnancy. *Abortion is legal in all of the United States, and has been since 1973.*

The following pages provide basic information about abortion for the woman who has an unwanted pregnancy. Chapter 11 "Abortion," provides more detailed information about abortion services, procedures, anesthesia, risks, and taking care of yourself after an abortion.

More than one and a half million abortions are performed each year on American women. In many cases the unwanted pregnancies are due to not using birth control. No birth control method is perfect, however, and even the most careful couple can end up with an unwanted pregnancy. It is not only young or unmarried women who choose abortion. Many married women and women in their forties have abortions as well. Abortion is not the best choice for everyone, and some religions and cultures forbid it. But many women choose abortion as the solution to an unwanted pregnancy.

Different Kinds of Abortion

There are four different kinds of abortions—early vacuum abortion, dilation and curettage (D&C), dilation and evacuation (D&E), and amnioinfusion abortion.

Abortions during the first three months of pregnancy are performed by the vacuum or D&C methods. They are safe and inexpensive, can be performed in a clinic or doctor's office, and can be done with local anesthesia (the woman remains awake). The woman can usually return to school or work the following day. Dilation and evacuation is a procedure similar to the early vacuum abortion, and is done primarily during the fourth month of pregnancy. The amnioinfusion abortion is done between the fourth and sixth month of pregnancy. It is performed in a hospital, and it may require that the woman stay for several days.

Time Pressure

If a woman is considering abortion, she should make the decision as early in the pregnancy as possible. Early abortion (within the first three months of pregnancy) is safer and cheaper than late abortion, and causes little or no time to be lost from work or school. If a woman waits too long to make up her mind, it may be too late for her to have an abortion at all.

Where to Get an Abortion

Early abortions are easily available in most areas of the United States. But women living in rural areas or in certain states may have to travel quite a distance. Later abortions (between the third and sixth month of pregnancy) come under state regulations, so services will be different in each state.

Abortion services may be listed in the telephone directory or Yellow Pages. The local Planned Parenthood clinic and the Health Department are also good sources of information about services in the area. Your doctor or health clinic may also know what is available.

If you are not sure what is available in your area, you can call the national office of Planned Parenthood in New York, or one of the regional offices (see telephone numbers at the end of Chapter 11). They will have a listing of abortion services in your area that meet their standards for quality of service.

An abortion service must be chosen carefully. Not all clinics or doctors offer all the methods. A good clinic will offer counseling as well as abortion, and will not pressure a woman to make a particular choice. A follow-up appointment will be scheduled for a few weeks after an abortion, and information about birth control will be given.

Abortion for Women under 18

According to federal law, abortion and other birth control services can be legally given to women under the age of 18. However, since other kinds of health care require the permission and signature of parents or a guardian, most hospitals and many doctors also require the parents' permission to give abortion services. Planned Parenthood and many other family planning clinics will provide abortion and birth control services to women under 18 without the parents' involvement.

Avoiding Future Unplanned Pregnancy

Right after an abortion is a good time for a woman to make plans to avoid an unplanned pregnancy in the future. The same clinic or doctor that does the abortion can help. No method of birth control is perfect, but almost any method is better than having an unwanted pregnancy. (See Chapter 9 for information about all the birth control methods.)

The waiting room at an abortion clinic.

UNWANTED PREGNANCY— A SERIOUS PROBLEM

Unwanted pregnancy is a serious national problem, affecting several million women in the United States each year. Fortunately, the risk of unwanted pregnancy is much less today than it was thirty years ago because of more effective birth control methods, increased public knowledge about reproduction, and better access to health care.

However, unwanted pregnancies still do occur and will continue to occur. A fertile woman of any age can experience an unwanted pregnancy, but women in their teens and early twenties have the greatest risk. More than a million American teenagers become pregnant every year, and the teen pregnancy rate in the United States is more than twice as high as it is in any of the western European nations or Canada. The reasons for this great difference are thought to be:

1. The other countries provide more and better sex education to their young people.
2. Health services (including family planning services) are more easily obtained in these countries.
3. The other countries use radio and television to promote responsible sexuality.

CAUSES OF UNPLANNED PREGNANCY

There are many different causes of unplanned pregnancy. The most common ones are described in this section.

Lack of Knowledge and Information

Some young people do not have any understanding of the human body, reproduction, and fertility be-

cause they have never received education in this area. The three main sources of information about sex and reproduction for children are parents, friends, and school programs. But many children are not informed. Unwanted pregnancy can be the result when they become sexually active.

Other young people are not aware of contraception. They may understand reproduction, but they don't have knowledge or information about birth control methods. Families and communities vary a great deal as to how much information about contraception is made available to their young people.

Another group of people who are at risk are people with mental limitations. Some mentally retarded men and women are not capable of understanding reproduction or of using birth control. Many others can understand but have not been given the information.

The majority of unwanted pregnancies, however, probably occur in situations where the partners were aware of contraception but did not use it. There are a number of reasons that this happens.

Lack of Access to Birth Control

In some cases, men and women would like to use contraceptives but aren't able to obtain them. The most common reasons for this are:

> They can't afford contraceptives.
> They can't get to a store or clinic.
> They are embarrassed or afraid of losing their privacy.

Lack of Awareness of Fertility

Some people see no need for birth control because they believe that one or both partners are not fertile. For example, if a girl is very young or if her periods are not regular, she and her boyfriend may assume she is not fertile, and pregnancy may be the result. Older couples also often take chances if the woman has had difficulty getting pregnant in the past, or if she is beginning menopause.

Inconvenience and Fear of Loss of Pleasure

Each birth control method has drawbacks as well as advantages. A woman may not use her birth control method because it is inconvenient to stop and insert a diaphragm, or she may forget to take the Pill. A man may not use condoms because he believes that they will reduce his pleasure and sensation.

Resistance to Birth Control

It is very common for people not to use birth control even when they do not want a pregnancy. This is particularly true for teenagers. In a recent survey of young women seeking abortions at a clinic, over 60 percent stated that they had not been using birth control, although they did know about it. Some of the reasons given by pregnant women for not using birth control are:

> "I thought it couldn't happen to me. I took a chance."
> "My boyfriend doesn't like it."
> "It's not 'natural.'"
> "I didn't think I would be having sex."
> "I didn't want to look prepared."

Experts believe that some unplanned pregnancies are the result of unconscious wishes. For example, at the conscious level, a woman may realize that a pregnancy at this time in her life is not desirable. But she may also have deep feelings of wanting to become a mother, or wanting to be pregnant. She may not be aware of these feelings. But because of them, she may take chances without being aware of it or without consciously intending to.

Choosing Not to Use Birth Control

The choice not to use birth control may be based on religious beliefs in which the use of some or all forms of contraception is forbidden. In other cases, people have moral or cultural values that disapprove of birth control. Men and women who choose not to use contraceptives are usually aware that an unplanned pregnancy could be the result.

Another reason some people do not use contraception is fear that certain methods can cause health problems. This is a mistake. Modern birth control methods are very safe—safer than pregnancy and childbirth, which also create health risks for most women. (See Chapter 9, page 187, for information on the safety of birth control.)

Failure of Contraceptive Method

Even when contraception is used, pregnancies still occur for a small percentage of couples. Incorrect use of the birth control method is often the problem. For example, a diaphragm that is not inserted properly, or pills that are not taken regularly, will not protect a woman from pregnancy.

Some methods have a higher risk of failure than others. For example, fertility awareness (natural birth control) is only about 76 percent effective, so some pregnancies can be expected by couples who use this method alone. (See Chapter 9, page 188, for a description of approved contraceptive methods and their risk of failure.)

Unwanted Sex

Some pregnancies are the result of unwanted sex, such as rape or coercion (when a woman is pushed into sex by threats or social pressure). Pregnancies in very young girls are sometimes the result of incest or other sexual abuse. Some women become pregnant from sexual intercourse that takes place when they are under the influence of alcohol or drugs. In these kinds of situations, women are not in a position to use contraceptive protection.

FOR FURTHER READING

ATLAS, STEPHEN. *Single Parenting: A Practical Resource Guide.* Englewood Cliffs, N.J.: Prentice-Hall, 1981.

MCGUIRE, PAMELA. *It Won't Happen to Me: Teenagers Talk about Pregnancy.* New York: Delacorte Press, 1983.

MCNAMARA, JOAN. *The Adoption Advisor.* New York: Elsevier-Dutton, 1975.

ROLES, PATRICIA. *Facing Teenage Pregnancy: A Handbook for the Pregnant Teen.* Oakbrook, Ill.: Eterna Press (P.O. Box 1344, Oakbrook, IL 60521), 1984.

RESOURCES

Information and referral services are available in your local community through the United Way agency, county or state Department of Social Services, and in the telephone book (the Yellow Pages usually have sections listing social services). In addition, the following national resources can be contacted:

Children's Defense Fund
122 "C" Street, N.W.
Washington, DC 20001
(202) 628-8787

A nonprofit organization that provides information about child abuse prevention, teenage pregnancy, foster care, health and welfare programs, and other matters concerning the well-being of children.

Parents Anonymous National Headquarters
6733 South Sepulveda
Los Angeles, CA 90045
(800) 421-0353 except in California
(800) 352-0386 in California
(213) 410-9732

A nonprofit organization that provides information and referrals to parents at risk of abusing their children and to adults who were abused as children.

8
Infertility

WHAT IS INFERTILITY?

Fertility is the ability to become pregnant and to give birth to a live baby (if you are a woman), and the ability to make a woman pregnant (if you are a man). **Infertility** is the inability to do this. Most adults assume that they are fertile, but the only way to know for sure is to produce a baby. The term **sterile** is used to describe a person who is permanently unable to reproduce for known reasons, such as having had a vasectomy. The term **infertile** is used for all persons who cannot reproduce, even if the reasons are not known.

    Primary infertility is used to describe persons who have never produced a pregnancy; **secondary infertility** refers to persons who have produced a pregnancy in the past, but are not fertile at present. Doctors define a couple as infertile if they have not been able to achieve a pregnancy after one year of trying. However, it is not unusual for a couple with normally functioning reproductive systems to take longer than a year to achieve a pregnancy.

HOW SERIOUS A PROBLEM IS IT?

It is estimated that in the United States 10 to 15 percent of couples who desire a pregnancy are infertile. The problem may be caused by the man, by the woman, or by a combination of factors involving both of them. Contrary to popular belief, infertility is not a problem primarily affecting women. Men are responsible for infertility in around half of all cases.

    More couples are seeking medical help for infertility every year. There are several reasons for this:

1. Couples are marrying and seeking pregnancy at a later age, when they are normally less fertile.
2. Increasing rates of sexually transmitted diseases

have caused higher rates of infertility, especially in women.

3. New and more effective treatments for infertility are available.

4. The number of babies available for adoption has decreased in recent years.

Infertility can cause great emotional and psychological stress for individuals and for couples. It is often a shock to learn of the problem, since most adults assume that they are fertile. Fortunately, there is a great deal of help available today to the infertile couple. Of all couples (or individuals) seeking medical help for this problem, 50 percent will achieve a pregnancy and have a baby. Of the couples seeking help who remain infertile, no cause for the problem will be identified in 10 percent of cases.

There are many different causes of infertility, some that can be treated with great success, and others that are very difficult to cure. The following pages describe the causes of infertility in men and in women, and tell about the ways it can be diagnosed and treated.

SPONTANEOUS CURES

Sometimes infertility problems go away with no treatment. This is called a **spontaneous cure**. Approximately 5 percent of couples who are infertile will achieve a pregnancy with no treatment at all after a period of time. Suprisingly, 15 out of every 100 couples who go for treatment for infertility will achieve a pregnancy without any help from the program. These unexpected success stories have been the source of many myths and beliefs about psychological and emotional causes of infertility. In fact, statistical chance probably deserves the credit; the couple kept on trying and eventually succeeded without special treatment.

HOW DOES INFERTILITY AFFECT PEOPLE?

Most people react with surprise when they learn that they may be infertile. In general, adults assume that they are fertile until proven otherwise. We are accustomed to taking all sorts of measures to prevent pregnancy, so we assume that when we do decide to have a baby, it will be easy to get pregnant!

Another common reaction is denial. Sometimes it is easier and more comfortable to believe that there is no problem, even when it is clear that there is one.

Infertility affects our basic image of ourselves —as men, as women, as a couple. It can make us anxious and insecure—even guilty—feeling that we are unworthy of a child, or that we are letting down our fertile partner. It is common to feel very angry when threatened with possible infertility, and it is also common to feel very sad.

If you think you may be infertile, what should you do?

1. Face up to the possibility of fertility problems, and begin to find out about solving them. Many couples are helped today, and recent scientific advances mean that even more will be helped in the future.

2. Remember that there are ways to become a parent even if you are infertile. Many families have found their solution in adoption or in other approaches such as artificial insemination. These approaches are discussed later in this chapter in the section on alternatives for the infertile couple.

3. Remember that both the discovery of infertility and the experience of trying to solve the problem put a lot of strain on the couple involved. This is an important time to be especially aware of your partner's feelings as well as your own, and not to neglect the relationship.

Infertility affects people in many different ways. In this chapter, we present information about the causes and treatment of infertility, and about the feelings and reactions that infertility may cause.

WHERE TO GET TREATMENT

The treatment of infertility is carried out by medical doctors. It is an area that requires specialized training for doctors already trained in gynecology and obstetrics. Male problems of infertility are also treated by urologists. Teaching hospitals (where medical students receive training) often offer an infertility clinic or program. Your family doctor can usually refer you to an infertility specialist.

It is important to find a doctor who specializes in this area, since it is a complex and rapidly changing field. Clinics or programs that use a team approach, where specialists from several disciplines work together on a couple's problem, offer excellent treatment. Treatment involves both the man and the woman, and requires that the couple share information about their sex lives (how often they have intercourse, and so on) as well as undergo examinations and tests. So it is important to find a doctor that both of you trust and feel comfortable with.

PHYSICAL EXAMINATION AND HEALTH HISTORY

The first step in evaluating a couple for infertility is a complete health history and physical examination for both the man and the woman. In addition to general health information, questions will be asked about the couple's sexual relationship, about past experiences of fertility or infertility, and about family patterns of fertility.

A thorough physical examination is done, by a gynecologist for the woman and by a urologist for the man. Examination of the woman includes a pelvic examination in which the vagina and cervix can be seen and the uterus and ovaries can be felt by the doctor. In the man, the penis, testicles, and prostate will be examined. (See Chapters 12 and 13 for more details about medical examination of the sexual organs.)

CAUSES OF INFERTILITY

General Causes

Age

Fertility for women starts when menstruation begins, commonly between the ages of 10 and 14, and ends at menopause, which usually takes place between the ages of 45 and 55. Men are fertile from the time of the first ejaculation (also usually around age 12) and, if there are no problems, they remain fertile until the end of life.

Older couples are less fertile and may take longer to create a pregnancy.

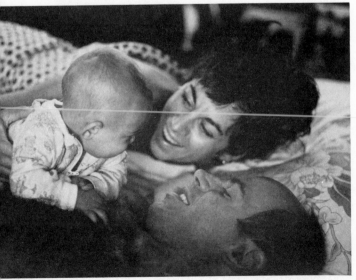

However, the degree of fertility varies over the lifetime. For both men and women, fertility is at its greatest during the teens and early twenties, and decreases a little each year after that. Around 80 percent of couples between the ages of 18 and 28 years of age will produce a pregnancy within a year if they have intercourse three or four times a week. For older couples the percentage achieving pregnancy in the first year will be lower, and the older they are, the longer it may take to start a pregnancy. No two couples are the same, however, and it is possible for young couples to be infertile and for older couples to have no problem conceiving quickly.

Frequency of Intercourse

In general, the more often a couple have intercourse, the more likely they are to produce a pregnancy. Sexual relations three or four times a week are considered the most effective pattern. Intercourse more often than that may lower the sperm count for the male, and if relations are less frequent they may not occur close enough to the time of the woman's ovulation.

Technique in Intercourse

Couples who do not have sexual intercourse at all, because of lack of desire or physical problems, are obviously unlikely to achieve a pregnancy. There are also many couples who do have sexual intercourse but are not aware that there are some positions and techniques that are more likely to result in a pregnancy than others. For conception to take place, the man must ejaculate within the woman's vagina. The position that is thought to be best for starting a pregnancy is when the man is on top and the woman's legs are flexed. It is helpful if the woman's hips are raised on a pillow, and if the man's penis remains inside the vagina for a few minutes after ejaculating. For the best chance of conception, the woman should remain in bed, on her back, for a half hour to an hour after intercourse. All douches and vaginal lubricant jellies and creams should be avoided.

Many of the couples who seek infertility services and then achieve a pregnancy without treatment (15 percent) are believed to be people who benefited by learning techniques for intercourse that seem to maximize chances of fertilization.

Effects of Contraception

The kind of contraception or birth control a couple has used in the past can affect their fertility when they are ready for a pregnancy. For example, women who have used the IUD (intrauterine device) are more likely to have problems getting pregnant than women who have used other methods. This is because IUD users are more likely to develop infections or inflammations of the uterus and Fallopian tubes, which often cause scarring and thus infertility. Barrier methods of birth control, such as the condom and the diaphragm used with spermicidal jellies or creams, are good methods for those who will want a pregnancy later. Because of the way they work, they protect women from infections and inflammations that cause infertility, at the same time they prevent pregnancy. Birth control pills are also recommended for women who will want a pregnancy in the future. Future fertility is important to consider when choosing a birth control method. (See Chapter 9 for information about all the birth control methods.)

Health Status

General health status affects fertility greatly. Good health is needed for maximum fertility. The couple seeking a pregnancy should pay attention to diet, nutrition, and general health. Malnutrition can cause infertility, and so can extreme physical or mental stress. Extremes of any kind can cause a problem. For example, some women runners develop temporary lack of menstruation as a result of excessive physical conditioning. Another example is the daily use of hot tubs or Jacuzzis by a man, which can make him temporarily infertile because of the effect of prolonged heat on the testicles. Infertility specialists can advise a couple about suitable diet and activities.

Alcohol and Drugs

Excessive drinking of alcohol can cause lack of desire for sex and reduced fertility for both men and women, and can cause impotence in men. The same problems can be caused by heavy use of "recreational" drugs. In addition, many prescription drugs can affect sexual behavior and fertility, and some can cause impotence in men. (See Chapter 3 for details on how alcohol and drugs can cause sexual problems.)

Radiation and Toxic Substances

Exposure to radiation can damage both women's ovaries and men's testes, causing infertility, which may be temporary or permanent. High levels of radiation can also cause genetic damage, which could result in problems with future pregnancies and higher risks of birth defects for any babies born.

There are also many toxic substances in the environment and in the workplace. The effects on fertility of many of these substances is not fully understood. But exposure to radiation and other toxic substances is a factor that must be considered when treating problems of infertility.

Psychological Causes

In the past it was believed that a high percentage of infertility problems were due to psychological problems of the woman, but this idea has not been supported by research results. It is very likely that what we now know to be problems of technique in intercourse or of stress were previously mistaken for psychological or emotional difficulties. As knowledge about the causes of infertility grows, the percentage of cases in which the causes are unknown or attributed to psychological problems continues to shrink.

Causes of Infertility in Men

After a thorough history and physical exam, semen analysis is the next step in diagnosis of infertility in men. Semen analysis measures the number of live, dead, and deformed sperm in a semen sample. When it is determined that there is a problem, such as absence of sperm or too few sperm, there are many different possible causes. The next section discusses these causes and their treatment.

Problems Related to Testicular Temperature

Many of the important causes of male infertility have one thing in common: They are conditions that cause the testes to be kept at a higher temperature than is normal, which slows down or

Frequent and prolonged hot-tub use can cause temporary infertility in men.

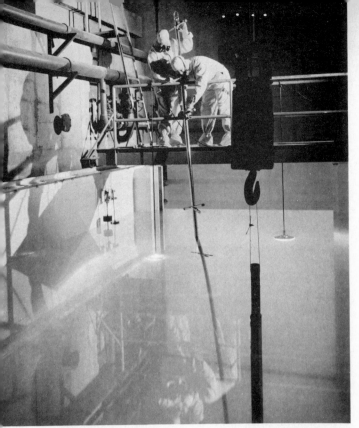

Exposure to radiation can cause infertility in both men and women.

even stops sperm production. Infertility caused by excess heat can be temporary. For example, prolonged daily use of a hot tub or Jacuzzi, or the wearing of tight underwear that holds the testicles close to the body, can cause poor-quality semen production, which will return to normal within a few weeks or months if the practice is stopped. Permanent sterility can also be caused by excess heat, as will be explained.

Varicocele

Close to 40 percent of all male infertility is caused by this relatively common problem. A **varicocele** is a varicose vein located in the testicles, more often on the left side than on the right. Approximately 15 percent of all men have this condition, which usually does not cause infertility and is not treated. When varicocele does cause infertility, however, by keeping the testes too warm to function properly, it can be treated with surgery to tie off the vein. A big improvement in sperm count and sperm motility (ability to swim) may be the result. After varicocele surgery, 53 percent of infertile couples are able to produce a pregnancy.

Lack of Function of the Testicles

Approximately 14 percent of male infertility is caused by failure of the testicles to produce sperm. There are a number of different causes for this. The three most common are:

1. *Undescended testicles:* Some boys are born with the testicles inside the abdomen, not in the scrotum (sac of skin that holds the testicles). Often the testicles will descend into the scrotum over time. If they do not, however, they will be permanently damaged by the higher temperatures inside the body, and this may cause infertility. (For more about undescended testicles, see Chapter 1.)

2. *Adult mumps:* When males get the mumps after puberty, the testicles can become severely inflamed. After recovery, the testicles may not function, leaving the man sterile. (See Chapter 13 for more on mumps and male fertility.)

3. *Klinefelter's syndrome:* This is a rare inherited condition involving abnormal sex chromosomes. Men with this condition often look like normal men, but they are usually sterile.

Hormonal (Endocrine) Problems

An estimated 9 percent of male infertility is thought to be caused by abnormalities related to the endocrine glands. These are diagnosed by tests of hormone levels and functions in the body. Infertility related to hormone problems in men can be treated medically, but so far there has not been a high success rate.

Blockage of Ducts

If the ducts (called the **vasa deferensia**) that carry the semen from the testicles to the penis are blocked, infertility will result because the sperm can't get through. This is the way the vasectomy works to provide birth control. (See Chapter 1 for information and pictures of this part of the male reproductive system, and Chapter 10 for information about vasectomy.) The ducts may be blocked for many different reasons. Among the most common are accidental injury from surgery or scarring from infections such as gonorrhea. This problem is diagnosed by a test in which dye is injected into the ducts and followed with X-rays to see if the tubes are clear. Blockage of the ducts is treated with surgery, which can be quite successful depending on how severe the problem is.

Retrograde Ejaculation

Retrograde ejaculation is a condition in which, when the man ejaculates, the semen passes into the bladder rather than out through the penis. Obviously, this causes infertility, since the semen does not arrive where it is needed. This problem is caused by a defect in the nerves that control the bladder and in the reflexes that normally act automatically to send the semen in the correct direction. The causes of this problem include prostate surgery, diabetes, and the effects of some drugs. The problem should be suspected if there is a lack of semen at ejaculation, and cloudy urine in the first urination after ejaculation. Retrograde ejaculation may be temporary or permanent, and treatment to date is not well developed. (For more details, see Chapter 13.)

Immunological Problems

It is possible for infertility to be caused by an allergic-type reaction, in which a man may develop antibodies that kill his own sperm. This usually happens as a result of injury or infection during which his semen comes in contact with body tissues, which develop a negative reaction. Treatment for this problem is not yet well developed.

Sexual Problems

It is estimated that 5 percent of male infertility problems are caused by sexual problems such as impotence or premature ejaculation. These difficulties prevent the sperm from being delivered within the vagina, where it is needed to start a pregnancy. The cause of impotence may be either physical or psychological. Premature ejaculation almost always has psychological causes. Fortunately, sexual problems that have a psychological basis can often be treated very successfully. (Chapter 3, "Human Sexual Behavior," contains more detailed information about these sexual problems and their treatment.)

Causes of Infertility in Women

Barriers to Fertilization

The Fallopian tubes   It is estimated that 20 to 30 percent of female infertility is caused by nonfunction in the Fallopian tubes preventing conception and pregnancy. (See Chapter 1 for a description and pictures of this part of the female reproductive system.) The most common problem is blockage of the tubes by scarring due to infection. This is why gonorrhea is a major cause of infertility. Chlamydia and several other types of pelvic infection can also cause this scarring. (See Chapters 12 and 14 for more about infections that can cause blockage of the Fallopian tubes.) Nonfunctioning Fallopian tubes can also be due to natural causes.

The treatment for this problem is surgery, which has become quite successful in recent years, depending on the specific problem. Approximately 50 percent of women treated with surgery today will be able to become pregnant.

Endometriosis   Another important cause of infertility is **endometriosis,** which affects women in their thirties more than younger women. It is a condition in which some pieces of the lining of the uterus (endometrium) travel out of the uterus and grow in the Fallopian tubes, in the abdomen, or even in other parts of the body. This lining material responds to the hormones that control the woman's menstrual cycle, and it bleeds when she has her period. This causes scarring, which, if it is in the Fallopian tubes or around the ovaries, can cause infertility. (See Chapter 12 for more on endometriosis.) This problem may be treated with hormones or surgery.

Cervical problems   Problems in the cervical area account for approximately 10 percent of infertility in women. Chronic cervical infection, growths, or scarring can all prevent the sperm from traveling through the cervix. (See Chapter 12 for more details on cervical problems.)

Another common difficulty is too little or poor quality mucus in the cervical area. The mucus may not support the sperm's travel, either because its texture is too thick or because its chemical makeup is hostile to the sperm. The woman may have an immune response in which she develops antibodies in the cervical area that attack and kill sperm.

The treatment of physical problems of the cervix is usually surgery. Mucus problems are usually treated with hormones.

Hormonal Problems

Ovulation problems   In couples seeking help with infertility, an estimated 20 percent of cases involve ovulation problems in the woman. There may be a complete lack of ovulation or a situation in which the woman ovulates irregularly, which reduces her chances of becoming pregnant. Lack of ovulation is treated with hormones to bring on ovulation and fertility.

Other hormonal problems   Endocrine problems can create infertility in other ways as well. Even if there is an ovum to be fertilized, the hormones in the woman's body may not provide the right environment for it to survive and grow. These problems are also treated with hormones to prepare the uterus for pregnancy.

Turner's syndrome   This is the most common genetic condition involving the sex chromosomes, but there are many different genetic problems that affect fertility, some of them extremely rare. Women with Turner's syndrome are born without ovaries, and thus are sterile.

Problems of the Uterus

Problems of the structure of the uterus can cause infertility. For example, the uterus may be tipped or bent severely out of the normal position. In some cases, a woman is born with a malformed uterus that cannot support a pregnancy. In addition, growths such as tumors, scar tissue, and adhesions from previous surgery can also cause infertility. These kinds of difficulties may prevent fertilization, or they may allow conception but then prevent the pregnancy from continuing because of lack of space or of a suitable environment for the growing fetus. The treatment of these conditions is usually surgery, which can help in many cases.

Problems of the Cervix

The structure of the cervix can also cause infertility, if it is malformed or closed off in some way. A woman may be born with a malformed cervix, or problems can be created as a result of a disease or medical treatment. In some cases these problems can be treated, usually by surgery.

Disease

The largest single cause of infertility in women is infectious disease. Gonorrhea and other organisms that cause **pelvic inflammatory disease** (PID) (see Chapter 12) can cause severe scarring of the Fallopian tubes and around the ovaries, if they are not treated early. These diseases often cause no symptoms in women until after they have already done damage. Women can avoid infertility in the future by learning to seek care early to prevent scarring caused by disease. Surgery is the most common treatment of these problems.

Immunological Problems

It is believed that immune-type reactions to sperm, in which antibodies attack and kill the sperm, exist in both men and women. The process is not yet well understood, but it appears to be an important factor in infertility. There are several approaches to treating this problem. Use of condoms during intercourse except on fertile days is recommended to reduce contact with sperm, which may reduce the immune response. Drugs can also be used to suppress the immune response in the woman's body.

Sexual Problems

Sexual problems that prevent the couple from completing normal intercourse certainly can be a cause of infertility. **Vaginismus** (see Chapter 3) is a problem in which a woman's vaginal muscles tighten in a spasm that makes intercourse very painful, or even impossible. Vaginismus may be caused by disease or injury that makes penetration of the vagina very painful, or it may be psychologically caused.

Lack of desire for sex can be a problem for women as well as for men. The result can be infrequent sex, or no intercourse at all, resulting in infertility. Lack of desire can be caused by health problems, the effects of drugs, or psychological causes.

If there is disease or other physical health problems, the treatment for sexual problems is medical. If the cause is psychological, effective treatment is also available from specialized therapists. (See Chapter 3 for information about sexual problems and treatments.)

DIAGNOSIS AND TREATMENT OF INFERTILITY

The preceding section presented information about the causes of infertility. The next section describes how infertility problems are diagnosed and treated.

Treating Male Infertility

In the past infertility was thought to be a female problem, and little attention was paid to problems of male infertility. Today it is known that approximately half of all infertility problems in couples are due to the male partner. Male infertility is not always a matter of the man producing no sperm. Often the problem is that he produces too few sperm (low sperm count), that the sperm he produces are defective, or that his sperm don't live long enough after ejaculation to start a pregnancy. The following section describes the tests and treatments for male infertility.

Semen Analaysis

Semen analysis, also called **sperm count**, is the technique for obtaining and studying the man's sperm. The semen is obtained by having the man masturbate and then ejaculate into a clean container. The semen must be delivered to the doctor's office or laboratory within an hour or two for examination. The semen will be studied for a number of factors that affect fertility:

1. *Sperm count:* How many million sperm there are per milliliter
2. *Motility:* The percentage of active sperm and their level of activity

3. *Morphology:* The normal or abnormal formation of the sperm
4. *Volume:* The total amount of semen in the ejaculate
5. *Liquefication:* The extent to which the semen is liquid or coagulated

Masturbation is the usual way to collect a semen sample. However, the man who chooses not to do this for religious or personal reasons can collect a sample by using the withdrawal method in intercourse, or by ejaculating into a condom during intercourse. These methods are less desirable for semen analysis but can be used.

Results of a semen analysis will vary over time. For this reason two samples are usually examined, taken a month or two apart. If the woman is treated for infertility over a long period of time, it may be a good idea for the man to be retested from time to time.

Postcoital testing

The postcoital test, also called the Huhner or PK test, is an examination of the semen, the cervical mucus, and the way the two interact together. It is performed several hours after the couple has had intercourse, during the woman's fertile period. A pelvic examination of the woman is performed, and samples of the cervical mucus and the ejaculate are taken. These are examined for sperm count and motility, and for the presence of living sperm penetrating the cervical mucus on their way toward the uterus. The possibility of immune system reactions can also be identified through the postcoital test.

Artificial Insemination (Husband)

The process of artificial insemination is one in which the man's semen is deposited in the woman's vagina by artificial means (other than intercourse). Usually this method of starting a pregnancy is used when the husband is infertile. The semen of another man who is fertile is used. (The method is described in detail later in this chapter.) We mention artificial insemination here because it is also used with the husband's semen in some infertility situations. Couples in which the man is fertile but has a sexual problem such as premature ejaculation, or where his fertility is reduced because of a large volume of semen, can be treated with artificial insemination, using the husband's sperm.

Treating Female Infertility

Diagnosis and treatment of female infertility is a much more developed field than is treatment of the infertile male. Many tests and treatments are available. Two possible explanations for this difference in the amount of treatment available for the two sexes are:

1. In the past, infertility was thought to be caused primarily by women, and thus they have been studied more.
2. Much more has always been known about women's reproductive systems than men's because of the need to care for women during pregnancy and birth, and for pregnancy prevention.

The following section describes some of the tests and treatments used with infertile women.

Checking Ovulation

Ovulation is defined as the production by the woman of a fertilizable egg, which is then pushed out of the ovary where it was formed, to journey down the Fallopian tubes. There are several ways to check if a woman is ovulating.

Basal body temperature   The most common way to check ovulation is by making a basal body temperature chart. This method, which has been in use since 1940, is simple and inexpensive. It is based on the fact that most women experience a shift in their basal temperature (temperature taken when resting) after ovulation. The temperature after ovulation is usually four-tenths to six-tenths of a degree Fahrenheit higher than it is before, and it remains higher until just before menstruation starts. It is important to note, however, that this test is not completely reliable. There are women who do not show a temperature shift who are ovulating, and there are some who have the temperature shift but do not ovulate. For most women, however, this is a good method.

The basal body temperature chart must be kept for several months before a clear pattern of temperature shifts can be seen. The woman uses graph paper, or a chart given to her by her doctor, to record her temperature (taken either by mouth or by rectum) every morning as soon as she wakes up—before she gets out of bed or even talks! She also records the days on which she has her period (menstruates) and when she has intercourse.

The couple and their doctor can use this chart to plan for the best times for the couple to have intercourse, and also to plan for the timing of other tests, many of which have to be done at a specific time in the woman's menstrual cycle.

Endometrial biopsy   The endometrial biopsy is a test in which a small sample of the lining of the uterus is obtained after the estimated date of ovulation. It is examined for evidence of hormones that indicate that ovulation has taken place. This test is used to confirm that ovulation is taking place, and

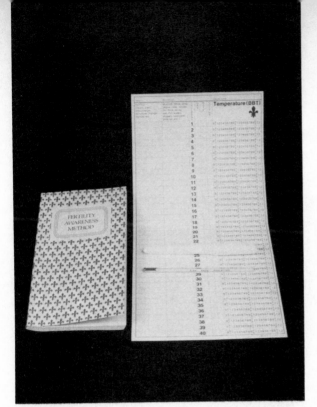

Keeping detailed daily records of a woman's temperature helps to diagnose and treat infertility.

also to study the quality of the body's response to ovulation and its preparation for possible pregnancy.

This test is performed in the doctor's office, with the woman in the position for a pelvic exam. A small instrument is inserted through the cervix to obtain the tissue sample. (For more on endometrial biopsy, see Chapter 12.)

Hormonal tests Ovulation may also be checked through analysis of the woman's blood. Levels of estrogen, progesterone, and other hormones in the blood help to chart the details of the woman's ovulation and the other phases of her menstrual cycle.

Cervical mucus reading Examination of the mucus at the entrance to the cervix can also provide a check on ovulation. Around the time of ovulation, the texture of the mucus, which is usually thick and nonliquid, changes. It becomes clear, thin, and watery—the proper texture for supporting the sperm in their entry into the cervix. This test is a good indicator of ovulation, particularly when combined with other measurements, such as basal body temperature. Women are also learning to use mucus reading as a natural form of birth control (see Chapter 9).

Stimulation of Ovulation

Treatment of the woman who is infertile because she is not ovulating has advanced a great deal in recent years. There are now several drugs that stimulate ovulation in a high percentage of women. If there are no other causes of the infertility as well (blocked tubes, for example), many of these women will become pregnant.

Since these drugs tamper with the complex endocrine system and can cause many possible side effects, this treatment is given only when all other possible causes of infertility have been eliminated. The couple who choose to undergo treatments for stimulation of ovulation need to discuss all the possible risks and benefits with their doctor. The treatments are expensive, and the chances of miscarriage, premature babies, and multiple births may be higher than normal.

Checking for Blocked Fallopian Tubes

There are several different methods for checking for blocked Fallopian tubes. The **hysterosalpingogram**, the **laparoscopy**, and the **hysteroscopy** are described in this section.

Hysterosalpingogram In this test a liquid dye that will show up on an X-ray is pumped gently into the uterus through the cervix. It fills the uterus and then, in cases where the tubes are open, travels out through the Fallopian tubes and spills into the abdominal cavity, where the body eventually absorbs it. As the dye travels, X-ray pictures are taken frequently. These show the outline of the shape of the uterus, the condition of the tubes, the location

Multiple births can result when women take fertility drugs.

of blockages (if any), and the area around the ovaries.

This is a very useful test, but it does subject the patient to low levels of radiation and to possible discomfort from cramping. An interesting side effect of the hysterosalpingogram is that women are more likely to become pregnant during the first few cycles after the test is performed. The reasons for this are not known, but may be the effect of the dye, under pressure, clearing and stimulating the tubal area.

Laparoscopy This test is performed by the same method that is often used in performing a tubal ligation (sterilization) on a woman. (It is described in Chapter 10.) With the woman under general anesthesia (asleep), a small incision is made in the woman's abdomen, below the navel. Through this incision a gas is pumped to fill the abdominal area and allow the organs to be seen clearly. Next, an instrument is inserted that allows the doctor to see the organs and to examine the ovaries, the Fallopian tubes, and the outside of the uterus. Endometriosis, adhesions, scar tissue, and many other problems can be identified through this test. Minor surgery can be performed at this time if needed.

Hysteroscopy In hysteroscopy, the doctor is able to see the interior of the uterus by means of an instrument inserted through the cervix. The walls of the uterus are pushed out by a transparent liquid solution pumped into the uterus. Abnormalities, growth, and other problems inside the uterus that may be causing infertility can be identified by this method. Some surgical treatment can be done during this examination, if needed.

MISCARRIAGES AND ECTOPIC PREGNANCIES

Ectopic Pregnancy

An **ectopic pregnancy** is a pregnancy that occurs outside the uterus. Most ectopic pregnancies are found in the Fallopian tubes, close to where they were fertilized. But they can also occur outside of the reproductive organs, in the abdominal cavity. (For more details about ectopic pregnancy, see Chapter 6.)

Ectopic pregnancies are doomed not to live and are extremely dangerous for the mother. In fact, they probably account for close to 10 percent of pregnancy-related deaths.

A woman who could be pregnant, and who develops abdominal pain and/or bleeding after the first menstrual period missed, should seek medical care immediately. These could be symptoms of an ectopic pregnancy.

An estimated 1 pregnancy in 200 is ectopic, and the rate of ectopic pregnancy in American women is increasing. The increased rate may be due to better diagnosis (more ectopic pregnancies are being diagnosed), or it may be associated with tubal damage caused by gonorrhea and other sexually transmitted diseases, which are increasing in prevalence. Surgery to open the tubes of infertile women may also contribute to the increased rate of ectopic pregnancy, as the way is cleared for the tiny sperm to get into the tubes, but the passage does not permit the much larger fertilized egg to pass into the uterus.

Around 70 percent of ectopic pregnancies are diagnosed before they rupture. The treatment is surgery to remove the fertilized egg. Sometimes the ovary and part or all of the Fallopian tube must also be removed. In cases where a rupture has occurred, emergency surgery is needed to save the woman.

Once a woman has had an ectopic pregnancy, her chances for normal fertility and childbearing are greatly reduced. Approximately 40 percent of women who have had an ectopic pregnancy will not be able to conceive again. The remaining 60 percent will get pregnant again, but approximately half of them will have another ectopic pregnancy or will miscarry.

Miscarriage (Spontaneous Abortion)

Spontaneous abortion, also called **miscarriage**, refers to the loss of a pregnancy due to natural causes, usually in the first three months. This is a very common event. (For more on miscarriage, see Chapter 6.) It is estimated that around 20 percent of all conceptions (pregnancies started) end with spontaneous abortion.

Many couples will experience a spontaneous abortion. It is not necessarily a sign that anything is wrong, and most will go on to produce a pregnancy that is carried through to a live birth. If a woman has three or more spontaneous abortions in a row, however, that is considered habitual abortion, and evaluation by a specialist may be advisable. However, a large percentage of those who have had three or more miscarriages will eventually carry a pregnancy to term without any treatment. Since spontaneous abortion is quite common, some couples experience several simply due to statistical chance.

Studies of women who habitually miscarry show that genetic problems cause 25 percent of the difficulty, physical or anatomic problems are responsible for 15 percent, and 23 percent can be blamed on hormonal problems. For the remaining

37 percent of cases, the causes have not been discovered. Immunological factors and certain infections may also contribute to spontaneous abortions, but little is known as yet about their influence.

The treatment of habitual spontaneous abortion depends on the cause of the problem. Difficulties that can be traced to endocrine (hormonal) problems of the woman are the most successfully treated. Drugs are used to bring the woman's complex hormonal system to normal functioning so that a pregnancy can be maintained. Physical problems (such as an abnormally shaped uterus) are also treated successfully in the majority of cases.

ALTERNATIVES FOR THE INFERTILE COUPLE

Adoption

Adoption is a choice that many infertile couples find to be a very satisfying way to build a family. Before modern medical treatment, it was really the only choice open for infertile couples. Social agencies that provide adoption services are available throughout the United States and can be located by calling your local Department of Social Services or United Way agency.

Adoption is not for everyone. Some people feel that they could never love a child who was produced by others as much as their own. Couples considering adoption need to discuss the decision carefully and to make sure that it is desired by both partners. A social worker at an adoption agency can help with this. (For a detailed description of the adoption process and the services available, see Chapter 7.)

There are not many babies available for adoption in the United States these days. Fewer unwanted babies are being born because of better birth control and the availability of abortion, and most unwed mothers today choose to keep their babies. Couples seeking to adopt may have to wait several years if they want a newborn infant in perfect health. It is much easier to adopt an older child, a child with health problems or handicaps, or a child of mixed racial background. Many couples have adopted babies born in other countries, and there are special adoption agencies that arrange these overseas adoptions.

We recommend that couples considering adoption contact an adoption agency rather than pursuing a private adoption. Adoption agencies are nonprofit social service organizations that work with both the natural parents and the adoptive parents to make sure a good match is made. They take responsibility for protecting the privacy of the people involved, and for making sure the legal aspects are taken care of correctly. The parents giving up the child can be sure that the adoptive family has been investigated and is a good family for their child. The adoptive family can be sure that the information they have about their baby is reliable, and that they are protected from legal or custody problems.

This may not be true in private adoptions arranged by lawyers, doctors, and others. A couple should be very careful about considering any form of private adoption, as the protections provided by an agency do not exist. Contracts or arrangements that require the adoptive couple to pay large sums of money are questionable and may be illegal. Direct adoptions arranged with the baby's natural parents are a very risky business.

Laws relating to adoption vary from state to state, and there is no regulation of adoptions done outside of adoption agencies. Sale of babies or children is, of course, illegal in all of the United States (see Chapter 7).

Many infertile couples make the choice to adopt.

Artificial Insemination

One simple, effective way of helping the couple in cases where the man is infertile, but the woman is not, is artificial insemination. Artificial insemination refers to a process that places a man's semen in a woman's vagina by artificial means (means other than intercourse). It is estimated that between 20,000 and 30,000 births each year in the United States are produced by artificial insemination.

Artificial insemination is a good choice if both partners are in favor of it. If either the husband or the wife is not comfortable with the idea, however, it should not be tried. Infertility itself is a very emotional subject that brings up many feelings in people. And artificial insemination, which involves children that are not entirely the biological product of the parents, can be especially sensitive. People react very differently to these ideas. Couples need to examine their feelings in depth and to respect the views of both partners in making a decision about artificial insemination.

Effectiveness

An estimated 70 percent of women receiving artificial insemination with donor (rather than husband's) sperm will become pregnant, usually within the first six months of treatment. Fertility drugs may be combined with artificial insemination to make the woman's ovulation more regular and predictable.

Procedure

Artificial insemination is a simple, painless procedure. The woman and the couple's doctor determine her probable date of ovulation using the basal body temperature chart and examination of the cervical mucus. Artificial insemination will be scheduled for the day before the estimated date of ovulation, and probably a second time within the next two days. At the doctor's office, with the woman in the position for a pelvic examination, the doctor inserts the sperm into the vagina, using a syringe. The woman remains in this position for approximately half an hour to allow the sperm the best chance for entering the cervix. Then she can get up and go home.

Donors

Artificial insemination by the husband (called AIH) and artificial insemination by a donor (called AID) both involve the same process. The semen containing the man's sperm is collected by having the man masturbate and ejaculate into a clean container. The ejaculated semen can be used immediately for artificial insemination, or it can be frozen and used at a later date. Fresh semen contains more living sperm than frozen and is the most effective, but babies conceived by either fresh or frozen semen seem to be equally healthy and normal. There is some variation in how well sperm tolerate freezing. Some men's semen can start a pregnancy after being stored for many years, but this is not true for most men.

The donor of sperm for artificial insemination is usually not known to the couple seeking a pregnancy. Arrangements for the donor are made by the doctor, who usually attempts to match the husband's physical characteristics (skin, eye, and hair color, and so on). A good donor is a healthy man with proven fertility. He should be screened for genetic diseases and AIDS, and his family's health history should be reviewed. The semen produced by the donor is also microscopically examined for infection or disease (such as gonorrhea) before it is used, since disease can be transmitted to the woman during artificial insemination.

Legal and Ethical Issues

It is recommended that the donor and the couple involved in artificial insemination remain unknown to each other. The husband is usually considered the legal father of a child produced by this means. But the legal aspects of artificial insemination are not well defined. A few states have laws specifically making the husband the legal father of such children, but most states have no laws on the subject. Some doctors and clinics handle the situation by having the couple sign a contract with them, spelling out the responsibilities and rights of each party. Husbands may be advised to go through legal adoption procedures as soon as the baby is born.

A reunion of families who produced babies through in vitro fertilization.

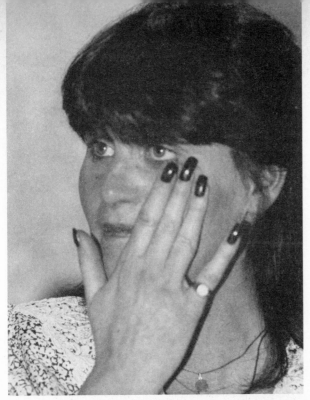 

Surrogate mother Mary Beth Whitehead bore a child for William and Elizabeth Stern.
When both she and the Sterns wanted to keep the baby, a court awarded the baby to the Sterns.

Because there are no national laws in this area, a couple considering artificial insemination should make sure that they know the laws of their state and that they agree on a plan for protecting the child's legal status.

Legal problems with artificial insemination have involved defective babies born by this means who are rejected by the couple, and questions of the husband's responsibility to support such children in cases of divorce. Court decisions have generally viewed the rights and responsibilities of husbands as being the same as those of a biological father. Legal problems can also develop if a person born by artificial insemination seeks to find out the identity of his or her biological father for medical or personal reasons.

There are many ethical issues for doctors and clinics that provide artificial insemination, and there is no legal regulation of their policies. There is no requirement that sperm donors or couples seeking children be investigated. Policies concerning artificial insemination for nontraditional families, such as single women and homosexual couples, are determined by the individual doctor or clinic.

In Vitro Fertilization

In vitro fertilization was first successfully used in humans in 1978. *In vitro* means "in glass" and refers to the fact that the ovum (the woman's egg) is removed from her body and is fertilized by sperm in a laboratory. One and a half to two days after fertilization, the embryo is returned to the woman's body and is placed in the uterus. The embryo then implants itself in the wall of the uterus and, if all goes well, develops into a normal fetus.

Since *in vitro* fertilization is a new and experimental treatment, it is available at only a few hospitals and clinics, and it is very expensive. It is primarily used for couples in which the wife's Fallopian tubes are blocked—where the woman is not fertile because the eggs produced by her ovaries cannot reach the uterus. *In vitro* fertilization allows the egg to get around the barrier of blocked Fallopian tubes by removing the egg (ovum) from the ovary and then returning it after fertilization to the uterus.

Research is continuing at a rapid rate in this area. Another new development involves implanting a fertilized egg produced by one woman into the body of another (see the next section on surrogate mothers). Many new approaches to *in vitro* fertilization and transfer of fertilized eggs (embryos) are being researched with animals, and in the future this new knowledge will be used to treat human beings. But such things move slowly because of concern about the legal, ethical, moral, and religious aspects of these scientific advances in control of human fertility.

Surrogate Mothers

Surrogate mothers are women who carry a pregnancy and bear a child for others. In recent years a few infertile couples have hired women to carry a pregnancy for them and to turn over the child to them when it is born. These are situations in which the woman is the infertile member of the couple. In most cases the woman hired has been artificially inseminated with the semen of the male member of the couple, so the child is biologically the product of the male in the infertile couple and of the surrogate mother. In several cases, relatives (such as a sister or mother of the infertile woman) have been the surrogate, which means that the baby born shares some inheritance with the infertile woman.

Like *in vitro* fertilization and artificial insemination, this new development is not yet regulated or controlled by law, and the legal status of children born to surrogates is not clear. Most couples and their surrogates have contracts drawn up by attorneys, but it is not clear that these contracts will hold up in court if the biological mother decides she wants the child.

Recent scientific developments also make it possible for a fertilized egg belonging to a couple in which the woman cannot carry a pregnancy for some reason to be implanted in the uterus of a surrogate mother. In this case the surrogate carries a pregnancy in which the fetus is biologically unrelated to her. This procedure is now available at some hospitals and clinics in the United States, but is still experimental and very expensive.

Life without Children

Infertile couples can also consider planning for a life without children. Many couples today who do not have infertility problems do not plan to have children. There are advantages to child-free living related to the extra time, resources, and energy the couple have available for other things. A childless couple have more time for each other, for work, and for activities they enjoy.

Childless couples also have many opportunities for involvement with children and young people. Close relationships with the children of relatives and friends are possible, and there are jobs such as child care and teaching that involve spending a great deal of time with children. In addition, there are many opportunities to work with children as a volunteer. Childless men and women can bring attention and love to children who badly need it. Local social service agencies, churches, and schools are good sources of information about volunteer opportunities with children.

For some people, there is no way to substitute for the children they want. But there are ways of overcoming the anger and sadness that infertility can bring. For some couples, counseling may be a good idea. It is possible to learn to live with the situation and to discover new paths to fulfilling the need to love and to nurture.

FOR FURTHER READING

BELLINA, JOSEPH, AND JOSELEEN WILSON. *You Can Have a Baby: Everything You Need to Know about Fertility*. New York: Crown, 1985.

MENNING, BARBARA ECK. *Infertility: A Guide for the Childless Couple*. Englewood Cliffs, N.J.: Prentice-Hall, 1977.

SILBER, SHERMAN J., M.D. *How to Get Pregnant*. New York: Charles Scribner's Sons, 1980.

RESOURCES

Information and referral services are available in your local community through the United Way agency, county or state Department of Social Services, and in the telephone book (the Yellow Pages usually have sections listing social services). In addition, the following national resources can be contacted.

National Committee for Adoption
P.O. Box 33366
Washington, D.C. 20033
(202) 328-1200

A nonprofit organization that provides information and referral to adoption services in your local area.

Resolve, Inc.
5 Water Street,
Arlington, MA 02174
(617) 643-2424

A nonprofit organization that provides information and education about infertility and infertility-related services (including surrogate parenting). Provides infertility counseling, referral, and support groups; has local chapters nationwide.

9
Contraception
(Birth Control)

WHAT IS CONTRACEPTION?

Contraception, also called birth control, refers to any action or device used to prevent conception (becoming pregnant). When a man or woman has sexual intercourse but deliberately avoids fertilization and conception, he or she is using contraception. Contraception can be "natural," involving no outside products or devices. An example of this is the withdrawal method, to be discussed below. Other kinds of contraception involve products that can be bought at a drugstore, such as the condom, which does not need a doctor's prescription. Products like the birth control pill require a visit to a clinic or doctor's office and a prescription. These methods are all temporary: They prevent conception

for a limited time. When the couple stop using them, the woman can become pregnant.

Sterilization is sometimes mentioned as a form of birth control, but it is very different from other birth control methods because it is permanent. A man or woman who has been sterilized—by vasectomy, tubal ligation, or other means—is infertile, not capable of reproducing. (See Chapter 10 for details on sterilization.)

Another term we often hear is **family planning**. This refers to any activities by a couple to control the number and timing of pregnancies.

HISTORY OF CONTRACEPTION

Since the beginning of recorded history, human beings have sought ways to limit births and population growth. Birth control has been practiced since antiquity. There is evidence that Egyptian women, thousands of years before Christ, used an early form of the intrauterine device (IUD) by placing a copper ring in the uterus. The withdrawal method has also been practiced in various cultures since antiquity. Abortion has been known almost universally throughout the world as a form of birth control. Some societies have even used infanticide, the killing of newborn babies, to keep their populations small.

Birth control in the United States has a long history. There were no restrictions on birth control products and information during the Colonial period and the early years of the country. After the Civil War, however, and up until a few years before World War II, there were many legal restrictions on birth control information and products. During this period most doctors did not provide family planning and birth control information or services to their female patients.

Starting in 1914, Margaret Sanger, the founder of modern birth control and family planning in the United States, campaigned to change the laws that made it illegal to distribute family planning information and to provide birth control services. As a public health nurse in New York City, she had seen many women die from illness brought on by too many pregnancies and from the complications of illegal abortions. Orphaned and abandoned children, as well as the poverty and suffering of families with more children than they could afford, also influenced her thinking.

Margaret Sanger, the founder of the family planning and birth control movement in the United States, in 1916.

The modern period of effective and widely available contraception in the United States began during World War II. The condom and the diaphragm were popular methods during the 1950s, and the contraceptive pill, which is used by more than 9 million women today, was first made available to the public in the early 1960s.

DECIDING TO USE CONTRACEPTION

Being Sexually Active

The purpose of contraception is to allow men and women who do not desire a pregnancy to enjoy sexual activity. But a high percentage of couples who do not want a pregnancy do not use birth control. There are many different reasons for this (see Chapter 7).

Taking Responsibility

If a woman begins menstruation at age 12 and enters menopause at age 47, she is capable of giving birth to more than 35 children during her fertile years. A man can father hundreds of children over a lifetime. It is important for each of us, once we become adults, to take responsibility for our powers of reproduction. If we don't do this, we can bring a great deal of misery and sadness to ourselves and to those we love. We can bring unwanted, unloved children into the world—children we may have no way of caring for. The fact that there are over one and a half million abortions performed every year in the United States shows how many unwanted pregnancies there are.

Only women can get pregnant, but both men and women have an equal role in creating life. They are both equal in the need to take the responsibility that comes with being a sexually active adult. It is one of the purposes of this book to help you take this responsibility.

Planning for Your Family

Birth control is not just for people who don't want any children. It is also for couples who do plan to have children, but want to be able to control *when* they have them and *how many* they have. Using modern family planning, it is possible for a couple to have the number of children they want and feel they can afford. They can have these children at the best possible time, when the parents are in good health and are able to give a baby all the love and care it needs.

Modern birth control allows couples to plan for the number of children they want and can afford.

Moral and Religious Concerns

There are great differences among people in their views on how sex, reproduction, and birth control should be handled. These moral and ethical differences are sometimes based in religion, sometimes in a person's culture, and sometimes in personal ideas or feelings about what is right. Many religions have specific instructions or rules about sexuality, reproduction, and birth control. This book is meant for everyone, regardless of beliefs. We are not trying to promote any specific way of handling these issues. It is our intention to provide information so that everyone who reads this book can make the best possible choices for herself or himself.

This section of the book, on birth control, tells about all the methods of birth control that are known to be effective, including methods like periodic abstinence. No matter what your religion or personal values, if you are interested in birth control or family planning, we think the next pages will have information that is useful to you.

Health Risks of Birth Control

Many people are concerned about the health risks of birth control. In the following pages, the safety and health risks of each method of birth control are presented, along with a description of each method. The health risks of most methods are very small. Since each person is different, however, some methods may represent a safer or better choice than others for a specific person.

One thing to remember is that *for almost every woman, any method of birth control, including abortion, has less risk of death than pregnancy and childbirth*, as Table 9–1 shows. The "no birth control" group in Table 9–1 shows the risk of death associated with pregnancy and childbirth for each age group.

Where Can I Get Birth Control?

For some forms of birth control, like periodic abstinence, all you need is knowledge about the method—then you can apply it yourself. There is nothing to buy, except maybe a special thermometer. Most forms of birth control, however, have to be purchased. Some are much more expensive than others. Some methods, like condoms or foam, can be purchased at any drugstore and do not require a prescription. There is no age requirement for buying contraceptives. Nonprescription contraceptives can also be ordered through the mail.

Many contraceptives, like the pill or the IUD, can be obtained only through a clinic or a doctor's office. These methods require a prescription. Obstetricians and gynecologists are specialists in this area, and most family doctors will also prescribe birth control products. Millions of Americans also use family planning clinics for birth control. There are many reasons for this—low cost, convenience, and privacy, to name a few.

Many private doctors and hospital clinics will not provide birth control services to persons under 18 years of age without the consent of a parent or guardian. Most family planning clinics, however, will provide services to young people without contacting their parents. The best way to be certain

TABLE 9–1 Deaths Associated with Pregnancy, Childbirth, and Use of Birth Control Methods (estimated deaths per 100,000 women per year)

Age 15–19	
No birth control	7.0
Birth control users	Less than 2.5
Age 20–24	
No birth control	7.4
Pill users who smoke	3.6
All other birth control users	Less than 1.6
Age 25–29	
No birth control	9.1
Pill users who smoke	6.8
All other birth control users	Less than 1.6
Age 30–34	
No birth control	14.8
Pill users who smoke	13.7
All other birth control users	Less than 2.1
Age 35–39	
No birth control	25.7
Pill users who smoke	51.4
Pill users who don't smoke	14.1
All other birth control users	Less than 2.9

Adapted from H. W. Ory, J. D. Forest, and R. Lincoln, *Making Choices* (New York: Alan Guttmacher Institute, 1983), p. 35. © The Alan Guttmacher Institute. Reprinted by permission.

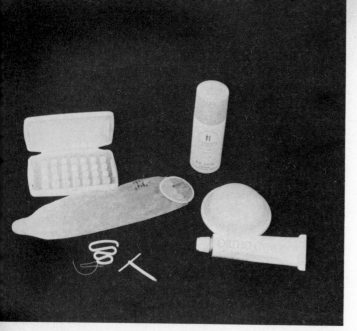

There are many birth control methods to choose from.

about the policy of any health care provider is to call and ask before making an appointment.

CHOOSING A METHOD OF BIRTH CONTROL

Many Choices

Men and women today have many choices in birth control. There are effective methods that are used by the man alone, by the woman alone, and by the couple together. Some methods, like the pill, protect you all the time, whether or not you have intercourse. Other methods are used only when you need them, at the time of sexual intercourse.

The many birth control methods can be divided into four basic groups:

1. Methods that work through **abstinence**—that is, through avoiding sexual intercourse at the times of the month that the egg could be fertilized
2. Methods that set up a **barrier** between the sperm and the woman's cervix and uterus, preventing fertilization
3. Methods that act on the body's **hormonal** system, blocking ovulation or otherwise making the user temporarily infertile
4. **Intrauterine devices,** which work in several ways, but primarily by irritating the tissues of the uterus and upsetting its chemistry so that the fertilized egg cannot implant in the uterus

All of the various methods are described in detail in the following pages. But first, let's look at another important question.

How Effective Are the Different Methods?

This is a very tricky question. All the methods discussed in this book are basically very effective, *if*

used properly. However, some are much easier to use properly than others. A great deal of research has been done to test the effectiveness of different methods, but the results vary. This is because people vary. A study of birth control effectiveness using unmarried teenagers will get different results from one using couples who have been married for five years. The types of relationships people are involved in, the frequency of intercourse, and the age of the individuals are some of the many factors that have an impact on contraceptive effectiveness.

American couples aged 18 to 28 who have intercourse without contraception three to four times a week for one year can generally expect the following rates of fertility:

50 percent will be pregnant in four months
66 percent in six months
80 percent by the end of the year

An estimated 10 percent of all couples are infertile, so this means that only ten percent of fertile couples will avoid pregnancy under these conditions. Couples in which one or both partners are older will have a slightly lower rate of conception.

Table 9–2 ranks the contraceptive methods from most to least effective, giving the estimated percentage of effectiveness under *ideal* conditions and under *average* conditions. The percentage figures mean the number of women out of every 100 who will avoid pregnancy over a year's time, using a particular method of birth control. Under poor conditions—when a couple cannot get access to their method, when sex cannot be anticipated, or when one or both partners is not motivated to use birth control—no method will be effective.

TABLE 9–2 Contraceptive Effectiveness

	Ideal Conditions	Average Conditions
Sterilization (tubal ligation or vasectomy)	99.6%	99.6%
Birth control pills	99.5	98
IUD	98.5	95
Condom	98	90
Spermicides (foams, creams, jellies)	95–97	82
Diaphragm (with spermicidal cream or jelly)	98	81
Withdrawal method (coitus interruptus)	84	77
Fertility awareness*	80–98	76
Douching	—	60
No birth control method	10	10

SOURCE: Adapted from Robert A. Hatcher, Felicia Guest, Felicia Stewart, Gary K. Stewart, James Trussell, Sylvia Ceral, and Willard Cates, *Contraceptive Technology 1986–87,* 13th rev. ed. (New York: Irvington Publishers, 1986), p. 102.

* Fertility awareness includes the basal body temperature method, the cervical mucus method, and the calendar method.

Looking at the "Average Conditions" column of Table 9–2, we see that 98 out of every 100 women using birth control pills will avoid pregnancy over the course of a year, and 2 will become pregnant. In the case of the diaphragm, 81 women will avoid pregnancy, but 19 will become pregnant.

Table 9–2 shows that the first three methods listed are much higher in average effectiveness than the other methods. The difference between them is that the top three methods protect people all the time, whether they have intercourse or not. If they do have intercourse there is nothing they have to do at that time to protect themselves. The other methods all require that the partners take some action or make a decision at the time of intercourse.

Couples who use a combination of two of the less effective birth control methods (such as condoms and spermicides) can achieve very good protection from pregnancy—much better than for one method alone.

Different Needs for Different People

There is no one method of birth control that is best for everyone. Each method has advantages and disadvantages; each has different risks and benefits. After reading the following pages, which describe the methods, you may still want to talk the situation over with an expert. The staff at family planning clinics are very familiar with the methods and are good at helping people to make a choice. Or your doctor can talk with you about it. You may want to talk with friends or relatives, but remember, your needs may be different from theirs. The

A teenage girl and her boyfriend get information at a family planning clinic.

method that is right for your sister, brother, or best friend may not be the best method for you.

It is important to consider your personal feelings and preferences, as well as those of your partner. Decisions about birth control need to be made in a thoughtful and rational way, but your feelings about the methods, even if they are not rational or logical, are also very important. If you don't like your birth control method, you may not use it, which could mean an unwanted pregnancy. Or you might use it, but end up losing your enjoyment or your desire for sex.

Birth control, like sex, works best when both partners agree and understand what they are doing. To be effective and not interfere with the enjoyment of sex, a birth control method must be acceptable to both partners.

NATURAL BIRTH CONTROL

Abstinence

The most natural form of birth control of all is **abstinence**, which means avoiding sexual intercourse. Abstinence has been used throughout history as a way of limiting births. Abstinence can mean no sexual activity at all for the partners, or it can mean "everything but" sexual intercourse. A couple can substitute oral sex, mutual masturbation, and other kinds of mutual sexual activity without fear of pregnancy. There are many possibilities for sexual activities that are satisfying to both partners but do not involve penis-in-vagina intercourse, or the risk of pregnancy. (For more on this, see Chapter 3.)

Periodic Abstinence

What Is It?

Birth control can also be carried out through **fertility awareness**—that is, by being aware of the woman's fertile days, and avoiding intercourse on those days. This approach is also called the **rhythm method** or **natural family planning**. This is a method that is acceptable to the Roman Catholic Church.

Where Do You Get It?

Natural family planning does not require a doctor's prescription or the purchase of any products (except maybe a special thermometer and temperature chart). But you do need a lot of information and, usually, some training in how to use this method. Family planning clinics, some doctors, and some religious groups can provide the information and training you will need.

How Does It Work?

There are three different approaches to determining when fertility occurs: the **calendar method,** the **basal body temperature method,** and the **cervical mucus method.** These are different ways of determining the dates of a woman's ovulation.

Calendar method To use the calendar method, a woman keeps a careful record of the dates of her menstrual cycle for several months. If her period is regular, it will not take many months, but if she is irregular she will need records for close to a year, and even then the calculations will be difficult. She then uses the following formula to calculate the days during which it is not safe for her to have intercourse.

1. Number the days of the cycle, starting with number 1 on the first day of bleeding and continuing until the expected date for the next period to begin.
2. The expected date of the next monthly period can be calculated by counting the number of days in previous monthly cycles. This method can work only if a woman's periods are reasonably regular. The shortest recorded cycle should be used as the basis for estimating when her next period is expected.
3. Count back 14 days from the end of the next expected cycle. This is the probable day of ovulation.
4. Add 4 days before the date of ovulation when the woman should also abstain. Ovulation may not occur exactly on the day calculated, and sperm can live for up to 2 days in the woman's body. So a woman can be impregnated from intercourse that took place as much as 2 days before ovulation.
5. Add 3 days after the date of ovulation; this is to take into account the fact that the egg can survive and be fertilized for 24 hours after ovulation, and the fact that ovulation may take place later than the expected day.
6. We now have calculated 8 days in which the woman should abstain from intercourse.
7. We see that the woman has 9 safe days at the beginning of her cycle, counting the ones in which she is menstruating. The safe period begins again 11 days before the cycle ends.
8. As you can see, long periods of abstinence are required with this method.
9. The number of safe days at the end of the cycle will be the same for all women, but the number of safe days at the beginning will vary as the length of the woman's cycle varies, so she should base her calculations on her shortest recorded cycle. A woman whose shortest cycle is 24 days will have only 5 safe days at the beginning of her cycle.

Figure 9–1 is an example of the safe and unsafe days for a woman with a 28-day cycle.

Basal body temperature method This method uses the basal body temperature (BBT), or the body's temperature when resting, to track ovulation. This can be done because the woman's temperature often drops one to two days before ovulation, and then rises for about three days thereafter. It then remains about one-half degree higher in the second half of the cycle. The temperature changes involved are very slight, and not all women have the marked rise in temperature at the time of ovulation. Most women, however, do have the slight shift from a lower temperature in the days before ovulation, to a higher one afterward. These changes are a natural part of the woman's cycle and do not represent a fever or illness.

Most women who use this method buy a special thermometer that makes it easier to see the very small changes in temperature. It is very helpful. The couple must abstain from intercourse from the time the temperature drops until after it has been elevated for three full days. After the woman has charted her temperature for a few cycles, if it is regular, she may be able to chart specific days of each cycle as safe or unsafe for intercourse (Figure 9–2). A woman who is not sure when she ovulates can avoid pregnancy by abstaining for the first half of her cycle, until after the three-day rise in temperature.

For the BBT method to be accurate, the woman must take her temperature every day, at the same hour in the morning, before sitting up or getting out of bed. An irregular schedule, colds, flu, or other problems can cause temperature changes that overshadow the changes caused by ovulation, so they cannot be detected. Also, not all women show these temperature changes. A woman who does not have them may or may not be ovulating.

Cervical mucus method The cervical mucus method tracks ovulation by watching for changes in the texture of the mucus (thick fluid) in the woman's cervical area. A woman desiring to use this method will need training in how to examine herself and the mucus. During most of the month there is little mucus in the area, and it is thick and cloudy in appearance. During the two to three days just before ovulation, the texture changes in a way that helps support the travel of the sperm through the cervix into the uterus. It becomes greater in quantity, clear, thin, and slippery, with an elastic quality, something like raw egg white. To use this method, women need to avoid intercourse during the first half of the cycle and until four days after the day with the largest amount of the thin mucus.

As with the rhythm and BBT methods, a chart should be kept for several months with the cervical mucus method, charting changes in the mucus texture until a clear pattern shows. At that time the woman may be able to predict her ovulation, and know when intercourse is safe and unsafe.

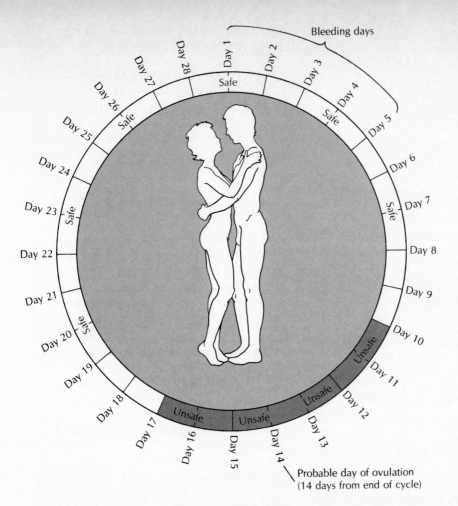

FIGURE 9–1. *Safe and unsafe days for intercourse for a woman with a 28-day cycle.*

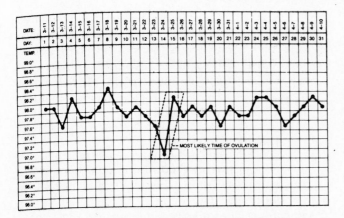

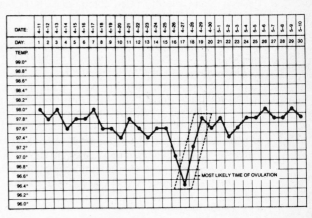

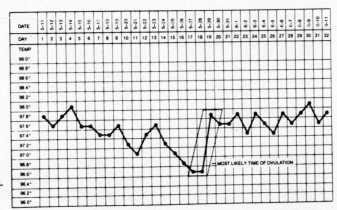

FIGURE 9–2. *Basal body temperature charts.*

How Effective Is It?

Table 9–2 on the effectiveness of the various birth control methods showed fertility awareness methods to be among the least effective of the major birth control methods. *Under average conditions, fertility awareness is estimated to be effective only 76 percent of the time.* It is not hard to understand why this is the case. Here are some of the reasons:

1. These are natural methods that do not interfere with the body's functioning. Since each body works a little differently, the signs and signals of ovulation vary, too, and can be hard to interpret.
2. These methods depend on regular, predictable cycles of menstruation and ovulation. Many women's cycles are not regular or predictable.
3. Fertility awareness requires a minimum of 8 days a month of abstinence from intercourse, and sometimes as much as 17 days a month. If a couple does not avoid intercourse during this period, pregnancy is likely.

Fertility awareness or natural family planning is the only choice for many couples whose religion or beliefs do not support the other methods. What can these couples do to increase the effectiveness of these methods?

1. First of all, *be very careful!* Since we know that no pregnancies result from abstinence, a couple should avoid intercourse whenever there is any question that the woman may be in a fertile stage. Unfortunately, this can mean that there are more days when sex is off limits than when it is O.K.
2. Effectiveness can also be increased by very careful charting and record keeping. Natural family planning methods depend on accurate records kept over long periods of time. They are ineffective if the basic information is not complete or correct.
3. Using two or three of the methods described instead of just one will also help. Since this approach provides several sources of information about ovulation, the understanding of when it occurs is more likely to be accurate.

What Are the Problems and Risks?

The major problem with fertility awareness methods is that there is a good chance you will get pregnant using them. There are no health risks to these methods, except those involved with being pregnant and giving birth. These risks are greater than with the other methods because your chances of becoming pregnant using these methods are higher. *Women who must not become pregnant for health reasons should not depend on these methods.*

A drawback to these methods for some couples is loss of sexual enjoyment. Using fertility awareness means that many days of the month are off limits for sexual intercourse. Couples who enjoy spontaneous sex, who don't like to plan it ahead, are placed under restrictions with this method.

The large amount of record keeping and paperwork involved may be a turn-off to some people. Others may not like to examine their cervical mucus, or may be on a schedule that makes it difficult to take their temperature under the correct conditions.

What Are the Advantages and Benefits?

Fertility awareness is a safe, inexpensive method of birth control. It does not require a doctor's prescription. It is acceptable to the Roman Catholic Church and to some other groups that do not support other methods of birth control.

The kind of record keeping and cooperation needed for a couple to use these methods may open up their communication about their sexual relationship, and might even make it better.

The detailed knowledge about the woman's body and her cycles is very helpful if infertility ever becomes a problem. Very similar records and techniques are used by couples who are *trying* to get pregnant.

Withdrawal Method

What Is It?

The withdrawal method, also known as **coitus interruptus,** is another form of natural birth control. This method allows the couple to have sexual intercourse without using any birth control products or devices. Withdrawal is one of the oldest known forms of birth control and has been widely used throughout the world.

How Does It Work?

To use this method, the couple have intercourse as usual. Then, when the man feels that he is about to ejaculate, he pulls his penis out of the woman's vagina and ejaculates outside it. This prevents the sperm from reaching the vagina.

How Effective Is It?

The withdrawal method can be about 84 percent effective under ideal conditions, but there are two things that can, and often do, go wrong that reduce its effectiveness to as low as 77 percent for the average couple. They are:

1. The man may not have the control needed to pull out before he reaches ejaculation, or he may not know in advance exactly when he will ejaculate.
2. The small amount of lubricating fluid that comes out of the man's penis as he gets sexually aroused

may have sperm in it, which will go into the woman's vagina when the penis does. If this is a second act of intercourse, and the man has ejaculated recently, there will definitely be sperm in this fluid.

Effectiveness can be increased by taking a few precautions and extra measures.

1. Wipe off the drops of lubrication that form at the head of the penis before beginning intercourse.
2. When ejaculating, keep the penis a good distance away from the vagina.
3. Keep spermicidal foam on hand to use after intercourse if withdrawal does not take place, and ejaculation occurs in the vagina.
4. Either avoid repeated acts of intercourse, or use contraceptive protection such as foam or a condom for the second or third acts, to control the sperm that will be in the lubricating fluid.

What Are the Problems and Risks?

There are no health risks involved in using the withdrawal method, except the risks related to pregnancy and childbirth if the woman gets pregnant. Withdrawal is not harmful to the man, although he may find it unpleasant.

The relatively low effectiveness rate is a problem with this method because the chances of unwanted pregnancy are increased. Most of the other problems with this method are psychological and emotional. Although some couples are comfortable with this method, others do not enjoy sex as much when they use withdrawal.

Breastfeeding provides some protection against pregnancy, but not enough to depend on.

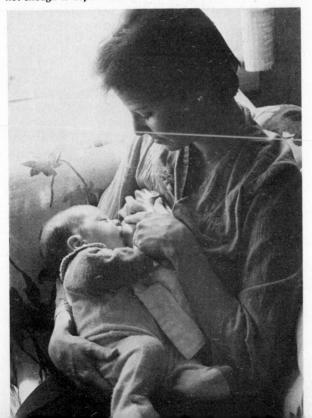

What Are the Advantages and Benefits?

The withdrawal method involves no health risks, costs nothing, and is far more effective than no birth control at all. It is always available, so it is good for emergency or unexpected situations where a couple may not have access to their usual method of birth control. It can also be the primary method of birth control for couples who are comfortable with it.

Breastfeeding

Breastfeeding a baby acts as a natural method of birth control, but it is not completely reliable. The same hormone that stimulates milk production also delays the woman's return to her normal menstrual cycle after childbirth. Women who do not breastfeed normally get a menstrual period two to three months after giving birth. Women who breastfeed usually do not get their period for several months (anywhere from 4 to 24 months). Unfortunately, most women do ovulate once before they get their first period, and some get pregnant at this time. So, although breastfeeding provides some protection from pregnancy, it is not something that the individual woman can count on as her only birth control method.

BARRIER METHODS

The Condom

What Is It?

The condom is a birth control method used by the man. It has been around for a long time—since the 1500s—and is very widely used throughout the world. The condom is a very thin latex sheath, shaped to fit snugly over the erect penis (Figure 9–3). It works by catching the semen when the man ejaculates and preventing it from coming in contact with the vagina.

Where Do You Get It?

Condoms can be purchased at almost any drugstore or pharmacy. Sometimes they are on display, and sometimes they are kept behind the counter so that you have to ask for them. In some states they are also sold in vending machines, and many magazines carry ads for companies that will ship them to you by a mail order. The fact that condoms do not require a doctor's prescription and are inexpensive and easy to buy makes them a very popular method.

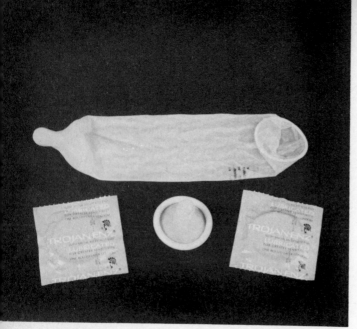

FIGURE 9–3. *The condom—rolled up and unrolled. Note the reservoir at the tip.*

In addition to latex condoms, which are the most commonly sold, there are also condoms made of animal tissue, called skin condoms. These are preferred by some people because they are thinner and thought to be more sensitive, so that they interfere less with the pleasure of intercourse. There are many brands and types of condoms sold; they come in colors, ribbed, lubricated, or dry, and with or without reservoirs at the tip to catch the semen. For added protection, the lubricating gel in some condoms contains a spermicide.

How Effective Is It?

Under ideal conditions, the condom can be about 98 percent effective, but under average conditions it is probably about 90 percent effective in preventing pregnancy. The condoms sold in the United States are carefully tested and are of high quality. When condoms fail as a method, it is usually due to human error. If a vaginal spermicide is used along with the condom, the protection against pregnancy is very great, equal to that of the birth control pill. Instructions on proper use of the condom are given in the next pages.

What Are the Problems and Risks?

There are almost no health risks to using the condom for birth control. A few people report irritation to the penis or vagina due to an allergy to latex, the material from which condoms are usually made. Skin condoms, made of animal tissue, are also available and might work for these couples.

Most of the problems with this method are matters of individual preference. Some people are very satisfied with this method, but others feel that the condom cuts down on the pleasurable sensa-

tions of intercourse, or that it is unpleasant to have to stop lovemaking to put the condom on.

What Are the Advantages and Benefits?

The condom is safe, very effective when used properly, inexpensive, and easy to obtain. It is not bulky and is easy to transport. It is not surprising that the condom is a favorite method of young people, of people who don't have intercourse very often, and of people who want to be protected in situations when intercourse is unexpected.

The condom has some other advantages that are often overlooked:

1. The condom is the best method to use when there is a chance that either partner may have a sexually transmitted disease (see Chapters 14 and 15) because it protects both the man and the woman from infection from the partner. It is a good method for a couple to use whenever one of them is being treated for an infection.

2. The condom may be helpful to the man with premature ejaculation problems, because it may reduce his sensations so that he can have intercourse longer before he ejaculates.

3. The condom may be helpful to some men who have difficulty keeping an erection because of past medical or surgical treatment. The tight rim at the base of the condom squeezes the penis slightly, reducing blood circulation. This helps blood to stay in the penis, maintaining the erection.

How Do You Use It?

The condom is put on by rolling it down onto the erect penis before intercourse and keeping it on until after ejaculation. Before the erection is completely gone, you must remove the penis from the vagina, holding the rim of the condom as you come out. If this is not done, the condom may slip off and spill in the vagina or nearby.

It is possible for a condom to rip, tear, or have a tiny hole in it, but this is very rare unless the condom is old. Condoms are good for three years after they are produced if they are stored properly. But an old condom or one that has been stored near heat (such as in a car) or carried in the pocket for long periods of time may be dried out and brittle, and may crack or tear.

Most of the unplanned pregnancies that result when couples are using the condom come from human error, not failure of the condom. Human error can be reduced if the following rules are followed carefully:

1. Use condoms every time you have intercourse.
2. Put the condom on before the penis ever gets near the vagina.
3. Leave a little extra space at the tip of the condom

for the semen if the condom doesn't have a bubble for it.

4. Keep a backup method such as foam available in case the condom breaks or leaks.

Diaphragm

What Is It?

The **diaphragm** is one of the barrier methods of birth control (Figure 9–4). It is used by the woman, and consists of a shallow, flexible latex cup, which is placed in the woman's vagina, covering the cervix, to hold a spermicidal cream or jelly in place. The jelly or cream coats the cervix and kills any sperm that get past the diaphragm rim. The diaphragm was invented in the early 1800s in Europe and was first brought to the United States by Margaret Sanger in the 1920s. Before the pill and the IUD became available in the 1960s, the diaphragm was the most widely used method of birth control in the United States.

Where Do You Get It?

The diaphragm requires a doctor's prescription and can be obtained from a family planning clinic, gynecologist, or some family doctors. An ex-

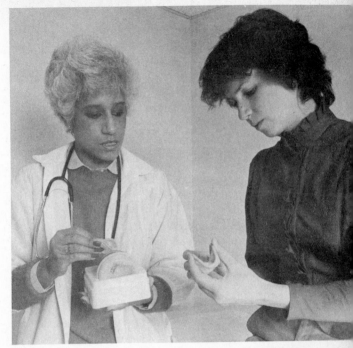

When used correctly, the diaphragm is a very effective birth control method.

amination and fitting is needed to determine the correct size for each woman. Most family planning clinics can give or sell you a diaphragm once you have been fitted; otherwise, you take the prescription to the pharmacy and buy the diaphragm there. A complete kit for using the diaphragm includes the diaphragm, a carrying case, spermicidal cream or jelly, and an applicator for putting in extra cream or jelly if needed. There is also a plastic inserter available for inserting the diaphragm, but it is not necessary.

How Does It Work?

Much like the condom, which is used by men, the diaphragm sets up a barrier between the sperm and the woman's cervix. Because the diaphragm covers quite a large area inside the vagina and gets moved around during intercourse, it is not effective without spermicidal cream or jelly. You could view the diaphragm as a latex cap that holds the spermicidal cream against the cervix.

The diaphragm with cream is most effective when inserted shortly before intercourse. The effectiveness may be less if it is inserted hours before sexual activity, but it can probably be used safely if it has been inserted up to six hours before intercourse. The diaphragm must be left in place for at least six hours after intercourse, in order to protect against sperm that may live for several hours in the vagina. More cream or jelly must be added, using an applicator, for each additional act of intercourse.

FIGURE 9–4. *The diaphragm is a shallow latex cup that covers the cervix.*

The diaphragm, if it fits properly, cannot be felt by the woman when she is wearing it, and she can wear it as much as is needed. Like a tampon, a diaphragm should not be left in the vagina for more than 24 hours at a time because of the danger of toxic shock syndrome (see Chapter 12). It should be removed, washed, and dried once a day. As soon as it is cleaned and new cream is added, it can be reinserted. But the constant wearing of a diaphragm is not recommended.

How Effective Is It?

Under ideal conditions, the diaphragm is about 98 percent effective in preventing pregnancy. Under average conditions, it seems to be around 81 percent effective. Why is there such a big gap between the ideal and average effectiveness rates? There seem to be several reasons, some involved with human failure and some with method failure. The diaphragm can fail if it does not fit properly, if it slips off the cervix during intercourse, or if it has rips or holes in it. Some of the common user-caused errors are the following:

1. The couple may not use the diaphragm *every time.*
2. The couple may run out of spermicidal cream or jelly.
3. Intercourse may take place more than six hours after the diaphragm was inserted.
4. The couple may not add more cream or jelly for each additional act of intercourse.
5. The woman may douche or remove the diaphragm less than six hours after intercourse.

What Are the Problems and Risks?

The diaphragm is a safe form of contraception, and it can be a very effective one. It does not create any serious risks to the health of the user, although a few people may be allergic to the latex used to make the diaphragm or to the ingredients in certain of the spermicidal creams or jellies. A rash or irritation to the penis or the vagina would be the sign of these problems. The spermicidal product is more likely to be causing the problem, so changing brands usually will resolve the situation.

A poorly fitted diaphragm is a problem. A diaphragm that is too small may slip out of place during intercourse, causing discomfort and not providing protection. A diaphragm that is too large will create a feeling of pressure in the vagina, may cause irritation to the bladder, and may make bladder infections more likely.

Another potential problem with this method is that it requires skill and practice to insert the diaphragm correctly. Although inserting the diaphragm becomes easier with practice, it is difficult at first to fold a three-inch cup with a spring rim, fill it with slippery jelly, and slip it into the vagina without spilling it or having it snap open (see Figure 9–5). A woman has to be serious about her desire to use birth control in order to learn this method.

To use the diaphragm properly, the woman (or her partner) has to reach inside the vagina to place the diaphragm, and then feel around with the fingers to make sure the diaphragm is in place. A woman who is not comfortable doing this is likely to avoid using the diaphragm when she has intercourse, in which case the method will not be an effective one for her. So the diaphragm is not the method for women who don't like to touch their vaginal area.

A woman using this method has to check frequently to make sure her diaphragm is in good condition, and must keep a supply of cream or jelly on hand. If intercourse is frequent, this can be a more expensive method than some others. The diaphragm itself costs little, but the supply of cream can be expensive over time.

What Are the Advantages and Benefits?

The diaphragm is a safe method of birth control that is effective when used properly. Because it is a barrier method, it does not affect the hormone system or a woman's fertility, so it is safe to use when nursing a baby.

The diaphragm may provide some protection from sexually transmitted diseases, since the cervix is covered, and because the spermicidal creams and jellies kill organisms that may cause disease.

This method is a convenient one for some people because the diaphragm can be inserted up to six hours before intercourse takes place. With some planning, the diaphragm can be in place before sex begins. It may be a good method for women who have intercourse only occasionally, since it can be used only when they need it. Women who are in a steady relationship and have regular sex may also like this method, because they can insert the diaphragm each night before they go to bed and remove it in the morning, whether or not they have had intercourse.

Another advantage to this method is that the woman gets to know her body and to feel comfortable with it. If inserting the diaphragm together is

FIGURE 9–5. *How to insert the diaphragm.*

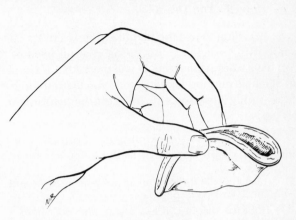

Step 1: Sperm-killing cream or jelly goes inside the dome of the diaphragm.

Step 2: Once you've covered the inside of the dome with cream or jelly, fold the diaphragm for insertion.

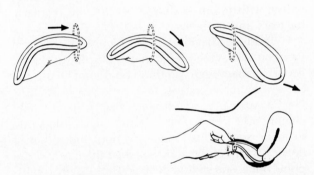

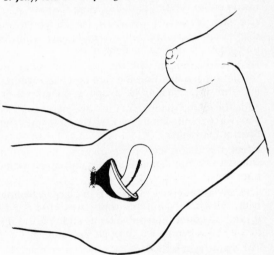

Step 3: Use your fingers to guide the diaphragm along the back wall of your vagina.

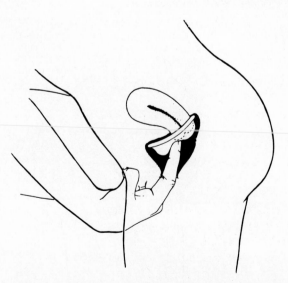

Step 4: Check for proper diaphragm placement. You should be able to feel your cervix through the dome of your diapgragm.

part of lovemaking for the couple, it may lead to better communication and understanding.

How Do You Use It?

Learning to use the diaphragm takes practice. Using it incorrectly, or not using it at all because you have trouble inserting it, will mean that it is not an effective method for you. Once you learn to do it, it takes only a few seconds to insert the diaphragm properly.

How to insert the diaphragm Correct insertion of the diaphragm involves the following steps:

1. Take the diaphragm out of its plastic case, and check for rips or pinholes.
2. Hold the diaphragm like a cup, and put about a tablespoon of cream or jelly into the center.
3. Using a finger, spread some of the jelly around the inside of the rim of the diaphragm.
4. Use one of several positions for inserting the diaphragm—standing with one foot raised (such as on a chair), squatting, or lying down.
5. Fold the diaphragm, with the cream still resting in the bottom, so that the sides are pinched together and the rim forms an "8" shape (see Figure 9–5).
6. Slide the folded diaphragm into the vagina as far as you can, pushing gently back, so that it follows the floor of the vagina.
7. When the diaphragm pops open to its original shape inside the vagina, it should end up covering the cervix.
8. Check whether the diaphragm is in place by feeling with a finger to see if the front part of the rim is tucked up behind the pubic bone, and that the tip of the cervix can be felt through the latex.
9. The diaphragm is held in place by a snug fit and by a vacuum, as it lies flat against the cervix.
10. When the diaphragm is properly in place and fits correctly, the woman should not be aware of it. There should be no pressure or pain.
11. Do not remove the diaphragm or douche until at least six hours after intercourse.
12. Use the applicator to add more jelly or cream for each additional act of intercourse.

When a woman is fitted for a diaphragm at a clinic or by a doctor, she is shown how to insert it and is given time to practice. She is checked to see if she is doing it correctly. Sometimes a return visit a few days later is a good idea, so the woman can be checked again.

When to use the applicator The applicator with extra cream is used each time if the couple makes love again with six hours. Since the diaphragm should not be removed during this period, more cream or jelly is put in the vagina using the applicator.

How to remove the diaphragm To take out the diaphragm, follow these steps:

1. Take a position like the one used for inserting the diaphragm.
2. Reach into the vagina with a finger and feel the front edge of the diaphragm tucked behind the pubic bone. Then hook the finger under the rim and pull down, breaking the suction that holds the diaphragm in place.
3. Gently pull the diaphragm out of the vagina (Figure 9–6).

Caring for the diaphragm A diaphragm should last about two years if you take care of it. After it is used, it should be washed with a mild soap and water, rinsed well, dried, put back in its plastic case, and stored away from heat. Powdering is not needed, but if it is desired use cornstarch. Talcum powder should not be used at all, since talc can be damaging if taken internally. A diaphragm will darken in color and may get brown spots on it over time. This does not mean there is anything wrong with it, but it should be checked regularly for tears and pinholes.

Products that contain petroleum jelly, such as Vaseline and some medications, may harm the latex of the diaphragm, so they should not be used at the same time.

A woman's diaphragm size will probably change over time, so she should check frequently to make sure it fits snugly, without more than a finger's width of distance between the rim and the pubic bone. She should get a new fitting after child-

FIGURE 9–6. *To remove the diaphragm, hook one finger underneath the rim and pull downward.*

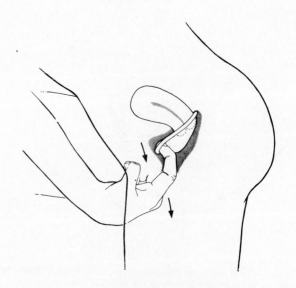

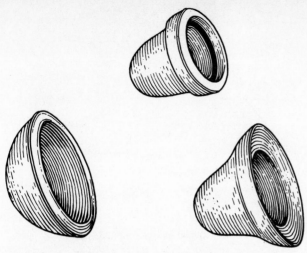

FIGURE 9–7. *Different kinds of cervical caps.*

birth or gynecological surgery, if the diaphragm is not comfortable, or if she is experiencing frequent bladder infections.

Cervical Cap

The cervical cap is a birth control device that is very similar to the diaphragm. It has been widely used in Europe and Great Britain for many years but until very recently it has been considered an experimental product by our government.

The cervical cap was invented in the early

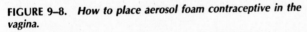

FIGURE 9–8. *How to place aerosol foam contraceptive in the vagina.*

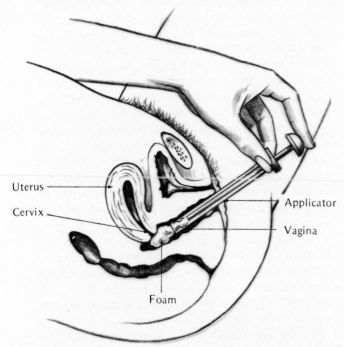

Uterus

Cervix

Applicator

Vagina

Foam

1800s in Europe. It consists of a latex or plastic cap, similar in appearance to a diaphragm but smaller, which fits tightly over the cervix (Figure 9–7). The early caps were custom-made for each woman, sometimes of gold and silver. They were used without spermicidal cream or jelly and were left in place for weeks without removal. Modern cervical caps are used with cream or jelly and are removed every 24 hours. Women can usually be fitted from standard sizes.

The cap is more difficult to insert and remove than a diaphragm, but it has the advantage of being smaller and less likely to be noticed during intercourse. Its safety and effectiveness appear to be similar to those of the diaphragm.

At present the cap is approved for use in the United States and is available from some clinics and private doctors.

Vaginal Spermicides

The next section presents information about several barrier methods of birth control, called vaginal spermicides.

What Are They?

These are all products that are put into the vagina, where they prevent pregnancy by killing the sperm in the area after the man ejaculates, so that the sperm cannot survive to pass through the cervix and uterus to impregnate the woman. Spermicides are available without prescription from pharmacies. There are many different products, but they all use the same chemical, nonoxynol-9, as a spermicide. Except for the sponge, all these products have to be reapplied with each act of intercourse.

Aerosol foam The foam comes in a pressurized container, which squirts the foam into an applicator. Using the applicator, the woman inserts the foam far back in the vagina before intercourse (Figure 9–8). More women use foam than any of the other vaginal spermicides. This product works by surrounding the cervix in a cloud of spermicidal foam, so that when the man ejaculates, the sperm are killed (most in less than a minute) and none get through to the cervix. Foam is believed to be the most effective of the products of this type, and many women find it the most convenient.

Spermicidal jellies and creams These are not the same jellies and creams that are sold for use with the diaphragm. These jellies and creams are meant for use alone, without a diaphragm. It is important to check carefully when buying these products at the drugstore, to make sure you have the right one. Each product has instructions printed on it explaining exactly how to use it. They usually come in tubes, like toothpaste, and are inserted in the vagina using an applicator. These products melt and then coat the cervix and nearby area with a sperm-killing chemical.

Suppositories and foaming tablets These products are placed in the vagina in solid form. Then they melt and spread to coat the cervical area. They depend on the heat and moisture in the vagina to work, so they may dissolve faster in some women than in others. There is a waiting time after they are inserted, before it is safe to have intercourse.

The sponge The sponge is a product that combines a spermicide with a disposable plastic sponge, which shields the cervix during intercourse and releases the sperm-killing chemical at the same time. It is shaped like a small, fat diaphragm, or a small doughnut with a dent instead of a hole (Figure 9–9). The woman wets it with water before use, to release the spermicide, and then inserts it before intercourse. The sponge is effective for 24 hours after it is inserted. Like the diaphragm, it must be left in place for at least six hours after the last act of intercourse. Using the sponge, sexual intercouse can be repeated as many times in a 24-hour period as the couple wishes, without changing the sponge or adding more spermicide. Repeated sex will be less messy, as the sponge will also absorb some of the semen.

Where Do You Get Them?

Vaginal spermicide products are sold without prescription in pharmacies and drugstores. Each product has detailed printed instructions on how it is to be used. These instructions must be followed if the product is to be effective. If you are not sure how to use any of these products, it is a good idea to check with your family planning clinic or doctor. Buying these products can be quite expensive, especially if you use them regularly over time. Besides figuring out which product works best for you, take a look at the price. In addition to the price of the tube, can, or package, how many times can it be used? What will it cost you for each time you have intercourse? There are big differences in cost between the products.

How Effective Are They?

The vaginal spermicides are about 95 to 97 percent effective under ideal conditions, and about 82 percent effective under average conditions,

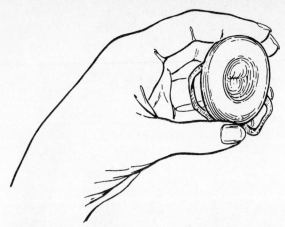

FIGURE 9–9. *The vaginal sponge contraceptive.*

which makes them less effective than the pill, IUD, or condom, but more effective than the fertility awareness methods. They are about the same as the diaphragm in effectiveness. Foam appears to be the most effective of the vaginal spermicides and is used by the most women.

Family planning specialists usually recommend foam as the most desirable of the spermicidal methods. These methods have not been popular in the past with family planning clinics and doctors, who usually recommend other methods. Their popularity is growing, however, as research shows that the spermicides can be a very effective form of contraception. Four million women in the United States are using them.

What Are the Problems and Risks?

There are no serious health risks in using vaginal spermicides, which is one reason they are popular. It is possible to be allergic to some of the ingredients in one product or another, or to find that it irritates the tissues, but the problem can usually be solved by changing to another brand.

The major problems with these products come with the suppositories and foaming tablets, because there is a waiting period before intercourse can take place, and because the products do not always foam or melt in a reliable way. Differences among women in the amount of moisture in the vagina, and so on, will affect the way these products function. The creams and jellies also require time to melt before intercourse.

The products that are effective only for a limited time, and that don't become effective until they have been in the body for a certain amount of time, can be difficult to use correctly. For some couples they will not be an effective method. Each product works a little differently, so it is important to read all the labels in order to find one that will work for you.

There are other possible disadvantages of using vaginal spermicides. For couples who have sex regularly, these methods can be quite expensive. Couples who have oral sex may find the taste or odor of these products unpleasant. Another possible drawback is the messiness of these products. The woman may need to use a tampon or sanitary pad after sex because of drippiness.

Because these methods can be purchased without a doctor's prescription, it is possible that women using them might be less likely to visit their clinic or doctor regularly to get an annual gynecological examination and pap smear. Women who do not get a checkup and pap smear (see Chapter 12) each year have a higher risk of developing cancer and other health problems.

What Are the Advantages and Benefits?

Vaginal spermicides are safe, convenient, and easy to get. When used properly, they are very effective. They don't require a trip to the doctor, and they don't involve hormones or foreign bodies, as the IUD does. They are safe to use while nursing a baby. If you use the foam, it is effective immediately, and you don't have to wait to have intercourse.

Another advantage of the spermicides is that the same chemicals that kill sperm also provide some protection for the woman against sexually transmitted diseases, including the AIDS virus.

These are good methods to keep on hand if you don't have intercourse often, or if you don't know when you might have it. They are also good methods to use as a backup, or in a time of transition. For example, if you forget to take your birth control pills, you can use foam for the rest of the cycle. Also, if a condom breaks or the withdrawal method fails, putting in foam after ejaculation is a good idea. There are no guarantees, since sperm can enter the cervix within seconds after ejaculation, but it is a lot better than doing nothing.

Another advantage of the vaginal spermicides is that they can be combined with another method, such as the condom, to produce a very high rate of effectiveness.

The sponge has advantages that none of the other spermicides do because its protection lasts 24 hours, and it can protect you for as many acts of intercourse as you have in that time period.

How Do You Use Them?

What all these products have in common is that they work because they contain a sperm-killing chemical. But they are different in the way they are used. The best advice we can give you is to *read the directions*, whichever product you are using. You can't use a foaming tablet the same way you use the foam. Each product is different. Also, *be careful what you buy*; there are many vaginal deodorants, douches, and other products on the market that are on the drugstore shelves right beside the contraceptives. It is easy to be confused by the similar packages and buy a product that is not a contraceptive at all!

Combined Methods

The individual barrier methods are not as effective in preventing pregnancy as methods like the birth control pill. But if two barrier methods, such as the condom and foam, are used together, the effectiveness rate is very high, similar to that of the pill or the IUD. Also, the barrier methods can be combined with other methods, such as the IUD, the pill, or fertility awareness, to give extra protection if it is needed.

HORMONAL METHODS

The Birth Control Pill

What Is It?

The birth control pill is a form of contraception that works by creating changes in the body's endocrine or hormone system. The woman takes small amounts of synthetic hormones (estrogen and progestin) in pill form, and these hormones interfere with her natural cycle, preventing ovulation and making conception impossible. Unlike the barrier methods described on the preceding pages, the pill works inside the body, causing changes in the body chemistry. For this reason, there are many possibilities for unwanted side effects. However, because the pill, when used correctly, is the most effective (98 percent) of all forms of birth control except sterilization, it is a very popular method.

The birth control pill was tested in Puerto Rico in the late 1950s and became available to the U.S. public in 1960. By the mid-1970s it had become the most popular form of birth control in the country, with approximately 8 million women using it each year. Since 1975 the use of the pill has dropped somewhat, with 6 to 7 million women using it today. The pill is also very popular in other countries, and it is estimated that over 50 million women are now using the pill worldwide.

Use of the pill is lower today than in the mid-1970s because of concern that some of the side effects of the pill may be dangerous to women who take it. A number of studies of the risks have been conducted, and more are underway. In fact, the pill

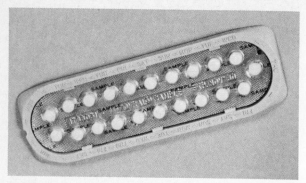

FIGURE 9–10. *One of the many brands of birth control pills.*

has been the subject of more research about its safety than any other drug prescribed in the United States. Because the risks are small for most women, and problems may not appear for years, very large numbers of women must be studied over long periods of time before we can be sure about all the effects of the pill. Details about the possible risks and problems of using the pill are given in the next few pages.

"The pill" is not just one product; there are over 25 different kinds of pills sold, produced by several different drug companies (Figure 9–10). The differences between these pills are in the amount and type of synthetic hormones they contain, in the way these hormones are combined, and in the pattern the woman follows in taking the pills (for example, whether she takes 21 pills and then stops for a week, or takes a pill every day and never skips a day.

The pills can be divided into two basic types: those that combine a synthetic estrogen and a progestin, and those that use progestin alone, which are sometimes called "minipills." The combined type is the type of pill most commonly prescribed, and many women are not aware of the minipill. The minipill was made available in the United States in the early 1970s, 12 years after the combined type of pill was introduced, and has not yet become as popular as the other kind. It works in a slightly different way, has a lower overall dosage of hormones, and is slightly less effective. The reason the minipill deserves our attention is that experts believe it may pose fewer health risks than the more popular combined pill. Research results comparing the safety of the two types of pills are not available yet, but women for whom the estrogen in the combined birth control pill is a problem should consider the minipill.

Where Do You Get It?

Birth control pills require a prescription, so you must visit a doctor or a clinic to get them. If you are going to use the pill for birth control, it is very important to have a physical examination and to report any health problems you may have or medications you may be taking. Because the pill works inside your body, rather than outside it like a condom or a diaphragm, it causes changes in your body chemistry, so you will need regular checkups with a doctor or clinic that knows your health history while you are taking the pill, just as you would if you were taking any other kind of prescription medicine. Once you have a prescription, birth control pills can be purchased at any pharmacy or at the clinic. It is a good idea to buy several months' supply at a time, since once you start taking them, you don't want to run out.

How Does It Work?

When a woman takes birth control pills, small amounts of synthetic estrogen and progestin hormones pass from her stomach and intestine into the bloodstream. These hormones are in addition to those normally produced in the body, and are kept at a constant level. Because of the steady supply of synthetic hormones to the brain, the pituitary does not produce its usual hormones to stimulate the ovary to produce an egg (Figure 9–11). The cycle of other hormonal shifts to prepare the uterus for the egg (see Chapter 1 for an explanation of the reproductive cycle in women) never gets started. For the woman using the pill, her natural cycle of ovulation and menstruation is replaced by a cycle produced and controlled by the pill. This is a cycle that does not include ovulation, although the woman does still menstruate. Since there is no ovulation, the woman cannot become pregnant. But if the pills are not taken regularly according to instructions, they may not override the woman's normal cycle, and she may ovulate and possibly become pregnant.

The minipill works differently, using only a synthetic progestin. The woman continues to menstruate on her own cycle, and she may still ovulate. But she does not get pregnant because the minipill produces changes in the lining of the uterus, the cervical mucus, and the action of the Fallopian tubes that create an environment that is hostile to sperm and to conception. The minipill is somewhat less effective in preventing pregnancy than the combined pill.

Both the pill and the minipill work by interfering with the natural cycles of the woman's hormone system. The effects are temporary; when she stops taking the pills, her system returns to normal and she becomes fertile again.

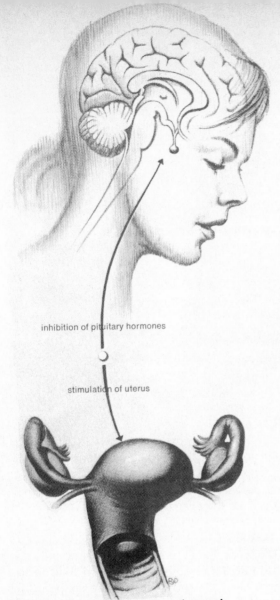

inhibition of pituitary hormones

stimulation of uterus

FIGURE 9–11. *How oral contraceptives work.*

How Effective Is It?

Used correctly, the pill is 99.5 percent effective in preventing pregnancy, which makes it the most effective of all the temporary methods of birth control. Only sterilization is more effective. Under average conditions the pill is still very effective (98 percent), although in some studies, groups of users such as very young women have shown a lower rate of effectiveness. As with all the other methods, effectiveness depends on the method being used properly. There may be minor differences in the effectiveness of the various types of pills, depending on the amount of synthetic hormone contained, and the minipill is believed to be a little less effective than the combined hormone pills. All in all, however, the pill is the most reliable method of birth control now available.

When the pill fails as a method, it is usually because it was not taken every day, consistently.

The pill must be taken daily over the whole cycle to provide protection on any day in that cycle. A single pill, taken before sex, after sex, or at any other time, does not provide any protection.

What Are the Problems and Risks?

There are a number of problems and risks in using the birth control pill, but the majority of women under 35 can take it safely. In considering the risks of any birth control method, we must compare them with the risks of being pregnant and giving birth, or of having an abortion. The pill would be considered an acceptable method for a woman if the medical risks are less than for either of these two situations. In the case of women who do not consider abortion as an option and would give birth if they became pregnant, the risks should be weighed against the dangers of giving birth.

Because the overall risks of taking the pill increase with age, a woman should stop using the pill for birth control before reaching the age of 45. Experts recommend that she stop by age 35 if she smokes.

The pill and cancer Although research into the health risks of the pill has been going on for twenty years, it will require more years before the effects of the pill over a lifetime can be known, and cancer often appears late in a person's life span. *From what is known at present, however, there does not appear to be an increased risk of developing cancer from taking the pill.* In fact, it appears that the pill may actually protect from the risk of certain kinds of cancer. Much has been written about the possible relationship between the pill and cancer, and the situation is difficult for the average person to judge. Research has shown that estrogen (one of the hormones in the pill) is linked to higher rates of cancer in people and animals under certain conditions. As research continues to explore possible linkages between cancer and the pill, women with a family history of breast cancer, or of certain other health problems that are linked to cancer, should be followed closely if they choose to take the pill.

The pill and circulatory/cardiovascular problems The most serious risks of illness or death caused by taking the pill are caused by blood-clotting problems. Most pill-related deaths are from blood clots. Blood-clotting problems are caused when chemical changes occur in the blood that cause it to form abnormal clots. These can cause illness, such as when they block a vein in the leg, or can be fatal if they block the flow of blood to the heart, lungs, or brain. For some women, using the pill increases the likelihood of having blood-clotting problems.

Blood clots also occur in women who are not taking the pill, and in men, although they are rare in young people. If the woman smokes in addition to taking the pill, this adds tremendously to her risk of circulatory and cardiovascular problems, especially after age 30.

There are other factors that also affect the risk of circulatory difficulties. A woman who has had any problems such as a stroke, a heart attack, or clots in any part of her body in the past should not take the pill. A woman who is overweight, or who has diabetes or high blood pressure, also has increased risk and should talk the situation over with her doctor.

High blood pressure High blood pressure develops in about 1 percent of women taking the pill. It is recommended that they get off the pill if this happens, even if the problem is not serious. The more years a woman uses the pill, the greater her risk of developing high blood pressure. If she has any history of blood pressure problems, this also makes it more likely. It is important for women who do take the birth control pill to have their blood pressure checked every 6 to 12 months.

Headaches Some women report more headaches or more severe headaches when they start using the pill. There are many different causes for headaches. The increased fluid retained in the body when taking the pill may be one cause. Mild headaches may be unpleasant but are probably not serious. *Severe headaches or more frequent headaches while taking the pill are an important symptom. A woman who has them should see her doctor immediately. They can be a warning sign of stroke or other serious cardiovascular problems.*

Effect on existing health problems Taking the pill may affect many health conditions that the woman had previously. If she is a diabetic, her blood sugar and insulin balance may change; therefore, her medication and diet may have to be adjusted. Women with an inherited tendency for high cholesterol and triglycerides (fats in the blood) may find that the pill makes the problem worse, especially if they are also smokers. Fibroid tumors of the uterus will often be stimulated to grow by use of the pill. Women who have been seriously depressed or suicidal in the past sometimes find that the pill increases their depression.

Several diseases that are affected by fluid retention may be made worse by taking the pill. Examples are epilepsy, migraine headaches, asthma, heart disease, and kidney disease.

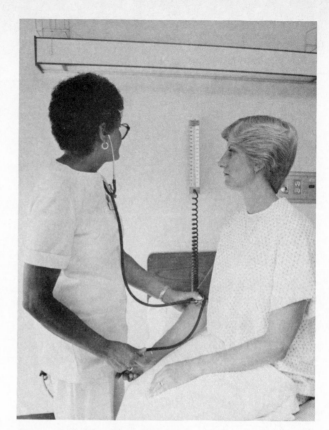

Women who take birth control pills should have their blood pressure checked every 6 to 12 months.

Women who wear contact lenses may find that the lenses don't fit as well after they start taking the pill. This is due to increased fluid in the body building up and changing the shape of the cornea of the eye.

Allergy to the pill is also possible, but there are very few confirmed cases.

The pill and other drugs When a person takes two different drugs at the same time, they may produce an effect called a **drug interaction.** This means that the two drugs together have an effect that is different from their separate effects. Drug interactions are the cause of many health problems. The pill does interact with a number of different drugs, and for this reason it is very important for any woman who is using the pill to report it whenever she seeks medical care.

The pill is known to interact with insulin, blood-thinning medications, and some tranquillizers, in ways that could be dangerous. Other drugs, such as tetracycline and other antibiotics, antihistamines, and other tranquillizers have an effect on the liver that could make the pill less effective. The pill may not be an effective birth control method if certain of these medications are taken.

Because of its effect in changing the body's blood-clotting system, women must normally stop taking the pill several weeks before any scheduled surgery. In the case of emergency surgery, it is important that the woman report that she is taking the pill.

As with any prescribed medication, the woman should share with her doctor all information about other drugs she may be taking, and she should ask about possible drug interactions. Pharmacists are experts on the subject of drug interactions, and are a good resource if questions come up about the pill and its possible interaction with other drugs.

Reproductive problems *Fertility:* In general, the use of the pill does not cause infertility problems. Although the woman does not ovulate when she is on the pill, her cycle generally returns to normal within three months after she stops taking the pill. It is usually recommended that women who want to get pregnant use another method of birth control for the first two months after they go off the pill, and not try to conceive until the third cycle. This is because there is a slightly greater risk of abnormal fetuses, miscarriage, and conceiving twins in the first two months after the woman goes off the pill.

A woman who starts to use the pill before she has developed a regular menstrual cycle may find that when she stops using the pill, there is a delay before she is able to become pregnant.

Pills during pregnancy: Neither the pill nor the minipill should be taken during pregnancy or when a woman suspects she may be pregnant. Babies born to women who have taken the pill during their pregnancy may be more likely to have abnormalities than other babies. The synthetic hormones in the pills are suspected of interfering with the development of the embryo, creating abnormalities.

Breastfeeding: The pill should not be taken by women who are breastfeeding infants. It causes a decrease in the amount and quality of milk produced. Some of the hormones in the pills will pass to the infant in the mother's milk as well, and it is not known what effect this might have on the child, either in infancy or in later years.

Vaginal problems: Research results are unclear, but many women report that they are more likely to develop vaginal infections when taking the pill. The most common type seems to be yeast infections (see Chapter 12). These minor infections are uncomfortable but can be treated. They are not transmitted to the partner, and are not a danger to health.

Sexual desire: Many women report changes in their desire for sex when taking the pill. Some re-port that they have increased desire and others that their interest in sex is less. It is not known whether the pill actually affects the sex drive or whether the psychological effects of the convenience of the pill and freedom from worry about pregnancy may be responsible for these changes.

Who Should Not Take the Pill

This section summarizes the information contained in the last few pages about the risks and dangers of using the pill. This time it is in the form of warnings about which women should *not* use the pill.*

WOMEN WHO SHOULD NOT TAKE THE PILL UNDER ANY CIRCUMSTANCES:

Women with any history or present problems of blood-clotting disease

Women with any liver damage or liver disease, including hepatitis or mononucleosis, within the last six months

Women who have known or suspected cancer of the breast

Women who are pregnant or suspect they may be pregnant

Women who have heart disease, coronary artery disease, or a history of stroke

WOMEN WILL PROBABLY BE ADVISED TO USE ANOTHER BIRTH CONTROL METHOD IF THEY HAVE ANY OF THE FOLLOWING CONDITIONS:

Past or present high blood pressure

Diabetes or a family tendency to diabetes

Gall bladder problems or surgery

Jaundice in the past

Sickle-cell disease

Smoking

Over 45 years of age

Over 40 years of age with another risk factor

Over 35 years of age and a smoker

Mononucleosis

Abnormal vaginal bleeding

Severe varicose veins

Long leg cast or major injury to the lower leg

Major surgery planned in the next four weeks

Migraine headaches

THE PILL MAY NOT BE THE BEST CHOICE FOR WOMEN WHO HAVE THE FOLLOWING CONDITIONS:

Headaches

Depression

Asthma

Epilepsy or seizure disorder

* These lists are adapted from Felicia Stewart, Felicia Guest, Gary Stewart, and Robert Hatcher, *Understanding Your Body* (New York: Bantam Books, 1987).

What Are the Advantages and Benefits?

The advantages and benefits of the birth control pill are tremendous. The pill is the most effective form of birth control that is currently available, short of sterilization. Despite its medical risks, it is safer than pregnancy and birth for most women.

The pill protects a woman at all times. She does not have to plan ahead for intercourse in order to be protected. It is a popular method with both men and women because it does not interfere in any way with the sexual act. The pill is also a method that the woman can use alone. It does not require the cooperation of her partner to be effective. The convenience of the pill is another advantage; there are no bulky products or equipment, and there is no mess, as with foams and jellies.

Many women like the pill because of its effects on their menstrual cycle. Their monthly periods are regular and predictable, and normally there is less blood flow than when the woman is not on the pill. Menstrual cramps are almost never a problem when a woman is on the pill, and premenstrual tension and bloating are usually less. Since the pill controls the monthly cycle, a woman can get on a pill schedule where she will never have her period over a weekend. By planning ahead, she can avoid getting her menstrual period during a specific time—for example, during exams or on vacation.

Other health-related benefits of taking the pill are that women are less likely to develop the following conditions:

Pelvic inflammatory disease
Ovarian cysts
Fibrocystic breast disease
Endometrial cancer
Ovarian cancer
Iron-deficiency anemia
Rheumatoid arthritis

Women with severe acne also find that it generally improves when they start taking the pill.

How Do You Use It?

Birth control pills are easy to use. They come in little packs, each containing a supply for one monthly cycle. There are two different kinds of packs: one with 21 pills, which is the most commonly used, and one with 28 pills. With the 21-pill cycle, the women takes one pill a day for three weeks, followed by one week of not taking the pill. During the week off the pill, she will get her period, approximately two days after her last pill. The 21-day cycle is popular because you always begin and end the pills on the same day of the week, so it is easier to remember your pill schedule. Women who take their first pill of a cycle on a Sunday and the last pill on a Saturday can be quite sure that their periods will not fall on weekends.

The 28-day pack of pills is very similar to the 21-day system. The woman takes 21 pills that contain hormones, and then an additional 7 pills (of a different color) that have no active ingredients. Then she starts a new cycle. Thus, the woman on 28-day pills takes a pill every day without break. She knows that she can expect her period during the time she is taking the 7 pills with no hormones. The purpose of these 7 pills is to help the woman keep the habit of taking a daily pill. Some women using the 21-day pack forget to restart their pills after a week of not taking them. The 28-day pack helps to prevent this problem.

The key to success in using the pill is forming the habit of taking the pill regularly. It is recommended that it be taken at the same time each day. Often the easiest way to form a habit is to link it to another regular habit, such as brushing your teeth each morning. Obviously, you have to remember to take the pill along on trips, and you have to plan ahead so that you don't run out. Most prescriptions for the pill let you buy enough for six months or a year at a time.

Even the best organized woman will forget a pill once in a while. If you forget one pill, take two the next day. If you forget two pills in a row, catch up by taking two each for the next two days, and use a back-up method such as the condom for the rest of the cycle. If you forget three pills in a row, your protection for that cycle is probably lost, so stop taking them and wait for your period. Then start again. Use another form of birth control, such as condoms or foam, until you start the pills again. If you are on the minipill, keep on taking the pills but use another method of contraception as well until after your next period.

If you decide to stop taking the pills for some reason, you can do so at any point in the cycle. Nothing bad will happen. However, you do need to begin using another method of birth control immediately. Whenever you stop the pill, no matter what point in the pill cycle you have reached, you will probably get your period about two days later. After that period, your body will return to its normal cycle.

Since the pills can be harmful to the fetus during pregnancy, it is very important to avoid a situation where you are taking the pill and there is a chance you might be pregnant. If you are sure you have taken all your pills, and you don't get your period, there is very little chance you are pregnant. But if you miss your period for two months in a row, get a pregnancy test at once. If you miss your period in a month in which you are not sure you took all the pills, you should also get a pregnancy test immediately.

When a woman who takes the pill decides she does want to become pregnant, she simply stops taking the pill. However, there is some question that babies conceived right after going off the pill may be more likely to be miscarried than other babies. It is recommended that the couple use another form of birth control through the first two cycles after the woman goes off the pill, and then begin trying to conceive on the third cycle.

The Morning-After Pill

What Is It?

The most common kind of morning-after birth control used to be a five-day treatment with the synthetic estrogen DES (diethylstilbestrol). A much larger amount of the hormone than is contained in birth control pills is used, and there are often side effects of nausea and vomiting. Ovral brand birth control pills are currently preferred as morning-after pills and seem to have fewer side effects. See the following paragraphs for information on how Ovral pills are used. Insertion of an IUD (intrauterine device) within five days after intercourse will also prevent pregnancy.

Where Do You Get It?

This treatment is available by prescription only. See your doctor or clinic if you think you need it. Treatment must take place within 72 hours after intercourse, so it is important to take action immediately. Doctors view this treatment as an emergency measure only.

How Does It Work?

The morning-after treatment works after fertilization and conception, but before the embryo is implanted in the uterus. This is the same time period in which the IUD has its contraceptive effect. The estrogen treatment upsets the body's normal hormonal balance and apparently creates a hostile environment in the uterus so that the embryo cannot implant and continue to develop. There is no long-lasting birth control effect from this treatment. If it is taken in time, it simply prevents pregnancy from intercourse that took place on one specific day.

How Effective Is It?

This treatment is extremely effective if it is begun within 48 hours after intercourse. It can be given up to as much as 72 hours after intercourse, but it is not as effective as when it is started earlier.

What Are the Problems and Risks?

Morning-after treatment with DES is a risky treatment. It should never be considered a routine form of birth control; it is meant only for true emergencies. In the past, when women have taken high doses of estrogen, it has created a higher risk of various kinds of problems, including cancer of the reproductive organs for children who are born to women who took the drug when they were pregnant. It also appears that women who took large amounts of this drug over a long period of time have a higher risk of developing reproductive system cancers. The morning-after DES treatment does not use as much hormone as these women took, and the treatment does not last a long time, so the risks should be lower. But we do not know what the long-term effects of taking the treatment might be.

If, by chance, a woman takes the morning-after treatment too late and her pregnancy is already implanted, she will probably be advised to consider abortion because of the risks of damage to the embryo caused by the treatment.

Another disadvantage of the morning-after treatment is that it will usually cause some discomfort, especially in the first two to three days of the treatment. Nausea and vomiting are common, and there may be abnormal bleeding and breast tenderness.

What Are the Advantages and Benefits?

Morning-after treatment with Ovral is rapidly replacing DES because it has been shown to be safer and to cause fewer side effects. In fact, the health risks of using Ovral for morning-after treatment seem to be minimal

This method is an effective way to prevent pregnancy after unprotected intercourse has occurred. It is a good emergency measure for women in situations where it is very important for them not to become pregnant, and where abortion is not an acceptable solution to an unwanted pregnancy. This method can also be used in situations where a woman or girl has been the victim of rape or other unwanted sex.

How Do You Use It?

The Ovral method requires that the woman take two Ovral pills within 72 hours (but preferably 12 to 24 hours) after intercourse, and take another two pills 12 hours later. Using this method, she receives a lower dose of hormones and is less likely to feel ill than with DES. The treatment is shorter and is believed to be as effective as DES in preventing pregnancy.

The DES morning-after method is usually in the form of pills taken over a period of five days. It can also be administered by injection. Since nausea and vomiting often occur during the treatment, the woman may have to make adjustments in her work or school schedule. This treatment is not available everywhere because it has not been approved by the Food and Drug Administration for use by the general public and because the Ovral method is now considered superior.

INTRAUTERINE DEVICES

What Are They?

Intrauterine devices (IUDs) are small plastic objects that are placed in the woman's uterus (Figure 9–12). It is believed that they prevent pregnancy by causing irritation and disrupting the normal chemistry of the lining of the uterus. Once a woman has one of these devices placed in her uterus, it remains there, perhaps for several years, and provides long-term protection against pregnancy. When she wants to become pregnant, the woman has the device removed.

Modern IUDs have been available since the late 1950s, but the use of intrauterine devices was known to the ancient Egyptians and to some other groups throughout history. Historically, putting objects in the uterus was used both to prevent pregnancy and to cause abortion if the woman was already pregnant.

It is estimated that 40 to 50 million women in the world today are using intrauterine devices; 3 to 4 million of these women are in the United States. IUDs are a popular birth control method for several reasons. First, they are inexpensive once they are inserted, as there are no additional birth control products to be purchased and kept on hand. Sec-

ond, like the pill, the IUD protects a woman at all times. She does not have to plan ahead for intercourse in order to be protected.

However, fewer women use IUDs in the United States than they did 10 years ago, because there is increasing concern about some of the health risks of using this method. Some clinics and doctors have stopped recommending IUDs for any of their patients. The problems and risks as well as the advantages and benefits of IUDs are described in the new few pages.

Where Do You Get Them?

The IUDs, like the pill and the diaphragm, can only be obtained from a clinic or a doctor. The IUD must be inserted by a trained clinician at the office. First, the woman must have a complete examination, as an IUD should not be inserted if she is pregnant or if she has recently had any kind of infection of the cervix or uterus. The size and placement of the uterus must be checked before a decision can be made about the type of IUD to use. Not every woman should use the IUD, and the clinician will help her decide if it is a good method for her. Sometimes there are problems such as fainting and weakness when the device is inserted, so it is important for the woman to be where she can be treated for these problems if necessary.

A follow-up visit is usually needed within the first month after the IUD is inserted. After that, if there are no problems, the woman only needs to come in for her usual checkups once a year or as often as her clinic or doctor recommends.

How Do They Work?

IUDs appear to affect the woman's body in many different ways that contribute to her protection against pregnancy, but not all of the effects are well understood. Research is going on in the United States and in other countries to increase understanding of the IUD's action, and to create better, safer IUDs.

Basically, the IUD works because the woman's uterus responds to an IUD as if it were a foreign body. The blood brings infection-fighting cells to the area, and the muscles contract to try to expel the foreign substance from the body. This infection-fighting response to the IUD also creates a hostile climate for a pregnancy to implant itself in the uterus.

In addition to the responses just described, which occur with any IUD, two kinds of IUDs have active substances in them as well, which make pregnancy even more unlikely. One kind has cop-

FIGURE 9–12. *Two types of IUDs (intrauterine devices).*

Family planning education in India. Intrauterine devices are used by an estimated 40 to 50 million women in the world.

per wire wrapped around it, which adds tiny amounts of copper to the environment of the uterus, causing chemical changes that are even more hostile to sperm and to pregnancy but are not noticeable to the woman. IUDs containing copper are associated with lower risks of pelvic infection than other IUDs. The other kind of active IUD has the hormone progesterone in it, which is slowly released into the uterine lining. This also helps to create a climate in the uterus that will not support pregnancy. The IUDs that contain progesterone affect the woman a little differently than the others. The hormone appears to reduce muscle cramps and the amount of blood lost during the menstrual period.

How Effective Are They?

The IUD appears to be effective in preventing pregnancy about 95 percent of the time under average conditions, and as much as 99 percent of the time under ideal conditions. This means it is more effective than either the diaphragm or the condom, but less effective than the pill. Like the pill, the IUD doesn't require the couple to plan ahead for intercourse or to take any special precautions at the time of sex. The protection of the IUD is automatic and continuous. This is probably a major reason that it is so effective. The IUD is a popular birth control method in some of the less developed countries where people don't have money to spend on birth control products, and health care is not easily available. This is because once the IUD is inserted, if all goes well, the woman doesn't need more medical attention or birth control supplies.

What Are the Problems and Risks?

The most serious risk of the IUD is that women who use IUDs are much more likely to get infections of the uterus and pelvic area than women who use other methods. These infections can lead to infertility. Using an IUD also increases the chances of ectopic pregnancy (see Chapter 6, page 124) and of serious illness and infection if the woman becomes pregnant while the IUD is in place.

There have been many health and fertility problems associated with IUDs in the United States, and a number of lawsuits have been filed against the companies that produce them. The best known cases involve the Dalkon shield, which has not been sold since 1975. Another IUD, the Saf-T-Coil, was taken off the market by its maker in 1983.

Warning: The Dalkon shield has been found to cause serious health risks for women. It is no longer sold, and has been removed from all women known to be using it. Any woman who thinks she may have the Dalkon shield should see her doctor immediately.

Cramps and Bleeding

The most common side effect of the IUD is increased cramping and bleeding at the time of menstrual periods. Approximately 15 percent of women who have the IUD inserted give it up within a year because of these problems. The body naturally rejects foreign substances, so it reacts to the IUD with cramps, which are an attempt to push it out of the body. The increased monthly bleeding is due to the irritation of tissues in the uterus, which reject the presence of the IUD. These same reactions are what make the IUD effective in preventing pregnancy. It is not unusual for a woman using an IUD to lose more than twice as much blood in her periods as she did before the IUD was inserted. This does not usually cause problems for women in good health, although there is a greater risk of becoming anemic, but it can be inconvenient because the bleeding may also continue for more days than before. Light bleeding or spotting between periods is also more common with the IUD than with other forms of birth control.

The most severe cramps and pain usually occur within the first few days after the IUD is inserted, but cramps each month just before the period starts are also likely to be more severe than before. Some women also notice cramps whenever they have contractions of the uterus, such as during intercourse or breastfeeding. Continuing severe pain is a sign of problems, and women who have this should see their clinic or doctor.

Infection

IUDs have the highest rate of infection of all the birth control methods (although death from IUD complications is very rare). One out of every 100 to 300 women using an IUD will be hospitalized for an infection every year. Women who have never had a pregnancy have an even higher rate of infection. See the sections on "Number of Partners" and "Fertility" on pages 211–212 for more information about women who are at high risk for pelvic infection with an IUD.

Infections that reach the uterus can be very serious, for several reasons. First, they can go into the Fallopian tubes and ovaries and cause illness, the need for surgery, and scarring that often results in chronic pain and infertility (see Chapter 8, "Infertility," and Chapter 14, "Sexually Transmitted Diseases"). Second, they can spread to the abdomen, damage other body organs, and even cause death.

A woman using an IUD should be very alert to signs of infection and seek treatment for them immediately, so that serious illness can be avoided. The warning signs of infection are:

1. Pain or tenderness in the abdomen
2. Chills or fever
3. Unusual vaginal bleeding or discharge
4. Pain during intercourse
5. Fatigue, muscle aches, or headaches

Sadly, a chronic low-level infection may never produce any of these symptoms and may remain undiscovered. A woman's Fallopian tubes may be damaged without her knowing it.

The treatment of infections usually includes antibiotics and rest at home, but hospitalization may be needed if the woman is extremely sick. The IUD is usually removed in these situations, and often cannot be replaced for some time because of the risk of reinfection. Infection is most likely to develop in the first weeks after an IUD is inserted or removed because the process may have transported bacteria into the uterus.

Pregnancy

The combination of using the IUD and becoming pregnant (which will happen to 4 or 5 women out of each 100 IUD users each year) produces several risks that can be very serious. About 50 percent of IUD users will have a miscarriage (spontaneous abortion), compared to around 20 percent of women in general, and the chances of getting an infection related to the miscarriage are high. *For IUD users, the combination of pregnancy and uterine infection creates a very high risk of death. The chances of dying from an infected spontaneous abortion are 50 times greater for women using the IUD than for other women.*

A woman who finds she is pregnant while using the IUD should see her clinician immediately. If she does not want the pregnancy and decides to have an abortion, it should be done as soon as possible, and the IUD can be removed at the same time. If she does want to continue the pregnancy, her clinician will recommend that the IUD be removed for her safety, but the process of removing it may also disrupt the pregnancy and cause her to abort. Babies have been delivered with the IUD left in place, but the danger to the mother is great.

Ectopic Pregnancy

Ectopic pregnancies are pregnancies that occur outside the uterus, usually in the Fallopian tubes. They are about 10 times more common among IUD users than other women, and may continue to be more common than average even after the woman stops using the IUD. An estimated 1 or 2 women out of every 1,000 IUD users will have an ectopic pregnancy each year. *Ectopic pregnancies are extremely dangerous to the life of the woman.* (See Chapter 6, page 124, for more on ectopic pregnancy.) This is because as the embryo attaches itself to the woman's body and grows, it can cause the tissues to rupture. There is danger of massive internal bleeding, which can cause death quite quickly.

A woman who has any of the danger signs of ectopic pregnancy should see her doctor immediately or go to a hospital emergency room.

The signs are:

1. Sudden intense pain in the lower abdomen
2. Light bleeding or spotting after a missed or very light menstrual period
3. Dizziness or fainting (which could be signs of internal bleeding)

Perforation of the Uterus

Another complication of the IUD is the possibility of perforation or puncture of the wall of the uterus by the IUD. This happens in 2 to 9 cases out of every 1,000 women using the IUD each year. Perforation is most likely to occur at the time of insertion of the IUD. The risk can be reduced by making sure you use a doctor or clinic that has had a lot of experience with IUDs. Women with a tipped uterus or one of unusual shape and women who have recently given birth (especially those who are breastfeeding) are more likely to have this problem than others. In rare situations, an IUD will puncture the wall of the uterus many months or even years after insertion. It may work its way out of the uterus altogether and come to rest in the abdominal cavity. In this location, obviously, it will not prevent pregnancy, and although there is no immediate danger to having the IUD free in the abdomen if there is no infection, most doctors and clinics will recommend that it be removed. Major surgery to open the abdomen may be required, or in some cases the IUD may be removed by a laparoscopy (see Chapter 10), which involves a small incision below the navel.

Expulsion

Somewhere between 1 and 20 percent of women will experience spontaneous expulsion of their IUD in the first year of use. The most likely time is with the first menstrual period after it is inserted. This means that the body, which rejects foreign substances, pushes the IUD out of the uterus through the cervix into the vagina. The expulsion may be painless and not noticed, or there may be cramps and bleeding. Many women lose their IUD without noticing it, and about one-third of all pregnancies among IUD users are caused by this. Detailed instructions on how to check to make sure the IUD is in place are given in the next few pages.

Other Problems

Some women become weak and faint during the insertion of an IUD. This is due to a shock reaction of the nervous system, which lowers blood pressure. It is less likely to happen if the woman gets a local anesthetic before the device is inserted. The reaction can be severe and in rare cases can cause convulsions or even cardiac arrest (the heart stopping). Clinics and doctors' offices are prepared for these reactions and can usually solve the problem quickly, although they may have to remove the IUD in these cases.

Removal of the IUD is usually uncomplicated and less painful than the insertion, but there can be problems if the string has gone up into the uterus, if the IUD has become embedded in the tissues of the uterus, or if the device has broken into pieces. There is an increased risk of infection for the first two weeks after the IUD is removed.

In addition to the greater risk of infections of the uterus mentioned earlier, the risk of minor infections of the cervix is also greater for IUD users than for other women. These can be treated with antibiotics without removal of the IUD, but they are likely to recur.

In rare cases, a woman may be allergic to her IUD. This is more likely in the case of the copper or progesterone-treated IUDs. This problem is solved by removing the device.

Reproductive Problems

Sex and the IUD In most cases the IUD will not affect the couple's sex life at all, but a few couples complain of irritation to the man's penis caused by rubbing against the string of the IUD, which hangs down out of the cervix. Sometimes this problem can be solved by having your clinician trim or reposition the string, or by melting the end of the plastic string so that it forms a ball and is not so bristly.

Number of partners IUDs are safest when used by a couple who have intercourse only with each other. Women who have several sexual partners at the same time, or over a period of a year, should think carefully about whether they want to use the IUD. Women using this method of birth control are more likely to develop serious pelvic infections when exposed to sexually transmitted diseases (see Chapter 14) than are women who use other methods. The chances of being exposed to a sexually transmitted disease are greater when a woman or her partner has intercourse with other people. Some birth control methods, such as condoms and diaphragms, actually provide a certain amount of protection against sexually transmitted diseases.

Fertility IUDs are a better method for women who do not want any more children than they are for women who plan to become pregnant in the future. Because of the higher risk of infection with the IUDs, women who use this method also run a higher risk of becoming infertile as a result of scarring caused by infection. It appears, also, that there may be some aftereffects of IUD use that make it harder to get pregnant even after the IUD is removed.

Many doctors and clinics will not recommend the IUD to women who have not given birth, both because these women have a higher risk of infection and because they are more likely to want children in the future.

The IUD and Cancer

Because the IUD causes chronic irritation of the tissues of the uterus, many women are concerned about the possible cancer-causing effects of this form of birth control. However, there have been no research results that show a higher risk of cancer for women who use the IUD in the more than twenty years that IUDs have been used in the United States.

Who Should Not Use the IUD?

This section summarizes the information contained in the last few pages about the risks and dangers of using the IUD. This time it is in the form of a warning about which women should not use the IUD.*

WOMEN WHO SHOULD NOT USE AN IUD UNDER ANY CIRCUMSTANCES:

Women who are pregnant
Women who have a pelvic infection (uterus or Fallopian tubes) or have had many in the past
Women who have had an ectopic pregnancy

WOMEN WHO ARE TAKING A RISK IF THEY USE THE IUD, AND WILL PROBABLY BE ADVISED TO USE ANOTHER BIRTH CONTROL METHOD:

Women who have had pelvic infections
Women with rheumatic heart disease
Women with diabetes
Women taking cortisone
Women with blood-clotting problems
Women who do not have access to emergency

* These lists are adapted from Robert Hatcher et al., *Contraceptive Technology, 1986–1987,* 13th rev. ed. (New York: Irvington Publishers, Inc., 1986), p. 193.

medical care (which might be needed because of the dangers of infection)
Women who want more children later on
Women who have more than one sexual partner
Women who can't or don't want to check the IUD strings

What Are the Advantage and Benefits?

The main advantage of the IUD is that it is 95 to 99 percent effective and that it protects a woman from pregnancy at all times, so she and her partner do not have to plan ahead for intercourse. An IUD can be an inexpensive method of birth control because there are no products to buy (but if the woman develops infections and needs medical treatment, the IUD can be quite expensive). If there are no problems, the only maintenance needed is regular checkups, watching for danger signs, and checking the string regularly to make sure the IUD is in place.

IUDs do not affect the body's hormone or chemical balance, so they do not interfere with the woman's monthly cycle, and they can be used while breastfeeding. In addition, copper-bearing IUDs have a mild antibacterial action.

Having an IUD inserted within five days of intercourse can also serve as a form of morning-after birth control. It can prevent the embryo from implanting in the wall of the uterus, so that no pregnancy can develop.

How Do You Use It?

The IUD is very convenient. Once it is inserted, there's really nothing for the woman to do except check the strings regularly, get checkups every six months or as often as recommended by her clinician, and watch for signs of infection or pregnancy.

To get an IUD, a woman goes to her family planning clinic or her gynecologist and gets a physical examination and health history. If she has had pelvic infections or an ectopic pregnancy, or if she has certain other health conditions, the IUD may not be recommended. Younger women, women who have not been pregnant, and women who have an unusual-shaped uterus usually have a harder time adjusting to an IUD, and are more likely to expel it.

There are several choices among IUDs: different sizes and shapes, IUDs that are treated with copper or progesterone. The woman makes her choice after discussion with her clinician about the advantages of each type. It is important for the woman to know which one she has, because some have to be replaced yearly, some every three years, and some can be left in place for a number of years. A final decision about the size of the device can only be made at the time of insertion, when the depth of the uterus is measured.

The IUD can be inserted at any time during the woman's cycle, but it is usually done during the woman's period or within a few days afterward, because it is definite that she is not pregnant at this time. The insertion takes a few minutes and is done in a medical examining room with the woman in position for a pelvic examination (see Chapter 12). The woman may receive an injection of local anesthetic into the cervix, as insertion is usually painful. First, a blunt rod is passed through the opening of the cervix to the back of the uterus, to determine its size. Final decisions about which IUD to use cannot be made until this measurement has been taken and the correct size for the IUD is known. Next, a narrow tube holding the folded IUD is inserted through the cervix. When the tube is withdrawn, the IUD unfolds and remains in the uterus, with the string passing down through the cervix.

The woman may feel intense cramping of the uterus at this time, and bleeding will soon start as well. These symptoms may last for a few days or even a few weeks as the body adjusts to the IUD. A checkup to make sure the IUD is in place will probably be scheduled for about two weeks after insertion, or after the next menstrual period.

The IUD is an effective means of birth control only if it is in place. For this reason, every woman who uses one must learn to check her IUD by feeling the strings. This should be done weekly or more often during the first few months, and monthly after that.

To check the strings, a woman should put one leg on a chair, squat, or use any other position where she can reach into her vagina. With the first and second fingers in the vagina, she should feel in the back for the cervix, which is a firm bump like the tip of your nose. The IUD strings should feel like plastic fishing line coming out of the cervix. The woman should also press gently on the opening of the cervix, which will feel like a dimple, where the string comes out. If she can feel the stiff plastic end of the IUD, then it is out of place, and the body is expelling it.

When a woman examines herself and can't find the strings, one of two things has happened. Either she has expelled the IUD without realizing it (which happens occasionally), and it is no longer in her body, or the strings have drawn up into the uterus. This could be a danger sign that the IUD has pierced the uterus and is slipping into the abdomen. If the strings are missing, the woman should get medical care to check if the IUD is still in her body. She should also begin using another form of birth control immediately.

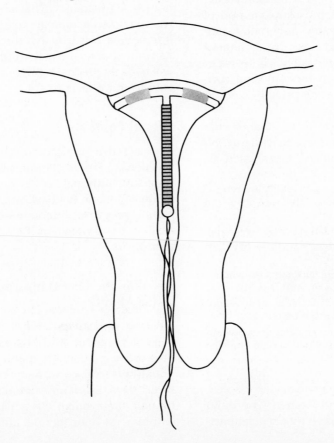

FIGURE 9–13. *An intrauterine device in place.*

Although there is little other than checking the strings that a woman must do when using the IUD, there are many things she can watch for that will make the IUD safer and more effective. Using condoms as added protection during the first three months after the IUD is inserted, and later, during the two or three most fertile days of the month, will give additional protection against pregnancy and infection. Keeping a careful watch for unusual pain, bleeding, or signs of early pregnancy is also important because early medical treatment can prevent many serious problems. If a woman is going to travel or live in remote areas where medical care is not easily available, she should check with her clinic or doctor. The IUD is not a good method for women who do not have access to emergency medical care.

Removal of the IUD when a woman no longer wants protection from pregnancy should be done by a health care professional. It is not a good idea for the woman to try to remove it herself, or to have her partner do it, even though the procedure is simple. The IUD may have become embedded in the tissues of the uterus, and there is a risk of damage to the woman's body or heavy bleeding if an untrained person tries to remove it.

THE IMPORTANCE OF BACKUP METHODS

Throughout this chapter we have recommended that couples use a second or backup method of birth control for extra protection at certain times. By doing this, they can come close to 100 percent protection from unwanted pregnancy. This is especially important for couples who would not consider abortion as a choice if their primary method of birth control were to fail.

Condoms, contraceptive foam, and/or the sponge should be kept on hand as a second method by all couples for use at high-risk times, such as:

1. When the woman is ovulating, if fertility awareness, the diaphragm, the IUD, foam, the minipill, or the condom is the primary method

2. The first month after a woman starts taking the pill, or any time she forgets to take the pill for two days or more

3. When the primary method fails, such as when a condom or diaphragm rips or an IUD is lost

4. When supplies run out unexpectedly, such as contraceptive cream or jelly for the diaphragm

5. For in-between times, when the couple is switching from one method to another, or right after the woman has given birth.

Condoms, foam, and the sponge are also excellent methods for men and women who don't have intercourse often, or don't have a regular partner. Besides being very effective, they are inexpensive, easy to buy, easy to use, and provide some protection against disease and infection.

METHODS THAT DON'T WORK!

In this chapter we have presented information about the methods of birth control that are available and are recommended because of their safety and effectiveness in preventing pregnancy. There is also a lot of inaccurate information passed around about prevention of unwanted pregnancy. In this section we talk about the methods you may have heard about, which *do not work*.

Doing "Everything But . . ."

In very rare cases pregnancies have been caused by ejaculation outside the woman's body, near the vaginal opening. This has happened to women who are virgins as well as others. Although it is very uncommon, a woman *can* become pregnant without ever having had intercourse.

"But We Only Did It Once"

Some people believe that a single act of intercourse, especially if it is the first time for the woman, will not cause pregnancy. They are wrong. Many young women have become pregnant after only one act of intercourse. It is true that the more times a woman has intercourse, the better the chances are that she will become pregnant. But once is enough, as many couples have discovered.

Special Positions

It is not true that having intercourse in certain positions, such as standing up, cannot make you pregnant. Although some positions, such as the woman lying on her back, may be most effective for getting pregnant, intercourse in any position can easily get you pregnant if it is the right time of the month.

Avoiding the One Dangerous Day of the Month

Most people assume that if a woman is going to become pregnant, it will happen within a few minutes or hours after the man ejaculates. But this is not always true, because sperm can live for two to three days inside the woman's cervix. So even though the woman's egg can only be fertilized within a 24-hour period after she ovulates, she could become pregnant from intercourse that took place days earlier.

Douching

Douching with water, vinegar, commercial douches from the pharmacy, Coca-Cola, or any of the other substances that you may have heard recommended is not effective birth control. Sperm can easily enter the cervix before intercourse is finished and before you have time to douche. Douching does create a hostile climate that will kill some of the sperm in the vagina. You should probably give it a try if, for example, you are using a condom for birth control and it breaks, but douching is nothing to count on if you want real protection from pregnancy.

Suppositories and Creams

There are many products on the shelves of pharmacies for women to use in the vagina, but not all of them are for birth control. Besides douches of various kinds, there are suppositories, jellies, and creams. *Be very careful when buying these products because some of them are contraceptives and some are not.* Many of these products have another purpose, like making a woman smell good or providing lubrication during intercourse, and provide nothing at all for birth control. Read the label carefully when buying any contraceptive product. It should say that the product is a *spermicide* and should give some information on how effective it is. If you are buying a spermicide, the foam products are considered the most effective.

Urinating after Intercourse

Urinating immediately after intercourse will not prevent pregnancy. It is recommended to women who have frequent urinary tract infections, because it seems to wash out the urinary tract and help prevent infection. But it won't have any effect on whether a woman gets pregnant.

Other Methods

Birth control is such an important human concern that throughout history people have experimented to find new methods. People are always sharing their latest invention—using Saran Wrap as a substitute for a condom, for example—with friends. But these experiments have not been tested for effectiveness of safety. In most cases they do not provide effective protection. Since you have a wide choice of contraceptives available today that have been proved effective and can be obtained easily, even by persons under 18 years of age, we strongly

recommend that the products described earlier in this chapter be used. *Don't take unnecessary chances with birth control. It is too important.*

METHODS OF THE FUTURE

The new developments in birth control that are expected to become available in the United States over the next few years will consist mostly of improved versions of existing methods, but a few completely new products are likely to appear. The following eight products could become available in the United States within the next three years.

IMPROVED PRODUCTS

1.   *Improved IUDs:* Smaller, safer IUDs and IUDs that can be left in place for 5 to 10 years
2.   *Improved barrier methods for women:* Improved versions of the sponge and the cervical cap, and possibly a disposable diaphragm
3.   *Improved long-acting injections:* Injections that prevent pregnancy for 30, 90, or 180 days have been tested for years, and new versions may be approved.

NEW PRODUCTS

1.   *Long-acting contraceptive implants:* Tiny rods implanted under the woman's skin, which slowly release synthetic hormones, providing pregnancy prevention for at least five years. These are successfully used in other countries now.
2.   *Vaginal rings:* Removable plastic vaginal rings (like the rim of a diaphragm) that release synthetic hormones. These are currently being tested in other countries.
3.   *New support for natural family planning:* A simple urine or saliva test to test for ovulation at home
4.   *Once-a-month contraceptive for women:* A contraceptive drug women could take once a month to bring on menstruation. Any pregnancy started that month would be aborted.

Other methods under investigation that may become available in the future include:

1.   Reversible sterilization for women and men
2.   Contraceptive drugs for men that suppress sperm production
3.   Antipregnancy vaccines for women
4.   Antifertility vaccines for men

Although a great deal of money is spent by drug companies and governments to develop and test new and more effective methods of birth control, some types of methods receive more attention and are more likely to become available eventually. Two important points are:

1. Contraceptive research has focused more on methods that are used by women than by men.
2. Contraceptive research has focused more on methods that can be sold commercially and make money than on simpler methods that would be free.

An example of a simple method is the application of heat to the testicles (such as with daily hot baths). This is a well known cause of temporary infertility in men and thus appears to have potential also as a method of male birth control. Yet this potential method (and other similar ones) seem to receive no attention.

FOR FURTHER READING

HATCHER, ROBERT A., FELICIA GUEST, FELICIA STEWART M.D., GARY K. STEWART M.D., JAMES TRUSSELL, SYLVIA CEREL BOWEN, AND WILLARD CATES, M.D. *Contraceptive Technology, 1988–1989* (14th rev. ed.). New York: Irvington Publishers, 1986.

RESOURCES

Information and referral services are available in your local community through the United Way agency, county or state Department of Health, Planned Parenthood, and other family planning agencies. Information on fertility awareness training can be obtained from Catholic churches or hospitals. In addition, the following national resources can be contacted.

Couple to Couple League International
P.O. Box 11184
Cincinnati, OH, 45211
(513) 661-7612

A nonprofit organization that provides information and referral for the symptothermal method of fertility awareness (natural family planning).

National Family Planning and Reproductive Health Association
122 "C" Street, N.W. Suite 380
Washington, DC 20001
(202) 628-3535

A nonprofit organization that provides information about family planning, abortion, and reproductive health matters.

Planned Parenthood Federation of America
810 Seventh Avenue
New York, NY 10019
(212) 541-7800

A nonprofit organization that provides information and education about family planning, abortion, and reproductive health matters, and referral to local Planned Parenthood affiliate clinics nationwide.

10
Sterilization

WHAT IS STERILIZATION?

Sterilization of a woman refers to a medical procedure that will cause her to be incapable of becoming pregnant in the future. Sterilization of a man refers to surgery that will make him unable to make a woman pregnant in the future. *Sterilization is permanent birth control.* In this chapter we describe the kinds of sterilization procedures available to men and women who choose not to have any more children.

Sterilization in both men and women involves cutting or tying off the tubes (Fallopian tubes in women, vas deferens in men) that carry the ovum and the sperm to the site where they can be fertilized. The surgery is called **vasectomy** for men and **tubal ligation** for women. Vasectomy and the several techniques used for tubal ligation are described in detail in the following pages.

Hysterectomy, or removal of the uterus,

which also causes a woman to be sterile, is described in another part of the book (see Chapter 12). It is not normally used for sterilization unless there is also a serious medical problem that makes removal of the uterus desirable.

DECIDING ABOUT STERILIZATION

Background

Sterilization is the most commonly used birth control method in the United States for couples over the age of 30. Just under a million sterilizations are done each year in the United States, about equally divided between men and women. It is estimated that in 1981 there were 13.7 million sterilized adults in the United States and over 100 million worldwide.

Although methods of sterilization have

Sterilization is chosen by couples who feel sure they have all the children they want.

been known since antiquity, the procedure did not take on a major role in family planning until after World War II. Since that time, the number of people seeking sterilizations has increased each year. Modern medical techniques make sterilization quite safe, and the laws have changed over the last forty years to make sterilization more easily available to men and women who want it.

Legal Issues

Sterilization is a permanent procedure that terminates a person's ability to reproduce. So the decision to seek sterilization is a very serious one, and the rights of men and women in this area are strongly protected by law. *According to today's laws, the decision to seek sterilization must be voluntary. No one can be sterilized against his or her will.* Before sterilization, each person must sign an informed consent form, to show that the procedure has been explained to him or her and that he or she understands the risks and benefits involved.

A man or woman seeking sterilization must be at least 21 years of age in most states, must be mentally competent, and must give informed consent to the procedure. Married persons can sign for their own sterilization without the consent of husband or wife (but it is recommended that they consult with their spouse on such an important decision). If a person plans to use federally financed health coverage, such as Medicaid, to pay for the treatment, there are strict regulations that require the person to wait 30 days after signing a consent form before the surgery can be performed. This is to protect people from being pressured into sterilization (which has been a serious problem for low-income and minority women in the past) or from acting in haste and taking an action they might regret later.

In the past, both the laws and the traditions of medicine limited sterilization to persons who had already had many children or who had health or mental problems that made having children undesirable. This is no longer true.

In the first half of this century, the laws of most states permitted the involuntary sterilization (sterilization without their permission) of mentally retarded and mentally ill persons, and of convicted criminals. Thousands of people, mostly living in hospitals or prisons, were sterilized. This practice is no longer carried out, but some states still have these old laws on the books. Court decisions over the last fifteen years make it clear that, today, only the individual has the right to make this decision; no one can force it on him or her. Most of the laws concerning sterilization are made by the states, so regulations are different from one state to another.

Effectiveness

Sterilization is almost 100 percent effective in preventing pregnancy. It is far more effective than any of the temporary birth control methods, including the pill. There are slight differences in the effectiveness rates of the different sterilization procedures, but the most important factor in effectiveness is the choice of an experienced doctor. Physicians who do many sterilizations each year have a much better record of effectiveness than those who only do a few.

Risks and Complications

Compared to other methods of birth control, sterilization is both safe and inexpensive, if you look at the costs and risks over a lifetime. Sterilization procedures have an extremely low risk of complications and death. Vasectomy, the procedure for men, is the safest. Complications from general anesthesia are responsible for most of the problems that develop with sterilizations, therefore, most of the risks of sterilization procedures can be avoided by using local anesthesia. The other problems that can develop are similar to those with any surgery, but are not frequent with sterilizations—the risk of infection, bleeding, or injury to organs near the site of surgery. Local anesthesia is always used for vasectomy unless there are special problems, and it is commonly used for most of the women's procedures. The specific risks and problems of each procedure are discussed later in this chapter.

Reversibility

Sterilization procedures are designed to be permanent. No one should choose sterilization unless he or she is certain that he or she will not want children in the future. However, there are many requests to have sterilizations undone (reversed) because people's feelings and life situations change over the years. Studies of attempts to reverse sterilizations have shown success rates of anywhere from 5 percent to 90 percent.

Even when a sterilization has been successfully reversed, the man or woman is likely to be less fertile than before. It is often difficult to start a pregnancy. As more experience is gained with reversing sterilizations, and as new techniques are developed, it is likely that the chances will improve. But for now, men or women planning sterilization cannot count on getting their fertility back through reversal of sterilization.

Commercial sperm banks advertise to men considering vasectomy that keeping frozen sperm samples is a way to preserve fertility in case children are desired at a later time. Unfortunately, frozen human sperm often does not keep well, and the chances of starting a pregnancy with sperm that have been frozen for several years is low. Although banking their sperm is an option for men considering vasectomy, at present it is not a dependable way to ensure future fertility.

Coming to a Decision

The decision to be sterilized is an important event in a person's life. It deserves a lot of time and careful thought. Since pregnancy can be avoided by other birth control methods, there is no reason to make a decision about sterilization in haste. It is important to know that sterilization (because it ends fertility) can affect the way a person feels about himself or herself as a man or a woman. It can also affect sexual feelings. So reaching a decision about sterilization involves more than rational, common-sense thinking about the situation. Feelings and emotions also must be taken into account—even if they don't seem to make sense. *Sterilization does not affect a man's or a woman's ability to have sex, or the hormone levels that help create desire for sex.* But for people who fear that sterilization will change them, or who are not comfortable with the idea, sterilization could have a negative effect on their sex lives.

Sterilization is available to all adults: single, married, with children and without. However, age and number of children are very important things to consider in coming to a decision. In general, the older the person and the more children he or she already has, the less likely the person is to regret the decision later. Younger people have more years ahead of them—years in which their life situation and their interest in having children could change a great deal. Each situation is different, and only the individual can know what is best for her or him.

A man or woman considering sterilization should also think about his or her relationships with the opposite sex. If the person is in a serious relationship, the partner's feelings certainly should be considered. In a long-term relationship, there may be a choice as to which partner will be sterilized. People who are not in serious relationships also need to think about long-term goals, about the kind of relationships they want for the future. Is it possible that a future partner might want children?

Some people choose sterilization for special reasons. They may carry genes for an inherited disease that they do not want to pass on, or they may have health or emotional problems that make having children unwise. Others choose sterilization for philosophical reasons, or because they prefer to adopt.

Sterilization is a serious decision. It is important to get all the facts and consider the outcome carefully.

Most people who choose sterilization are satisfied with their decision afterward and do not develop emotional or sexual problems resulting from the procedure. The people who are most likely to have problems afterward or to regret their decision are those who were not really comfortable with the idea in the first place. No one should be sterilized unless it is his or her own choice, and no one should do it for a partner, against her or his own best judgment.

It is also important to keep in mind that relationships change over the years, and that close to half of all marriages in the United States end in divorce. Although it is rare, children may also die. A decision about sterilization should be made looking far into the future, not just at today's situation.

STERILIZATION FOR MEN: VASECTOMY

The Vasectomy Procedure

Vasectomy is a minor surgical procedure in which the two tubes (called the vas deferens) that carry sperm from the testicles to the urethra are cut and tied, causing sterility. It is a short (20 to 30 minute or less) operation, which is performed in a doctor's office or a clinic under local anesthesia (similar to the Novocain used by dentists). As Figure 10–1 shows, the doctor makes either one or two half-inch incisions in the scrotum, and gently lifts out the vas deferens. A short section (half an inch to an inch) is cut from each of the two tubes. The ends are tied off and may be cauterized (sealed by burning). The tied-off tubes are returned to the inside of the scrotum, and the incision is closed with a few stitches. After a resting period of 15 to 30 minutes, the man can go home. He can usually return to his normal activities within one to two days. If his stitches are not the absorbable type, he will need to return to have them removed within a few days.

Although he can have sexual intercourse as soon as it is comfortable, the man is not yet sterile, and the couple must still use another birth control method (see Chapter 9). Some sperm are stored in the body beyond the point of the vasectomy, and these remaining sperm must be flushed from the body (10 to 20 ejaculations) before the man will be

FIGURE 10–1. *The vasectomy procedure.*

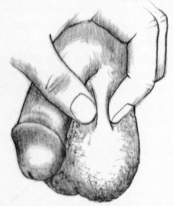

(1) Locating vas deferens

(2) Vas deferens exposed by small incision in scrotum

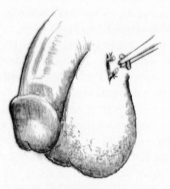

(3) A small section of vas deferens removed and ends tied and/or cauterized

(4) Incision in scrotum closed

(5) Steps 1-4 repeated on right side

sterile. The man cannot consider himself sterile until he has had two successive sperm counts that show no sperm in his ejaculate.

Effectiveness

The vasectomy is a very effective form of sterilization. The failure rate for vasectomies is approximately 1.5 pregnancies per 1,000 procedures (over a lifetime).

Risks and Complications

Serious complications from vasectomy are very rare, and no deaths from the procedure have been recorded in the Western Hemisphere. Approximately 5 men out of 100 will experience some kind of complication after vasectomy. Almost all of these problems are minor, most commonly the development of a blood clot (hematoma) in the area of the incision, and infection. The blood clots usually dissolve without treatment, and infections are treated with antibiotics. Epididymitis, which is inflammation of the ducts that carry sperm from the testicle to the vas deferens, sometimes occurs but usually goes away within a week. It is treated with rest, cold packs, and wearing a support. A granuloma or lump of scar tissue sometimes develops, but it usually does not require treatment.

Between one-third and one-half of all men having vasectomies develop antibodies to their own sperm. There is no evidence that this is harmful.

Vasectomy does not affect a man's hormones or his sexual abilities in any known way. His ejaculations remain the same. Any changes (positive or negative) in sexual behavior and feelings after a vasectomy are probably due to the psychological reaction of the man or his partner to the surgery, rather than to the vasectomy itself. In surveys of British and Canadian men who had had vasectomies, over 98 percent reported that they had no regrets about their decision, and 73 percent reported increased sexual pleasure since the surgery. Decreased sexual pleasure was reported by 1.5 percent of the men, and the rest reported no change.

There is a small chance that the vas deferens may grow back together, causing the man to be fertile again. Some doctors recommend a sperm count every year to protect against this possibility.

Advantages and Benefits

The most important advantage of vasectomy is that it is the safest, easiest to perform, and cheapest of all the sterilization methods (for both sexes). Vasectomy surgery for a man also produces less discomfort and loss of time from work or other activities than does tubal ligation for a woman.

Vasectomy gives men permanent control over their fertility, which is an advantage if they are sure they do not want to father more children. Women may appreciate the fact that a man has had a vasectomy, as it relieves them of responsibility and worry about unwanted pregnancy.

Preparation for Vasectomy

A physical examintion and a medical history will be taken before the vasectomy is performed. A blood-clotting test may be done. Any infections or problems in the area of the penis and testicles will be noted, and treated if necessary, before surgery. Some problems, such as previous hernia surgery or an undescended testicle, may make the vasectomy difficult to perform, and hospitalization may be needed. But for most men the vasectomy will be simple outpatient surgery, under local anesthesia.

The following steps are involved in preparing for the vasectomy:

1. Be absolutely sure that you and your partner understand the procedure and the fact that it is permanent.
2. You may be asked to cut or shave the hairs from around the scrotum and penis.
3. Shower or bathe before the surgery, washing the area carefully.
4. Arrange to have someone drive you to and from the surgery.
5. Take along an athletic supporter to wear after surgery.

After the Vasectomy

Some swelling and pain can be expected after surgery. The scrotum may turn black and blue in the area of the incision. Any pain should be mild and can be treated with an aspirin substitute. Aspirin should be avoided.

Pain and swelling can be kept to a minimum by using ice packs and by avoiding activity for the first 48 hours after surgery. Wearing jockey shorts or an athletic supporter 24 hours a day also helps, and can be continued for as long as it feels good. After 48 hours, it is all right to return to normal activities, but heavy lifting, straining, and extreme physical activity should be avoided for a week or so.

Sexual intercourse can be resumed within two or three days, or as soon as the man feels it would be comfortable. But activities that rub, stretch, or irritate the area of the incision should be avoided, and if the man feels discomfort, he should stop. The contraceptive effects of the vasectomy have not yet begun, so it is important to keep using a birth control method.

The man will return to the doctor's office for a checkup sometime within one to six weeks after the vasectomy. Depending on the kind of stitches used, he may need to return to have them removed as well. He will also need to return twice for a sperm count, in order to be sure he is sterile. To get a sperm count, the man brings in a fresh sample of semen (usually obtained by masturbation), which is examined under a microscope for the presence of sperm. Between 10 and 20 ejaculations are usually needed after vasectomy to clear all the sperm that are stored beyond the site of the vasectomy from the man's body.

Serious complictions are very rare, but the man should see his doctor immediately if he develops any of these symptoms after surgery: a fever of 100.4 or greater, bleeding from the incision site, or severe pain and swelling.

STERILIZATION FOR WOMEN: TUBAL LIGATION

Tubal Ligation Procedures

Tubal ligation is a surgical procedure in which the Fallopian tubes are blocked, causing sterility. The woman's ovaries continue to produce an egg each month, but it is only able to travel partway down the Fallopian tube. It remains there and eventually

is absorbed by the body. A tubal ligation takes 20 to 30 minutes to perform, and recovery from the procedure is rapid. There are many different approaches to blocking the tubes, including tying off, cutting, removing a section of the tube, and cauterization (burning and sealing the tissue with an electrically heated instrument) (Figure 10–2). Many doctors use a combination of these methods.

Tubal ligations can be divided into two general groups: **abdominal tubal ligations**, in which the approach is made through the abdomen, and **vaginal tubal ligations**, in which the approach is made through the vagina.

Effectiveness

The tubal ligation is a very effective form of sterilization, and produces far more protection from pregnancy than any of the temporary birth control methods, including the pill. The failure rates for the different types of tubal ligations vary, with the estimated failure rate for the laparoscopic method being 2.0 pregnancies per 1,000 procedures, calculated over a lifetime. Most of the pregnancies that are discovered after tubal ligation are pregnancies that were started just before the surgery took place. Other failures are caused by incomplete closing of a tube, accidental tying off of a ligament instead of a tube, or (very rarely) presence of a third tube.

The best protection against the risk of an ineffective tubal ligation is careful selection of the doctor who does the procedure. Doctors who do

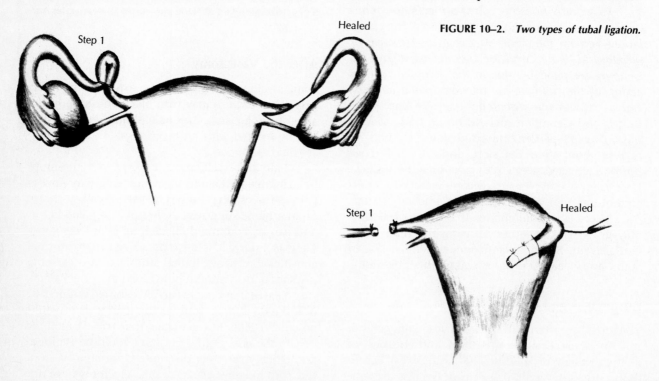

Step 1

Healed

FIGURE 10–2. *Two types of tubal ligation.*

Step 1

Healed

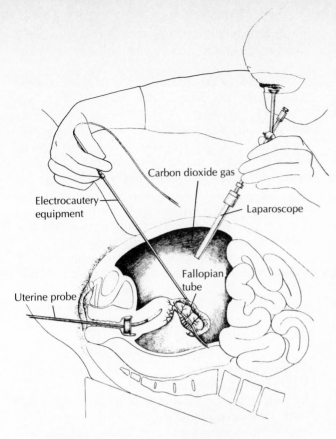

FIGURE 10–3. *Laparoscopy.*

many procedures over the course of a year have a lower rate of failure and of complications than those who do few.

Abdominal Tubal Ligations

The three major kinds of abdominal tubal ligations are the **laparoscopy,** the **minilaparotomy,** and the **laparotomy.** With the minilaparotomy and the laparoscopy, the surgery can be performed at a hospital or an outpatient surgical center, but the woman does not have to stay overnight. With the laparotomy, the woman will need to spend a few days in the hospital.

Laparoscopy

Laparoscopy (also called "band-aid sterilization") is the most commonly performed sterilization procedure for women (Figure 10–3). This procedure approaches the tubes by means of a small incision (approximately one inch) just below the navel. Carbon dioxide gas is pumped into the abdomen through this incision to create space so that the Fallopian tubes can be easily located and seen. Next, a long slender instrument called a laparoscope is inserted. This instrument lights the interior of the abdomen; the doctor can look through it to see the inside of the abdomen and the Fallopian tubes. An electric cauterizing instrument is inserted through the same incision, or through another small (half-inch) incision in the lower abdomen. This instrument is used to burn and seal a section of each tube. The tubes may also be sealed by the use of plastic clips or rings. To assist the doctor in locating and reaching the tubes, an instrument called a uterine probe is inserted through the vagina and cervix into the uterus. Using the probe, the doctor can move the uterus and bring the tubes closer to the incision. Local or general anesthesia can be used; using local anesthesia lowers the risk of complications.

A very similar procedure (called **postpartum tubal ligation**), which does not require the use of the laparoscope, can be done just after a woman gives birth. At this time the uterus is enlarged and located high in the abdomen so that it can be easily reached. A small incision is made just below the navel, and through it the doctor can reach the tubes and close them off. Postpartum tubal ligations are becoming less common because they have a higher failure rate than other tubal ligation procedures. This is because the woman's body, as it heals and repairs itself after childbirth, sometimes also causes the Fallopian tubes to grow back together, making the woman fertile again. Another reason women are choosing to wait until a few months after childbirth to get a sterilization is that they may want to be sure first that the new baby is doing well.

Minilaparotomy

The minilaparotomy involves a small (one- to one-and-a-half-inch) incision an inch or so above the pubic bone. The Fallopian tubes are drawn up through this incision, closed off, and then returned to the abdomen. The uterine probe, used in laparoscopy, is also used with this procedure. This surgery is generally done with local anesthesia. Recovery from this type of tubal ligation is rapid. Usually the woman can return to normal activities within two days. The scar will not be visible when wearing a bikini. This approach to tubal ligation is relatively new to the United States but is widely practiced in other countries. It is becoming popular here because it is simple, can be done with local anesthesia, and has a low rate of complications.

Laparotomy

Tubal ligation can also be performed through a standard laparotomy, or opening of the lower abdomen through a five-inch incision. This incision may be vertical, with one end toward the navel and the other just above the pubic bone, or it may be horizontal, stretching across the lower abdomen. A laparotomy may be desirable if the woman needs surgery for another reason and requests that a tubal ligation be performed at the same time, or if she has had previous surgery or scarring that makes doing the tubal ligation difficult. General anesthesia is used with this procedure, and a three-day stay in the hospital is usually needed. Recovery time is longer than for the other sterilization procedures.

Vaginal Tubal Ligation

The vaginal tubal ligation (**culpotomy**) is performed with the woman in the position for a pelvic examination. An incision is made just below the cervix in the cul de sac of the vagina (Figure 10–4). Through this opening, the Fallopian tubes are located and closed off. This procedure has the advantages of leaving no visible scar and of short recovery time. However, it also has a higher complication rate than the abdominal tubal ligation because the vagina is host to many bacteria, which increase the risk of infection after the surgery.

Risks and Complications

The risks and complications of tubal ligation are different for each method. The laparoscopy and minilaparotomy have the lowest complication rates of all the methods. Vaginal tubal ligation has a complication rate about twice as high as the abdominal methods, because of the many organisms that live in the vagina and increase the chances of infection. For this reason, the vaginal tubal ligation is not as commonly performed as the other procedures. The death rate from complications of tubal ligation is

FIGURE 10–4. *Location of incision for vaginal tubal ligation.*

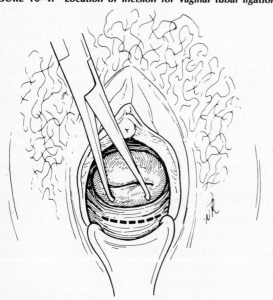

low, approximately 2.5 per 100,000 procedures for laparoscopy and slightly higher for the other methods.

Complications related to use of general anesthesia make up most of the problems that may develop in relation to a tubal ligation. Local anesthesia is safer than general, but both are very safe for a healthy woman. Smokers, women with asthma or heart disease, and overweight women have a higher risk of anesthesia-related complications.

Although such damage is very rare, injury to the internal organs is possible during tubal ligation. It this happens, a second surgery to repair the tissues or to stop bleeding could be needed.

Infection is another possible complication. It is most common with the vaginal tubal ligation, but can occur with any of the procedures. This can usually be treated with antibiotics, but if it spreads to the abdominal cavity or forms abscesses, hospitalization and further surgery could be needed.

Not all of the tubal ligation procedures can be performed on all women. Extremely overweight women and women who have scarring from abdominal surgery or infections in the past may have to have the laparotomy procedure. In 7 out of 1,000 laparoscopies, unexpected problems, such as scarring, are found, and the tubal ligation cannot be completed as planned. The surgery can be stopped at that point, or the doctor can go ahead and complete the tubal ligation using another method, such as laparotomy.

After tubal ligation, a woman continues to get her menstrual period as before, although in some cases it becomes irregular.

Advantages and Benefits

Tubal ligation is a very inexpensive, safe, and convenient means of birth control for women who are certain that they do not want to give birth to more children. For healthy women older than 35 to 40, the health risks of tubal ligation are lower than the risks of continued use of the pill or of pregnancy and childbirth.

Another important advantage of tubal ligation is that it frees the woman from worry about unwanted pregnancy. For some women, this freedom from worry allows them to enjoy sexual activity more than in the past. *Tubal ligation does not affect a woman's hormones or her ability or desire to have sex in any known way. Her vagina and uterus are not affected. Any changes (positive or negative) in sexual behavior or feelings after tubal ligation are probably due to the psychological reaction of the woman or her partner to the surgery, rather than to the surgery itself.*

All the sterilization procedures except laparotomy can be performed on an outpatient basis at a hospital or surgical center, using local anesthesia. Tubal ligations done by laparotomy (the five-inch incision) must be done in a hospital operating room and may require the woman to remain in the hospital for several days.

Preparation for Tubal Ligation

The first step in preparing for a tubal ligation is to be absolutely certain that you and your partner understand about sterilization and feel sure that this is the right plan for you. You can change your mind at any time before the surgery.

If you decide on a tubal ligation, your doctor will take a medical history and perform a physical examination, including a Pap test (see Chapter 12), blood count, and urinalysis. Further tests may be ordered as well, such as tests of bleeding and clotting times, and a chest X-ray. Present or past health problems, such as a history of pelvic infections, previous abdominal surgery, being seriously overweight, hiatal hernia, and asthma and heart disease may affect the type of procedure recommended. If a vaginal tubal ligation is planned, antibiotics or special douches may be prescribed for a few days before the surgery.

Women taking the birth control pill will probably be asked to stop about a month before surgery. Women using the IUD may be advised to have it removed before tubal ligation. In these cases it is important for the couple to use another birth control method during the weeks before surgery. Condoms, foam, or the diaphragm are all convenient and effective methods (see Chapter 9).

In planning for the surgery, a woman needs someone to drive her to and from the clinic or hospital, and a flexible schedule for the first week or so after the tubal ligation. She should not drive a car for at least 24 hours after surgery because of the lingering effects of sedatives or anesthesia. Women have different experiences with regard to how fast they recover from surgery. Recovery time will be longer if general anesthesia is used. Some pain and discomfort can be expected from the incision, and, if laparoscopy was the method, from the pressure of the gas that was used to inflate the abdomen. This pressure is usually felt as pain in the shoulder and chest area, and it goes away within one to two days, when the gas is absorbed.

After the Tubal Ligation

Most women can go home within one to four hours after laparoscopy or minilaparotomy tubal ligations. The vaginal tubal ligations may require a one- or two-day stay in the hospital, and tubal ligations performed by laparotomy may require more. The laparotomy procedure requires several weeks of recovery time, but for the other methods, recovery is rapid. A flexible schedule should be kept for a week, since women recover at different rates. No heavy lifting should be done for at least a week.

A follow-up visit to the doctor's office will be needed to check the incision. The doctor may use dissolving stitches or the kind that need to be removed at the office. Women who have the abdominal tubal ligation should avoid sexual intercourse until it is comfortable (usually within a week). Tubal ligations are effective immediately after surgery, so there is no need to use another form of birth control. The vaginal tubal ligations require the couple to avoid sexual intercourse for four to six weeks to allow time for the incision to heal. Vaginal bleeding or spotting may occur for a few days after surgery with both methods.

Follow your doctor's advice about showers and baths after surgery; it is usually all right to start showering immediately, but with some of the procedures you may be asked to wait.

Most women getting tubal ligations do not develop complications after surgery. However, women should contact their doctor or clinic immediately if they have any of the following symptoms:

1. A fever higher than 100.4 degrees Fahrenheit
2. Fainting spells
3. Continuing or severe pain in the abdomen
4. Bleeding from the site of the incision

FOR FURTHER READING

GREENFIELD, MICHAEL, AND WILLIAM M. BURRUS. *The Complete Reference Book on Vasectomy.* New York: Avon Books, 1973.

STEWART, FELICIA, M.D., FELICIA GUEST, GARY STEWART, M.D., AND ROBERT HATCHER, M.D. *My Body, My Health: The Concerned Woman's Book of Gynecology.* New York: Bantam Books, 1981.

RESOURCES

Information and referral services are available in your local community through the county or state Department of Health, and Community Hospitals. In addition, the following national resources can be contacted.

Association for Voluntary Surgical Contraception
122 East 42nd Street, 18th floor
New York, NY 10168
(212) 251-2555
A nonprofit organization that provides information and education about surgical contraception.

11
Abortion

Abortion is the ending of a pregnancy before the fetus has developed enough to live outside the woman's body. The term **abortion** usually refers to a medical procedure to end a pregnancy. However, many pregnancies are also lost through natural or **spontaneous abortions** (also called **miscarriages;** see Chapter 6), in which the woman's body rejects the pregnancy. The following pages describe the kinds of medical abortions available to a woman if she wishes to end a pregnancy. For information about other choices for a woman with an unwanted pregnancy, see Chapter 7, "Unplanned and Unwanted Pregnancy."

Every year over one and a half million American women have abortions. Most women seeking abortions are young, unmarried, and in their teens and twenties. The majority have not been using birth control. Since no birth control method is perfect, however, some women seeking abortions have been careful users of contraception. All fertile couples who are having intercourse are at some risk (if only a small one) of an unwanted pregnancy, and some users of abortion services are married women and women in their thirties and forties.

The most common reason for choosing abortion is an unwanted pregnancy, but many abortions are performed for other reasons. The woman may have health problems that make pregnancy and childbirth very dangerous for her. Or a woman who wants children may have learned through amniocentesis (see Chapter 6) that she is pregnant with a child with serious deformities or defects such as Down's syndrome. Some abortions are performed on women who have become pregnant as a result of rape or incest.

Abortion is not the best choice for everyone, and some religions and cultures forbid it. But for many women it can be the best solution to a problem pregnancy.

BACKGROUND INFORMATION

Abortion has been practiced since prehistoric times. It is found today in all the countries of the world. More than a third of the world's population lives in countries like the United States, where abortion is legally available to women on request. In other countries, abortion is limited to cases where there is a serious social or medical reason. Less than 10 percent of the world's population lives in countries where abortion is completely illegal, and in these places abortions are still performed illegally.

Abortion is legal in all the United States, and has been since 1973. Because of a U.S. Supreme Court ruling, the states are not allowed to restrict the offering of abortion services during the first three months of pregnancy. Abortions done in the third to the sixth month of pregnancy can be regulated by the state, so the availability of these late abortions is different in different states. Abortions are not generally available after the sixth month of pregnancy, except when there are serious health problems.

Before 1973, complications from illegal abortions were a major cause of illness and death for women in the United States. Since abortion has become legal, women can obtain the service from properly trained health care professionals under safe conditions. The rate of complications today is extremely low, making abortion much safer than pregnancy and childbirth in almost every case.

ABORTION METHODS

There are four different abortion methods used in the United States today: **early vacuum abortion, dilation and curettage (D&C), dilation and evacuation (D&E),** and **amnioinfusion abortion.** More than 90 percent of abortions are performed early, during the first 12 weeks of pregnancy.

Early Vacuum Abortion

Most of the abortions performed in the United States (over 80 percent) are done by the early vacuum method. It is used to terminate pregnancies up to 12 weeks from the first day of the woman's last monthly period (the first three months of the pregnancy). This method of abortion is extremely safe and effective, and can be performed in a clinic or doctor's office. Local anesthesia (numbing of the cervical area) is usually all that is needed. General anesthesia (in which the woman is asleep during the abortion) is also available if a woman chooses a hospital or surgical center for the abortion.

The abortion is done with the woman lying in the position for a pelvic examination (see Chapter 12). When local anesthesia is used, the first step is the injection of a local anesthetic (similar to the Novocain used by dentists) into the cervix and the surrounding area. The woman will probably not feel the needle, but she may feel mild cramping as the liquid is injected. The anesthetic takes effect quite

The decision to choose abortion deserves careful thought.

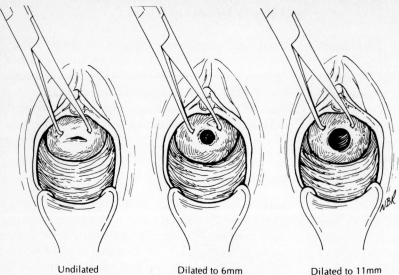

Undilated   Dilated to 6mm   Dilated to 11mm

FIGURE 11–1. *Dilating rods are used to enlarge the opening in the cervix.*

fast, and within minutes the abortion can begin.

A plastic or metal dilating rod is inserted in the cervix to widen the opening for the vacuum tube (Figure 11–1). Several rods of increasing size may be used, depending on the size of the vacuum tube needed (Figure 11–2). The smallest vacuum tubes (called **cannulas**) are needed for the earliest abortions, and larger ones are used as the pregnancy advances. The cannula is then inserted into the uterus through the enlarged opening in the cervix. The cannula is attached to a small machine that works like a vacuum cleaner, sucking up the contents of the uterus and carrying them out of the woman's body (Figure 11–3). This process takes only a few minutes. It removes the embryo or fetus and all the other tissue and blood that the woman's body has produced to support the

pregnancy (Figure 11–4). This material can weigh as little as one or two ounces for an abortion performed at five or six weeks, or as much as a pound for an abortion performed at three months. Next, a **curette**—a sharp, spoon-shaped instrument—may be used to check the inside of the uterus, to make sure all the tissue has been removed.

When the abortion is over, most clinics require the woman to rest for an hour or so before going home. If general anesthesia was used, she may have to wait longer, because it will take time for the drugs to wear off.

As far as pain goes, different women report different experiences. Most women who have local anesthesia say the discomfort during the dilation and suction parts of the abortion can be similar to menstrual cramps. Some women say this part of

FIGURE 11–2. *Instruments used in early vacuum abortions.*
A. Tenaculum *(clamp used to hold the cervix steady)*
B. Cannula *(vacuum tube)*
C. Curette *(spoon-shaped scraping instrument)*
D. Dilating rods of different sizes

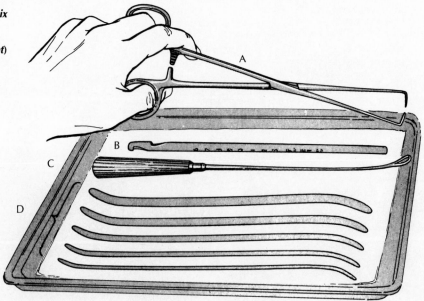

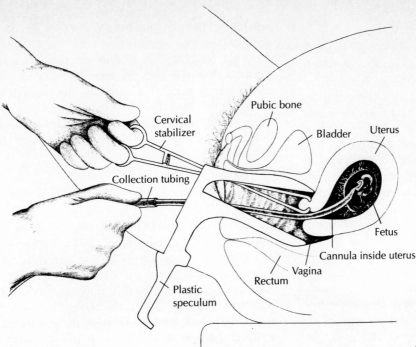

FIGURE 11–3. *An early vacuum abortion in process.*

the procedure is briefly painful. Cramps may last for an hour or two after the abortion is over, then gradually decrease. After an early vacuum abortion, a woman can plan to return to work or school the following day or, if necessary, later on the same day, after a few hours of rest.

Menstrual Extraction

Menstrual extraction refers to the use of the early vacuum aspiration method to remove the contents

of a woman's uterus at the time her menstrual period is expected, or within a week or two after. In the past, when pregnancy tests were not effective until two weeks after a period was due, some women who thought they might be pregnant used this method. Today there are blood tests for pregnancy that will work a week after conception (a week before the woman's period is due), so there is no need to guess. If these early tests show the woman is not pregnant, she does not need extraction. If she is pregnant, she can get an early vacuum abortion.

FIGURE 11–4. *An early vacuum abortion completed.*

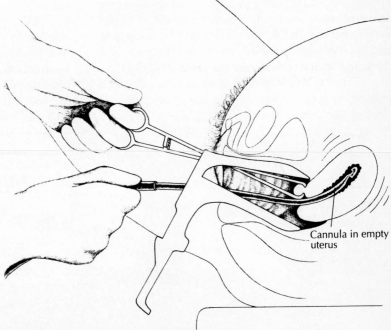

Dilation and Curettage

Dilation and curettage (also called a D&C) is a commonly used surgical treatment of women in which the uterus is scraped by a long-handled spoon-shaped instrument called a curette. The contents of the uterus are removed and can then be examined for signs of disease or other problems. (For a full description of the treatment, see Chapter 12).

The D&C can also be used as an abortion method, and it was the most commonly used method in the United States when abortion first became legal in 1973 (because it was an effective method that was familiar to all women's doctors). Today, the vacuum abortion method has almost completely replaced the D&C because it is safer, quicker, less painful for the woman, and just as effective. A woman seeking an early abortion today is not likely to have a D&C unless she has other health problems for which the D&C is needed.

Dilation and Evacuation

The dilation and evacuation method (D&E) is similar to the early vacum abortion, but is done later in the pregnancy, from 13 to 16 weeks of pregnancy (the second trimester), and in some cases up until the twenty-fourth week of pregnancy. With these later abortions, general anesthesia (sleep) is usually used. The cervix must be dilated much more in order to remove the larger contents of the uterus, and surgical instruments must be used in addition to the vacuum tube. The procedure takes much longer than the early vacuum method, from 15 to 30 minutes.

To prepare for the abortion, the woman's cervix may be dilated using **laminaria rods** (thin sticks made of dried seaweed), which are inserted in the cervix the day before the abortion. The laminaria rods gently swell as they absorb the body's moisture, and widen the cervical opening (Figure 11–5).

Drugs will probably be used as well to induce contractions of the uterus (like labor contractions) toward the end of the abortion. The contractions will loosen the placenta from the wall of the uterus, so that it can be removed.

Although the D&E abortion takes longer to perform than the early vacuum abortion, and usually requires general anesthesia, the woman's recovery time after the abortion is about the same. Once she is released from the hospital or surgical center, she should be able to return to her usual activities without delay.

Amnioinfusion Abortion

Amnioinfusion abortions can only be done after about 15 weeks of pregnancy, as the amniotic sac must be large enough to be worked with easily. Since most abortions are done much earlier, this type of abortion represents only 6 percent of all abortions done in the United States.

In the amnioinfusion abortion, the doctor insertes a hollow needle through the woman's abdominal wall and through the wall of the uterus, removes some of the amniotic fluid, and injects a liquid into the amniotic sac that surrounds the fetus (Figure 11–6). The liquid injected may be one of several different solutions. These solutions all have the same effect; they make the uterine environment toxic for the fetus, and they send a message to the woman's body that the pregnancy cannot survive. The woman then goes into labor and expels the fetus through the cervix and vagina in the same way as she would a spontaneous abortion or miscarriage.

General anesthesia is not needed, but local anesthesia is used at the site where the needle goes into the abdomen. Anesthesia is usually not needed during labor and the expulsion of the fetus.

This type of abortion is done in a hospital and requires a stay of anywhere from 12 to 48 hours. The length of time the woman will spend in the hospital depends on how quickly she begins labor after the amnioinfusion. Labor does not usually begin for several hours. A drug (oxytocin) may be given to bring on labor contractions or to make

FIGURE 11–5. *Use of laminaria to dilate the cervix.*

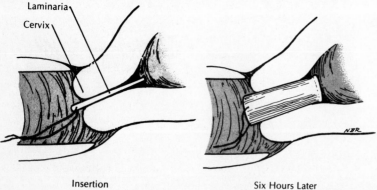

Laminaria
Cervix

Insertion   Six Hours Later

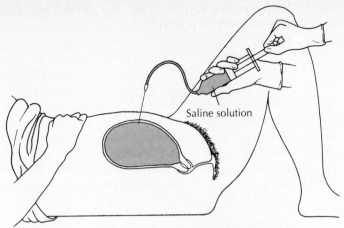

Saline solution

FIGURE 11–6. *An amnioinfusion abortion.*

them stronger. Laminaria rods (see previous section) may be inserted in the cervix to dilate the opening.

Nurses will assist the woman when she begins to expel the fetus and placenta. But women should be prepared for the fact that with a late abortion of this type, the fetus (although it could not live outside the uterus) is very recognizable as a baby. In very rare cases, where the pregnancy was more advanced than anyone realized, fetuses have been born alive. Such fetuses rarely survive outside the uterus.

In most cases the placenta will also be expelled at this time, but if it is not, the doctor may need to use instruments to reach into the uterus and dislodge it. After the abortion is complete, the woman will remain in the hospital for three to four hours, and then be able to return home. She may need to rest for a day or two before returning to her usual activities.

Other Kinds of Abortion

Hysterotomy and Hysterectomy

In rare cases, abortion may be performed through a hysterotomy, which is the removal of the fetus and other contents of the uterus through the abdomen, as with a caesarean section. This may be done when a late abortion is needed and other surgical treatment is planned at the same time, such as tubal ligation (sterilization), or when amnioinfusion does not work. Women who have medical problems that make it unsafe for them to use the amnioinfusion abortion may receive this method.

Hysterectomy, in which the whole uterus is removed at the same time the abortion is performed, is also done rarely, usually in situations where a serious disease or medical problem is involved. Both these treatments require hospital-ization and general anesthesia (sleep). (For information about hysterectomy, see Chapter 12.)

Prostaglandin Suppositories

A relatively new abortion method approved for use in the United States is a vaginal suppository containing the hormone prostaglandin. As it dissolves, the hormone enters the woman's system through the walls of the vagina and causes labor contractions. The woman expels the fetus through the vagina, as she would with a spontaneous abortion or miscarriage. This method has not been widely used in the United States, and there is not much information yet about its safety.

RU 486

RU 486 is a very promising new drug which, taken in pill form, causes abortion in women during the first six weeks of pregnancy. It belongs to a class of synthetic hormones called antiprogester-ones and is very effective in causing abortion in the first weeks of pregnancy. In addition, it seems to cause little discomfort or side effects. RU 486 was approved for use in France during 1988, but is not likely to be marketed in the United States in the near future. The drug has captured worldwide attention because of its potential for providing a cheaper, safer, more private alternative to the surgical abortion methods now available.

RU 486 appears to work by preventing the corpus luteum from producing the progesterone needed to support the embryo during the early weeks of development in the uterus. It is not 100 percent effective; women who take the drug and do not abort must undergo surgical abortion.

Folk Remedies to Cause Abortion

There are many different herbs, tonics, and other folk remedies that women have used in the past to try to cause an abortion. Some are given as teas and others as douches. *None of these methods is as safe or effective as an early vacuum abortion, and most are totally ineffective. Some can make a woman very ill, and a few can be fatal. These treatments are not recommended.*

Two other very dangerous folk remedies to cause abortion have almost disappeared in this country, thanks to the availability of safe legal abortions today. Attempts to puncture the amniotic sac with a sharp object such as a knitting needle pushed through the cervix, or to cause abortion by inserting a bit of cloth or another foreign body into the uterus, have been responsible for the deaths of many women in the past. Serious infection, hemorrhaging (excessive bleeding), and damage to internal organs are the major risks from these "remedies." Furthermore, these treatments often do not end the pregnancy, although they may damage the fetus. DANGER! DO NOT ATTEMPT TO USE THESE METHODS!

ANESTHESIA

A woman seeking an abortion often has a choice of anesthetics. She may get local anesthesia, with which she remains awake but feels little or no pain in the area being treated (similar to the use of Novocaine by the dentist). Or she may get general anesthesia, in which she is asleep during the treatment. Local anesthesia is given by an injection in the cervical area. General anesthesia will be given by an intravenous solution in the arm and, after the woman is asleep, by a gas administered through a mask over her nose.

Most early abortions are performed with local anesthesia, which is convenient and inexpensive. It can be safely given in a doctor's office or clinic, whereas general anesthesia can be safely administered only in a hospital or surgical center, which will charge more for the abortion. General anesthesia also requires more tests before the abortion (which will cost money), and it has aftereffects that may leave the woman feeling unwell for a day or two. Local anesthesia has no aftereffects. However, if the doctor also gives a sedative to make the woman feel more relaxed, it will cause drowsiness (a sleepy feeling), which may last for a few hours after the abortion. Local anesthesia is safer than general anesthesia, but both methods are very safe for a healthy woman.

CHOOSING AN ABORTION SERVICE

In many parts of the United States, women have a lot of choices—clinics that specialize in abortions, doctors who perform abortions at their offices, and hospitals. But in other areas, women will find that abortion service is not available, and they may have to travel long distances to get an abortion.

Information about abortion services in your area can be obtained from Planned Parenthood or other women's health services, or from the local health department. Your gynecologist, family doctor, or local hospital may also have the information. Planned Parenthood keeps a list of abortion services offered throughout the United States that meet their standards for safety and quality of care. The address and telephone number for the Planned Parenthood national office is at the end of this chapter.

CAUTIONS

1. Do not use an abortion service that does not have a 24-hour emergency telephone number. Complications are rare after an abortion, but it is important to have emergency care available.
2. Do not use a clinic or doctor's office for a general anesthesia abortion. This can be done safely only in a hospital or surgical center.

An **abortion clinic** is likely to be your choice for an abortion if you want the following:

1. Early vacuum abortion
2. Local anesthesia
3. Low cost
4. The support of being with other women also getting abortions

A **doctor's office** can offer these same services, and may provide more personal attention and care. A **hospital** or **surgical center** will be needed if you are seeking:

1. General anesthesia
2. A late abortion (D&E or amnioinfusion)

Both late abortions and general anesthesia are much more expensive than the other methods.

If You Are Under 18 Years of Age

According to federal law, abortion and other birth control services can be legally given to women under the age of 18. Since other kinds of health care require the permission and signature of a parent or guardian, however, many hospitals and doctors also require the parent's permission to give abortion services. Planned Parenthood and many other family planning clinics will provide birth control and abortion services to women under 18 without involving their parents. The best way to find out the policy of a particular doctor or clinic is to telephone and ask before making an appointment.

PROBLEMS AND RISKS

Abortion is a medically low-risk procedure, safer in almost every case than it would be to continue the pregnancy and give birth. Fewer than 5 percent of women getting early vacuum abortions experience a minor complication from the treatment, and fewer than 1 in 100 has a serious problem. Late abortions are not as problem-free, so the overall rate for minor complications from abortion is about 12 women out of each 100. Pregnancy, childbirth, and abortion are all quite safe for most women, but in fact, a woman who carries out a full-term pregnancy has a 25 times greater risk of death than a woman who has an early abortion (in the first eight weeks of pregnancy). Early vacuum abortion is the safest of all the treatments, and the health risks of abortion increase the later the procedure is done. So if you choose to have an abortion, it is wise to have the abortion as early in the pregnancy as possible.

Who Should Not Have an Abortion?

Almost every woman can consider abortion as a choice. In general, any health problems that might be made worse by abortion would be threatened even more by a full-term pregnancy and delivery. However, some health problems, such as the following, may require special medical care:

1. Active pelvic infection
2. Allergy to anesthesia or other drugs
3. Severe health problems such as bleeding disorders, heart or kidney disease, diabetes, and others
4. Emotional or mental problems
5. Rh negative blood type

For this reason, a careful medical history should be taken before an abortion. The woman should be sure to report all allergies and all drugs she is taking, as well as any physical or mental health problems.

Complications

Serious complications and death from abortion are very rare. Most problems are mild and can be treated easily. Infection and incomplete abortion are the two most common complications.

Infection

Infection of the uterus and Fallopian tubes can develop after an abortion, especially if the woman already had an infection of the vagina or cervix before the abortion. If there is a chance that the woman has been exposed to gonorrhea, she should be tested for this disease before getting an abortion. Signs of infection after abortion are:

Fever
Abdominal cramps
Discharge from the vagina
A feeling of fatigue

The symptoms may appear as soon as 24 hours after the abortion or as late as several days after. Early treatment is very important with any uterine infection. If the infection spreads into the Fallopian tubes and the abdomen, scarring may develop that can cause infertility. Most uterine infections can be treated successfully with antibiotics.

Incomplete Abortion

An incomplete abortion is one in which not all the pregnancy tissue was removed from the uterus. It is a common cause of infection after abortion. The signs of incomplete abortion are severe abdominal cramps and continuing symptoms of pregnancy, such as nausea and breast soreness. Some women, however, have no symptoms at all. If the abortion was incomplete, this will be discovered at the follow-up visit two weeks after the abortion. It is very important to keep the follow-up appointment, even if you feel fine.

If an incomplete abortion is found, the treatment must be done a second time to remove the remaining tissue. A second vacuum abortion or a dilation and curettage (D&C) may be done.

Hemorrhage

Hemorrhage (excessive bleeding) is another possible complication of abortion. It is rare with early vacuum abortions and with local anesthesia, but the risk increases with late abortions and with the use of general anesthesia. In most cases, hemorrhage occurs during the abortion and can be treated immediately. Hemorrhage is more likely if the woman has been taking blood-thinning medications or large doses of aspirin. Excessive bleeding is rare after an abortion and may be a sign of an incomplete abortion or of injury to the cervix or uterus.

Injury to the Cervix

In rare cases the woman's cervix may be injured by the clamp that is used to hold it in early abortions, or by strong labor contractions in amnio-infusion abortions. The tearing may cause bleeding and may require stitches. Injury to the cervix can cause infertility problems and increase the chances of miscarriage and premature delivery in the future.

Perforation of the Uterus or Cervix

Perforation of the uterus or cervix is another rare complication, in which the instruments used

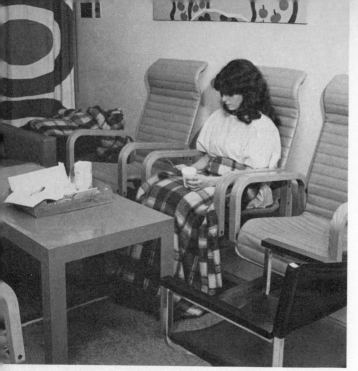

Most women can return to their normal activities with only a brief rest after an abortion.

in the abortion puncture the wall of the uterus or cervix. These punctures usually heal themselves without causing a problem, but if any nearby organs such as the bladder or intestines are punctured, surgery is necessary to repair the damage.

Infertility

Many women worry that an abortion may cause them to be infertile in the future. Complications of abortion (especially infection) can cause infertility. However, the rate of infertility problems for women who have had one abortion does not seem to be any higher than it is for women who have never had one. To keep the risk of future infertility as low as possible, women should seek the earliest possible vacuum abortion, and should get treatment immediately if there are any signs of infection.

AFTER THE ABORTION

Taking Care of Yourself

Most women are able to return to their normal activities almost immediately after an abortion, but it is wise to avoid strenuous exercise for a few days. Cramps and bleeding may continue for about two weeks, but the cramps should not be severe, and the bleeding should not be more than on the heaviest days of the menstrual period. If there is severe pain and continued heavy bleeding, contact your clinic or doctor immediately.

The following are some do's and don't's for good self-care during the first two weeks after an abortion:

1. Take your temperature twice a day for one week after the abortion. Get medical care if it goes over 100.4 degrees.
2. Keep the two-week follow-up appointment.
3. Do not douche.
4. Take showers, not baths.
5. Use sanitary pads, not tampons.
6. Avoid sexual intercourse.

The reason for avoiding douches, baths, tampons, and sexual intercourse is that there is an increased risk of infection of the uterus immediately after an abortion, since the opening in the cervix is dilated. Any foreign material in the vagina can make infection more likely. Uterine infections can cause infertility as well as illness if they are not treated early.

A woman's normal menstrual period should return between four and eight weeks after the abortion. A few women develop breast milk after a late abortion. If this happens, wear a tight bra day and night for a few days, avoid any stimulation of the breasts or nipples, and cut down on fluids.

Caution: If a woman develops any of these danger signs after an abortion, she should contact her doctor or clinic immediately for treatment:

1. Fever of 100.4 degrees Fahrenheit or higher
2. Severe cramps or abdominal pain
3. Bleeding that is heavier than her heaviest menstrual flow, or lasts more than three weeks
4. Unusual or unpleasant-smelling vaginal discharge
5. If her next menstrual period does not begin within eight weeks
6. If signs of pregnancy such as nausea and breast tenderness continue

Birth Control

It is possible to become pregnant within a week or two after an abortion. A woman who wants to avoid another pregnancy should make plans for future birth control at the same time she gets the abortion. The birth control pill can be started immediately after the abortion. Condoms, foam, or a diaphragm can be used as soon as the woman begins having intercourse again. See Chapter 9 for information on the various birth control methods.

Women who are certain that they do not want to bear more children may consider sterilization for themselves or their partner at the time of an abortion. Information about sterilization procedures can be obtained from the clinic or doctor who does the abortion. In some cases it may be possible for a woman to have both procedures done at the same time. See Chapter 10 for information on sterilization.

Repeat Abortions

No birth control method is perfect, so there is always the risk of another unwanted pregnancy for fertile women. Some clinics report that as many as 20 percent of their patients have already had at least one previous abortion. *Effective birth control is better for a woman's physical and emotional health than repeated abortions.*

There is some concern that repeat abortions can cause infertility problems and add to the risks of pregnancy and childbirth. This does not appear to be true for early vacuum abortions. Late abortions are more likely to create fertility problems for the woman in the future, and repeated late abortions could be quite damaging to her health.

Emotional Reactions

Having an abortion is a difficult emotional experience for some women. But for most, the main feeling is relief. It is normal for a woman to have strong feelings after an abortion, such as:

Anger: Toward herself for not having used contraception; toward her partner for getting her pregnant

Sadness: At the loss of a possible baby; at the lost chance to be a mother

It is normal for a woman to have mixed feelings after an abortion and to need to talk about it to a trusted friend.

Relief: To know that a situation that she could not handle has been avoided

If a woman has considered her situation carefully and decided that abortion is the best plan, she will probably be comfortable with her decision. *Studies of the emotional and psychological health of women who have had abortions show that they are about the same as other women who have not had them.*

Women who are more likely to have emotional problems after an abortion are:

Women who had trouble deciding whether they wanted an abortion or not

Women who did not want an abortion but were pushed into it by family members or by their partner

Women who have had emotional or mental problems in the past

A pregnancy is an important event that changes a woman's life in many ways, whether she goes through with it and becomes a mother or whether she has an abortion. So it is normal that whatever decision the woman makes, she will have strong feelings.

FOR FURTHER READING

CORSARO, MARIA, AND CAROLE KORZIENOWSKY. *A Woman's Guide to a Safe Abortion.* New York: Holt, 1983.

RESOURCES

Information and referral services are available in your local community through Planned Parenthood and other family planning clinics, the county or state Department of Health, and community hospitals. In addition, the following national resources can be contacted.

National Abortion Federation
900 Pennsylvania Ave, SE
Washington, DC 20003
(800) 772-9100
(202) 546-9060
A national nonprofit federation of abortion service providers, which provides information about abortion and referral to local abortion services.

Planned Parenthood Federation of America
810 Seventh Avenue
New York, NY 10019
(212) 541-7800
A nonprofit organization that provides information and education about family planning, abortion, and reproductive health matters, and referal to local Planned Parenthood affiliate clinics nationwide.

12
Women's Health Problems

PREVENTING PROBLEMS

General Health

Good general health helps prevent all kinds of health problems, including women's reproductive health problems. There are seven important areas of our lives that affect health greatly and over which we have some control:

1. *Nutrition:* Adequate nutrition is necessary for good health.

2. *Weight:* Being seriously overweight or underweight puts a strain on the body and increases health problems.

3. *Exercise:* Regular exercise is necessary for good health.

4. *Smoking:* Smoking has been proved to cause major health problems and contribute to others.

5. *Substance abuse:* Heavy use of alcohol and/or drugs can cause some health problems and contribute to others.

6. *Stress:* Stressors like exhaustion, overwork, anger, and tension can cause some health problems and contribute to others.

7. *Hygiene:* Good hygiene can prevent many health problems.

Hygiene

In the modern days of wonder drugs we sometimes forget the importance of good hygiene or cleanliness in preventing health problems. Daily baths or showers, frequent hair washing, and careful attention to cleaning the genitals and anus (rectal opening) all help to prevent infections and illness. Washing the hands after using the toilet and before eating also provides a lot of protection.

Vaginal Hygiene

The vagina is a self-cleaning organ, which does not usually need any special cleaning or douching. The fluid from the walls of the vagina and the mucus secreted by the cervix normally keep the vagina clean. The mucus, semen, menstrual blood, and discarded cells from the walls of the vagina are all expelled from the vagina naturally by the force of gravity. Many different bacteria and organisms live in the healthy vagina, including some organisms that can cause vaginitis. They usually cause no problem. When the balance of these organisms is upset, however, vaginal infections develop and create problems. Regular douching is not recommended because it can upset this natural balance. It is best to douche only when it is recommended as part of medical treatment of an infection.

Vaginal hygiene sprays and special scented douches have no health purpose. Some of these products can be irritating to vaginal tissues and can cause problems. A woman who has a problem of vaginal odor or discharge should see her doctor or clinic to find out what the problem is and have it treated.

Breast Self-Examination

Breast self-examination is an important way for women to protect themselves from cancer. It is recommended that women begin to examine their breasts regularly each month as soon as they begin menstruation, and continue all their lives. Although the risk of cancer is low for women in their teens and twenties, it can occur, and it is good to form a habit of self-examination and get to know how your own breast tissue normally feels. Starting at age 35, regular self-examination becomes very important for women, as breast cancer is more common among older women. In fact, breast cancer is the most common cause of death among American women aged 40 to 45.

Most breast lumps are discovered first by women through self-examination, and it is believed that women who regularly examine their breasts are more capable of identifying small changes in their breasts than is a doctor or other health care professional who examines the woman only once a year. Since 80 to 90 percent of breast lumps are benign (not cancerous), most of the lumps women discover are not serious. But it is important to have them checked.

Breast self-examination is a simple procedure, which takes only a few minutes and should be done every month. The best time to do it is approximately one week after the beginning of the menstrual period, because this is a time when estrogen levels are low and the breasts are least swollen and tender.

There are two steps to self-examination:

1. Looking at the breasts in the mirror
2. Examining the breasts by feeling them with the fingers

Step 1: Looking in the mirror   This part of the examination can be done sitting or standing. Looking in the mirror with her arms at her sides, the woman observes her breasts for any changes in appearance since the last month (Figure 12–1). She looks for changes in the shape of the breasts, changes in the direction the nipple points, and changes that make one side different from the other. Any area that looks pulled in or dimpled and any areas of rough, reddened skin should be noted. Next, the woman raises her arms over her head and looks again for changes. Then she puts her hands on her hips and presses down, tightening the pectoral muscles, and checks again for changes. The final step is to squeeze each nipple gently to check for any discharge.

Step 2: Examination by touch   For the second part of the exam, the woman lies down on her back. Placing one hand behind her head, she uses the other hand to gently feel the breast, using the flat of the fingers. Using a planned pattern (such as a pinwheel), she feels every area of the breast by placing the flat of the fingers on the breast, pressing firmly, and then moving the whole hand in a small circular movement, so it slides over a small section of the breast. It is important to check every part of the breast, including the area close to and behind the nipples and the "tail" of the breast tissue that extends into the armpit. The woman should also feel under her arms for enlarged lymph nodes, which feel like a round, firm bump and may be sore. The same examination can be done a second time in a standing or sitting position, which puts the breasts in a different position and may make it easier to find some lumps.

Learning breast self-examination is important for women of all ages.

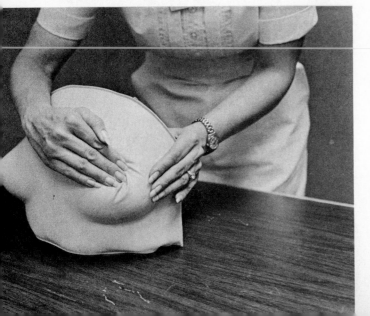

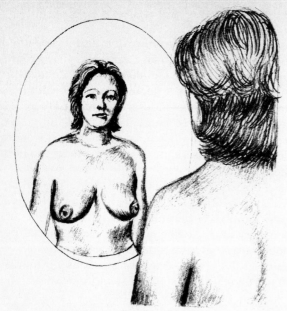
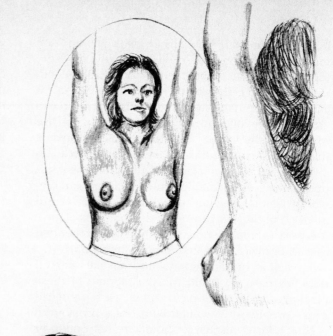

Step 1: Looking at the breasts in the mirror

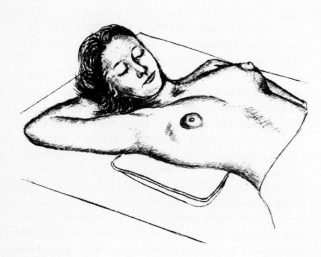
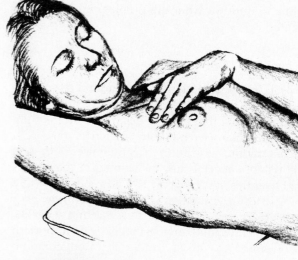

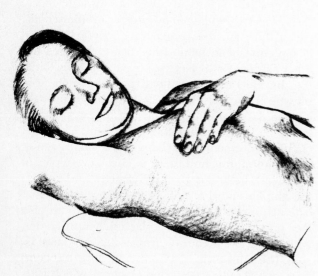
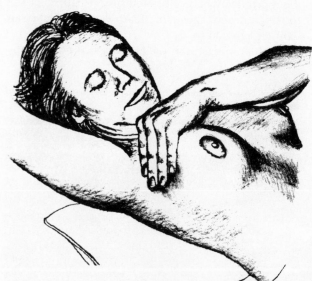

Step 2: Examining the breasts by touch

FIGURE 12–1. *Breast self-examination.*

What Am I Looking For?

Women's breasts come in many different textures; some are naturally lumpy or grainy in spots. Regular self-examination allows a woman to get to know the texture of her breasts so that she can recognize changes. The woman is looking for lumps, bumps, and thickened or stringy spots that are new or different from the last time she examined her breasts. They are most likely to occur in the upper quarter of the breast closest to the armpit, so this area should get special attention. A lump may be large or small, round or irregular in shape, and may be fixed in one place or movable. Some lumps seem to swell to a larger size before a menstrual period, and to shrink afterwards.

What Do I Do if I Find Something?

A woman sould see her doctor or clinic if she finds any of the following:

A dimple or identation on the breast
A noticeable change in breast shape or size
Discharge from the nipple
A new lump or bump in the breast
Swollen lymph nodes under the arm

There is usually no serious problem, but it is important to have these changes checked. In general, lumps that feel like fluid-filled sacs, those that move easily within the breast, and those that change size during the monthly cycle are likely to be harmless cysts rather than cancer. New lumps that are small, hard, and unmovable should be seen by a doctor as soon as possible. (See the section on breast problems later in this chapter for more details.)

GETTING HEALTH CARE

When to Get Care

All women should have a gynecological examination and Pap smear (see pages 244–246) when they become sexually active, or by age 20 at the latest. After that, they should be tested every year (although the American Cancer Society suggests that certain women who are at low risk for cancer do not need a Pap smear more often than every three years). *After 40, all women should have an examination and Pap smear every year.* Depending on age, health problems, and family health history, many women will find that their health care provider recommends that they be seen more often.

Women should also seek medical care if they have any symptoms of illness or infection of the reproductive organs. Fever, abdominal pain, abnormal bleeding, and inflammation of the vulva, vagina, or cervix all are signs that medical care is needed. Also, any growths, lumps, blisters, or ulcers on the vulva or in the vagina call for a visit to the doctor or clinic, as do all breast lumps.

When a woman believes she may be pregnant, she should get a pregnancy test as soon as possible and should begin prenatal care if she is planning to continue the pregnancy. Early prenatal care is very important to protect the health of both the fetus and the mother (see Chapter 6).

Choosing a Doctor or a Clinic

A woman has many choices about how and where she will get medical care. She can choose a doctor in private practice or group practice, she can use a clinic operated by a hospital, or she may join an HMO (health maintenance organization) that will provide all her care. There are also community health clinics and family planning clinics (such as those run by Planned Parenthood) that many women choose for care. Clinics are usually less expensive than seeing a private doctor. In some areas there are city or county health clinics with free or very low cost care. Doctors, hospitals, and clinics are listed in the Yellow Pages, but it is best to find one that has been recommended by someone who has used it. The time to look for a doctor or clinic is *before* you need one. It is not easy to search for the right kind of care when you are sick or in an emergency. Hospital emergency rooms are great in an emergency, but they are not the best place to get other kinds of care because they are expensive and do not offfer follow-up services.

The most frequent reason that women of childbearing age see a doctor is for reproductive health services. Family planning services, prenatal care, vaginitis, and urinary tract infections are among the most common reasons for women to seek care. For this reason, many women view the doctor who provides their obstetrical care (care related to pregnancy and childbirth) and gynecological care (care related to women's reproductive health problems) as their family doctor. The doctors most commonly used for these services belong to one of four different specialties:

> *Obstetrician/gynecologist:* The **ob-gyn** has had three to four years of specialty training after medical school, including a year and a half each of obstetrics (a specialty in pregnancy and childbirth) and gynecology (a specialty in women's reproductive health problems).
>
> *Family practice doctor:* The **family practitioner** has had at least three years of specialty training after medical school, including at least three months of

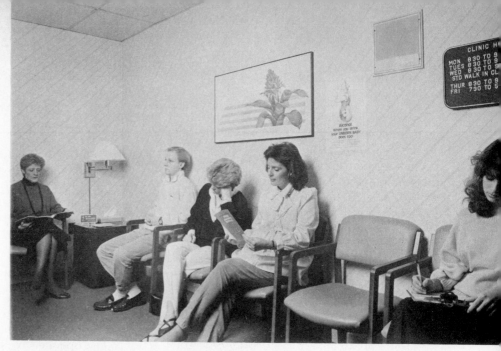

Clinics are usually less expensive than private doctors.

training in obstetrics and gynecology. This new kind of specialist focuses on treating the whole family.

Internist: The internist has had at least three years of specialty training after medical school, which may or may not have included three months of training in obstetrics and gynecology. Not all internists do gynecological checkups.

General practitioner: The general practitioner is a medical doctor or a doctor of osteopathy. He or she does not usually have any specialized training in obstetrics and gynecology, but may have a lot of experience.

When a woman gets her care from a doctor who is not a specialist in women's health, she will be referred to another doctor who is a specialist when it is necessary.

It is becoming more and more common today for women to receive part of their health care from other health professionals, such as **nurse practitioners, nurse midwives,** and **physician's assistants.** These health care providers work under the supervision of a doctor and have special training. Many women report that they are very satisfied with these new caregivers, who often have more time to explain things and answer questions than the doctor has. Most of these new providers are women, whereas most physicians are men (although this is changing). Some women feel more comfortable getting their gynecological care from another woman and have more confidence that a woman can understand their problems. *What is most important is to choose a health care provider who has the right training and experience to give the best possible care.*

The Gynecological Examination

Getting regular gynecological checkups and seeing a health care provider whenever a problem develops are important habits for all women to develop, regardless of age.

The gynecological examination consists of four parts: the health history, general physical examination, breast examination, and pelvic examination (including the vulva, vagina, and cervix). It is something that some women dislike and tend to put off, even when they have a health problem that needs attention. Going for the first gynecological examination can be especially scary, particularly if you don't know what to expect. Embarrassment, loss of privacy, and fear of pain are some of the feelings women often have. Some women may also feel that gynecological care is only for married women or those who are sexually active. This is not true. All women have reproductive systems, including a vagina, uterus, and breasts, and problems can develop in women who are not sexually active as well as in others. The doctor cannot usually tell if a woman is sexually active from a pelvic examination, but it is often (not always) possible to tell if she is a virgin.

A gynecological examination should not be painful unless there is severe infection or other problems. The exam is not so embarrassing once a woman knows what to expect and finds a doctor or clinic with which she feels comfortable. A friendly, helpful, and supportive atmosphere in the office and the examining room really helps, and many doctor's offices and clinics have it.

Most women become accustomed to the examinations over time and don't avoid them. After a few years of annual checkups, family planning visits, vaginal infections, and even prenatal care and childbirth, a pelvic examination is no longer such a big deal. Also, a pelvic examination can be a positive experience because the woman can be reassured that she is free from disease or infection, and she has a chance to ask her caregiver any questions she may have.

The next section describes the four parts of the gynecological examination.

Health History

For the health history, you will be asked to fill out a form or answer questions about the following things:

The current problem, if any

Menstrual periods and problems, if any

Use of birth control

Past pregnancies and births, and any problems with them

Past illnesses

Hospitalizations and surgery

Family history of illness, especially cancer, diabetes, and high blood pressure

Past and present use of medications, including allergies to drugs

Physical Examination

Most gynecological examinations include at least a partial physical examination as well. Usually weight and blood pressure are taken, and a urinalysis and blood count may be done also. The doctor or other caregiver (usually a nurse practitioner) will generally listen to your heart and lungs, check your eyes, nose, and throat, and perhaps examine your thyroid gland (in the neck) and your abdomen.

Breast Examination

Breast self-examination was described earlier in this chapter. The health care provider follows the same steps in examining the breasts. If you have questions about how to examine your breasts or about the way your breasts feel when you examine them, this is the time to ask.

Pelvic Examination

The pelvic examination is done on a special table with stirrups at the end in which your heels rest. The woman lies on the table with her heels in the stirrups, her knees flexed, and her hips at the lower edge of the table. The purpose of this is to make the examination as easy and comfortable as possible and to allow the examiner to see the area clearly. Examining tables can be set up in several ways, and the woman may be lying down (as shown in Figure 12–2) or propped up during the examination. Many women prefer to be propped up so they can see what is going on. Ask your health care provider to adjust the table if it is not right.

Preparation Women should not douche for at least 24 hours before a pelvic exam, as this may make it difficult to determine if there is infection and may affect the results of the Pap test. It is also important to empty the bladder just before the examination.

To prepare for the pelvic exam, the woman is asked to remove all her clothing below the waist. The lower half of her body is covered with a sheet, which is draped over her knees. Her examiner is most likely to be a doctor or a nurse practitioner. Those who specialize in women's health and do a great many pelvic examinations usually create the least discomfort when examining, and are best able to spot abnormal conditions. If there is no infection or inflammation, the pelvic examination should be painless. If the examiner is a man, a female nurse or

FIGURE 12–2. *The pelvic examination.*

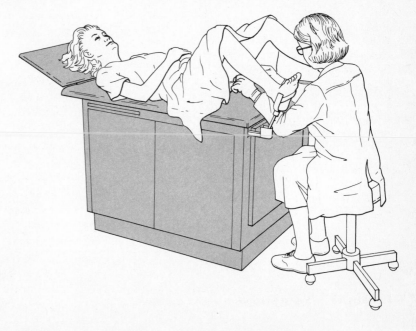

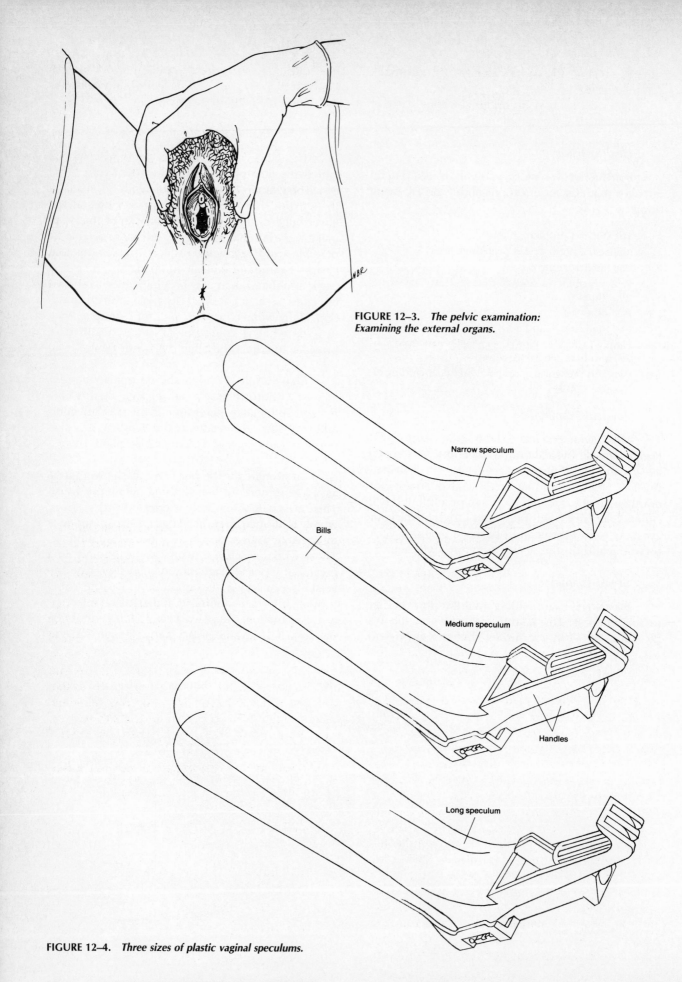

FIGURE 12–3. *The pelvic examination: Examining the external organs.*

Narrow speculum

Bills

Medium speculum

Handles

Long speculum

FIGURE 12–4. *Three sizes of plastic vaginal speculums.*

assistant may be present for the comfort and protection of both doctor and patient.

Once you are on the table, it is important to relax as much as possible, particularly the vaginal and abdominal muscles. The more relaxed the woman is, the easier and more comfortable the examination.

The pelvic exam takes only a few minutes and consists of four different steps.

External examination The doctor or nurse practitioner looks at the vulva, vaginal lips, clitoris, urethral opening, and outside of the vagina for evidence of infections or other problems (Figure 12–3). If you have any painful, irritated, or itching spots or bumps here, this is a good time to ask about them, as they could be missed unless you point them out. The examiner may also test the strength of the vaginal muscles by placing one or two fingers in the vagina and asking you to cough or bear down. This is to see if there is any muscle weakness or a hernia in the upper or lower vagina. If you have had problems of loosening of the vaginal muscles during sex, loss of bladder control, or the vagina protruding out of its opening, be sure to mention it.

Speculum examination In the second step, the examiner gently inserts a metal or plastic **speculum** into the vagina, and opens it. This allows a good view of the cervix and the upper part of the vagina. This part of the examination should not be painful, but there is a feeling of pressure as the vaginal walls are pushed apart by the speculum. The more relaxed you are, the less this will bother you. If there is pinching or pain, speak up, because this should not happen. The examiner has several sizes of speculums, and a smaller one may be more comfortable (Figure 12–4).

During the speculum exam, the doctor can see if there is infection, ulceration, or any other problem in the vagina or on the cervix (Figure 12–5). The Pap smear is taken at this time, and samples of vaginal and cervical mucus can be taken for laboratory tests and cultures to identify disease organisms. If you are wearing an IUD, the examiner can see if it is in place (by the string that hangs out of the opening in the cervix). If there has been a recent miscarriage or if you are pregnant, the examiner may be able to tell this by the condition and color of the cervix. The examiner may also be able to tell if you have ovulated in the last day or two by changes in the cervical mucus. If your practitioner does not offer you a mirror, you may want to ask for one so you can see your cervix and vaginal walls for yourself. This may make it easier to understand any problems you may have and how to care for them.

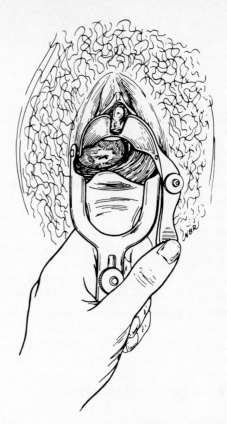

FIGURE 12–5. *The pelvic examination: Using a speculum to view the cervix.*

Bimanual examination The third step in the gynecological exam is called the bimanual exam. First the speculum is removed, and then the examiner inserts two fingers into the vagina until the cervix can be felt. With the other hand, she or he presses down on the abdomen (Figure 12–6). Using this method, the examiner can feel the location, size, and shape of the uterus, ovaries, and other pelvic organs. The uterus is loosely held in place by ligaments and can usually be moved by the examiner. Normally it is located at the upper end of the vagina and tilts slightly forward. But in some women it may be tilted backwards (**retroverted**), or **prolapsed**, which means dropped downward

FIGURE 12–6. *The pelvic examination: Bimanual examination.*

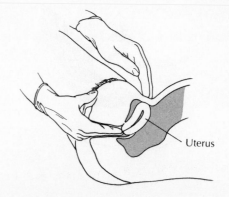

Uterus

slightly into the vagina. There are natural differences between women in the size and shape of the uterus, with sizes ranging from that of a lime to the size of a pear. After several pregnancies, the uterus may remain permanently larger than before. If the uterus is enlarged because of pregnancy or growths such as fibroid tumors, the examiner will discover it during the bimanual exam. The uterus may be tender if there is an infection within it.

The bimanual exam is also used to check the ovaries and Fallopian tubes, which are located on either side of the uterus. The Fallopian tubes are very soft and cannot usually be felt, but if they are infected they may be swollen and tender. The ovaries, which are small, egg-shaped lumps about one and a half inches long, can usually be felt and are often sensitive. This part of the examination can be difficult because the woman must relax her abdominal muscles to allow the examiner to feel the area of the ovaries, and she may feel a little discomfort when the examiner puts pressure on them. The size and shape of the ovaries changes during the menstrual cycle, as eggs are produced. The purpose of this part of the examination is to identify any abnormal enlargement of the ovaries, such as cysts or other growths.

Rectovaginal examination   The fourth step in the gynecological exam is the **rectovaginal exam,** in which the examiner places one finger in the vagina and one in the rectum (Figure 12–7). This allows him or her to feel the thin layers of tissue between the vagina and the rectum to make sure there is no weak spot or hernia (called a **rectocele**). The rectal exam also may detect hemorrhoids, polyps, or other growths. A rectal exam alone is used in some

situations to examine the uterus and ovaries of a woman or girl who is a virgin and has a small hymenal opening. Some women find the rectovaginal exam a little uncomfortable, but it takes only a minute to perform and can give the examiner important information about health.

Vaginal Self-Examination

In the past few years, many women have learned to examine their own vaginas and cervixes. There are benefits to becoming more familiar with your own system and learning what is normal for you. Self-examination is easily done with a friend's help but can also be managed by a woman alone with a little practice. The best way to learn is from another woman who has been trained in vaginal self-examination. In some communities there are women's self-help groups where women can learn self-examination and share the knowledge they have gained about their bodies. The equipment needed is a **speculum,** which can be purchased at a pharmacy that carries medical supplies, a flashlight or other movable light source, and a long-handled mirror. The first step is for the woman to become familiar with the speculum so that she knows how to open and close it and how to lock it into position. She may want to lubricate the speculum with a lubricating jelly or warm water. The woman then lies in the position for a pelvic exam at the doctor's office, with her head and shoulders propped up so she can see. She inserts the speculum into the vagina and locks it in the open position. Then, observing the vagina through the mirror, she manipulates the speculum to bring the cervix into view (Figure 12–8). Having the flashlight or a lamp focused on the mirror allows her to reflect light into the vagina so she can see more clearly. When she has finished examining the area, the woman removes the speculum (closing it first) and washes it with antiseptic soap.

The Pap Smear

The **Pap smear** is a laboratory test of cells that have been gently (and painlessly) scraped from the woman's cervix. It detects cancer of the cervix and also identifies abnormal cells that could develop into cancer over time. It can also aid in identifying other noncancerous infections. *A regular Pap smear is considered a very important part of health care for all adult women. Deaths from cervical cancer have been greatly reduced since this test became available.* A Pap smear every year is recommended for most woman, starting at age 20 or when they become sexually active. But if the woman is in a high-

FIGURE 12–7. *The pelvic examination: Rectovaginal examination.*

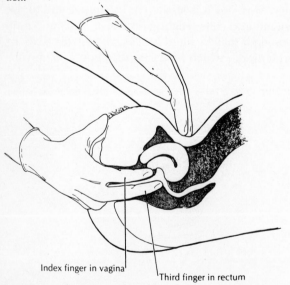

Index finger in vagina

Third finger in rectum

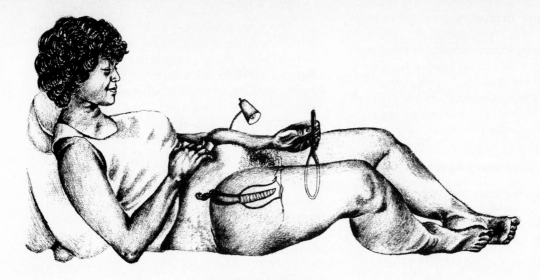

FIGURE 12–8. *Vaginal self-examination.*

risk group for cervical cancer or if her test results have been abnormal, she will need to be tested more often. Follow the advice of your doctor or clinic on how often you need to get a Pap smear.

The Pap smear is performed during the speculum exam. A small wooden paddle is used to gently scrape the tissue at the mouth of the cervix (Figure 12–9). The cells scraped off are put on a laboratory slide and sent for examination.

The results of a Pap test are reported in Table 12–1 as Classes I through V. Class I results are normal or negative, meaning that cancer was not found and the cells in the area are normal. Class V results are positive for cancer, meaning that cancer cells were found, and the disease may be invasive. A biopsy of the cervix is needed to be sure. Classes II, III, and IV are intermediate results, showing inflammation, abnormal cells, precancerous cells, or carcinoma in situ (a localized cancer on the surface of the cervix). Results showing abnormal cells are also called cervical intraepithelial neoplasia, or CIN. It is believed that if women with CIN are not treated, 30 to 50 percent of them will eventually (after about 5 years) develop invasive cancer of the cervix. Invasive cancer is cancer that spreads deeply into the cervix and possibly to other parts of the body. If women with abnormal or precancerous results on

their Pap smears are treated, cancer is prevented in almost every case.

If your Pap results are Class I, normally you will not be notified unless you call the doctor's office or clinic to check. Simply plan to return for the next Pap smear in a year or whatever time period was recommended. If your Pap result was between II and V, you will be called or sent a letter to return to your doctor or clinic for further diagnosis and treatment. Approximately 45 out of each 1,000 Pap smears show inflammation or abnormal cells and fall into Classes II through V, but in most cases the woman does not have cancer.

If you do have an abnormal result on a Pap smear, the first step is to return to the doctor's office or clinic, where you will be checked for infections or other problems that could have caused the abnormal result. Depending on what is found,

FIGURE 12–9. *The pelvic examination: The Pap smear.*

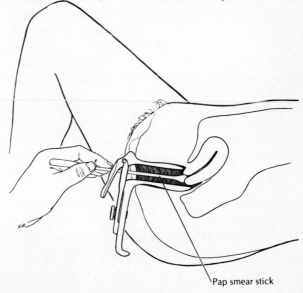

Pap smear stick

TABLE 12–1 Pap Smear Classifications

Class I	Normal	Normal cells or mild inflammation
Class II	Abnormal	Inflammation or abnormal cells
Class III	Abnormal	Abnormal cells (precancerous)
Class IV	Cancerous	Carcinoma in situ (localized cancer)
Class V	Cancerous	Cancer (biopsy needed to confirm if it is invasive)

SOURCE: Adapted from Bruce D. Shepard and Carroll A. Shephard, *The Complete Guide to Women's Health* (New York: New American Library, 1985), p. 204.

you may be asked to return in a few months for another Pap test and checkup, or your doctor may investigate further with a colposcopy, a biopsy of the cervix, or other treatment. Most abnormal Pap results are not cancer, and many women have normal results when retested a few months later.

More details about abnormal Pap results and about cervical cancer and how it is treated are presented later in this chapter.

Other Diagnostic Tests and Procedures

There are many different tests and procedures that may be performed in a doctor's office or clinic to help diagnose gynecological problems or to treat them. Some of the more common ones are described next.

Urine Tests

Urine tests are used for many purposes. There are urine tests for pregnancy and diabetes that may be done right at the office. More commonly, however, a urine sample is sent to a laboratory for analysis. Bladder and kidney infections and many other kinds of problems can be identified through urine tests. The doctor must be specific about which tests he or she wants done.

It is important to follow the instructions for giving a urine sample carefully, as it is easy for women to collect a bit of menstrual blood or vaginal discharge along with urine. This can contaminate the urine and affect the accuracy of the test results.

Cultures

Often a small sample of vaginal discharge, mucus from the cervix, pus, blood, or urine is sent to a laboratory for culture. A **laboratory culture** means that the laboratory attempts to grow bacteria or other organisms in the sample in order to identify the disease that is causing problems. The sample is placed in a warm environment on a jelly that contains nutrients it needs to live. Within a few days it can be examined to identify the organisms. Since different kinds of organisms require different environments to thrive, the doctor must be specific about which organisms the laboratory should attempt to culture. If a woman believes she may have been exposed to a certain disease, such as gonorrhea, she should mention this.

Some organisms are very difficult to identify and to culture, and culturing viruses takes extra time and special techniques. Nevertheless, cultures are one of the best ways to obtain a definite diagnosis of infection.

Blood Tests

There are hundreds of different tests that can be performed on a blood sample. The most common test is the **blood count**, which detects anemia. Finger or ear lobe prick tests are often used for a blood count. Most other blood tests require more blood, which is taken from a vein, usually in the inner elbow, and sent to a laboratory. Many kinds of diseases, including syphilis, can be diagnosed through blood tests. The state of the person's metabolism, the functioning of the liver and kidneys, levels of different hormones, even information about the person's genetic makeup can be obtained from blood tests. But the doctor must order the specific tests needed; if the appropriate tests are not ordered, the problem may not be detected.

Colposcopy

Colposcopy is a relatively new method of examining the cervix for abnormal cells using a **colposcope**, which looks like a small pair of binoculars mounted on a tripod. The instrument allows the surface of the cervix to be examined in detail using a lens that magnifies it from 10 to 20 times, along with special lighting.

Colposcopy is used to examine the cervix after an abnormal Pap smear result, and can help to locate accurately areas of abnormal cells for biopsy (see next section). Regular colposcopic examination is recommended for DES daughters (see details later in this chapter).

The examination is painless and is done in a doctor's office with the woman in the position for a pelvic exam and a speculum holding the vagina open. It takes 10 to 20 minutes to complete, which can be a long time for the woman to remain still with a speculum in place.

Since colposcopy is a new technique, many doctors have not been trained in its use. Only a person who has received training can interpret the findings properly.

Biopsy

A biopsy is the taking of a small sample of tissue from a growth, lump, wart, sore, or ulcer to be examined under a microscope by a pathologist (a specialist in examining abnormal or diseased tissue). The purpose is to arrive at an exact diagnosis of the problem. Biopsies are frequently used to determine if cancer is present, but they are used to diagnose other kinds of problems as well.

There are many different ways of taking a tissue sample for biopsy, depending on where it is located on the body and what types of cells are involved. Sometimes the whole lump or sore area

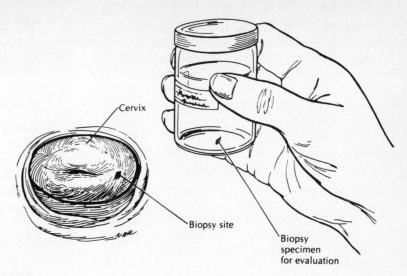

FIGURE 12–10. *A cervical biopsy.*

will be removed for examination; at other times a small sample will be taken.

A **cervical biopsy** refers to one or more small samples taken from abnormal areas on the surface of the cervix using a small instrument like a paper punch (Figure 12–10). Since the cervix is not very sensitive to pain, there should be only a feeling of cramping when the biopsy is taken. Light bleeding or spotting may occur after the biopsy, and it is recommended to avoid douching, intercourse, and tampons for a week to prevent infection and heavy bleeding.

An **endocervical biopsy** or **curettage** refers to obtaining a sample of tissue from inside the cervical canal by inserting a small spoon-shaped scraping instrument called a curette (see Figure 11–2) into the cervix and scraping a few long, shallow slivers of the tissue surface for examination. This may cause cramping but should not be very painful because there are few pain nerves in the cervix.

An **endometrial biopsy** refers to obtaining a

sample of tissue from the endometrium or lining of the uterus. This is done by inserting the curette through the cervix into the uterus and scraping off a few shallow strands of the lining for examination (Figure 12–11). This procedure is similar to a D&C (described later in this chapter), except that only a few sample areas of the uterus are scraped. Local anesthesia is often used for endometrial biopsy to reduce pain. An endometrial biopsy can also be obained by **vacuum scraping**. Using a vacuum aspirator like the ones used for early vacuum abortions or a syringe, a sample or the entire endometrium can be removed for examination. Local anesthesia is usually used for the vacuum procedure to reduce cramping and pain.

Cauterization and Cryosurgery

Cauterization (also known as cautery, heat cautery, and burning) and **cryosurgery** (also known as cryotherapy, cold cautery, and freezing) are two methods used to destroy abnormal cells and tissue

FIGURE 12–11. *An endometrial biopsy.*

on the cervix and in the vagina. They are also used in some cases to treat warts in the vagina and on the vulva, chronic cervicitis, and endometriosis affecting the cervix and vagina. Cautery works by burning or freezing the abnormal tissue, which is then replaced by new growth of normal cells. It is often very effective.

This treatment can be done in a doctor's office or clinic and does not require anesthesia. Heat cautery is the older method and the one for which more doctors have the training and equipment. A metal probe is touched to the area to be treated; when electricity is run through it, it heats up and burns the tissue. The treatment lasts only a few seconds but can be painful depending on what part of the body is treated.

Cryosurgery is a newer method requiring more sophisticated equipment, which not all doctors or clinics have. Compressed nitrous oxide or carbon dioxide gas is piped into an instrument that looks like a gun. The tip of the instrument is pressed against the area to be treated; when the gas is released into the gun, it quickly cools the tip, which freezes the tissue touching it. Freezing takes about two minutes and usually feels cold, but not very painful. Cryosurgery is less destructive and more easily controlled than heat cautery, and is less painful as well. The risk of damaging the surrounding normal tissues and causing scarring is also less.

Both procedures destroy the surface layers of tissue. When the cervix is treated, there is a heavy, watery vaginal discharge, which usually lasts about a week after cervical treatment. Women are advised not to have intercourse, use tampons, or douche for 10 to 14 days after treatment to give the area time to heal. A scab forms to cover the area for about a week after treatment, and if this is disturbed by intercourse or anything else in the vagina, heavy bleeding may develop. Complete healing takes place after several weeks.

Complications from cautery, though rare, can include infection or bleeding after treatment, excessive damage to tissues during treatment, and scarring of the cervix which could lead to fertility problems.

REPRODUCTIVE CYCLE PROBLEMS

Menstrual Problems

Menstrual problems of various kinds are among the most common health problems for women. Most women have menstrual periods for over thirty years and experience several different kinds of menstrual problems over time. Fortunately, most of these problems are temporary and are not serious threats to the woman's health. But some of the problems, such as **menstrual cramps** and **premenstrual syndrome** (**PMS**), do cause women a lot of discomfort and time lost from work, school, and other activities.

Menstrual Cramps

Menstrual cramps are painful muscle spasms in the lower abdomen, which occur during menstrual bleeding. They are usually worse during heavy bleeding. Almost all women have had menstrual cramps at some time. Most of the time, cramps are perfectly normal and not a sign of illness or medical problems; however, IUD (intrauterine device) problems, pelvic infection, fibroid tumors of the uterus, and endometriosis can also cause severe cramps. This section discusses menstrual cramps that are not related to medical problems; information on cramps caused by disease and medical problems is found in this chapter under the name of the medical condition or problem.

Many young women have severe menstrual cramps for the first few years after their periods begin. The problem usually becomes less severe when they reach their mid-twenties or after their first pregnancy. The cramps usually occur during the first day or two of menstrual bleeding and may be so severe that the woman cannot attend school or work, but must rest at home. With strong cramps, the woman often has other symptoms such as backache, leg pain, diarrhea, nausea, vomiting, dizziness, and loss of appetite.

The causes of menstrual cramps are not well understood. Several factors may contribute to the problem, including high levels of prostaglandin hormones, a narrow opening in the cervix, and a relative lack of blood supply to the muscles of the uterus (caused by the intensity of the cramps).

Usually the pain of menstrual cramps can be treated effectively, and women do not need to lose time from their regular activities. Aspirin and ibuprofen (sold as Nuprin and Advil), both of which have antiprostaglandin effects, are effective against cramps, especially if the woman starts the medication *before* severe cramping develops. Very severe cases may require a prescription medication. Biofeedback and relaxation training (available through psychologists and pain clinics) also can be helpful to women with severe cramps.

Besides taking pain-killing medication, there are a number of ways to reduce the pain of menstrual cramps through self-care:

1. Take calcium and magnesium supplements starting a few days before your period is due.
2. Lie down to rest, and experiment to find the most comfortable position (usually with knees pulled up).

3. Take warm baths or apply heat to the abdomen and lower back.

4. Take a single shot of hard liquor; it helps to relax uterine muscles (but don't drive afterwards).

5. Have an orgasm, either with a partner or by masturbation; it reduces the congestion of blood and fluid in the pelvic area.

6. Use meditation or relaxation exercises to relax the body and mind.

7. Investigate the herbal teas thought to help with menstrual pain (available in health food stores).

Note: Women who take birth control pills almost never have serious menstrual cramps.

PMS (Premenstrual Syndrome)

Premenstrual syndrome is the name for a set of symptoms that many women develop a few days before their menstrual periods. It is most common among women in their thirties and forties. The symptoms may begin as early as ten days before the next period, or may be noticed only in the last two or three days before the period begins. The most common symptom is swelling and fluid retention, which is believed to be due to high levels of the hormone estrogen in the second half of the cycle. Some women will gain five or six pounds of excess water in their tissues during this time. The excess water retained is thought to be responsible for most of the other symptoms of PMS, which include swollen legs and breasts, pelvic aching, headache, nervousness, irritability, and loss of ability to concentrate. The symptoms usually disappear rapidly once menstrual bleeding begins.

In women who have PMS, the symptoms may be quite mild and easily tolerated, or they may be severe enough to keep the woman out of work or school. The severity of the symptoms may vary from one month to the next. Very severe PMS symptoms can make a woman appear temporarily to be highly emotional (even unstable or irrational). This can be so frightening and embarrassing that women may avoid work, school, or social events when they have the symptoms or when they fear they might have them.

Since there is no one medical explanation for all cases of PMS, there is no single effective treatment. The medical treatments for PMS include water pills (diuretics), tranquillizers, and hormones (progesterone to balance the suspected high estrogen levels). These treatments, however, especially water pills, can have side effects that can cause more problems. When water pills are taken over any period of time, they may cause the body to become low in potassium salts. These must be replaced with potassium-rich foods such as bananas and cranberry juice, or by potassium supplements.

In most cases, once women recognize and understand PMS, it can be managed effectively through self-care, so prescription medications are not needed.

Self-care for PMS is as follows:

1. Avoid salt and salty foods for at least a week before your period is expected (longer if symptoms start earlier).

2. Eat potassium-rich foods such as bananas, cranberries, and other fresh fruit.

3. Drink lots of water.

4. Take vitamin B6, along with a B complex vitamin.

5. Get plenty of exercise and rest.

6. Avoiding caffeine and alcohol may help.

7. Investigate diuretic teas at the health food store, and read up on which foods and vitamins are natural diuretics.

8. Talk with other women about PMS; many women have it, and each one finds her own way of managing it.

9. Have an orgasm, either with a partner or by masturbation; it helps to reduce the congestion of blood and fluid in the pelvic area.

Irregular Periods

Regular menstrual periods average 24 to 32 days from the first day of one period to the first day of the next. Bleeding lasts from 3 to 7 days, and between 1 and 4 tablespoons of menstrual blood and tissue are usually lost. Most women have some variation in their menstrual cycle, with some cycles being a few days longer than others. A woman's cycle is considered normal and regular as long as:

1. It is predictable within a few days.

2. It does not last more than seven days.

3. It does not cause the loss of more than four tablespoons of blood and tissue.

Many women suffer from premenstrual tension and irritability.

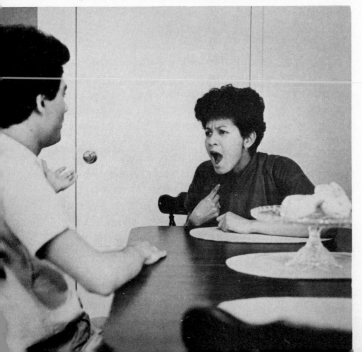

Any vaginal bleeding that is not part of the woman's normal menstrual pattern should be reported to her health care provider. In most cases it is nothing serious, but unusual vaginal bleeding is the most common sign of cancer of the uterus, so it should always be reported. Cancer of the uterus is very rare for women under 30, but becomes more common as women get older. *A woman who has any bleeding at all after menopause should seek medical care immediately because of the risk of uterine cancer* (unless she is taking hormone replacements, which produce a cycle of regular menstrual bleeding).

When a woman's menstrual pattern is unpredictable and irregular, the cause is often a hormone imbalance and lack of ovulation. Hormone imbalances are very common in early adolescence, when the menstrual cycle first begins, and in midlife when menopause takes place. Emotional stress, exhaustion, malnutrition, and excessive exercise or athletic training can also cause lack of ovulation and irregular periods. Irregular bleeding can also be caused by pelvic infection, polyps in the uterus, an IUD, thyroid deficiency, ectopic pregnancy, and problems with birth control pills.

Treatment for irregular bleeding may include treatment with Provera, a synthetic hormone, which brings on menstrual bleeding and causes a complete shedding of the lining of the uterus. Surgical treatment (D&C) is also often used to diagnose problems in the uterus. The complete shedding or removal of the endometrium (the uterine lining) either through treatment with Provera or through a D&C often solves bleeding problems. If the problem is caused by hormone imbalance, hormone treatment (progesterone) may be given for a few days each month to bring on a period. If the bleeding is not a sign of a serious problem, no treatment may be given. Women taking birth control pills who experience irregular bleeding can usually be helped by adjusting the dosage of hormones, most commonly by changing to another pill.

Spotting between Periods

About 10 percent of women have a day or two of spotting or light bleeding between periods. This is believed to be caused by hormone changes that take place at the time of ovulation. Spotting caused by ovulation is harmless and is not considered a medical problem. If the next menstrual period begins almost exactly 14 days after the spotting, it is probable that the spotting is related to ovulation.

Bleeding after Intercourse

Bleeding after intercourse is a sign of inflammation of the cervix. There are many possible causes for this. Most are not serious, but a woman with this symptom should seek medical care.

Delayed Periods with Heavy Bleeding

Delayed periods with heavy bleeding are usually caused by lack of ovulation. If the woman does not ovulate, the uterus does not receive the correct hormone signals to start her menstrual period on schedule. The uterine lining continues to build up for several more weeks, and then finally bleeding begins. The bleeding may stop after a few days and then start again, and the total blood loss may be more than the woman usually has. This pattern is common for women a few years before menopause, when they may not be ovulating. It can also be a sign of miscarriage.

Regular Heavy Bleeding

Heavy bleeding (also called **hypermenorrhea**) with each period is normal for some women and is not considered a problem unless the woman loses so much blood that she becomes anemic. However, heavy bleeding can also be a sign of infection or other problems. Possible causes of heavy bleeding are the IUD, uterine infection, polyps or fibroid tumors of the uterus, and adenomyosis (a condition in which the uterine lining grows into the muscle of the uterus). Women with blood-clotting problems or who are taking blood-thinning medications may also have very heavy bleeding. Women with heavy bleeding should get a blood count for anemia every six months.

Regular Light Bleeding

Some women lose very little blood in each period (called **hypomenorrhea**), especially if they are taking the pill. This is not a problem. There is a lot of variation between women in the amount of uterine lining, and a pattern of light bleeding is normal.

No Menstrual Bleeding

Lack of menstrual bleeding is divided into two types: **primary amenorrhea**, which refers to a woman who has never had a menstrual period, and **secondary amenorrhea**, which refers to a woman who had menstrual periods in the past, but whose periods have stopped.

A woman who has not had a menstrual period by the age of 18 is considered to have primary amenorrhea. She should seek medical care to discover if there is a problem. In most cases the woman will find that her system is normal, but she may have an inherited tendency to begin her periods late. Other possibilities are abnormalities such as imperforate hymen or abnormal chromosomes (see Chapter 1).

When a woman who has had periods in the past stops menstruating, and she is under 45 years of age, the first possibility to investigate is pregnancy. If the woman is not pregnant, lack of menstruation is probably caused by temporary suppression of brain hormones needed to bring on ovulation and a menstrual cycle, usually caused by factors in the woman's life-style. Emotional stress, serious illness, travel, depression, and malnutrition, as well as excessive dieting, exercise, or physical training, can all cause menstrual periods to stop temporarily. Women experiencing major changes in life-style, such as moving away from home, often stop having their periods for a few months. In these cases hormone treatment can be used to bring on ovulation and regular periods, but it is usually not necessary. In most cases the woman's body will return to normal after temporary stress without medical treatment. In rare cases lack of menstrual bleeding is caused by other medical conditions, such as a pituitary gland tumor (usually noncancerous).

Most women have a few times in their lives when they miss periods and are not pregnant. But a woman who knows she is not pregnant and does not get her period for several months should seek medical care to find out the reason.

Menopause Problems

Menopause, which occurs between the ages of 45 and 55 for most women, is a natural part of the aging process, which ends the reproductive years and the menstrual cycle. Menopause is not a disease or an illness; but it does cause major changes in the woman's body, which take place slowly over a period of several years. Sometimes these changes cause unpleasant or uncomfortable symptoms such as hot flashes, which usually disappear when the menopausal changes are complete. In addition, after menopause a woman's body chemistry is different, putting her at higher risk for certain health problems. In general, health problems are more common after menopause because the woman is older, and older people are more likely to develop health problems of many kinds.

This section describes health problems related to menopause; Chapter 1 gives a more complete description of the menopause process and its effects on the body.

Signs and Symptoms of Menopause

End of menstruation As a woman begins menopause, her menstrual cycle changes. In some cases her periods become lighter and less frequent until they stop altogether. For many other women the periods become irregular and may be either heavier or lighter than before. *Approximately half of all women have no identifiable problems with menopause. Their only symptoms are changes in the menstrual cycle, followed by the end of menstrual bleeding.* Many women, however, experience a variety of other symptoms with enough intensity to cause problems. About 15 percent of women have symptoms that are severe enough to require treatment.

Hot flashes and night sweats A hot flash is a sudden rise in body temperature that lasts for one to three minutes and is accompanied by feelings of hotness, sweating, and flushing. It is caused by the lower levels of estrogen found during and after menopause. The symptoms become milder or disappear if estrogen replacement therapy is given. Night sweats are similar and seem to be caused in the same way. They may be severe enough to wake the woman up several times a night and to drench her nightclothes and sheets with sweat. They also diminish with estrogen treatment.

Emotional changes In the past many experts believed that the body changes and hormone shifts of menopause caused depression and emotional problems for a high percentage of women. In fact, most women do not experience more emotional problems than usual during this time, and there is no evidence that menopause causes severe, long-lasting depression or mental illness. However, hor-

For many women menopause is no problem.

mones do have a powerful effect on emotions and feelings as well as on the body, so it is not surprising that emotional upset and discomfort may be more common for some women during the hormone changes of the menopausal years, just as it is during the teens, when the complex cycle of menstrual hormones is established.

Pelvic relaxation syndrome Pelvic relaxation syndrome describes a number of health problems, such as prolapsed uterus, cystocele, and rectocele, that are caused in part by the aging process. They affect about half of all women who have passed menopause. (These conditions and the treatments for them are described later in this chapter.)

Osteoporosis Osteoporosis is a condition in which the bones become brittle and thin, sometimes so weak that they can fracture from the stress of normal walking. It is most commonly found in postmenopausal women and is caused by loss of calcium from the bones. Osteoporosis is a major cause of illness and disability for older women and can lead to complications causing death. Slow loss of calcium from the bones during the adult years is normal for both men and women and does not usually cause problems. Many different factors contribute to the rate of calcium loss.

The major factors that appear to increase risk of osteoporosis are:

1. Insufficient calcium in the diet
2. Lack of exercise
3. For women, reduced estrogen levels
4. Smoking
5. Excessive alcohol consumption
6. Stress

Pregnancy and breastfeeding can also cause loss of bone density if the woman does not have an adequate diet.

After menopause women lose calcium from their bones because the lower levels of estrogen affect the body's ability to utilize calcium. It is estimated that without estrogen replacement therapy, approximately 30 percent of postmenopausal women will develop osteoporosis. Women who have had the ovaries removed before menopause have a similar risk. Over time the bones will become porous and break easily. Fractures of the hip and spine are especially common. Complications following fractures due to osteoporosis are a major cause of death in older women. Slender, small-boned women with fair skins seem to be most at risk for osteoporosis. Black women have a heavier bone structure and a much lower risk.

The major techniques for preventing osteoporosis after menopause are:

Adequate calcium consumption and exercise in childhood and adolescence when bones are growing, which is very important because this determines how dense the bones will be when the woman goes into menopause. A dense, heavy bone structure is stronger and can withstand more loss of calcium without risk of fractures.

Consuming 1,000 to 1,500 milligrams of calcium per day (throughout a woman's adult lifetime, not just after menopause) in foods such as milk and cheese, or in calcium supplements. The average American diet does not contain enough calcium to prevent osteoporosis in women.

Weight-bearing exercise such as walking or jogging, which slows loss of calcium from the bones.

Estrogen replacement therapy after menopause, which slows loss of calcium from the bones.

Vaginal dryness Lower levels of estrogen affect the skin all over the woman's body, causing it to become dryer and thinner than before. In some women these changes cause the vagina to become dry and easily irritated, resulting in painful intercourse and more frequent vaginal infections. This problem can be treated by using a water-soluble

Some older women choose estrogen replacement therapy to help prevent osteoporosis and other health problems.

lubricant such as KY jelly with intercourse, which will provide the moisture the body has stopped producing. Another choice is to use a lubricant containing estrogen or to take estrogen replacement therapy. The use of estrogen will cause the vaginal walls to thicken and provide more natural lubrication.

Estrogen Replacement Therapy

What is it? Estrogen replacement therapy (ERT) is the taking of estrogen as a supplement to replace that which is no longer produced by the woman's own body. It is a very popular treatment for menopausal women, and millions of American women are using it. ERT is, available in pills, by injection, and in creams. Progesterone, another female hormone, is usually contained in the supplement as well to balance the estrogen and counteract the possibility of negative side effects. Some estrogen pills also contain a male hormone, testosterone, which is believed to increase the sex drive in women as well as men. ERT is prescribed at different dosages and in combination with other hormones, depending on the specific case. The estrogen doses in ERT are much lower than those in birth control pills.

The most common use of ERT is to reduce the uncomfortable symptoms of menopause, such as hot flashes and vaginal dryness, and to prevent the development of osteoporosis (described previously). ERT is also used with younger women who have had their ovaries removed (oophorectomy). Without ERT, these women would go into menopause immediately.

How effective is it? ERT has been shown to be effective in reducing hot flashes and vaginal dryness problems, as well as in preventing loss of calcium from the bones (if used as part of a treatment plan that includes adequate nutrition and exercise). It does not cause replacement of bone, but it helps to prevent the loss of bone if it is started shortly after menopause.

ERT appears to have several other positive effects, but not all experts agree on these. ERT appears to cause the skin of the face seem fresher, thicker, and more youthful. It also may help menopausal women who suffer from emotional distress by relieving insomnia (inability to sleep) and promoting restful sleep. An intense feeling of itching all over the body called **formication**, which a few women experience with menopause, is often relieved by ERT. In many cases it appears that ERT increases the sex drive, but this has not been clearly established by research, and it appears that each woman may react differently.

What are the problems and risks? Women who take ERT may experience some mild effects of estrogen similar to those from birth control pills (see Chapter 9). There are also many women who should not take ERT because it may make other medical conditions worse. This list is also similar to the one for the birth control pills, but it should be noted that women of menopausal age are much more likely to have these health problems than younger women.*

WOMEN DEFINITELY SHOULD NOT TAKE ERT IF THEY HAVE ANY OF THE FOLLOWING CONDITIONS:

> Present or past blood-clotting disorders
> Stroke
> Abnormal vaginal bleeding
> Cancer of the breast or reproductive organs

Women who have serious medical problems, such as heart disease, vascular disease, diabetes, liver disease, high blood pressure, or sickle cell anemia, must weigh the possible effects of ERT carefully, and must be sure to discuss the decision with all the clinicians involved, especially those who provide medical care for their other problems.

In addition, ERT may not be advisable for women with fibroid tumors of the uterus, epilepsy, asthma, varicose veins, or a family history of diabetes. It also appears that women who take ERT are at higher risk for gallbladder disease and possibly for migraine headaches. When surgery is planned, ERT should usually be suspended for four weeks before the operation to avoid the risk of complications due to blood clots.

At present, it is unclear whether ERT increases the likelihood of developing cancer. Women who are taking ERT or who are considering it should follow new research findings as they come out, since the situation is not clear. Estrogen taken alone has been found to be responsible for increased risk of endometrial cancer (cancer of the lining of the uterus). This is due to overstimulation of growth of the uterine lining after menopause, without the cleansing effect of a monthly period. This risk is prevented, however (and is actually reduced), when progesterone is taken along with the estrogen to balance it, creating a body chemistry more like that before menopause.

It also appears that ERT may cause certain kinds of cancers of the reproductive organs to grow more quickly. Conditions that are stimulated by the body's natural estrogen before menopause, such as uterine fibroids and fibrocystic breast disease, also

* These lists are adapted from Felicia Stewart, Felicia Guest, Gary Stewart, and Robert Hatcher, *Understanding Your Body* (New York: Bantam Books, 1987).

may become worse during ERT. Without ERT, menopause usually brings a time of relief from these estrogen-related problems.

At present, the benefits of ERT are seen as greater than the risks for many postmenopausal women, and it may be desirable for them to continue the treatment throughout their lives. Each woman's health situation is unique, however, and ERT is not recommended for all women. In addition, health status changes over time, so women on ERT should see their physician regularly.

INFECTIONS

Vaginitis

What Is It?

Vaginitis refers to an infection or inflammation of the vagina, which may have a number of different causes. The symptoms include pain, itching, vaginal discharge, and odor. The three most common kinds of infections of the vaginal area are produced by three different types of organisms: **bacteria, trichomonas,** and **yeast (candida)**. Most women have one or more of these organisms present in the vagina all the time, but normally they do not create health problems. Poor general health, exhaustion, a new sexual partner, or other changes can create an imbalance in the woman's system that allows the organisms to multiply and cause illness. Some women find these infections tend to develop at certain points during their menstrual cycle.

Infected men may develop similar symptoms to women and can transmit the organisms to any woman with whom they have intercourse. Both men and women often carry the organisms of infection without symptoms, and may transmit infection without being aware that they have it.

How Serious Is It?

Vaginal infections from bacteria, yeast, or trichomonas can be extremely uncomfortable and bothersome, but they are not a serious threat to the life or health of a woman. Vaginitis caused by these organisms does not affect the uterus or Fallopian tubes and will not develop into pelvic inflammatory disease or cause sterility. However, other infections such as chlamydia and gonorrhea (see Chapter 14), which may produce similar vaginal symptoms, can develop into serious internal infections and may cause sterility.

What Are the Signs, Symptoms, and Treatments?

The symptoms of vaginal infection are usually pain, itching, and a vaginal discharge which may have an unpleasant odor. Each of the three major kinds of infection has slightly different symptoms and requires different treatment. Reinfection is common for all three.

Yeast infections (candida) Yeast infections, also called **candida, candida albicans, monilia,** and **fungus,** are the most common vaginal infections and are caused by a yeast fungus that is normally found in the vagina and digestive tract of women. Infection develops when the body chemistry is out of balance. If the acid/alkaline balance (also called the Ph balance) of the vagina is not sufficiently acid, good conditions for the growth of yeast organisms exist, and the yeast may overgrow, causing the symptoms of infection. Treatment seeks to kill enough yeast organisms to bring the vagina back in balance, not to eliminate them completely.

Poor general health, exhaustion, diabetes, pregnancy, use of birth control pills, and treatment with antibiotics are all conditions that make yeast infections more likely. Some women tend to develop them shortly after the menstrual period, because the menstrual blood is alkaline and affects the Ph balance of the vagina.

The symptoms of yeast infection are a thick white vaginal discharge with a curdlike or "cottage cheese" consistency. Severe itching, redness, and inflammation around the labia and sometimes on the upper thighs is also common. Yeast infections are easy to diagnose both from the symptoms and by examining the vaginal discharge under a microscope. They can also be cultured.

The treatment is antibiotic suppositories or creams applied to the vagina (or penis, if a man is infected) daily for a week or more. A number of different drugs are effective and may be prescribed, including miconazole, nystatin, candicidin, and clotrimazole. Boric acid in capsules (600 milligrams) used daily as a vaginal suppository for two weeks also seems to be effective. This treatment does not require a prescription, but the woman may have to make the suppositories herself from boric acid and size 00 gelatin capsules if they are not available from a pharmacy.

Reinfection with candida is common, and some women find that they develop a new infection shortly after treatment is ended, or every month after their periods. There are several self-help remedies that seem to reduce the chances of developing yeast infections in women who get them often, and seem to help to cure infections when they do develop. Drinking cranberry juice, eating yogurt, and avoiding sugar are helpful to many women. Plain (unflavored) yogurt is also used as a vaginal cream to help restore the chemical balance of the vagina.

Trichomonas infections Trichomonas infection is caused by a one-celled organism called a trichomonad, and is usually transmitted from one person to another by sexual intercourse. The trichomonad can live for a few hours outside the body, so it can also be passed on by sharing towels, bathing suits, or other items with an infected person.

The symptoms of trichomonas are a frothy, thin, gray, or greenish-white vaginal discharge, which may have an unpleasant smell; itching and redness in the vaginal area; and pain on urination. Diagnosis of trichomonas infection is made by the symptoms, physical examination, and examination of a sample of vaginal fluid under the microscope. Trichomonas can also be diagnosed through a culture.

Trichomonas infection is most effectively treated with Flagyl (metronidazole) taken by both the woman and her partner. However, this drug has several negative side effects, including possible nausea, diarrhea, and dryness and/or a metallic taste in the mouth. If alcohol is taken while the drug is in the system, many people experience nausea, vomiting, and headache. In addition, this drug may depress the number of white blood cells in the body (which are needed to protect against infection), and a white cell count is needed if a second course of the drug is given. Another form of treatment is the use of antibiotic suppositories or medicated douches. This is sometimes effective but does not provide treatment for the partner. Persons who prefer not to take Flagyl and pregnant women (who should not take Flagyl) might consider this approach.

Bacterial infections Bacterial infections of the vagina are also called **hemophilus, corynebacterium,** and **gardnerella.** The terms **bacterial vaginosis** and **nonspecific vaginitis** are also used to describe vaginal infections for which the exact cause is not known. These are believed to be bacterial infections in most cases. The symptoms are a yellow to gray-green vaginal discharge, which may be thick or watery and which often has an unpleasant smell (often described as a "fishy" smell). Pain on urination, vaginal itching, and painful intercourse are also symptoms.

Diagnosis of bacterial infection is made by the symptoms, by physical examination, and by laboratory tests.

A number of drugs and treatments are used. Flagyl (metronidazole) taken by both the woman and her partner is the most effective, but may produce unpleasant side effects (discussed previously). Tetracycline and other antibiotics are also prescribed for both partners but are not always effective. In some cases the infected woman is treated with medicated creams, jellies, or suppositories containing sulfa or other antibiotics. This treatment seems to reduce the symptoms, but there is a question as to whether it eliminates the infection. There is no effective way to treat infected men with creams or jellies (since the infection is inside the urethra), so reinfection of the couple is likely with this approach unless the man uses a condom in intercourse.

Often, male sexual partners of infected women do not have symptoms of infection. The use of condoms (even if also taking antibiotics) is recommended to protect the man and the woman from possibly infecting and/or reinfecting each other (creating an infection that bounces back and forth between them). If a man who has no symptoms uses condoms for 15 successive ejaculations, it is thought to "clear" his system of possible infection.

Cervicitis

What Is It?

Cervicitis is an inflammation of the cervix that is often caused by an infection such as chlamydia, another sexually transmitted disease, or trichomonas. Injury to the cervix from intercourse, from the insertion of an IUD, or from childbirth can also cause cervicitis. Irritating substances such as the chemicals found in deodorized tampons or commercial douches can also cause the problem.

How Serious Is It?

Cervicitis is a very common condition that is not serious in most cases. However, it can be a symptom of a more serious problem such as gonorrhea, chlamydia, or precancerous abnormal cell growth, and it should be evaluated and treated by a doctor.

What Are the Signs and Symptoms?

A swollen, red cervix, which may be painful to the touch, is the major symptom of cervicitis. Mild cervicitis often produces no noticeable symptoms at all, however, and the woman may first be told of it during a medical checkup. The symptoms of severe cervicitis are increased vaginal discharge, which may have a foul smell; pain during intercourse or when the cervix is touched; and bleeding or spotting, especially after intercourse. Cervicitis can also cause abdominal pain or aching and the urge to urinate frequently.

Cervical eversion and cervical erosion Cervical eversion refers to a condition in which the

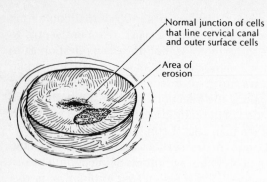

Normal junction of cells
that line cervical canal
and outer surface cells

Area of
erosion

Cervical Erosion

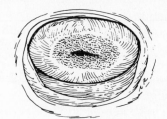
Cervical Eversion

FIGURE 12–12. *Cervical erosion and cervical eversion.*

cells that normally line the opening of the cervix also grow outside the opening along the surface of the cervix (Figure 12–12). These mucus-secreting cells are different in appearance from the normal surface of the cervix and are slightly more likely to become infected. Cervical eversion is usually not considered a problem and is not treated. The term **cervical erosion** is also used to describe patches of these mucus-secreting cells when they appear on the surface of the cervix. A doctor may describe them as similar to ulcers, but they are usually not a problem; they are a normal development, which most women will have at some time. Cervical eversion is found more commonly among DES daughters, women who take birth control pills, and young women who have never been pregnant.

CIN (cervical intraepithelial neoplasia or cervical dysplasia) CIN refers to the growth of abnormal cells on the surface of the cervix. It can be detected by a Pap smear (described earlier in this chapter) and, over time, can develop into cancer.

What Is the Treatment?

Treatment of cervicitis depends on the cause of the inflammation. If it is due to an infection such as a sexually transmitted disease, the cervicitis should disappear when the infection is treated, usually with antibiotics. With chronic mild cervicitis it is sometimes impossible to tell what organism in the vagina is causing the irritation. Sulfa or antibiotic creams or douches may be prescribed to reduce the populations of bacteria in the vagina, allowing the cervix to heal. Another treatment for mild cases is the use of douches or creams that affect the Ph (acid/alkaline) balance of the vagina, creating an environment that is hostile to infectious bacteria. Cautery or cryosurgery (described earlier in this chapter) is also sometimes used to treat severe cervicitis if it does not respond to other treatment. (The treatment of cancer of the cervix is described later in this chapter.) Good general health and nutrition, sufficient rest, and avoidance of

stress are all important in keeping the body's defenses strong against inflammations like cervicitis.

Urinary Tract Infection (UTI)

What Is It?

Urinary tract infection (UTI) is one of the most common health problems of women and can cause a great deal of discomfort. *E. coli*, a type of bacteria found in the rectum and in feces, is the organism most commonly found in urinary tract infections. Several different names are used for UTIs depending on the part of the urinary tract in which they are found. **Urethritis** is the name for inflammation of the urethra, the one-and-a-half-inch tube that leads from the bladder to the vulva. **Cystitis** is the term used for inflammation or infection of the bladder, and **pyelonephritis** is the name for infection of the kidneys (Figure 12–13).

FIGURE 12–13. *A woman's urinary system.*

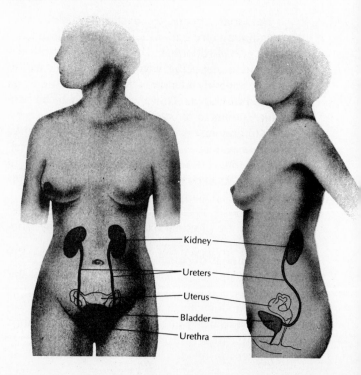

Kidney

Ureters

Uterus

Bladder

Urethra

UTIs usually develop after irritation or injury to the urethra, which provides an opportunity for bacteria to enter the urethra and move up into the bladder. Some of the causes of injury or irritation are as follows:

1. Frequent or vigorous sexual intercourse, especially after a period of little or no sexual activity (this is why bladder infections are sometimes called **honeymoon cystitis**)

2. Lack of sufficient lubrication, or positions in intercourse where the penis rubs against the urethra

3. Failure to urinate frequently enough or to drink enough water (so bacteria multiply in the bladder)

4. Pressure on the bladder or urethra, such as from pregnancy or from too large a contraceptive diaphragm (which may prevent the bladder from emptying completely)

5. Bubble baths, feminine hygiene sprays, scented douches, and vaginal deodorants (all contain ingredients that may irritate the urethra)

6. Catheterization, which is the insertion of a small plastic tube (catheter) through the urethra into the bladder to drain the bladder or to obtain a urine sample (used mostly after surgery)

7. Poor hygiene (it's especially important to wipe front to back after a bowel movement to avoid fecal matter coming into contact with the vagina or urethra)

8. Bicycle riding

Diabetic women are also at high risk for UTIs because their systems frequently suffer from chemical imbalance. Women after menopause have more frequent UTIs, probably because their vaginal and urethral tissue are drier and more easily irritated.

How Serious Is It?

Infections of the urethra and the bladder are usually not serious and are easily treated. But some women get the infections frequently, which can be very inconvenient and uncomfortable. Kidney infections are more serious, and since they do not always cause noticeable symptoms, they may go untreated for long periods of time and cause permanent kidney damage, which is a cause of high blood pressure and other problems.

What Are the Signs and Symptoms?

The first symptoms of urinary tract infection are usually burning and urgency in urination. This can be extremely uncomfortable and often creates the sensation of needing to urinate all the time, but not being able to. There may also be aching, cramps, or tenderness in the lower abdomen. The urine may look cloudy, may have blood or mucus in it, and may have an odd smell. If the infection has progressed to the kidneys, there may be pain in the back, fever, and feelings of being ill.

Diagnosis of UTI can usually be made from the symptoms. If there is infection, examination of the urine under a microscope will show bacteria and white blood cells, which are not normally present in urine. A culture can be done to identify the organism that is causing the infection. In addition to the more common organisms, gonorrhea and other sexually transmitted diseases can also cause UTI.

What Is the Treatment?

Medical treatment A woman may have the symptoms of UTI but not actually have an infection. By drinking large quantities of water and acidifying the urine by drinking cranberry juice or taking vitamin C, she may be able to make the symptoms disappear. If the symptoms don't go away within 48 hours, however, the chances are good that infection has set in. Sulfa drugs and broad-spectrum antibiotics are commonly used to treat urinary tract infections. The symptoms of infection normally go away within a couple of days, but it is important to keep taking the medication for as long as instructed. Some health care providers prescribe a single dose of antibiotic in pill or injection to treat UTIs. Pyridium (phenazopyridine hydrochloride) may also be prescribed to reduce the burning and pain on urination. This medication has a soothing effect on the bladder and urethra, and will turn the urine a dark orange color. This change of color is harmless and temporary.

If a woman has frequent infections, her doctor may want to do tests to look for problems in her entire urinary system. An **intravenous pyelogram (IVP)**, which is an X-ray of the urinary tract, or a **cystoscopy**, which is an examination of the inside of the bladder, may be recommended.

Self-care The best approach to UTIs is to prevent them, and there are many things women can do to decrease the chances of developing urinary tract infections. The following list shows some methods for preventing infection and helping to speed recovery when infection is present.

1. Drink plenty of water every day (six to eight glasses) and don't put off urinating.

2. Avoid irritating the urethra; use extra lubrication if needed for intercourse, and choose positions that don't put constant pressure on the urethra.

3. Urinate just before and immediately after intercourse. An empty bladder is less likely to be irritated, and urinating after intercourse helps to wash out bacteria that may have been introduced into the urethra.

4. Avoid birth control methods that place pressure on the urethra. For some women, the diaphragm or even the sponge creates pressure. Spermicides kill

bacteria as well as sperm, so using them may help a woman avoid UTIs.

5. Drink cranberry juice daily and take vitamin C supplements; both change the Ph balance of the urine to make it more acid. Acidic urine is hostile to the growth of bacteria. Citrus fruits and juices have the opposite effect and should be avoided.

6. Take a shower or bath every day, and make sure your partner does so as well.

7. Always wipe from front to back after using the toilet to prevent bacteria from the rectum coming in contact with the urethra.

8. Avoid caffeine, alcohol, and strong spices, all of which are irritating to the bladder and urethra. If you can't give them up, dilute them with large quantities of water.

Many women who are prone to catch frequent UTIs can tell when an infection seems to be coming on and can prevent it from developing by flushing the system with lots of water and following the preceding list of suggestions.

Pelvic Inflammatory Disease (Pelvic Infection)

What Is It?

Pelvic inflammatory disease (PID) and pelvic infection are general terms for inflammation or infection of a woman's pelvic organs. PID includes inflammations of various parts of the pelvic anatomy, including:

Endometritis: Infection of the lining of the uterus
Endoparametritis: Infection of both the lining and the muscle wall of the uterus

Salpingitis: Infection of the Fallopian tubes
Oophoritis: Infection of the ovaries

Additional problems that are included under PID are:

Tubo-ovarian abcess: A walled-off pocket of pus and infection in the area of a woman's Fallopian tubes and ovaries
Pelvic peritonitis: A generalized infection of the lower abdomen, caused by the spread of infection from the reproductive organs

PID is a common illness, affecting close to a million women each year. The disease is twice as common as it was twenty years ago. PID can be caused by a large number of organisms, including gonorrhea, chlamydia, and mycoplasma. It usually begins as an infection of the cervix. If it is not treated, it moves upward into the uterus, and from there it can progress through the Fallopian tubes to the ovary and into the abdomen (Figure 12–14).

Although the vagina, like the skin, is host to a variety of organisms that do not usually cause illness, the cervix represents the passageway to the interior of the body, which is normally sterile. Once disease organisms pass the cervix, the body is less able to fight them, and infection can develop and spread rapidly.

PID is most commonly caused by a sexually transmitted disease organism, and gonorrhea is responsible for almost half of the PID in the United States. PID infections can also be transmitted by insertion of an IUD, pelvic surgery such as an abortion or D&C, childbirth, or miscarriage. Women

FIGURE 12–14. *How pelvic infection spreads.*

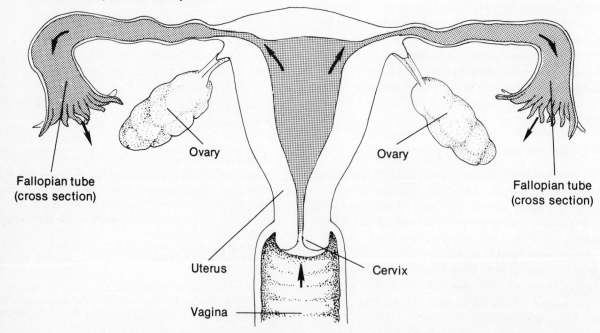

have an increased risk of pelvic infection if they use an IUD and if they are exposed to infection during menstruation. In both cases the reason is that bacteria can enter the uterus more easily at these times. Having many sexual partners also increases the risk.

How Serious Is It?

PID is a very serious illness. If it is not treated it can lead to illness, infertility, chronic health problems, and (in rare cases) death. PID is the most common cause of infertility in American women. The inflammation of the Fallopian tubes and the scars left by infection often close off the tubes so that fertilization and pregnancy cannot take place. Women who have had PID are also more likely to have an ectopic pregnancy (see Chapter 6). When severe PID infection does not respond to treatment, surgery may be necessary, and a woman may lose one or both Fallopian tubes, the ovaries, and (less commonly) her uterus. Women who have had PID have a higher risk of getting repeat infections. Also, damage to the pelvic organs, scars, and adhesions may cause continuing pelvic pain long after the infection is cured.

What Are the Signs and Symptoms?

PID infections are divided into three types, **acute, chronic** and **silent.** Acute PID is a serious infection, that may cause some or all of the following signs and symptoms:

> Sudden high fever or a low-grade fever which may come and go
> Chills
> Abdominal, back, or leg pain
> Pelvic cramps and aching
> Unusual vaginal discharge or bleeding
> Feelings of illness or unusual tiredness
> Pain during or after intercourse
> Swollen abdomen or pelvic lymph nodes
> Abdominal tenderness (sensitive to pressure or jarring)
> Pain or difficulty urinating
> Pain when having a bowel movement

Acute PID needs immediate medical treatment.

Chronic PID is long-lasting, low-level pelvic infection which may cause few symptoms but have a very negative effect on the woman's general health. It may develop after a severe infection that does not completely disappear when treated. Women who have chronic PID often find that they are more likely to develop symptoms when they are tired or run down, or have another infection. Chronic PID can be difficult to cure. Repeated or chronic infections are often caused by a sexual partner who has not been treated and is reinfecting the woman.

Silent PID is pelvic infection that produces no noticeable symptoms. It is very common for women to have no symptoms of chlamydia or other pelvic infections until the disease is far advanced and has done considerable damage to the pelvic organs. *Women who have any reason to believe that they may have been exposed to a sexually transmitted disease or may be developing a pelvic infection should seek medical care immediately.*

What Is the Treatment?

The best teatment for PID is to avoid getting the infection in the first place. The instructions in Chapter 14 on how to avoid sexually transmitted diseases also apply to avoiding PID. PID is treated with antibiotics but is not always easily cured. Symptoms such as pelvic pain sometimes persist after the disease is cured, and it is common for infection to recur. The choice of the specific antibiotic to be used is based on the organisms that are causing the infection. It is common to find several different organisms involved in a single case of PID, and it is often difficult to identify which ones are causing the illness. Laboratory tests often take several days or even weeks to give results, and antibiotic treatment is usually started before the test results are back (because it is so important to catch the infection as early as possible). Medications may be changed or adjusted after laboratory test results come back. *As with all sexually transmitted diseases, all sexual partners of a woman with PID must be treated at the same time.*

Hospitalization is needed under certain conditions, such as:

1. If abscesses have developed
2. If the diagnosis is not clear (PID symptoms can be confused with appendicitis)
3. If the woman is pregnant
4. If the woman is unable to tolerate antibiotic pills and needs intravenous medication

Exploratory surgery, such as laparoscopy or laparotomy (see Chapter 10), may be needed to identify and treat the problem if the infection is life-threatening, has caused abscesses, or is not responding to treatment. In rare cases, removal of some or all of the pelvic organs may be necessary.

Toxic Shock Syndrome

What Is It?

Toxic shock syndrome (TSS) is a rare but serious illness thought to be caused by toxins (poisons) produced by the staphylococcus aureus bacteria. This potentially serious problem is most often developed by menstruating women who are using tampons. It is believed that the bacteria grow in menstrual blood trapped in the vagina when a woman leaves a tampon (or a similar object such as a contraceptive sponge) in place for a long period of time. The bacteria may enter the woman's bloodstream through the walls of the vagina if there are any scratches or breaks in the mucus membrane.

Toxic shock syndrome has been found in men and children as well as women, since the illness can develop in anyone who has an open sore or wound through which the bacteria can enter. But the vast majority of cases have been menstruating women with staphylococcus infections of the vagina that caused no symptoms and were not noticed until TSS set in.

How Serious Is It?

TSS is a very serious illness with a death rate of over 10 percent for those hospitalized for the infection. It is very rare, however, with only about 3 out of each 100,000 women of menstruating age needing hospitalization for TSS each year. The disease has only been identified in recent years, and understanding about it is still limited. It is likely that not all the cases in the United States are being reported. There may be many mild cases in women who are never hospitalized or who never seek medical care. The disease is being studied by the Centers for Disease Control in Atlanta, Georgia, and all identified cases should be reported there.

What Are the Signs and Symptoms?

The symptoms of TSS are likely to develop while a woman is menstruating, and the illness usually comes on very rapidly.

The warning signs are the following:

1. A sunburn-like rash
2. Fever (101 degrees Fahrenheit or more)
3. Diarrhea
4. Vomiting
5. Muscle aches

A woman who develops these symptoms while menstruating should get medical care immediately.

What Is the Treatment?

Medical treatment TSS is usually treated effectively with penicillin or another antibiotic, but some strains of the infection are resistant to penicillin and can be difficult to treat. Because this serious disease develops very fast, it is important to get medical care immediately if you develop the symptoms.

Self-care and prevention The best protection for women against TSS is not to use tampons at all. The disease is extremely rare, however, and most women need not worry about developing it. There are a number of actions women can take to reduce the chances of TSS infection.

1. Avoid "superabsorbent" tampons (like Rely tampons, which were taken off the market because of their link to TSS). Use medium or regular tampons rather than super sizes.
2. Avoid scratching or irritating the mucus lining of the vagina when the vagina is dry or there is little bleeding (if the tampon sticks to the walls of the vagina or shreds when you try to take it out, the vagina is too dry).
3. Don't use tampons 24 hours a day (wear a pad for a few hours each day, perhaps at night).
4. Change tampons more frequently than is necessary.
5. Wash hands before inserting tampons, and make sure the tampon and applicator aren't dirty or contaminated.
6. Don't use tampons if you have had TSS, if you believe you have had mild TSS symptoms, or if staph bacteria have been found in your vagina.

CYSTS, TUMORS, AND CANCERS OF THE REPRODUCTIVE SYSTEM

Fibroid Tumors of the Uterus

What Are They?

Fibroid tumors are firm, dense, slow-growing tumors that develop in the walls and along the surface of the uterus. They are very rarely cancerous (less than 1 case out of 200) and do not usually require any treatment if they are not causing problems. Other names for fibroid tumors of the uterus are **myoma, fibromyoma,** and **leiomyoma.** Fibroid tumors are the most common cause of an abnormally enlarged uterus (not due to pregnancy), and 20 to 50 percent of all women have some fibroid growths. Fibroids are most commonly found in women in their thirties and forties, but they do develop in younger women as well. For reasons that are not known, fibroid tumors are more common in black women than in others.

How Serious Are They?

Fibroid tumors are usually not a serious problem. Most women who have them have no symptoms, and the tumors are discovered during a medical checkup. If the tumors are not causing

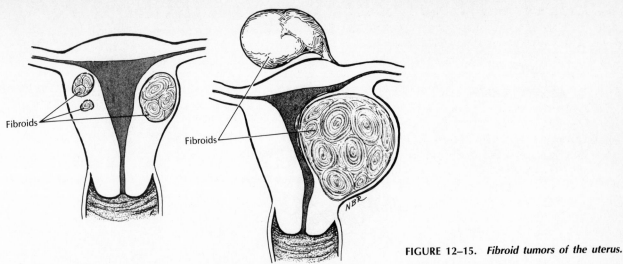

FIGURE 12–15. *Fibroid tumors of the uterus.*

problems, there is usually no reason to remove them. In most cases they grow slowly and tend to shrink after menopause. There is a very small risk that fibroid tumors may be cancerous or may become cancerous over time. If the tumors are large, they can cause problems with pregnancy. In rare cases, large fibroids can require emergency surgery if their blood supply is cut off and the tissue starts to die.

What Are the Signs and Symptoms?

Fibroid tumors grow within the muscle wall of the uterus and on the inner and outer surface as well. They may also grow away from the uterus, fed and supported by a stalk of tissue, as shown in Figure 12–15. A fibroid tumor growing outside the uterus on a stalk may be difficult to distinguish from a tumor of the ovary. It is common to have several fibroid tumors clustered together. Small tumors usually cause no symptoms for the woman and will be diagnosed only when they are large enough to be felt as lumps or bumps on the uterus when the woman has a medical checkup. If the tumors grow on the inside surface of the uterus, they may not be felt during a pelvic examination, but they may cause abnormal bleeding, difficulty in getting pregnant, and miscarriages.

Larger tumors may cause feelings of heaviness and pressure in the lower abdomen, stress incontinence, and heavy bleeding and cramps during menstrual periods. In the rare cases where a fibroid is cut off from its blood supply and starts to deteriorate, severe abdominal pain may develop.

Diagnosis of fibroid tumors is usually made by a physical exam, but X-ray of the abdomen, sonogram (see Chapter 6), hysterosalpingogram (see Chapter 8), and D&C (see details later in this chapter) are also all used to identify the problem. If it is not possible to decide if a pelvic lump is an ovarian tumor or a fibroid tumor of the uterus, exploratory surgery is sometimes needed.

What Is the Treatment?

The causes of fibroids are not known, but it is known that high levels of estrogen in the body stimulate rapid growth. Pregnancy, use of the birth control pill, and use of estrogen replacement therapy after menopause all cause increased fibroid growth in some women. Once a woman develops fibroids, usually during her reproductive years, they continue to grow slowly until she reaches menopause. At that time, because of naturally lower levels of estrogen in the body (if she is not taking estrogen replacement therapy), they will tend to shrink and may almost disappear.

If a fibroid tumor has reached around three and a half inches in size or is causing health problems, surgery is usually recommended to remove it. This can be done by **myomectomy,** the removal of the tumor from the wall of the uterus (Figure 12–16), or by **hysterectomy,** the removal of the entire uterus. Both surgeries require hospitalization for several days, an abdominal incision, and several weeks of recovery time. Since fibroid tumors tend to recur, hysterectomy is often recommended for women who do not plan to have more children. Women who have a myomectomy and later become pregnant will probably have to deliver the baby by caesarean section.

Cancer of the Reproductive Organs

Cancer of the reproductive organs accounts for 41 percent of all cases of cancer but only 28 percent of cancer deaths in women. The difference is caused by the fact that some kinds of cancers are more easily diagnosed and cured than others. According

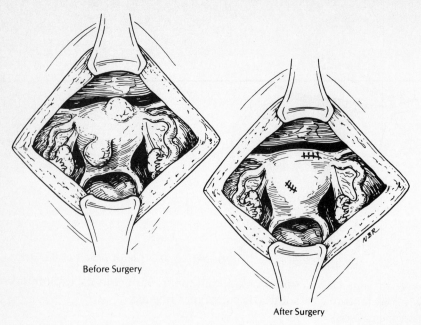

Before Surgery

After Surgery

FIGURE 12–16. *Myomectomy (surgery to remove fibroid tumors).*

to the American Cancer Society's estimated figures for 1987 (Figure 12–17), 27 percent of all new cases of cancers in women will be breast cancer. The disease is quite common, and it is estimated that 1 in 11 women will develop breast cancer at some point during their lives. Fortunately, the survival rate has improved in recent years. If the cancer is localized in the breast, 96 percent of women are well five years after treatment. If the cancer has spread beyond the breast, the survival rate after five years is 70 percent. (See the section titled "Breast Problems" later in this chapter for information about the symptoms and treatment of breast cancer.)

Uterine cancer (which includes cancers of the uterus, cervix, and endometrium) was expected to cause 10 percent of new cases in women in 1987. In cases that are detected and treated early, 80 to 90 percent of women are well five years after treatment. The overall survival rate is only 65 percent, however, because it includes many women who were not diagnosed and treated early. (The next section of this chapter provides for information about the symptoms and treatment of uterine cancer.)

Cancer of the ovaries was expected to cause only 4 percent of new cancers in women in 1987, but 5 percent of deaths. This disease is now the leading killer among cancers of the woman's reproductive system. Although it is rare, the cure rate is not good, with only about 35 percent of women with ovarian cancer found to be well five years after treatment. The poor survival rate for ovarian cancer is in part due to the fact that the disease usually produces no symptoms until it is far advanced. Further, the ovaries are difficult to examine. In addition, many older women (who are most at risk for the disease) no longer obtain regular pelvic exam-

inations because they have had hysterectomies. As long as a woman has ovaries, a regular pelvic exam is needed to check them. (Information about the symptoms and treatment of ovarian cancer is provided later in this chapter.)

Reproductive cancers in women cannot be completely prevented, but in most cases they can be cured if treated early.

Women can do several things to lower the risk of developing cancer and to increase their chances of survival if it does develop.

1. Monthly breast self-examination is very important for all women.

2. Regular gynecological checkups, including a Pap smear and a breast examination, are also very important for all women, including those who have had hysterectomies or mastectomies.

3. Women should be aware of the symptoms of cancer and should seek medical care in between checkups if suspicious symptoms develop.

4. There are also many life-style factors that affect the likelihood of developing cancer. Some of the factors affecting reproductive cancers in women include:
    A. Diet and nutrition: Obesity (overweight) increases the risk of breast, uterine, and other cancers. A high-fat diet may increase the chances of breast and other cancers.
    B. Smoking: Increases the chances of developing lung cancer and some other cancers.
    C. Radiation: Exposure to X-rays increases the risk of cancer (and fertility problems).

Uterine Cancer

What Is It?

Uterine cancer includes cancers of the cervix, the endometrium (lining of the uterus), and the

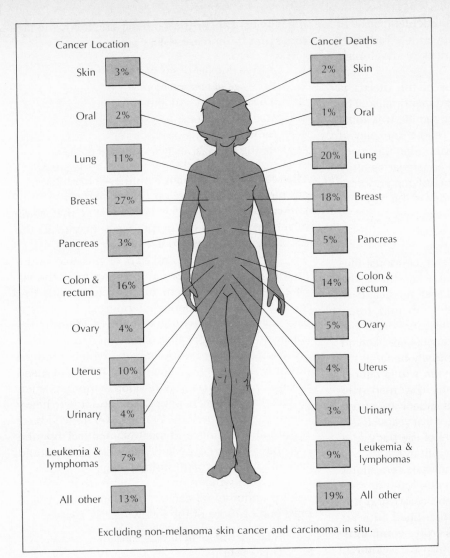

Cancer Location		Cancer Deaths	
Skin	3%	2%	Skin
Oral	2%	1%	Oral
Lung	11%	20%	Lung
Breast	27%	18%	Breast
Pancreas	3%	5%	Pancreas
Colon & rectum	16%	14%	Colon & rectum
Ovary	4%	5%	Ovary
Uterus	10%	4%	Uterus
Urinary	4%	3%	Urinary
Leukemia & lymphomas	7%	9%	Leukemia & lymphomas
All other	13%	19%	All other

Excluding non-melanoma skin cancer and carcinoma in situ.

FIGURE 12–17. *Estimated new cancer cases and cancer deaths in women by location (1987).*

uterus itself, and makes up 11 percent of all cancers among women. Cancer of the ovaries is discussed separately in the section of this chapter called "Cysts and Tumors of the Ovaries." Cancers of the vulva, vagina, and Fallopian tubes are less common and are not discussed in this book.

Cancer of the cervix is a progressive disease that usually begins as mildly abnormal cells (which many women develop) on the cervix. In some women these abnormal cell changes continue over months and years until true cancer develops. Fortunately, thanks to the Pap smear (described earlier in this chapter) and better gynecological care, cervical cancers can usually be identified early, while they are still restricted to the cervix (carcinoma *in situ*). Invasive cancer of the cervix, which is harder to treat, is less common today than in the past as a result of early diagnosis and treatment. Carcinoma *in situ* is most common among women from ages 25 to 40; invasive cancer of the cervix is most often found in women over age 45.

There are two types of cancers of the uterus.

The most common is endometrial cancer (about 96 percent), which develops in the endometrium (the lining of the uterus that is shed monthly by menstrual bleeding). The remaining 4 percent of cancer of the uterus develops in the muscle and other tissues of the uterus itself.

Uterine cancer rates have risen in the United States over the last 25 years, and the disease is now more common than cervical cancer. There are several possible causes for this, including the increasing proportion of the population that is elderly and at higher risk for the disease, and the tremendous reduction in the numbers of cervical cancer cases, which has come about as a result of early detection. In addition, high levels of estrogen in the body that are not counterbalanced by progesterone seem to be linked to a higher risk of developing uterine cancer. Use of birth control pills or estrogen replacement therapy for postmenopausal women should not create this risk, but some other kinds of hormone treatment and natural hormone levels within the body can do so.

There are no known environmental causes of uterine cancer, but excessive exposure to radiation is thought to increase the chances of developing the disease over time.

Over 80 percent of cancer of the uterus is found in women who have passed menopause. The disease is rare in women under age 40. It is most often discovered when women report unexpected vaginal bleeding, months or years after the menstrual cycle has ended. The Pap smear is only around 50 percent effective in identifying endometrial cancer. An endometrial biopsy is the test that is used to check for this kind of cancer.

How Serious Is It?

Any form of uterine cancer is a serious, life-threatening condition. A woman who thinks she may have uterine cancer should seek medical care immediately, because early detection and treatment are the key to successful elimination of the disease. Left untreated, uterine cancers are likely to spread to other organs and eventually be fatal.

The cure rate for carcinoma *in situ* is almost 100 percent, and 80 to 90 percent of women who are diagnosed early with cervical cancer are cured (have no recurrence of cancer after five years). If the disease has spread to other parts of the body (the lymph nodes, vagina, uterus, or other areas), the chances of cure are lower. Precancerous conditions (where abnormal cells that could develop into cancer in the future are found) of the cervix and the endometrium are frequently identified during checkups. Treatment of precancerous conditions can almost always prevent cancer from developing.

When endometrial cancer is treated early, over 80 percent of women are cured (free from cancer signs or symptoms after five years). The more advanced the disease, and the more it has spread to other parts of the body, the less the chances of complete cure. The disease can recur after the uterus is removed (often in the vagina or lower abdomen), and frequent checkups are needed even after treatment is completed.

What Are the Signs and Symptoms?

Early cancer of the cervix (carcinoma *in situ*) is usually a silent disease, with no signs or symptoms. This is the reason that an annual gynecological checkup and Pap test are so important. Over 90 percent of cases are easily identified with a Pap smear. More advanced cervical cancer may cause abnormal bleeding from the vagina, either between periods or after intercourse (but usually the cause of such bleeding is much less serious).

Certain women have a higher risk of developing cervical cancer than others. The following factors seem to increase risk:

1. A large number of sex partners
2. Early age of first intercourse
3. A history of venereal warts
4. Many pregnancies
5. Having genital herpes
6. Having had a sexually transmitted disease

The reasons that women with these characteristics are more likely to develop cervical cancer are unknown at present, but it is suspected that some infections, such as the herpes virus, may make the development of cancerous cells more likely.

The most important sign of possible endometrial cancer is abnormal bleeding from the vagina. Around 80 percent of all women with this form of cancer experience it. Abnormal bleeding is easy for postmenopausal women to identify, because any bleeding at all is unexpected (unless they are taking estrogen supplements, which produce monthly bleeding). Women who have not been through menopause may develop symptoms such as bleeding between periods or prolonged heavy bleeding during periods. Women over 40 who have abnormal bleeding and postmenopausal women who have any unexpected bleeding at all should seek medical treatment immediately.

Certain women are at a higher than average risk for endometrial cancer. They are women who have one or more of the following risk factors:

1. A family history of uterine cancer
2. Overweight
3. High blood pressure
4. Diabetes
5. Infrequent menstrual periods
6. Infertility
7. Menstrual periods continuing after age 50
8. Prolonged treatment with estrogen (other than the birth control pill)

What Is the Treatment?

As usual, the best treatment is prevention. In the case of uterine cancer, we do not know how to prevent it completely, but there are excellent means for identifying precancerous conditions (often during routine checkups). By treating precancerous con ditions early, cancer itself can usually be avoided.

Cervical cancer is treated in a variety of ways depending on the severity of the condition, the woman's age and plans for future childbearing, and other factors. There are a number of treatments available from which the woman and her doctor can choose. If there are abnormal cervical cells that are considered precancerous, minor surgery, including cryosurgery or cauterization, is commonly used. **Conization,** which is surgical removal of the area around the opening of the cervix (described earlier in this chapter), is another treatment of precancerous cervical conditions. Hysterectomy is also often recommended for women with precancerous conditions if they do not wish to have more children, because it gives the best protection against developing cancer.

If true cancer has developed, a hysterectomy is usually needed, and if it is suspected that the disease may have spread beyond the cervix, radiation treatment may be needed as well. Radiation and chemotherapy may also be used in combination with surgery or alone to treat this condition; an individualized treatment plan is needed for each woman.

When carcinoma *in situ* is treated with conization instead of hysterectomy (usually because the woman wishes to have more children), the cancer returns in around 10 percent of cases. Frequent checkups are needed if this method is used.

Treatment of endometrial cancer is planned differently for each individual woman based on evaluation of the type of cancer, how far it has spread, and other health factors. For cancers detected early, which have not spread beyond the uterus, a hysterectomy with removal of the uterus, Fallopian tubes, ovaries, and cervix is the usual treatment (see the section on hysterectomy later in this chapter for more on the different types of hysterectomies). If cancerous cells have been found in lymph nodes or other areas outside the uterus, radiation is often used in addition to surgery. Radiation may be given before surgery or after, and may involve beaming the treatment to the lower abdomen and pelvis from outside the body, or temporarily implanting tiny radioactive devices inside the uterus. Hormonal drugs and chemotherapy are also used to treat some women. After treatment is completed, a woman who has had uterine cancer must have frequent checkups to make sure the disease does not recur.

Cysts and Tumors of the Ovaries

What Are They?

Ovarian cysts are fluid-filled areas that grow within the ovary. Tumors are solid growths. Most ovarian cysts are found in women during their reproductive years and are produced by the normal functioning of the ovaries; they are not cancerous. These are called **functional cysts,** of which there are two types: **follicle cysts** and **corpus luteum cysts.** Other kinds of ovarian cysts and tumors are much less common and can be found in women of any age. The great majority of ovarian growths (also called neoplasms) are benign (noncancerous) when found in young women, but in women over age 50, close to half are found to be malignant (cancerous).

Follicle cysts are created when the egg is developing. They normally rupture at ovulation, releasing the egg. Occasionally, the cyst does not break open and continues to grow. Corpus luteum cysts develop after the egg follicle ruptures. The remaining tissue usually produces hormones for the remainder of the menstrual cycle and then stops functioning and is absorbed back into the ovary. Sometimes this material continues to grow and is called a corpus luteum cyst. Women with **polycystic ovaries** have many small follicle cysts on both ovaries.

How Serious Are They?

Functional cysts are not usually a serious problem. They are called *functional* because they are part of the normal functioning of the ovary and they develop to a certain degree in every monthly cycle. In most cases they produce no symptoms and are identified only during medical checkups. They usually disappear without treatment after one or two menstrual cycles. Women taking birth control pills almost never develop functional cysts because the pills suppress the functioning of the ovaries. If a functional cyst becomes too large and starts to cause pain or bleeding, or to press on other body organs, surgery may be needed to remove it.

Most other ovarian growths are not cancerous and often do not cause symptoms or need treatment. Ovarian cancer, however, although it is not as common as some other reproductive cancers such as breast cancer, is a major killer, with only 35 percent of women surviving for five years after diagnosis. For this reason, early diagnosis and treatment of suspicious growths on the ovaries is of great importance.

What Are the Signs and Symptoms?

Most ovarian cysts and tumors cause no symptoms and are discovered only during medical checkups when the ovary is found to be enlarged. If there are symptoms, they may be similar to the signs of ectopic pregnancy and may include pain on the right or left sides of the lower abdomen, a feeling of presure or fullness in the area, and bleeding from the vagina.

What Is the Treatment?

If the cyst or tumor is less than 3 inches in diameter, if it is not causing symptoms, and if the woman is in her reproductive years, the usual treatment is to wait for a month to see if the growth will start to shrink and dissolve on its own. Birth control pills or similar hormones may be given for a month or two to suppress the functioning of the ovaries. Functional cysts or tumors should regress with this treatment.

If the growth is larger than three inches in diameter, causes pain or bleeding, or occurs in a woman who has passed menopause, the chances of cancer or other serious problems are higher, and exploratory surgery is usually done immediately to biopsy the growth and determine the type of cyst or tumor. A pregnancy test, sonogram, and X-ray of the abdomen are other diagnostic tests that may be done to determine whether the problem could be an ectopic pregnancy or a growth on the uterus instead of an ovarian problem. Sonograms may also be able to distinguish between a fluid-filled cyst and a solid tumor. Exploratory surgery may be done through a laparoscopy or laparotomy (see Chapter 10, for an explanation of these surgeries). Noncancerous cysts and tumors can usually be removed surgically without removing the ovary. In the case of very large growths, the ovary may be taken out as well, but the woman's remaining ovary is usually able to produce sufficient hormones. If the remaining ovary is not damaged and the woman was fertile before the problem developed, she should continue to be fertile, producing eggs with the remaining ovary.

Ovarian cancer has a high fatality rate, in part because it often is well advanced before the woman has symptoms. Even if only one ovary has been affected, it is usually treated by removing both ovaries, the Fallopian tubes, and the uterus. Radiation or chemotherapy may be needed as well. Some doctors recommend that women over 45 have their ovaries removed (if they are having abdominal surgery for another reason) to prevent the risk of ovarian cancer. Unfortunately, removal of the ovaries can cause other problems, so women who are considering this procedure should investigate the risks and benefits carefully. A woman who has had a hysterectomy but still has her ovaries still needs regular pelvic exams to check for ovarian problems.

Bartholin's Gland Cysts

What Are They?

The Bartholin's glands are two small glands located on either side of the entrance to the vagina.

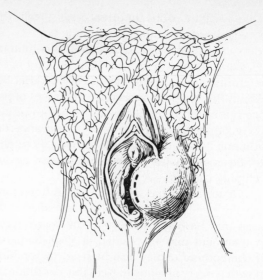

FIGURE 12–18. *An infected Bartholin's gland.*

They secrete a small amount of fluid during sexual excitement. The Bartholin's glands cannot be seen or felt under normal conditions, but it is not uncommon for one or both to develop a cyst if the duct that carries fluid produced by the gland becomes clogged. Approximately 2 percent of women seen for gynecological examinations have a small Bartholin's gland cyst. The glands can also become infected and abscess, although this is not common (Figure 12–18). Disease organisms apparently enter the gland through the ducts that carry fluid out.

How Serious Are They?

Bartholin's gland problems are not serious, but they can produce a lot of discomfort and can interfere with sexual enjoyment. Small cysts in the gland are usually not a problem. If they become large, they can be uncomfortable and interfere with sexual intercourse. An infected Bartholin's gland can be extremely painful if an abscess develops. Women who have had one infection tend to have recurrences.

What Are the Signs and Symptoms?

Symptoms of a Bartholin's cyst are a firm, small lump just outside the vaginal opening (Figure 12–18). Such lumps are usually not tender or sore, but may be irritated by intercourse. An infection and abscess will produce redness, soreness, and a hot feeling, as well as a painful, tender lump that can swell rapidly to a size as large as a lime.

What Is the Treatment?

Small Bartholin's cysts usually cause no problems and are not treated. When there is a large cyst, usually the whole gland is removed surgically. This can be done at a surgical center or hospital, usually with general (sleep) anesthesia.

An infected or abscessed Bartholin's gland may be treated in one of several ways. Antibiotics may be given to combat the infection, the abscess may be lanced and drained, and minor surgery may be done to prevent the abscess from recurring. An incision to drain the abscess may be done at the doctor's office under local anesthesia, or in a surgical center or hospital under general anesthesia. Usually a wick of gauze or other material will be left in the incision for a few days to assure continued drainage. Often the incision will be stitched around the edges (called *marsupialization* of the gland) in order to prevent the duct from healing closed, so that an abscess or cyst cannot form again.

Surgical treatment of Bartholin's gland problems is minor surgery and involves few risks except for the risks associated with anesthesia. However, the glands are located in a sensitive area of the body, and may be painful, swollen, and tender for two to three weeks after surgery until recovery is complete.

BREAST PROBLEMS

Swelling and Tenderness

Most women experience some swelling and tenderness of the breasts during the few days before their menstrual period begins. This is caused by hormonal changes that cause the body (including the breasts) to retain fluid. Pregnant women also often have these symptoms.

In addition, as many as 30 percent of women between the ages of 35 and 50 develop a condition called **fibrocystic breast syndrome,** which is really not a disease but a naturally occurring condition possibly related to an excess of the hormone estrogen. Fibrocystic breast syndrome is most likely to develop in a woman who is not ovulating, so that her body is not producing other hormones, such as progesterone, to balance the estrogen in her body. The condition improves or disappears after menopause when estrogen levels are lower (unless the woman takes estrogen supplements). A woman with fibrocystic breast syndrome has many small cysts in her breast tissues, which swell up in the days before her period, when the body retains more water. These cysts are different from other breast lumps in that they change size during the menstrual cycle. They are at their smallest at the end of menstrual bleeding and at their largest just before the next period begins. Large cysts caused by this

condition are discussed later in the section on breast lumps.

Breast swelling and tenderness is only a minor problem for most women, but for some the swelling can be so great that the breasts ache, feel very heavy, and are painful to the touch. Lymph nodes under the arms may also ache. Fortunately, there is a great deal that women can do to reduce these symptoms through self-care. (See information on prevention of premenstrual syndrome (PMS) earlier in this chapter.) The same techniques will help to prevent or reduce premenstrual breast swelling and tenderness. In addition, several changes in diet have been shown to be effective in reducing the number and size of fibrocystic lumps. The most important one is avoidance of caffeine. Caffeine (and similar compounds) is found not just in coffee, but in tea, colas, and chocolate as well. Most women who avoid caffeine get some relief from fibrocystic breast syndrome within one or two months. Some notice a change immediately. Avoiding smoking also seems to help. Vitamin B complex and vitamin E supplements have also been shown to be helpful. A well-fitting bra with good support also helps to reduce symptoms.

Medical treatment for breast tenderness includes pain relievers such as aspirin, Motrin, or Tylenol; diuretics (water pills); and treatment with hormones such as progesterone. Diuretics can cause health problems by reducing potassium in the body, which must be replaced by eating potassium-rich foods such as bananas and cranberries, or by taking potassium supplements. The hormone drugs that suppress the woman's monthly cycle also have a number of side effects.

Discharge from the Nipples

Discharge from the nipples may occur at many different points in a woman's life and can be due to many different causes. Many pregnant women notice a small amount of discharge from the nipples. This is usually perfectly normal but should be mentioned to the doctor or other prenatal caregiver at a checkup. A milky discharge in a woman who has not just delivered and is not nursing a baby is known as **galactorrhea.** It may be (but is not necessarily) caused by elevated levels of a hormone called prolactin. An increase in prolactin may be stimulated by a number of factors, including certain drugs such as tranquillizers, antidepressants, and antihypertensives (drugs for high blood pressure). Chest surgery, shingles, tumors of the pituitary gland, and hypothyroidism (low-functioning thyroid) can also cause this condition, as can prolonged stimulation of the breasts as part of sexual activity.

Growths in the breast that can cause breast discharge include fibrocystic breast disease, papilloma (a noncancerous tumor of the breast duct), and breast cancer. Infection can also be a cause. A discharge from both nipples is likely to be related to elevated prolactin, while a discharge from only one breast is more likely to be caused by a growth or an infection.

There is a great variation in the appearance of the fluid discharged from the breasts; in galactorrhea (prolactin-caused discharge) it may be clear or milky in appearance, whereas with fibrocystic disease or infection it may be yellow or green, and in the case of papilloma or breast cancer it may be bloody.

Treatment of breast discharge depends on the cause of the problem. Any woman with a discharge from the nipples should seek medical care, as it can be a symptom of serious illness. Fortunately, in most cases it is not.

Breast Lumps

This section is divided into two parts, "Benign (Noncancerous) Lumps" and "Breast Cancer."

Benign (Noncancerous) Lumps

What are they? Benign breast lumps are usually caused by fibrocystic breast disease, described earlier. There are two types, **cysts,** which are fluid-filled sacs of tissue that often swell and shrink during the menstrual cycle, and **fibroadenomas,** which are made up of a solid mass of tissue and are less likely to change during the monthly cycle. Both types of growths are common in women in their reproductive years, particularly during the thirties and forties, but fibroadenomas are more common in adolescents. After menopause, both cysts and fibroadenomas tend to shrink and may even disappear.

How serious are they? Cysts and fibroadenomas are very common and are not a serious health problem. They can cause considerable discomfort or even be disfiguring if they grow very large, but if this happens they are not difficult to treat. What makes cysts and fibroadenomas an important health problem is that breast cancer creates lumps that are very similar. For this reason, all breast lumps should be examined by a medical care provider.

What are the signs and symptoms? Cysts and fibroadenomas are generally painless, movable lumps, which may be round or irregular in shape and may be clustered, several together. Cysts may feel like liquid under pressure, like small water bal-

loons. Fibroadenomas are firmer and may have a stringy texture. Women who have fibrocystic disease may have breasts that feel both stringy and lumpy all over. During breast self-examination they try (it can be very difficult) to identify *new* lumps or *changes* in the texture of the breast (see breast self-examination techniques earlier in this chapter). If a woman finds a lump in her breast and she is not in a high-risk group for breast cancer (see next section), she may choose to wait a month to see if it changes size with her menstrual cycle, in which case she can be reasonably sure it is not cancerous. If she seeks medical treatment immediately, she may be asked to return after a few weeks to check for changes.

Most breast lumps are first noticed by women themselves, but there are other ways in which they can be diagnosed. Some are identified by health care practitioners during checkups. Others are identified by an X-ray of the breasts, called mammography.

What is the treatment? The first step with cysts and fibroadenomas is to evaluate them to be sure they are not cancerous. If a cyst is suspected, a needle aspiration is usually performed to attempt to draw out the fluid. For a needle aspiration, the doctor inserts a fine needle into the breast, punctures the cyst, and tries to draw out fluid (Figure 12–19). Sometimes a local anesthetic is used to deaden the nerves where the needle goes in, but needle aspiration is not normally a very painful procedure. If all the fluid can be withdrawn, the cyst usually collapses and disappears. The fluid can be sent to a laboratory for testing for cancer

FIGURE 12–19. *Needle aspiration of a cyst in the breast.*

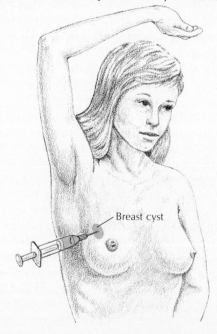

Breast cyst

cells, but cysts of this type are almost never cancerous.

If a lump cannot be aspirated, or if it is not completely gone after aspiration, the next step is biopsy, which is the removal of a sample of the lump for laboratory examination. There are several types of biopsy, the simplest of which is needle biopsy. Needle biopsy can be performed in a doctor's office. A local anesthetic is injected under the skin, and then a large needle is used to punch out a section of the breast lump, which is then sent to a laboratory. Other biopsies require a one- to two-inch incision in the breast through which a sample or all of the breast lump can be removed for examination. General anesthesia (sleep) or local anesthesia may be used for this procedure, which is done in a hospital or outpatient surgery center and usually does not require the woman to stay overnight.

Laboratory tests on a breast biopsy can take more than a week to complete. In some cases women are asked to sign consent for a mastectomy to be done at the same time as the biopsy, if the biopsy proves to be cancerous. In these cases a quick examination of a sample of the tumor is performed, while the surgeon and the patient wait, and then a mastectomy is performed if cancer is present. This approach is not recommended because the quick laboratory results obtained are not as accurate or complete as the tests that take longer. There is a small chance that a mastectomy might be done unnecessarily.

Breast Cancer

What is it? Breast cancer is the most common cancer affecting women, causing 27 percent of all cancer in women, and approximately 110,000 new cases in the United States each year. Over 37,000 women die each year from breast cancer, and an infant girl born today has a 1 in 11 chance of developing the disease.

Breast cancer is usually found as a small lump of cancerous cells growing in a woman's breast. It may spread to the lymph nodes under the arm, and can metastasize (spread) to start cancerous growths in other parts of the body as well. Breast cancer is rare among younger women, but becomes increasingly common after age 40. The causes are not known, but some women are much more likely to develop it than others.

How serious it it? Breast cancer is a very serious disease, which is usually fatal if it is not treated. It is the most common cause of death for women between the ags of 40 and 44 in the United States and a major health threat for all women over 40. Fortunately, when breast cancer is treated be-fore it spreads to other parts of the body, 96 percent of the women treated are cured. (Cancer cure rates are measured by whether the person is alive without cancer symptoms five years after treatment.) If breast cancer has spread (metastasized) to other parts of the body, the survival rate is much lower. For this reason early diagnosis and treatment of breast cancer are very important.

What are the signs and symptoms? While most breast lumps are not cancerous, a persistent lump in the breast, especially one that does not change with the woman's menstrual cycle, may be cancer. Other signs to watch for are:

An unusual thickening or swelling of part of the breast

Redness or scaliness of the skin on the breast or nipple

Dimpling of the skin on the breast or changes in breast shape

Retraction or inversion of the nipple or nipple pain or tenderness

Discharge from the nipple.

In the early stages breast cancer is usually a small and painless lump. A woman may not notice it unless she does a careful breast self-examination each month.

Some women have a higher risk of developing breast cancer than others. The following factors have been shown to put women in the high-risk group:

Previous breast cancer
Female relatives who have had breast cancer
First menstrual period before age 12
Menopause after age 55
Never gave birth
First child born after age 30
Noncancerous breast disease
Overweight
Cancer of the uterus

Women who have a mother or sister who developed breast cancer before menopause have an eight times greater risk than others.

There has been concern that long-term exposure to estrogen drugs such as birth control pills and to estrogen replacement therapy (ERT) after menopause may create a higher risk of breast cancer. Birth control pills have been in use in the United States for over twenty years now, and so far there is no evidence that they increase the risk of breast cancer. Estrogen replacement therapy has been suspected of increasing risk, but this has not been established. Recently another hormone, progestin, has been added to estrogen replacement therapy to help prevent increased risk of cancer. It is believed that this new type of ERT does not cause increased risk.

Successful treatment of breast cancer depends on early diagnosis. If all cases of breast cancer were treated early, few women would die from the disease. There are three steps women can take to identify breast cancer early, when treatment is very successful:

1. *Monthly breast self-examination by all women over age 20.*
2. *Yearly professional examination of the breasts for all women over 40 by a health care provider who specializes in women's health care. Examination every three years for women under 40.*
3. *Yearly mammography for all women over 50; mammography (X-ray of the breasts) every one to two years for women 40 to 50.*

In addition, a single mammography is recommended for all women between the ages of 35 and 40 to serve as a baseline for comparison of future X-rays. Mammography can detect changes in breast tissue and lumps that are too small to identify with the fingers. It is a very important tool in early detection of breast cancer.

What is the treatment? There are four major treatments for breast cancer:

1. Surgery, usually a mastectomy (removal of the breast)
2. Radiation
3. Chemotherapy (treatment with drugs)
4. Hormone therapy

It is common for a woman to receive two or more of these treatments in combination, depending on the type of cancer she has and the extent to which it has spread outside the breast.

Mastectomy and lumpectomy Mastectomy is a general term used for surgical removal of the breast. There are several different kinds of mastectomies that remove different amounts of the tissue. **Lumpectomy** refers to surgical removal of the cancerous lump and the tissue surrounding it only, leaving the rest of the breast in place (Figure 12–20). Lumpectomy combined with other nonsurgical treatment is used to treat women who have breast cancer in the very early stages, and it appears to be as effective as mastectomy in these cases. Figure 12–20 shows the three kinds of mastectomies most commonly performed:

(A) The **simple mastectomy**, in which only the breast is removed

(B) The **modified radical mastectomy**, in which the breast and some lymph nodes are removed

(C) The **radical mastectomy**, in which the breast, the muscles underlying it, and all the lymph nodes that drain the breast are removed

In the past, the radical mastectomy was performed on almost all women with breast cancer because it was believed to give the greatest protec-

FIGURE 12–20. *Four types of surgery for breast cancer.*

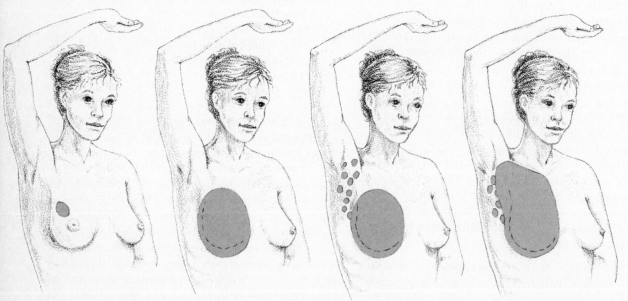

Lumpectomy: Only the tumor and surrounding tissue is removed

Simple mastectomy: The entire breast is removed

Modified radical mastectomy: The breast and lymph nodes are removed

Radical mastectomy: The breast, lymph nodes, and underlying muscles are removed

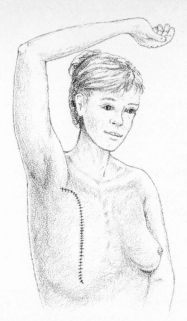

FIGURE 12–21. *A mastectomy scar.*

tion against recurrence of the disease. However, the radical mastectomy also created health problems for many women, including permanent swelling of the arm on the side treated (due to loss of lymph nodes which drain fluid from the arm) and partial loss of ability to move the arm. In recent years it has been shown that most women do as well with the simple or modified procedures, and some can even be treated with a lumpectomy. Simple or modified mastectomies are now the most commonly performed surgery. These procedures are less likely to cause health problems and are less disfiguring than the radical mastectomy.

Mastectomy leaves a long, 6- to 8-inch vertical scar, and a permanently changed body (Figure 12–21). Surgical reconstruction of a breast through plastic surgery using tissue from other parts of the body is a possibility for many women. For others there is a choice of breast prostheses made of soft plastic, silicone, or polyester. Prostheses can be created in exactly the size, shape, and weight of the missing breast. Women with mastectomies can wear normal clothing, including bathing suits. Some women choose not to wear a prosthesis.

Radiation   Radiation therapy is used either before or after surgery to kill cancer cells in the area of the breast or the lymph nodes under the arm.

Chemotherapy   Chemotherapy is used primarily to kill cancer cells related to the breast cancer that may be found throughout the body. In the past it was thought that a cancerous tumor in the breast had to grow for a while before it spilled cells out to other parts of the body. Now there is evidence that, with some kinds of cancer, the cells are found throughout the body from the beginning. Chemotherapy is often used in addition to surgery.

Hormone therapy   Hormone therapy in the treatment of breast cancer is used to suppress estrogen in the woman's system, because estrogen seems to encourage the growth of certain types of cancers (although it is not known to cause them to appear in the first place).

Choosing Treatment

A woman who is diagnosed with breast cancer usually has several choices of treatment. Knowledge about which treatments are most effective is still growing rapidly, and there is often disagreement within the medical field about them. Trying to make a decision can be very confusing, but there are two important rules to follow in coming to a decision:

1.   *Don't rush into anything.* Take the time needed to find out about all the choices for treatment. Don't sign consent for a mastectomy at the same time a biopsy is done. Then, if the lump is cancerous, you can consider all your options and make an informed choice.

2.   *Get expert opinion.* Seek out specialists in breast cancer at hospitals that specialize in cancer or at university medical schools. Read up on the latest treatments and research results. Get a second or third opinion.

Emotional and psychological issues   Breast cancer is very frightening for women. The fear of cancer is one of the reasons many women don't examine their own breasts regularly and don't seek medical care when they find a breast lump. Besides the fear of possible death from cancer, most women fear losing a breast to mastectomy. A woman's breasts are part of her feminine appearance and her identity as a woman, as well as being a source of pleasure for her and for her sexual partner. Many women also fear sexual rejection by their partner or by future partners.

Even though breast cancer is frightening, there is nothing to be gained by denial or by avoiding medical treatment for the problem. Recovery from the disease depends on early treatment. There are now several hundred thousand women in the United States who have had mastectomies. There are also support groups, such as Reach to Recovery (sponsored by the American Cancer Society) made up of women who have had mastectomies who help others adjust to the changes. They can have a very positive effect on a woman's recovery and adjustment. There are also specialty stores that supply custom-made breast prostheses, and specially

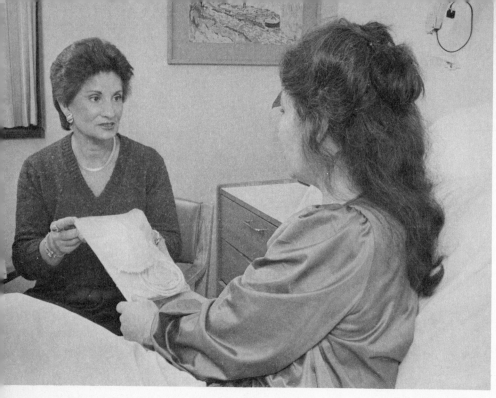

A Reach-to-Recovery volunteer visits a mastectomy patient.

designed lingerie and bathing suits are also available.

The discovery of breast cancer is a tremendous threat to a woman's physical and emotional being, but each year thousands of women are getting treatment, recovering, and being able to carry on normal lives. When emotional recovery is difficult or prolonged, counseling can be very helpful and supportive.

PELVIC RELAXATION SYNDROME

What Is It?

Pelvic relaxation syndrome is the name given to a set of symptoms related to relaxation of muscles and ligaments in the pelvis that hold the reproductive organs in place. Some of the conditions caused by pelvic relaxation syndrome are:

1. Vaginal hernias, such as:
    Cystocele: hernia of the wall of the bladder into the vagina
    Urethrocele: Hernia of the urethra into the vagina
    Rectocele: Hernia of the wall of the large intestine into the vagina
2. Vaginal prolapse: Dropping of the upper part of the vagina toward the vaginal opening
3. Prolapsed uterus: Dropping of the cervix and uterus toward the vaginal opening

About half of all women have some degree of pelvic relaxation after menopause, although few have serious enough problems to require treatment. Many women also develop pelvic relaxational problems during the reproductive years, as a result of conditions such as:

1. Giving birth to many children
2. Vaginal or abdominal surgery
3. Overweight
4. Conditions such as a chronic cough or chronic constipation, which causes straining of abdominal and pelvic muscles.

The tendency to develop pelvic relaxation syndrome may also be inherited.

How Serious Is It?

Pelvic relaxation syndrome is not a serious problem for most women. In some cases, however, it can cause extreme discomfort and be a danger to health. For example, cystocele and urethrocele are common causes of stress incontinence, a condition in which the woman cannot hold her urine. Rectocele can cause chronic constipation. The vagina and uterus can drop so far that they protrude outside the body through the opening of the vagina.

What Are the Signs and Symptoms?

Many women develop some symptoms of pelvic relaxation syndrome after menopause, when muscles and tendons naturally start to relax as part of the aging process. Other women may start to notice symptoms after childbirth or after vaginal or abdominal surgery. Symptoms of cystocele, urethrocele, and rectocele may include stress incontinence or difficulty having a bowel movement. Symptoms of vaginal or uterine prolapse may be a heavy feeling or feeling of pressure in the pelvis. The feeling is usually more noticeable at the end of the day, particularly after standing for hours. It may add to a sense of tiredness. The cervix may be noticeably lower, so that the woman or her sexual partner notices a barrier or a change in the space inside the vagina during intercourse. In severe cases the woman may find that part of her vagina or uterus actually protrudes from her body when she strains her abdominal muscles, for example in having a bowel movement. The problem can be diagnosed by the woman's symptoms and a pelvic exam.

Urinary Incontinence

Urinary incontinence is the problem of not being able to hold one's urine. It is quite a common problem for women, with almost one-third of the women seen at one gynecology clinic reporting that they had this problem at some time during their lives. The most common cause is relaxation of the pelvic muscles, which hold the bladder, urethra, vagina, and uterus in place. If these muscles are weak, the woman may suffer from stress incontinence, or losing urine when physical stress is placed on these muscles (for example, when coughing, sneezing, laughing, or running). Urgency incontinence, which is less common, refers to involuntary loss of urine, acompanied by a strong urge to urinate. This can develop during urinary tract infections when the bladder and urethra are very irritated, or can be a symptom of emotional stress and anxiety. Some women report feeling that they lose urine when they have an orgasm during sexual intercourse. This feeling is thought to be due to fluid (not urine) expelled by some women at the time of orgasm when the Grafenberg spot or G spot (see Chapter 3) is stimulated. Urinary incontinence is not usually a serious problem, although it can be embarrassing and inconvenient.

What Is the Treatment?

Most of the problems associated with pelvic relaxation are mild and do not require treatment. Mild problems, including cases of stress incontinence, can often be improved with exercises to improve the strength of the pelvic floor muscles (see Kegel's exercises, discussed below). Severe cases may require surgery to repair hernias of the vaginal wall; to reposition the bladder, urethra, and vagina; and/or to tighten relaxed muscles and ligaments. In approximately one-third of women who have surgery for stress incontinence, the problem recurs within a few years. Hysterectomy is sometimes done as part of surgery to repair a prolapsed uterus

or vagina, particularly if the woman does not wish to have more children or if there are other medical problems that make a hysterectomy desirable.

If surgery is not desired or not desirable because of other medical conditions, a prolapsed uterus or vagina can sometimes be held in place by a pessary, a rubber ring or loop that rests behind the pubic bone and extends up into the back of the vagina (behind the cervix) to hold it in place. This device must be removed every few weeks for cleaning and can cause vaginitis. It is not likely to be recommended for women who are sexually active.

Kegel's Exercises

Kegel's exercises were developed by Dr. Arnold H. Kegel to help women suffering from mild stress incontinence to regain control over their urination by strengthening the pubococcygeus muscle. This muscle runs from the pubic bone in front to the end of the spine, or coccyx, in the back, around the urethra, vagina, and rectum (see Chapter 1, Figure 1–3). The strength of this muscle allows a woman to control her bladder and also affects the muscular tone of her vagina during sexual intercourse. Kegel's exercises are often prescribed as preparation for childbirth and for tightening pelvic muscles after delivery. They are used in sex therapy to help women who have difficulty enjoying sex or having orgasms to tighten the muscles at the entrance to the vagina, which increases the sensations of intercourse.

To identify the pubococcygeus muscle, a woman should stand or sit over the toilet with her legs spread and try to start and stop the flow of urine several times. The muscle required to do this is the one to work on.

To strengthen this muscle, the woman should try to tighten it as much as possible, hold for five seconds, and then slowly release. She should practice this exercise in sets of 10 several times a day and should expect improvement in ability to control urine within a few weeks. Many women report increased sexual pleasure as well. This exercise can be practiced any time in any position and will not be noticed by other people, so it is easy to do while driving a car, at the office, or resting at home.

ENDOMETRIOSIS

What Is It?

The lining of the uterus, which is shed each month as menstrual blood, is called the endometrium. Endometriosis occurs when patches of endometrial tissue are found outside the uterus, usually on and around the ovaries and on the outer surface of the uterus. These patches of tissue respond to the same hormonal cycles that cause the woman to have menstrual periods. They grow and thicken during the month and bleed during the woman's period. These monthly changes and bleeding outside the uterus often cause severe pain, especially during the few days before the menstrual period begins and during the period. Endometriosis is also an important cause of infertility.

The number of cases of endometriosis has increased greatly in the last forty years. It is estimated that 5 to 20 percent of all women have some endometriosis. The disease is most common among women in their late twenties and thirties who have not had a child. The increase in numbers of women with the disease is believed to be related to recent changes in society, specifically the pattern of women pursuing careers and delaying childbearing until their thirties. Once endometriosis develops, it gradually worsens over time unless the woman either becomes pregnant or enters menopause. Both pregnancy and menopause suppress the hormonal cycles that feed the growth and spread of endometriosis.

How Serious Is It?

Endometriosis is a common cause of chronic pelvic pain, painful menstrual periods, and painful sexual intercourse. It is estimated to be the cause of 6 to 15 percent of infertility cases in women. Over time, the disease can cause considerable damage to the tissues surrounding the uterus, Fallopian tubes, and ovaries, and can spread to the outer surface of the large intestine, the bladder, and other areas of the abdomen. In rare cases endometriosis has caused problems by migrating to other parts of the body, including the nose and the lungs. Adhesions and other scar tissue can develop, causing pain and other problems in the functioning of the bladder and bowels. In rare cases, large cysts formed by endometrial material can rupture, spilling blood into the abdomen and causing acute illness requiring emergency surgery.

What Are the Signs and Symptoms?

It is believed that many women have mild cases of endometriosis but are not aware of it because it causes no symptoms. The amount of pain a woman experiences from endometriosis seems to depend on the location of the patches of endometrial tissue. The most common symptoms are severe pain in the few days before a menstrual period and during the first few days of bleeding. Painful intercourse is also a common complaint. This seems to be due to patches of endometrial tissue in the ab-

domen between the back of the uterus and the colon and around the base of the uterus (Figure 12–22). Pain is caused when the man's penis touches the back of the cul de sac or moves the cervix. It is typical for these painful symptoms to increase slowly over the years. Inability to become pregnant is another common symptom.

The cause of endometriosis is not known. The most accepted theory is that bits of the endometrium escape from the uterus through the Fallopian tubes and attach themselves to tissues outside the uterus. As these tiny patches of tissue thicken and bleed in response to the hormones that guide the menstrual cycle, they cast off cells that spread the disease to other parts of the abdomen.

Symptoms of endometriosis are often similar to those for pelvic inflammatory disease. The only way a definite diagnosis of endometriosis can be made is through surgery. Laparoscopy (see Chapter 10) is commonly used to look at the pelvic organs and to remove small deposits of endometrial tissue.

What Is the Treatment?

The treatment of endometriosis depends on how serious the symptoms are, the woman's age, and her plans for childbearing. If the symptoms are mild and infertility is not a problem, no treatment may be needed. For serious symptoms and infertility caused by endometriosis, there are two approaches to treatment: use of hormones and surgery.

Hormonal therapy for endometriosis has the goal of suppressing the functioning of the ovaries, (as birth control pills do). This reduces the spread and symptoms of the disease. Hormone therapy creates a hormone balance similar to pregnancy or

FIGURE 12–22. *Common locations of endometriosis.*

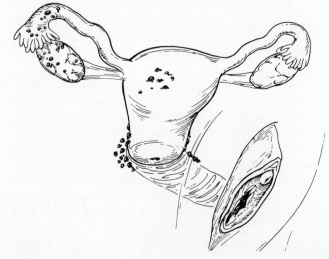

menopause in the woman and maintains it for nine months to a year. Most women's symptoms are much improved after this treatment, and as many as 40 percent of those who were infertile before as a result of endometriosis may be able to conceive after this treatment. These treatments have possible side effects and risks which a woman considering them should discuss in detail with her doctor. Endometriosis will recur in almost 20 percent of women within a year after treatment.

Surgery for endometriosis involves opening the abdomen and removing as much of the endometrial material and scar tissue as possible. Women who do not plan to have more children may be advised to have a hysterectomy (removal of the uterus) and possibly an oophorectomy (removal of the ovaries) as well. (These two surgeries are discussed later in this chapter.)

PELVIC PAIN AND PAINFUL INTERCOURSE

Normal Discomfort

Pain in the lower abdomen or pelvic area is a common reason for women to seek medical care and a good indicator that there may be a health problem. Most women occasionally experience discomfort in the pelvic area. Menstrual cramps, ovulation, and intestinal problems such as constipation and diarrhea can cause temporary discomfort from time to time. But when a woman experiences unusual discomfort, pain that does not go away, or pain along with other symptoms of illness, she should seek medical care.

Vaginal Pain

Pain around the entrance to the vagina can have several causes. Often it is noticed because it makes sexual intercourse painful. Vaginal infections such as yeast and trichomonas, herpes, allergic reactions to soaps or douches, and sensitivity to contraceptive products such as foams or jellies are all common causes of vaginal pain.

In addition, intercourse can be painful and the vaginal tissues can become irritated if there is not enough lubrication of the vagina. A woman's body may not produce enough natural lubrication for many resons, including lack of sexual arousal or beginning intercourse before arousal is complete, the use of antihistamines and other medications, and low levels of estrogen (sometimes found in women after menopause, nursing mothers, and during certain phases of the menstrual cycle).

When lack of lubrication is the problem, the first thing to try is a longer period of foreplay. Contraceptive products such as jellies, creams, and foams, or a water-soluble lubricating jelly used during intercourse will also help. For women who have passed menopause, dryness due to low estrogen can be prevented by using an estrogen vaginal cream or by estrogen replacement therapy. If dryness is due to insufficient arousal, the couple can solve the problem by taking more time to stimulate the woman before beginning intercourse.

Vaginal pain can also be the result of vaginismus (muscle tightness or spasms that make intercourse difficult or impossible). This problem seems to be linked to painful or traumatic sexual experiences in the past. The treatment is counseling and exercises to do at home (see Chapter 3) to help the woman overcome fear and become accustomed to vaginal penetration.

Frequent and prolonged sexual intercourse, especially when a woman is not accustomed to it, can cause pain and soreness in the vagina. This goes away within a day or so if the vagina is given a rest.

Urethral Pain

Pain around the urethra (urinary opening) during intercourse can be caused by many of the same things that irritate the vagina: lack of lubrication, vaginal infections, or lack of estrogen. In addition, positions for intercourse that cause the penis to rub directly against the urethra, as well as urethral and bladder infections, may cause pain.

Deep Pelvic Pain

Pain deep in the pelvic area may have many causes and may be linked with the woman's reproductive system, with the urinary system, or with the intestines. Problems that cause pain in this area often cause pain during intercourse as well, especially when there is deep thrusting of the penis. Common causes of deep pelvic pain during intercourse are:

Infections of the cervix, uterus, tubes, or ovaries
Fibroid cysts of the uterus
Endometriosis
Ovarian cysts
Scar tissue
A narrowed or shortened vagina after hysterectomy

These conditions are all discussed elsewhere in this chapter. In addition, bladder infections and various intestinal problems can cause pain in this area.

Pain of Unknown Cause

In some cases no cause can be found for pelvic pain, but it still persists. A woman in this situation should seek a second or third opinion if the pain is causing problems for her. Surgery does not usually help unless a specific problem has been found which can be treated, but surgery may be offered to help find a problem, such as endometriosis.

Some pelvic pain, like pain in other parts of the body such as headaches and backaches, may be caused by stress, emotional turmoil, and exhaustion. In these cases, counseling to identify the sources of stress and to learn how to minimize its effects may be helpful.

DES EXPOSURE

What Is DES?

DES stands for **diethylstilbestrol,** the first synthetic estrogen, which was developed in the 1930s and came into use for medical purposes in the early 1940s. The drug (along with two similar products, dienestrol and hexestrol) was sold under more than two hundred brand names, mainly in pill form but also as an injectable drug and cream. Its first use was to suppress milk production in women after childbirth and to reduce the estrogen deficiency symptoms of menopause. In 1942 the drug was also approved by the Food and Drug Administration for use on pregnant women to prevent miscarriage. Between 1942 and 1971 approximately two million pregnant American women were treated with DES, although there was never any evidence that the drug did help to prevent miscarriage. In the early 1970s it was discovered that the daughters born to women treated with DES during pregnancy were more likely to have defects of the reproductive system and to develop reproductive system cancer than were other women. Since that time, an increased likelihood of reproductive health problems for DES sons, and possible increased risk of reproductive cancer for DES mothers, have also been identified. Because of these findings, the use of DES on pregnant women is no longer approved by the FDA (since 1971).

How Does It Affect People?

There are three groups of people at risk for health problems related to the use of DES during pregnancy—the mothers, their daughters, and their sons. For daughters and sons, the chances of DES-caused health problems are greater if they were exposed to the drug during the first five months of the pregnancy. DES daughters are potentially the most severely affected group.

DES Daughters

DES daughters have higher rates of several reproductive health problems than other women their age.

1. They have a 1 in 700 to 1 in 7,000 risk of developing a form of vaginal cancer (clear cell adenocarcinoma) which is extremely rare in other women. Most of the cases identified so far have developed when the women were between the ages of 14 and 24. Clear cell adenocarcinoma is treated with surgery. Normally, the uterus, cervix, and part of the vagina must be removed. Plastic surgery may be needed later to rebuild portions of the vagina. Fortunately, most women who have developed this condition have recovered and are free of cancer.

2. It appears that DES daughters are more likely than other women to develop cervical dysplasia, a condition of abnormal cell growth on the surface of the cervix. Women with cervical dysplasia are more likely to develop cervical cancer than others.

3. An estimated 40 percent of DES daughters have abnormalities of the cervix and uterus (a cervical collar or hood and a narrow or T-shaped uterus are the most common). These abnormalities do not cause any known sexual or health problems but may contribute to the higher infertility and miscarriage rates of DES daughters.

4. DES daughters are more likely than other women to have cervical and vaginal adenosis, a condition in which the surface of the cervix and parts of the vagina are covered with glandular cells that are usually found only inside the cervix. This condition is usually harmless but is suspected of increasing the chances of cancer developing later.

5. DES daughters appear to have a much higher rate of menstrual and fertility problems, including menstrual irregularity, infrequent ovulation, and much higher rates of miscarriage.

DES Sons

The problems of DES sons have not received as much study, but it has been found that they have much higher rates of undescended testicles (see Chapter 1) and that a substantial percentage, perhaps as high as one-third, have some kind of abnormality of the penis or testicles such as testicular cysts, underdeveloped penis or testicles, or hypospadias (abnormal location of the urinary opening on the penis). DES sons also appear to be more likely to have a low sperm count or abnormal sperm cells than other men. This could cause infertility. There is no evidence that DES sons have a higher risk of cancer.

DES Mothers

It has been considered that DES mothers (the women who took DES during pregnancy) might have a higher risk of cancer of the breast, cervix, and ovaries than other women. However, several research studies have found no evidence of this.

What Is the Treatment?

The first step for anyone who suspects that he or she may be a DES mother, daughter, or son is to check the medical records to be sure. DES mothers should inform their children. The second step is to locate a physician who is knowledgeable about DES and has had some experience with other cases. For women, this will be an obstetrician/gynecologist; for men, it may be a pediatrician or a urologist. Anyone who has been exposed to DES needs a special medical evaluation and more frequent checkups than average.

The long-term effects of exposure to DES are not yet known. DES mothers may experience higher rates of reproductive cancers in old age. DES daughters and sons may develop cancers or other problems in the future. All persons exposed to DES should have annual checkups by a specialist familiar with DES cases and should follow the research findings about DES-related problems as they develop in the coming years.

SURGERY

Women in the United States need to be careful to avoid medical overtreatment. The U.S. health care system, although it is the best in the world in some respects, has a pattern of overtreating some women's health problems, often by surgery. In fact, most of the surgery performed in this country is done on women. Five of the seven most commonly performed operations are done exclusively on women. Women should think carefully and get several opinions before agreeing to any surgery, particularly surgery of the reproductive organs.

In the past some experts thought that a woman's reproductive organs had no function after menopause, and that their removal would simply eliminate possible sites for cancer in the future. Using this logic, surgery was often performed when less radical treatment might have been enough. Today we are aware that removal of the uterus and the ovaries can affect a woman's future sexual functioning, and it is suspected that her emotional well-being and possibly her general health can be affected as well. It is most important for each woman to find out all the possible treatments available to her when surgery is suggested, so that she can make an informed decision about which treatment is best for her.

D&C (Dilation and Curettage)

What Is It?

Dilation and curettage, commonly known as D&C, is the most common surgery performed in the United States. In fact, around 4 percent of all women in the United States undergo a D&C each year, and most women will have at least one D&C during their lifetime. D&C is minor surgery, with few medical risks. It involves dilation of the cervix and the scraping of the inside surface of the uterus with a spoon-shaped scraping instrument called a curette.

When Is It Needed?

D&C is performed for two major purposes. First, D&C provides the best method of diagnosing the cause of abnormal bleeding from the uterus. Abnormal bleeding can be a sign of uterine cancer, uterine polyps (small noncancerous growths on the inner wall of the uterus), or a hormone imbalance causing overgrowth of the lining of the uterus. Prolonged heavy bleeding can cause anemia and other health problems for women.

The second use of the D&C is to remove extra tissue that is sometimes left behind in the uterus after pregnancy and childbirth or after miscarriage. Bits of this placental tissue remaining in the uterus can cause serious bleeding, infection, and illness if they are not removed. In the past, D&C was used for early (first three months) abortions, but it has been replaced by the vacuum abortion method, which is faster and involves fewer risks. The vacuum procedure, which removes the lining of the uterus and any other contents, is also used instead of a D&C by some doctors to diagnose abnormal bleeding.

How Is It Performed?

D&C is performed in a hospital or outpatient surgery center. It does not usually require the woman to stay overnight. General (sleep) or spinal anesthesia is normally used, although it is possible to do the 10- to 20-minute surgery with local anesthesia. The procedure is very similar to an early abortion (described in Chapter 11). Normally, the woman will not be required to shave her pubic hair.

The surgery is performed with the woman in

position for a pelvic examination. After a thorough pelvic examination, the doctor inserts a speculum to hold the vagina open and attaches a tenaculum (clamp) to the cervix to steady it. Next, a slender instrument with a blunt end, called a uterine sound, is inserted through the cervix to the top of the uterus to measure its length. Following this, the opening of the cervix is dilated (made larger) by inserting a series of dilating rods (see Figure 11–2) through the mouth of the cervix to enlarge the opening. This is also sometimes done by inserting laminaria rods (slender sticks of dried seaweed) in the cervix the day before the D&C. As they absorb moisture from the body, the laminaria swell, gently and painlessly enlarging the cervical opening over a number of hours. When the woman comes in for surgery, the cervix is already dilated.

Once the cervical opening is enlarged to about half an inch in diameter, a slender instrument with a spoon-shaped end, called a curette, is inserted into the uterus and used to scrape the inner surface gently, removing the soft lining that is normally shed as a menstrual period (Figure 12–23). The tissue removed is saved for laboratory analysis. Scraping can take anywhere from 2 to 15 minutes, depending on what is found. Small uterine polyps can be removed at this time, and uterine fibroids can be diagnosed. Removal of fibroids usually requires additional surgery.

When surgery is over, the woman can usually leave the hospital or surgical center within an hour or two after she awakens from anesthesia. The general anesthesia used for a D&C is light, and the aftereffects do not last as long as the types used for major surgery. If local anesthesia was used, the woman may have been given sedatives as well and may have to wait for the effects to wear off. The woman will need a ride home from the hospital and should not plan to drive for 24 hours.

Recovery from a D&C is very quick. Some women experience mild abdominal cramps for a few hours and light bleeding for a few days after surgery, but the discomfort is usually minor. Most women can return to their normal activities within a day or two. Women are usually asked to avoid using tampons, douching, and having intercourse for the first two weeks after surgery to reduce chances of infection pasing into the uterus through the open cervix. After two weeks the cervix will have returned to normal.

A checkup one to two weeks after surgery is needed to make sure the cervix is closing properly and to check for possible infection. Laboratory results are usually available after a week, and your doctor may telephone with them or discuss them with you at the office. Cancer is not commonly found.

What Are the Risks?

The risks of serious complications from a D&C are very low; there are, however, a few women for whom D&C is considered risky. Conditions that

FIGURE 12–23. *Dilation and curettage (D&C).*

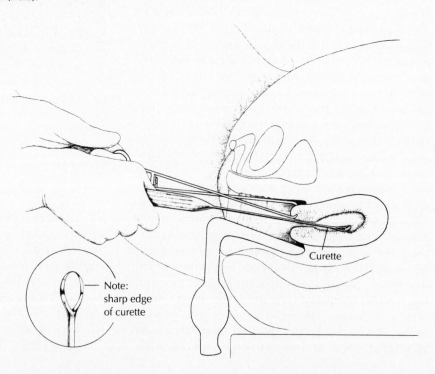

Note: sharp edge of curette

Curette

can make D&C unwise or unsafe include the following:

> Infection of the cervix, uterus, or Fallopian tubes
> Possible wanted pregnancy (D&C will act as an abortion)
> Serious medical problems, such as heart disease, that increase the risk of anesthesia
> Blood-clotting problems

The most common complication of D&C is infection. The uterus, Fallopian tubes, and ovaries can become infected by organisms transported into the uterus during surgery. This is most likely to happen if infection already exists in the vagina or cervix. For this reason, any known infections should be treated *before* surgery to minimize risks.

There is also a risk of hemorrhage or uncontrolled bleeding after D&C, although this is rare. Injury to the walls of the uterus or the cervix during surgery, a polyp or fibroid that is only partially removed, or blood-clotting problems can all be causes of hemorrhage.

It is possible, though exceedingly rare, for the uterus to be perforated (punctured) during D&C and for the bladder or intestines to be damaged as well. Uterine perforations usually heal themselves without problems, but an injury to the bladder, blood vessels, or intestines usually requires more surgery to repair.

A very rare complication of D&C is called **Asherman's syndrome**. In Asherman's syndrome a layer of scar tissue forms inside the uterus so the lining of the uterus (endometrium) cannot develop normally. This can cause infertility and prevent menstrual periods. This problem is more likely to develop if the uterus is infected at the time of surgery and then damaged by scraping too deeply.

Whenever general or spinal anesthesia is used, there is an additional risk of complications from these drugs.

The warning signs of problems after surgery include:

> Heavy bleeding (requiring more than one pad in one hour, or heavier than the heaviest day of the menstrual period and lasting for 6 to 12 hours)
> Severe and persistent abdominal cramps or pain
> A fever of 100.4 degrees Fahrenheit or higher
> Faintness, dizziness, or weakness
> Foul-smelling vaginal discharge

Does It Affect Sexuality?

D&C does not have any permanent effects on a woman's sexuality. She should avoid intercourse for about two weeks after surgery, as explained earlier.

Hysterectomy

What Is It?

Hysterectomy is surgery to remove a woman's uterus. Sometimes the ovaries and Fallopian tubes are also removed. It is the second most commonly performed operation in the United States (after D&C). Over 660,000 women in the United States have hysterectomies every year; if the current rate of operations continues, over 50 percent of women will have hysterectomies before they reach age 65.

Hysterectomy has been studied extensively because it appears that many of the operations done in the past were not necessary. There is evidence of overtreatment, particularly of certain groups of women. Women who live in parts of the country where there are many surgeons, and women who are poor and attend clinics where medical students are trained, are much more likely to receive hysterectomies than other women.

When Is It Needed?

THE SITUATIONS IN WHICH HYSTERECTOMY IS NEEDED TO SAVE A WOMAN'S LIFE ARE THE FOLLOWING:

> Invasive cancer of the vagina, cervix, uterus, Fallopian tubes, or ovaries
> Severe, uncontrollable hemorrhaging
> Severe, uncontrollable pelvic infection

CONDITIONS FOR WHICH A HYSTERECTOMY MAY BE DESIRABLE FOR SOME WOMEN ARE:

1. *Carcinoma* in situ *of the cervix:* Abnormal cells (dysplasia) and carcinoma *in situ* (cancer on the surface of the cervix) are conditions that are often treated with hysterectomy in women who do not plan to have more children. Other choices that leave the uterus in place are cryosurgery or conization of the cervix; both these treatments are described earlier in this chapter.

2. *Uterine fibroids:* If a woman has large uterine fibroids (especially if they cause excessive bleeding, back pain, or pelvic pain), hysterectomy may be needed. Other choices are a myomectomy to remove the fibroids but leave the uterus, and hormone treatment (because fibroids are stimulated by estrogen).

3. *Chronic pelvic infection:* If pelvic infections become chronic or recurrent and cause a great deal of pain and time lost to illness, a hysterectomy may become desirable. The other choice is continued treatment with antibiotics and pain-killing drugs.

4. *Endometriosis:* If the symptoms of endometriosis become so severe that the woman is disabled by the discomfort for several days each month, hysterectomy may be needed. The other choice is hor-

mone treatments, because endometriosis is stimulated by estrogen.

5. *Bleeding problems:* If uterine bleeding is continuous and heavy, it may sap the woman's health and cause anemia. There are many possible causes for this. Hysterectomy may be needed if the problem persists after treatment for possible hormone imbalance or infection has failed, and after endometrial biopsy and/or a D&C. Removal of an IUD can sometimes solve the problem. If bleeding is not severe, iron supplements can help prevent anemia.

6. *Prolapsed uterus:* If a prolapsed (dropped) uterus is causing severe pain, pressure, or difficulty in urinating or passing a bowel movement, a hysterectomy may be desirable, but most women with this condition do not need surgery.

HYSTERECTOMY SHOULD BE AVOIDED FOR THE FOLLOWING CONDITIONS:

1. *To prevent cancer:* When you do not have cancer or a precancerous condition of the cervix or uterus, hysterectomy and the health problems it can cause creates more risk than the chances of getting cancer.

2. *For sterilization:* Safer, easier, and cheaper methods exist (see Chapter 10).

3. *For pelvic pain of unknown cause:* Hysterectomy may not relieve the problem.

4. *For abortion:* Safer, easier, and cheaper methods exist (see Chapter 11).

5. *For cervicitis:* Hysterectomy is not needed.

6. *For uterine fibroids, prolapsed uterus, endometrio-*

sis, or irregular bleeding: If the condition is not causing discomfort or health problems, hysterectomy is not needed and the risks of surgery and anesthesia should be avoided.

Hysterectomy (or any surgery) should be performed only when it is needed. The risk of complications and of permanent effects on the woman's health (to be discussed) should be weighed against the possible benefits. Fortunately, hysterectomies are not usually needed on an emergency basis; in most cases the woman has time to think about her decision. She has time to get a second or third opinion from other doctors and time to read about hysterectomy and its effects. Sometimes there are other treatment choices that are not as extreme as hysterectomy. And sometimes waiting a few months may change the way the woman feels about the problem, or the condition itself may improve.

How Is It Performed?

There are different kinds of hysterectomies, as shown in Figure 12–24.

1. **Complete hysterectomy** (the most common procedure) refers to the removal of the uterus and cervix, leaving the Fallopian tubes, ovaries, and vagina.

2. **Complete hysterectomy with bilateral salpingo-oophorectomy** refers to the removal of the uterus, cervix, Fallopian tubes, and ovaries. In some cases, only one tube or ovary may be removed.

FIGURE 12–24. *Four types of hysterectomies (shaded areas indicate organs removed).*

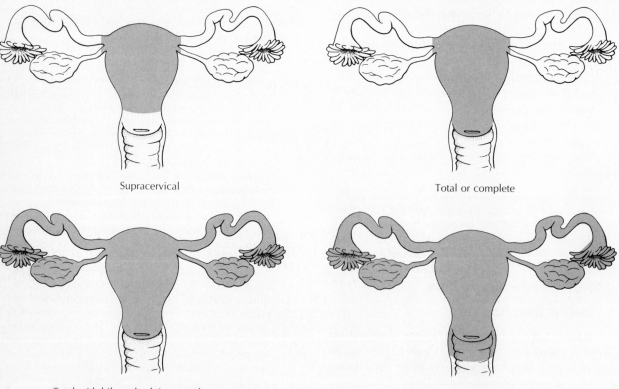

Supracervical

Total or complete

Total with bilateral salpingo-oophorectomy

Radical

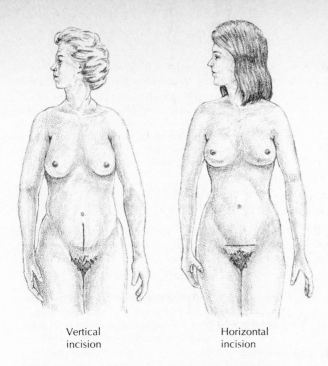

Vertical
incision

Horizontal
incision

FIGURE 12–25. *Abdominal hysterectomy: Two types of incisions.*

3. Less common types of hysterectomy are the **subtotal** **hysterectomy**, in which the uterus alone is removed and the cervix is left and the **radical hysterectomy**, in which the uterus, cervix, and tubes (and usually the ovaries) are all removed, along with the upper part of the vagina. The subtotal hysterectomy is not often used today because the cervix has no known function after the uterus is removed, and cancer of the cervix may develop later. The radical hysterectomy is used in cases of early invasive cervical cancer.

The woman's body can be approached in two different ways in performing a hysterectomy. In an **abdominal hysterectomy** (which is the most common) a five-inch incision is made in the woman's abdomen. This may be a vertical incision going from the navel to the pubic bone, or a horizontal incision across the lower abdomen just above the pubic hairline (Figure 12–25). If there are old abdominal scars, the surgeon may follow them and remove the old scar tissue.

The **vaginal hysterectomy** is performed through the vagina and is used only when the ovaries and tubes do not need to be removed (Figure 12–26). It is popular because it does not leave a scar that can be seen and because recovery is faster, since the abdominal wall has not been cut. There is more risk of infection with a vaginal hysterectomy, however, because of the many organisms that live in the vagina.

Recovery from Hysterectomy

A hysterectomy is major surgery and usually requires four to six days in the hospital. Full recov-

ery takes six to eight weeks for most women, but some women will take less time and some will need more. Many women feel tired for as long as six months to a year after the surgery. It is very important to take the time needed to recover; not to overdo; and to follow the surgeon's instructions about when to begin lifting, bathing, and sexual intercourse.

The **danger signs** that women should watch for after coming home from the hospital are:

Fever of 100.4 degrees Fahrenheit or higher
Severe pain
Heavy vaginal bleeding (soaking one pad in an hour)
Pain, bleeding, or other problems with urination
Lack of a bowel movement (for three days or more)
Pain, swelling, or tenderness in the leg
Chest pain, coughing, or difficulty breathing

During the first two weeks after surgery the woman will need to rest and avoid all lifting. She will not be able to do housework or care for children without help during this time. Showers are usually all right, but baths should be avoided. During the second to the fourth week the woman can gradually begin to do more of her usual activities.

At a postoperative checkup, usually done about four weeks after surgery, it can be decided when a woman will be ready to return to her normal activities, including work (usually about six weeks after surgery). Sexual intercourse can usually be resumed four to six weeks after surgery, although some couples begin sooner. If a woman's job is strenuous or involves heavy lifting, she may

FIGURE 12–26. *Vaginal hysterectomy: Location of the incision.*

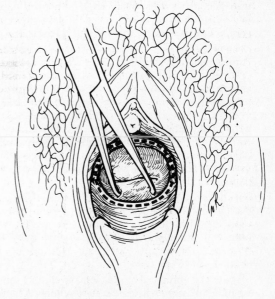

need to limit her work to part time for a few weeks after her return.

A woman who has had her ovaries removed will begin menopause immediately after surgery. Some women experience hot flashes from estrogen deficiency while they are still in the hospital. Estrogen replacement therapy (ERT) is usually prescribed to prevent the unwanted symptoms and risks of estrogen deficiency. Even women who have not had their ovaries removed may experience temporary symptoms of low estrogen. This is believed to be due to reduced blood flow to the ovaries during surgery. These symptoms usually disappear on their own within a few weeks or months, when the woman's ovaries begin to function again.

What Are the Risks?

The risk of death or serious complications from hysterectomy depends on the age and general health of the woman. For healthy women under 45, the death rate from the surgery is about 1 per 2,000 cases. It is higher for older women and women with serious health problems, especially high blood pressure.

Over 40 to 50 percent of women develop some complication from the surgery. The most common are:

1. *Infection:* Infections of the bladder and kidney, and of the incision site, are the most common complications. They are treated with antibiotics and usually clear up easily, but they may cause a longer hospital stay. Vaginal hysterectomies have an infection rate that is one and a half times as high as for the abdominal procedure.

2. *Hemorrhage:* Excessive bleeding can occur during surgery, and about 15 percent of all women require transfusions for this. In about 1 percent of cases heavy bleeding may develop 7 to 10 days after surgery, requiring hospitalization and transfusions.

3. *Urinary problems:* Problems with urination are common after hysterectomy and are a major cause of longer hospital stays because women must be kept in the hospital while a catheter (a thin plastic tube inserted through the urethra into the bladder to drain it) is needed to help them urinate. About 5 percent of women still cannot urinate on their own 12 days after hysterectomy. Normally these problems clear up within a few weeks after surgery, but in 1 out of 200 cases the surgery causes permanent damage to the urinary system.

4. *Intestinal problems:* If the intestines are damaged during surgery or if scar tissue from the hysterectomy grows in such a way that it interferes with intestinal functioning, more surgery may be needed to correct the problem. This occurs in about 1 out of 200 cases.

5. *Blood clots:* Abnormal blood clots develop in about 1 percent of women having hysterectomies. A blood clot can cause death if it breaks loose and travels through the bloodstream to the lungs or the brain.

6. *Other damage to the reproductive system:* In rare cases the vagina may be shortened or narrowed as a result of surgery, or the ability of the ovaries to produce hormones may be permanently damaged. Chronic vaginal discharge caused by problems in healing a vaginal incision also develops in a few cases.

7. *Emotional problems:* Some women experience bouts of depression in the weeks and months after hysterectomy. There are several possible reasons for this, including the stress of the surgery, the illness that preceded it, and the enforced rest and inactivity that comes after it. Further, removal of the uterus may cause a woman to feel that she is no longer feminine and womanly. In addition, many women experience rapid hormonal changes caused by the surgery, which may contribute to emotional upset. The age of the woman, her general health, and her family situation all make a difference in how likely she is to be depressed after surgery. If feelings of loss or depression are severe or last for more than two months, counseling can be very helpful.

Does It Affect Sexuality?

Little is known about sexual changes for women who have had hysterectomies, and more research is badly needed. Many women report less sexual desire and less enjoyment of sex after hysterectomy. Many others report better sexual experiences after surgery. Thus, it is not possible to predict how hysterectomy will affect sexuality for a specific woman.

Physical changes After hysterectomy, a woman is missing some organs in her abdomen that she previously had. The size and shape of her vagina may have changed slightly, and in most cases she no longer has a cervix. After such major surgery, some women may be afraid or may not wish to have sex at first for fear that they will be injured. At the least, when a woman begins to have intercourse after surgery, things will feel a little different. She may have a little pain and discomfort from sex until the internal healing is complete and she and her partner have adjusted to the changes in her body. These physical changes should not have a negative impact on sexuality once a couple has had a chance to adjust. Some women report that certain internal sensations of excitement or pleasure are gone after surgery and that their orgasms have changed. This is understandable because sexual activity does affect the uterus, causing increased blood flow and contractions at the time of orgasm. Fortunately, there are so many nerve endings in the woman's genital area that changes in sexual sensation do not mean a loss of ability to enjoy sex or to have orgasms. But the focus of sensation may move from one area to another.

Hormone changes If the ovaries are removed along with the uterus, the woman who has not already passed menopause will immediately begin it. The lower estrogen levels will cause physical changes and may affect sexuality. If one ovary or even part of an ovary is left, it usually will produce enough hormones to prevent premature menopause. Premenopausal women who do not have their ovaries removed may also experience a temporary loss of estrogen due to shock to the ovaries caused by surgery. These menopausal symptoms are usually temporary but can affect a woman's sexuality while they are present. Removal of the ovaries in women who are past menopause may also have hormonal effects, since the ovaries continue to produce low levels of several different hormones after menopause.

Fertility changes After hysterectomy a woman is sterile and can never become pregnant again. This change may have a profound emotional and psychological effect on the woman and on her sexual partner. The positive or negative feelings that each has about this change will affect how they feel about each other sexually. Couples who feared unwanted pregnancies often find that their sexual relationship is better after hysterectomy. Couples who are saddened by the loss of fertility may find sex less enjoyable than before.

Psychological and emotional changes Most women have strong feelings about hysterectomy and its effects. They may desire the surgery to end pain and discomfort or the risk of serious illness and possible death. At the same time, they may fear that losing the uterus makes them less feminine and perhaps less desirable to men. Their feelings may be conflicted, and in many cases women may not be aware of all their feelings. Emotional and psychological factors are probably more powerful than physical and hormonal changes in determining how a woman reports the effects of surgery on her sexuality.

Relationship changes The decision to have a hysterectomy is an important one in the life of the woman and often for her partner as well. How the couple handles this critical time is likely to affect their feelings for each other and thus to affect their sexual relationship. Consideration, understanding, patience, and gentleness on the part of both the man and the woman are likely to have a positive effect on sexual adjustment after surgery.

Conization

What Is It?

Conization, also known as **cone biopsy**, is a surgical procedure in which a cone-shaped section is removed from the cervix. It can be performed in an outpatient surgery center or a hospital. Conization is performed when there are abnormal or precancerous cells on the cervix. It serves two purposes. First, the tissue removed is sent to the laboratory for pathology analysis. Second, the coniztion often removes all the abnormal cell areas of the cervix so that no further treatment is needed. Conization removes more tissue than a cervical biopsy or cryosurgery, but much less tissue than a hysterectomy.

When Is It Needed?

Conization may be performed when a woman has mild to severe cervical dysplasia, CIN, or carcinoma *in situ* (discussed earlier in this chapter). The usual first step in diagnosis is colposcopy. When abnormal cell growth is mild and appears only on the surface of the cervix, it is usually treated with cryosurgery. But if the condition is more serious or appears to be located inside the entrance to the cervix, so that the full extent of the disease is not certain, conization may be chosen because it removes more cervical tissue, including the lower portion of the entance to the cervix. This material can then be evaluated by a pathologist, and if all abnormal tissue has been removed by the conization, further treatment may not be needed. If invasive cancer is found, a hysterectomy is needed. If the abnormal cells are carcinoma *in situ*, a hysterectomy may be chosen, especially if the woman does not want more children. When more children are desired, in many cases it is safe to wait a few years after conization before doing the hysterectomy, provided the woman is careful to get frequent checkups to make sure the condition has not become worse.

How Is It Performed?

Conization is usually performed under general anesthesia (sleep) in a hospital or outpatient surgery center. With the woman in position for a pelvic examination, the surgeon uses a speculum to hold the vagina open so the cervix can be seen. Then, using a scalpel, he or she carves out a cone-shaped portion of the cervix (Figure 12–27). Stitches are used to reduce bleeding, but the enlarged opening in the lower part of the cervix is not closed. It is not usually necessary to remain overnight in the

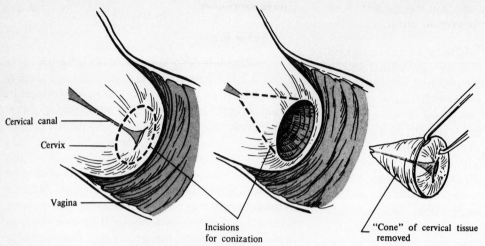

Cervical canal

Cervix

Vagina

Incisions
for conization

"Cone" of cervical tissue
removed

FIGURE 12–27. *Surgical conization of the cervix.*

hospital, although some physicians prefer to keep their patients overnight because of the risk of hemorrhage. Most women can return to their normal activities within 5 to 10 days, although bleeding and vaginal discharge may continue for several weeks after surgery. Sexual intercourse can usually be resumed three to four weeks after surgery.

What Are the Risks?

Hemorrhage or heavy bleeding is the most common complication of this surgery, creating problems for 1 in 10 women. Hospitalization, blood transfusion, or further surgery may be needed if hemorrhage develops. Bleeding problems are most likley to occur during surgery or a week to 10 days later, when the dissolving stitches placed in the cervix begin to disappear. Less common complications are infection and perforation (puncture) of the uterus. In addition, there is a small risk of serious health problems whenever general anesthesia is used.

The long-term effects of conization on the woman's fertility can also be serious. Because the cervical canal has been shortened, it may not be strong enoug to remain closed during pregnancy and may cause miscarriage or spontaneous abortion. This condition, called **cervical incompetence,** is more common in women who have had conization surgery. In addition, the loss of many of the glands located in the opening of the cervix that produce cervical mucus may cause difficulties in getting pregnant. Scar tissue in the cervical opening can also seal it off, preventing menstrual blood from flowing. Scar tissue can make childbirth more difficult by inhibiting dilation of the cervix. In spite of these risks, conization is often chosen by women who want more children, because the alternative,

hysterectomy, would make them permanently sterile.

Does It Affect Sexuality?

Intercourse must be avoided for several weeks while recovering from surgery. Conization is not believed to have any permanent effects on sexual functioning.

FOR FURTHER READING

GRAY, MADELINE. *The Changing Years: The Menopause without Fear.* New York: Doubleday, 1981.

MILLETTE, BRENDA, AND JOELLEN HAWKINS. *The Passage through Menopause: Women's Lives in Transition.* Reston, Va.: Reston Publishing Company, 1983.

SHEPHARD, BRUCE D., AND CARROLL A. SHEPHARD. *The Complete Guide to Women's Health* (rev. ed.). New York: New American Library, 1985.

STEWART, FELICIA, M.D., FELICIA GUEST, GARY STEWART, M.D., AND ROBERT HATCHER, M.D. *My Body, My Health: The Concerned Woman's Book of Gynecology.* New York: Bantam Books, 1981.

WATSON, RITA ESPOSITO, AND ROBERT C. WALLACH. *New Choices, New Chances: A Woman's Guide to Conquering Cancer.* New York: St. Martin's Press, 1983.

RESOURCES

Information and referral services are available in your local community through the county or state Department of Health, community hospitals, and the United Way agency. In addition, the following national resources can be contacted:

American Cancer Society
90 Park Avenue
New York, N.Y. 10016
(212) 599-3600

A nonprofit organization that provides information and education on cancer, through local chapters, some of which provide free services to cancer patients. (Contact the local chapter.)

American Diabetes Association National Service Center
1660 Duke Street
Alexandria, VA 22314
(800) 232-3472
(703) 331-8303

A nonprofit organization providing information, education, and referral to diabetes-related services.

Cancer Information Hotline
(800) 4CA-NCER

A hotline maintained by the National Cancer Institute to answer questions and provide information about cancer to patents, health care providers, and researchers.

Hill Burton Program
U.S. Dept. of Health and Human Services
(800) 638-0742

in Maryland (800)492-0359

A government service that provides information and referrals for free medical care in your local area.

13
Men's Health Problems

PREVENTING PROBLEMS

General Health

Good general health helps to prevent the development of all kinds of health problems, including men's reproductive health problems. There are seven important areas of our lives that affect health greatly and over which we have some control:

1. *Nutrition:* Adequate nutrition is necessary for good health.
2. *Weight:* Being seriously overweight puts a strain on the body and increases health problems.
3. *Exercise:* Regular exercise is necessary for good health.
4. *Smoking:* Smoking has been proved to cause some health problems and contribute to others.
5. *Substance abuse:* Heavy use of alcohol and/or drugs can cause some health problems and contribute to others.
6. *Stress:* Stressors like exhaustion, overwork, anger, and tension can cause some health problems and contribute to others.
7. *Hygiene:* Good hygiene can prevent many health problems.

Hygiene

In these days of wonder drugs and technical advances in health care, we sometimes forget the importance of good hygiene or cleanliness in preventing health problems. Daily baths or showers, frequent hair washing, and careful attention to cleaning the genitals (sex organs) and anus (rectal opening) all help to prevent infections and illness. Washing the hands after using the toilet and before eating also provides a lot of protection.

Genital Hygiene

Men's genitals, the penis and scrotum, do not usually require any special care. A daily bath or shower will keep them clean. Men who are not circumcised (who have not had the foreskin of the penis surgically removed) should take care to pull back the foreskin and wash the skin underneath when bathing. This is not necessary for uncircumcised infants and young boys.

Self-examination of the Testicles

Self-examination of the testicles is an important preventive health practice for men. **Cancer of the testicles** is rare and makes up only 1 percent of all cancer in men, but *it is the most common type of cancer in men between the ages of 20 and 35.* There has been a great deal of publicity and public education about the importance for women of monthly breast self-examination to identify possible cancerous lumps, but *most men are not aware that they should examine their testicles each month—to identify testicular cancer at the early stage.*

When treated early, testicular cancer is usually cured; but if it spreads beyond the testicles (frequently to the lungs), it may cause death. Although cancer of the testicles is less common in men over 35 and very rare in teenagers, all men should perform a monthly self-examination starting at age 14 or 15.

How to Examine the Testicles

Self-examination of the testicles is simple and easy to learn, and it takes only a few minutes. The testicles should be examined once a month after a warm bath or shower. Warm temperatures cause the skin of the scrotum (the sac of skin that holds the testicles) to relax, making it easier to feel the organs inside and to find anything unusual. The first step is to stand naked in front of a mirror and look for any swellings or bumps on the scrotum (Figure 13–1). The second step is to examine the entire surface of each testicle, gently and carefully, using both hands. With the thumbs in front and the first two fingers in back, gently slide or roll the testicle so that all surfaces are felt. The testicle normally feels like a firm slippery egg with a completely smooth surface, except for a cord or ridge that runs up the back. This is the epididymis, a tube that carries the sperm from the testicle to the urethra.

What Am I Looking For?

Testicular cancer usually appears as a small, firm, painless, pea-sized lump on the side or front of the testicle.

What If I Find Something?

A lump or any unusual growth or change in the testicles or scrotum should be examined by a doctor at once. There are many kinds of problems and infections that can cause pain, swelling, and changes in the testicles (see details later in this chapter). Most are not cancerous, but it is always wise to have any problems with the testicles checked. Monthly self-examination is useful because it allows each man to become familiar with what his testicles and scrotum feel like normally, so that it is easier to identify changes.

Cancer of the testicles is curable if treated early, usually by surgical removal of the testicle. Fortunately, the disease usually attacks only one side, and the man's other testicle remains normal. Since one testicle is all that is needed to provide a normal amount of hormones and sperm, the man's future sexual functioning need not be affected. If a man is concerned about the appearance of his testicles, a plastic prothesis (replacement) for the missing testicle can be inserted in the scrotum.

FIGURE 13–1. *Self-examination of the testicles.*

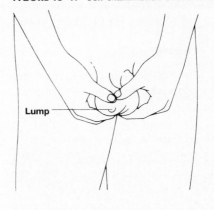

Lump

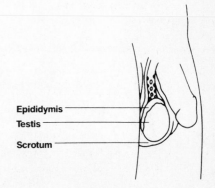

Epididymis
Testis
Scrotum

Getting Health Care

When to Get Care

Any lumps, bumps, or sores on the male genitals should be examined by a doctor. Other symptoms of infection or disease are:

1. Pain or difficulty urinating
2. A discharge from the penis
3. Swelling and inflammation of the penis or testicles
4. Swollen or tender lymph nodes in the pelvis or groin
5. A rash on or around the genitals
6. Hernia symptoms

Changes or difficulty with sexual functioning can also be a symptom of health problems.

Unlike women, most men do not need frequent medical care for their reproductive systems. Common reasons for seeking reproductive health care for men are:

1. Prostate problems (common after age 55)
2. Infections (often caused by sexually transmitted organisms)
3. Trauma (bumps and bruises)

Most men see a doctor only when they have a problem, but regular checkups, including examination of the genitals, are good health protection. All men over 45 should also have a yearly examination of the prostate gland to check for prostate cancer.

Choosing a Doctor or a Clinic

A man has many choices as to where to get health care. He can choose a doctor in private practice or group practice, a clinic operated by a hos-

Prostate problems are a common complaint of men over 55.

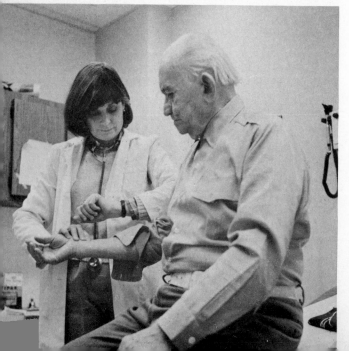

pital, or a health maintenance organization (HMO), which will provide all his care. Some areas also have community clinics, which are less expensive than seeing a private doctor. In some areas there are also city or county public health clinics, which provide free or very low cost care. Doctors, hospitals, and clinics are listed in the Yellow Pages, but the best way to find one is through a personal referral from someone who has used the facility and recommends it. The best time to look for a doctor is *before* you need one. It is not easy to search for the right kind of care when you are sick or in an emergency. Hospital emergency rooms are great in an emergency, but they are not the best place to get other kinds of care because they are expensive and do not offer follow-up services.

The doctors who most commonly provide men's and boy's reproductive health care belong to several different specialties:

Urologist: The urologist has had one to two years of general surgery training after medical school, followed by three to four years of specialized training in urology, which is the study of both the genital and urinary systems of males (and the urinary system of females). The urologist specializes in the reproductive health and urinary problems of males, although he or she also treats women.

Family practice doctor: The family practitioner has had at least three years or specialty training after medical school, focused on treating the medical needs of the whole family. She or he has usually had some training in urology.

Pediatrician: The pediatrician has had at least three years of training in the health problems of infants and children after completing medical school, including the study of the genital and urinary problems of male infants and young boys.

Internist: The internist has had at least three years of specialty training after medical school, which may or may not have included some training in urology.

General practitioner: The general practitioner is a medical doctor or a doctor of osteopathy. He or she does not usually have any specialized training in urology, but may have a great deal of experience.

If a man gets his medical care from a doctor who is not a specialist in urology, he will be referred to a specialist by his doctor when it is necessary. Almost all surgery on the reproductive systems of men and boys is performed by urologists, except for circumcision of infants, which is usually performed by an obstetrician or a pediatrician.

The Urological Examination

A complete examination of the male reproductive and urinary systems is called a **urological** examination. A regular checkup that includes a urological examination is a good habit for all men to develop, regardless of age. The urological examination consists of a health history, a physical examination of the abdomen and genitals, and a rectal examination to identify problems with the prostate gland. The examination is something that some men dislike and tend to put off, even when they have a health problem that needs attention. Going for the first urological examination can be upsetting, especially if you do not know what to expect. Embarrassment about such a personal examination, dislike of losing privacy, and fear of becoming aroused during the examination are common feelings for a man facing his first examination. Fortunately, the examination is not so embarrassing once a man knows what to expect, is not a sexually arousing experience, and should not be painful unless there is severe inflammation or other problems. A friendly, helpful, and supportive atmosphere in the office and examining room really helps, and many doctors' offices and clinics have such an atmosphere.

The following sections describe the various parts of the urological examination.

Health history   For the health history, you will be asked to fill out a form or answer questions about the following things:

> The present problem
> Past illnesses and surgeries
> Present medications
> Allergies
> Smoking, alcohol, and drug use
> Exposure to industrial chemicals and dyes
> Family history of illness, especially cancer, diabetes, heart problems (including high blood pressure), lung disease, kidney problems, and bladder problems
> Urinary symptoms such as frequent urination, difficulty in urinating, burning or pain, loss of control, or discolored urine

Physical examination   The urological examination may include or be part of a general physical examination. Weight, blood pressure, urinalysis, and blood count may all be obtained. In addition, the doctor or other health care provider (such as a physician's assistant or nurse practitioner) will listen to your heart and lungs, check your eyes, ears, nose and throat, and possibly examine the thyroid gland (in the neck).

Abdominal examination   The abdomen is examined with the man lying down so that his muscles are relaxed. The kidneys and bladder are examined by touch as the doctor presses down on the abdomen with the fingers, and feels under the ribs. In addition to examining the kidneys and bladder, other problems in the abdominal area may be identified. Another part of the examination, called **percussion**, may be performed with the man sitting or standing. The doctor taps on the upper back just under the shoulder blades and on the abdomen. If excess blood or fluid has collected in the kidney area, this can help the doctor to discover it. Percussion is normally painless, but it can be painful if the kidneys or prostate are seriously infected and inflamed.

Genital examination   The genital examination is usually performed with the man in a standing position but may also be done lying down. The doctor checks the surface skin of the penis. If the man is not circumcized, the foreskin is retracted (pulled back) to see the condition of the underlying skin. The urinary opening is also examined, and the urethra, which runs along the underside of the penis, is felt for lumps or inflammation. The tissue between the anus and the scrotum and penis is examined. The skin of the scrotum is checked carefully, and then the testicles and epididymis (the tube that carries sperm from the testicles to the seminal vesicles) are examined by touch for inflammation or growths. A flashlight may be used to pass light through the scrotum to help identify fluid-filled cysts such as hydrocele (see details later in this chapter). If there is a hernia, with abdominal contents descending into the scrotum, it can be identified at this time. Some men have hernias that show up only when there is pressure on the abdomen, for example when lifting, coughing, or straining. The doctor may ask the man to cough, to see if the pressure produces evidence of a hernia. (See further discussion of hernias later in this chapter.)

Rectal examination   The rectal examination is almost always part of a urological checkup and takes only a few minutes. Although some people find it uncomfortable, it is not painful unless there is severe inflammation. The examination is usually performed on a man in one of three ways: with the man standing and bent over the examining table (see Figure 13–2), lying on his back with the knees spread and flexed, or lying on his side with the knees pulled up to the chest. The doctor looks at the skin in the rectal area and presses the tissue around the anus to check muscle tone and to identify hemorrhoids and other problems. Then a gloved finger is inserted into the anus to feel for muscle tone (tightness). Nerve reflexes may be tested by a quick squeeze of the end of the penis, causing the rectal muscles to contract. The finger is used to sweep along the inner surface of the rectum to check for growths and other problems. The

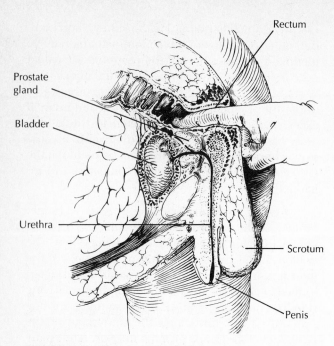

Labels on figure: Rectum, Prostate gland, Bladder, Urethra, Scrotum, Penis

FIGURE 13–2. *Rectal examination.*

prostrate gland, which is located at the base of the bladder, wrapped around the urethra, is examined next. It is located a few inches up from the anus against the wall of the rectum, on the side closest to the abdomen.

The prostate is a plum-shaped organ, usually about two inches in diameter, which normally has a firm, rubbery texture. When the prostate is located, the physician uses the finger to examine the size, shape, and texture of the gland to check for growths and inflammation. The prostate examination is not painful unless the gland is very inflamed and tender. If the man has infrequent sex or an infection, fluid may build up in the prostate, giving it a mushy texture.

A sample of the fluid secreted by the prostate may be needed to check for infection or other problems. It is obtained by prostate massage, which the doctor performs as part of the rectal examination. Gently pressing and massaging the prostate a few times with the finger will cause a few drops of prostate fluid to be expressed from the gland. This fluid then travels down the urethra and out the penis, where it is collected for laboratory analysis. The prostate is not particularly sensitive, and the massage is not generally considered sexually stimulating.

Diagnostic tests and procedures There are many different tests and procedures that may be performed in a doctor's office or clinic to help diagnose problems of the male reproductive system. The three most common types are described next.

Urine tests Urine tests are used for many purposes, including the identification of urethral, bladder, and kidney infections and the detection of diabetes. Most tests are done at the office, but in some cases the urine sample is also sent to a laboratory for further analysis.

Cultures A small sample of urine, blood, pus, urethral discharge, or prostate fluid may be sent to a laboratory for culture. The laboratory attempts to grow bacteria or other organisms found in the sample in order to identify the disease that is causing problems. Since different organisms need different environments to grow, the doctor must be specific about which organisms the laboratory should attempt to grow in culture. If a man believes he may have been exposed to a certain disease, such as gonorrhea, he should mention this.

Some organisms are very difficult to identify and to culture. Culturing viruses such as herpes take extra time and special techniques. But cultures are one of the best ways to obtain a definite diagnosis of an infection.

Blood tests There are hundreds of different tests that can be performed on a blood sample. The

A blood test is needed to diagnose many diseases.

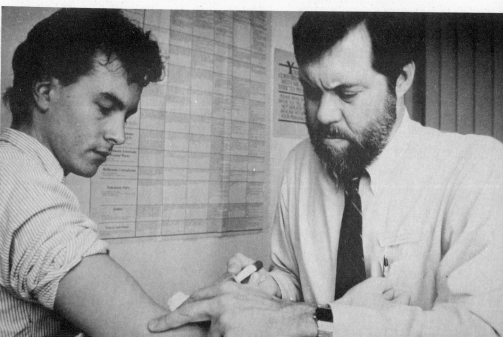

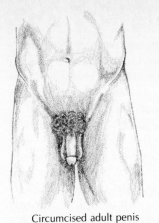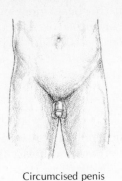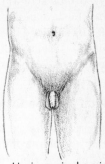

Circumcised adult penis　　　Uncircumcised adult penis

Circumcised penis
(9 year old boy)

Uncircumcised penis
(9 year old boy)

FIGURE 13–3. *Circumcised and uncircumcised penises (adult and child).*

most common is the blood count, which detects anemia. The finger or earlobe prick is often used for a blood count. Most other blood tests require more blood, which is taken from a vein, usually in the inner elbow, and sent to a laboratory. Many kinds of diseases, including syphilis, can be diagnosed through blood tests. The state of a person's metabolism, the functioning of the liver and kidneys, levels of different hormones, even information about the person's genetic makeup can be obtained from blood tests. But the doctor must order the specific tests needed. If the right tests are not ordered, the problem may not be detected.

CIRCUMCISION

What Is It?

Circumcision is the surgical removal of the foreskin of the penis. It is most commonly performed on newborn infants, but a male can be circumcised at any age (Figure 13–3). Circumcision is minor surgery and is a common practice in most hospitals in the United States. An estimated 80 percent of newborn American males are circumcised, usually by an obstetrician. As for any operation, the parents' written consent is needed.

When Is It Needed?

Circumcision of all male infants is part of the practice of the Jewish and Islamic religions. However,

circumcision is also a common practice across all groups in the United States because of health beliefs and cultural preferences. In contrast, only a small minority of newborns are circumcised in European countries. The American Academy of Pediatrics took the position over fifteen years ago that the routine circumcision of newborns is not medically justified; that is, the health risks of the surgery are greater than the potential health benefits.

In the past it was believed that circumcision of newborns provided some protection from cancer of the penis (a rare disease) in later years and possible protection from cancer of the cervix for sexual partners. It now appears that this is not true. Good hygiene is important for both circumcised and uncircumcised men in the prevention of penile cancer.

In rare cases, older boys and adult men may need circumcision as a result of health problems such as phimosis, a condition in which the foreskin cannot be drawn back to uncover the glans of the penis because of infection and inflammation.

How Is It Performed?

Circumcision of infants is usually performed at the hospital within a few days of birth by a pediatrician or an obstetrician. The surgery is minor, takes only a few minutes, and is usually performed without anesthesia. It involves cutting away the extra skin that covers the glans of the penis. There is a little bleeding, but in newborns stitches are not usually required.

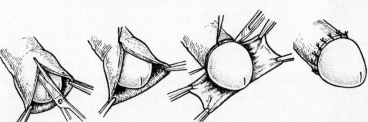

FIGURE 13–4. *The procedure for circumcision of an adult.*

Circumcision of the adult is usually performed by a urologist or a surgeon, in a hospital, under local anesthesia (similar to the Novocaine used at the dentist's office) or general anesthesia (when the patient is "asleep" during the surgery). Stitches are needed to control bleeding (Figure 13–4).

What Are the Risks?

The risks involved in circumcision of the newborn male are pain from surgery without anesthesia, the chance of serious infections or bleeding (1 out of 500), and loss of the protective covering of the glans (head) of the penis. In very rare cases penises have been permanently damaged by the cutting of too much tissue. The circumcised baby has a higher risk of developing inflammations of the urinary opening at the end of the penis, because the area is not protected from wet diapers by the foreskin. This inflammation can cause scarring that partially closes off the urinary opening, making additional surgery necessary.

Circumcision of the adult involves more risks, but it is still minor surgery. Bleeding or infection can develop, and scar tissue may form that can make erections difficult or painful. This can cause pain during intercourse. Fortunately, these problems are usually temporary and can be treated successfully. There are additional health risks if general anesthesia is used.

Lifting heavy objects can bring on hernia problems for men.

Does It Affect Sexuality?

Circumcision does not in any way affect a man's ability to have sexual intercourse or make a woman pregnant. It is not believed to have any effect on a man's enjoyment of sex or sexual sensation, although the skin of the glans of the penis is tougher (since it is exposed) than that of an uncircumcised man. The question of whether the foreskin, or lack of it, has an effect on enjoyment of sex by female partners has not been studied. Some men and women find either the circumcised or the uncircumcised penis more attractive to look at, but this preference is probably based on what they are accustomed to seeing.

INGUINAL HERNIA

What Is It?

A **hernia** is a weak spot in a muscle wall which allows internal tissues to bulge out. Hernias can develop in many parts of the body. An **inguinal hernia** is located in the groin. It is an opening in the muscles that support the bottom of the abdomen through which intestinal tissue can descend. All men have two small openings in these muscles where the spermatic cord connecting the testicles with the urethra passes through. These are the openings through which the testicles pass from the abdomen to the scrotum shortly before birth. In some boys or men these openings may be larger than they should be, allowing intestinal tissue to pass through to create a bulge of tissue in the groin or in the scrotum. In other cases, these openings may be stretched or enlarged by lifting heavy objects or by chronic straining with constipation. Generally a man will have a hernia on only one side, but it is possible to have two, a condition called a **double hernia**. Inguinal hernia is a very common problem in men, and hernia repair is one of the most commonly performed surgeries in the United States.

How Serious Is It?

An inguinal hernia is a health problem that can cause a great deal of discomfort or can be almost unnoticed. Many men have hernias that go untreated for years. Inguinal hernia is not a serious threat to health unless intestinal tissue gets trapped outside the abdomen by tightened muscles (an **incarcerated hernia**). In this case, the blood supply to the trapped tissue may be cut off. When this happens (a **strangulated hernia**, which is rare), emergency surgery is needed to avoid problems that could be fatal.

What Are the Signs and Symptoms?

An inguinal hernia can develop slowly over time without noticeable symptoms, and may only be identified during a medical checkup. Some male babies are born with inguinal hernias. The problem can also develop suddenly, especially when lifting a heavy object; the man may feel a tearing sensation in his groin, followed by a bulging of tissue in the area within a few days. Many hernias do not cause much discomfort and may be ignored for years; others may cause so much discomfort and inconvenience that the man seeks treatment immediately.

What Is the Treatment?

The treatment for inguinal hernia is surgery to repair the defects in the abdominal muscles. The surgery is usually performed in an outpatient surgical center or at a hospital under general anesthesia (sleep) or spinal anesthesia. It can also be done under local anesthesia. An incision is made in the groin area to allow the surgeon to move any intestinal tissue that is outside the abdomen back into the abdomen, and to sew up the muscles in the area of the hernia. Recovery is rapid, with the man walking the day after surgery, but some activities, such as lifting, must be avoided for several weeks.

Early treatment is recommended for a hernia even if it is not causing serious problems, because of the danger of strangulation. It is safer and better to have hernia repair surgery before a dangerous emergency develops.

Some men who wish to avoid surgery wear a **truss,** a supportive garment that puts pressure on the site, keeping intestinal tissue from protruding through the hernia. Although the truss may relieve the symptoms, it will not cause the hernia to go away, and it may continue to grow larger. Complications can develop even if a truss is worn.

Hernias can recur after surgical treatment, but this is not common.

PROSTATE PROBLEMS

Enlarged Prostate

What Is It?

The **prostate gland** is a plum-shaped organ, normally about two inches in diameter, located at the base of the bladder (Figure 13–5). Prostates vary in size, and a very enlarged one in an older man may be as large as a baseball, whereas a small prostate in a young man may be just a little over an inch in diameter. The urethra passes through the center of the prostate, and the seminal vesicles are located just above it. It is within the prostate gland that the sperm from the testicles combine with fluid from the prostate and enter the urethra, creating semen, the sperm-containing fluid that is ejaculated. An enlarged prostate (also known as **benign prostatic hypertrophy**) is a natural overgrowth of prostate tissues that occurs in most men as they get older. The cause appears to be natural changes in the body's hormone balance that begin around age 30, causing the prostate to begin to grow slowly.

Men commonly start to have problems with an enlarged prostate at around age 55, but difficulties can develop earlier. Almost all men will develop health problems related to an enlarged prostate if they live long enough, and many of them will eventually need surgery.

How Serious Is It?

An enlarged prostate is not a serious problem for most men, but it can cause illness in some cases. An enlarged prostate presses on the urethra and can make it difficult for the man to urinate. If it prevents complete emptying of the bladder, over time the bladder may become permanently enlarged and lose the muscular ability to contract. In addition, urinary infections are more likely to develop if the bladder does not empty completely each time the man urinates. Occasionally an enlarged prostate will cut off the man's ability to urinate altogether, a condition called **acute urinary retention.** The bladder overfills, causing feelings of pressure and discomfort, but the man is not able to urinate (Figure 13–6). Emergency medical treat-

FIGURE 13–5. *Location of the prostate gland.*

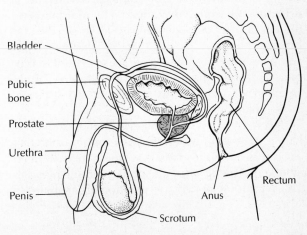

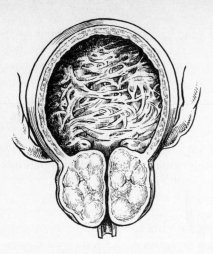

FIGURE 13–6. *An enlarged prostate can prevent urination.*

ment (called **catheterization**) is required, in which a catheter (a thin rubber tube) is passed through the penis up the urethra to the bladder, allowing the bladder to empty.

The pressure of urine backed up into an overfilled bladder can, over time, cause damage to the ureters (the tubes that carry urine down to the bladder from the kidneys) and to the kidneys themselves. Although serious complications of an enlarged prostate, such as kidney damage or kidney failure, are rare, they can develop silently without noticeable symptoms other than difficulty urinating. For this reason, men who have difficulty urinating (even if they feel they can live with it and don't need treatment) should be checked by a doctor to make sure no serious problems are developing.

What Are the Signs and Symptoms?

The major symptoms of an enlarged prostate are frequency of urination and difficulty urinating. The first symptom is usually the frequent need to urinate, and a man may find himself having to get up several times each night. A man may also notice a decrease in the force of urination and in the size of the stream. He may have difficulty getting started, and the stream may stop and start while he is urinating. He is forced to spend a lot more time on the act of urination because it goes so slowly, and he may have the feeling that his bladder is not completely empty after he finishes. These symptoms are annoying and inconvenient, but if there are no other problems many men put up with them rather than face surgery.

Another, less common symptom is acute urinary retention, in which the man cannot urinate at all. If this continues for a few hours, he will need emergency medical treatment to drain the bladder. The symptoms of urinary retention are inability to urinate, a feeling of urgent need to urinate, lower abdominal pain and pressure, and occasionally pain up the sides and in the kidney area. Men who have a history of difficulty in urinating may develop retention suddenly for no apparent reason, or as a result of consuming certain foods or drugs that cause inflammation of the tissues in the prostate area. Alcohol, spicy foods, allergic reactions, and certain drugs can all cause the prostate tissues to swell so that urination is made impossible and urinary retention develops. Some over-the-counter drugs such as antihistamines, nasal sprays, and eyedrops contain drugs that can cause urinary retention. So do some nonprescription sleeping pills (because they contain antihistamines). If in doubt, ask the pharmacist. If retention was caused by diet or drugs, it may not recur if the man avoids the substance that is causing the problem. Otherwise, if a man has developed urinary retention once, it is likely to happen again, and surgery may be needed.

An enlarged prostate can be identified by a physician during rectal examination. However, a large prostate which causes no symptoms and shows no signs of being diseased does not need treatment. On the other hand, a relatively small prostate may cause symptoms and problems and may need treatment.

Symptoms similar to those of enlarged prostate can also be caused by nerve damage (for example, damage due to diabetes or spinal cord injury) that affects the functioning of the bladder and urethra, and by certain drugs that affect the nervous system. Temporary urinary retention often develops after surgery in the pelvic area. The mechanics of urination are complex and involve many systems of the body. For this reason, when a man complains of difficulty in urination, his physician must rule out other possible causes of the problem before it can be assumed that the prostate is the only cause.

What Is the Treatment?

The most common treatment for health problems caused by an enlarged prostate is surgery to remove a portion of the gland and relieve pressure on the urethra. At present there is no effective treatment for the problem without surgery. There are drugs that are used to relax muscles and make urination easier, but they are usually only a temporary measure. In the future, hormonal treatments may become available. Surgery is needed if the enlarged prostate has caused any of the following problems:

1. Multiple urinary tract infections

2. Urinary backup, creating pressure and potential damage to the bladder and kidneys

3. Recurring urinary retention

When the only problems are difficulty and slowness in urinating, the man has a choice of putting up with the inconvenience caused by the prostate or having surgery (which involves some health risks).

Prostate surgery The most commonly performed surgery to reduce the size of an enlarged prostate is called **transurethral resection of the prostate** and is performed on 90 to 95 percent of cases. This procedure removes prostate tissue through the urethra under general (sleep) or spinal anesthesia. In transurethral resection, only tissue inside the prostate gland is removed (similar to removing the pulp from inside an orange).

The steps of the procedure are as follows:

1. A small telescope is inserted through the urethra to examine the bladder, prostate, and urethra.

2. The urethra is dilated (expanded) using metal dilating rods.

3. A slender surgical instrument called a resectoscope is introduced through the urethra to the area of the prostate. This instrument has a metal loop on the end that can be used to cut or to coagulate (to stop bleeding by applying heat) and a telescope through which the surgeon can see the area. The resectoscope is used to delicately chip and cut away the excess prostate tissue.

4. The next step is to flush out all the cut-away tissue and to coagulate any areas that are bleeding. Throughout the surgery the prostate area is kept filled with fluid to hold the walls of the organ apart so the area can be seen and treated.

This operation requires a short hospital stay. The man is likely to be uncomfortable the first day or two after surgery. He can usually return home as soon as the urinary catheter (inserted after surgery) is removed, usually within one to three days. There is a two- to four-week recovery period. Intercourse, strenuous physical activity, and heavy lifting must be avoided for a month. Driving and light activity can usually be resumed in one to two weeks.

Antibiotics are usually given for 5 to 10 days after surgery to prevent infection, and the man is advised to drink a lot of fluids for several weeks to keep the bladder and urethra flushed out. Alcohol should be completely avoided for three weeks.

Transurethral resection of the prostate is usually very effective in relieving urinary symptoms. In a small number of cases the tissue may grow back, and a second operation may be needed.

Prostate surgery is also performed by an **open prostatectomy,** in which the surgeon enters the body through the abdomen or groin area to remove all or part of the prostate. This approach is used when the prostate is exceptionally large or when there are other medical problems. It has a longer recovery period but can produce as good results as transurethral resection.

Risks and benefits Men who have prostate problems need to weigh the benefits of surgery carefully against the risks to future health and sexual functioning. The American health care system, although it is the best in the world in some respects, has a tendency to overtreat some health problems, often with surgery. Older people, because they have more health problems, are especially at risk of overtreatment. Men should think carefully, find out all the possible treatments, and get several medical opinions before agreeing to any surgery.

The average risk of death from transurethral resection is 4 in 1,000, which is high, but it must be remembered that the surgery is usually performed on older men, who are likely to have other health problems as well. The risk of death is lower for younger, healthy men. There are several specific risks to prostate surgery in addition to the usual risks of infection and bleeding (which are part of any surgery) and of complications from anesthesia. The risks are as follows:

1. Urethral stricture (urinary opening narrowed by scar tissue): 6 percent

2. Permanent incontinence (inability to control urine): less than 1 percent

3. Permanent impotence (inability to have an erec-

Prostate surgery does not usually interfere with a man's ability to enjoy sex.

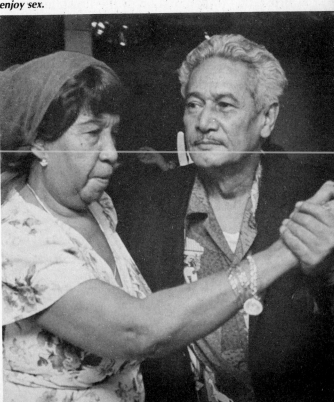

tion): 5 percent (estimated 2 percent due to damage caused by the surgery, and 3 percent caused by psychological factors)

4. Retrograde ejaculation (ejaculation into the bladder rather than out the penis): 40–50 percent

Retrograde ejaculation results from damage to a muscle within the prostate that automatically closes off the opening to the bladder when a man is about to ejaculate. If this muscle does not work, the ejaculate is forced up into the bladder rather than down the penis. This changes the sensations of ejaculation somewhat and makes a man sterile, because the sperm cannot be deposited in the female partner's vagina.

Does It Affect Sexuality?

Many men fear that prostate surgery will make them impotent. As the preceding figures show, however, only about 2 percent of men are rendered physically impotent by surgery for an enlarged prostate (although prostate surgery for other problems, such as cancer, causes higher rates of impotence).

Most men who do have surgery for an enlarged prostate are very satisfied with their sexual abilities after surgery. Many do have retrograde ejaculation, but most report that it does not interfere with sexual pleasure or orgasm, although it does alter the sensations somewhat.

Living with an enlarged prostate and doing without surgery does not cause problems with sexual functioning. Men who choose to put off prostate surgery and tolerate urinary symptoms do not usually find their sex lives affected.

Prostatitis (Inflammation of the Prostate)

What Is It?

Prostatitis (an inflamed prostate gland) has several causes. Unlike an enlarged prostate, which normally affects older men, prostatitis is most common among men from 18 to 45. It may be a temporary condition caused by extreme changes in the amount of sexual activity, in which the prostate become swollen and sore from being much more active than usual, or from suddenly stopping all sexual activity when the body is accustomed to frequent sex. Infrequent sex or no sex over time can also cause prostatitis. In some sensitive people, inflammation of the prostate can also be caused by consumption of alcohol or spicy foods. Acute prostatitis refers to inflammation of the prostate accompanied by symptoms of illness such as fever, and is usually caused by bacteria or other organisms. Chronic prostatitis refers to low-level inflammation

of the prostate that continues over a long time. It can be difficult or impossible to cure. Often the cause cannot be determined.

How Serious Is It?

Prostatitis is a very common condition in men, one that affects most men at some point in their lives. It is not usually a serious threat to health, but it can cause a great deal of inconvenience and discomfort and can interfere with the ability to enjoy sexual activity. Chronic prostatitis can be a drain on a man's overall level of health, energy, and well-being. Acute prostatitis can be life-threatening if it is untreated and abscesses (pockets of pus and infected material) form on the prostate. These abscesses can burst, causing severe pelvic infection.

Prostatitis can be an indicator of many different kinds of problems, from minor infections to serious sexually transmitted diseases.

What Are the Signs and Symptoms?

The major symptom of prostatitis is a painful and swollen prostate. Since the prostate is located deep within the pelvis, a man cannot feel it directly, but the inflammation is likely to press on the urethra, causing frequent urination and pain on urination. There may also be generalized aching and pain in the pelvic or groin area, which may extend down to the penis. Ejaculation may be painful, and there may be a loss of interest in sex. A urethral discharge may be present. Low back pain can also be a symptom of prostatitis. When the prostate is examined by a doctor through rectal examination, it will feet hot, swollen, and mushy in texture, and it may be lumpy. The doctor's touch is likely to be painful. Fever, chills, and feelings of illness may also be present. If infection of the urethra, bladder, or kidney is also present, the urine may be cloudy and may have an odd color or smell. In chronic prostatitis the symptoms may be milder but may include a discharge from the urethra.

Diagnosis of the problem may involve laboratory tests and cultures of urine, prostate fluid, and blood to identify the organism causing the infection. In many cases of prostatitis no infecting organism is found, and the cause of the inflammation cannot be located. Viral infections are thought to be responsible for some of these.

What Is the Treatment?

The treatment for prostatitis depends on what has caused it. Any man who develops the symptoms of prostatitis should seek medical care because it could be a sign of a serious problem. In addition, if a minor problem is left untreated, it could become chronic and be much more difficult to get rid of in the future.

Inflammation that is due to excess sexual activity will resolve itself and disappear with a few days' rest from sex. Inflammation that is caused by an absence of sex or infrequent activity results from overfilling of the prostate with fluid meant for ejaculation. The man's body rids itself of some of the excess fluid naturally through nocturnal emissions, commonly called wet dreams (loss of semen during sleep), but in some men the fluid still builds up. The solution in these cases is more frequent and regular sexual activity resulting in ejaculation, either with a partner or through masturbation (self-stimulation). This will keep the prostate flushed out, and the inflammation will disappear.

Inflammation that is caused by consumption of alcohol or certain foods is effectively prevented by avoiding these substances.

Acute prostatitis is usually caused by an infecting organism. Antibiotic treatment is usually begun immediately and is very effective. In most cases the symptoms of illness should disappear within a few days, and complete recovery should take place within a few weeks.

Chronic prostatitis is difficult to treat because the cause of the inflammation is usually not known. There are several different approaches to treatment. Regular sexual activity with ejaculation (either with a partner or by masturbation) may be recommended to flush out the congested prostate. *If sexually transmitted infection is present (including chlamydia), the man should always wear a condom during intercourse with a partner. The purpose is to avoid passing on infection and to avoid possible reinfection if the partner already has the infection.* Regular massage of the prostate by a physician can also reduce congestion but is probably less effective than sexual activity resulting in ejaculation. If an unidentified infection is suspected, a long course of antibiotics, lasting for months or perhaps for a year, may be prescribed. This appears to cure the condition in some cases.

In rare cases, severe chronic prostatitis may be treated with surgery, usually a transurethral resection (the same operation that is performed for an enlarged prostate). However, this surgery cannot always remove all the inflamed tissue, so the problem may continue afterward. Since this surgery carries a small risk of incontinence and impotence, and causes sterility (because of retrograde ejaculation) in many cases, it is not usually recommended.

Does It Affect Sexuality?

Prostatitis definitely affects a man's sexual life because it can cause painful ejaculations, general discomfort in the pelvic area, and in some cases a loss of interest in sex (probably due to discomfort). Fortunately for most men, their prostate problems are temporary and can be treated and cleared up in a short time. Men with chronic prostatitis must take care of their general health and learn to avoid situations that cause prostate problems to flare up.

Cancer of the Prostate

What Is It?

Cancer of the prostate is a very rare disease in boys and young men and a very common disease in older men. Autopsies of men dying from other causes show that around 30 percent of all men over age 50 have some cancer cells in the prostate. The older the man, the more likely he is to have prostate cancer, and it is estimated that between 67 and 80 percent of men over age 80 have the disease. In most cases prostate cancer tumors are small and slow-growing, taking up only a little space inside the prostate. They cause no health problems or symptoms and thus are not usually diagnosed or treated. In a small percentage of cases, however, prostate cancer grows and spreads, causing serious illness and the risk of death. Around 27,000 men die each year from prostate cancer, and the disease is responsible for an estimated 10 percent of all cancer deaths in men (Figure 13–7).

There are several different types of prostate cancer. Some of them are not likely ever to cause problems, and others tend to spread rapidly through the body. Since the disease usually has no symptoms until it is far advanced, many men do not learn that they have cancer until it is too late to cure it. A yearly prostate examination is recommended for all men over 45 to identify prostate cancer in the early stage.

The causes of prostate cancer are not well understood, but it appears that several different factors may increase the chances of getting the disease, including the following:

1. Genetic (inherited) factors
2. The body's hormone balance, especially the amount of testosterone
3. A high-fat diet
4. Exposure to substances in the environment (men who work with batteries or in the textile, rubber, and fertilizer industries appear to have higher risk, as do city dwellers compared to rural residents)
5. Certain viruses

How Serious Is It?

Because prostate cancer can be fatal, it must be considered a serious disease. Most men who

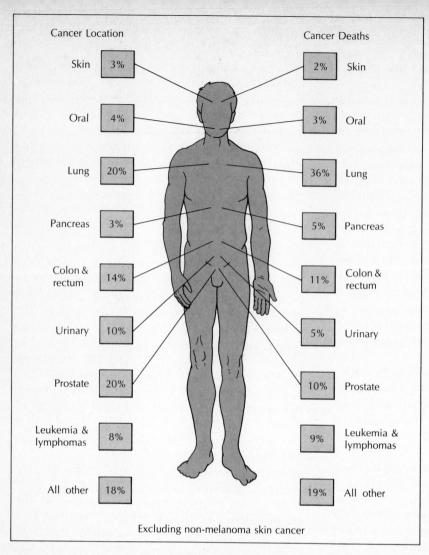

Cancer Location		Cancer Deaths	
Skin	3%	2%	Skin
Oral	4%	3%	Oral
Lung	20%	36%	Lung
Pancreas	3%	5%	Pancreas
Colon & rectum	14%	11%	Colon & rectum
Urinary	10%	5%	Urinary
Prostate	20%	10%	Prostate
Leukemia & lymphomas	8%	9%	Leukemia & lymphomas
All other	18%	19%	All other

Excluding non-melanoma skin cancer

FIGURE 13–7. *Estimated new cancer cases and cancer deaths in men by location (1987).*

have it, however, die of something else, often without ever knowing that they have prostate cancer. The different kinds of prostate cancer have different patterns of growth. In general, a single small tumor inside the prostate tends to grow slowly and rarely causes problems. Cancer cells disseminated throughout several areas of the prostate are considered more likely to grow rapidly and to spread beyond the prostate. Once cancer has spread beyond the prostate to the lymph nodes, to other parts of the pelvis, or throughout the body, it can be difficult or impossible to cure. Although there is no known way to prevent prostate cancer from developing, reducing the amount of fat in the diet is recommended. A yearly prostate examination is the best way to identify prostate cancer early and determine if treatment is needed. If the disease has been diagnosed, then frequent checkups are needed to make sure it does not grow or spread.

What Are the Signs and Symptoms?

Prostate cancer in the early stages has no symptoms and is most often identified through a prostate exam or during surgery for an enlarged prostate. If the tumor or tumors have grown quite large, pressure on the urethra may cause difficulty in urinating or may shut off the flow of urine. If the disease has metastasized (spread) to other parts of the body (often the bones of the pelvis and spine), there may be pain in these areas as well as feelings of tiredness and illness, and weight loss.

What Is the Treatment?

There are several types of treatment for prostate cancer, and the decisions about whether to treat the disease or not, and which kind of treatment to use, are made on the basis of several considerations, including the following:

1. How likely the cancer is to grow and spread
2. The age, health, and life expectancy of the man
3. Whether the cancer is causing symptoms that need treatment
4. Whether a complete cure is possible

If the man is very elderly, or if he has other health

problems that will limit his life to a few more months or years, the cancer may not progress enough to create problems for him during his remaining life. A younger man with prostate cancer, who is otherwise in good health and can expect to live for many years, is more likely to need treatment. If he remains untreated, the disease may cut his life short.

No treatment   Prostate cancer is not usually treated if there is a single small tumor of a slow-growing type in the prostate because this type of cancer almost never grows enough to cause problems. This type of cancer is discovered in around 15 percent of men undergoing surgery for an enlarged prostate. Other, faster growing types of cancer also may not be treated if the man is very elderly or if he has other health problems that will limit his life.

Surgical treatment   The most common treatment for prostate cancer is surgery to remove the entire prostate (called a **radical prostatectomy**). This treatment is effective if the disease has not spread beyond the prostate. The lymph nodes in the pelvic area may be biopsied or removed before prostatectomy is planned, to make sure that the cancer has not spread to other parts of the body. Even if the cancer has spread, a prostatectomy may still be done, but it will probably be combined with other treatment such as radiation or hormone therapy as well.

Prostatectomy is a different operation from the transurethral resection used for an enlarged prostate, and the side effects are also different. In a prostatectomy the entire prostate gland is removed, and the urethra is attached to the bottom of the bladder, where the prostate was located. Because it is necessary to remove all of the tissue in the area, certain important nerves and muscles can be lost in prostatectomy, causing the man to be permanently impotent. In the past, radical prostatectomy meant permanent impotence in almost every case. Today, however, men can choose a surgical approach called a **nerve-sparing radical prostatectomy**, which leaves the nerves needed for erection and potency in place. An estimated 50 percent of men remain potent after the nerve-sparing procedure. Critics of this procedure claim that not removing the nerves may reduce the chances of curing the disease. In addition to the risk of impotence, some men are not able to control their urine completely after radical prostatectomy. Six months after surgery, 10 to 15 percent of men still have a little leakage of urine. For most of them, it is so little that it does not cause a problem.

Radiation therapy   Radiation is often used to combat cancer that has spread beyond the prostate. It may be used in addition to surgery or alone and may be applied from outside the body by a beam aimed at the prostate, or by implanting tiny seeds of radioactive material directly into the gland itself.

Hormone therapy   The growth of some prostate cancers apparently requires the hormone testosterone, and it has been found that eliminating that male hormone from the system often causes the disease to shrink rapidly and almost seem to disappear. Testosterone is produced in the man's testicles, and the ways to eliminate it from the system are called **surgical castration** and **chemical castration**. Surgical castration is a procedure in which the testicles are removed from the scrotum. The man is sterile after this procedure and is likely to become permanently impotent as well. The production of testosterone in the man's body can also be reduced or eliminated by chemical castration, the giving of a continuous dose of the female hormone estrogen, which prevents the man's body from manufacturing testosterone.

Both chemical and surgical castration will have feminizing side effects; that is, they will make a man less masculine in appearance. Under this treatment, the man's sex drive is likely to become less or go away altogether, he is likely to become impotent, he may start to grow breasts (gynecomastia), and his skin will become smoother and more like a woman's in appearance. In spite of these serious side effects, castration is sometimes chosen by the man and his physician because the treatment can be life-saving.

Chemotherapy   Advanced prostate cancer that does not respond to the hormone therapy just described is sometimes treated with other drugs. These cancer-fighting drugs are mostly experimental, but several have been found that can be helpful and can prolong survival in some cases.

Does It Affect Sexuality?

Cancer of the prostate does not cause problems for most of the men who develop it; in fact, it usually causes no symptoms at all and is not treated. If the man has surgery to remove the prostate (radical prostatectomy), however, he may become permanently impotent. If he has surgical or chemical castration, he is also likely to lose his desire for sex.

PROBLEMS OF THE TESTICLES AND SCROTUM

Mumps Orchitis

What Is It?

Mumps orchitis is a complication of the childhood viral disease, mumps. Mumps used to be a common infectious disease of childhood, but it is now rare in the United States because a vaccine is available with which most children are immunized. Mumps is caused by a virus that produces fever, feelings of illness, and swelling of the salivary glands, especially the parotid glands located just behind the angle of the jaw. Mumps is found throughout the world, and most children will become infected if not vaccinated. The disease occurs rarely in adults because most are immune as a result of vaccination or of having been infected in childhood, but when an adult man gets mumps it can have serious effects.

How Serious Is It?

Mumps is rarely serious for male or female children. It causes a week or two of illness, but most recover without problems. When adult men and boys past puberty are infected with mumps, however, about 20 to 35 percent will develop mumps orchitis (inflammation of the testicles caused by the mumps virus), usually just on one side. About 30 percent of these men will suffer permanent loss of the ability to produce sperm in the affected testicle. If both testicles are affected, the man may become completely sterile. Although the affected testicles stop producing sperm and shrink in size, they usually continue to produce the male hormones needed to maintain a man's normal appearance and sexual ability.

What Are the Signs and Symptoms?

The symptoms of mumps orchitis usually develop three to four days after the onset of the disease. One or both testicles becomes swollen, tender, and painful to touch. The swelling usually lasts about a week. If the testicle is damaged by the infection, it will start to shrink in size one to two months later.

What Is the Treatment?

The best treatment of mumps is to avoid it by making sure all children are vaccinated against it. In the years before the vaccine was invented, parents used to try to make sure their male children were exposed to the disease in early childhood, so that they would be immune by the time they reached puberty.

Once the viral infection has set in, there is no medical cure, and treatment involves making the person as comfortable as possible until he recovers (after about a week). In the case of mumps orchitis, the man will need to remain in bed. A heating pad or hot water bottle may provide comfort. Supporting the testicles on a soft towel or wearing an athletic supporter may also help. Medication for pain and fever may be needed.

Does It Affect Sexuality?

Mumps in adult men can cause sterility if both testicles are damaged, but it does not nor-

Mumps is rarely dangerous for children, but it can cause serious problems for teenage boys and adult men.

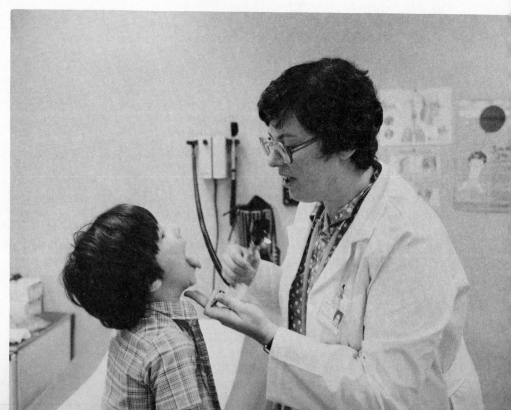

300

mally cause problems with the man's ability to have sexual intercourse. Fortunately, the disease usually affects only one testicle, and the man remains fertile. A testicle damaged by mumps will atrophy over time (shrink and become noticeably smaller), but it will usually continue to produce male hormones. Even when both testicles are affected and the man is made sterile by mumps, his desire and ability to have sex are rarely affected.

Epididymitis

What Is It?

Epididymitis is the most common infection of the scrotum. It consists of painful swelling of the epididymis, the tube that runs along the back of each testicle and carries sperm from the testicle to the vas deferens (the tube that carries sperm to the urethra). It can develop on one side or can involve both testicles. Epididymitis is usually due to infection that develops when organisms infecting the urethra or prostate travel down the vas deferens into the epididymis. It is a very common condition, especially for men with prostate problems. Epididymitis is rare in children, and is most commonly caused by sexually transmitted diseases in young men and by prostate infections in older men.

How Serious Is It?

Epididymitis can be very painful and can cause illness requiring several days to a week of bed rest, but most men recover from it without ill effects. In severe cases or if the disease is untreated, scarring of the vas deferens and epididymis may occur, which can block off the tubes either partially or completely and can cause sterility. If the infection is not completely cleared up, epididymitis can become a chronic low-level infection with occasional flare-ups.

What Are the Signs and Symptoms?

The symptoms of epididymitis are pain and swelling in the epididymis, often beginning when a man already has an infection of the prostate or urethra. Fever, feelings of illness, difficulty in urinating, pain when urinating, and pus in the urine are also symptoms. Physical strain, extreme sexual excitement, or the pressure of backed-up urine can all contribute to the chances that infective organisms will travel to the epididymis.

When infection of the epididymis begins, the swelling can be felt separate from the rest of the testicle, but as inflammation progresses the whole area will swell and become tender (although the testicle itself rarely is infected).

It can be difficult to differentiate epididymitis from torsion of the testicles (discussed later in this chapter), a condition in which a testicle twists and its blood supply is cut off. Both conditions cause a swollen and painful testicle, but in the case of epididymitis, symptoms of infection are also present and there is no evidence that blood flow to the area is cut off. Torsion of the testicle is a more common cause of testicular swelling in children, but swelling in adult men is more likely to be caused by infection.

What Is the Treatment?

Treatment for epididymitis is with antibiotics to eliminate the infection. Blood, urine, and prostate secretions may be tested and cultured to identify the organism causing infection so that the most effective drug can be used. *If the infection is sexually transmitted, the man's partner(s) must also be treated.*

Bed rest is usually needed in the three to four days when infection is acute, wearing an athletic supporter may help, and heat or ice packs may reduce discomfort. Lidocaine (an anesthetic) can be injected locally into the spermatic cord just above the testicle to reduce pain. Physical strain and sexual activity can make the symptoms worse and must be avoided during the illness. Most men recover from the acute phase within a few days, but swelling and pain may persist in the epididymis for as long as two weeks, and it may be a month or so before the epididymis completely returns to normal.

Frequent reinfections can be prevented by tying off the vas deferens on the affected side. This prevents infecting organisms from reaching the epididymis. The man will remain fertile as long as the other side is functioning normally.

Does It Affect Sexuality?

Severe epididymitis on both sides can cause sterility as a result of blockage of the epididymis and the vas deferens with scar tissue. Less severe infection or infection on one side only may permanently reduce a man's fertility and can also, in rare cases, make him completely sterile. Sexual activity must be avoided during the acute phase of the illness, but after recovery there are no permanent physical effects on a man's sexual ability.

Torsion of the Testicles

What Is It?

Testicles hang free within the scrotum, suspended from the spermatic cord, which contains the vas deferens and the blood supply. When a testicle becomes twisted on this cord, the blood supply is cut off and the testicle rapidly (within one to two hours) becomes swollen and painful. This condition is called **torsion of the testicle**. If the testicle does not untwist itself and is not treated within a few hours, the testicle will be destroyed and the ability to produce sperm and male hormones will be permanently lost in that testicle. Torsion is most common in boys 5 to 20 years of age but occasionally occurs in babies and in adult men. The tendency to develop this problem appears to be inherited and is related to what is called the "bell clapper deformity," which simply means that the way the man's testicles and spermatic cord are constructed makes it more likely that they will become twisted. Anyone who has had torsion on one side is at high risk of having it on the other side.

How Serious Is It?

Torsion of the testicles is very serious because it can cause the complete loss of the functions of one or both testicles. If a man loses the function of both testicles, he will be sterile and will require hormone therapy for the rest of his life in order to maintain normal masculine appearance and sexual ability. The damage caused by torsion can take place within as few as four hours, usually before the boy or man has sought medical treatment. If treatment for torsion takes place within 12 hours after onset of symptoms, the chances of saving the testicle are good. Treatment between 12 and 24 hours after onset may be successful, but treatment that is begun 24 hours or more after onset is not likely to save the testicle. In most cases of torsion, the testicle is lost because people are slow to recognize the severity of the problem and to seek medical care. In addition, the problem is sometimes incorrectly diagnosed as an infection and is not treated properly.

What Are the Signs and Symptoms?

The symptoms of torsion of a testicle are the sudden onset of swelling and severe pain in one side of the scrotum, particularly in a boy below the age of puberty. Pain in the lower abdomen, nausea, and vomiting may also occur. The whole testicle will be swollen, in contrast to the early stages of epididymitis when just the epididymis is swollen. Reportedly, torsion is most likely to occur after exposure to the cold and during sleep.

The major problem in diagnosing torsion is differentiating it from epididymitis, an infection of the epididymis. Since blood flow to the testicle is cut off by torsion but not by infection, several tests of blood flow to the testicle are used to diagnose the problem. They include the use of a special stethoscope (Doppler stethoscope) with ultrasound and a "nuclear scan," which involves injection of an extremely small dose of radioactive material into the bloodstream so that blood flow in the scrotal area can be observed on a scanner.

If torsion is not treated, the testicle will become extremely painful and swollen for a few days, reaching a size as large as a grapefruit in some cases. Then the swelling will slowly subside over a few months, and eventually the testicle will shrink to about the size of a pea.

What Is the Treatment?

Torsion of the testicle can be successfully treated in over 90 percent of cases if the correct treatment is begun within a few hours after onset of symptoms. Unfortunately, most boys and men do not get early treatment, and the testicle is destroyed.

Within the first few hours after torsion occurs, it may be possible for a physician to untwist a testicle without surgery. This is attempted with local anesthesia. Testicles almost always twist in a certain direction, so the physician attempts to rotate the testicle back in the other direction. If the treatment is successful, blood flow to the testicle will improve rapidly, and the pain and swelling will be relieved.

In most cases, surgery is needed to untwist the testicle and to fix it in place with a few stitches so that it cannot rotate again. This is minor surgery that only takes a few minutes but is usually performed under general (sleep) anesthesia.

Surgery may be needed after the acute phase of torsion even if it was not treated, because the testicular tissue has died. It may be necessary to remove the damaged testicle to avoid additional health problems. *It is important for all boys and men who have had torsion of one testicle to have the other testicle stitched into place as well, to prevent possible torsion on the other side in the future.*

Does It Affect Sexuality?

As explained before, most cases of torsion of the testicle result in loss of the function of the testicle. The testicle no longer produces sperm or male hormones. If only one testicle is affected, the man's single remaining testicle can produce a normal amount of male hormones, but he may become infertile.

The development of infertility in the remaining testicle is believed to be due to an autoimmune response built up in the body as a result of the destruction of the other testicle. In these cases the man's body creates cells that attack his own sperm cells, killing them.

If both testicles are destroyed by torsion, the

man has essentially been castrated. He will be sterile and will need to take hormone supplements all his life to maintain normal masculine appearance and sexual ability. If he does not take hormone supplements, he will gradually lose interest in sex, will lose the ability to have erections, and will develop a more feminine appearance.

Hydrocele, Varicocele, and Spermatocele

What Are They?

Hydrocele, varicocele, and spermatocele are three conditions affecting the scrotum that are usually quite harmless and do not normally require treatment. **Hydrocele** refers to a collection of excess fluid in the sac surrounding the testicles. **Varicocele** refers to an enlarged vein (varicose vein) protruding into the scrotum, usually just behind and above the testicles. It is estimated that 10 percent of men between ages 15 and 25 have a varicocele. **Spermatocele** refers to a small cyst filled with spermatic fluid, which is usually located just above the testicles.

How Serious Are They?

Hydrocele is not usually problematic unless the scrotum is made so enlarged and heavy by the extra fluid that it is uncomfortable or unsightly. The excess fluid can be drained periodically by needle aspiration, if necessary, or the condition can be permanently corrected by minor surgery.

Varicocele is not a threat to the health of a man, and usually has no symptoms, but it is a major cause of infertility in men (see Chapter 8). The presence of large blood vessels in the scrotum can raise the scrotal temperature enough to slow sperm production, resulting in infertility. When this is a problem, the protruding veins can be closed off through a minor surgical procedure. In most cases the man's sperm count will improve, although his fertility may never reach normal levels. When varicocele is the cause of infertility in a couple, 50 percent are able to start a pregnancy after surgery.

Some physicians recommend surgery on all varicoceles as soon as discovered, to prevent possible future infertility.

Spermatocele causes no health problems and does not require treatment unless it is annoying to the man, in which case it can be removed by minor surgery.

What Are the Signs and Symptoms?

The symptoms of hydrocele are an enlarged scrotum, in which one or both of the testicles feel as if they are larger than normal because they are surrounded by excess fluid (Figure 13–8). The sac of fluid may be soft or firm but is not tender or sore. A bright light held behind the scrotum passes through the fluid-filled sac. When a needle is used to aspirate (draw out) the fluid, it is a clear yellow liquid.

The symptoms of varicocele are a firm, lumpy (like a bag of worms) knot of blood vessels located in the scrotum above and behind the testicles, more frequently on the left than on the right. The knot becomes larger and firmer with physical straining or long hours of standing, and recedes and becomes softer when lying down. It may be tender. In rare cases, if the lump grows too large, it may exert pressure on other blood vessels serving the testicles.

The symptoms of spermatocele are usually a small painless cyst located above the testicles. It is usually not noticed by the man and is often identified during a medical checkup. It does not usually cause any problems and does not require treatment unless it is bothersome to the man.

What Is the Treatment?

These conditions usually do not require treatment. When they do, minor surgery is used.

Do They Affect Sexuality?

Varicocele is a major cause of infertility in men, but fortunately it is easily treated. None of the three conditions has any physical effect on a man's

FIGURE 13–8. *Hydrocele and spermatocele.*

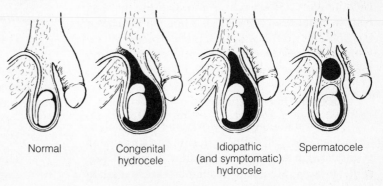

Normal

Congenital hydrocele

Idiopathic (and symptomatic) hydrocele

Spermatocele

sexual desire or ability. A man may want the conditions treated because he feels they are unattractive.

Cancer of the Testicles

What Is It?

Cancer of the testicles is a very rare disease, with only about two to three new cases per 100,000 men found each year in the United States. Testicular cancer develops most often in men aged 20 to 35, but it can occur in older men and in boys who have passed puberty. Men and boys with testicles that have never descended into the scrotum have a slightly higher risk of developing this rare cancer than others.

How Serious Is It?

Cancer of the testicles is a very serious disease because if it is not identified and treated early, it can spread through the body and cause death. *It is the most common type of cancer for men aged 20 to 35.* In 99 percent of cases only one testicle is cancerous. Fortunately, most cases of testicular cancer can be cured, if diagnosed early.

What Are the Signs and Symptoms?

The most common symptom of cancer of the testicles is a small, hard, painless, pea-sized lump located on the front or side of the testicle. It is much easier for a man to identify a lump that should not be there if he practices regular self-examination of the testicles (see description earlier in this chapter) so that he knows how they normally feel.

Other symptoms can be a feeling of heaviness of the scrotum, aching in the groin, and accumulation of fluid in the scrotum. These symptoms are usually caused by other health problems, but in a few cases the cause is identified as cancer.

What Is the Treatment?

There are several different types of cancer that affect the testicles, and the treatment is different for each. In almost every case, removal of the diseased testicle is necessary. If there is a chance the cancer has spread into the lymph glands of the pelvic and groin area, they may be removed as well. Chemotherapy and radiation may also be used.

Does It Affect Sexuality?

Removal of one testicle does not usually damage a man's sexual ability or desire, and fortunately testicular cancer affects both sides in only 1 percent of cases. Men with testicular cancer usually have decreased fertility, and removal of one testicle may contribute to this problem.

Other parts of the treatment, however, may cause problems. Removal of the lymph glands in the pelvic and groin area often causes reduction in the amount of seminal fluid (from the remaining testicle and the prostate gland) expelled at ejaculation, and in many cases there is a complete lack of fluid, causing a "dry ejaculation." Men with no fluid at ejaculation are sterile, and those with a reduced amount have reduced fertility. Chemotherapy and radiation can cause loss of desire for sex, impotence, and lack of fertility, but these effects are usually temporary. The man's sexual capacity should return and fertility may return when the treatment ends.

PROBLEMS OF THE PENIS

Phimosis

What Is It?

Phimosis is a condition in men who have not been circumcised in which the foreskin cannot be drawn back from the head (glans) of the penis. The problem is usually caused by poor hygiene and chronic infection, which causes the foreskin to become scarred and contracted. Circumcised men who have some foreskin left can also develop the problem. It is rare in men who bathe daily and keep their genitals (particularly the area under the foreskin) clean. A related condition, called **paraphimosis,** develops when the foreskin is pulled back from the glans and is so tight that it cannot be returned.

In most newborn babies who are not circumcised, the foreskin cannot be fully retracted. This is not a problem because there is no infection, and the foreskin grows, stretches, and detaches from the glans during the first few years of life. Eventually it slides over the glans easily. By age 3, over 90 percent of foreskins can be retracted. In a few cases retraction does not become possible for several more years, but it is not usually a problem.

How Serious Is It?

Phimosis is not usually a serious health problem. If left untreated, the infection could, over time, cause damage to the penis and to general health. In the case of paraphimosis, if the foreskin is too tight, it can cut off circulation to the head of the penis.

What Are the Signs and Symptoms?

The symptoms of phimosis are usually redness, swelling, and tenderness of the foreskin and glans, along with a discharge of pus from under the foreskin. The man or boy may not have noticed that the foreskin cannot be pulled back. In paraphimosis, the foreskin has been pulled back and is so tight that it won't return to its normal position. It has a rubber band effect right behind the glans, causing redness, swelling, and aching of the tip of the penis.

What Is the Treatment?

Good hygiene, including daily baths or showers in which the foreskin is retracted and the area under it is washed, will prevent almost all cases of phimosis in adolescent and adult men. All uncircumcised male children should be taught the importance of including the area under the foreskin in bathing. In infants and young boys where the foreskin does not fully retract, such cleansing is not necessary and should not be attempted.

When phimosis does develop, the infection that is normally present is treated with antibiotics. This usually brings quick relief from the symptoms. If it is necessary, the foreskin can be slit to make it looser and to allow drainage. Once the infection is cleared up and the swelling reduced, a circumcision may be done to prevent the problem from recurring.

Does It Affect Sexuality?

Erections are painful and sometimes impossible when phimosis is present since the foreskin does not retract to allow the penis to lengthen and expand. Sexual intercourse would be difficult or impossible under these conditions. Fortunately, phimosis is usually easy to treat, and recovery is rapid. In most cases there is no permanent damage to the penis or the man's sexual abilities.

Priapism

What Is It?

Priapism is an uncommon health problem in which the penis remains erect over a long period of time (hours or days) and the erection will not subside. It is usually a painful condition that is not associated with sexual desire or excitement, although it may develop after prolonged sexual stimulation. It is thought that priapism develops when there is a defect in the functioning of the circulatory or nervous systems that prevents blood in the penis from draining normally. In about 60 percent of cases, the cause is not known. In the other cases, diseases such as leukemia, sickle-cell disease, and pelvic tumors or infections have been identified as the cause. Other potential causes are injuries to the penis or to the spinal cord, and certain medica-

tions. Most cases of priapism resolve themselves within a few hours and cause no problems, but if the erection persists for more than a few hours, emergency medical treatment is needed to prevent tissue damage and possible future impotence.

How Serious Is It?

Priapism can be a very serious condition if it persists over many hours, because the tissue inside the penis will be damaged, resulting in permanent impotence (which may be either partial or complete). Priapism that is treated within a few hours may have no permanent effects. If the condition persists for a few days, however, the chances of permanent damage are very high. *Priapism is a medical emergency. Any man or boy who has the condition should seek medical care immediately.*

What Are the Signs and Symptoms?

The main symptom of priapism is a painful erection that lasts several hours without subsiding and takes place when the man is not feeling sexual desire or excitement.

What Is the Treatment?

The goal of treatment for priapism is to reduce the erection as quickly as possible and to keep it from recurring. Minor surgery is required in most cases. However, a combination of sedatives, pain-killers, and ice cold saline enemas is effective in some cases. If this treatment is not effective, the blood in the corpus cavernosa of the penis is drained by insertion of a needle. Surgery may also be performed to create a temporary drain either into a nearby vein or into another part of the penis. (See Chapter 1, Figure 1–6, for a drawing showing the corpus cavernosa.)

Does It Affect Sexuality?

It is fortunate that priapism is a rare condition, because many men are left partially or totally impotent by it as a result of damage inside the penis. The quicker the recovery, the better chance a man has of avoiding damage and impotence.

Peyronie's Disease (Twisted Penis)

What Is It?

Peyronie's disease is a condition in which the penis develops a curvature that is more pronounced when the penis is erect. The curvature is caused by the growth of fibrous plates of tissue (like scar tissue) under the skin of the penis. Peyronie's disease can be a cause of painful erections, and in some cases the severely bent angle of the penis leads to an inability to have intercourse. The cause of this condition is not known, but it is most frequently seen in middle-aged men.

How Serious Is It?

Peyronie's disease is a mild condition that is not a cause of death or serious illness. But it can cause difficult or painful intercourse and, in a few cases, the inability to have intercourse.

What Are the Signs and Symptoms?

The major symptom of this condition is a slowly increasing bend or twist in the angle of the penis, which becomes more noticeable when erect. If the angle is severe, erections may be painful. Flat plates of dense, heavy tissue can be felt under the skin of the penis (Figure 13–9). The condition usually develops slowly, over months or years, and often recedes and disappears in the same way. The disease does not progress to a serious stage in all men. Many develop mild symptoms, which do not cause serious problems and which never get any worse.

What Is the Treatment?

There is no known treatment that is effective in curing this condition. Often, however, the disease disappears over time without treatment. For this reason, because most men who have the problem still have normal sexual functioning, they are usually advised to wait for a year or so to see if the condition goes away without treatment. Severe cases, which prevent sexual activity and persist over months or years, can be treated with surgery, but the results are not often completely satisfactory. The fibrous tissue can be removed and replaced with skin grafts, and in some cases a penile prosthesis (described later in this chapter) may be implanted.

Some of the nonsurgical treatments that are used are radiation therapy; the injection of steroids, dimethyl sulfoxide (DMSO) or hormones into the area; and vitamin E and potassium pills. There is no evidence that any of these treatments is effective.

Does It Affect Sexuality?

In most cases of Peyronie's disease, sexuality is not affected, but an advanced case can have a very negative effect on a man's ability to have sexual relations and to enjoy them. The man's erection may be painful, and his penis may be bent at such an angle that it is not possible to penetrate his partner's vagina. Fortunately, most cases do not progress to this point, and men with only mild symptoms can usually adjust and continue to have satisfying sexual relations.

Bruises and Blood Clots

Like other parts of the body, the penis can be bruised and even fractured (although there is no bone in the penis). A fracture of the penis (which is uncommon) occurs when the erect penis is bent violently, tearing the walls of tissue inside. The result is internal bleeding and a painful injury. Surgery is sometimes needed.

After trauma to the penis or after physically rough intercourse, a man may find a painful, dark bruise on the penis. It is also possible for blood clots to develop in the veins just under the skin of the penis, creating a hard lump. Sometimes a vein may be clotted over several inches and may feel like a hard rigid cord under the skin. Bruising and blood clots under the skin of the penis are not serious problems, but they can be painful and can take many weeks to heal. Similar symptoms could be the sign of a more serious health problem, so if a man has a serious bruise or blood clot on the penis, he should have it checked by a doctor.

Bumps, Rashes, and Sexually Transmitted Diseases

There are many kinds of lumps, bumps, sores, and rashes that can develop on the penis. Most are not serious. Lichen planus and pityriasis rosea both cause itchy and scaly skin outbreaks, but they are not transmitted from one person to another and generally disappear over time, without treatment. Fungus infections such as yeast and ringworm often develop in the groin area and can affect the penis, especially if the man is not circumcised. Many kinds of sexually transmitted diseases cause

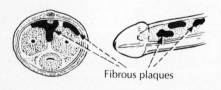

Fibrous plaques

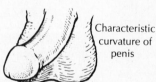

Characteristic curvature of penis

FIGURE 13–9. *Peyronie's disease.*

similar symptoms. (They are described in Chapter 14.) Since skin rashes on the genitals can be symptoms of serious sexually transmitted diseases, it is important to have them checked by a doctor, especially if you know or suspect that you may have been exposed to a disease.

Cancer of the Penis

What Is It?

Cancer of the penis is a very rare disease in the United States, amounting to fewer than 4 in 1,000 new cases of cancer and fewer than 2 in 1,000 cancer deaths in men. Most cancer of the penis involves the glans and foreskin and tends to develop in older men. The cause is not known, but poor hygiene and chronic infection or inflammation of the area seem to be associated with it.

How Serious Is It?

Although penile cancer is usually slow to grow and spread to other parts of the body, it is considered a very serious illness because it can cause death if left untreated, and because treatment in some cases involves amputation of part or all of the penis.

What Are the Signs and Symptoms?

The major symptom of cancer of the penis is a sore or growth on the penis that will not heal. It is most likely to be found on the skin of the glans or the inner surface of the foreskin, but it can also appear on the shaft of the penis. It can be a lump, a growth, or an ulcer and may appear similar to the symptoms of several sexually transmitted diseases. Identification of the specific disease causing the symptoms is made by biopsy and laboratory studies.

Other symptoms can be pain or bleeding from the site, pain or difficulty on urination, and a discharge from the penis.

What Is the Treatment?

There are several ways to treat cancer of the penis. Small growths or ulcers can be treated with chemotherapy, either in locally applied cream or in pills or injections. Radiation can also be used to shrink the growth. Larger tumors are surgically removed or treated with lasers to prevent spread of the disease. The surgical procedure is to amputate the penis at a point a little less than half an inch below the edge of the growth. The tip of the penis is then closed with flaps of extra skin, and a new urethral opening is made so the man can urinate normally. In most cases the man will still be able to control his urine after this surgery, and his ability to have an erection and to ejaculate will also remain. He can resume sexual intercourse when recovered, but his penis will be shorter. In very advanced cases of the disease, the entire penis may be amputated and a new opening for the bladder made in the groin. If the disease has spread to the lymph nodes of the groin or abdomen, more surgery and radiation treatments may be needed.

Does It Affect Sexuality?

Any disease that affects the penis affects a man's sexuality. Fortunately, cancer of the penis is very rare and tends to develop in older men who may be less active sexually. The original symptoms of a growth or ulcer near the head of the penis can make sexual intercourse difficult, painful, or unpleasant. Treatment with radiation or chemotherapy is a slow process that may temporarily have a negative effect on sexual interest and ability. Partial amputation of the penis leaves the man with a shortened penis, and complete amputation ends his ability to have normal sexual intercourse but does not end his interest or desire for sex. To continue sexual activity, he must learn other means of satisfying his partner and himself (see Chapter 3).

IMPOTENCE

What Is It?

Impotence is the inability to have an erection sufficient to penetrate the vagina of the partner. There are many different causes for impotence, which may be temporary or permanent. Most men experience occasional temporary impotence at some point in their lives as a result of such things as exhaustion, heavy drinking, or lack of attraction to the partner. However, approximately 10 million American men are believed to be chronically impotent.

What Causes It?

Impotence can be divided into two kinds: **psychogenic** (caused by psychological or emotional factors) and **organic** (caused by problems in the body's functioning). In the past it was believed that 90 percent of impotence was psychogenic, but recent advances in diagnosing and treating the problem show that perhaps 50 percent of impotence is psychological or emotional, and the other 50 percent organic. Organic impotence is more likely to be found in older men, but psychogenic impotence is found in men of all ages.

This section of the book deals only with organically caused impotence. For information about psychogenic impotence, see Chapter 3.

There are many causes of organic impotence:

1. Central nervous system damage or disorders
2. Diabetes
3. Alcoholism
4. Hormone disorders
5. High blood pressure
6. Circulatory system disorders
7. Infection, surgery, and injury
8. Effects of drugs

Details about these causes are given in Chapter 3.

Diagnosing Impotence

Tremendous progress has been made in recent years in determing the specific causes of impotence so that effective treatment can be planned. However, the exact mechanisms by which erections occur are still not completely understood. If a man gets any erections at all, including morning erections, which are unrelated to sex, the cause of his impotence is not physical.

One simple test to determine whether impotence is psychological or has to do with organic problems in body functioning is the "postage stamp test." In the normal course of sleep each night, men who are not organically impotent get from three to five erections (of which they are not usually aware) lasting 20 to 40 minutes each. If a man sticks a ring of postage stamps around his penis before going to sleep at night, these erections (if they occur) will be strong enough to tear the stamps at the perforations so that the ring will come off. If no erections occur, the ring will be intact. This test is not 100 percent reliable, and a man who tries it might want to use it for several nights in a row.

The same type of test (with better equipment) can be done at a doctor's office under supervision and is probably more accurate. Other tests that can be done to determine the cause of impotence are checks of blood pressure and pulse within the penis and of penile arteriography (in which dye is injected into the arteries that supply the penis with blood. Then the blood supply can be checked with a scanner). The bulbocavernosus reflex latency test (in which a nervous system reflex is checked by applying electrical or other stimulation to the penis) and cavernosography (in which the blood in the corpus cavernosum of the penis is injected with dye so that the drainage system of veins in the area can be seen and studied) are two other techniques.

What Is the Treatment?

The treatment of organically caused impotence depends on the cause of the problem. If the cause is prescribed drugs or substances such as alcohol, discontinuing use of them should solve the problem (unless, as in the case of chronic alcoholism, permanent damage has been done to the system). In the case of necessary medications such as drugs for high blood pressure (hypertension), a change in the amount or type of drug used may help.

Hormone imbalances can usually be treated with hormone replacement therapy; surgery might be required if the imbalance is due to a tumor or other abnormality of hormone-producing glands. Surgery to restore potency by undoing the effects of circulatory system damage such as atherosclerosis has not yet been very successful, but new approaches are being developed.

A temporary drug treatment (papavirine) is available (on an experimental basis in the United States), which a man can inject into the penis each time he wants an erection. The drug causes increased blood flow to the penis and produces an erection in about two-thirds of impotent men. The erection lasts several hours and does not go down after ejaculation. This treatment is growing in popularity for men who have intercourse once a week or less often, but is not as practical for those who want an erection more frequently, because it requires an injection each time. The drug is not available everywhere because it is not yet approved by the Food and Drug Administration.

At present the most effective treatment for impotence that is permanent and total (caused by defects in the nervous system or the circulatory system, or by chronic disease) is the use of penile implants.

Penile Implants

Penile implants are rigid or inflatable rods implanted inside the penis to provide the stiffness and rigidity of an erection and make intercourse possible. *It is estimated that over 100,000 men have had penile implants inserted since 1979, and the number is rising each year.* Most forms of health insurance, including Medicare, pay for penile implants. Most of the men receiving implants are over 50 years of age, although quite a few men in their forties have them also. Diabetes is the cause of impotence in 27 percent of the men receiving implants.

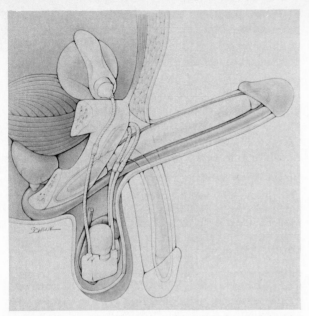

FIGURE 13–10. *One model of an inflatable penile prosthesis.*

Penile implants (also called **penile prostheses**) come in two basic types: rigid or semirigid (malleable) and inflatable. Both kinds consist of two silicone rods placed inside the penis in the corpus cavernosum, which is the space that normally fills with blood to provide an erection. The prostheses come in a number of sizes to fit all men. The rigid or semirigid (malleable) prosthesis is chosen by about 60 percent of men receiving prostheses because it is the simplest, least expensive, and least likely to break down. In some cases it can be inserted during outpatient surgery, using only local anesthesia. The main disadvantage of the rigid or malleable implant is that it gives the man a permanent erection, which he may find embarrasing or inconvenient at times. One form of semirigid or malleable implant has an inner core of steel or silver wire that can be bent so that the penis can be tucked into a comfortable, nonerect position when not in use for sex. Other forms have a hinge device that allows the penis to bend so it will not show under clothes. With these devices, however, the penis will still be somewhat enlarged and rigid.

The inflatable prosthesis comes in several models, the best known of which is pictured in Figure 13–10. There are three main parts to the system: the penile implants; a bulb filled with fluid, which is placed in the abdomen; and a pump, which is placed in the scrotum. The penile implants serve as reservoirs for fluid, which can be pumped in when an erection is wanted and drained out when sexual activity is completed, leaving a soft, flaccid penis. The man squeezes the pump 10 to 15 times when he wants to inflate the

rods in the penis, and presses a button on the pump when he wants the rods to deflate.

The inflatable prosthesis is more expensive and more complicated to install, usually requiring a hospital stay and general (sleep) anesthesia. Because it is more complicated, it is more likely to break down and require additional surgery at a later date. The estimated life span of an inflatable prosthesis is three to five years.

The advantages of the inflatable prosthesis are that it is more natural looking, more comfortable, and more convenient because an erection is produced only when needed. It also gives a more "natural" erection, since it inflates the thickness as well as the length of the penis. Couples who have tried both the rigid and the inflatable implant report that the inflatable prosthesis is the more satisfying for sexual intercourse.

A third type, called the inflatable or liquid malleable prosthesis, has a fluid reservoir and pump contained in the implant. When an erection is desired, fluid is pumped up from the end closest to the body into the middle and outer parts of the prosthesis. The liquid malleable implant provides an erection similar to the rigid or malleable prosthesis.

Choosing a penile prosthesis can be difficult. A man who is considering a prosthesis should talk with a physician who can discuss all the types that are available. He also may want to get a second or third opinion. He should be aware that new models are continually being developed. If the man is married or has a permanent sexual partner, he will probably want to involve the partner in making the decision as well. Not all doctors are trained to do the surgery to implant all models, but they should be able to discuss the features of each and refer the man to another physician if necessary.

Implantation of a penile prosthesis is minor surgery, which carries the risks of infection and reaction to anesthesia associated with all surgery. Other complications can be discomfort from the prosthesis, particularly if it is incorrectly placed or the wrong size. Men can begin sexual intercourse as soon as three weeks after the implant, but it may not be completely comfortable until 6 to 12 weeks after surgery.

LACK OF EJACULATION

What Is It?

The ability to have an erection and the ability to ejaculate are separate functions in men, controlled by different parts of the nervous system. It is possible for a man to have erections and be able to have intercourse but be unable to ejaculate. A man may have a complete lack of ejaculation or what is called **retrograde ejaculation,** in which he ejaculates but the fluid goes the wrong way—up into the bladder rather than down the urethra and out through the penis. In this case the sensation of having an ejaculation is there, but nothing comes out. If a man cannot ejaculate, he is sterile.

What Causes It?

The most common physical cause of lack of ejaculation is probably the effect of surgery that damages nerves in the lower abdomen and pelvic area. Medications and drugs (including alcohol) can also affect the nervous system in such a way that they prevent the complex ejaculatory response. In addition, injuries to the spinal cord, especially those that paralyze the lower body, often cause loss of ejaculation, although the man often still has erections. Prostate surgery causes retrograde ejaculation in many cases because a small valve that normally closes at ejaculation and prevents semen from going into the bladder is damaged or removed. Like impotence, lack of ejaculation can also be caused by psychological or emotional factors. In these cases a man often is not able to ejaculate with a partner, but may ejaculate when masturbating or may have nocturnal emissions (wet dreams). If lack of ejaculation has physical causes, such as nerve damage as an aftereffect of prostate surgery, the man will not ejaculate under any conditions.

What Is the Treatment?

Treatment of lack of ejaculation depends on the cause. Medications can be discontinued or changed, or recreational drug use can be stopped. If the problem is psychological, psychotherapy or sex therapy may help (see Chapter 3). If the problem is caused by nerve damage or by surgical removal of needed valves or organs, there is no treatment that can restore the ejaculatory function.

Does It Affect Sexuality?

Lack of ejaculation definitely affects a man's sexual experience. How it is affected depends on the exact nature of the problem, whether the man still enjoys the sensations of orgasm, and whether he is concerned about being fertile.

Inability to ejaculate means that the man is sterile, because the sperm do not leave his body. He may have erections and be able to engage in sexual intercourse, but the sensations of ejaculation will be missing (in the case of complete lack of ejaculation) or changed (in the case of retrograde ejaculation). The sensation of orgasm is still there for many men (including those with retrograde ejaculation), but most report that it feels somewhat different. Most men with retrograde ejaculation caused by prostate surgery do have orgasms and report that, once they grow accustomed to the change, their sexual relations are very satisfying.

FOR FURTHER READING

BROOKS, MARVIN B. *Lifelong Sexual Vigor. How to Avoid and Overcome Impotence.* New York: Doubleday, 1981.

ROWAN, ROBERT L., M.D. *Men and Their Sex.* New York: Irvington Publishers, 1982.

SILBER, SHERMAN J., M.D. *The Male: A Comprehensive and Clearly Written Guide to the Male Sexual System.* New York: Charles Scribner's Sons, 1981.

RESOURCES

Information and referral services are available in your local community through the county or state Department of Health, community hospitals, and the United Way agency. In addition, the following national resources can be contacted:

American Cancer Society
90 Park Avenue
New York, NY 10016
(212) 599–3600
A nonprofit organization that provides information and education on cancer through its local chapters, some of which provide free services to cancer patients. (Contact the nearest local chapter.)

American Diabetes Association National Service Center
1660 Duke Street
Alexandria, VA 22314
(800) 232–3472
(703) 331–8303
A nonprofit organization providing information, education, and referral to diabetes-related services.

Cancer Information Hotline
(800) 4CA–NCER
A hotline maintained by the National Cancer Institute to answer questions and provide information about cancer to patients, health care providers, and researchers.

National High Blood Pressure Information Center
U.S. Department of Health and Human Services
120/80 National Institutes of Health
Bethesda, MD 20892
(301) 951–3260

Hill Burton Program
U.S. Department of Health and Human Services
(800) 638–0742
in Maryland: (800) 492–0359
A government service that provides information and referrals for free medical care in your local area.

14

Sexually Transmitted Diseases

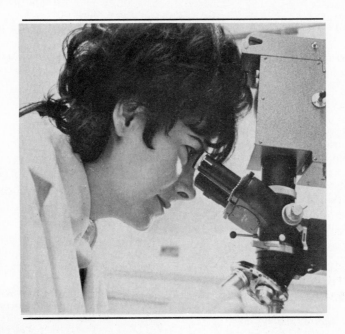

DEFINITION

Sexually transmitted diseases (STDs) are infectious illnesses that are passed from one person to another through sexual intercourse or other kinds of intimate contact. Another name for STDs is **venereal diseases.** In most cases they are transmitted from contact of the mucous membranes, which means that the mouth, rectum, and eyes, as well as the penis and vagina, are places where STD organisms can be passed from one person to another.

A few STDs are serious and can be life-threatening or cause sterility, but most are minor illnesses, which can be cured with medical treatment. For a detailed discussion of acquired immune deficiency syndrome (AIDS), see Chapter 15.

Some diseases, like **hepatitis,** are not considered STDs because in most cases they are transmitted in other ways, but they can be transmitted through sexual contact as well. Other conditions such as **yeast infections** (also known as candida) can develop in the reproductive tracts of men and women without sexual contact, but if the person who has the condition is sexually active, it can spread to the partner.

The incidence of sexually transmitted diseases has increased tremendously in the United States since the late 1960s. **Gonorrhea** is the most common serious infection, with an estimated 2.5 million cases a year. **Chlamydia,** which causes similar health problems, is believed to affect an equally large number of women and men. Genital herpes (which is not a serious condition for most people) is even more common, affecting approximately 20 million Americans at present and continuing to spread rapidly.

There are many reasons for the increase in STDs. The "sexual revolution" has meant that men and women have more sexual partners over a lifetime, which increases the chances of infection. The mobility of the population means that infections are quickly spread from one part of the country to another. In addition, birth control methods have changed, and the condom and diaphragm, which provide some protection against STDs, have become less popular in recent years.

HOW TO AVOID SEXUALLY TRANSMITTED DISEASES

There are many ways to reduce the chances that you will catch a sexually transmitted disease.

1. *Keep the number of sexual partners low.* The fewer sexual partners you have, the less chance that you will come in contact with an STD. People who do not have a sexual partner or who have only one partner (who does not have sex with others) have the lowest risk.

2. *Avoid sex with strangers.* People you don't know are less likely to warn you if they have an STD, and you are less likely to know about it. People who use prostitutes are taking a big chance (as are prostitutes themselves).

3. *Use barrier or spermicidal contraception.* The condom provides the best protection for both the man and the woman against STDs. The chemicals in spermicides such as foam or the jelly used with diaphragms also kill some disease organisms. Intrauterine devices (IUDs) should be avoided because they can make infections worse for the woman if she does get an STD. (See Chapter 9 for information on contraceptive methods.)

4. *Get medical treatment immediately if there is any chance you have been exposed.* See a health care provider immediately if you develop any signs of infection after sexual contact. Seek health care also if you have any reason to suspect that your partner may be infected, even if you have no symptoms. *Serious STDs like gonorrhea sometimes cause no symptoms, but still cause damage and can be passed on!* Remember the STD organisms can be located in the mouth, throat, and rectum as well as in the sexual organs.

5. *Maintain good general health and hygiene.* A person in good health has more resistance to all kinds of diseases, including STDs. Daily baths or showers help, as does keeping the sexual organs clean. Frequent douching for women is not recommended because it can upset the natural chemical balance of the vagina, which helps to protect against infection. Women should always wipe from front to back after using the toilet to avoid spreading germs from the rectal area to the vagina.

6. *Avoid infection from close contact with persons who have an STD.* Almost all cases of sexually transmitted diseases are passed on by sexual contact. It is not easy to catch them by any other means. However, some disease organisms can live for a few hours outside the body on bathing suits, towels, underwear, and even toilet seats. Never share bathing suits or towels with an infected person and never let a child do this. Directly touching an area such as a herpes sore can also transmit the infection. Each disease is different, and your doctor can advise you about what precautions should be taken if you live with or are close to someone who is being treated for an STD.

7. *When getting checkups, tell your health care provider if you may have been exposed.* Having laboratory tests for STDs when you get your regular checkups is good protection against dangerous silent infections.

8. *Be aware that having an STD once does not protect you from getting it again.* STDs are not like measles or chicken pox; you do not develop immunity after having one. You can be infected over and over again if you are exposed.

STDS AND THE LAW

The federal government requires that the states report all known cases of gonorrhea, syphilis, and AIDS (acquired immune deficiency syndrome) because they are a danger to the health of the public. Granuloma inguinale, chancroid, and lymphogranuloma venereum (which are very rare in the United States today) and hepatitis B (which is transmitted

Singles bars are popular places to meet new sexual partners.

sexually as well as by other means) must also be reported to the federal government.

Reporting of these diseases is done through state and local departments of public health, and each state handles things differently. Private doctors, hospitals, and clinics are required to report all cases of these diseases to the health department. However, not all cases get reported.

After receiving a report, the local health department may want to interview the infected person to find out with whom he or she has had sexual contact. The purpose of this is to prevent the STD from spreading further and to make sure that all persons who have been exposed get treatment. This is very important because serious illness, infertility, and even death can result from these diseases. Health departments keep the names of persons who have been reported confidential and are usually able to interview sexual contacts without identifying the infected person.

Even if the health department does not get involved, it is very important for people who have an STD to let all their sexual partners know about the illness. It may be embarrassing or upsetting to do it, but the future health and even the lives of other persons could be at stake.

GONORRHEA

What Is It?

Gonorrhea is caused by *Neisseria gonorrhoeae*, a bacteria that is transmitted from one person to another during sexual intercourse. It usually affects the reproductive organs but can also be found in the mouth and throat or the rectum (usually as a result of oral or anal intercourse) and can be passed on to the eyes as well.

The chances of catching this infectious disease from a single sexual encounter with an infected person are high, close to 100 percent for women having intercourse with an infected man, and 20 to 25 percent for men having sex with an infected woman.

How Serious Is It?

Gonorrhea is a very serious disease because if it is not treated, it can spread from the reproductive system throughout the body causing systemwide infection, which can involve the heart, the nervous system, and the joints. Untreated gonorrhea in women often produces pelvic inflammatory disease (PID) when it spreads up from the cervix into the uterus, the Fallopian tubes, and the ovaries. When pelvic inflammatory disease develops from gonor-

rhea infection, it results in blockage of the Fallopian tubes and sterility in 15 to 40 percent of cases. In men, infection of the prostate or the epididymis (tubes carrying sperm from the testicles) may develop. Gonorrhea is especially dangerous because, in an estimated 80 percent of women and 10 to 20 percent of men, it is a silent disease with no noticeable symptoms. Severe health damage, including permanent sterility, often occurs in women who are not aware that they have an infection. Women who have gonorrhea at the time they give birth may transmit the infection to the baby's eyes.

Gonorrhea is rarely fatal, but it is a major cause of illness, hospitalization, and loss of time from work and school. It is the most frequently reported communicable disease in the United States.

What Are the Signs and Symptoms?

In men, the most frequent symptoms of gonorrhea infection are a discharge from the penis, a burning sensation in the urethra, and pain when urinating. A few men may be infected but have no symptoms. Infections of the throat or rectum often have no symptoms and may not be diagnosed.

In women, unfortunately, as many as 80 percent of gonorrhea infections have no symptoms. Many are diagnosed during routine checkups or during medical treatment for other problems, long after they have caused damage to the woman's body. For this reason, women who believe that they could have been exposed to gonorrhea should ask for a gonorrhea culture each time they go to the doctor or clinic for family planning, a checkup, or a Pap smear.

In women who do have symptoms, there may be a vaginal discharge or, less commonly, pain and burning on urination and pain in the urethra. If the gonorrhea has developed into pelvic inflammatory disease, pain or aching of the lower abdomen may be present, as well as fever and feelings of being ill.

Diagnosis of gonorrhea is made by a culture, which takes two days to develop. Cultures should be taken from the genitals and also from other sites in the body where there has been sexual contact, such as the throat and the rectum.

When gonorrhea is found in young children, sexual abuse by an adult is often the cause.

What Is the Treatment?

Gonorrhea is usually treated very successfully with antibiotics, usually penicillin and tetracycline. Some medications can be given as a single injection; others are in pill form and must be taken over time. Penicillin-resistant strains of gonorrhea must be treated with another drug, and so must people who are allergic to penicillin. If severe pelvic inflammatory disease and systemwide infection have developed, hospitalization is necessary for treatment. Gonorrhea located in the rectum or throat reacts differently to drugs and may require different medication. Gonorrhea patients often have other STDs as well, such as chlamydia, which require treatment at the same time.

All recent sexual partners of a person with gonorrhea must be examined, tested, and treated. All persons treated for gonorrhea need to be retested after treatment to make sure the infection is gone. Sexual intercourse must be avoided or condoms must be used until the person is cured of the infection.

CHLAMYDIA AND OTHER NONGONOCOCCAL INFECTIONS

What Are They?

A number of different organisms, including chlamydia, cause illnesses similar to gonorrhea in both men and women. Often, two or more organisms are involved at the same time, and chlamydia or another infection may be present at the same time as gonorrhea. Chlamydia is found in about 40 percent of all cases of urethritis (in men) and cervical infection and pelvic inflammatory disease (in women). Infections from chlamydia and other nongonococcal (not gonorrhea) organisms are very common and are found more often than gonorrhea in some parts of the country. Chlamydia was identified as a common STD only a few years ago, and not all doctors and clinics have the facilities to do the laboratory tests to diagnose it. Even with the proper facilities, these infections are sometimes difficult to diagnose.

How Serious Are They?

Chlamydia and other nongonococcal infections are generally less serious for men than gonorrhea, but for women they can be just as dangerous. They take longer to develop, are more likely to have no symptoms, and are often difficult to cure. In men they cause inflammations of the urethra, the prostate gland, and the epididymis (the tubes that carry sperm from the testes to the urethra). In women, infection starts at the cervix and may travel to the uterus, Fallopian tubes, and ovaries. Pelvic inflammatory disease may develop and cause scarring, and this scar tissue may cause sterility by blocking the Fallopian tubes. Babies born to women with these diseases often develop infections of the eyes

and respiratory tract, including pneumonia. In fact, it has recently been noted that as much as 30 to 50 percent of pneumonia cases in infants under six months of age may be caused by chlamydia infections passed on from the mother during childbirth.

Women with chlamydia and other nongonococcal infections are more likely to have abnormal Pap smear results than others.

What Are the Signs and Symptoms?

An estimated 25 percent of men with chlamydia have no symptoms. Those who do have symptoms complain of frequent and painful urination and of a urethral discharge. The discharge is likely to be less than with gonorrhea and may be noticeable only when first getting up in the morning. Prostate problems or inflamed testicles may also be symptoms if the infection has progressed to those areas.

These infections have no symptoms in 80–90 percent of infected women as well, but when symptoms exist, there is vaginal discharge and, if the infection has progressed, lower abdominal pain, fever, and feelings of being ill.

What Is the Treatment?

The usual treatment for chlamydia and other nongonococcal infections is the antibiotic tetracycline in pill form given to the infected person and to his or her partner. Erythromycin is also used. Approximately 80 percent of cases are cured after one week of antibiotic treatment. Those that are not are given a second course of treatment. Sexual intercourse should be avoided until the treatment is completed. Reinfection is likely unless all partners are treated.

HERPES

What Is It?

Herpes is an infectious disease caused by the **herpes simplex virus,** which enters the body through the mucous membranes or skin and causes blisters and sores on the skin. Once a person has been infected with herpes, the virus remains in the body permanently (locating itself in nerve cells at the base of the spine), although it may not cause symptoms for months or years at a time.

There are two types of herpes simplex viruses (HSVs). HSV I is transmitted by normal human contact and is the cause of cold sores and fever blisters affecting the face, lips, and mouth. HSV II (also known as **genital herpes**) is transmitted primarily

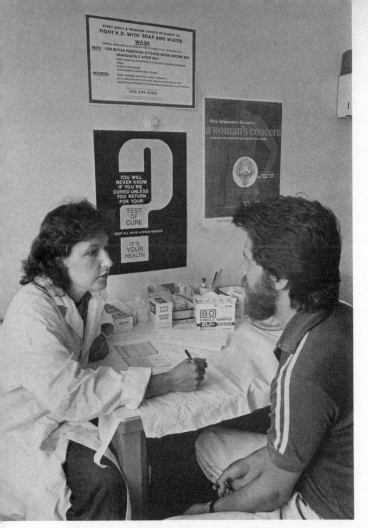

Herpes is a common sexually transmitted disease.

by sexual activity and creates similar blisters and sores in the genital area. Both HSV I and HSV II are found throughout the world, and in some populations close to 100 percent of the people have been exposed to HSV I by age 5. HSV II is not quite so widespread, but one study done at a prenatal clinic in the United States showed 61 percent of women aged 35 to 44 had been infected. Older persons have higher rates of herpes of both types because they have lived longer and thus have had more opportunity to be exposed to the disease.

Although HSV I generally is restricted to the face and mouth, and HSV II is the cause of nearly 90 percent of genital herpes, either virus can spread to other parts of the body. Type I infections are most frequently found in children, and Type II infections are most common after sexual activity is begun because they are transmitted primarily by sexual contact. Adults who have never been sexually active rarely have HSV II.

HSV II is a rapidly spreading STD in the United States, with an estimated 20 million Americans now carrying the virus and at least half a million new cases identified each year.

The following section presents information about HSV II (genital herpes).

How Serious Is It?

Genital herpes is a chronic disease for which there is no known cure. However, there is effective treatment for the sores that break out. Genital herpes is usually a mild disease and rarely requires hospitalization, but it can be very painful and can cause a great deal of time to be lost from work or school if it recurs frequently. It is not known why one person will have recurrences of the infection every few weeks, whereas another may never have a problem after the first outbreak. The discomfort of the sores and the fear of infecting others can cause infected men and women to reduce the frequency with which they have sexual intercourse. This incurable and unpredictable disease can cause psychological and emotional problems for some men and women.

The most serious complication of genital herpes is the risk for pregnant women of infecting the baby during childbirth. Herpes infections in the newborn can be fatal. If a woman has an active infection at the time the baby is due, caesarean section is used to deliver the baby. This protects the baby against infection because the baby does not pass through the cervix and vagina, where the sores are located. In a few cases, however, the infection may travel through the cervix to the fetus, and the baby may be born infected. Some women who have HSV II have no symptoms and are not aware of the disease. In rare cases, giving birth to an infected baby may be the first time they learn of the problem. It is very important for pregnant women who think they may have been exposed to herpes to share this information with their doctor.

Genital herpes virus is also believed to be related to higher rates of cancer of the cervix in women, and possibly to higher rates of miscarriage and premature delivery.

What Are the Signs and Symptoms?

First Infection

Genital herpes infection usually develops within three to seven days after sexual contact with an infected person, but it can develop as late as 22 days after the contact. The first infection with HSV II usually causes a lot of discomfort, as the following description of the symptoms shows. The infected person may lose several days from work or school. One or more fluid-filled blisters appear in the genital area. After two to three days the blisters break, becoming painful skin ulcers or sores. The sores heal by themselves within two to three weeks. The first infection with HSV II usually also includes swelling of the lymph nodes in the pelvic area and flu-like symptoms of low fever, headache, and feelings of illness. Urination may be painful if urine comes in contact with the open sores. Sores in women may develop on the lips of the vagina, near the rectum, on the upper thighs or buttocks, or inside the vagina and on the cervix. It is possible to be unaware of the illness if the sores occur only within the vagina.

In men, the ulcers develop on the penis or scrotum, near the rectum, on the upper thighs, and on the buttocks. In rare cases they may develop inside the urethra (which carries urine and semen through the penis), causing painful urination.

In severe infection, both women and men may find that the nerves in the pelvic area may be temporarily affected, causing inability to urinate, constipation or diarrhea, or a numb sensation in the lower back or pelvic area. In rare cases, meningitis (inflammation of the membranes surrounding the brain and spinal cord) may develop.

HSV II infections are usually found in the genital area, but they can also be transmitted to the mouth and throat and the rectum by oral and anal intercourse. Infection of the eyes can also develop if a person touches the eyes with contaminated hands.

Genital herpes is usually diagnosed by physical examination and the patient's report of the symptoms. It can also be diagnosed through laboratory tests of cells scraped from the sores.

Later Infections

After the first infection has cleared up, the infected man or woman will have no symptoms of the disease. In most cases, however, the disease will recur, with new blisters and sores. The symptoms will be milder than with the first infection and will heal more quickly, within one to two weeks. A typical pattern for later infections is to develop the blisters five to eight times a year. Some men and women, however, never experience later infections, whereas others continue to develop new blisters every few weeks. Good general health and nutrition, and keeping the stress level low, help to provide some protection against recurrences of the illness. The infection is more likely to develop when the person has a cold, a fever, gets sunburned, or is under stress or exhausted. Some women develop the infection right before or after their monthly periods, or if they have a vaginal infection.

No Symptoms

Most of the time, a man or woman with HSV II infection has no symptoms at all, but the virus is still in the body, in a dormant or resting phase. *Genital herpes is transmitted to another person when the disease is active (when there are blisters or sores present). When there are no symptoms, the infected person is not likely to pass the disease on to the partner.* It is not common, but it is possible for there to be an active sore (such as on a woman's cervix) of which the person is not aware. In such a case the disease could be passed on unknowingly.

How Do I Avoid Getting Herpes or Giving It to Others?

At present, there is no cure for genital herpes. The best treatment is to avoid catching it in the first place. If you already have herpes, it is important to avoid passing it on to your partner or to family members. The chances of getting herpes can be kept low if the suggestions listed earlier in this chapter under "How to Avoid Sexually Transmitted Diseases" are followed. If your partner has herpes and you don't, you must be very careful to avoid sexual contact when he or she has a blister or sore. If you decide to have sex anyway, use a condom *and* a spermicidal cream, jelly, or foam that contains Nonoxynol–9, a product that kills other organisms beside sperm and may help to prevent infection. Since it is possible (though not common) to pass herpes to others through sharing towels, bathing suits, and so on, when you have active sores you should keep towels separate. Wear cotton underpants in bed if you share your bed, and do not share bathing suits or underwear with others. Avoid touching the sores on yourself or your partner, and wash your hands thoroughly if you do. Herpes virus can enter the skin through small cuts or breaks in the skin, as well as through mucous membranes. Keep the hands especially clean when touching the eyes or putting in contact lenses.

Pregnant women with herpes must inform their doctor of this fact so that they can be sure the baby is not infected during childbirth. If the woman has active sores at the time she delivers, a caesarean section will be needed. HSV II infection in a newborn can cause blindness, brain damage, and even death.

What Is the Treatment?

There is no cure for genital herpes at this time. The treatments that do exist are intended to lessen the severity of the symptoms of the illness and make the infected person more comfortable. Researchers are working on possible immunizations or cures and are looking for more effective ways to treat herpes. Experimental treatments are being tested by some doctors and clinics.

The most effective treatment now available for the symptoms of herpes is acyclovir (sold as Zovirax), which comes as an ointment, in pill form, and as an intravenous drug. This is a prescription drug that has the effect of shortening the time the symptoms last, and helping the sores to heal quickly.

The other treatments for herpes infection are aimed at alleviating the symptoms. They include pain-killing gels, sitz baths, keeping the area dry with cornstarch and loose-fitting clothing, and taking aspirin or aspirin substitutes. Antibiotics may help prevent secondary infection from developing, but they will not help with the herpes infection. Rest and good nutrition help, and some people believe that extra doses of vitamin C are helpful. There are a number of home remedies that people have developed to reduce the discomfort, such as wet compresses containing various herbs, aloe gel, and so on. Each person needs to explore what helps him or her to feel most comfortable, but keeping the area clean and dry at all times is helpful.

Because women with genital herpes appear to develop cervical cancer at higher rates than other women, it is important for them to get a Pap smear (see Chapter 12) at least once a year, and more often if their doctor recommends it.

SYPHILIS

What Is It?

Syphilis is a life-threatening sexually transmitted disease caused by the organism *Treponema pallidum*. It can be difficult to diagnose because the disease has several stages, each with different symptoms. If syphilis is not treated, it can result in serious damage to the nervous system, brain, and heart and can also end in death.

Syphilis is known throughout the world and reached its peak of infection in the United States during World War II. Today, syphilis is a rare disease in the United States, with approximately 10 new cases of syphilis each year per 100,000 people. The disease is uncommon today for two reasons; first, the discovery of antibiotics that can treat the disease effectively, and second, the requirement in most states that couples getting married take a blood test for syphilis. The recommended practice of testing all pregnant women for syphilis has also helped to prevent spread of the disease. Syphilis is still considered an important disease, however, because it is very infectious, can be fatal, and is transmitted by pregnant women to their infants.

Syphilis is very easily transmitted, with a 50 to 60 percent chance of catching the infection from a single sexual encounter with an infected person. The disease is about twice as common among men as among women, and about one-half of the new cases of syphilis discovered each year in the United States are in homosexual men.

How Serious Is It?

Syphilis is a very serious sexually transmitted disease because of the enormous damage it can do to the body, the fact that it can be passed on to unborn children, and the fact that it causes death. Untreated syphilis, in the late (tertiary) phase, causes brain damage, mental illness, paralysis, blindness, deafness, damage to the heart and circulatory system, and eventually death. Untreated syphilis is the cause of some of the saddest cases in mental hospitals and nursing homes today. The infected person can still be cured even in the late stages, but damage already done to the brain, nervous system, and other parts of the body cannot be undone.

What Are the Signs and Symptoms?

The symptoms of syphilis are different for each stage of the disease. They are described next.

Primary Syphilis

Primary syphilis refers to the body's first set of reactions to a new infection, which usually develop within 10 to 90 days after exposure to an infected sexual partner. The only symptom of primary syphilis is usually a **chancre** (pronounced "shanker"), which is a painless skin ulcer, usually in the area of the genitals but also sometimes appearing on the mouth, hands, anus, or any other area that may have been in contact with the infected person during sexual activity. There is usually only a single chancre, which (if not treated) will last for two to six weeks and then heal itself. Infected men will usually notice the ulcer, which is likely to be on the penis, but only 10 percent of infected women will be aware of this primary stage because the ulcer often develops inside the vagina and is not noticed. There may be a slight swelling of lymph nodes at this stage of the illness, but it is usually not severe enough to cause concern.

The infected person is extremely contagious to others while he or she has the chancre. It is possible for more than one chancre to develop and for the ulcer to look like one of the other sexually transmitted diseases. Only laboratory tests can tell for sure if the person has syphilis.

Secondary Syphilis

The second stage of infection begins about six to eight weeks after the exposure to the disease. In about one-third of cases it overlaps with the primary (chancre) stage. A tremendous variety of symptoms may develop. Infected persons may run a low fever and have a tired, flu-like feeling, with aches and pains and a loss of appetite. A large amount of the hair on the head may fall out. About three-quarters of patients will have some kind of skin rash or outbreak, half will have enlarged lymph nodes, and a third will have inflammation in the throat. Some people develop hepatitis at this stage, and in rare cases deafness or inflammation within the eyes can occur.

There are several different types of skin rashes that are typical of this stage. The most common form is scattered small, red, pimple-like outbreaks found all over the body, including the soles of the feet and the palms of the hands. Other possible types of rashes are a pink measles-like rash on the trunk of the body and the inner arms, or a scaly psoriasis-like outbreak over some or all of the body. All these rashes are infectious, and the disease can be transmitted to another person during this stage.

The secondary stage of the infection lasts from two to six weeks if it is not treated. The illness may recur several times over a two-year period.

Latent Syphilis

When the symptoms of secondary syphilis go away, the infected man or woman enters the third stage, the latent stage of the disease. For about one-third of syphilis victims, the disease remains latent for the rest of their lives, and they never have any more symptoms of the illness, although laboratory tests of their blood will continue to show infection. Even though during this stage there are usually no signs or symptoms of the disease, the infected man or woman continues to be infectious to people with whom he or she has sexual contact, and the woman can still infect her unborn child. After four years with no symptoms, people in the latent state of the illness do not usually infect their partners, but women who become pregnant can still infect their babies.

Late Syphilis

The final stage of syphilis, called late or tertiary syphilis, develops anywhere from 2 to 30 years after the original infection in two-thirds of infected people if they are not treated. This stage has many different signs and symptoms. If infection travels to the brain and spinal cord, the symptoms include mental illness, paralysis, seizures, and the loss of memory and of the ability to speak and write. Blindness, deafness, and loss of sensation in various parts of the body are also common. Gummas, which are noncancerous growths of the skin, bone, or body organs, may also develop. Late syphilis can also cause damage to the circulatory system, producing aneurysms (ballooning weak spots) in the arteries. The result of these severe symptoms of late syphilis is often death.

Congenital Syphilis

Congenital syphilis is the term used to describe the illness in babies who are born with the disease as a result of the mother's infection. These infants develop the symptoms of secondary syphilis, including rashes, and are highly infectious to others. By age 2, if untreated, they begin to develop abnormalities of the bone and enlargement of the liver and spleen. Certain deformities of the head and face, especially the nose and mouth, are characteristic of congenital syphilis.

Diagnosis

Diagnosis of syphilis can be difficult because of its many different stages and symptoms. Different kinds of laboratory tests are needed at different stages of the disease. The most common tests for syphilis are blood tests such as those taken before getting a marriage license. Diagnosis can also be made by the symptoms, by laboratory examination of cells taken from skin ulcers or rashes, and by tests of fluid from the lymph glands and spine.

What Is the Treatment?

Syphilis is curable, but damage already done to the body by the infection cannot be reversed. Penicillin in special long-lasting, high-potency forms is by far the most effective treatment for syphilis. If the disease is still in the primary stage, it is relatively easy to cure. In later stages, however, the treatment takes longer and may be more difficult. Persons allergic to penicillin are given tetracycline, or in some cases erythromycin.

In all cases, the infected person must be followed carefully and retested after treatment to make sure the disease is cured. The person who has had syphilis will continue to get positive results on certain blood tests for syphilis for years after treatment.

All sexual partners must be treated for syphilis at the same time to prevent reinfection, and sexual intercourse should be avoided until treatment is completed. Cooperating with health officers who trace persons with whom you have had sexual contact is also important to keep this life-threatening disease from spreading and harming others.

CYTOMEGALOVIRUS (CMV)

What Is It?

Cytomegalovirus is a member of the herpes virus family. It is found throughout the world, and most people carry the virus in an inactive form in their bodies. Although most people have been exposed to cytomegalovirus, the virus does not usually cause illness. Cytomegalovirus appears to be transmitted by close human contact, and it is believed that sexual contact is one of the major ways in which the virus is transmitted from one person to another.

How Serious Is It?

Cytomegalovirus is an important cause of birth defects and illness in newborn babies who are infected by the mother while in the uterus. One in 100 babies born in the United States has a health problem or defect that is caused by the virus. Ten percent of all babies have the virus at birth, but in most cases it does not cause problems.

For most people, the virus remains in a latent or inactive form in the body throughout life and appears not to cause problems. When cytomegalovirus does cause illness, it is most commonly found in two groups: newborn babies and people with poorly functioning immune systems. It can be fatal for both. Men and women who receive organ transplants are given drugs to suppress their immune responses and have a high risk of developing a cytomegalovirus-caused illness.

What Are the Signs and Symptoms?

The presence of cytomegalovirus in the body can be diagnosed through blood tests that show antibodies, and through location of the virus in body fluids. In most cases the infected person will have no signs of illness. Those who do become ill usually develop fever, sore throat, feelings of being ill, and inflammation of the liver. The symptoms are often confused with those of mononucleosis. The illness generally lasts about four to six weeks, and the person is fully recovered after eight weeks.

Newborns with cytomegalovirus-caused health problems may have enlarged liver and spleen, an abnormally small head, mental retardation, damage to the nervous system, and other serious defects, which may be fatal.

What Is the Treatment?

At present there is no effective treatment for cytomegalovirus infection, nor is there a vaccine to protect against getting it in the first place. Research is underway to gain a better understanding of the disease and its effect on the body. Fortunately, cytomegalovirus does not create problems for most people.

LESS SERIOUS STDS

Vaginitis

Vaginitis is described briefly in this part of the book because it is frequently passed on by sexual contact, although it also develops in women who are not sexually active. More detailed information about vaginal infections is given in Chapter 12. Vaginitis refers to an infection or inflammation of the vagina, which may have a number of different causes. The three most common kinds of infections of the vaginal area are produced by three different types of organisms: bacteria, trichomonas, and yeast (candida).

Vaginal infections from bacteria, yeast, or trichomonas can be extremely uncomfortable and bothersome, but they are not a serious threat to the lives or health of women or men. Vaginitis does not affect the uterus or Fallopian tubes and will not develop into pelvic inflammatory disease or cause sterility.

The symptoms of vaginal infection are usually pain with intercourse, itching, and a vaginal discharge, which may have an unpleasant odor. Each of the three major kinds of infection has slightly different symptoms and requires different treatment. Reinfection is common for all three.

Antibiotics such as Flagyl (metronidazole) are the usual treatments for these infections and may be given in pill form or as vaginal creams or suppositories. Sexual partners must be treated at the same time to avoid reinfection.

Venereal Warts

What Is It?

Genital warts, also known as condyloma acuminata are painless, dry, skin-colored growths that develop in the genital area or near the anus. They are caused by the human papilloma virus (HPV) and are similar to the warts found on other parts of the body.

Genital warts are found throughout the world and are transmitted by sexual contact. The number of cases in the United States has increased tremendously over the last twenty years, with an increase greater than 450 percent in the number of cases seen by private doctors.

How Serious Is It?

Genital warts are quite common and can be difficult to eliminate. Even when the warts themselves have been removed, the virus that can cause them remains in the body. It is important to see a doctor immediately when symptoms of genital warts develop because early treatment is easier and more effective. Early treatment is also important because growths that look like warts could be symptoms of a serious illness such as syphilis or cancer. Genital warts are related to a higher risk of abnormal Pap smear results and to an increased likelihood of cervical cancer. For this reason an annual Pap smear is essential for any woman who has had venereal warts.

What Are the Signs and Symptoms?

Symptoms of genital warts generally develop one to three months after exposure, but may not appear for as much as 20 months. The infected person can transmit the disease before the warts develop. Genital warts start off as small, painless, flesh-colored lumps just like warts on other parts of the body. As they grow, they may link together to form large warts with a rough cauliflower-like surface. Like warts on other parts of the body, they may grow either fast or slowly and may disappear after a time without treatment. In women the warts may develop on the vulva, in the vagina, and on the cervix. Warts on the cervix may be flat and not visible to the eye; they may have no symptoms. In men, warts may appear on any part of the penis or scrotum but are usually found on or near the glans. Warts can also develop in the urethra, particularly in men, which can be uncomfortable and difficult to treat. Warts may develop around and inside the anus in both men and women. This appears to be caused by anal intercourse in most cases and is far more common in homosexual men than in others. Infection in the mouth and throat can develop from oral intercourse.

In general, genital warts are not painful and do not cause feelings of illness. If they are not treated early, however, they may grow large and may become irritated and uncomfortable as well as being unpleasant to look at. Warts can have a negative effect on sexual enjoyment in addition to being infectious to others.

Genital warts grow more rapidly under certain conditions: Warmth, moisture, poor hygiene, and pregnancy are all conditions that encourage growth. There seem to be more problems with genital warts in warm, humid climates.

How Do I Avoid Getting Warts or Giving Them to Others?

The best protection against getting warts is to follow the suggestions for avoiding STDs (see details earlier in this chapter). Avoid sexual contact with anyone who has warts or who has been exposed. If you do have sex with such a person, use a condom. Keeping the genital area clean and dry at all times will also help. It is believed that genital warts must be transmitted by skin-to-skin contact, and not all people who have been exposed develop them. Once infected, a person can spread the disease to other parts of the body by touching the infected area.

What Is the Treatment?

Genital warts can be removed, but the best results are obtained if the disease is treated early, before there are many large warts. The most common treatment for genital warts is with Podophyllin, which is applied weekly to the warts at your doctor's office or clinic until they disappear. This treatment may take several weeks or months and does not always work. The drug has some toxic effects on the body, and the skin around the warts should be protected by a layer of vaseline or a similar product. Additionally, the drug must be washed off the skin several hours after it is applied, and should not be used over a long period of time. Pregnant women cannot use this treatment, as it may cause damage or even death to the fetus.

Trichloracetic acid and 5-fluorouracil cream are two other products that are also used by some doctors to treat warts. Other treatments include removing them by freezing (cryotherapy), by burning (electrocautery), and by surgery. The symptoms will be eliminated only if *all* the warts are removed and infected sexual partners are also treated. Even then, the warts will recur in some cases.

Pubic Lice

What Is It?

Pubic lice are small parasites, similar to head lice and body lice. They are also known as **crabs, pediculosis pubis,** and **phthirus pubis.** The lice are found in the pubic hair and are usually transmitted through sexual contact. They are very small grayish creatures shaped like tiny crabs. Their eggs, also called nits, are tiny, pearly white bumps, each of which is attached to a hair shaft near to the skin. The lice live on human blood, and their bites cause itching.

How Serious Is It?

Pubic lice cause itching and can be uncomfortable, but the condition is not difficult to cure and does not cause illness. Although other kinds of lice can carry serious illness, pubic lice have not been known to carry any disease to their human hosts. A rash or skin irritation may develop from scratching the bites.

What Are the Signs and Symptoms?

The main symptom of pubic lice is itching in the pubic area, but not everyone notices it. Red or bluish spots may show where the louse has bitten. A skin rash or irritation may develop as a result of scratching the bites.

The lice are usually transmitted from one person to another by sexual contact, but they can be spread through shared clothing or by sleeping in the same bed. They die within 24 hours if they are not in contact with humans. Pubic lice are usually found in the body hair around the genitals and anus, but they may spread, especially in very hairy persons, to hair on the chest and stomach and under the arms. In some cases the lice also infest the eyebrows and eyelashes.

Adult lice live three to four weeks, and the females can lay up to 26 eggs. The eggs take 10 days to hatch, and the louse develops into an adult over a 15-day period. Symptoms of the infestation may be noticed within a day or two after sexual contact or not until several weeks later.

What Is the Treatment?

Infestation with pubic lice is easily cured with a prescription lotion, cream, or shampoo called Kwell, which contains the pesticide Lindane (gamma benzene hexachloride). There are other, safer products sold in pharmacies (Vonce, R.I.D., and A–200 Pyrinate) that do not require a prescription and are usually equally effective. Kwell should not be used by pregnant women or very young children. Spending time in a very hot sauna also kills lice. Even after the eggs are dead, they will remain firmly attached to the hair shaft. The best way to remove them is with a special fine-toothed comb sold at pharmacies for this purpose.

Treatment is effective only if sexual partners are treated at the same time and if all infested clothing and bedding is washed in hot water or dry cleaned.

Molluscum Contagiosum

What Is It?

Molluscum contagiosum is a mild virus infection of the skin that causes small, flesh-colored or pearly pimple-like growths with indented centers.

The disease is most common in children, who transmit it to each other by skin contact, and can be found on any part of the body. But it is also sexually transmitted, in which case the outbreaks are in the area of the genitals, buttocks, and upper thighs.

How Serious Is It?

Molluscum contagiosum is a mild infection with no serious complications. It does not cause discomfort and usually cures itself within a few years.

What Are the Signs and Symptoms?

The only symptom of the disease is the skin outbreaks, which develop a few days to three months after exposure to the infection. The individual bumps last for about two months each, but new ones continue to break out. The problem can usually be diagnosed by physical examination; laboratory tests of samples from the skin can also be done. It is important to be seen by a doctor for any kind of skin outbreak in the genital area, even if you think it is a mild condition like molluscum contagiosum, because some similar skin outbreaks are symptoms or signs of serious illness.

What Is the Treatment?

In most cases, if the disease is causing no problems, your doctor will recommend no treatment at all because it will go away by itself in a few years and is not a risk to health.

If the disease is treated, drugs such as cantharone can be used, or the papules can be removed surgically.

Scabies

What Is It?

Scabies (*Sarcoptes scabiei*) is a skin parasite that is transmitted by sexual contact or by other close personal contact, including shared clothing or beds. The scabies organisms feed on skin tissue. The tiny mites burrow under the surface of the skin, laying eggs there which hatch and produce more mites, which make new burrows. The infestation causes intense itching, especially at night.

How Serious Is It?

Scabies does not cause serious illness, but it can be extremely uncomfortable because of the intense itching. Scratching can cause the skin to become inflamed, and other skin infections may develop. The disease can be difficult to diagnose, especially when other infections have set in, be cause it may look similar to a number of other skin problems.

What Are the Signs and Symptoms?

The signs of scabies are the burrows, which may be one-eighth to one-quarter inch long. It may be possible to see the mite, a tiny brown and white speck at one end of the burrow. Once the person becomes sensitized, the burrows will become red and irritated, and a red itchy rash and bumps will develop. Scabies are usually located on the hands, especially between the fingers; on the wrists, elbows, and underarms; around and under the breasts; and on the genitals and buttocks. They are not usually seen on the face or head. If scabies appear on the penis, they may show up as red, inflamed welts or ridges.

The first time a person gets a scabies infection, he or she will not usually develop symptoms for a month or more, although the person can pass on scabies to others during this period. After a month the body becomes sensitized to scabies, and itching and discomfort will develop around the burrows. Exzema and hives may also develop as a reaction. Sensitivity to scabies remains, and if a person is infested a second or third time, there is no waiting period; the person will react with itching immediately.

The life span of the female scabies mite is about 40 days, during which she lays two to three eggs a day in her burrow after fertilization by the male, which lives on the surface of the skin. The eggs hatch after three to four days and become adult after nine more days.

Diagnosis of the disease is by physical examination, by the symptoms, by examining the mites under a microscope, and by laboratory tests performed on skin scrapings taken from the burrows and rashes.

Infested persons can pass scabies on to others at any time, even before they are aware that they have the disease. Poor hygiene and crowded living conditions create an environment in which scabies can be transmitted easily. Although sexual contact is believed to be the main source of the spread of the disease, close contact over time with family and friends, especially sharing the same bed, can also be enough to spread scabies.

The symptoms of scabies often persist for months after treatment, even though the disease has been cured.

What Is the Treatment?

Scabies are effectively treated with Kwell, a prescription medication containing the pesticide Lindane (gamma benzene hexachloride). This medication should not be used by pregnant women and small children. Other products used to cure scabies are Eurax (crotamiton) and sulfur cream. All sexual partners and infested family members must be treated at the same time to avoid reinfestation. Clothing and bedding must be washed in hot water or dry cleaned. The mites can survive for two or three days away from the human body.

After the scabies is cured, the skin is likely to remain irritated. Calamine lotion or aloe vera applied to the skin, as well as antihistamines, may help. Ointments containing cortisone should be avoided.

UNCOMMON STDS (CHANCROID, LYMPHOGRANULOMA VENEREUM, AND GRANULOMA INGUINALE)

What Are They?

Chancroid, lymphogranuloma venereum, and granuloma inguinale are three sexually transmitted diseases that cause skin ulcers in the genital area and inflammation of the lymph nodes in the pelvis and groin. All three are rare in the United States. The diseases are known throughout the world and are found more commonly in the less developed nations, particularly those with warm climates.

Chancroid is caused by the bacteria *Hemophilus ducreyi*, lymphogranuloma venereum by *Chlamydia trachomatis*, and granuloma inguinale, also known as donovanosis, by the organism *Calymmatobacterium granulomatis*.

How Serious Are They?

If not treated, the ulcers caused by these diseases can destroy tissue in the genital area, leaving large scars, which can cause health problems and problems with sexual functioning. If the diseases are treated early, they can usually be cured without permanent damage to health. Good hygiene and general health are important factors in reducing the risk of becoming infected.

What Are the Signs and Symptoms?

The main symptom of these diseases is the appearance of slow-growing skin ulcers in the genital area after exposure to an infected person. The ulcers may or may not be painful. New ulcers may develop on skin that touches the infected area. In many cases the pelvic lymph nodes become infected and are enlarged, tender, and painful. The nodes may abscess, forming new ulcers, which are difficult to heal. If untreated, the ulcers can cause destruction of tissues in the genital and anal area, obstructing the openings of the vagina, urethra, and rectum.

What Is the Treatment?

All three diseases are curable if treated with antibiotics, although they may be difficult to cure if they have been left untreated for a long time. If ulcers have developed from abscesses of the lymph nodes, these may continue after the disease is cured and require further treatment. Surgery may be needed to correct damage to the genital and rectal area.

HOMOSEXUAL MEN AND STDS

Homosexual (gay) and bisexual men are at risk of transmitting the same STDs as heterosexuals during sexual activity. In addition, they are at risk of transmitting a number of other diseases that are not likely to be passed on in sex between men and women. Contact with many partners and the use of anal intercourse (particularly oral–anal intercourse) are major causes of this. Use of latex condoms provides the best protection against infection. (Homosexual women, also called lesbians, appear to be less likely to develop STDs than either homosexual men or heterosexual couples.)

The diseases that homosexual men have a high risk for contracting are mainly of two types: intestinal infections and viral hepatitis.

Intestinal Infections

The risk of intestinal infections with both bacteria and parasites is high for homosexual men because of the likelihood of contact with feces during anal sex. Intestinal infections (including shigellosis, amoebiasis, giardia, campylobacter, and cryptosporidiosis) are not usually considered sexually transmitted diseases. They are generally transmitted by food or drink that has been contaminated with the organisms (which grow in human and animal digestive tracts and are found in feces). These diseases are often found in gay men, however, and cause such symptoms as diarrhea, abdominal pain, inflammation of the intestines and rectum, and rectal discharge.

Sexually transmitted intestinal infections can cause a lot of discomfort and illness, but they can usually be treated effectively once they are diagnosed. Few deaths are caused by these infections, but complications can develop and hospitalization may be needed in a few situations.

Homosexual men are at risk for several sexually transmitted diseases that do not usually affect heterosexual couples.

Viral Hepatitis

Viral hepatitis (including type A—infectious hepatitis, type B—serum hepatitis, and type non-A/non-B hepatitis) is also transmitted by homosexual contact, although they are not considered sexually transmitted diseases. Hepatitis A is thought to be transmitted through contact with the partner's feces, and hepatitis B through contact with the partner's blood. Anal sex and any sex that causes damage to tissue and bleeding can create the opportunity for infection to be transmitted. Hepatitis symptoms generally develop one to three months after exposure, causing nausea, vomiting, loss of appetite, feelings of being ill, pain in the abdomen, and jaundice (yellowing of the whites of the eyes and the skin). Dark-colored urine and light-colored feces may occur, along with an enlarged and sensitive liver.

There are no drugs or treatments to cure hepatitis at present. The infected person will generally be ill for a few weeks and recover on his own, given rest and proper care. Few deaths are caused by hepatitis, but complications can set in that require hospitalization. A vaccine that gives immunity from hepatitis B has been developed and is recommended for homosexuals because of their high risk.

Hepatitis can be transmitted to others even when the infected person shows no signs of illness. In a few cases, people become chronic carriers of hepatitis B and can transmit the disease to many others over a period of years.

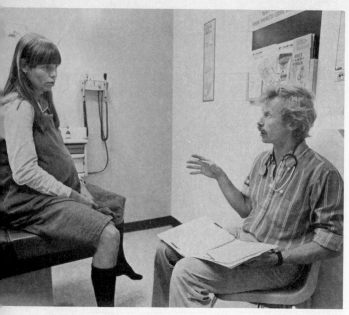

Some sexually transmitted diseases can be transmitted to the baby during childbirth and can cause serious illness.

Getting Good Medical Care

Sexually active gay men should be particularly careful to get frequent checkups and prompt medical care when needed because of the high risk of contracting STDs. In gay men STDs are often found in the anus or in the mouth and throat as well as on the genitals. Proper diagnosis and treatment may not take place if the doctor or other caregiver is not aware that the sick person is a homosexual or is not familiar with the sexual practices and diseases common to gay men. In large cities there is often a special clinic in the Health Department that treats gay persons. This can be a good source of care.

Wherever you go for treatment, it is important to be open about your life-style and sexual habits, even if it is embarrassing. Don't let fear or embarrassment keep you from getting the care you need. Your future health is too important.

STDS AND PREGNANCY

STDs are known to be a major cause of infertility. But they can also cause problems for the pregnant woman and her expected child, mainly by infecting the baby during childbirth. Most STDs do not affect the baby while it is in the uterus. They are transmitted by contact with the cervix and the walls of the vagina during childbirth. For this reason, caesarean section is often used for births where there is a chance that the infant may become infected.

It is important for all pregnant women to be examined and tested for STDs, especially since some of them have no noticeable symptoms and may not even be aware of the illness. Testing early in pregnancy and again a month or two before the baby is due is a good idea, since STDs can be picked up during pregnancy as well as before. The following STDs (which are described in detail earlier in this chapter) are known to cause problems in pregnancy and childbirth.

> *Gonorrhea:* Causes eye infection in newborns, can cause blindness.
>
> *Chlamydia:* Causes eye infections and pneumonia in newborns, can cause blindness.
>
> *Herpes:* Can cause blindness, brain damage, or even death in newborns.
>
> *Syphilis:* Increases chances of miscarriage or stillbirth, causes birth defects and congenital syphilis infection.
>
> *Cytomegalovirus:* Causes serious birth defects in newborns.
>
> *Venereal warts:* Often grow rapidly during pregnancy, can make delivery difficult, can infect baby's larynx.

FOR FURTHER READING

CORSARO, MARIA, AND CAROLE KORZENIOWSKY. *STD: A Commonsense Guide to Sexually Transmitted Diseases.* New York: Holt, Rinehart and Winston, 1982.

RESOURCES

Note to readers: Additional information and referral services are available in your local community through the county or state Department of Health. In addition, the following national resources can be contacted:

Herpes Resource Center
American Social Health Association
P.O. Box 100
Palo Alto, CA 94306
(415) 328–7710

A non-profit organization that provides information and referral for services and self-help groups in your local area.

Sexually Transmitted Disease Hotline
(800) 227–8922

Provides information and referral for treatment of sexually transmitted diseases.

15
AIDS
(Acquired Immune Deficiency Syndrome)

AIDS is a fatal sexually transmitted disease, first identified in the late 1970s, which is spreading rapidly in many parts of the world. By the end of 1988, an estimated 5 to 10 million people in the world had been infected, 1 to 2 million of them in the United States. It is not known what percentage of those who are exposed will eventually become ill from AIDS, but so far the number of new AIDS cases is more than doubling every year. Sexually transmitted diseases can spread through the population very fast, and it is possible that within a few years AIDS could become a major killer in the United States and in the rest of the world.

It is very important that all people, espe-cially families with children and couples planning to have children, become aware and informed about AIDS and its prevention. Young people just beginning their sexual lives are especially at risk of contracting this fatal sexually transmitted dis-ease if they are not well informed. We urge every-one to read this chapter carefully and then watch for new developments in prevention and treat-ment in the news media. The information con-tained here was up to date as of December 1988, but there are new developments every month in the war against this disease.

AIDS will only be eliminated when it can be prevented or cured. Prevention can contain and eventually eliminate the disease, either by educating people in how to protect themselves from exposure to the virus, or by development of a vaccine that provides immunity, or both. To date, no effective vaccine has been developed, nor is there any treatment that can cure the disease. Since prevention by vaccine and medical cure of the disease are both solutions that are not likely to become available for a few years at least, education for prevention is the key to stopping AIDS at present.

WHAT IS AIDS?

AIDS stands for **acquired immune deficiency syndrome,** the name of a new and fatal disease first identified in the late 1970s. It is believed to have first appeared in Central Africa. AIDS is a rapidly spreading epidemic, affecting many parts of the world, particularly the United States, Africa, Europe, and South America.

The organism that causes the disease is a recently discovered virus, which has been named **HIV (human immunodeficiency virus).** The virus breaks down the body's immune system, making the person vulnerable to many kinds of illnesses. People who develop AIDS usually die within a few years. Although AIDS seems to be fatal to all people who develop the disease, it is not known what percentage of people infected with the virus will become ill with AIDS, nor is it known how long the virus may lie dormant in the body before causing illness.

In the United States AIDS has primarily affected male homosexual adults, and there are 9 male AIDS patients for every female with AIDS. AIDS cases among children, however, are 55 percent males and 45 percent females. In African countries where AIDS is prevalent, the disease appears to be equally common in men and women.

HOW MANY PEOPLE HAVE BEEN INFECTED?

As of December 1988, over 130,000 cases of AIDS had been reported to the World Health Organization (WHO), but the organization estimated that the true number of cases worldwide as of that date was probably in excess of 350,000. The WHO estimated that over 400,000 new cases of AIDS would appear during 1989 and 1990, and that 5 to 10 million people worldwide had been infected with the virus.

As of January 9, 1989, the Centers for Disease Control (CDC) in the United States had received reports of 81,876 cases of AIDS in adults and teenagers, and 1,355 cases of children with AIDS. About 62 percent of these AIDS cases were homosexual or bisexual men, and around 20 percent were intravenous drug abusers. The remainder were sexual partners of the aforementioned two groups, or people who had received transfusions contaminated with the virus, or babies born to AIDS-infected mothers.

Forty-five percent of all cases of AIDS were located in two states: New York and California. The CDC estimated that 20 to 50 percent of homosexual and bisexual men in the United States had been infected with the virus, and 5 to 65 percent of intravenous drug users. Blacks and Hispanics make up 40 percent of all AIDS cases, although they are less than 20 percent of the United States population. It has been estimated that less than 1 percent of the general population has been exposed to AIDS; however, rates of infection vary depending on the region of the country, lifestyle, and age.

It is believed that for every AIDS case reported there are three to five more persons suffering milder symptoms of the same illness. These persons are

Research has not yet found a cure for AIDS.

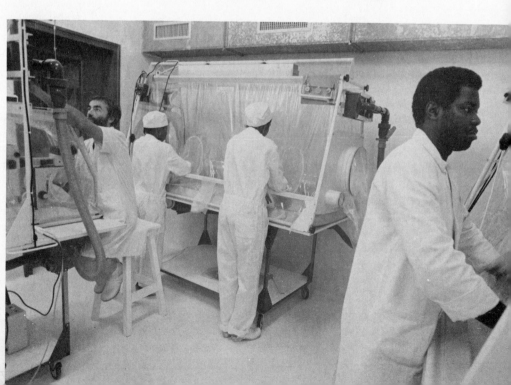

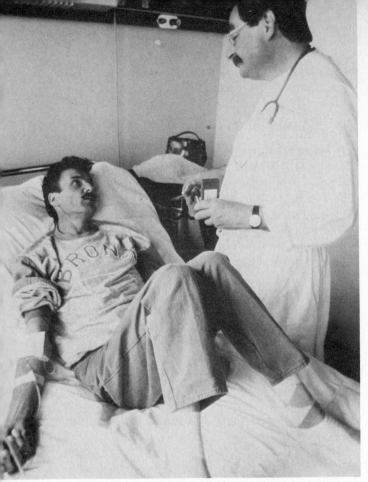

An AIDS patient and his doctor.

said to have ARC, or AIDS-related complex. It is estimated that anywhere from 1 to 2 million Americans have been infected with the AIDS virus, but it is not known if they will all become ill. So far, it appears that 20 to 30 percent of them can be expected to develop AIDS within five years of becoming infected. Whether some people who have been infected will never become ill is unknown. Such people do appear to be infectious to others even if they are not ill.

WHAT ARE THE SIGNS AND SYMPTOMS?

The Centers for Disease Control have defined AIDS broadly as the presence of a disease that indicates an immune deficiency in people under 60 years of age who have no other diseases or conditions that could cause or explain this deficiency. Diseases regarded as important indicators of AIDS include potentially fatal "opportunistic" infections, Kaposi's sarcoma (a form of cancer), and central nervous system infection with the HIV virus. Information about each of these diseases is presented next.

The general symptoms of possible AIDS infection include:

1. Weight loss greater than 10 pounds in one or two months

2. Prolonged loss of appetite
3. Unexplained recurring fevers, chills, and night sweats lasting more than several weeks
4. Swollen lymph nodes in the neck, armpits, or groin lasting more than two weeks
5. Continuing unexplained fatigue
6. Continuing unexplained diarrhea or bloody stools
7. White coating or spotting on the tongue, unusual blemishes in the mouth, sore throat, difficulty swallowing
8. Continuing dry cough not due to smoking, cold, or flu
9. Unexplained bleeding from any opening in the body

Each of these symptoms could also be associated with a number of other health problems, so the appearance of one or more does not mean that a person is likely to have AIDS. A person who develops any of these symptoms, however, should seek medical care immediately, and if AIDS infection is a possibility (if the person may have been exposed) it is important to seek care from a doctor or clinic experienced in diagnosing and treating AIDS.

Opportunistic Infections

The presence of opportunistic infections is a major symptom of immune system deficiency. These are infections caused by organisms that normally surround us in the environment without causing illness. In the person with a weakened immune system, the organisms take the opportunity to move into the body and multiply; thus, they are known as **opportunistic infections.** The opportunistic infections typically seen in AIDS patients are caused by viruses (such as herpes), fungi (such as candida or thrush), protozoa (such as amoeba), and mycobacteria (organisms that cause tuberculosis and other diseases).

The illnesses that develop may have a wide variety of symptoms and range from mild to severe and life-threatening. Some viral infections have symptoms similar to those of mononucleosis, with fatigue, fever, loss of appetite, sore throat, and swollen lymph glands lasting for several weeks. Fungus infections of the mouth and digestive tract (known as **thrush**), and of the lungs are also common. Protozoa infections such as **Pneumocystis carinii** are also frequently found and may cause pneumonia, diarrhea, and inflammation of the brain.

Kaposi's Sarcoma

Kaposi's sarcoma is a form of cancer in which tumors grow in the walls of the blood vessels. In persons with AIDS it usually first appears as pain-

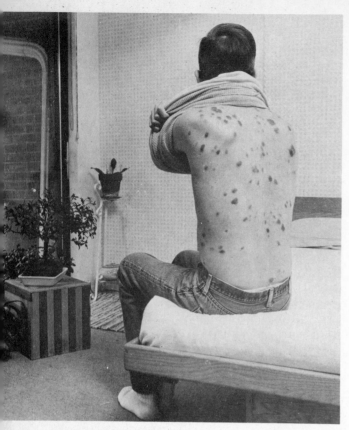

A man with Kaposi's sarcoma.

less purple or brownish raised spots or lumps on the skin or on the mucous membranes of the mouth. The tumors may also develop inside the body, in the digestive tract or other body organs.

In the past, Kaposi's sarcoma was found only in elderly men of Jewish or Mediterranean descent, and usually developed only on the legs. In these men the cancer was a slow-growing, nonfatal illness, which was treated effectively with radiation or chemotherapy. More recently, Kaposi's sarcoma has appeared as a symptom of AIDS infection in people of all ages and ethnic backgrounds. In AIDS cases it seems to appear on all parts of the body, grows more quickly, and is less easily treated.

Central Nervous System HIV Infection

In some persons with AIDS the virus attacks the central nervous system (CNS). The symptoms can be mild and may include depression, sadness, lack of energy, and sometimes memory loss. In severe cases the person's mental functioning can be very much impaired. When these symptoms were first noticed in AIDS cases, they were thought to be caused by emotional distress related to the seriousness of the disease. Many AIDS patients do suffer from depression for this reason, but in other cases the problems are caused by HIV infection of the central nervous system.

ARC (Aids-Related Complex)

Persons who are made ill by AIDS virus infection but do not meet the Centers for Disease Control definition of the disease are said to have ARC, or AIDS-related complex. They are usually not as ill as AIDS patients, but they may be too sick to work or perform their usual activities. The symptoms of illnesses that they develop are due to suppression of the immune system and may include opportunistic infections that are not as severe as those in AIDS cases, or infections that do not meet Centers for Disease Control criteria for AIDS. The symptoms of ARC are similar to those of AIDS, which are listed earlier in this chapter. People who have any of these symptoms should see their health care provider immediately.

HOW DO I FIND OUT IF I HAVE BEEN INFECTED? (HIV ANTIBODY TESTING)

Infection with the AIDS virus is diagnosed indirectly through tests that identify antibodies to the virus. Antibodies are substances produced by the body's immune system to fight off infection. If a person has antibodies to the HIV virus in his or her blood, it indicates that he or she has been exposed to and infected with the virus. But the presence of antibodies to the AIDS virus does not mean that the person has AIDS or ARC. Most people who test positive for the antibodies are not ill (although they are probably carrying the virus and able to transmit it to others).

HIV antibody testing can be obtained by anyone who is concerned that he or she might have been exposed to the disease. Local health departments, private physicians, and clinics serving homosexuals (gays) or drug abusers generally offer testing. Anyone who is not sure where to obtain testing in his or her community should call the local health department for a referral.

Unfortunately, the tests that are now available are not completely reliable, which means that a small number of people (approximately 1 in 100) will get results that are false positive (results that indicate the person has been exposed when this is not so). Testing a second time can usually solve this problem. In addition, people who have been exposed to the virus may get negative test results (showing no exposure) for a number of different reasons, including the fact that it takes the body time to develop the antibodies that show up on the test. If a second test taken six months later is also negative, a person can feel confident that he or she has not been exposed.

HIV antibody testing has been approved by the Food and Drug Administration for use by blood banks to protect blood supplies. Testing has been routine at blood banks and companies that process blood products since 1985, and some blood products also receive a special heat treatment to eliminate contamination. There is little need to worry about becoming infected with AIDS through transfusions of blood or blood products received after 1985.

It is possible to be tested for HIV antibodies anonymously (the results are reported only to the person tested, using an identification number instead of a name). This means that the test results will not appear on any medical or other records associated with the person's name. This can be important if there is a possibility of job discrimination or other problems if the test result is positive. People concerned about keeping their test results private may prefer to use a clinic that provides anonymous testing rather than their regular doctor, clinic, or HMO. The regular care provider can always be notified of the test results later if necessary.

HOW DO I AVOID GETTING AIDS OR GIVING IT TO OTHERS?

Although AIDS infection so far has been concentrated in certain groups, everyone who is sexually active with a partner in the United States needs to learn about this disease, what the risks are, and how it can be prevented. The following people are at high risk of contracting AIDS virus infection (based on groups of people who have become ill with the disease so far):

1. Homosexual (gay) and bisexual men
2. Intravenous drug users
3. Hemophiliacs and other blood transfusion recipients who received transfusions before 1986
4. Sexual partners of members of any of the above groups
5. Babies born to women who are members of any of the above high-risk groups

Although this list may sound like a limited group to which no one in your family belongs, it is important to remember that anyone who has been a sexual partner of a member of one of these groups (since the late 1970s) is at high risk. If your sexual partner has had sex with anyone from one of these groups, he or she is at risk and so are you.

AIDS is transmitted by the exchange of body fluids such as blood, semen, saliva, urine, and feces.

Homosexual intercourse appears to be the most common way the disease has been transmitted in the United States so far, but it can also be passed on by sexual contact between men and women. The most important ways in which the AIDS virus is transmitted are:

1. Intimate sexual contact with an infected person
2. Sharing needles with an infected person
3. When an infected woman gives birth

Since 1985 transfusions of blood or blood products are no longer an important source of risk.

Safe Sex

To protect themselves and their partners from AIDS, all sexually active people in the United States (men and women, homosexual and heterosexual, young and old) are being advised to practice "safe sex." This means avoiding all sexual practices that could transmit the disease. (A side benefit of safe sex is that it also prevents transmission of most other sexually transmitted diseases.)

People who live in parts of the country where few AIDS cases have yet been found should still follow safe sex practices. It takes only one sexually active person to introduce the disease, which can easily be contracted elsewhere and brought to the community.

The basic rules for avoiding STDs are listed in Chapter 14. There are additional guidelines for avoiding contracting or transmitting the AIDS virus. *The basic idea is that any activity that allows for possible contact between the body fluids or feces of one person and the mouth, anus, vagina, bloodstream, cuts, or sores of another is considered unsafe at this time if there is a possibility that one or both partners has been exposed to the AIDS virus.*

The recommended safe sex practices are as follows:*

SAFE SEX PRACTICES

1. Massage, hugging, body-to-body rubbing
2. Dry social kissing
3. Masturbation (touching your own genitals)
4. Acting out sexual fantasies (which do not include any unsafe practices)
5. Using vibrators or other sex toys (but not sharing them)

LOW-RISK SEX PRACTICES

1. Wet (French) kissing (to be avoided if either partner has any sores in the mouth)

* These lists are adapted from Betty Clare Moffatt et al., *AIDS: A Self-Care Manual* (Santa Monica, Calif.: IBS Press, 1987), p. 125.

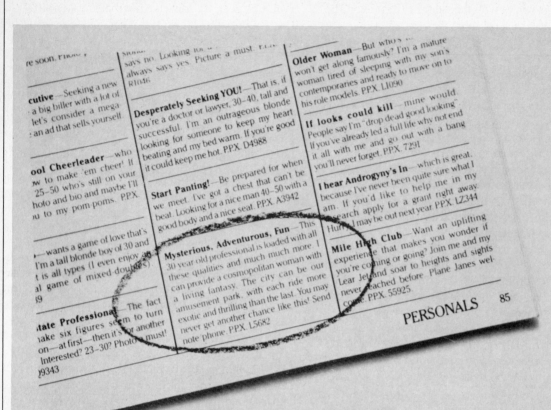

"I got AIDS through the personals."

A great way to meet someone new?
Well, someone new means someone you don't know. And no matter how tall, attractive, and successful someone sounds, he could be carrying the AIDS virus.

And it's not just the Personals. Whether you meet someone in a bar, on line at a movie, or in your health club, they could be infected.

So what should you do? Never leave the house? That would be stupid. But it's just as stupid to sleep with anyone whose sexual or drug use history you don't know.

Right now there's no cure for AIDS, and no vaccine to prevent it.

Remember, you don't have to have sex. But if you do, using a condom is a must,

AIDS because it's one thing that can help protect you from getting AIDS.

If you think you can't get it, you're dead wrong.

2. Mutual masturbation (touching each other's genitals) (use plastic gloves if there are any cuts on the hands)

3. Vaginal intercourse using a condom (anal intercourse with a condom is more risky)

4. Oral sex (mouth to penis) using a condom

5. Oral sex (mouth to vagina) using a thin piece of rubber between the mouth and vagina (higher risk during menstruation)

6. Skin contact with semen or urine, if there are no breaks in the skin

UNSAFE SEX PRACTICES

1. Vaginal or anal (more risk) intercourse without a condom

2. Unprotected penetration of the vagina or anus with a finger or hand

3. Unprotected oral sex

4. Semen in the mouth (or urine or feces)

5. Mouth-to-anus contact

6. Blood contact of any kind

7. Sharing sex toys (or needles for drug use)

The only people who do not need to practice safe sex are:

1. People who are not sexually active with a partner

2. Couples who are both virgins when they begin their relationship, have no other sexual partners afterward, and have not shared a needle or received a blood transfusion since before 1980

3. Couples who have been in a monogamous relationship (no other partners for either) since before 1980, neither of whom has shared a needle or received a blood transfusion during that time

Special Precautions for Those Who May Be Infected

AIDS can also be transmitted by nonsexual means, and persons who have AIDS, ARC, or a positive HIV test, or who are in the high-risk group for AIDS infection, should also take the following precautions:

1. Do not donate blood, plasma, sperm, body organs, or other tissues.

2. Do not share toothbrushes, razors, or other personal care items that could be contaminated by blood.

3. If you are a drug user, do not share needles or leave your equipment lying around where someone else might use it.

4. Avoid pregnancy if you are a woman in the high-risk group or are sexually involved with a man who is high-risk. AIDS-infected mothers may pass on the disease to their babies.

When a person is seriously ill with AIDS (as with some other diseases), special precautions must be taken in the hospital and at home to avoid spreading the infection by contact with body fluids.

Prevention at Home, Work, and School

AIDS is not easy to catch. It is not transmitted by casual contact and is not carried in the air or on clothing. Although the virus has been found in saliva and tears, it does not seem to be easily transmitted through these fluids. Shaking hands or working in an office with a person with AIDS is not going to expose you to infection, but situations where there is contact with body fluids may create a risk (for example, nursery school teachers or ambulance personnel).

Preventing transmission of AIDS at home, work, and school depends on following the precautions listed earlier for at-risk people and on using common sense and good hygiene. There is no problem sharing space with infected persons, including bathrooms and kitchens, as long as basic rules of hygiene are followed by all, including the following:

1. Wash hands after using the toilet.

2. Wash hands before touching or preparing food.

3. Use gloves and disinfectant (one part of household bleach to nine parts of water is sufficient) to wash bathrooms and to clean up messes or spills involving blood, feces, urine, or vomit.

4. Wash all kitchen and serving utensils after each use with hot water and soap.

5. Wash and disinfect any tools or spaces that come in contact with blood.

6. Wash, disinfect, and cover all wounds with a bandage to prevent blood contact.

Neither the families nor the medical personnel who care for persons with AIDS seem to be at risk of contracting the disease, so it appears that daily casual contact does not cause risk, and even personal care of persons with AIDS can be managed without risk if the rules of hygiene are followed.

For those who have questions about what is safe and what is not, the local health department, your own doctor, or the AIDS hotline (see telephone number at the end of this chapter) are all good sources of advice.

TREATMENT FOR AIDS AND ARC PATIENTS

There is a great deal of work being done in the medical community to develop effective treatments for persons ill with AIDS and ARC and to prevent new cases. Public education about the risks of AIDS has already had an impact in this country, and it appears that the rate of spread of the disease in the

A training meeting for AIDS support-group leaders.

homosexual community has slowed. Unfortunately, the infection is still being transmitted rapidly among intravenous drug users and their families. As more women become infected, growing numbers of AIDS-infected babies are being born. In addition, prisons in some parts of the country appear to be high-risk places for spread of the disease.

Current research is focused on preventing AIDS through development of vaccines and helping AIDS and ARC patients by developing treatments to strengthen the damaged immune system. Several drugs are being tested on an experimental basis.

Opportunistic infections, Kaposi's sarcoma, and other problems brought on by immune system weakness are treated with existing drugs and methods. Opportunistic infections can often be effectively treated, but the damage to the immune system is such that the AIDS patient is likely to have repeated infections. Over time, the person's health becomes so weakened that an opportunistic infection is likely to be fatal.

Many persons with AIDS or ARC and their families have formed groups to share information about AIDS and its treatment, and to provide emotional support for each other. Such groups can be very helpful and can be located through local AIDS treatment programs or clinics and through gay-oriented social service programs. Since the homosexual community has been struck hardest by this disease, it has developed the most programs to advise and help AIDS patients and their families.

Most of these services are available to nonhomosexuals and their families as well.

SERVICES FOR THOSE WHO TEST POSITIVE FOR AIDS ANTIBODIES

Men and women who have received positive results on an AIDS antibody test are usually offered some counseling at the clinic where the test is performed. At present, people who test positive must assume that the virus will remain in their bodies for the rest of their lives, and that they may be infectious to sexual partners and others. Understandably, many people need services to help them understand and live with this difficult situation. The stress of living with the possibility of developing AIDS can be damaging to health, relationships, and emotional well-being. In addition, the person may have to make major adjustments in sexual practices to avoid infecting others. The person who tests positive is also waiting for new medical developments that may be helpful in preventing development of the disease. In response to these needs, some communities have developed self-help, education, and support groups for persons who have tested positive and their families and partners. Like support groups for AIDS patients, such services can be located by contacting health care programs that test for AIDS or care for AIDS patients, and gay-oriented social service programs.

FOR FURTHER READING

BENZA, JOSEPH F., JR., AND RALPH D. ZUMWALDE. *Preventing AIDS: A Practical Guide for Everyone.* Cincinnati, OH: Jalsco, Inc. (P.O. Box 30226, Cincinnati, OH 45230), 1987.

MOFFAT, BETTY CLARE, JUDITH SPIEGEL, STEVE PARRISH, AND MICHAEL HELQUIST, EDS. *AIDS: A Self Care Manual.* Santa Monica, CA: IBS Press (744 Pier Avenue, Santa Monica, CA 90405), 1987.

RESOURCES

Information and referral services are available in your local community through the county or state Department of Health, United Way agency, and gay and lesbian service agencies. In addition, the following national resources can be contacted:

National AIDS Hotline
U.S. Public Health Service
Centers for Disease Control
(800) 342–AIDS and
(800) 442–2437
(202) 646–8182

Provides information about AIDS and referral for services in your local area.

The Fund For Human Dignity
The Educational Foundation of the Lesbian and Gay Community
666 Broadway
New York, N.Y. 10012
(800) 221–7044
(212) 529–1600

A nonprofit organization that provides a national crisis line for gay and lesbian information, AIDS counseling, and referral to services in your local area.

Bibliography

CHAPTER 1: THE HUMAN BODY

BOSTON WOMEN'S HEALTH COLLECTIVE. *The New Our Bodies, Ourselves*. New York: Simon and Schuster, 1984.

DEMAREST, ROBERT J., AND JOHN J. SCIARRA. *Conception, Birth and Contraception*, 2nd ed. New York: McGraw-Hill, 1976.

GEER, JAMES, JULIA HEIMAN, AND HAROLD LEITENBERG. *Human Sexuality*. Englewood Cliffs, N.J.: Prentice-Hall, 1984.

HAEBERLE, ERWIN J. *The Sex Atlas*. New York: Seabury Press, 1978.

KASE, NATHAN G., AND ALLAN B. WEINGOLD, EDS. *Principles and Practice of Clinical Gynecology*. New York: Wiley, 1983.

MONEY, JOHN. *Sex Errors of the Body: Dilemmas, Education, Counseling*. Baltimore, Md.: Johns Hopkins University Press, 1968.

SILBER, SHERMAN J. *The Male: A Comprehensive and Clearly Written Guide to the Male Sexual System*. New York: Charles Scribner's Sons, 1981.

SILVERSTEIN, ALVIN. *Human Anatomy and Physiology*. New York: Wiley, 1980.

CHAPTER 2: CONCEPTION: HOW HUMAN LIFE BEGINS

DANFORTH, DAVID N., AND JAMES R. SCOTT, EDS. *Obstetrics and Gynecology*, 5th ed. Philadelphia: Lippincott, 1986.

GARREY, MATTHEW M., A. D. T. GOVAN, C. HODGE, AND R. CALLANDER. *Obstetrics Illustrated*, 2nd ed. London: Churchill Livingstone, 1974.

GUTTMACHER, ALAN F. *Pregnancy, Birth, and Family Planning*. New York: New American Library, 1987.

HYDE, JANET SHIBLEY. *Understanding Human Sexuality*, 3rd ed. New York: McGraw-Hill, 1986.

LESKO, WENDY, AND MATTHEW LESKO. *The Maternity Sourcebook*. New York: Warner Books, 1984.

PREVITE, JOSEPH. *Human Physiology*. New York: McGraw-Hill, 1983.

SAMUELS, MIKE, AND NANCY SAMUELS. *The Well Pregnancy Book*. New York: Simon and Schuster, 1986.

SHEPHARD, BRUCE D., AND CARROLL A. SHEPHARD. *The Complete Guide to Women's Health*, rev. ed. New York: New American Library, 1985.

STEWART, FELICIA, FELICIA GUEST, GARY STEWART, AND ROBERT HATCHER, *My Body, My Health: The Concerned Woman's Book of Gynecology*. New York: Bantam Books, 1981.

CHAPTER 3: HUMAN SEXUAL BEHAVIOR

BARBACH, LONNIE. *For Yourself: The Fulfillment of Female Sexuality*. New York: Doubleday, 1975.

————. *For Each Other: Sharing Sexual Intimacy*. New York: Doubleday, 1982.

BERKOW, ROBERT, ED. *The Merck Manual*. Rahway, N.J.: Merck, Sharpe & Dohme Research Laboratories, 1977.

BOSTON WOMEN'S HEALTH COLLECTIVE. *The New Our Bodies, Ourselves*. New York: Simon and Schuster, 1984.

CALDERONE, MARY S., AND ERIC W. JOHNSON. *The Family Book about Sexuality*. New York: Harper and Row, 1981.

FREEDMAN, G. R. *Sexual Medicine*. London: Churchill Livingstone, 1983.

GAGE, WILLIAM E., ED. *Sex Code of California: A Compendium of Laws and Regulations*, 3rd ed. Sacramento: Planned Parenthood Affiliates of California, 1981.

GEER, JAMES, JULIA HEIMAN, AND HAROLD LEITENBERG. *Human Sexuality*. Englewood Cliffs, N.J.: Prentice-Hall, 1984.

HAEBERLE, ERWIN J. *The Sex Atlas*. New York: Seabury Press, 1978.

HOLMES, RONALD M. *The Sex Offender and the Criminal Justice System*. Springfield, Ill.: Charles C. Thomas, 1983.

JOHNSON, ERIC W. *Love and Sex in Plain Language*, 4th rev. ed. New York: Harper and Row, 1985.

KNOBEN, JAMES E., AND PHILIP O. ANDERSON, EDS. *Handbook of Clinical Drug Data*, 5th ed. Hamilton, Ill.: Drug Intelligence Publications, 1983.

MASTERS, WILLIAM H., VIRGINIA E. JOHNSON, AND ROBERT C. KOLODNY. *Human Sexuality*, 2nd ed. Boston: Little, Brown, 1985.

MONEY, JOHN. *Sex Errors of the Body: Dilemmas, Education, Counseling*. Baltimore, Md.: Johns Hopkins University Press, 1968.

POMEROY, WARDELL B. *Boys and Sex*. New York: Delacorte Press, 1968.

SILBER, SHERMAN J. *The Male: A Comprehensive and Clearly Written Guide to the Male Sexual System*. New York: Charles Scribner's Sons, 1981.

STRONG, BRYAN, SAM WILSON, MINA ROBBINS, AND THOMAS JOHNS. *Human Sexuality: Essentials*, 2nd ed. St. Paul, Minn.: West, 1981.

CHAPTER 4: TALKING TO YOUR CHILD ABOUT SEX

GRAMS, ARMIN. *Sex Education: A Guide for Teachers and Parents.* Danville, Ill.: Interstate Printers and Publishers, 1970.

PLANNED PARENTHOOD FEDERATION OF AMERICA (FAYE WATTLETON WITH ELISABETH KIEFFER). *How to Talk with Your Child about Sexuality.* New York: Doubleday, 1986.

CHAPTER 5: SEX AND THE LAW

GAGE, WILLIAM E., ED. *Sex Code of California: A Compendium of Laws and Regulations,* 3rd ed. Sacramento: Planned Parenthood Affiliates of California, 1981.

GEER, JAMES, JULIA HEIMAN, AND HAROLD LEITENBERG. *Human Sexuality.* Englewood Cliffs, N.J.: Prentice-Hall, 1984.

HOLMES, RONALD M. *The Sex Offender and the Criminal Justice System.* Springfield, Ill.: Charles C. Thomas, 1983.

MASTERS, WILLIAM H., VIRGINIA E. JOHNSON, AND ROBERT C. KOLODNY. *Human Sexuality,* 2nd ed. Boston: Little, Brown, 1985.

MEISELMAN, KAREN C. *Incest.* San Francisco: Jossey-Bass, 1978.

STRONG, BRYAN, SAM WILSON, MINA ROBBINS, AND THOMAS JOHNS. *Human Sexuality: Essentials,* 2nd ed. St. Paul, Minn.: West, 1981.

CHAPTER 6: PREGNANCY AND CHILDBIRTH

DANFORTH, DAVID N., AND JAMES R. SCOTT, EDS. *Obstetrics and Gynecology,* 5th ed. Philadelphia: Lippincott, 1986.

HYDE, JANET SHIBLEY, *Understanding Human Sexuality,* 3rd ed. New York: McGraw-Hill, 1986.

GARREY, MATTHEW M., A. D. T. GOVAN, C. HODGE, AND R. CALLANDER. *Obstetrics Illustrated,* 2nd ed. London: Churchill Livingstone, 1974.

GUTTMACHER, ALAN F. *Pregnancy, Birth, and Family Planning.* New York: New American Library, 1987.

LESKO, WENDY, AND MATTHEW LESKO. *The Maternity Sourcebook.* New York: Warner Books, 1984.

PREVITE, JOSEPH. *Human Physiology.* New York: McGraw-Hill, 1983.

SAMUELS, MIKE, AND NANCY SAMUELS, *The Well Pregnancy Book.* New York: Simon and Schuster, 1986.

SHEPHARD, BRUCE D., AND CARROLL A. SHEPHARD. *The Complete Guide to Women's Health,* rev. ed. New York: New American Library, 1985.

STEWART, FELICIA, FELICIA GUEST, GARY STEWART, AND ROBERT HATCHER. *My Body, My Health: The Concerned Woman's Book of Gynecology.* New York: Bantam Books, 1981.

CHAPTER 7: UNPLANNED AND UNWANTED PREGNANCY

ALLEN, JAMES E. *Managing Teenage Pregnancy: Access to Abortion, Contraception, and Sex Education.* New York: Praeger, 1980.

ASHDOWN-SHARP, PATRICIA. *A Guide to Pregnancy and Parenthood for Women on Their Own.* New York: Vintage (Random House), 1977.

BOLTON, FRANK G., JR. *The Pregnant Adolescent: Problems of Premature Parenthood.* Vol. 100, Sage Library of Social Research. Beverly Hills, Calif.: Sage, 1980.

COSTIN, LELA B. *Child Welfare: Policies and Practices,* 2nd ed. New York: McGraw-Hill, 1979.

KADUSHIN, ALFRED. *Child Welfare Services,* 3rd ed. New York: Macmillan, 1980.

MCNAMARA, JOAN, *The Adoption Advisor.* New York: Hawthorn Books, 1975.

ZUCKERMAN, ERVA. *Child Welfare.* New York: Free Press, 1983.

CHAPTER 8: INFERTILITY

FENTON, JUDITH ALSOFROM, AND AARON S. LIFCHEZ. *The Fertility Handbook.* New York: Clarkson N. Potter, 1980.

HARRISON, MARY. *Infertility: A Couple's Guide to Causes and Treatments.* Boston: Houghton Mifflin, 1977.

KASE, NATHAN G., AND ALLAN B. WEINGOLD, EDS. *Principles and Practice of Clinical Gynecology.* New York: Wiley, 1983.

MENNING, BARBARA ECK. *Infertility: A Guide for the Childless Couple.* Englewood Cliffs, N.J.: Prentice Hall, 1977.

SILBER, SHERMAN J. *How to Get Pregnant.* New York: Charles Scribner's Sons, 1980.

CHAPTER 9: CONTRACEPTION

ALAN GUTTMACHER INSTITUTE, *Making Choices: Evaluating the Health Risks and Benefits of Birth Control Methods.* New York: Alan Guttmacher Institute, 1983.

COREA, GENA, *The Hidden Malpractice: How American Medicine Treats Women as Patients and Professionals.* New York: William Morrow and Company, Inc., 1977.

HATCHER, ROBERT A., FELICIA GUEST, FELICIA STEWART, GARY K. STEWART, JAMES TRUSSELL, AND ERICA FRANK. *Contraceptive Technology 1984–85,* 12th rev. ed. New York: Irvington Publishers, 1984.

HATCHER, ROBERT A., FELICIA GUEST, FELICIA STEWART, GARY K. STEWART, JAMES TRUSSELL, SYLVIA CEREL, AND WILLARD CATES. *Contracep-*

tive Technology 1986–87, 13th rev. ed. New York: Irvington Publishers, 1986.

KASE, NATHAN G., AND ALLAN B. WEINGOLD, EDS. *Principles and Practice of Clinical Gynecology*. New York: Wiley, 1983.

NOFZIGER, MARGARET. *A Cooperative Method of Natural Birth Control*. Summertown, Tenn.: The Book Publishing Company (156 Drakes Lane), 1976.

SEAMAN, BARBARA, AND GIDEON SEAMAN. *Women and the Crisis in Sex Hormones*. New York: Rawson Associates, 1977.

STEWART, FELICIA, FELICIA GUEST, GARY STEWART, AND ROBERT HATCHER. *My Body, My Health: The Concerned Woman's Book of Gynecology*. New York: Bantam Books, 1981.

CHAPTER 10: STERILIZATION

GREENFIELD, MICHAEL, AND WILLIAM M. BURRUS. *The Complete Reference Book on Vasectomy*. New York: Avon Books, 1973.

HATCHER, ROBERT A., FELICIA GUEST, FELICIA STEWART, GARY K. STEWART, JAMES TRUSSELL, AND ERICA FRANK. *Contraceptive Technology 1984–1985*, 12th rev. ed. New York: Irvington Publishers, 1984.

HODGSON, JANE E., ED. *Abortion and Sterilization: Medical and Social Aspects*. New York: Grune and Stratton, 1981.

KASE, NATHAN G., AND ALLAN B. WEINGOLD, EDS. *Principles and Practice of Clinical Gynecology*. New York: Wiley, 1983.

STEWART, FELICIA, FELICIA GUEST, GARY STEWART, AND ROBERT HATCHER. *My Body, My Health: The Concerned Woman's Book of Gynecology*. New York: Bantam Books, 1981.

CHAPTER 11: ABORTION

HATCHER, ROBERT A., FELICIA GUEST, FELICIA STEWART, GARY K. STEWART, JAMES TRUSSELL, AND ERICA FRANK. *Contraceptive Technology 1984–1985*, 12th rev. ed. New York: Irvington Publishers, 1984.

HODGSON, JANE E., ED. *Abortion and Sterilization: Medical and Social Aspects*. New York: Grune and Stratton, 1981.

KASE, NATHAN G., AND ALLAN B. WEINGOLD, EDS. *Principles and Practice of Clinical Gynecology*. New York: Wiley, 1983.

STEWART, FELICIA, FELICIA GUEST, GARY STEWART, AND ROBERT HATCHER. *My Body, My Health: The Concerned Woman's Book of Gynecology*. New York: Bantam Books, 1981.

CHAPTER 12: WOMEN'S HEALTH PROBLEMS

AMERICAN CANCER SOCIETY. *1985 Cancer Facts and Figures*. New York: American Cancer Society, 1985

———. *1987 Cancer Facts and Figures*. New York: American Cancer Society, 1985.

BOSTON WOMEN'S HEALTH COLLECTIVE. *The New Our Bodies, Ourselves*. New York: Simon and Schuster, 1984.

BRODY, JANE. *The New York Times Guide to Personal Health*. New York: Avon Books, 1982.

CUTLER, WINNIFRED BERG, CELSO-RAMON GARCIA, AND DAVID A. EDWARDS. *Menopause: A Guide for Women and the Men Who Love Them*. New York: Norton, 1983.

KASE, NATHAN G., AND ALLAN B. WEINGOLD, EDS. *Principles and Practice of Clinical Gynecology*. New York: Wiley, 1983.

SHEPHARD, BRUCE D., AND CARROLL A. SHEPHARD. *The Complete Guide to Women's Health*, rev. ed. New York: New American Library, 1985.

STEWART, FELICIA, FELICIA GUEST, GARY STEWART, AND ROBERT HATCHER. *My Body, My Health: The Concerned Woman's Book of Gynecology*. New York: Bantam Books, 1981.

CHAPTER 13: MEN'S HEALTH PROBLEMS

ACADEMY OF PEDIATRICS. "Care of the Uncircumcised Penis" (pamphlet). Elk Grove, Ill.: Academy of Pediatrics Publications Department. (P.O. Box 927, Elk Grove Village, Ill. 60007), n.d.

AMERICAN CANCER SOCIETY. *1985 Cancer Facts and Figures*. New York: American Cancer Society, 1985.

———. *1987 Cancer Facts and Figures*. New York: American Cancer Society, 1985.

AMERICAN MEDICAL SYSTEMS (public relations materials). Minnetonka, Minn.: American Medical Systems (11001 Bren Road East, Minnetonka, MN 55343), n.d.

BRODY, JANE. *The New York Times Guide to Personal Health*. New York: Avon Books, 1983.

CHALFIN, STUART. M.D. F.A.C.S. Personal communication, February 20, 1986.

RAND, CYNTHIA S., CAROL-ANN EMMONS, AND JOHN W. C. JOHNSON. "The Effect of an Educational Intervention on the Rate of Neonatal Circumcision." *Obstetrics and Gynecology* 62, no. 1 (July 1983).

ROWAN, ROBERT L. *Men and Their Sex*. New York: Irvington Publishers, 1982.

SCOTT, F. BRANTLEY, IRVING J. FISHMAN, AND J. KEITH LIGHT. "A Decade of Experience with the Inflatable Penile Prosthesis." World Journal of Urology 1 (1983): 244–250.

SCOTT, ROY, R. FLETCHER DEANE, AND ROBIN CALLANDER. *Urology Illustrated*, 2nd ed. New York: Churchill Livingstone, 1982.

SILBER, SHERMAN J. *The Male: A Comprehensive and Clearly Written Guide to the Male Sexual System*. New York: Charles Scribner's Sons, 1981.

SMITH, DONALD R. *General Urology*, 11th ed. Los Altos, Calif.: Lange Medical Publications, 1984.

U.S. DEPARTMENT OF HEALTH AND HUMAN SERVICES. *Testicular Self-Examination* (pamphlet). Washington, D.C.: U.S. Public Health Service, National Institutes of Health (NIH Publication No. 85–2636), n.d.

CHAPTER 14: SEXUALLY TRANSMITTED DISEASES

BOSTON WOMEN'S HEALTH COLLECTIVE. *The New Our Bodies, Ourselves.* New York: Simon and Schuster, 1984.

BRODY, JANE. *The New York Times Guide to Personal Health.* New York: Avon Books, 1982.

HOLMES, KING K., AND PER-ANDERS MARDH. *International Perspectives on Neglected Sexually Transmitted Diseases.* New York: McGraw-Hill, 1983.

KASE, NATHAN G., AND ALLAN B. WEINGOLD, EDS. *Principles and Practice of Clinical Gynecology.* New York: Wiley, 1983.

MELTZER, ALAN S. *Sexually Transmitted Diseases: Guidelines for Physicians and Health Workers.* St. Albans, VT: Eden Medical Research, 1981.

NOBLE, ROBERT C. *Sexually Transmitted Diseases: Guide to Diagnosis and Therapy,* 3rd ed. New Hyde Park, N.Y.: Medical Examination Publishing Company, 1985.

SHEPHARD, BRUCE D., AND CARROLL A. SHEPHARD. *The Complete Guide to Women's Health,* rev. ed. New York: New American Library, 1985.

STEWART, FELICIA, FELICIA GUEST, GARY STEWART, AND ROBERT HATCHER. *My Body, My Health: The Concerned Woman's Book of Gynecology.* New York: Bantam Books, 1981.

CHAPTER 15: AIDS (ACQUIRED IMMUNE DEFICIENCY SYNDROME)

AMERICAN PUBLIC HEALTH ASSOCIATION. "Aids Update." In *The Nation's Health.* Washington, D.C.: American Public Health Association, January 1988.

LANG, JENNIFER, JUDITH SPIEGEL, AND STEPHEN M. STRIGLE, EDS. *Living with AIDS: A Self-Care Manual.* Los Angeles, AIDS Project of Los Angeles (3670 Wilshire Blvd, Suite 300, Los Angeles, CA 90010), 1984.

MOFFAT, BETTY CLARE, JUDITH SPIEGEL, STEVE PARRISH, AND MICHAEL HELQUIST, EDS. *AIDS: A Self-Care Manual.* Santa Monica, CA: IBS Press (744 Pier Avenue, Santa Monica, CA 90405), 1987.

U.S. AIDS PROGRAM. "AIDS Weekly Surveillance Report." Atlanta, Ga.: Centers for Disease Control, January 9, 1989.

U.S. DEPARTMENT OF HEALTH AND HUMAN SERVICES. *Report of the Surgeon General's Workshop on Children with HIV Infection and Their Families.* Rockville, Md.: U.S. Department of Health and Human Services, U.S. Public Health Service, Health Resources and Services Administration, Bureau of Health Care Delivery and Assistance, Division of Maternal and Child Health (DHHS Publication No. HRS-D-MC 87–1), 1987.

WORLD HEALTH ORGANIZATION. "Global AIDS Epidemic in 1987–88" (Press Release No. WHO/34). Geneva: World Health Organization (WHO Media Service, 1211 Geneva 27, Switzerland), December 16, 1987.

WORLD HEALTH ORGANIZATION. "1988 Was Year of Global Mobilization against AIDS" (Press Release No. WHO/52). Geneva: World Health Organization (WHO Media Service, 1211 Geneva 27, Switzerland), December 20, 1988.

Acknowledgments

PHOTOGRAPHS

Chapter 1: 1 Statue of *The Mediterranean* by Aristide Maillol (c. 1901). Bronze, 41" high. The Museum of Modern Art; gift of Stephen C. Clark. **3** Alan Carey/The Image Works. **11** Arlene Collins/Monkmeyer Press. **16** Jim Anderson/Woodfin Camp & Associates. **18** Ken Karp. **20** (top) Ken Karp, Sirovich Senior Center. **20** (bottom) Abigail Heyman/Archive Pictures.

Chapter 2: 22 Nancy Durrell McKenna/Photo Researchers. **24** Harriet Gans/The Image Works. **25** Courtesy of Dr. Landrum B. Shettles. **26** Suzanne Szasz/Photo Researchers. **33** Nancy Durrell McKenna/Photo Researchers.

Chapter 3: 34 Laima Druskis. **35** (top) Suzanne Szasz/Photo Researchers. **35** (bottom) Susan Dryfoos/Monkmeyer Press. **36** (top) David S. Strickler/Monkmeyer Press. **36** (bottom) Phiz Mezey/Taurus Photos. **37** Roswell Angier/Archive Pictures. **39** Ken Karp. **41** Alan Carey/The Image Works. **42** Ken Karp. **43** Ken Karp. **44** Lily Solmssen/Photo Researchers. **59** (top) Frank Siteman/Taurus Photos. **59** (bottom) Stephen Capra. **61** Mary Evans Picture Library/Photo Researchers. **62** Frank Fournier/Woodfin Camp & Associates. **63** Frank Siteman/Taurus Photos. **64** Teri Stratford. **65** Susan Rosenberg/Photo Researchers. **67** Lynne Jaeger Weinstein/Woodfin Camp & Associates. **68** Stephen L. Feldman/Photo Researchers. **70** Frank Siteman/Taurus Photos. **71** Charles Gatewood/The Image Works. **73** Eugene Gordon. **74** Eric Kroll/Taurus Photos. **75** UPI/Bettmann Newsphotos.

Chapter 4: 78 Monique Manceau/Photo Researchers. **79** Mimi Forsyth/Monkmeyer Press. **80** (top) Randy Matusow/Monkmeyer Press. **80** (bottom) Ken Karp. **81** Suzanne Szasz/Photo Researchers. **82** Richard Frieman/Photo Researchers. **83** Paul Conklin/Monkmeyer Press. **84** Renee Lynn/Photo Researchers. **85** Courtesy of Atari. **87** Barbara Rios/Photo Researchers. **88** (top) Lynn McLaren/Photo Researchers. **88** (bottom) Phiz Mezey/Taurus Photos. **89** Alice Kandell/Photo Researchers. **90** Ulrike Welsch/Photo Researchers. **91** (top) Ken Karp. **91** (bottom) Frank Siteman/Taurus Photos.

Chapter 5: 93 Blair Seitz/Photo Researchers. **95** Mimi Forsyth/Monkmeyer Press. **97** Barbara Rios/Photo Researchers. **98** Ed Lettau/Photo Researchers. **99** Ed Lettau/Photo Researchers. **101** Robert Goldstein/Photo Researchers. **103** Bettye Lane/Photo Researchers. **104** Freda Leinwand/Monkmeyer Press. **105** Frank Siteman/Taurus Photos.

Chapter 6: 107 Nancy Durrell McKenna/Photo Researchers. **109** Ira Berger/Woodfin Camp & Associates. **110** Teri Stratford. **112** Teri Stratford. **115** Ken Karp. **116** Teri Stratford. **117** American Cancer Society. **121** Teri Stratford. **123** Mark Antman/The Image Works. **125** Suzanne Szasz/Photo Researchers. **126** Sepp Seitz/Woodfin Camp & Associates. **128** George Gardner/The Image Works. **129** Sepp Seitz/Woodfin Camp & Associates. **130** Laima Druskis. **132** Abigail Heyman/Archive Pictures. **133** Chuck Fishman/Woodfin Camp & Associates. **135** Chuck Fishman/Woodfin Camp & Associates. **136** Elizabeth Crews/The Image Works. **137** Elizabeth Crews/The Image Works. **138** (top) Abigail Heyman/Archive Pictures. **138** (bottom) Abigail Heyman/Archive Pictures. **140** Teri Stratford. **149** Abigail Heyman/Archive Pictures. **150** Bob Daemmrich/The Image Works. **151** Ethan Hoffman/Archive Pictures. **152** Mimi Forsyth/Monkmeyer Press. **153** Alan Carey/The Image Works. **154** Linda Ferrer/Woodfin Camp & Associates. **156** Elizabeth Crews/The Image Works.

Chapter 7: 158 The Children's Defense Fund. **159** Erika Stone/Photo Researchers. **160** Erika Stone/Photo Researchers. **161** Polly Brown/Archive Pictures. **163** Polly Brown/Archive Pictures. **164** Polly Brown/Archive Pictures. **165** Linda Ferrer/Woodfin Camp & Associates. **166** Erika Stone/Photo Researchers. **167** (top) David M. Grossman/Photo Researchers. **167** (bottom) Elizabeth Crews/The Image Works. **169** Bettye Lane/Photo Researchers.

Chapter 8: 171 Michael Kagan/Monkmeyer Press. **173** Mark Antman/The Image Works. **174** Mimi Forsyth/Monkmeyer Press. **175** NASA Lewis Research Center. **179** (top) Teri Stratford; materials courtesy Planned Parenthood, New York City. **179** (bottom) Erika Stone, Photo Researchers. **181** Alan Carey/The Image Works. **182** IVF Australia. **183** UPI/Bettmann Newsphotos.

Chapter 9: 185 Lynn McLaren/Photo Researchers. **186** UPI/Bettmann Newsphotos. **187** Freda Leinwand/Monkmeyer Press. **188** Teri Stratford; materials courtesy Planned Parenthood, New York City. **189** Blair Seitz/Photo Researchers. **193** Shirley Zeiberg. **195** Susan Rosenberg/Photo Researchers. **209** United Nations/ILO.

Chapter 10: 217 Eric Kroll/Taurus Photos. **218** Paul Conklin/Monkmeyer Press. **219** David Grossman/Photo Researchers.

Chapter 11: 226 Ed Lettau/Photo Researchers. **234** Erika Stone/Photo Researchers. **235** Ken Karp.

Chapter 12: 236 Deborah Kahn/Stock, Boston. **237** J. P. Laffont/Sygma. **240** Blair Seitz/Photo Researchers. **249** Ken Karp. **251** Chester Higgins, Jr./Photo Researchers. **252** Chester Higgins, Jr./Photo Researchers. **272** American Cancer Society.

Chapter 13: 286 Jeffrey W. Myers/Stock, Boston. 288 Ken Karp. 290 Jim Wilson/Woodfin Camp & Associates. 292 Ellis Herwig/ Taurus Photos. 295 Eric Kroll/Taurus Photos. 300 Ken Karp.

Chapter 14: 311 American Cancer Society. 312 Alan Carey/The Image Works. 315 Hazel Hankin/Stock, Boston. 323 Ken Karp. 324 Peter Menzel/Stock, Boston.

Chapter 15: 325 Dion Ogust/The Image Works. 326 Claude Poulet/Gamma-Liaison. 327 D. Gutekunst/Gamma-Liaison. 328 Alon Reininger/Woodfin Camp & Associates. 330 AP/Wide World Photos. 332 Alon Reininger/Woodfin Camp & Associates.

ILLUSTRATIONS

Figures 1–2B, 1–4, 1–5, 1–7, 9–3, 9–8, 10–1, 10–2. James Geer, Julia Heiman, and Harold Leitenberg, *Human Sexuality,* pp. 27, 29, 30, 31, 34, 35, 36, 131, 132, 136, 138. Reprinted by permission of Prentice-Hall, Inc., Englewood Cliffs, N.J. © 1984.

Figures 1–2A, 1–6A, 6–1, 6–15. David A. Schulz, *Human Sexuality,* 3rd ed., pp. 103, 106, 137, 145. Reprinted by permission of Prentice-Hall, Inc., Englewood Cliffs, N.J. © 1988.

Figures 1–3, 9–2, 10–3, 11–3, 11–4, 11–6, 12–1, 12–4, 12–8, 12–23. Federation of Feminist Women's Health Centers, *A New View of a Woman's Body* (New York: Touchstone Books, 1981), pp. 25, 26, 28, 30, 40, 107, 132, 133, 135, 144, 146.

Figures 1–6, 1–9, 1–10, 1–11. Sherman J. Silber, *The Male: A Comprehensive and Clearly Written Guide to the Male Sexual System,* pp. 4, 145, 148, 149, 150. Reprinted with permission of Charles Scribner's Sons, an imprint of Macmillan Publishing Company, and Grafton Books, a division of the Collins Publishing Group. Illustrations by Scott Barrows. Copyright © 1981 Sherman J. Silber, M.D.

Figures 1–12, 3–1, 3–2, 3–3. Erwin J. Haeberle, *The Sex Atlas* (New York: The Continuum Publishing Corporation, 1978), pp. 20, 38, 39, 60, 61, 62, 63. Reprinted by permission.

Figure 1–13. The Boston Women's Health Book Collective, *Our Bodies, Ourselves: A Book By and For Women,* 2nd ed., rev. (New York: Touchstone Books, 1979), p. 36. Copyright © 1971, 1973, 1976 by Boston Women's Health Book Collective, Inc. Reprinted by permission of Simon & Schuster, Inc.

Figures 1–14, 9–5, 9–6, 10–4, 11–1, 11–2, 11–5, 12–3, 12–5, 12–6, 12–7, 12–9, 12–10, 12–11, 12–12, 12–13, 12–15, 12–16, 12–18, 12–22, 12–26, 12–27. Felicia Stewart, Felicia Guest, Gary K. Stewart, and Robert Hatcher, *Understanding Your Body* (New York: Bantam Books, 1987), pp. 19, 129, 132, 133, 134, 246, 292, 301, 319, 320, 322, 326, 332, 333, 363, 367, 373, 405, 423, 425, 428, 532.

Figures 2–1, 2–3, 2–5, 2–6, 2–8, 2–9, 2–10, 2–11, 6–6, 9–4, 9–11, 9–13. Robert J. Demarest and John J. Sciarra, *Conception, Birth, and Contraception* (New York: McGraw Hill, 1976), pp. 44, 46, 52, 53, 61, 63, 67, 68, 86, 87, 99, 107, 115. Reprinted by permission. Copyright 1976.

Figures 2–2, 2–4, 2–7, 6–3, 6–4, 6–5, 6–7, 6–8, 6–11, 6–12, 6–14, 6–16, 6–17. Mike Samuels and Nancy Samuels, *The Well Pregnancy Book* (New York: Summit Books, 1986), pp. 54, 56, 62, 63, 237, 242, 280, 282, 284, 292, 296, 297, 299, 329, 336, 339, 349. Copyright © 1985 by Mike Samuels, M.D., and Nancy Samuels. Reprinted by permission of Summit Books, a division of Simon & Schuster, Inc., and the Elaine Markson Literary Agency. Artist Wend Frost.

Figure 3–4. Lonnie Barbach, *For Each Other: Sharing Sexual Intimacy* (New York: Signet Books, 1982), p. 69. Copyright © 1982 by Lonnie Barbach. Reprinted by permission of Doubleday, a division of Bantam, Doubleday, Dell Publishing Group, Inc.

Figures 6–9, 12–13. Bruce D. Shephard and Carroll A. Shephard, *The Complete Guide to Women's Health* (New York: New American Library, 1985), pp. 140, 162. Copyright 1982, 1985 by Bruce D. Shephard, M.D., and Carroll A. Shephard, R.N. Reprinted under an arrangement with New American Library, a division of Penguin Books USA, Inc.

Figure 6–15. Neg. no. 296628, 296629, 296630, 296631 courtesy Department of Library Services, American Museum of Natural History.

Figures 9–7, 9–9. Robert Hatcher, Felicia Guest, Felicia Stewart, Gary K. Stewart, James Trussel, Sylvia Cardl, and Willard Cates, *Contraceptive Technology, 1986–1987* (New York: Irvington Publishers, 1986), pp. 221, 224.

Figures 13–4, 13–6, 13–8. Roy Scott, R. Fletcher Deane, and Robin Callander, *Urology Illustrated* (Edinburgh, London, and New York: Churchill Livingstone, 1975), pp. 221, 285, 326. Reprinted by permission.

Figure 13–2. Donald R. Smith, *General Urology,* 10th ed., p. 41. Copyright © Lange Medical Publications, 1981. Reprinted by permission.

Figure 13–10. Courtesy of American Medical Systems, Inc., Minnetonka, Minnesota.

Index